973.92   1
  S847p   v.5
Stevenson--The papers of Adlai E.
  Stevenson

                MAY 3 0 1975

Books by Walter Johnson

THE BATTLE AGAINST ISOLATION

WILLIAM ALLEN WHITE'S AMERICA

THE UNITED STATES: EXPERIMENT IN DEMOCRACY
(with Avery Craven)

HOW WE DRAFTED ADLAI STEVENSON

1600 PENNSYLVANIA AVENUE: PRESIDENTS AND THE PEOPLE, 1929–1959

THE FULBRIGHT PROGRAM: A HISTORY
(with Francis J. Colligan)

Edited by Walter Johnson

SELECTED LETTERS OF WILLIAM ALLEN WHITE

ROOSEVELT AND THE RUSSIANS: THE YALTA CONFERENCE
By Edward R. Stettinius, Jr.

TURBULENT ERA: A DIPLOMATIC RECORD OF FORTY YEARS, 1904–1945
By Joseph C. Grew

THE PAPERS OF ADLAI E. STEVENSON

Volume I: Beginnings of Education, 1900–1941
Volume II: Washington to Springfield, 1941–1948
Volume III: Governor of Illinois, 1949–1953
Volume IV: "Let's Talk Sense to the American People," 1952–1955
Volume V: Visit to Asia, the Middle East, and Europe — March–August 1953

The Papers of Adlai E. Stevenson

WALTER JOHNSON, *Editor*

CAROL EVANS, *Assistant Editor*

C. ERIC SEARS, *Editorial Assistant*

The Papers of

Advisory Committee

Adlai E. Stevenson

VOLUME V

Visit to Asia, the Middle East, and Europe
March—August 1953

LITTLE, BROWN and COMPANY • Boston • Toronto

FIRST EDITION

T 02/75

The photo of Nehru receiving Stevenson is courtesy of Press Information Bureau,
Government of India. All other photos are courtesy of William Attwood.

The editors gratefully acknowledge the permission of the following authors, publishers, individuals and institutions to reprint selected materials as noted:

Archibald S. Alexander, George V. Allen, American Universities Field Staff,
William Attwood, Barry Bingham, Chester Bowles, Julian P. Boyd, Arnold C. Brackman, Ellis O. Briggs, Bethia S. Currie, Foreign Policy Association, John Kenneth
Galbraith, Raymond A. Hare, John Keswick, Theodore Kollek, *Life* magazine, *Look*
magazine, the *New Republic, New Statesman,* the *New York Times,* Praeger Pub-
lishers, the Regents of the University of California, Leo Rosten, Gregg Sinclair,
Syracuse University Press, Gerald Templer, and Woodruff Wallner, for all items
from their publications and writings as detailed in the footnotes.
Columbia Broadcasting System, Inc., for a quotation from a radio interview of
Governor Stevenson by Edward P. Morgan on February 14, 1953. Copyright ©
1975 CBS, Inc. All rights reserved.
Harper & Row, Publishers, for quotations from *What I Think* by Adlai E.
Stevenson. Copyright 1954, © 1955, 1956 by R. Keith Kane.
Harper & Row, Publishers, for excerpts from *As We Knew Adlai: The Stevenson
Story by Twenty-two Friends,* edited and with preface by Edward P. Doyle. Copy-
right © 1966 by Harper & Row, Publishers, Inc.
Harper & Row, Publishers, for permission to reprint *Call to Greatness* by
Adlai E. Stevenson. Copyright 1954 by Adlai Ewing Stevenson.

LIBRARY OF CONGRESS CATALOGING IN PUBLICATION DATA

Stevenson, Adlai Ewing, 1900–1965.
  The papers of Adlai E. Stevenson.

  Includes bibliographical references.
  CONTENTS: v. 1. Beginnings of education, 1900–
1941 — v. 2. Washington to Springfield, 1941–1948. —
v. 3. Governor of Illinois, 1949–1953. [etc.]
  1. Stevenson, Adlai Ewing, 1900–1965. I. Johnson,
Walter, 1915–   ed.
E748.S84A25 1972   973.921′092′4 [B]   73-175478
ISBN 0-316-46758-8 (v. 5)

Designed by Barbara Bell Pitnof

*Published simultaneously in Canada
by Little, Brown & Company (Canada) Limited*

Foreword

"It seems to me that it's terribly important for anyone who is speaking or writing about contemporary affairs to understand something of . . . this revolution that's going on in the colonial areas of the world, and in Asia particularly," Adlai Stevenson told Edward P. Morgan on February 14, 1953.[1]

Although Stevenson had been a frequent visitor to Europe, he had never traveled in Asia and the Middle East. He wanted to observe at first hand the rebellion against white Western colonialism that had been remaking the face of this part of the world since the close of World War II. Many of the new nations that had emerged from the disintegration of old empires remained uncommitted in the cold war between the Soviet Union and the United States. With their anti-Western feeling, their demand for a better way of life, and their insistence on being recognized as equals by Westerners, many nations of Asia were adding a new dimension to world politics.

It was this new dimension that Stevenson wanted to study. Although he had been an active participant in the founding of the United Nations at San Francisco, head of the American delegation at the United Nations Preparatory Commission in London, and a member of the American delegation at the United Nations Assembly meetings in 1946–1947, his exacting duties as governor of Illinois had temporarily re-

---

[1] Radio interview, Edward P. Morgan collection, Wisconsin State Historical Society.

moved him from active participation in the rapid and complicated changes that were altering the postwar world.[2]

In the decade of the 1950's, Stevenson was one of the few American statesmen who had an understanding of Asia. The lasting impressions that Stevenson brought home from his 1953 trip "appeared in the themes he developed in the next few years," Herbert J. Muller wrote. Muller added: "The chief concerns that Stevenson brought back from his travels sprang from a livelier, fuller awareness of the revolution of rising expectations, the need of understanding and sympathizing with it, and the increasing danger of the immense gulf between the wealthy Western democracies and the impoverished non-Western peoples. He tried to drive home the elementary truths that the world's ills were not all caused by aggressive communism, and that we lacked the resources to remedy them all. Immediately we needed to think afresh about our policy regarding China." [3]

This current volume of *The Papers of Adlai E. Stevenson* is a day-by-day description of how this statesman educated himself through grueling days and nights of intensive interviewing and observation. (He bemoaned the precious hours lost at formal receptions and dinner parties.) It reveals how he gained a deeper understanding of his times and with it a continuing growth in his stature as a statesman-educator.

Julian Boyd wrote: "Stevenson's manner of informing himself about world conditions reveals the essential integrity of the man just as his speeches, his letters, his conversations, and all of his human relations did — a complex and highly civilized human being with a passionate concern for the plight of his fellow man. The punishment that Stevenson gave himself and his aides on this trip is a measure of his humanity as well as his desire, as a responsible political figure, to be accurately informed." [4]

Adlai E. Stevenson's own words — in letters, postcards, speeches, press conferences, and his abortive attempts at keeping a diary — are presented in the volumes of *The Papers of Adlai E. Stevenson*. These

[2] Adlai E. Stevenson throughout his lifetime was constantly increasing his knowledge and understanding of men and events. For example, during the years from 1927 to 1941 (except for 1933–1934, when he was in Washington) his association with the Chicago Council on Foreign Relations and his friendships with many faculty members of the University of Chicago, including Samuel Harper, professor of Russian history; Bernadotte E. Schmitt, Distinguished Service Professor of European history; and Robert M. Hutchins, president of the university, contributed significantly to Stevenson's intellectual development.

[3] Herbert J. Muller, *Adlai Stevenson: A Study in Values* (New York: Harper & Row, 1967), pp. 154, 156.

[4] Letter to Walter Johnson, March 2, 1970.

volumes are a documentary biography of Stevenson and, at the same time, a documentary history in his own words of the extraordinary, and often bewildering, changes that remolded the United States and the world during his lifetime from 1900 to 1965.

In selecting the materials from Stevenson's papers to be published in these volumes the editors decided to emphasize the material that helped answer such questions as: How did he educate himself? How did he become the man he became? What were the key influences in his life? How did he understand his times? How did he articulate the problems of his times?

Look magazine kindly granted us permission to reprint the articles that Adlai E. Stevenson wrote about his 1953 trip. Generally, Stevenson wrote about more than one country in each of his articles for *Look*. We, however, have separated the material so that what he wrote about a given country concludes his visit to that country. Every day of the trip Walter Johnson dictated the events of the day and these discs were transcribed by Phyllis Gustafson and Mrs. Kay McQuaid at the Stevenson office in Chicago. A copy of this diary is in the Stevenson papers at the Princeton University Library. We have drawn heavily from this record, as well as from the diary that William Attwood kept of the trip.

Barry Bingham wrote a series of articles while on the trip for his newspaper, the Louisville *Courier-Journal*. Bingham also wrote "With Adlai in Asia," in *As We Knew Adlai: The Stevenson Story by Twenty-two Friends,* edited and with preface by Edward P. Doyle, foreword by Adlai E. Stevenson III (New York: Harper & Row, 1966), pp. 188–198. In the same volume, William Attwood, "Pencils, Pads, and Chronic Stamina," pp. 154–168, and William McCormick Blair, Jr., "A Dazzling Decade," pp. 235–243, contain material about the trip. Attwood also wrote "Seeing the World with Stevenson: Twenty Questions and Their Answers," *Harper's,* November, 1953, pp. 560–562, and "What Asia Thinks of Adlai," *Look,* June 20, 1953, pp. 69 ff. In various countries, the *New Republic* had correspondents describe the Stevenson visit. These have been most useful.

We are grateful to *Look* magazine, the *New Republic,* the Louisville *Courier-Journal,* and Harper & Row for permission to quote from this material. We are especially indebted to Harper & Row and Atheneum for permission to reprint Stevenson's book *Call to Greatness* — his most thoughtful writing to come out of his trip of self-education.

We are grateful to William Attwood and William McCormick Blair, Jr., for reading the entire manuscript of Volume V, and to Barry Bingham for reading the manuscript through the chapter on Pakistan. In addition, Professor Stuart Gerry Brown read the entire manuscript as did the members of the Advisory Committee to *The Papers of Adlai E. Stevenson*. Their suggestions have been most valuable.

We are grateful also to the following for reading those sections of the manuscript of which they have special knowledge: Professor Norton S. Ginsburg, Professor William R. Polk, Albert Ravenholt, Professor Robert Van Niel, Professor Walter Vella, Professor Jagdish Sharma, General Maxwell D. Taylor, Ambassador Ellis O. Briggs, Ambassador George V. Allen, Ambassador Raymond A. Hare, Ambassador Edwin F. Stanton, Sir Gerald Templer, and the Right Honorable Malcolm MacDonald.

The major repositories of the papers of Adlai E. Stevenson are:

(1) Princeton University Library. Since the majority of the papers are at Princeton, the editors will identify the location of only the material that is *not* at Princeton.

(2) Adlai E. Stevenson collection, Illinois State Historical Library (A.E.S., I.S.H.L.).

(3) Elizabeth Stevenson Ives collection, Illinois State Historical Library (E.S.I., I.S.H.L.).

Handwritten letters or postcards that are in the possession of individuals will be so designated. Since Stevenson did not have a secretary on the 1953 trip, we have tried to unearth a representative selection of his many handwritten postcards and letters. We are grateful to those individuals — and particularly to Mrs. Edison Dick — who have searched in their files for this material. Mrs. Dick submitted extracts to the editors from handwritten letters and postcards. She has indicated with ellipses material that was deleted by her and has omitted the salutation and closing of each letter.

When he wrote by hand, Stevenson had several idiosyncrasies. He spelled "it's" without the apostrophe; he used "thru" for "through," etc. We have left them as he wrote them and have not added a *sic*.

Ordinarily, Stevenson signed letters with his full name. Some, to close personal or political friends, were signed "AD" or "ADLAI." In cases where we have had to work with carbon copies, it is impossible to know how they were signed. Hence, signatures have been omitted from such items. Whenever we have located the original, and he signed it otherwise than with his full name, we have included the signature.

Under the legal agreement between Walter Johnson and Adlai E. Stevenson III, Borden Stevenson, and John Fell Stevenson, Adlai III agreed to read each volume before publication. If he objected to the inclusion of any particular item of his father's papers, and Walter Johnson refused to accept the objection, the matter in dispute went to Judge Carl

McGowan for final — and irrevocable — decision. Adlai III objected to nothing included in Volume V.

We are most grateful to Governor Stevenson's sister, Mrs. Ernest L. Ives, for her infinite patience and her considerate help at all stages in the preparation of this volume, including the excellent photographs she provided.

Little, Brown and Company, Mrs. Eugene Meyer, Mrs. Marshall Field III and the Field Foundation, Mrs. John French, Mr. and Mrs. Harold Hochschild, Arnold M. Picker, Robert Benjamin, Newton N. Minow, James F. Oates, Jr., Francis T. P. Plimpton, Benjamin Swig, Philip M. Klutznick, Mrs. John Paul Welling, William McC. Blair, the late R. Keith Kane, Simon H. Rifkind, Wilson W. Wyatt, the late Wiliam Benton, Daggett Harvey, Mr. and Mrs. Edison Dick, William McCormick Blair, Jr., Lloyd K. Garrison, J. M. Kaplan, Jerrold Loebl, Hermon D. Smith, Edward D. McDougal, Jr., Glen A. Lloyd, Mr. and Mrs. Gilbert Harrison, Irving B. Harris, Edwin C. Austin, Archibald Alexander, Jacob M. Arvey, Paul Ziffren, Frank Karelsen, George W. Ball, C. K. McClatchy, Maurice Templesman, Barnet Hodes, and Scott Hodes generously provided funds to defray the editorial expense of these volumes. The University of Hawaii kindly assisted us in defraying the cost of typing the manuscript.

We are grateful to Roger Shugg, of the University of New Mexico Press; Larned Bradford, of Little, Brown and Company; and Ivan von Auw, of Harold Ober Associates, for their encouragement and support.

WALTER JOHNSON
CAROL EVANS
C. ERIC SEARS

Contents

CONTENTS

Illustrations

With President Tito of Yugoslavia.

Visiting Tito's island retreat at Brioni with Borden Stevenson and Mr. and Mrs. William Attwood.

Surrounded by young Yugoslavs in Belgrade.

With Queen Elizabeth at Goodwood racecourse in Sussex, England.

The Papers of Adlai E. Stevenson

One

Out of a Job and Time to Travel

*A*dlai E. Stevenson described his 1953 tour through thirty countries in Asia, the Middle East, and Europe as "fascinating, fatiguing — and fattening."

And William Attwood, European editor of Look, *who was one of Stevenson's traveling companions, remarked:*

> It was interesting — too damned interesting. It was the kind of once-in-a-lifetime trip that is wonderful in retrospect, but time has not yet had a chance to blur the memory of more than five months of hectic days and sleepless nights and stifling weather and too many airports. The trouble with travelling with Stevenson is that he sets the pace. And Stevenson has one incurable defect: he suffers from chronic stamina.[1]

Early in August, 1952, several weeks after Governor Stevenson had been drafted by the Democratic National Convention, he decided "if elected, to make a quick journey to Japan, Korea and India 'to see for myself,' meet the people with whom I would have to deal, and to give the best possible evidence of our profound concern for the Orient." Then, Stevenson wrote in February, 1953:

> We kept the plan secret, fearful that it might be construed as a political gesture. This may have been a mistake, and while I

[1] "Seeing the World with Stevenson: Twenty Questions and Their Answers," *Harper's*, November, 1953, pp. 56–62.

[3]

cannot approve the General's speech about going to Korea and the implication of early settlement or the misleading use that was made of it, I think he did the right thing to go out there and that we will all benefit from his first-hand information. I only wish that time and circumstances had permitted him to travel further.[2]

Time and circumstances permitted Stevenson to do just that, since, as he said to the Gridiron Club on December 13, 1952, "A funny thing happened to me on the way to the White House!" He was free to travel to Asia and the Middle East to see and to listen. It was a part of the world to which he had never been. He told a press conference on January 5, 1953, a week before he retired as Illinois's chief executive, that American preoccupation with Asia was indicated for many years to come. "I can see no political significance in the trip," Stevenson added. "It will obviously enhance what authority I might have for writing in the future." [3]

On Monday, January 12, Governor Stevenson left the executive mansion for his home in Libertyville. He had established an office at 11 South La Salle Street, Chicago, as a place "to deposit myself, my secretary, Carol Evans, and my papers." [4] A few days later he stopped off in New York City to accept an invitation from Gardner Cowles to write a series of articles on his world trip for Look. *Then on January 21 he arrived at the home of Mr. and Mrs. Ronald Tree on Heron Beach, St. James, Barbados, in the British West Indies for his first real rest since the campaign. It was not, however, all basking in the sun, since he wrote the introduction to his book,* Major Campaign Speeches, *which Random House published while he was in Asia.*

And, as was his inveterate custom, he wrote many handwritten letters and postcards. The two that follow are samples.

To Mrs. Ernest L. Ives [5]

January 21, 1953

Dear Buff —

Arrived here this AM after 3 very busy days in N.Y. I've loafed all day today & hope to be able to get at my work tomorrow, but I'm fearful that this luxurious and languid place was not contrived for work!

[2] *Major Campaign Speeches of Adlai E. Stevenson, 1952,* with an introduction by the author (New York: Random House, 1953), p. xxvii.
[3] Chicago *Sun-Times,* January 6, 1953.
[4] Ibid.
[5] This handwritten letter is in the Elizabeth Stevenson Ives collection, Illinois State Historical Library (E.S.I., I.S.H.L.).

While unpacking in Libertyville I couldn't find the box of my liquor treasures that were in the cupboard in the closet in my room in the Mansion. I asked Ernest [Ives] to pack them up for me for Libertyville and I'm fearful that something went wrong. Let me know if he knows.

I had a fearful time trying to dispose of my belongings and I'm afraid the Fields will rebel come summer when they move in with all their troops.[6]

I hope all is well with Tim.[7] I'll be back in N.Y. about the 11th of Feb. to finish up my "publishing" contracts & make a speech; then to Wash. for 2 or 3 days with the Senators, Congressmen et al & home for the last preparations for the great hegira commencing Mar 1.

Love and heartfelt thanks for your heroism in "my last hours" in Spfd. I don't yet know how you got it all done —

AD.

On January 12, the day that Adlai Stevenson left Springfield, he invited Walter Johnson, professor of history at the University of Chicago, to join him on his world tour. Two years before, as chairman of the Fulbright Educational Exchange Program, Johnson had visited many of the countries of Asia and the Middle East. Stevenson explained that he wanted Johnson to help him gather information particularly from intellectuals and the opposition in a given country for a book that he might write. William McCormick Blair, Jr., Stevenson's assistant in Springfield, handled the planning of the trip and then managed the tour with skill and incredible patience.

To Walter Johnson [8]

January 21, 1953

Dear Walter:

Bill [Blair] may have reported to you that I signed up with Look for six or eight articles during the journey and have reached an agreement with Harpers for the book reserving the option not to write one at all.

[Gardner] Cowles of Look insists on sending his foreign editor, William Attwood, and a photographer along,[9] but I've decided I should like

---

[6] Marshall Field IV, publisher of the Chicago *Sun-Times,* and his family rented Stevenson's home in Libertyville.

[7] Timothy Ives was just completing his Air Force training and was soon to leave for Korea as a fighter-bomber jet pilot.

[8] This handwritten letter is in the possession of Walter Johnson.

[9] A photographer did not accompany the group. Instead, Attwood either hired a photographer in each country or took the photographs himself.

you to go too in case I attempted the book. It is quite alright with them and although a party of six is inconveniently large we can break up when need be and two could go ahead as an "advance party," or stay behind to clean up the loose ends on the material gathering. Attwood is an attractive young man — early thirties, Princeton, good linguist, has lived much abroad and seems a likely companion. He came back from Paris for the meeting in N. Y.

So gird your loins and sharpen your pencils, my friend, and we'll be off around Mar. 1, returning in July — if the schedule works out OK.

I'm fearful that I'll get nothing done in this never never land!

Yrs

ADLAI

On St. Valentine's Day, Stevenson as titular head of the Democratic party delivered the principal speech at the Jefferson-Jackson Day dinner in New York City. Then, from February 15 to 17, he was in Washington visiting with Democratic senators and congressmen and workers at the Democratic National Committee. Arthur Krock remarked that Stevenson's problem was "how politically to survive on a national scale during the term of President Eisenhower." Unlike Wendell L. Willkie, who did not maintain good relations with Republican congressional leaders after his defeat in 1940, Governor Stevenson "has made it plain that he intends to do this very thing with the Congressional Democrats and the state leaders." In addition, Krock noted that the world-circling trip would not only keep Stevenson in the news, but on his return it would afford him opportunities to hold a national audience through speaking and writing. Moreover, during the five months that he was away, the Eisenhower Administration would have laid the foundations of its program and "built enough super-structure to present whatever political target it may." As a result, his first opposition speech in September could be made "on sound evidence that then will be available to him." [10]

When Stevenson visited Capitol Hill, secretaries and clerks turned out in large numbers to greet him, and the formal reception at the House of Representatives was attended not only by Democrats but by Republicans as well. "His charm, high intelligence, humor and wit, and the fact that Stevenson is one of those rare politicians who gain abiding national stature despite emphatic defeat at the polls, somewhat explain the magnitude and bi-partisan nature of this triumph," Krock observed. [11]

[10] New York *Times,* Sunday, February 22, 1953.
[11] Ibid.

The visit also included a briefing session at the Department of State and a luncheon at the White House with President Dwight Eisenhower. The following day, the President wrote his defeated opponent that he had "thoroughly enjoyed" the meeting. "I hope you find your trip interesting and informative. Whenever you may be visiting any old friend of mine, I would consider it a favor if you would extend him my warm greetings," the President added. He then repeated his request of the day before that Stevenson visit him on his return "to give me, at first hand, your impressions." At that time, as well, the President wrote perhaps "we can discuss further your offer to help in the promotion of true bipartisanship in our international affairs."

To Dwight D. Eisenhower

February 24, 1953

My dear Mr. President:

Thank you so much for your very gracious letter. I, too, enjoyed and profited from our meeting and I shall always be grateful for your courtesy and hospitality.

I shall certainly take advantage of your invitation to call again on my return from my journey, although I am afraid that I shall have little to add to your information.

Respectfully yours,

Lloyd K. Garrison of Paul, Weiss, Rifkind, Wharton & Garrison, of New York City, was in charge of negotiating contracts with Look *for Stevenson's articles and with Harper & Brothers for a possible book. The* Reader's Digest *was considering reprinting Stevenson's article "What I Learned About America," which was to appear in* This Week, *March 29, 1953.*

To Lloyd K. Garrison

February 24, 1953

Dear Lloyd:

So many thanks for your letter. I return the authorship letter regarding Readers Digest. Just do as you think best — for it will always be better than I think best!

I feel that I should have paid you up to date before departing for your extraordinary services in this unfamiliar jungle. Just send along a statement to Miss Evans, care of me at 11 South LaSalle at your convenience and if there is enough money in the till in my absence she will pay it. If not, it will be attended to on my return.

I have been in a more acute frenzy than usual to get off on this journey and attend to a myriad of things here, but it seems almost hopeless.

Love to Ellen [12] — and by the way, you both would look awfully good if I found you lurking behind a column in the Colosseum in Rome looking for savage elephants!

Yours,

While Stevenson was to be away, his former secretary Mrs. Margaret Munn arranged to have the Dalmatian Artie — King Arthur — taken care of.

To Margaret Munn [13]

February 24, 1953

Dear Margaret:

In my state of disorder you couldn't have thought of anything more indispensable than a compass.

The situation is as always — I don't know which way I am going or where I've been. But somehow I suppose we'll get off on the journey. We miss you mightily and come the return, we must have a reunion.

Give Artie my love and tell the wretched dog that I miss him more than he probably misses me — and that goes for you too — !!

Yours,

To Mrs. Ernest L. Ives [14]

February 24, 1953

Dear Buffie:

I have been in an utter frenzy trying to get cleaned up here to leave on my journey. Please tell Ernest that if Miss Evans needs any money or help or anything I hope he will take care of it in my absence and I can reimburse him later. I think I have things in fairly good shape, but I can never be sure.

I shall be at the Fairmont Hotel in San Francisco some time between 8 and 9 o'clock on Sunday evening, March 1, and sail Monday afternoon. I will pray that Tim [Ives] makes contact all right and will take

[12] Mrs. Garrison.

[13] This letter is in the possession of Mrs. Munn. The last six words were handwritten.

[14] The original is in E.S.I., I.S.H.L.

him along with me on my rounds, lunch and so forth, in San Francisco.

I think you have been so heroic about him and his military career thus far that I hate to think that you are softening now. It is easy enough to say that there is nothing you can do and therefore why be miserable. Knowing the power of thought and suggestion as you do, I am sure you will master it promptly which is the kindest thing you can do for him.

I should think you and Ernest would accept the Brooks invitation,[15] although I may not get to England myself by that time. It has been impossible to keep the schedule with any finality beyond Karachi, but we will try to keep you informed as we progress. As of now, it looks as though we would come out of the Middle East and reach Rome about June 20. Borden is planning to go abroad as soon as college is out the first of June and travel about until I turn up.[16] You know how difficult it is to arange their plans for them with any definiteness, but I have urged him to keep in touch with you. He might very well want to go over with you and stay with you until I arrive if various plans with his college mates do not pan out.

I was glad to hear that you had seen the specialist [17] and I hope you can get some genuine rest before the excitement of the summer. I should think Ernest would be delighted with the prospect and would also feel much more fit after more weeks there in the lovely spring.

I shall certainly try to remember to send you some envelopes for the doctor.[18] It seems a cheap way to pay the bills, but, well, you know my predicament what with the ghastly traveling, official requirements and writing.

Love,

On February 26, in Los Angeles, Stevenson attended a day-long conference of Democratic party leaders from eleven Western states. That evening he spoke to more than one thousand party members at a $100-a-plate fund-raising dinner. After his appearance, Earl C. Behrens wrote: "Adlai E. Stevenson . . . may not know it but his fellow Demo-

[15] Sir Basil Brooke, prime minister of Northern Ireland, and Lady Brooke were old friends of the Iveses.

[16] Borden Stevenson was a sophomore at Harvard College. He joined his father's group in Egypt.

[17] Mrs. Ives had developed an arthritis-like condition which prevented her lower jaw from closing properly. She was to consult an orthodontist in Chicago.

[18] Mrs. Ives's doctor was a stamp collector. He told her that he would not send her any bills "if you will give me all the stamps from the letters and postcards Adlai sends home from his trip." Letter, Mrs. Ives to Walter Johnson, January 6, 1967.

crats in California want him to take another try at the presidency in 1956. . . . Stevenson is recognized as the most brilliantly articulate losing candidate for the presidency who has hit the American political scene for a long time." [19]

Before arriving in San Francisco on March 1, Stevenson, William McCormick Blair, Jr., and Miss Carol Evans spent two days at Palm Springs where Stevenson tried to catch up with some of the correspondence that had piled in on him since his defeat. He had been answering some of this correspondence ever since election day, but he never was able to reply to it all. While he was on his trip, Miss Evans acknowledged the remainder of the letters.

To Leland Stowe [20]

February 27, 1953

Dear Leland:

I am mortified that I have not acknowledged your exquisite and touching letter of November 5 long before this. Perhaps I was saving the best for the last; but at all events I have read it now, and while I can hardly believe that I am endowed with the qualities or the destiny you suggest — I like it! Knowing the difficulties that confronted me and the accumulated frustrations and anxieties, it seemed to me that there could be no compromise or equivocation, and that the only possible satisfaction I could get out of the campaign would be the manner in which it was conducted. That it pleased you and your wife and earned your respect is a rich reward.

It is hard for me to see the future and my political role. For the moment I shall travel and then look at it all again some time in the fall or winter. It has been impossible for me to develop any positive passion for office, and I have occasional misgivings as to whether I have the proper equipment for successful political competition. I agree emphatically that no man is sufficiently and completely qualified for that ghastly job. But I am rambling — and I must leave for Japan!

With heartfelt thanks.

Cordially yours,

P.S. I hope we can talk of these things some time.

David L. Cohn, freelance writer and author of many books, including Where I Was Born and Raised (*Boston: Houghton Mifflin, 1948*), *frequently sent Stevenson drafts for speeches.*

[19] San Francisco *Chronicle*, March 2, 1953.
[20] Director of the News and Information Service of Radio Free Europe in Munich.

To David L. Cohn

March 1, 1953

Dear Dave:

I am dictating this note before leaving the West Coast to thank you for the superb script you sent me for the New York speech. As you doubtless noticed, I lifted a bit and will continue to nibble on it in the future.

I am asking Miss Evans to enclose a copy of my itinerary so far as we have worked it out.

The meeting in Los Angeles was most successful, and while our organization is woefully weak here, there is a lot of disorganized public support and enthusiasm which has hopeful aspects.

With warm thanks and best wishes always.

Yours,

On Sunday evening, March 1, Stevenson, his nephew Lieutenant Timothy Ives, and Blair arrived at the Fairmont Hotel in San Francisco. They were joined by Barry Bingham, editor and publisher of the Louis-ville Courier-Journal, *and Walter Johnson. After a visit with Pierre Salinger, of the San Francisco* Chronicle, *Stevenson appeared on a television interview program.*

Before retiring, the group spent an hour with Ambassador and Mrs. Henry Grady, who had recently returned from Iran. Stevenson quizzed Grady about the respective power of the shah and Prime Minister Mohammed Mossadegh, who had recently nationalized the British-controlled oil company.[21]

Before breakfast the next morning Stevenson wrote to his old friend Jane Dick, of Lake Forest.

To Mrs. Edison Dick [22]

March 2, 1953

. . . The L.A. affair was a sell out and I'm so relieved you thought well of the speech knowing the circumstances of its preparation. The 2 days in Palm Springs — dreadful place — night clubs and neons — were OK and I got my "desk" cleaned up with Miss E. [Carol Evans] who'll stay there a few days to get the letters out. I think they netted

[21] Later, while in Asia, Stevenson decided not to visit Iran since the internal power struggle between the shah and Mossadegh made the situation too delicate.

[22] This handwritten letter is in the possession of Mrs. Dick.

over $50,000 at L.A. — so I feel I've done my bit along with $135,000 in N.Y. toward eliminating the deficit.[23]

But the mail! Horrors — it follows us everywhere and a vast pile was awaiting us in S.F. last night. We arrived just in time to go on a TV program, then a party at Ambassador [Henry] Grady's house, now a reception in the hotel for all comers and it will be a mob scene — then a lunch on the boat, then newsreels, and then, pray God, the Golden Gate and a few days of peace before the commotion starts in Honolulu.

The Stevenson group had breakfast with George Miller, California Democratic state chairman, Mrs. India Edwards, of the Democratic National Committee, and a number of other party leaders. Immediately afterwards nearly a thousand people jammed the Gold Room of the Fairmont to honor Stevenson. It was obvious from the enthusiasm for him, as the San Francisco Chronicle *noted that day, that California Democrats had been reechoing the sentiments of his Los Angeles speech: "Out of power, the Democratic party must assert its pioneering concern for urgent human needs and bring to bear upon them its imaginative genius, kindled and warmed as always by the quality of human sympathy which has been our special distinction and strength; which has made ours the party not only of heart to feel, but of the head to do."*

The crush at that reception was such that no reception line was possible. Although Stevenson had been assured that he would not have to make a speech, to the delight of those present he stood on a chair and spoke for a few minutes. He urged everyone to support the Eisenhower Administration in the national interest of the United States. As he finished, he said that he had thought he was going on his trip as a private citizen but now he believed that he was "a trained donkey." When this elicited an enthusiastic response, his eyes twinkled and he added: "I don't mind being a donkey."

Following the reception, the Stevenson group went aboard the S.S. President Wilson, where George Killion, president of the American President Lines, had a buffet lunch for some thirty people. After lunch, when Stevenson went on deck, he was besieged by amateur photographers. Autograph collectors crowded around, as well, and he obliged all. One eight-year-old told him that his entire class had voted for him, and a three- or four-year-old called him "Mr. Eisenhower" and

---

[23] When he returned from the trip he spoke at many additional fund-raising affairs and the deficit from the 1952 campaign was finally eliminated.

asked for an autograph. *This brought gales of laughter from Stevenson, and an autograph.*

On the five-day journey to Hawaii, Stevenson spent much time answering the torrent of letters and telegrams that had awaited him in Los Angeles and San Francisco. He also read books and articles about the countries he was to visit. With his companions he discussed the questions to be asked in each country. He insisted, as he had in his public statements, that he was going as a private citizen to talk to all sorts of unofficial people: journalists, educators, trade union leaders, writers, students, and businessmen. Each of the group would gather information to help him gain as perceptive a view of each country as was possible in such a brief visit. He expressed some momentary irritation that the Department of State had insisted on alerting every embassy of his impending arrival. He explained that he was determined not to be drawn into an endless round of official receptions and dinners.

As he talked about traveling as a private citizen to listen and learn, it was obvious that he had only the slightest inkling of what lay ahead. He did know that thousands of letters from around the world had poured into his office bemoaning his defeat.

One from Norway written on February 10, 1953, stated:

> Like all the other thousands of Norwegians who followed your campaign more intently than has ever before been the case with a foreign political campaign, I was entirely captivated by the plain and direct way in which you brought the true democratic message home to each of us, pointing to the very core of democracy, the conscience of the single individual and, consequently, to the co-responsibility of each of us whenever engaged in the discharge of some petty electioneering duty as well as in our personal everyday dealings. . . .

And a letter from England, February 1, said:

> For how many years did many of us reflect cynically and sadly upon the unhappy truth of John Stuart Mill's contention that completely equalitarian democracy would mean collective mediocrity! How overjoyed we were to realize, when you appeared on the political scene, that this need not always be the case! . . .

Although Stevenson had seen many of these letters, he did not seem to realize how widely his speeches had been printed in the press of the world. As he was soon to learn, his reputation as an articulate spokesman, sensitive and sympathetic to the problems of people everywhere, had indeed preceded him.

As he continued to emphasize how he wanted to meet the common people, it was suggested that when he reached Japan he should walk in his bare feet through a paddy field. His eyes twinkled and he remarked: "Oh, I wouldn't dare. I might meet Eleanor Roosevelt coming across the field."

He also talked about his luncheon at the White House with President Eisenhower. It had been amiable, but the President had not asked him to undertake any mission for him. This was as Stevenson wished it, and he was determined that the people he talked to in various countries should understand that he was not traveling as the President's emissary. At the same time, he was not traveling as his critical opponent.[24] He made it clear that he did not want to embarrass Eisenhower during his first months in office, and, moreover, he wished to know more about the problems of Asia and the Middle East at first hand before criticizing the Republicans' conduct of foreign policy.

William Attwood, who joined the group in Honolulu, has written:

> Stevenson traveled as an American first and a Democrat second. He calmed world-wide apprehension about the new administration by stressing the policies most Democrats and Republicans have *in common:* resistance to aggression, support of the United Nations, assistance to our friends, peace without appeasement. He spoke in calm, confident, eloquent tones about his country and his faith in the good sense of the American people. He never concealed his contempt for McCarthy and his methods — but he cautioned our neighbors not to exaggerate one man's influence nor to confuse Senator Joe with Uncle Sam.[25]

Stevenson had just received the news that Stalin had suffered a stroke, and there was much speculation as to whether the Soviet Union would change after Stalin. At one point at lunch, Stevenson said: "Wouldn't it be 'wonderful' or 'awful' if we had peace — the stock market would fall and twelve million people would be unemployed." Captain Joseph D. Cox, at whose table he dined, interjected, "But we could blame the depression on Stalin." Stevenson chuckled and observed: "Oh, we Democrats will do better than that, don't worry."

At that lunch a radiogram arrived from a ship in the area, the S.S.

---

[24] Barry Bingham, "With Adlai in Asia," in *As We Knew Adlai: The Stevenson Story by Twenty-two Friends,* edited and with preface by Edward P. Doyle, foreword by Adlai E. Stevenson III (New York: Harper & Row, 1966), p. 189.

[25] "Seeing the World with Stevenson," p. 62.

Sonoma. *Stevenson read it aloud to the amusement of those at the table: "Wish you a pleasant trip and hope we get the opportunity to vote for you again."*

After lunch, while Stevenson was reading in his deck chair, a lady came up to him, introduced herself and said that she worked for Louella Parsons. "Who?" asked Adlai. "Louella Parsons," she repeated. "Who is she?" asked Adlai. When the lady left, Stevenson turned to Blair, who by now was convulsed with laughter, and said: "Who the hell is Louella Parsons?" As Blair has written, Stevenson had an "abysmal ignorance in those days of show business and show people." [26]

On the next to the last evening aboard ship, Stevenson reminisced about some of the letters he had received since his defeat. There were quite a number from ladies who extended invitations to him to visit, including one who enclosed a voluptuous photograph. Stevenson took from his briefcase a handwritten letter of some sixty pages. It was written in diary form from September to election day. The writer each day analyzed a Stevenson speech and the state of the world at that particular moment. Stevenson talked of the possibility that some of these letters might be assembled in book form. Blair commented that such a book should open with the telegram that came the day after the election: "You are better in defeat than Eisenhower is in de head."

That evening a cable arrived from Frank Fasi, Democratic National Committeeman of Hawaii, asking Stevenson to appear on his television program on Sunday. Stevenson's instant reaction was "no." But Blair told him he could not speak to a meeting of the Princeton Club that evening and refuse the request of the National Committeeman. Finally, he capitulated and told Blair to wire that "I'll be on for fifteen minutes." Blair also persuaded him not to agree to a cocktail party at the home of the Walter Dillinghams — in those days practically a command performance in Hawaii. Blair pointed out that the Dillinghams had sent their Christmas cards in October urging a vote for Eisenhower. "Moreover," he added, "it would not be fair to all the Democrats of Hawaii to go to such a party." Stevenson agreed, but since they were old friends he remarked that he would see them alone.

The last day aboard a host of radiograms came from Honolulu extending invitations to speak. One was from the Territorial Legislature. Stevenson grumbled a bit and said what a fine vacation this trip was turning out to be. For nearly an hour he kept insisting that Blair should wire a refusal. The rest of the group were equally insistent that he had to do it. Blair and Johnson told him that the Democratic party in the Islands was just becoming a real political force for the first time and

[26] "A Dazzling Decade," in *As We Knew Adlai*, p. 236.

needed the prestige of his speaking to the Legislature. Bingham pointed out that this would be the last time he would be speaking to an American audience and some leading Democrats for five months. When Bingham reached the word Democrats, Adlai beamed and observed that that would be a "great tragedy." Finally, he told Blair to send a message saying: "If you insist, I will speak." Blair adroitly persuaded him to accept the wording: "If it is imperative, I shall be happy to speak."

The Honolulu Star-Bulletin *sent a lengthy radiogram asking Stevenson for his views on some dozen questions. The message closed with: "Hope the weather is fine. Aloha." Stevenson replied: "Aloha. Weather wonderful. Aloha."*

Then he returned to writing letters and postcards.

To Mrs. Ernest L. Ives [27]

March 7, 1953

Dear Buffy —

Its been a restful voyage, even tho I've been at my desk most of the time trying to clean up the monstrous accumulation of mail mostly from the West Coast where my followers were many and aggressive. Tomorrow we reach Honolulu and I must step again into the clamor, entertaining and "appearances." I'm afraid that will be the case all the way, but we are determined to do all we can to minimize it — otherwise I'll need a sanatorium or another vacation when I get back.

I talked with Borden & J.F. [John Fell] from Palm Springs, also Adlai came to Chi to see me off. The prospects for B. [Borden] going abroad are very good. His mother even reacted well to Adlai's suggestion that J.F. should accept his school friends invitation to stay with them in England or that he should be on the "Experiment in International Living" and stay with a French family. B. wants to fly with a friend in time for the coronation, stay with Mary Spears [28] in London, for a few days & then go with his friend to Paris where the latters family live and then travel about Fr. or Italy a little until I get there. As you know its hard to plan all details by phone so I said Ok & that I would let him know when I was reaching Rome and he could meet me there. Later it occurred to me that it might be well for him to travel in the Near East with me & I wrote him that I would let him know when I got to Egypt or somewhere in the Middle East.

Just keep in touch with him about your own plans so that he can hook up with you if his plans are changed for any reason.

[27] This handwritten letter is in E.S.I., I.S.H.L.

[28] Lady Mary Spears of London, England, novelist and aunt of Stevenson's ex-wife Ellen Borden Stevenson.

You will have heard from Tim by this time. He met me at the Airport in S.F., stayed the night with me at the hotel and the next frenzied day, "Just like the campaign," and saw me off following a big farewell luncheon given by the Pres. of the Line on the ship. He was <u>fine</u> — looked fine, if a little white, spirits high and full of enthusiasm and expectation. He thinks he will be in Tokyo before I leave & if so I'll report again. As for his state of mind you have nothing to worry about; he also seems to me very level headed and sensible & I'll bet he's a sound man & officer.

I've had to write more than 100 post cards & letters ack. things on this journey & have had time for almost none of the preparation & reading I had planned —

Love,
AD.

To Mrs. Edison Dick [29]

March 7, 1953

Calif. was a clamorous chaos; the journey in a beautiful suite, courtesy of the Co.! [American President Lines] has been perfect, except that I've been obliged to work most of the time — not the reading and preparation for the journey I planned but acknowledging another avalanche of correspondence that awaited me on the ship. Some I'm returning for the files; most of it I've disposed of. Tomorrow Hawaii and more chaos and "appearances." Will it ever end — and when it does how discontented will the Discontented Dragon be!

The Perils of Publicity is fine,[30] but it needs some smoothing — too many "One must think of one's" — etc. — a form that always sounds to me a bit stilted. I don't know what to do or when I'll have time to work on it. I'll carry it along a bit and then perhaps send it back to [Lloyd] Garrison — untouched! — I'm anxious to know about Whistle Stopping, the letters etc etc.[31] And I shudder to think of the work I've left for you.

---

[29] This handwritten letter is in the possession of Mrs. Dick.

[30] Mrs. Dick had written the first draft of an essay that Stevenson might rewrite and publish. As Mrs. Dick wrote Walter Johnson on May 7, 1967, it was "a supposedly humorous short piece on the pitfalls to a human being that are brought on by sudden and extraordinary fame and adulation." "The Perils of Publicity" was never published.

[31] As a Christmas gift in 1953 for her fellow workers, Mrs. Dick had published her experiences in the 1952 presidential campaign under the title *Whistle Stopping with Adlai* (privately published, 1953). She was also selecting, for inclusion in a book, letters written to Stevenson after his defeat. The project was later abandoned.

. . . My team is fit — except for Bill [Blair] who is definitely not a sailor, but what a masterful manager.

To Benjamin H. Swig [32]

March 7, 1953

Dear Mr. Swig —
We're *rolling* along and full of happy memories of San Francisco — and, as always, gratitude to you!

Stevenson, while governor of Illinois, had attended the First Presbyterian Church of Springfield. The Reverend Richard Paul Graebel, pastor of the church, sent Stevenson copies of his recent sermons.

To the Reverend Richard Paul Graebel [33]

March 7, 1953

We're rolling along on the first leg of this appalling journey — and I've just read those first two sermons of the year again. Thanks — and thanks again for all the light and insight and heart you gave me. I yearn, curiously enough, for Spfd & my old job and dear friends.

ADLAI

Early on Saturday morning, March 7, the Stevenson party joined Captain Cox on the bridge and watched the sun rise and then Diamond Head loom in the distance. At 8 A.M., when the S.S. President Wilson docked, the official welcoming party, the reporters, and the hula dancers poured on board. Mrs. Harriet B. Magoon, secretary to Mayor Johnny Wilson, stepped in front of the Royal Hawaiian Band and sang "Ke Kali Nei Au." As the leis piled higher and higher around Stevenson's shoulders he looked at his companions and said: "I'm going under, boys." As the leis kept coming he added: "This is too many flowers. It looks like my funeral." Mrs. Charles Kauhane, wife of the Democratic minority leader of the House of Representatives, came to his rescue and began peeling some of the flowers off and draping the leis over his arm.

[32] Owner of the Fairmont Hotel, San Francisco. This handwritten postcard is in the possession of Mr. Swig.
[33] This handwritten postcard is in the possession of Mr. Graebel.

After greetings from Governor Samuel W. King, former Governor Oren E. Long, John A. Burns, chairman of the Democratic Central Committee, Gregg M. Sinclair, president of the University of Hawaii, and other leading Democrats, including John Akau, Jr., Masato Doi, Mrs. Haili Among, H. Tucker Gratz, Robert G. Dodge, and William H. Heen, the group was taken in a motorcade to the Royal Hawaiian Hotel.

At 10 A.M. Stevenson met with the Oahu members of the Hawaii Statehood Commission. Governor King explained that they feared that if Hawaii's entrance as a state was put in the same "package" as Alaska, the bill would not pass. While Hawaii had worked hard on behalf of Alaska, former Governor Long urged that Hawaii should be considered separately and judged on its own merits. President Gregg Sinclair observed: "We have fifty-five years of pupilage behind us. We have asked for statehood many times. We have passed every test. . . . We feel strongly that it is about time our case is settled."

Stevenson explained that he thought the "package" approach was the most desirable. "You know my position has been for statehood for both territories, and that has been the stand of the Democratic party. . . . You say you are for statehood for both territories. I should think the better way would be to bring joint pressure to accomplish the objectives of both territories, with Hawaii participating in behalf of Alaska."

"We would be very happy," Mr. Long replied, "to have them both become states together in a single bill, but we do not think this will happen."

Stevenson was then asked to cable two congressmen, Sam Rayburn and John McCormack — the Democratic leaders in the House of Representatives — urging that they support Hawaiian statehood separately from the question of Alaska. Stevenson replied that he would give the request serious thought and "perhaps" he would "be able to send back a message." [34]

Following this meeting the Stevenson group toured Pearl Harbor and then lunched with Admiral Arthur W. Radford and his staff. The discussion focused mainly on the sources of oil and military supplies for mainland China and North Korea.

Late that afternoon hundreds of people attended a Democratic fundraising luau at the Chinese-American Club. Stevenson attacked the roast pig, lobster, squid and other delicacies with gusto, avoiding the poi, however. Then, as William Attwood, who had just joined the group,

---

[34] He finally decided he could not support the strategy of admitting the two territories by separate bills. Statehood was defeated until Alaska was admitted in a separate bill in 1958 and Hawaii followed a year later.

noted in his diary, Stevenson proceeded "to wow hundreds of Democrats . . . with a gag-studded ad lib talk." [35]

Early the next morning, after breakfast at the Outrigger Canoe Club, the great Olympic swimmer Duke Kahanamoku, Charles Amalu and "Steamboat" Mokuahi took the Stevenson party out in a canoe to enjoy the waves of Waikiki. Later that morning the group was driven across the Pali Pass, saw the breathtaking view of the Winward side of Oahu and swam and lunched at the Kailua beach home of H. Tucker Gratz.

Returning, the party was driven around the coast and stopped for twenty minutes at the Diamond Head home of the Dillinghams. From there Stevenson rushed to the television program of Frank Fasi, where among other things, he remarked that the TV lights were "hotter than the Hawaiian noonday sun." Dinner that evening was with the Princeton Alumni Club. The members were almost totally Republican and hostile to Hawaiian statehood. In his impromptu remarks, Stevenson mentioned that he had once been president of the Princeton Club in Chicago but that he had ceased attending after entering politics because the members were "so Republican."

Back at the hotel Stevenson answered more of his correspondence. As he was leaving the suite, he remarked that if he saw another lei he would "throw up." When he reached the entrance of the hotel, the manager placed one over his head. At the airport some two hundred Democrats were there to see him off. Once again there were more leis.

After climbing aboard the Pan American Clipper, Stevenson peeled off the leis, sank back in his seat, and sighed. "Well," he said, "that's that." What he meant, William Attwood wrote later, was: "No more receptions, no more flashbulbs, no more speeches, no more handshaking, no more politics." [36]

Nine and a half hours later, on March 10, he breakfasted at Wake Island (March 9 got lost as the plane crossed the international date line). There was still plenty of evidence of the war around — tanks, blockhouses, and derelict Japanese freighters. Stevenson was inquisitive about everything and clambered with great agility around the guns Japan had captured at Singapore. Back on the plane, Stevenson spent the hours to Tokyo reading material on Japan.

He later wrote of the beginning of his journey:

[35] Although none of those in his party realized it at the time, Stevenson tried out a number of phrases and concepts that he would use a few days later in his speech to the America-Japan Society.

[36] "What Asia Thinks of Adlai," *Look*, June 30, 1953.

REPORT BY ADLAI STEVENSON [37]

In flight, mid-Pacific

As a boy, I collected stamps and dreamed of far places and strange peoples. Now fortune has granted me a journey of exploration around this shrunken world, and during the next few months I will visit lands in which dwell a billion of our neighbors.

What are these billion neighbors doing and thinking about the Red Shadow? Can we avoid the lunacy of atomic war? What about Korea? Has Stalin's death really changed Soviet strategy? What mistakes are we making? Are we winning or losing the global struggle for men's minds and hearts? And what more can we do — or should we do?

These and many more questions kept me awake in the Clipper after we took off from Honolulu for ancient Asia. My thoughts ranged back to the night ten years ago when I took off from Pearl Harbor in a huge, noisy Navy seaplane bound for our outpost on Midway Island. Japan was our enemy then; Russia our ally. Now my companions and I were flying to a friendly Japan and Russia was the free world's foe.

Looking back through history, it is plain to see that the center of gravity in world affairs has been moving westward from the Tigris and Euphrates valleys, the fertile crescent of the Middle East, to Egypt, to Athens, to Rome, through the Europe of Charlemagne, to England, which kept the Pax Britannica for 100 years. And now in our time, out of the violent convulsions of two world wars, North America — the United States — has suddenly emerged as this center of gravity, albeit unconsciously and unintentionally.

A great destiny, yes, but not a happy fate. For further west lies Asia, home of more than half of the earth's inhabitants. And Asia is in the torment of rebirth, groping and struggling and experimenting with new concepts of freedom, of nationalism, of democracy — and communism.

So I decided to go to Asia first, then the Middle East, and to come home through the more familiar lands of Europe.

---

[37] *Look*, May 19, 1953. This is the introduction to his first article, which also included his visits to Japan, Korea, Formosa and Hong Kong. That material is reprinted after the editorial description of the visit to each.

Two

Japan

MARCH 10-14;

MARCH 18-19, 1953

W*hen Stevenson stepped out of the Pan American Clipper in Tokyo at 3:00 P.M. on March 10, he was met by what the Tokyo Eve-ning News described as "the vortex of a shoving, jabbing, prodding, maelstrom of animate flesh." As the crowd surged around Stevenson, everybody seemed to have cameras. He blinked, flashed his quick grin, and remarked: "Japan looks more like a photocracy than a democracy to me."*

The Evening News headlined the arrival of "Citizen Adlai" and wel-comed him by reprinting his speech accepting the Democratic nomi-nation. "Once in a while, much too rarely," the paper wrote, "expres-sions of certain basic philosophical principles are made in such a lucid convincing manner as to make the words more memorable with time. Adlai Stevenson . . . rendered an address which was, we firmly believe, one of the most cogent interpretations of the true spirit of democracy — humility coupled with recognition of obligation to serve the general welfare — that has been heard in many years." [1]

Cars from the American embassy drove the party to Frank Lloyd Wright's Imperial Hotel and then to the embassy for a briefing by Am-bassador Robert Murphy and his staff. It was one of the most informa-tive briefings of the entire trip. Stevenson himself busily jotted down notes and asked a number of questions. The political attaché discussed Prime Minister Shigeru Yoshida's Liberal party (which at that point

[1] Hessell Tiltman, " 'Citizen Adlai' in Japan," *New Republic*, March 30, 1953, pp. 8–9, has a fine summary of reactions to the visit.

was so rent with factionalism that Yoshida was fighting to save his post), *the Progressive Reform party, the right- and left-wing Socialist parties, and the Communist party. It was emphasized that many intellectuals seemed to be moving toward the Marxist-oriented* (*but not Soviet-controlled*) *left Socialist party. The party, with its stand for neutralism and opposition to the rearmament of Japan, had wide appeal. Their firm stand against amending the constitution to permit rearmament placed the United States in an unenviable position, Ambassador Murphy observed. During the occupation we had insisted on the no-rearmament clause in the constitution and now we were pressing for the opposite.*

There was considerable discussion in depth about the economic situation with emphasis on the problems of too many people, too little land, too few resources, and Japan's pressing need of expanding its world markets. When it came time for the public affairs officer, Saxton Bradford, to speak, he observed that it was difficult to chart the attitudes of any public. Stevenson interrupted: "Yes, I know. I tried that and I failed."

At one point Bradford stated that many Japanese intellectuals were a generation behind thinkers in Europe and the United States. They had been isolated from outside contacts by their militarist governments since the early 1930's and by our military occupation. As a result, many Socialists, labor leaders, writers, and teachers were talking the language of the political radical of a generation ago. And they had little or no knowledge of Stalinist Russia. Instead, they remembered the pre-Stalinist Marxist slogans and responded emotionally to the old fighting phrases. Stevenson was intrigued with this analysis and asked Johnson to pursue it further with Bradford and some Japanese intellectuals.

The public affairs officer concluded his briefing by remarking that when he had come into the room before we arrived to check the map that was facing us he found a sign which read "Adlai for '56." Stevenson responded: "I'm against your public relations program."

Stevenson held a brief press conference at the insistence of Japanese reporters and foreign correspondents immediately after the briefing. He made it clear that it would be pretentious for him to speak about Japan.

It was remarks like this during his visit that prompted Ernie Hill to write to the Chicago Daily News *that Stevenson had resolved "that he will not become the new American pop-off." Stevenson declined daily, Hill added, "to harangue the Eisenhower Administration . . . or 'expert' the world situation on a day-to-day basis. . . . For that and other reasons, he made a tremendous hit in Japan and Korea. He is regarded here as a statesman with intellect and wit."* [2]

[2] Chicago *Daily News,* March 19, 1953.

When a reporter asked why he was taking the trip, Stevenson explained that circumstances over which he had had no control had made him unemployed and afforded the chance to travel as a private citizen. And, he added: "I came to inspect Asia, which has a great bearing on the present world situation and the future of America."

To the question whether the death of Stalin would mean that the Soviet Union would be easier to work with, Stevenson pointed out that he was out of touch with developments. It would be unwise, however, to assume that Stalin's death meant any abrupt alteration in Russian foreign policy.

When he was asked what he thought about Japan's building up its military strength, he replied that free nations must be strong to meet the challenge of Soviet aggression. He expressed the hope that the Japanese people would conclude that their best interests coincided with those of the United States. But as to the specific question of Japan's rearmament, he said: "I am not in a position to comment on the issue. I think the Japanese will pass the best judgment on it." [3]

Barry Bingham wrote: "Adlai had to be amazingly nimble at press conferences to avoid the booby traps that were laid for him. The remarkable thing was that he managed to say so much of substance without once crossing the line of propriety on American foreign policy he had drawn in his own mind." [4]

After the press conference the Stevenson group dined with Foreign Minister Katsuo Okazaki and twenty Japanese officials and businessmen. "Nobody learned anything," William Attwood noted in his diary. After this affair, Attwood, Bingham and Johnson avoided as many formal dinners and receptions as possible in order to gather information. Although Stevenson and Blair could not avoid them, Hessell Tiltman, Tokyo correspondent for the Manchester Guardian, wrote: " 'Citizen Adlai' kept the time-wasting to a minimum." [5] And Ernie Hill reported: "While Stevenson was forced to attend a certain number of protocol functions . . . his aides were out talking with rank and file." [6]

The morning after arrival — March 11 — Stevenson and Blair went to the U.S. Far East Command for a briefing on the Korean situation. Attwood talked to a number of reporters and he, Bingham and Johnson interviewed many callers at the Imperial Hotel who wished to see Stevenson.

[3] *Mainichi,* March 11, 1953.

[4] "With Adlai in Asia," in *As We Knew Adlai: The Stevenson Story by Twenty-two Friends,* edited and with preface by Edward P. Doyle, foreword by Adlai E. Stevenson III (New York: Harper & Row, 1966), p. 193.

[5] " 'Citizen Adlai' in Japan," p. 8.

[6] Chicago *Daily News,* March 12, 1953.

Stevenson's aides followed the practice here and in other countries of interviewing a wide range of people, reporting what they learned to Stevenson, and recommending that he himself interview some of those who seemed to be the best informed. For instance, most of the morning of March 11, Johnson spent interviewing Wolf Ladejinsky, formerly of the Department of Agriculture, who had been in Japan since 1945 and had been influential in the Japanese land reform program. He discussed the new political power of the farmer, problems created by the expanding birth rate, and the economic situation in general. He emphasized that the difficulties facing Japan were compounded because the United States had helped arouse greater expectations of freedom, democracy, and a better life. If these were unfulfilled, then there would be "immense resentment, disillusionment and restlessness."

When this interview was completed, Johnson arranged for Stevenson and Ladejinsky to have a conference together later.

The Stevenson group lunched with General Mark Clark and afterwards visited the Tokyo General Hospital to talk with some of the Korean war wounded. On the way to the hotel, Stevenson remarked that he was tired. Attwood wrote in his diary: "If he tries to keep up this pace he's going to crack before the trip's over — and already cables, invitations to speak, letters, dinner invitations are pouring in from all over S. E. Asia. It's tough being a reporter when you're also a VIP."

Back at the hotel, Stevenson plunged into a conversation with Donald Kingsley, the director of the United Nations Korean Reconstruction Agency. Kingsley stressed that it would be a waste of time to increase the army of South Korea unless it was backed up by a viable economy. He explored in some detail what this involved and also discussed President Syngman Rhee's hatred of Japan.

At six P.M. Stevenson held a press conference in reverse with a number of foreign correspondents. He asked all the questions. There was a discussion of the attempt to oust Prime Minister Yoshida, concurrence that the United States was pushing Japan too fast and too hard on rearmament, and agreement that President Rhee's stubborn hostility to Japan made economic development in Korea difficult. "His tireless questioning," Hessell Tiltman wrote, "indicated he was interested in about everything." [7]

Stevenson and Blair dined with Progressive party leader Mamoru Shigemitsu, Bingham and Attwood were the guests of foreign correspondents at a family-type geisha house, and Johnson dined with Ukai Nobushige, professor of political science at Tokyo University. He analyzed the reasons why many writers and teachers believed Japan should

[7] "'Citizen Adlai' in Japan," p. 9.

[25]

be uncommitted in the struggle between the United States and the Soviet Union, the danger that rearmament might enable the extreme rightist militarists to regain power, and the restlessness among a large number of university graduates who could not find employment. He also stated that many intellectuals feared that the election of Eisenhower would mean more militarism in the United States. Since they did not approve of militarism in Japan, they did not like it in the United States. He added that the election of Richard M. Nixon in their minds represented McCarthyism taking over the government.

Meanwhile, after dinner, Stevenson and Blair joined Bingham and Attwood at the geisha house. "Stevenson had hesitated about coming until he learned that this type of house was as proper as a vicarage," Attwood wrote in his diary. "At 11 we put on our shoes and tottered away. At the door, the owner bowed very ceremoniously and bade us farewell in English: 'Take it easy.' I wish we could. If we keep up this pace — or Adlai anyway — we'll all be in Tokyo General Hospital within a week."

The next morning Stevenson, Blair, and Bingham called on the prime minister and other officials. Attwood interviewed Professor Lawrence Battistini, who had been in Japan for the past seven years. He had prepared a memorandum for Stevenson which insisted that the United States was losing out ideologically all over Asia heavily because we were identified with militarism and colonialism. Later, when Attwood gave Stevenson the statement, Attwood remarked that some of the conclusions sounded pretty heretical. "What's the matter with heresy?" Stevenson inquired. "We need it."

Meanwhile, Johnson spent the morning talking with Robert A. Scalapino, professor of political science at the University of California, Berkeley. (Stevenson had read with profit an article of his entitled "Reflections on American Relations with Japan," prepared for an Institute of Pacific Relations Conference held in Honolulu in January, 1953.) Johnson and Scalapino had a widely ranging discussion of the Japanese social structure, the trade unions, the right-wing movements and the Communist party, both of which were strongly nationalistic and antiforeign.

At noon the entire Stevenson group went to luncheon at the America-Japan Society. The largest crowd in the society's history (over eight hundred) came to hear Stevenson's only public speech in Japan. Takashi Komatsu, president of the society, in introducing Stevenson, said that words were inadequate to express what was in their hearts for him. He then quoted from Stevenson's message of concession to Presi-

dent Eisenhower on election night as an outstanding example of the give and take necessary for a democracy. Stevenson's speech follows.

THE IMPORTANCE OF ASIA
IN THE STRUGGLE OF THE FREE [8]

Mr. Komatsu, President Saito, Ambassador Murphy, Count Kabayama, distinguished guests, and my friends of the Japanese-America Society: I was going to say my fellow Democrats and then I was reminded that perhaps the election was over. I was profoundly flattered by the chairman including me at the top of their list of visitors to this famous organization. I also noted that most of them were Republicans. Well, I have my reward at last — I was at the bottom in November and now I am at the top. But I had to come all the way to Tokyo, and Tokyo doesn't vote apparently.

Mr. Komatsu has told you about his long residence in my state and that he attended both high school and college in Monmouth, Illinois. This is a very happy circumstance, because if you should ask me any questions about Illinois, I would immediately refer them to Mr. Komatsu, who doubtless knows more about my beloved state than many of its residents.

I am sure that those of you who didn't hear what I have had to say will realize that's your good fortune.[9] Indeed, I had thought not to speak at all during this journey and I believe that what's happened here today confirms my every intention, but I must thank you from the bottom of my heart for your invitation to come here and for your presence in such large numbers, and I don't even blame the Republicans for the interference. In fact I think the intercession was more divine than human or Republican — and there's quite a difference between Republicans and divinity.

I should like also to thank the photographers for turning off the lights; this is the first time I have been able to see across the hall.[10] Indeed I had about come to the conclusion that the new society in Japan was a "photocracy," not a democracy.

On this matter of speaking, when you are supposed to be looking and listening, rather recalls to me a remark, which many of you perhaps will

[8] The text is from the America-Japan Society *Bulletin*, February-March, 1953.

[9] The public address system failed at this point. The engineer could not repair it, so Stevenson spoke without it.

[10] The U.S. Army had installed huge lights to film the speech. When some in the Stevenson party objected because the lights disturbed everyone, they were turned off.

remember, that Disraeli made many years ago. When a young member of the House of Commons came to him and said, "Mr. Prime Minister, do you think I should engage actively in the debate?" the Prime Minister made an appraising study of this man's callow countenance and said, "No, I don't think you should, it would be better if the House wondered why you didn't talk rather than why you did." This may teach you a lesson about asking itinerant visitors such as myself to speak before your Society.

It may be true, as Mr. Komatsu has pointed out so generously, that I used to be a politician. However, you need have no fear on that account you are now about to be exposed to a political speech. I am not a politician but only a traveler. Indeed, when I was in Hawaii the other day, some graduates from my university, Princeton, presented me with a scroll. It was a charming scroll full of agreeable sentiments, and concluded with the remark, "now that your political career is over." Well, I thanked them as graciously as I could for such a considerate epitaph. It is rather better to know when your political career is over than merely suspect it. I couldn't but think of the old professor at Columbia University whom Nicholas Murray Butler used to talk about, who lived to a ripe old age. President Butler didn't like him very much and when he died, he was asked by the faculty to write his epitaph, and some of you may remember it ran like this: "Here lies the body of Professor George Johnson, died at forty, buried at eighty."

Instead of making a speech at all, what I propose to do today is simply to try to outline, and perhaps for my own satisfaction as much I hope as for yours, some of the reasons that have caused me to take up my present occupation of world travelling.

But one of the reasons that I shall pass over lightly, is a certain event that overtook me on my way to the White House; and the second reason, of course, is like all of us who have worked in government and in politics, we defer going back to working for a living as long as we can. I thought some of you might want to know what made me seize this opportunity to set off on a trip around the world in the first place and to start it with a visit to Japan, in the second.

It goes without saying, of course, that I am traveling as a private citizen with no official, or, indeed, semi-official mission to accomplish. But perhaps all the more on that account the reasons that impelled me to come straight to Asia rather than Europe and to plan my journey with most of the emphasis on the Orient might be of interest, because they are reasons which, I think, are those the great majority of my fellow countrymen would share. It goes without saying also that I have long wanted to see Japan with my own eyes. I heard tales of it from my infancy from my father, who came and stayed here before the turn of the century. I am distressed that our visit is so short, but perhaps it's better on the whole because your hospitality and courtesy has been so gracious that perhaps if my visit were to be longer I should never go home at all.

To speak these days of the increased importance of the Orient to the United States is, of course, to deal in a cliché of the most resounding sort. In fact to use another ponderous bromide, we are living in the age of communication and all parts of the world are increasingly important to all other parts. However, there is, I think, a special significance for all of us, and one felt especially keenly by all of you here today, in the increased importance of the relations between our two countries in particular. Though we celebrate its centenary this year, it's only a moment in historical time since the day the Black Ships of Commodore Perry sailed into Edo Bay. That moment marked the final meeting of eastern and western civilizations in their courses around the globe. It was a moment that could not, indeed cannot, for in a sense we are still living in it, ever come again. It was and is a unique moment in world history and one that brackets Japan and America together indelibly in a relationship that no other two nations in the world can ever hope to share.

We think sometimes of the migration of the center of gravity in historical times. The center of gravity in world affairs moved from the Tigris and the Euphrates Basin to the Egypt of the Pharaohs; to the great Attic civilization of Greece, thence to Rome; and, moving ever westward, to the France of Charlemagne; to London and then, only in our time, that great leap across the Atlantic to the United States of America. Moving ever westward . . . Japan on the rim of the Pacific, lies, once distant, but now closer and closer toward the center of gravity in world affairs. It's obvious to anyone, I suppose, that Asia is in what might be called this era of decision, this area of decision as well, in our modern world. Evidences of that, some tragic as in Red China, or in war-wrecked Korea, some heartening, as in the Philippines, India, Pakistan, confront us on all sides.

But what seems to me to be more pertinent at the moment, here in Tokyo for the first time is that we in the United States and Japan are also, in this centennial year of Japan's re-emergence into the community of nations, at a crucial time of decision. In a very real sense, this nation is the one in whose hands the destiny of Asia and thus of the world may rest. Whether it is to be a free or a slave world is, of course, the decision that we all face in this era of decision. But the point I should like to make is that Americans, all of them, not just sightseeing travelers such as myself and my associates, are aware of Japan's critical importance in the way that the decision will finally be made.

What we Americans foresee is, of course, not only a free world but especially a community of Pacific nations to balance the great free community of European nations to both of which, and to one no more than the other, the countries of the Western Hemisphere belong. Well, that sums up, if I may say so, as best I can on short notice and in short order the basic reasons that set us forth on this trip in a westerly direction. We have a billion neighbors in the world. It was to see some of our billion neighbors of the free world that I thought it a suitable time to travel a bit, and yet as I take it for granted that my basic assumption about Asia in general and Japan in particular are shared by most Americans, I assume that it is my job on this trip less to tell Asians about Americans than to find out something about Asians to tell Americans when I get back. To say that we have a basic awareness of Asia's importance is not, I regret to admit, to say that we have any considerable part of the knowledge we must develop as to how we can best build our Pacific community and make it live up to its undreamed of potentialities.

I felt at the outset, as we used to say, "this trip was necessary," if only, as I say, to diminish my own ignorance. If I can bring some information that will do the same for any of my fellow countrymen, I shall feel that it has all been well worth while.

The question that history asks and which Japan as well as America must answer is whether this idea, this ancient idea, of individualism — the idea of personal freedom for you and for me — is equal to the idea of collectivism — the idea of personal subordination to the state; whether the idea of maximum personal liberty is equal to the idea of maximum personal discipline.

This old contest between freedom and despotism, which is renewed in every generation, is acute within ours, and likewise the conflict between national independence and national subordination.

I don't think that war is an inevitable part of this gigantic contest. Even the most ambitious and ruthless men don't deliberately invite destruction on the basis of their power. They can throw, to be sure, the iron dice, but they cannot foretell the fortunes of war.

We who are free must have great strength in order that weakness will not tempt the ambitious, as we have seen all too well in Korea latterly, and, even in our time, throughout Europe in this bloody generation. The measure of the strength we must have is not what we would like to afford but what the adversary compels us to afford.

No one can predict, and it would be foolish to try to predict, how and when the peaceful purposes of our power will succeed in creating durable peace. But are our efforts conditional upon assurance of prompt success? To answer "yes" to that question would be to accept the certainty of eventual defeat.

Coexistence is not a form of passive acceptance of things as they are. Coexistence means waging the contest between freedom and tyranny in peaceful terms by peaceful means. It will involve negotiation and adjustment — compromise, if you please, but not appeasement — and I, for one, would never shrink from these if they would advance the security of the world.

Though our progress may be slow, it can be steady and it can be sure. A wise man does not try to hurry history. Many wars have been avoided by patience and many have been precipitated by reckless haste.

In Europe, our efforts to build patiently for peace, as you well know, are meeting with success. The Marshall Plan has brought, as we all know, a striking improvement in the political and economic conditions. The North Atlantic Treaty Organization is building a strong system of military defenses. Europe is not yet wholly secure against subversion within or attack from without, but this goal of security is, at least, in sight.

I wish I could say the same for Asia, but there would be no greater disservice to our people at home than to underestimate the gravity of the dangers in this area, and perhaps for many, many years to come.

Across the continent of Asia more than a billion of the world's peoples are churning in one of history's greatest upheavals and convulsions. All the struggles of man over the centuries — economic, political and spiritual — have come together in Asia and now seem to be reaching a climax.

The causes behind that upheaval are many and varied. But there is nothing complicated about what the people want, at least that's what we think. What they want is simply a decent living — and they want some measure of freedom for themselves and their countries.

The word used most frequently by Asians to describe their aspirations, as we understand it, is the word nationalism. Nationalism to Asians means, I suppose, a chance to stand on their own feet, a chance to govern themselves, a chance to develop their resources for their own welfare. It means the end of legalized inferiority. It means pride, spirit and faith.

And this type of nationalism is not inconsistent with closer cooperation among nations nor with the need for an enforceable peace. I suspect that many Asians actually regard freedom and national independence as the doorway to international order — just as we do.

Russia's interest here in Asia is nothing new.

The expansionist aims of Russia didn't change with the passing of the Czars. But today the glove of a revolutionary ideology covers the steel hand of imperialist expansion.

The strategy, it seems to us, of communism in Asia is to pose as the champion — the only champion — of the Asian peoples. Communism has not created the cause or the forces behind this vast upheaval. Rather it is attempting to give direction to these long incipient forces. It seeks to impose its own label on the multiple revolutions going on in Asia today by identifying itself with the deeply felt needs and hopes and wants of peoples.

There is an important difference, it seems to me, between communism as we view it and communism as some of the people in Asia view it. When we in the United States think of communism we think of what we are going to lose. And when many of the Asiatics think of communism they think of what they are going to win — especially if they believe that they have nothing to lose.

It's important, then, that we in America and in Japan know these things and think about them, for we shall never be able to cope with communism unless we understand the emotional basis of its appeal. They have failed to incite the workers to revolution in Western Europe. They have failed to turn the western allies one against the other.

But the communists may well believe that in the aspirations and the grievances of the East they have the key to world power. They hope, and perhaps even expect, that we cannot rise to this challenge in the East.

Furthermore, they may not feel the same need for quick and tidy solutions that is felt in certain quarters in America. They may believe that they can afford to have a patience equal to the enormity of the stakes involved.

And the stakes are nothing less than the overwhelming preponderance of power, for with more and more of Asia under the iron fist, they could turn with new energy and vast new resources in an effort to win a bloodless victory in a weakened and frightened Europe.

These expectations define the dimensions of the threat we face and of the tasks which lie ahead of us — tasks which can be met only by disciplined, resourceful, imaginative, and reasoned effort. It is an effort which has, it seems to us, two parts: defense, first, and development.

There is active fighting, as we all know, in Malaya and Indochina. What will the defensive task require in these areas, and in Japan, in the Philippines, Formosa, India and elsewhere? What contributions, what commitments to the security of this area should the U.S. make, and can it make these commitments effectively to the emerging system of Pacific defense? These are some of the questions, the hard, the ugly questions, that we must all face before disaster and not afterward.

In Korea the United Nations took a long step toward building a security system in Asia. As an American I am proud that we had the courage to resist that ruthless, cynical aggression; and history will never record that Korea was a "useless" war, unless today's heroism is watered with tomorrow's cowardice.

I believe we may in time look back at Korea and the events of this post-war period here in Japan, our reconciliation and community of friendship and common peaceful purpose, as a major turning point in history — and a turning point which led not to another terrible war, but to the first historic demonstration that an effective system of collective security is possible.

Having failed to defeat us on the field of battle, the enemy in Korea now seeks to defeat us by exhausting our patience. But the contest with tyranny is not a hundred-yard dash — it is a test of endurance.

This defensive effort in Korea and elsewhere in Asia and this miracle of Japanese-American relations are building a shield behind which we have the opportunity to assist in that other great task — the task of development. By working with each country to expand the production of its goods, goods which are needed by other countries in the region, a self-generating and self-financing cycle of trade and development can be initiated, which will reduce and can eventually eliminate the need for the more direct and, perforce, temporary forms of American aid. At the same time, we can enlarge our export markets and develop new sources of the products we need to import. These programs are in accordance, it seems to me, with our best traditions. And I think I can assure our friends in Asia that America will never seek to dominate their political and their economic development. We think of this in terms of partnership. We will not try to make their societies over in the image of our own. On the contrary, we respect the integrity of their institutions and the rich values of their cultures. We expect to learn as well as to teach.

Technical assistance programs are primarily concerned with the material needs and wants of individual men and women. Yet we do not make the mistake of believing that the answer to communist materialism is simply a different brand of materialism.

The answer to communism is, in the old-fashioned phrase, good works — good works inspired by love and dedicated to the whole man. The answer to the inhumanity of communism is humane respect. And the men and the women of Asia desire not only to rise from wretchedness of the body but from abasement of the spirit as well.

In other words, I suggest that we must strive for a harmony of means and of ends in our relations with Asia — and indeed with the rest of the world. The means of our cooperation, to be sure, are primarily material.

If we believe this threat in Asia is dangerous to us, then it is in our own self-interest to help the Asiatics defend and develop, adjusting our policies to the constantly changing circumstances in a world of accelerating change. But we must not, in our necessary concern for the urgent tasks of defense and development, permit, if you please, the means to obscure the ends. That end is the widening and the deepening of freedom and of respect for the dignity and the worth of men, Asiatic or Occidental.

Some may say to you that this is visionary stuff. To this I would reply that history has shown again and again that the self-styled realists are the real visionaries — for their eyes are fixed on a past that cannot be recaptured. The summons of the twentieth century is a summons to our vision, to our humanity, to our practicality. If these provide the common purpose of America and of Japan, of our joint enterprise, of our progress together, we need have no fear of the future. Because the future will belong to free men.

This lovely land and this government and these friendly people whose destiny, whose hopes, are linked inextricably with our own . . . to them I am profoundly grateful for their welcome here in Tokyo. We in our country ask of no nation anything for ourselves; we ask nothing we could not ask for humanity itself. We know how sorely tried this great country is, how appalling are the economic obstacles it faces, but we know, and Japan knows, that security and peace in this tormented world is not a gift but a prize. In the struggle for that prize I pray that Americans and Japanese will rub shoulders for generations to come.

And, in conclusion, may I add but another word, and that is that before I set off on this long journey I lunched with the President of the United States. He asked me particularly to bring his good wishes, his respect and his friendship to our friends throughout the world. I know of no better place than this meeting of Japanese and Americans here in Tokyo to bring you the greetings of the President of the United States. Thank you.

Japanese reporters commented delightedly after this speech that Stevenson, unlike so many American visitors, was not patronizing or im-

patient. And the Nippon Times *wrote: "It is reassuring that an American leader of Mr. Stevenson's caliber has added his voice to the growing recognition of the important role of Asia in the world wide struggle to keep freedom alive."* [11]

Reporters clamored for copies of the speech. It required considerable time to supply them with the verbatim text because Stevenson had continued to make changes in his manuscript up to the moment of delivery.

During the afternoon Stevenson interviewed a number of people in his room, and later the entire party dined with Ambassador Murphy and his guests, who included Prime Minister Yoshida and several ambassadors.

At seven the next morning, Stevenson and Kenneth Young, chief of the Northeast Asia Division of the Department of State, visited the huge fish market, where Stevenson sampled raw fish, and then the vegetable market, where he ate with delight some beautiful strawberries. At nine the Stevenson group flew in the ambassador's plane to the airfield near Osaka. Walter Nichols, Japanese-speaking public affairs officer of the U.S. Information Agency, joined Stevenson as interpreter. En route by car to Kyoto, Stevenson asked to see an industrial plant. He walked into the Kanebo Spinning Company, unannounced, and toured the plant with the assistant manager as his guide. Stevenson busily asked questions about wages, working conditions and pricing. Meanwhile, photographers who had met him at the airport were taking pictures.

He reached the Miyako Hotel in Kyoto in time for lunch and immediately thereafter, trailed by three cars of newspapermen, he visited the Detached Palace, built in 1590. The next stop was a Buddhist temple, the Nishi Hongwanji. After touring the temple he had tea and cakes with a group of priests. The abbot gave Stevenson an oblong lacquered object. He looked puzzled and turned to his aides. "Boys," he whispered, "what the hell do you suppose this is?" They shrugged. He turned to the abbot and said warmly: "Sir, I haven't the faintest idea what you've given me, but never in my whole life have I been so touched." After the ceremony he drove to the famous Heian Shinto Shrine. By this time, the head of the tourist section of the Kyoto municipality had joined him, along with more photographers and reporters.

Before retiring that evening, Stevenson wrote his daily quota of postcards and some letters.

---

[11] Cited in Tiltman, " 'Citizen Adlai' in Japan," p. 8.

To Mrs. Ernest L. Ives [12]

[no date]

Dear Buff —

So far so good — altho I'm getting a little tired already. We flew here in Ambassador [Robert D.] Murphy's plane after some hectic days in Tokyo. I saw everyone — Jap. & Am. — and will see the Emperor when I go back to Tokyo before leaving for Formosa.

Tomorrow we go to Korea — [General] Mark Clark is sending his plane for me and I have no complaints about the reception I've had here!

The journey out was Ok, but I had to work on the horrible accumulation of correspondence on the ship most of the time.

This is a lovely old city — full of shrines & antiquities but Tokyo is hideous.

Love to Ernest & I pray your jaw is mending! [13]

Love
AD

At eight the next morning he visited with a small group of students and faculty at Doshisha University. The students explained the attraction of Communism for many of their contemporaries, and they complained of the friction and disorder in Japanese politics under the democratic system that the United States had "imposed." One student asked Stevenson what he had meant by the phrase in his speech before the America-Japan Society "don't rush history" and then demanded, "Just what is democracy, anyway?"

Stevenson replied for some five minutes, demonstrating not only that he could be gracious but that he could be blunt. During the last two world wars, he explained, the problem of the freedom of the individual was central to the conflicts. This was a great concept, he added, but it was an idea that could not be forced on people. On the other hand, the Communists had imposed their ideas by force on a number of nations. Democracy, he continued, "is honest disagreement. It is the right to hold the opinion you believe in, and to fight for it with self-respect and determination. The virtue of democracy is not cold order. It is the heat of men's minds rubbing against each other, sending out sparks. It is liberty with responsibility. It is a struggle that never ends and is always worth the fight." [14]

[12] This handwritten letter is in the Elizabeth Stevenson Ives collection, Illinois State Historical Library. It is postmarked March 14, 1953.

[13] Mrs. Ives's orthodontist had prescribed an appliance to try to correct her jaw condition, but had not resorted to surgery.

[14] See Barry Bingham, "East Asians Seem to Have Made Stevenson Symbol of What They Want America to Be," Louisville *Courier-Journal*, May 3, 1953.

For Japanese students to have freedom, he continued, would require constant struggle and they should not be so impatient as to go to either the extreme right or the extreme left whenever a problem occurred. He added that he was greatly disturbed that so many Japanese intellectuals were not offering leadership. "The trouble with intellectuals," he said, "is that they see so much they do not always see things very clearly and, as a result, the intellectual is apt to be wobbly."

After leaving the university he visited the United States Cultural Center in Kyoto, and then took off, at noon on March 14, on a military plane for four and a half days in Korea.[15]

On March 18 he returned to the Tokyo airport at nine P.M. and went immediately to the hotel. At breakfast the next morning some of the group, including Stevenson, were a bit shaky, having been sick most of the night. But with his "chronic stamina," he was off early to borrow a cutaway from the ambassador for his visit to the emperor. After this protocol visit, Stevenson and Wolf Ladejinsky spent hours in the countryside inspecting Japanese farming at first hand. They were accompanied by Stevenson's nephew, Lieutenant Tim Ives, and Miss Ellen Davies and Miss Bertrande Benoist, who had been seated with him at the captain's table aboard the S.S. President Wilson.

Meanwhile, others in the group continued to interview knowledgeable people. Bingham and Attwood met with individual Japanese and American reporters, including Wu Tang, of the Pan Asia Newspaper Alliance, and Robert Eunson, of the Associated Press. Johnson met with Professor Allen Cole, of the Fletcher School of Law and Diplomacy, who was studying social mobility and the Japanese class structure. Through Cole, Johnson met Miss Yoko Matsuoka, a freelance journalist, who discussed the changed status of women since 1945 and the strong opposition among women to rearmament. Johnson also talked to Hessell Tiltman, Tokyo correspondent for the Manchester Guardian, about Formosa and explored with him the reliability of some of the information Stevenson had received on Japan. Johnson followed the same procedure with sociologist Herbert Passin, who had been in Japan for seven years and was currently doing research on a Social Science Research Fellowship.

During the afternoon Gordon Bowles, of Tokyo International House, arranged for Stevenson and Johnson to meet with a group of seven Japanese intellectuals, including Yoshishige Abe, president of Peers College; Shigeru Matsumoto, managing director of International House; Yoshisaburo Matsukata, director of the Kyodo News Service; and Masao Maruyama, professor of political science at Tokyo University.

There was general agreement that the occupation had made many

[15] This visit is discussed in Chapter Three.

important contributions to Japan, but that it had pushed too much and now there was the added danger of the United States pushing too fast on rearmament. Young people were vigorously opposed to this, as were women. One of the group explained that young people were shocked by the defeat of Japan in view of the way they had been taught that Japan was divine and invincible. Their disillusionment over the defeat had made them passionately in favor of peace.

There was irritated objection from the group to President Eisenhower's campaign statement that "Asians should fight Asians." [16] The implication was, they insisted, that Asians should be mercenaries for the United States. Instead, they believed that "Asians should assist Asians" in economic development. (Stevenson had heard already from Ambassador Murphy and others of the bitter reaction to Eisenhower's remark.)

One of those present stated that the United States was not at all well known in Japan. The picture many people had was of the pre–New Deal nation. There would be more respect for American leadership if Asians knew about the growth of trade unions, the social security system, the extension of governmental controls over the economy, and the widespread improvement in the standard of living of so many Americans since the Great Depression.

At six o'clock that evening a group of Japanese editors and publishers held a party in Stevenson's honor. Stevenson did the questioning, but, as Attwood noted in his diary: "All were rather circumspect." One editor did remark, however, that "all too frequently the United States supported people who can speak English instead of people who have quality regardless of their command of the language."

Before leaving Tokyo, Stevenson dined with some of the younger members of the embassy staff, including Saxton Bradford and Wolf Ladejinsky. They spoke of the apprehension felt throughout Asia at what the Eisenhower-Dulles policies might be. For this reason, they told Stevenson, he would receive a great welcome especially in Southeast Asia where he was regarded as a symbol of a temperate, nonaggressive policy with the emphasis more on economic assistance and less on military considerations. Stevenson's reaction to all this was one of embarrassment. He pointed out that the times were so critical that it was more important to help Eisenhower than to criticize him unless his policies were obviously against the national interest.

Following dinner, Stevenson boarded a Northwest Airlines flight that took off for Taiwan (Formosa) at one A.M., March 20.

After Stevenson had left Japan, Hessell Tiltman wrote:

[16] New York Times, October 3, 1952.

. . . Stevenson covered an immense amount of useful ground and impressed all comers with his unusual combination of modesty and competence. . . . Japanese with whom I talked were immensely impressed by the grasp of essentials, breadth of outlook and "world eye" displayed by the visitor. . . .

"Citizen Adlai," the most important private citizen seen in Tokyo since the Pacific war, lived up to the advance billing. If his world-trip may be regarded as a pilgrimage, then the ex-Governor of Illinois is the ideal of what an American pilgrim should strive to be — modest, reticent, eloquent when necessary, competent, essentially democratic, and — so far as the circumstances made possible — accessible. . . .[17]

Stevenson wrote of his visit to Japan:

REPORT BY ADLAI STEVENSON [18]

The first glimpse of Asia was miles of neat seaweed gardens in Tokyo Bay, a reminder that, in vast areas of the earth, there is neither land nor water to waste, and the principal preoccupation of scores of millions is how to keep alive. Then, suddenly, Tokyo spread out endlessly below us along the confusing coast and away toward the steep mountains.

At the airport, there were bows, handshakes, smiles, flowers and speeches of welcome while the cameras clicked all about. Shades of the campaign!

Friends extricated us from the welcome for the long drive into the city, past miles of factories, unpainted shacks, new gas stations, tea-houses, pinball parlors, mazes of people and youngsters everywhere playing the nation's most popular sport, baseball. (It has been soberly suggested that night games might help solve the overpopulation problem.)

Tokyo, the world's third largest city, is drab and formless. There are great new buildings, starkly functional, but most reconstruction has been haphazard and flimsy. For the modern Japanese are a pragmatic people: their concern now is recovery and survival, not urban beautifications. But in the old imperial capital of Kyoto, we saw much of the beauty of the past preserved in scores of shrines, palaces, gardens and monuments, and were entertained by the delightful abbot of the great Buddhist temple.

The most striking impression of rural Japan is that there are no farm-

[17] " 'Citizen Adlai' in Japan," pp. 8–9.

[18] *Look*, May 19, 1953. This first article also included his report on Korea, Formosa, and Hong Kong. That material is reprinted after the editorial description of the visits to the respective countries.

ers as we know them, just gardeners who fertilize with human excrement and meticulously tend every inch of precious ground by hand. The average farm is only two and one-half acres, compared to 155 in the United States. Houses are clustered to conserve land. Such gardening produces remarkable results. In the great market in Tokyo, I saw wondrous vegetables and fruits — strawberries three inches long, white radishes three feet long.

Japan has a population of 84 millions, which is increasing a million a year, and they say you can travel from north to south by jumping from roof to roof. Even with rice and wheat yields two to three times higher than those of the rest of Asia, and with intensive fishing of her waters, Japan must import a fifth of her food.

The lot of the Japanese farmer is improving. In 1945, two-thirds were tenants, but now, thanks to the postwar land-reform program, 90 per cent have obtained what farmers want the world over — a piece of land of their own. There is little support for communism among the hardworking farmers, 90 per cent of whom are literate.

I talked and talked with businessmen, educators, students, shopkeepers, missionaries, newspapermen, with our able representatives, Gen. Mark Clark and Ambassador Robert Murphy, with the Prime Minister and Foreign Minister, with Shigemitsu, the Progressive party leader, with Socialists of the Right and Left. Finally, I called on the Emperor. In a borrowed cutaway!

The story they all told was: Too many people, too little land, too few resources.

But the energy and resourcefulness of this remarkable people cannot be discounted. The merchant fleet, destroyed in the war, is being rapidly replaced, power resources enlarged, more land reclaimed. Businessmen are actively canvassing world markets: they want trade, not aid. Yet without outlets on the mainland of Asia or more access to the markets of Southeast Asia and the United States, Japan may need help for years to come. Last year's trade deficit was $756 million, made up by the U.S. in payments for support of troops, offshore procurement and soldier spending.

Politically, the Japanese are suffering the pains of democracy's adolescence. Liberals, progressives and socialists are split and squabbling — mostly over greater centralization and rearmament. The Communists are relatively weak, and no organized extreme right-wing group exists — as yet — but I found a strong streak of theoretical Marxism and pacifism. And no wonder. Disastrous defeat, the atomic bomb and our postwar occupation, policy designed to eradicate militarism, have all had an effect. Today, there is little popular support for expanding the

100,000-strong National Security Forces into a U.S.-financed army, but thoughtful Japanese do not overlook the covetous Russians and Chinese nearby.

Is the new Japan reverting to the ways of the past?

I suppose the only answer is "yes and no." No doubt the occupation policies will be modified in the direction of greater centralization, both political and economic. Yet, in spite of alarms in some quarters, I could detect no present danger of the prewar authoritarianism that led Japan to disaster.

The painfully emerging Japanese version of democracy may not be wholly to our liking, but the sooner we get over the idea that we can remake ancient societies in our image the better. As long as extremism in Japan gets no stronger, we will be able to work with this great and sorely pressed people. We need their friendship and they need ours.

Three

Korea

MARCH 14-MARCH 18, 1953

At noon on March 14 Stevenson left Japan on a military plane for Korea. Joining him on the flight were Robert Shakne, of the International News Service, and Robert Tuckman, of the Associated Press. Stevenson's aides were given noncombatant identification cards which listed their simulated rank as "major to colonel." Stevenson's rank was "brigadier general to general." When one aide congratulated him on being a general, he remarked that he had not done well, really, as he had had a simulated rank of colonel in World War II and ten years was a "hell of a long time to wait to make general."

On the flight Stevenson studied carefully a memorandum prepared by Donald Kingsley of the United Nations Korean Reconstruction Agency. Kingsley maintained that while the United States had to continue military pressure in Korea and elsewhere on the periphery of Soviet expansion, such pressure could never be more than a primary step. "Ideas, when related to the legitimate aspirations of men, have never been defeated militarily," he wrote. In Asia the Communists promised the people three basic things: (1) land reform — an end to landlordism and the right of the peasant to the fruits of the land he works; (2) national and cultural independence from Western colonialism; and (3) peace.

The United States, he added, could not meet these challenges "by lectures on freedom of speech, constitutional rights, the American standard of living, television or free elections. None of these has any real meaning out here. . . . What, I believe, we can do is to meet and defeat the Communists in the area where they are weakest — namely, in that of performance." Throughout Asia and the Middle East, he continued, "It is the problem of assisting these people to improve their own living standards, while assuring them of their independence. In the simplest terms, what they want is respect and rice. If we can solve this problem we can stop Communism." He recommended that economic aid programs be handled by the United Nations, since the people of Asia did not fear the UN, "while they do fear the 'Eisenhower Era' and a new imperialism."

When the plane touched down at Pusan at 2:30 P.M., Stevenson looked out the window and glimpsed a Korean military band, a Republic of Korea honor guard, Korean dignitaries, and hundreds of American G.I.'s with cameras. "Oh God," he said. "Don't they know I lost the election?"

As he stepped from the plane, so many bouquets were thrust at him that he had to keep passing them back to the rest of his group. The R.O.K. band played "The Stars and Stripes Forever," cameras clicked, and Stevenson made a brief statement to the Korean dignitaries and the newsmen. Thousands upon thousands of schoolchildren lined the dusty road into Pusan and there were "Welcome Stevenson" banners sprinkled throughout the crowd. Blair said to Stevenson, "It's just like the campaign, except the crowds here are more enthusiastic."

At the embassy, which was housed in a warehouse, Ambassador Ellis O. Briggs and his staff, including Niles Bond, Arch Calhoun, Sidney Mellen and Holland Bushner, briefed Stevenson on the political and economic situation. Briggs, although he made it clear that he was well aware of the efficiency of the Rhee government in staging "spontaneous" demonstrations, said that he was nevertheless astonished at the warmth of the reception. He added that there was no doubt that the people were flattered by his visit to Pusan and had been disappointed that President Eisenhower had not stopped there the past December. And Briggs observed that his dominant impression of Korea was "the astounding cheerfulness and valor of the people." [1]

The Korean government Briggs described in terms of pieces of old string and old tape all held together with chewing gum. United States assistance and Syngman Rhee kept it together. Rhee, the ambassador said, was a dedicated, complex, fascinating and clever man, fighting for Korea every minute of the day. The United States had frequent conflicts with him over policy and did not always emerge victorious in the disputes. The relationship of the embassy to the president, Briggs described in terms of an old New Yorker cartoon showing a solicitous

[1] Barry Bingham, "The Best Thing about Korea Is the Spirit of Its People," Louisville *Courier-Journal*, April 5, 1953.

mother telling her child: "It's broccoli, dear," and the child replying, "I say it's spinach, and I say the hell with it." [2]

The major difference with Rhee was over his insistence that there had to be a united Korea to the Yalu River. He was stubbornly opposed, Briggs said, to the proposal of the United Nations the past autumn which would bring a settlement at the 38th parallel.

Other members of the embassy staff pointed out that the political situation in South Korea was stronger than the economic. Rhee was brighter and more agile than his opponents. There was widespread corruption, elections were rigged, and the security police were hardly respectful of dissent. When the seventy-seven-year-old Rhee went, they added, the huge military machine that the United States had trained might take over.

Briggs remarked that in view of the bankruptcy of the country and the poverty of the people, the cheerfulness and friendliness of the people "pepped up" the embassy staff whenever they began to feel grim about the future of Korea. It was emphasized that under our military occupation at the close of the war, estates owned by Japanese were divided among the peasants. But Korean landlords had successfully prevented any land reform on Korean-owned land. The briefing closed with the observation that under Japanese rule for some forty years, the Koreans had had no political experience and few Koreans had been trained as government administrators or as managers and technicians.

At this point, Stevenson told Ambassador Briggs that this had been "the best and briefest briefing" that he had ever had.[3]

Immediately after the briefing, Stevenson visited with the acting prime minister, Paik Tu Chin, and Foreign Minister Dr. Chŭng Hwan Cho. When the photographers finished taking pictures, Stevenson met with some thirty members of the National Assembly, including Speaker P. H. Shinicky, leader of the Rhee opposition. Attwood wrote in his diary: "Stevenson did his usual expert job of ad libbing a few courteous remarks in such a way as to make them sound fresh and full of feeling." Stevenson explained that Pusan's reception had touched and surprised him since it was the kind reserved usually for heads of state, a post he had tried to achieve but had not been successful. He then paid tribute to the sacrifice and valor of the Korean people.

---

[2] Reprinted in *The New Yorker Twenty-fifth Anniversary Album, 1925–1950* (New York: Harper, 1951), p. 4.

[3] Ambassador Briggs wrote: "Having been exposed for many years to horrible endless indoctrination furnished visitors who obviously would have preferred almost any other form of torture, I vowed when I myself became Chief of Mission to make capsules out of haymows, even if dozens of nutritious seeds, mice and grasshoppers were demolished in the process." Letter to Walter Johnson, June 1, 1967.

After this meeting, the Stevenson party dined at Ambassador Briggs's residence. Following dinner, a group of Korean dancers performed some traditional folk dances. "Korean dancing is crude by comparison with the ordered posturings of the Japanese performance," Barry Bingham wrote. "It is also hot with color and emotion. Though it owes allegiance to a storied past, it is definitely free and uninhibited." [4]

Early the next morning, Sunday, March 15, Stevenson, Bingham and Blair flew to Cheju Island to see the training program of the R.O.K. army. Mrs. Briggs and Attwood visited Ewha University, which was housed in a cluster of wooden shacks until it could return to Seoul. Attwood met with the ambassador for lunch to seek further information on political and economic conditions. Meanwhile, Johnson interviewed Sir Arthur Rucker of the United Nations Korean Reconstruction Agency to explore further plans for rebuilding devastated Korea. During the afternoon Johnson met with Niles Bond, Arch Calhoun, and others of the embassy staff, and later with George Paik, president of Chosun Christian College, to explore the educational needs of the country.

When Stevenson returned that afternoon he had a lengthy conversation with Dr. Howard A. Rusk, who was investigating health and welfare needs for the private American-Korean Foundation. He also talked with representatives from the Netherlands, Australia, and the Philippines, who were serving on the United Nations Commission for the Unification and Reconstruction of Korea.

At six the next morning Stevenson flew with Ambassador Briggs and Major General C. J. Ryan, head of the U.S. military advisory group to the R.O.K. army, to the R.O.K. officer training camp at barren Kwangju. By noon the plane reached Seoul, where a band, a R.O.K. honor guard, U.S. and R.O.K. soldiers, and hordes of photographers were waiting. Stevenson was driven to President Rhee's house through streets lined with children and soldiers and strung with banners: "Adlai Stevenson Forever a Friend of Korea," "Unify Korea," and "Drive Back the Chinese Reds."

Over cups of tea President Rhee insisted that now was the time to drive the "Reds" back to the Yalu River. At one point he said, "The Democrats saved Korea. I hope now the Republicans will finish the task." Stevenson smiled and said, "I hope so too." After tea, as Rhee and Stevenson posed for the ubiquitous photographers, Rhee remarked that all photographers were a nuisance, but that the Japanese were absolutely the worst, aggressive and without manners.

[4] For a description of the various dances the Stevenson party saw in Asia, see Barry Bingham, "Asian Panorama, with Dancing Figures," *Virgina Quarterly Review*, Vol. 30, No. 3, Summer, 1954, pp. 392–401.

Stevenson lunched with the mayor of Seoul at the residence for visitors maintained by the U.S. Army and spent the afternoon at several Air Force units observing their operations and hearing reports of pilots returning from bombing North Korea. The airmen made no secret of their frustration in not being allowed to pursue enemy MIG's across the Yalu River. "Throughout the day," Attwood wrote in his diary, "Stevenson was his usual brisk, alert, cheerful self, seemingly interested in every detail of what was told him, and always ready with a smile and a greeting for anyone who came up to say hello."

Dinner that evening was at the home of President and Mrs. Rhee. Included in the party were General Paik Sun Yup, the thirty-two-year-old head of the R.O.K. army; the prime minister; the ambassador; General Maxwell D. Taylor; and General C. J. Ryan. Stevenson plied Rhee with innumerable questions. The president insisted that he had tried to establish amicable relations with Japan but that he had been treated "shabbily." He denounced the Japanese for their treatment of Koreans living in Japan, and he accused Japanese fishermen of encroaching on Korean waters. Then Rhee insisted that Korea could not have a viable economy unless the country was unified to the Yalu River. He also said most firmly that South Korea should have an army of one million. (At that point it was about 450,000.)

At the other end of the table, Mrs. Rhee talked of the immense need of American help in training government administrators. In addition to experts to run an efficient government, Korea was in dire need of secretaries and file clerks. She explained that she worked every day on the president's correspondence and had only one secretary who could use both Korean and English. Her file clerks, she added, "didn't know how to file anything."

After dinner Stevenson visited with newspaper reporters at the local press club. Before retiring, as Attwood wrote in his diary, "Johnson sat up with Stevenson another half hour taking notes on the Rhee talk. Tired as he is, Stevenson somehow manages to keep going and never shows fatigue in public."

At eight the next morning, March 17, the Stevenson party, in uniform and accompanied by General Taylor, flew to the forward lines. During the course of the day he visited — sometimes by two-seater helicopters — the First Marine Division, the First R.O.K. Division, the First Commonwealth Division, and the U.S. Army Second Division. The Chinese forces were dug in well, and as Attwood wrote in his diary: "Everywhere there was far less disposition to bomb Manchuria or forge ahead to the Yalu than we found among the airmen."

At the U.S. Second Division the Stevenson group donned helmets and armored vests, drove in jeeps to the front, and trudged up a ridge through trenches to look out on the Chinese lines about a thousand yards away. (At this point in the Korean conflict, ground action generally was limited to artillery fire during the day and night patrols into no-man's-land.) Stevenson stayed for nearly half an hour visiting with the soldiers stationed at the command post. Then, when a mortar exploded several hundred yards away, General Taylor hustled him down the ridge and back to a safer base. At one point, Stevenson remarked that being able to get around to so much of the front was one of the compensations of having been defeated in November. (President Eisenhower had not been allowed to go forward of division headquarters the past December.)

"All of us were dust-caked, grimy and bone-tired," Attwood wrote in his diary after the group flew back to Seoul. Stevenson quickly showered, changed, and attended a reception in his honor given by the mayor of Seoul. Dinner that evening was with General Taylor and two of his corps commanders — Lieutenant General I. D. White and Lieutenant General Reuben E. Jenkins. In a brief welcoming speech, Taylor facetiously reproached Stevenson for having attended Princeton, since Field Marshal Sir Bernard Montgomery had only heard of Harvard, Yale and McGill. Stevenson replied that this confirmed everything he had heard about "Monty," and recounted Winston Churchill's remark when a member of the House of Commons criticized Montgomery for entertaining a German prisoner-of-war general at dinner: "No worse fate could befall an enemy officer." Attwood noted in his diary: "Taylor and Stevenson are both men who love to use the language well and the exchange of pleasantries and compliments was on a high, polished plane."

Taylor assured Stevenson that he and the other two generals were at his disposal, and a frank, high-level discussion ensued. Stevenson said that he was puzzled. Eisenhower had himself "over a barrel" by having promised a quick solution in Korea during the campaign. Stevenson mentioned that at home many thought that increasing the R.O.K. army was a way out. Others wanted to go all-out even if it meant a full-scale war with China. "What will be the cost of an all-out attack?" Stevenson asked. "What will be the cost of a stalemate?"

Taylor cautioned that his opinions were personal and not for publication. The R.O.K. army had been greatly overrated by newspapers, he said. They were an excellent defensive force, he continued, and increasingly could assume more front-line duty, but only if the current stalemate continued.

Taylor then stated that the forces under his command could not launch a crippling attack. Such a blow would require stripping other vital areas of troops or an all-out mobilization at home. In addition, if we were to attack we had to consider all the consequences. How far should we go? To the Yalu and dig in there on an even more extended line than at present? Or keep going? If the attack was made, it would have to be an enveloping amphibious operation, which would necessitate preliminary bombing of Manchurian air bases to protect our shipping. All were difficult political decisions, he added, but they had to be known before any military action could do more than plunge ahead blindly.

Taylor, in response to a question from Stevenson about the Republican slogan "Unleash Chiang Kai-shek," said that to land Nationalist troops on the China coast would mean that the United States would have to equip and support them. Talk of invading the mainland was mostly talk and impractical, he asserted. If the United States wanted to take on China, then our aim should be to destroy the bulk of the Chinese army which was now in Korea. He repeated that an offensive to knock China out of Korea could only be done at enormous cost in men and money.

He remarked that it all added up to a pretty black picture, but he wanted to leave Stevenson with at least one optimistic note. In Berlin, when the Russians had realized that we would not be dislodged and would persist with the airlift, they ended the blockade. In other words, they pulled out of a situation that was unprofitable to them. In Korea, the Chinese, he said, were "hurting" more than we were. How long they wanted to keep it up was anybody's guess, but there was a chance that a little more patience on our side might produce results.[5]

It was an unpleasant situation but, at that moment, not the bloody mess some thought it was. Usually more soldiers were hurt in jeep accidents behind the lines than in combat. "You're safer here with the army than back in Springfield," he asserted. In response to a question from Stevenson as to the possibility of a split between China and the Soviet Union, Taylor thought that it was possible and would be immensely worthwhile.

"Taylor said all this with great coherence and eloquence," Attwood wrote in his diary. "His thinking is methodical and careful and I know he impressed Stevenson."

When Taylor finished answering questions, Stevenson chuckled reflectively and remarked that this conversation bore out many things he had said during the campaign as to the need for patience and restraint and the realization that there was no easy solution to Korea.

When Stevenson returned to his billet about 10 P.M., General Ryan

[5] Peace talks were taking place at this time. On July 26 an armistice was signed at Panmunjom ending the fighting.

*was waiting to tell him more about the R.O.K. army. As Attwood wrote
in his diary: "He thinks Stevenson is great because he's spent more time
looking at the R.O.K. army (says Ryan) than any other visitor to Korea."*

At 7:15 the next morning Stevenson visited a Korean orphanage. En
route a U.S. Army officer described the work of UNCACK — the United
Nations Command Civil Assistance and Economic Aid Korea. At the
moment there were over 300,000 out of a population of 750,000 on relief
in Seoul. In addition to furnishing food, clothing and medical supplies,
UNCACK was in charge of sanitation.

Although the children at the orphanage had not been told that Stevenson was coming for a visit, their intelligence seemed to be excellent.
When he arrived there were crudely lettered signs, "Welcome Stevenson." After visiting with the children they sang "God Bless America,"
"Old MacDonald Had a Farm," and "My Bonnie Lies over the Ocean."

From the orphanage he drove to the airport, where he and his aides
donned immersion suits, Mae West belts, and crash helmets. (The departure for the aircraft carrier Oriskany was delayed a few minutes because Stevenson had difficulty being shoehorned into his suit.) As he
approached the carrier, which was pitching in a heavy sea, the pilot of
Stevenson's plane explained to him that his code name was "Wheelchair" and the code name of the Oriskany was "Jehovah." At lunch
aboard, Stevenson told Admiral Joseph J. (Jocko) Clark, commander of
the Seventh Fleet, that flying to Jehovah had been "quite a morale-
builder."

He watched both jets and propeller planes land and take off for
missions in North Korea at thirty-second intervals. Then at lunch Admiral Clark, a true believer in General Douglas MacArthur's maxim
"There is no substitute for victory," expressed his views in firm language.

When he flew back to Seoul, Stevenson and Ambassador Briggs paid
a farewell visit to President Rhee. On his return to the airport, Stevenson held a brief, noncommittal press conference and flew off to
Tokyo. Aboard the plane, Attwood and Stevenson discussed the article
he would write for Look. "I think he wishes he hadn't consented to
write during the trip," Attwood noted in his diary. "He also wishes he
had altered the schedule so as to permit longer stops, with rest periods
at each place. This would have meant going to fewer countries. But the
State Department, who knows what an asset he is to U.S. policy abroad,
is anxious to utilize him as much as possible and obviously pressed him
to go to as many places as he could fit into the period of the trip. I fail
to see why he should be stuck with this itinerary. . . . Fortunately,
Blair has wired Washington that Stevenson will accept no engagements
(to speak, etc.) unless they are first cleared with him. Apparently the

Department has been making these dates, figuring he would be too gracious to turn them down."

Stevenson wrote of the visit to Korea:

REPORT BY ADLAI STEVENSON [6]

More questions than answers awaited me in Korea.

There were, I found, two Koreas. One of the fighting men, of Old Baldy, the Iron Triangle, MIG Alley, of napalm and rotation — the Korea of stalemate, frustration and expense so well known to Americans. And another — of the South Koreans — ragged, crowded, impoverished, yet buoyantly cheerful. The second Korea was the one that greeted us as we stepped off the plane at Pusan. Along the dusty roads into the teeming, ramshackle city, people by the thousands and schoolchildren in their black uniforms were lined up, smiling, shouting and waving Korean and American flags.

I saw much of this jagged, naked land, which early French missionaries likened to "a sea lashed by a heavy gale." I watched the rigorous training of Republic of Korea soldiers on windswept Cheju-do Island and barren Kwangju. I visited air bases, flew on to an American aircraft carrier off the east coast, taxied by helicopter to three division headquarters and puffed up a mountainside for a look at the front-line trenches — and the tough enemy dug in like moles.

Back of our lines I saw schools and universities carrying on in shattered buildings and hillside caves. I saw refugees by the thousands, living in wretched shacks and squalor.

There were long talks with our sensible Ambassador, Ellis Briggs, with countless American and Korean officials, with officers, soldiers and airmen of many nations. I talked and traveled with thoughtful, articulate Gen. Maxwell Taylor, with his corps commanders and with Vice-Admiral Joseph J. (Jocko) Clark, commander of the Seventh Fleet.

Not a word did I hear about an ammunition shortage anywhere from anyone.

Three times, I conferred with that uncompromising, emotional and engaging old patriot, President Rhee, a dedicated man with a single purpose: Drive to the Yalu and unite Korea.

Unless all Korea is united — the resources and industry of the North and the population and agriculture of the South — we shall have at best an ally with a strong heart and a weak back. But assuming the country could be united right up to the Yalu — what then? How is that long frontier at the junction of the Bamboo and Iron Curtains going to be

[6] *Look,* May 19, 1953.

defended from infiltration or new invasions? And, politically, who is going to succeed old Syngman Rhee? Would eager, able young generals backed by a huge army fill the vacuum with a military dictatorship?

So far as America is concerned, talk of pulling out altogether is, of course, nonsense from any point of view. The burden of fighting, I found, was rapidly shifting. ROK divisions held more than half the line, and thanks to American instructors and training methods, they were turning out battle-ready soldiers and officers faster than we could equip them.

What I saw in the crude, improvised ROK training camps — the spirit, the concentration, the discipline — was exciting and infectious. As we passed through classrooms at Kwangju, hardly an eye wavered in our direction. And they were learning fast.

I came away from tortured Korea both exhilarated by one of the best and best-led armed forces in U.S. history, by the fine co-ordination and the historic significance of sixteen nations joined in a common cause, and by the courage, endurance and cheerfulness of the Korean people. But I was depressed by the appalling problems, economic, political and military, that face this devastated country — yes, and that face *us*, perhaps for years to come. From the multitude of relief agencies that are ministering to the bewildered Koreans, I got the reliable impression that it would take a billion dollars of investment to help Korea achieve anything like a viable economy.

It has been a strange war. U.N. soldiers, mostly ROKs, have gone to their death nightly on routine patrols. Our troops long since substituted the goal of rotation for victory. Frustrated pilots have returned to their bases with tales of chasing MIGs up to the Yalu, then turning back in the teeth of flak guns they could see but weren't allowed to hit. Why not at least hit whatever hits us?

We flew away from Seoul in the early morning after visiting an orphanage in an old Buddhist temple. I'm haunted still by the faces of those shivering, smiling children lined up on the frosted ground singing *God Bless America* as we drove away.

In the plane, on the way to Formosa, I wrote some notes. Here they are:

> Korea may be a turning point in world history — the first great collective stand against a new Attila and new Genghis Khan, in partnership. There are four alternatives: 1. Withdraw. 2. Negotiate a settlement. 3. Attack. 4. Stalemate.
>
> 1. To pull out now is unthinkable.
> 2. A negotiated settlement is a possibility. Communist truce pro-

posals could be sincere. Even as they gave up the Berlin blockade and other unprofitable ventures, the Communists may want to end this deadlocked war. But we should not mistake a change of tactics for a change of heart. Conversion to communism and not co-existence with the free world will still be the goal.

What would they settle for? A unified Korea with a democrat-ically elected government? With Stalin's death, we may soon know if they mean business — or merely want to soften us up before applying greater pressure in Korea or elsewhere. In the latter event, we must consider the third alternative — attack.

3. With larger forces, we could fight up to the waist of the pen-insula by frontal attack and amphibious end runs — and even on to the Yalu — but only if the American people are prepared for a much greater effort, for stripping our defenses in other vital areas, for forgetting about rotation and peacetime comforts. Are we pre-pared to pay the heavy price that would cost us in casualties?

4. Stalemate is not so much an alternative — it's what we are stuck with. But trading casualties, even at ten to one, with an enemy that doesn't care is bad business.

After four stirring days in Korea, I have but one conviction: There is no easy way out of this war until Moscow and Peking have had enough. I am glad I said just that during the campaign last fall.

Perhaps patience is the price of world power, and the cheapest and the best solution. Maybe, as I have said before, "Korea can't be settled in Korea"; perhaps we will have to learn to live with it, even as the British learned to live with the "Northwest Frontier." Maybe we will have to learn to think of Korea not as a point of decision but as a checkpoint of Communist expansion, at least until we have regained the ideological offensive in Asia and the Red Shadow recedes. You can shoot Communists, but you can't shoot poverty, ignorance and communism.

Four

Taiwan

MARCH 20 – MARCH 22, 1953

*A*t six A.M. *on March 20, after a five-hour flight from Tokyo, the plane landed in Okinawa for refueling. Four hours later the plane landed at Taipei, Formosa, where an enthusiastic crowd of Americans and Chinese (some waving a Northwestern University banner) greeted Stevenson. "Mr. Stevenson's rousing welcome was one of the warmest accorded to a 'private citizen' of a foreign country," the New York* Times *reported.*[1] *"The red carpet was rolled out for Adlai Stevenson," Barry Bingham wrote. "He has not been considered a very sympathetic figure by Chiang Kai-shek and his supporters; but they recognize that Stevenson has the ear of many Americans."* [2]

As Stevenson walked off the plane, he waved to the crowd and said: "I am greatly impressed. But I am not running for any office on this island."

He was driven to a huge government guesthouse which had been the residence of the governor-general when the Japanese controlled the island. Shortly after arrival he attended a short briefing at the embassy by Ambassador Karl Rankin and his staff. The ambassador emphasized that although many of the six million native Taiwanese looked back on the "good old days" of the Japanese occupation, there really was no desire to have them return. The influx since 1949 of over two million Nationalist troops, officials, and supporters, he added, had seriously upset the economy. The U.S. Mutual Security Agency was spon-

[1] March 21, 1953.
[2] "A New Kind of Chinese Wall," Louisville *Courier-Journal,* April 12, 1953.

soring a modest industrialization program to help absorb some of the newcomers. The ambassador claimed that the great bitterness of the Taiwanese toward mainland Chinese that had erupted in a bloody revolt in 1947 now seemed to be disappearing.

Following the briefing, Stevenson went to see Generalissimo Chiang Kai-shek. Stevenson thanked President Chiang for the warm welcome at the airport, and Chiang replied that he was the most distinguished American ever to visit Taiwan and that they had been deeply impressed by his campaign speeches. The remainder of the half-hour interview was recorded in shorthand by a Chinese official:

MINUTES OF TALK BETWEEN PRESIDENT CHIANG KAI-SHEK AND MR. ADLAI STEVENSON [3]

Time: March 20, 1953, 11 A.M.
Place: The President's Office, Taipei

THE PRESIDENT: What is your opinion of the situation in Korea?

MR. STEVENSON: We were in Korea altogether four days. During this period, we visited a recruiting center, an officer training camp, the front held by the 1st Corps, 7th Fleet units off the Eastern shore and the 5th Air Force. Our troops are in good condition but they are facing a stubborn enemy, who has dug in and built a front 25 miles deep. The cost would be tremendous if our forces should try to rip a hole on the enemy line. I hope your raids along the mainland coast could take some pressure off the Korean front.

THE PRESIDENT: Hit and run raids on the mainland coast may be helpful to a certain extent to the progress of war in Korea. But no effective purpose will be served unless a full-scale invasion of the mainland is launched. While you were in Korea, did you see some of the anti-Communist Chinese prisoners of war?

MR. STEVENSON: Yes, I visited one camp on the Cheju Island, which housed those prisoners who do not want to be repatriated against their will. They gave me a rousing welcome with a chorus and musical instruments. It seems they are all friends of yours.

THE PRESIDENT: Anybody who comes out of Communist China of his own will is our friend.

MR. STEVENSON: Do you think the Korean war has hurt Communist China? Some people say that there has been no effect. And do you

[3] This English transcription was prepared under the supervision of Walter Johnson.

think the Chinese people have no complaint against the Chinese Communist participation in the war in Korea?

THE PRESIDENT: Of course, the Chinese people are against the Communist participation and the prolongation of the war. However, the heavy casualties in Korea will not have much effect on the Communists. China is a vast manpower reservoir. The Communists have now planned and started to build up a reserve force of 20,000,000 men. On the other hand, the war does drain on Communist economy and finance.

MR. STEVENSON: Don't you think the Korean war also drains on Soviet Russia's economy?

THE PRESIDENT: I think not. So far as manpower is concerned, the people getting killed in Korea are Chinese and Koreans; there is not a single Russian. In respect to material, what the Russians have given the Communists to fight in Korea in artillery, tanks, airplanes and other weapons amounts to only 15% or 10% of their production. Besides, the Russians are not giving anything free of charge. They get back raw materials, food, and even human labor in exchange. And in such exchange, they always gain.

MR. STEVENSON: In your opinion, then, what should be the best way for us to follow in Korea? To keep the stalemate as now or to push ahead to a military victory?

THE PRESIDENT: Elimination of the Chinese Communists on the mainland is a prerequisite to the final solution of the Korean war. Minus this, Russia will remain a strong power and the war in Korea will go on. So the recovery of the China mainland is an imperative necessity.

MR. STEVENSON: Our forces are fighting the Communist forces in Korea and destroying them. Since frontal attack will be too costly, the military authorities are thinking of landing behind the enemy line, thus encircling the enemy divisions in the forward positions. Another more ambitious plan is to push our armed forces right to the bank of the Yalu River.

THE PRESIDENT: In my opinion, the Korean problem cannot be solved in Korea alone even if the United Nations forces are pushed to the bank of the Yalu River. It must be viewed as part of the entire Far East problem. Today, Communist troubles in the Far East countries all stem from Communist China. So long as the China mainland remains Communist, its manpower, natural resources and the vast territory will be all available to Soviet Russia as its capital for aggression.

Only by depriving the Russians of the China mainland may its aggression be brought to an halt.

MR. STEVENSON: Everyone will agree with you that the ideal thing is to detach China from Russia. But the question is how? By invasion?

THE PRESIDENT: When I am talking about depriving Russia of the China mainland, I have no illusion that Communist China would do so by its own will. This is an impossibility. In my opinion, to eliminate the Chinese Communists requires the unity of the anti-Communist forces of the world under the leadership of the United States, with Free China bearing the blunt [brunt] of the task. When I say American leadership, I am not asking American forces to join our fighting against the Communists. We need only American support in supply and the acquiescence of other Western countries when we start the invasion of the mainland.

MR. STEVENSON: Do you think that with American support in logistics your army is strong enough for a successful invasion of the mainland?

THE PRESIDENT: In comparison with the Communists, our armed strength is only one-fifth of theirs. But my past experience convinces me that I shall win. For armed strength is only one factor in the type of war we are fighting here. Another equally or even more important factor is the support of the people. I am sure that 95% of the population on the mainland are anti-Communist and will support us when we start fighting back.

MR. STEVENSON: Will the Communist troops defect?

THE PRESIDENT: Yes, when they are pretty sure that we are going to stay. That will take three to six months, during which we must win several battles. This also applies to the people. Because of Communist reprisal and tight control, they will not show their true feelings until they are sure that we shall be able to protect them.

MR. STEVENSON: What is your opinion on blockade or embargo against Communist China?

THE PRESIDENT: A thorough embargo may be as effective as a blockade. It will deal a severe economic blow to the Communists. For up to date, Communist China still depends on the Western countries for most of the things which they must import. Soviet Russia is exploiting Communist China rather than supplying her. Furthermore, Russia is even getting certain material from the West through Communist China, such as Ceylon's rubber, Britain's machinery, and oil products from other countries.

[56]

MR. STEVENSON: If you have more ships, will you be able to impose an effective blockade?

THE PRESIDENT: China mainland has a very long coast. To blockade the entire coastline is not possible. However, with more ships, we can impose an effective blockade along the stretch between Swatow and Shanghai. But in my opinion, no blockade will be really effective in hitting the Communists if Hong Kong and Shanghai are not included. These two ports are handling the most important supplies for Communist China. Besides, most ships plying between Western countries and these two ports are unfortunately those belonging to either Britain or the United States. Of course, the latter do not fly the American flag. They fly the flags of other countries. This is one point we have to keep in mind when we talk about a blockade.

Note: These minutes have not been checked with either President Chiang or Mr. Stevenson and therefore cannot be considered final.

Following this talk with the president, Stevenson called on Premier Chen Cheng. Amidst pleasantries, the premier stated that they of the Nationalist government had made terrible mistakes when they were in charge of the mainland. Here in Formosa, however, he said, they were changing the situation and were going to prove that they were fit to rule when they got back on the mainland.

As Stevenson drove to Ambassador Rankin's residence for lunch he was struck by the contrast between the lush vegetation of the Formosan mountains and the gaunt, eroded mountains of Korea. Among those at lunch were the foreign minister, George K. C. Yeh; General Sun Li-jen, commander of the army; General Chou Chih-jou, chief of the General Staff of the Ministry of National Defense; General W. C. Chase, chief of the U.S. Military Advisory Group; Dr. H. G. Schenck, head of the Mutual Security Agency Mission; and Howard P. Jones, counselor of the embassy.

After lunch the Stevenson group went to inspect an army training program. Also there to see the demonstration were newspaper publisher Roy Howard, Alfred Kohlberg of the China lobby, and radio commentator Tex McCrary. "The troops would have looked better if we hadn't seen the ROKs first," Attwood wrote in his diary. "The Chinese seemed slack and inattentive compared to the Koreans and lacked the fire in the eye. I must say there was little spark in our eyes either: Stevenson got about two hours sleep last night, the rest of us around four or five."

Meanwhile, Howard P. Jones and Johnson discussed the political sit-

uation on Taiwan. Jones talked at length of K. C. Wu, governor of the province of Taiwan. Wu had recently resigned as governor but Chiang had given him a leave for rest. (Wu was not in Taipei while Stevenson was there.) Wu had been struggling without success, Jones said, to curb the security police and establish a rule of law. Jones also discussed the power struggle between Premier Chen Cheng and the Generalissimo's eldest son, General Chiang Ching-kuo. The latter had been gaining control of the Kuomintang party machinery, was head of the political department of the army, and was the supervisor of the raids and guerrilla activities on the mainland.

Then William Sponsler, of the embassy staff, discussed a helpful memorandum that he had prepared for Stevenson. He explained that it was U.S. policy to help the island become self-supporting. But this ran into conflict with the principal goal of the Nationalist government, which was to return to the mainland.

Late that afternoon the Northwestern University Alumni Club, the Chinese Association for the United Nations, the National Bar Association, the Rotary Club, and the International House Association held a reception in Stevenson's honor. At the close of the reception Stevenson was sufficiently fatigued to agree to have a quiet dinner at the government guesthouse.

On Saturday morning, March 21, the Stevenson party had a lengthy session with officials of the Mutual Security Agency. Dr. H. G. Schenck explained that the Joint Commission for Rural Reconstruction (JCRR) would be the agricultural division of the MSA in any other country. In Taiwan, however, it was partially independent, since it had originated on the mainland in 1948. There were three Chinese and two Americans on the commission. The MSA did, however, control the budget of the JCRR. Up to date, the land reform program under the JCRR had reduced rents from 50 to 60 per cent of the crop to a maximum of 37.5 per cent. Land confiscated from the Japanese had been sold to tenants at reasonable prices. Currently the large estates of Formosans were being purchased and sold in small parcels to tenants. The JCRR was also providing greater incentives and working capital for farmers.[4]

Other members of the MSA staff described the technical assistance program to train public health workers and technicians for industry. The rehabilitation activities to expland harbors, power plants, textile factories and attempts to develop fertilizer plants were described in de-

[4] En route to Taiwan, Stevenson had read an enlightening article on the JCRR and the general situation by Albert Ravenholt, "Our Opportunity on Formosa," *Reporter,* December 9, 1952, pp. 14–18.

tail. *Martin Wong, who was deputy secretary-general of the Council for U.S. Aid in the Nationalist government, concluded the discussion by saying: "We know that this is our last chance here on Formosa and we feel that through the cooperation that exists with the MSA we are going to demonstrate that we can do a real job."*

Stevenson then met with Dr. Chiang Monlin, Dr. T. H. Shen, T. H. Chien, William H. Fippin, Raymond H. Davis — the commissioners of the JCRR. The chairman, Dr. Chiang, said:

"Mr. Stevenson: This is your first trip to Free China. But we all feel a sort of intimacy toward you. That sort of intimacy comes from your great speeches in which you have personified before the world the high ideals of the American people that not only transcend the traditional party lines but also the national boundary lines.

"These great personified ideals echoed far and wide in the hearts of millions of people throughout the world.

"We hope you will find your counterpart spirit, however modest it may be, in the program of the Joint Commission on Rural Reconstruction (JCRR).

"The JCRR program is based upon two fundamental principles. 1. Social justice, or in other words, fair distribution. 2. Material well-being, or in other words, increase of production.

"We are endeavoring to strike a balance between the two. For working for social justice, or fair distribution, alone it would be but an equalization of poverty. On the other hand, if we work for production alone, it would widen the gaps between the haves and have-nots.

"The most important work for social justice is land reform which is to be completed by the end of this year. The land problem has caused recurrent agrarian revolutions throughout Chinese history since the first century A.D. Many a powerful dynasty was swept away by the tides of agrarian revolution.

"The most fundamental work for increase of production is irrigation, fertilizer and pest control.

"By carefully working out a coordinated plan of distribution and production, we will have the key to the solution of the agrarian problem, in this part of the world.

"We cast our eyes upon the stars. We set our feet to the grassroots. It has been our policy that we learn from the farmers, but not to teach them according to our fancies.

"We have set up high ideals but our ways of implementation are practical. I hope, Mr. Stevenson, this will meet your approval. As to the practical implementation of JCRR program, allow me to pass it to Mr. Davis and Mr. Fippin."

The commissioners described in detail their work with local farm groups and explained how in one village an irrigation pump was being installed, in another a fish pond was being developed, and in still another hog cholera was being controlled. (The JCRR, they explained, was then involved in some 608 projects.) In all their activities, whatever they did had to be supported by the local people and part of the cost had to be contributed by the people involved. Along with the insistence that there had to be a felt need on the part of rural people, the JCRR insisted that there had to be a fair distribution of the results of the given activity. One commissioner stated: "The JCRR approach of working with the local people was vital. Furthermore, more important than this was the joint approach of the JCRR in terms of Americans and Chinese working together and pooling their different cultural and educational backgrounds for a mutual program."

After this discussion, Stevenson visited a health station which had been constructed and equipped by the local community raising half the costs and the JCRR contributing the remainder. He drove a few miles out of Taipei and inspected a rural marketing cooperative that had been organized by local farmers to buy fertilizer and sell rice. This co-op was also experimenting in the breeding of Berkshire boars. When Stevenson saw one huge boar, he said: "I saw this fellow at the Illinois State Fair last year."

At this point, Stevenson saw a temple next to the co-op. He insisted on visiting it, accompanied by hordes of children. Afterward he went to see a farmer who raised fish for sale, had a water buffalo, and farmed some ten acres. This put him in a category above an ordinary Formosan farmer. Stevenson talked to the farmer, who was surrounded by his twelve children and grandchildren, and asked how old he was. The farmer replied, "Fifty-two." "That's my age," Stevenson said. "But I haven't forgotten that a minute ago your children were referring to you as an old man."

After lunch with members of the JCRR, reporters and photographers arrived at the guesthouse for the largest press conference ever held on Formosa. Stevenson remarked that he had been encouraged by what he had seen of the government's attempt, especially through the JCRR, to live down the past and make Formosa a laboratory of better government. "Everything I have seen or heard indicates conspicuous improvement," he added. "It is always a mistake to confuse bigness with greatness. This is a laboratory of better government and a healthy economic setup. The fact that it is small does not mean it is worthless."

Asked to comment on President Eisenhower's statement that the Seventh Fleet patrolling the Formosan Straits would "no longer be em-

ployed to shield Communist China" from attacks from Formosa, Steven-son replied that he had not realized the statement was necesary. "I did not think the Seventh Fleet was used to protect the mainland. Most of the people back home had the impression that Nationalists had been making raids on the mainland despite the Seventh Fleet." [5]

Another reporter asked what his future political plans were. He said: "I think maybe I won't have any problem at all. If I travel as much and as fast as I've been doing, I'll never get home at all."

When one reporter pressed him for his views on the military effectiveness of Chiang Kai-shek's forces, Stevenson chuckled and said: "I am no military expert. The highest military rank I ever achieved was as an apprentice seaman in the United States Navy in World War I."

One reporter wondered if he planned to remarry. Stevenson replied: "I'm available but I haven't had many applications." The next question disrupted the press conference. A Chinese reporter said that he understood Stevenson was going to marry Margaret Truman. Stevenson, with a twinkle in his eyes, said to the interpreter: "Ask him if he still beats his wife." Those who understood English burst into laughter, while those who did not looked more and more puzzled as the interpreter labored diligently for two or three minutes trying to explain what the remark actually meant. When the interpreter finally gave up in despair, that ended the press conference. Later, a foreign correspondent apologized on behalf of the press corps for the "irreverent" questions about matrimony, but Stevenson replied that the reporters were more embarrassed by it than he was.

As Stevenson left the conference room and walked upstairs, Blair and Johnson reminded him that they had tried to caution him that American humor did not translate easily or well. He nodded his head in agreement and said that he would try to restrain himself in the future. (Although he did try, it was against his nature. His humor was not contrived, it was not something that he strove for. It sprang from a deep, spontaneous source.)

Later that afternoon Stevenson and Blair talked to the head of the Kuomintang and visited an arsenal. Bingham and Attwood called on former Premier Chang Chun, who insisted that they could return to the mainland — with U.S. logistical support — without risking World War III with the Soviet Union. The Russians might intervene only if U.S. combat troops were landed, but the Nationalist official insisted that U.S. troops would not be needed.

[5] The New York *Times*, March 22, 1953, printed a portion of the press conference. In fact, under President Truman, raids from Formosa against the mainland had occurred.

Following this conversation, they met with a well-informed U.S. official who stated that Chiang in fact had only about 150,000 combat troops. In the United States, he added, the China lobby had put over a big hoax by talking of 600,000 troops.[6] He stated that the Nationalist troops in Burma were not being brought to Formosa because Chiang wanted them there in case of an invasion of the mainland. He added that intelligence information from the interior of China was not reliable.

Meanwhile, Johnson talked to a faculty group at the National University of Taiwan about elementary, secondary, and higher education on the island.

Among the letters awaiting Stevenson on his arrival in Taiwan was one from a student who had recently returned from the United States. The letter had been "startling." [7] Among other things, it stated: "I am very glad that you are coming to Formosa, for I know you are not like many others who are so easily satisfied with what is on the surface. The officials will tell you what they want you to know and show you what they want you to see. . . . I am in a position to find out a few things which probably are not available to Americans. Therefore, I humbly offer you my service, limited as it is."

Stevenson asked Johnson to interview the writer of the letter. In the subsequent conversation, the student explained that her father had formerly been a high government official, who was now deeply discouraged about the lack of free speech on Taiwan. The father's concern over the ruthlessness of the Generalissimo's son, Chiang Ching-kuo, permeated the discussion. (Stevenson never met Chiang Ching-kuo on the visit.) The student said that the father felt that the JCRR was doing constructive work and would continue to do so provided it did not "get in the way" of the personal desires of the Generalissimo's family. Then, the student added: "Governor Stevenson has been given a good reception in Formosa not because they like him but because they fear that he may be in power in 1956."

Stevenson dined that evening at the home of the Generalissimo. After dinner he invited Stevenson, Foreign Minister George Yeh, Ambassador Rankin, and an interpreter to withdraw to a private room. Barry Bingham joined the group, and he wrote the following report of the hour-and-a-quarter discussion:

[6] See Ross Y. Koen, *The China Lobby in American Politics* (New York: Macmillan, 1960).

[7] Johnson wrote that word in his diary at the time. It was startling in view of the security police and the intense thought control exercised. It took immense personal courage for the student to write the letter and give the phone number.

The Governor opened the discussion by saying that America and Free China share the objective of controlling Communist aggressive power, and he asked the President's opinion on how the purpose could best be accomplished, taking into account America's heavy commitments, both military and economic, throughout the world.

Chiang replied that the only way to destroy Communist power is to attack it at its roots. This entails an attack on mainland China, coordinated with increased military pressure in Korea and Indo-China. This would cause the Chinese Reds to pull back their best forces to meet the mainland challenge. Chiang could accomplish this purpose successfully, he said, if America would agree to divert to him 20 per cent of the military support we are now sending to our own and allied forces in Korea.

The Governor pointed out that a full offensive in Korea might take a 100 per cent increase in our military contribution there. Chiang then expressed the view that if such an increase were necessary to insure the success of a Korean offensive, it would be better not to do it at all, since no real decision could ever be forced in Korea without an attack on the mainland.

The Governor asked for enlightenment as to why Communism has established a grasp on the masses of the Chinese people, who are predominantly agrarian, whose traditions are opposed to Communist tenets, and in the absence of an overwhelming Soviet military force in China. He pointed out that in Eastern Europe, the satellite countries are held only by sheer physical force exerted by the Red Army.

Chiang answered that China was now more tightly held by Communist power than any country in the world. The Communists have some 5,000,000 men in China to control the population. No Chinese is allowed to move more than a mile from his home without a permit, which he must be prepared to show whenever challenged. Even in Soviet Russia itself, he asserted, there is not such a thorough system of police control. Even so, the Chinese people have not generally accepted Communism and will not accept it as long as a "beacon" is held out to them from Taiwan. Chinese over 30 will never succumb to Communism. The younger people are under increasing danger of being absorbed by the system.

The Governor pursued the point of how Communism makes its appeal to the masses in the Far East. He assumed that its attraction was partly due to a sense of want among millions of people, a want not only for material things, but for justice and a sense of participation in a decent society. He added that land reform was apparently widely used as a propaganda weapon by the Communists, as well as nationalism and a promise of escape from colonialism. China, he noted, had not been under the domination of a foreign power, yet Communism had managed to identify itself in China with a promise of freedom from oppression.

Chiang asserted that the Governor and many other Westerners are wrong about the basis for the Communist movement in China. Its appeal has been political rather than economic, he insisted. The Chinese are the easiest people in the world to satisfy economically. As long as they have something to eat, they are not inclined to blame their government. It was the exercise of political force that captured China, a naked power play, and not a promise of better economic standards. Communism in China pretended to support the tenets of democracy. Then it proceeded to undermine any attempts by the Nationalist Government to institute democratic reforms.

As an example, Chiang cited the land reform program, "land for the tiller," which had been proposed in the early Twentieth Century by Dr. Sun Yat-sen. When Chiang attempted to put this program into practice, the Communists sabotaged every effort. On Taiwan it had only been possible to put land reform into effect because the Communists were outlawed. Communists use democratic freedoms to destroy democratic practices.

Chiang then reminisced at some length about his years of fighting against Communism from 1925 to 1945. He said his group used to have a saying to the effect that to beat Communism you need to use 30 of 100 troops for military purposes and 70 for political purposes. When he captured a new area from the Communists, he would use this ratio in consolidating his success. Until 1945 he had fought the Communists without cessation. Then came the period from 1945 to 1948 when an effort was made to work out a compromise with the Communists. This led to the fall of China.

Foreign Minister Yeh put in that the Chinese people now have seen a demonstration of Communism in action, and they are ready to revolt against it. There have been many little agrarian rebellions on the mainland, he declared, but the outside world has not heard of them. The Chinese now see that the Communists are "much worse than we were, much more corrupt, much more authoritarian."

The Governor asked how long Chiang could retain his army in a state of effectiveness, while remaining on Taiwan. He noted that the troops are growing older. Chiang replied that he could keep them at a high point of readiness for not more than three years. He added that every year that passes will make it more difficult to rally resistance on the mainland, as the Communists are systematically destroying all seeds of opposition leadership. If he can make his campaign soon, he declared, he could establish a firm footing on the mainland in three months, and large scale defections from the Communist ranks would then begin.

The Governor brought up the point that you cannot kill Communism with bullets. A military victory could not be the whole story. It is necessary to release men's minds as well as their bodies from slavery.

Chiang announced that Communism must be fought with bullets first. Only after its military strength is broken can programs be introduced to win the ideological conflict.

The Governor mentioned the Communist problem in other Asiatic nations, naming Indo-China, Thailand, Malaya, Indonesia, Burma. Chiang asserted that here again the only way to solve the problem is to strike at the central force of Communism on the Chinese mainland. This would relieve pressure elsewhere in Asia, he continued, as all the other Communist movements are directed by Chinese in the various countries and operated under the supervision of Mao Tse-tung. This is true, he said, of the Huks in the Philippines, the Communist movements everywhere in Southeast Asia, and also in Korea and Japan.

The Governor expressed some surprise at the statement about Chinese leadership of the Communist movement in Japan. He was assured that Chinese are the ringleaders, that they operate under Japanese names, and that it is not possible to tell a Chinaman from a Japanese by outward appearance. He pressed for a figure on the number of Chinese in Japan, and the Foreign Minister furnished an estimate of 30,000.

The Governor turned to India, and asked Chiang what he thought would be the result of Communist pressure there. Chiang answered that India would be easier for the Communists to take over than Indo-China, where there are French fighting forces. He added that Moscow could put India into its pocket whenever it so desired. It has not yet been absorbed because at present it suits the Kremlin better to permit Indian neutralism than to take over the subcontinent, which would alarm the non-Communist world and create a stronger and more united resistance.

The Governor mentioned that although Nehru's policy externally is "soft" toward Communism, he understands that internal policy in India is tough on subversion and that India jails more political prisoners than possibly any other country.

The Foreign Minister put in that India has a long tradition of revolt and civil disobedience, as expressed in one form by Gandhi, that Indian jails have always been full, and that such methods have no effect on Communist strength in India. Chiang added that direction of the Indian Communist movement has recently been transferred from Mao's hands to the direct supervision of the Kremlin, which is a unique distinction in Asia.

Chiang stated that strength must be developed against Communism at three vital points in Asia, Korea, Japan, and Nationalist China. By using this concentration of strength against the common enemy, the power of Communism elsewhere in Asia can be broken.

Chiang then told of the propaganda themes that he is using to fight Communism among the Chinese. One is land reform, which is effectively demonstrated on Taiwan. Another is nationalism, which he uses to stress the thought that mainland China is under the domination of a ruthless foreign power which is determined to destroy Chinese culture and traditions. After a pause for translation, he added a third propaganda point, democracy, in the sense of self-government for the Chinese people.

The Governor expressed the view that the demonstration being carried out in Taiwan will be of great value in winning back the support of the Chinese people. He thanked the President for the frank expression of his views, not only on China and the Soviet Union but on India.[8]

Bingham told the rest of the Stevenson group: "Throughout the talk, from the beginning, Stevenson was asking the questions. The Generalissimo tried to sound him out on what he thought and where he stood on a question, but Stevenson adroitly ducked these by replying with another question."

When Stevenson returned to the guesthouse at 10:30 P.M., General Sun Li-jen, commander of the Nationalist army, talked to him alone for an hour. He was ill at ease and spoke in a low voice since he clearly feared that the room was equipped with microphones. He spoke highly of General Joseph Stilwell's work in China during World War II.[9] He said that General George C. Marshall had been absolutely right during his official mission to China in 1946 when he had criticized the Nationalist government as corrupt, inefficient, and without popular support.[10] The general added that the secret police were maintaining rigid thought control on Taiwan and that Chiang and his son were ruthless and relentless in suppressing any opposition to themselves. While he said that they did have a good army — he agreed that the number had been grossly exaggerated in America — the United States would have to mobilize if it was really going to help them invade the mainland. The general added that he thought they could get somewhere on the mainland but that their present leadership was "bad." It was still the old

[8] This transcription was written immediately following the discussion by Barry Bingham. A copy is in the possession of Walter Johnson. Bingham recalled: "It had to be written from memory as it was not considered good form to take notes. I believe the Governor found it a fairly accurate record of the conversation, however." Letter to Carol Evans, May 22, 1972.

[9] See Theodore H. White and Analee Jacoby, *Thunder out of China* (New York: William Sloane Associates, 1946).

[10] For a discussion of this mission see Tang Tsou, *America's Failure in China, 1941–50* (Chicago: University of Chicago Press, 1963).

regime concerned with personalities and personal power, he concluded, rather than with the nationalism and democracy of Sun Yat-sen's revolution.

It was interviews like this that led Frank Robertson, correspondent for the Christian Science Monitor, *to write: "Adlai E. Stevenson is having the problems and challenges of this complex section of the Far East presented to him at a rate that would confuse and confound most men. Yet one gathers that the Democratic leader is getting a clear picture and that he has the subject in focus."* [11]

After breakfast on March 22, Stevenson left Taipei for Hong Kong.

Stevenson wrote of his visit to Formosa:

REPORT BY ADLAI STEVENSON [12]

We dropped into beautiful Formosa through a slot in green mountains intricately carved with paddy terraces. Here on a mountainous island less in area than one half of one per cent of the vast Chinese mainland which he dominated for 25 years, Chiang Kai-shek has rallied remnants of the Kuomintang party and of his once enormous Nationalist armies.

Back home, Chiang's government is often pictured either with a halo or a forked tail. On this lush last foothold of Free China, a reformation is taking place, aided by U.S. dollars disbursed under the scrutiny of some 2000 Americans. The refreshing thing is that many Chinese leaders — military and civilian — candidly admit the evils and errors of the past and agree that the forked tail had wagged the halo right off. They don't underestimate the job of reselling the new regime to the world.

I was overwhelmed by my welcome — a bedroom as big as a tennis court, an elaborate civil reception, two long talks with President Chiang and an elegant Chinese dinner at his villa in the lovely foothills back of Taipei. I began to wonder if they knew I had *lost* the election!

My visit to Formosa was a little baffling. *I came expecting to find a strong army and weak government. I left with the reverse impression.*

The effort to establish here among some six million Formosans and nearly three million mainland refugees a laboratory model of good government seemed to me both sincere and demonstrably effective. Production of rice is above prewar; with the help of American engineers, important hydroelectric projects are afoot; bridges, roads, factories are multiplying; public-health work is vigorous; 84 per cent of the children are in school; teachers, nurses, skilled workers are being

[11] "Stevenson in Hong Kong and Formosa," *New Republic,* April 13, 1953, p. 8.
[12] *Look,* May 19, 1953.

trained; living standards are already higher than prewar; **land rents** have been reduced and a land-reform program is succeeding.

I was deeply impressed with the work of the Joint Commission on Rural Reconstruction, a mixed Chinese and American group of technicians headed by the distinguished philosopher Dr. Chiang Monlin. It has two guiding principles — increased production and social justice through fairer distribution. As Dr. Chiang told me, "Agrarian revolutions have destroyed many powerful Chinese dynasties, but they all failed; a land reform that doesn't increase production just equalizes poverty."

There are many difficulties too — lack of capital, a big army to support, little private enterprise, underpaid teachers and civil servants and, as usual in the Orient, too many people living in too small an area.

And there are less obvious but more alarming problems — personalized government, one-man rule in place of a rule of law; palace intrigues, secret police, constant political indoctrination in the army, and what some Chinese call "Russian methods," to insure absolute loyalty to the regime.

Perhaps I could summarize it this way: A great effort at economic and social reform, with lingering reminders of an obsolete past.

But what of the army and the invasion of the mainland? We inspected infantry training and maneuvers with live ammunition. Our guides were Gen. Chou Chih-jou, the chief of staff, and Maj. Gen. Sun Li-jen, commander of the army and a fine patriot. The soldiers looked sharp and disciplined, though modestly equipped. (Maybe they would have looked still better if I had not seen the ROKs.)

But, all told, there are no more than 200,000 trained combat troops available on Formosa; a few thousand more are on the Nationalist islands near the mainland. And there's another important fact we tend to overlook: This army is getting old. Already the average age of enlisted men is 28. In three years, as Chiang himself told me, their combat effectiveness will begin to deteriorate.

This helps explain the almost pathetic impatience of the Chinese Nationalist leaders to return to the mainland. It pervades every discussion, affects every judgment. All admit we would have to equip them, transport them and provide the air cover and logistical support. But Chiang insisted to me that he won't need a single American infantryman; that with increased allied pressure in Korea and Indo-China he could hold a beachhead; that 95 per cent of the Chinese people are anti-Communist and will support him; that after a few months and a few victories, even the Communist soldiers will start defecting. And so Chiang believes he would soon be on his way to the reconquest of China and the extermination of the Communist threat in Asia.

The single-mindedness of this spare, nervous man with bony jaw and piercing eyes reminded me of Syngman Rhee. Each thinks only of the liberation of his own country — with our help. Each is confident of success if we will do this or that. Each insists his war is the important one and the logical place for the decisive effort. And neither seems much concerned about America's other vast commitments or the global nature of the conflict.

"Elimination of the Chinese Communists on the mainland," Chiang said, "is prerequisite to final solution of the Korean war. The Korean problem cannot be solved in Korea alone, even if the United Nations push to the banks of the Yalu River. Only by depriving the Russians of the China mainland may aggression be brought to a halt."

But up in Korea, they said that the place to destroy the Reds was right there where their army was concentrated — not in uncertain scattered blows at the vast mainland.

Chiang has no patience with the long view of things. He says communism must be fought with bullets first; only after its military strength is broken can programs be introduced to win the ideological struggle. Even as President Rhee wants no armistice or settlement that will leave him with a divided country, I gathered that Chiang is fearful of any Mao-Kremlin split which would leave him sitting on Formosa.

Chiang told me he could win on the mainland even if outnumbered five to one. But I also heard that rugged Kwangtung and Fukien provinces opposite Formosa are already fortified, that a radar net has been installed along the coast and that the Reds can now rush reinforcements to any beachhead in a week.

And what if Chiang failed? Would we send Americans into the vast morass of the China mainland to bail him out? Where would they come from — Korea? And if his army is lost in the great mainland gamble, who would defend Formosa? For Formosa must be held.

After Korea and Formosa, I left for Hong Kong in confusion twice confounded, but with at least the definite feeling that: 1. The Chinese are making an impressive demonstration of good administration on Formosa. 2. There is dissatisfaction at many levels with police-state methods. 3. The Nationalist Army is not so strong as people think.

I must add that I never expect to be received more graciously and eagerly anywhere.

Five

Hong Kong

MARCH 22 – MARCH 26, 1953

During the flight from Taiwan to Hong Kong on March 22, Stevenson remarked in a quizzical tone that the longer he was in Asia the "mushier" and more complex all the issues seemed to be. "That's what happens to good reporters who try and delve into their subject and understand it," Attwood wrote in his diary. "He is certainly not taking this assignment lightly and his pieces are going to be the product of a lot of thinking as well as leg work — we won't have the pat answers or the neat formulas for cold war victory — but maybe we'll have a mirror that will accurately reflect at least part of the outlines of this troubled world."

At noon, as the plane approached Hong Kong, Stevenson joined the pilot in the cockpit to have a better view of the spectacular harbor. When he landed, there was a brief press conference. He was told that the night before, three Americans had been seized by Communist officials from their boat off the Portuguese colony of Macao. Stevenson remarked that he did not like kidnappers. When he was asked whether Chiang Kai-shek's forces were in a position to invade the China mainland, he repeated the remark made in Taiwan, that since he had never been higher than an apprentice seaman he was in no position to comment. When questioned as to the impact of Stalin's death on world politics, he replied that he did not know what the intentions of the Russians were but that it would be a mistake to diminish our efforts to strengthen the free world.

Albert Ravenholt, a member of the American Universities Field Staff who had been in China a number of years before the 1949 Communist victory, wrote in the Chicago Daily News *that Stevenson "has been cautious in all of his statements since arriving in this region. This partly reflects Stevenson's own hesitation in the face of a mass of impressions, personalities and sometimes conflicting information. It also reflects his unusual sense of responsibility. He seems to recognize far more than the great majority of American political leaders who have visited here the manner in which Asians may interpret his remarks."* [1]

A motor launch took Stevenson from Kowloon to Victoria Island and he and his party were driven across the mountain to a lovely villa, overlooking Repulse Bay, that had been placed at his disposal by Paul McNutt, former governor of Indiana and commissioner to the Philippine Islands, and C. V. Starr, an insurance magnate.

Albert Ravenholt joined Stevenson for lunch. Stevenson discussed what he had learned in Taiwan, and then the conversation turned to the People's Republic of China. Stevenson quickly accepted a suggestion of Ravenholt's that he bring some knowledgeable people to the villa for informal seminars on mainland China.

When Stevenson asked him whether a landing from Taiwan was feasible and whether people on the mainland would defect, Ravenholt replied that widespread defections would require good organization and an appealing ideology but the Nationalists had neither. As the result of a question from Stevenson, Ravenholt talked at length of an area some hundred miles from Hong Kong which he knew well. Mao Tse-tung's forces at first had arrested only those associated with the Nationalist government. Gradually Communist cadres entered the area and, in February, 1950, they started to liquidate the landlords and moneylenders associated with the old order. The cadres worked carefully to get the community to pass judgment on the man being tried and to join in executing him. Later, Ravenholt added, the liquidating of urban people associated with the old order started on a massive scale.

That afternoon, with Ravenholt as guide, he visited the fishing village of Aberdeen, walked on sampans and junks, and then prowled through the fish market. Later Stevenson and his companions were driven to the teeming Chinese quarter of the city of Victoria and they tramped through back alleys and chatted with shopkeepers. At one point Stevenson exclaimed: "Now, we're really seeing something. I'm getting more out of this than interviewing Chiang!" [2] *Attwood wrote in his diary*

[1] Chicago *Daily News*, March 30, 1953.

[2] William Attwood, "Seeing the World with Stevenson: Twenty Questions and Their Answers," *Harper's*, November, 1953, p. 57.

after this tour: "He's a very ebullient guy when having a good time, and thoroughly fascinated by new sights, sounds and smells."

Dinner and the evening were spent quietly without any officials at the villa. After discussing ideas for the first Look *article, Stevenson wrote a number of postcards and letters.*

To Mr. and Mrs. Howard Brinton [3]

[no date]

Dear Mr. & Mrs Brinton

Of all the things I wanted to do and *didn't,* I think the visit to your "camp" was the most disappointing — not just because of my friend John Forbes,[4] not because of the refugee problem of which I heard a good deal, but because of my long esteem for the Friends and their heroic work. Besides I wanted to meet you! But my visit was hopelessly short. Thanks —

To T. S. Matthews [5]

March 23, 1953

Dear Tom — Your letter caught up with me in Formosa — and a breath of England,[6] even in March — was welcome indeed. Lord knows when I'll get there — probably not until the end of June or early July — if at all! At the moment the latter seems most likely. I've "finished" Japan, Korea and Taiwan and they've all but finished me. Perhaps after a couple of more tranquil days here in Hong Kong with the evening just over the hill I'll feel better about it all — and I think you can count on that evening but the date will have to await the myriad miles and ordeals in between. How does one express coherent, orderly, confident views about this vast, tortured, teeming, frightened segment of our world. Anyway I've got to and soon — if superficially to earn my fare — and with a mind full of mush how I dread it!

AES

On Monday, March 23, after a leisurely breakfast and shopping for gifts to send home, Stevenson met with U.S. Consul General Julian F. Harrington and his staff. They explained that an attack on Hong Kong

[3] Mr. Brinton, a retired educator, was a representative of the American Friends Service Committee of Japan. This handwritten postcard is in the possession of Professor John Forbes, Blackburn College, Carlinville, Illinois. It is postmarked March 23, 1953.

[4] The Brintons' son-in-law.

[5] Editor of *Time* magazine, 1949–1953, and a Princeton classmate of Stevenson's. This handwritten letter is in the possession of Mr. Matthews.

[6] Mr. Matthews was on assignment in London.

was not anticipated since it was important to the People's Republic as a listening post to the outside world and as a source of foreign exchange which they received for selling food to the city. Since the British had been putting more and more strategic goods on the prohibited list, trade with mainland China had been declining. At the moment, China was getting most of her goods from Europe on Polish ships that unloaded in Chinese ports.

Back at the villa, Stevenson's party at lunch included Ravenholt, Howard Boorman, political officer at the U.S. consulate general; Richard Harris, correspondent for The Times *of London; and novelist Preston Schoyer, formerly a professor of Yale University in China. Stevenson proceeded to pump these "old China hands" until late afternoon. Harris insisted that, whether Communist-dominated or not, China would be difficult to work with for the next century. Boorman added that China had the same concept now that it had before the Western nations opened it up in the nineteenth century — a firm belief that it was the center of the cosmos.*

He and the others discussed how Mao's forces had broken the old framework of society and were substituting the concept of loyalty to the community for loyalty to the family. New marriage laws, allowing equality for women, were striking at the heart of the old family system and drawing women into the mainstream of Chinese life. Most people now, it was added, had greater security than in the past. Moreover, although masses of Chinese were annoyed at Communist invasion of their privacy, there was pride that for the first time since Westerners had known China it now had a strong centralized, effective government — "a government that governed."

When Stevenson asked whether any invasion from Formosa was feasible, the general response was that although masses of Chinese feared Mao's government, they were impressed with it. Chiang Kai-shek's system of personal rule could not be reimposed now that the people had tasted rule by law — even Communist law. Chiang was still discredited in China and most of Asia, and basic reforms as well as idealism were necessary for the Nationalists to have any attractiveness. In other words, it was emphasized, until there was something better than personal government by the Chiang family there would be little encouragement for people to defect from the Communists.

Boorman then stated that in analyzing the China problem or the Asia problem, Americans assumed that if a problem existed there must be a solution to it. This simply was not true in Asia. Pat answers would not work, and it was a serious mistake to try to solve problems in Asia "the American way."

When the question was posed as to the chance of a break between Mao's China and the Soviet Union, there was agreement that this was not possible at the moment. But they pointed out that the situation was far different from Eastern Europe where the Red Army was the power factor that enabled the Communists to gain control. In China, Mao had patiently built his own Communist party and army over the past twenty-five years or so, and sometimes he had been in opposition to Russian policy. The Soviet Union, for instance, between 1945 and 1947 had not really wanted Mao to have a unified China. But Mao's organizational ability and fortuitous circumstances led to what the Russians had not expected. The group added that the facts did not prove that the Russians understood China — Communist-led or otherwise.

Early that evening Stevenson spent an hour with John Keswick, head of the British trading firm Jardine Matheson, who had been Admiral Lord Louis Mountbatten's adviser on China during World War II. When Stevenson asked him to justify the trade of Hong Kong with the People's Republic, Keswick replied that Hong Kong had to live. But, he added, British control of contraband was effective. He then stated that he did not think an economic blockade of China would make the Chinese fight any less in Korea. If they were driven to the Yalu River, he doubted that this would accomplish much of anything, since "you cannot defeat Communism in Asia by bayonet and blockade." Moreover, he stated, "It is impossible for the white man to impose his creed on Asia."

When asked his opinion of the possible success of an invasion from Taiwan, Keswick was most emphatic. Chiang's Nationalists were "not the answer to China," since they did not have "what it takes." Chiang, he stated, was Humpty Dumpty and all the U.S. Army and all the U.S. horses could not put Chiang together again.

A base on Taiwan to contain further Chinese expansion was quite a different thing from talk of invading from Taiwan, he contended. The U.S. had to continue its policy of ringing the Soviet Union with bases from Western Europe, through the Mediterranean, the Persian Gulf, and around to Japan. This was essential to maintain order, but it was not sufficient. In addition, there had to be economic assistance to enable people to eat and live decently, and then there had to be a political program so that people would gain a new self-respect. "A philosopher," he remarked, "is far better for this than a general." And, he added, there had been a political-philosophical vacuum in China into which Mao's Communism moved. Mao supplied the country with a unifying "religion" added to the deep spirit of Chinese nationalism.

When Stevenson asked him how he justified British recognition of Mao's government, Keswick said that avoiding World War III depended

*upon the coexistence of Communist and free nations. "If we live up to
our principles, actually live up to them, and carry them out in action,
we will win," he added. As he took a sip of Scotch, he said: "If I may
say so, you are being too logical about the problems out here. . . . The
situation is illogical and you have to deal with it illogically." Then he
remarked that it was a great mistake in American history that the U.S.
did not join the British in recognizing the People's Republic.*

*Stevenson countered by remarking that it was "perfectly silly" for the
British to have a chargé d'affaires in Peking when British soldiers were
fighting Chinese soldiers in Korea. Keswick immediately replied that
it was "perfectly silly" for the U.S. then to have an ambassador in Moscow — "you're really fighting Russia in North Korea." As Stevenson began to say we were not fighting Russia in Korea, Keswick interrupted:
"Look, I would vote for you in the U.S., but not on that one."*

*Then he handed Stevenson a book entitled "What I Know about
China, by John Keswick." When Stevenson opened it, it had nothing in
it but blank pages.[7]*

*Early the next morning, Stevenson, Bingham and Blair drove to the
frontier and watched travelers and goods go back and forth across the
border. Meanwhile, Attwood and Johnson prepared outlines of what
they thought should go into the first article for* Look.

After lunch Stevenson began going over his own notes for the Look
*article and he also answered some correspondence. At every stop, in
addition to letters from local people, there were a great many from the
United States. Professor Arthur M. Schlesinger, Jr., of Harvard University, for instance, sent him regular reports on political developments and
usually included clippings from newspapers.*

To Arthur M. Schlesinger, Jr.[8]

March 24, 1953

Dear Arthur —

Its been a fascinating and exhausting journey. We've "done" Japan,
Korea, Formosa and Hong Kong — and they've about done me! . . .
I'm awfully eager to avoid speeches with so much to see, hear and do.[9]
At the moment I'm looking down on Repulse Bay, junks, sampans and

---

[7] However, Keswick later wrote several articles about China in the *Royal Central
Asian Society Journal*, 1964–1966.

[8] This handwritten postcard is in the Schlesinger papers, John F. Kennedy Library.

[9] Mr. Schlesinger had enclosed with his letter a request from a friend that
Stevenson make a speech when he reached his country.

beauty beyond description, but the Reds are just over the hills and this morning I drove up to the border to have a look at them —

Yrs

ADLAI

To Ernest L. Ives [10]

March 25, 1953

Dear Ernest —

Thanks for your letter and I'm glad to hear that Buffy is determined to get to the bottom of her trouble. I'll hold the thought! I saw Tim [Ives] in Tokyo and he was in fine form. Yesterday we heard that he had to pay up some of our left over bills & I hope somehow to reimburse him. While in Korea I was told they were not using the fighter-bombers much just now, but of course if a push starts they'll be very active again. Its wicked looking country for fighting — very mountainous but our Army is the best fed and cared for in history and the "morale" is excellent. Its been a great adventure, but I got a little tired before we reached here — Hong Kong — where we have lived in a luxurious private home and recovered a bit. Today I must write my first piece for the magazine if I can untangle this mass of notes & pull myself together. Love to Buff.

ADLAI

Stevenson's writing of the first draft of his article was interrupted by a reception in his honor at the American Club and dinner at the home of Consul General and Mrs. Harrington. But early the next morning, March 25, Attwood wrote in his diary: "Stevenson settled down to work on his piece, groaning and muttering like any professional writer. He had my outline, copies of all these notes, Johnson's stuff, his own and a lot of material in handout form."

Generally on the trip, Stevenson wrote his first draft in longhand, and Attwood typed it and edited it. Stevenson would edit this into a third and sometimes fourth draft. After one day's hectic rewriting, Stevenson apologized to Attwood for being so meticulous. "I'm afraid I'm too legalistic," he explained. "But I want each word to express just what I mean." [11] Attwood observed: "I have seen a lot of professional

---

[10] This handwritten letter is in the Elizabeth Stevenson Ives collection, Illinois State Historical Library.

[11] William Attwood, "What Asia Thinks of Adlai," *Look*, June 30, 1953, p. 73.

writers sweating over their prose. Seldom have I met one as consci-entious and attentive to detail." [12]

During the afternoon of March 25, Albert Ravenholt brought another group of "old China hands" to be interviewed. Included were Colonel David D. Barrett, a retired U.S. Army officer who had been chief of the American mission to Mao's government in Yenan in the 1940's; Carl D. Barkman, of the Netherlands foreign service; Captain David Galula, of the French army and currently assistant military attaché at the French consulate in Hong Kong; and Ralph N. Clough, political attaché at the U.S. consulate general.

Barkman told Stevenson that while there did not seem to be any signs of a split between Russia and China, one should never forget that the Chinese Communists were Chinese nationalists. He recommended that Western nations explain to China that they did not care whether China was Communist or not. Their only concern was whether China became imperialistic.

Colonel Barrett discussed how Mao's forces, since driving Chiang off the mainland, had been attacking the United States in violent language as a "fascist-oriented, imperialistic nation." He added that up to 1949 all of the Chinese Communist leaders he had known despised the Russians as "savages and imperialists." He emphasized that Mao should not be underestimated. He was intelligent and had great appeal to the people.

Captain Galula stated that it was nonsense to think that there were cliques of Communist generals struggling with each other for power. Moreover, unlike what had happened in the Soviet Union or in Communist parties in Western countries, there had been no purges of top leaders in China's party. He also said that Chiang's forces could not reconquer the mainland using a purely military approach. It would have to be a political as well as a military war. The Chinese Communists, he added, had learned to send political cadres into every captured community. These cadres sought out people who would work with them and gradually mobilized the full resources of the community behind their efforts.

Mr. Clough agreed that political organization was essential to a successful military operation. During the past eighteen months, he observed, Nationalist General Li Mi had been attacking China from northern Burma, but he had not learned the lesson that he had to win support of the people in the community he invaded. As a result, when the Communists counterattacked, Li Mi's army, with no popular sup-

[12] "Seeing the World with Stevenson: Twenty Questions and Their Answers," p. 59.

port, had to retreat to Burma. Captain Galula interjected that in Indo-china the French so far had failed to organize the population. As a result, after the French conquered an area and then moved on, the enemy moved right back and organized the people against the French.

There was general agreement that Chiang Kai-shek had only about forty thousand active guerrillas on the mainland. This, Stevenson was told, was Chiang's own confidential figure and when he stated there were six hundred thousand guerrillas this was for propaganda purposes.

At the close of the conversation, all five experts agreed that although nationalism had not yet come to the fore among the Chinese Communists, they were in fact vigorous nationalists and they were Asians.

That evening and all the next morning until he departed for Manila, Stevenson wrote and rewrote his article for Look. *As a result of his experience with Stevenson in Hong Kong, Albert Ravenholt wrote:*

> Adlai E. Stevenson has embarked upon his new role as leader of the "constructive opposition" by first seeking an answer to the thorniest problems confronting the United States abroad. . . . Stevenson's success may determine whether the Democratic party now can rise to the challenge and offer the American people meaningful alternatives by which to judge the foreign policy of the Eisenhower administration. . . . Stevenson's fact finding trip through Asia is emphasizing one of America's major national handicaps. This is the failure of its political parties to develop the staff of trained specialists needed to evolve policies that take account of America's world-wide involvement.[13]

Stevenson wrote of his visit to Hong Kong:

REPORT BY ADLAI STEVENSON [14]

I found Hong Kong to be a lovely harbor bustling with sampans, junks, steamers and warships, which no longer deserves its wicked reputation as the port of entry for strategic goods to China.

The British have finally cracked down and little of military value goes up the Pearl River to nearby Canton except pharmaceuticals (mostly antibiotics made in Europe). Trucks, steel and rubber now go straight to Red Chinese ports like Tientsin. Probably 50,000 tons a week reach China, mostly in fast new Polish ships especially built for the Red China trade.

Western businessmen are still trading with China. Switzerland is the

13 Chicago *Daily News,* March 30, 1953.
14 *Look,* May 19, 1953.

financial clearing house. While I was in Hong Kong, a Dane arrived from Peking where he had just closed a deal for 25 million dollars' worth of pharmaceuticals — probably to be purchased in Germany, France and Belgium and shipped in a Polish vessel from a Dutch port.

We are entitled to stricter control of such commerce by our allies.

Meanwhile, Hong Kong is glutted with two million refugees from the mainland and suffering from declining trade.

A sturdy Scottish police inspector took me up to the border — the Lo Wu bridge over the Sham Chun River — and we stood by the barrier watching people come and go and coolies stagger back and forth with Chinese goods for Hong Kong — soybeans, embroidery, camphor crystals — and goods for China — aluminum paste for paint, office supplies, hand wrenches from Germany, photographic paper. From the Chinese side of the bridge, a loud-speaker blared Communist songs — Red guards took our pictures!

Why don't the Reds try to take this allied bridgehead to China?

For the moment, China has good reasons for leaving Hong Kong alone. An attack might touch off World War Three. Capture of the city would only burden China with another dead port and several million mouths to feed. As it is, Communist agents can come and go freely and the colony must live off mainland food — the sale of which provides the Reds with a steady source of valuable foreign exchange.

Hong Kong is a two-way listening post and I heard much that was sobering about Red China from American, British and other allied sources. The consensus was that it's dangerous to assume that most Chinese are praying for Nationalist liberation. The masses hunger for security — for land and a chance to work it unmolested — and this government is the first in a long while that has been able to enforce its authority in all of China.

Order has admittedly been imposed by executions, "brain washing" and terror techniques; but life has been cheap in China for a long time and the Communists have shrewdly allowed the people themselves to settle old grudges and do as much of the dirty work as possible. They have also introduced agricultural reforms, youth movements and new marriage laws (and don't underestimate the power of "emancipated" Chinese women!). The Communists pay their soldiers and employees well.

It would be foolhardy to expect millions to defect to Chiang — whom many associate with warlords, landlords and disorder. Nor has Chiang the trained personnel to move into each town, take over administration and indoctrinate the people with new hope — the democratic equivalent of the Communist teams that appear too effective.

Must we therefore sit back while the Reds tighten their grip on this enormous mass of land and people from which, as Chiang says, all the Communist trouble in Asia stems?

An "old China hand" put it this way: "The terror hurts, Korea hurts, at least economically; the guerrillas are busy; even the efficiency of the Communists — rigid tax collection, for example — is distasteful to the easygoing Chinese. Trouble will breed more trouble, repression more repression. Industrialization in a hostile world will be difficult; there may be a showdown with Russia over who gets what out of Manchuria. Finally, Mao is not a fool and he will quit in Korea when it no longer pays off, even as the Russians eventually gave up the Berlin blockade."

If a U.S.-backed invasion of the China mainland by Chiang's forces is not just a military diversion to weaken the Reds in Korea but the initial instrument of liberation in China, then there is much more planning and preparation, political as well as military, to be done. The stakes are high; so is the price of failure.

Patience, firmness and confidence in our cause are not words that fire imaginations or light torches. But what we should realize is that we must somehow match the patience and persistence of communism in an area where time is measured not in months or even years but in decades and generations.

Our policy — in the future, I hope, as in the past — is to halt the further armed expansion of communism in Asia — Korea, Indo-China, Malaya — and to match its appeal to the masses with something better. My first impression is that we are on the right course; that we are succeeding, slowly and painfully to be sure, but better than many frustrated and impatient Americans think.

Six

The Philippines

MARCH 26–MARCH 30, 1953

During the four-hour flight from Hong Kong to Manila, Stevenson continued to work on his article for Look. Occasionally strangers would come to his seat to say hello. Attwood noted in his diary: "For a public figure, he is certainly one of the most unassuming and unpretentious men I have ever met, with never a disagreeable word for or about anybody. His only discernible changes of mood range from briskness to apparent distraction."

When he landed early in the evening there was a boisterous welcoming crowd of reporters, photographers, diplomats and Filipino officials. For several minutes the newsmen pressed him with questions. He was asked to comment on Eisenhower's statement during the campaign that "Asians should fight Asians." [1] Stevenson replied that the Korean war "is not a matter of race — it has to do with principles."

The ambassador, Admiral Raymond Spruance, who had known Stevenson when the latter was assistant to Secretary of the Navy Frank Knox, 1941–1944, drove the group to his home for dinner. Before dinner Stevenson had a lengthy talk with forty-six-year-old Ramón Magsaysay, who was campaigning for the Nacionalista party nomination for president.

Magsaysay had achieved fame and prominence as a guerrilla leader during the Japanese occupation of the Philippines. After the war he was elected to Congress. In 1950, when U.S. Secretary of Defense General George C. Marshall had warned President Elpidio Quirino to stop the

[1] New York Times, October 3, 1952.

[81]

corruption in the Philippine army or there would be no further U.S. aid, Magsaysay had been made minister of defense. He reorganized the army and launched an effective campaign to defeat the Communist-led guerrillas — the Hukbalahaps. But a month before Stevenson reached Manila, Magsaysay had resigned over the widespread corruption in Quirino's government and in protest at the failure of the president to institute social and economic reforms to alter the evils that had bred the guerrilla movement.

At dinner Stevenson sat next to Senator José Laurel, Nacionalista party leader, who had been defeated by Quirino in 1949 in a corrupt election.[2] Among the others at dinner were President Quirino's foreign secretary, Joaquin Elizalde; Ford Wilkins, publisher of the Manila Bulletin; and William Lacy, counselor of the embassy.

After dinner Stevenson and Magsaysay resumed their earlier conversation. Magsaysay expressed his concern that Quirino again would attempt to intimidate voters and commit vote frauds in order to win. The United States, the Nacionalista leader insisted, should warn the president that all aid would be canceled unless the elections were honest. If the U.S. was not firm about this, he added, there would be trouble and some uprisings if Quirino stole the election. He stated that the people of the barrios hated Quirino and his corrupt government.

He reminded Stevenson and the ambassador that in 1950 when he became minister of defense, Quirino had refused to discharge two corrupt generals until Secretary of Defense George C. Marshall threatened to stop all funds unless the army was reformed. Therefore, Magsaysay reiterated, Quirino should be warned that there would be no more U.S. money until we knew that the election would be honest.[3] After Magsaysay departed, the ambassador explained that Magsaysay's analysis of the situation was accurate and that he was the one political figure of any stature who was both dynamic and incorruptible.

The next morning there was a briefing at the embassy by Spruance; Lacy; R. R. Renne, chief of the Mutual Security Agency; Ralph Busick, public affairs officer; and other members of the staff. It was pointed out that there were probably 3500 armed Huks remaining in central and southern Luzon, who as a result of Magsaysay's work as

2 Senator Laurel's articles "Bread and Freedom" started in the Manila *Sunday Times*, March 29, 1953. He advocated Magsaysay's election to bring bread and freedom to the people. He warned that Quirino could not win reelection without greater crimes than he had perpetrated in 1949.
3 For an analysis of Magsaysay's winning campaign, see Peggy Durdin, "A Filipino Emerges as a New Asian Leader," *New York Times Magazine*, November 22, 1953, pp. 17ff.

minister of defense were not the serious threat the Communist-led guer-rillas had been in 1949 and 1950.

There was considerable discussion of the report of a mission ap-pointed by President Truman and headed by former Under Secretary of the Treasury Daniel W. Bell.[4] *The report of the mission, issued in 1950, had recommended (1) a revision of the tax structure to increase the proportion of taxes collected from high incomes and large estates and steps to stop widespread tax evasions by the rich; (2) an increase in agricultural production, to be achieved by breaking up large estates and selling the land to the tenants, establishing rural credit facilities to re-duce excessive interest rates, opening new land for homesteading, and improving research and extension services; (3) industrial development, including expansion of power and transportation facilities; (4) social reforms, including a minimum wage for all workers, the right to orga-nize free trade unions, adequate health, education and housing; and (5) reform of public administration to insure honesty and efficiency in the government.*

One of the embassy officials pointed out that the Quirino government would not bring about land reform, since the landlords were his main supporters, and the lack of land and a decent return for a day's labor enabled the Huks to appeal to the peasantry. He added that although the tax situation was somewhat better since the Bell Mission, tax eva-sion by the wealthy was still widespread.

R. R. Renne explained that the Mutual Security Agency was trying to implement the Bell report through road- and dam-building, by increasing food production through better fertilizer, irrigation, and seeds, and by encouraging pioneer settlement on the island of Mindanao. The MSA had also made a contract with Cornell University to provide spe-cialists for the College of Agriculture at Los Baños and with the Uni-versity of Michigan to supply specialists to the University of the Philip-pines to train public administrators. There was also a discussion of the feudalistic class structure inherited from the long Spanish domination of the Islands and the difficulties this posed for basic and needed re-forms.

After the briefing, Stevenson paid a courtesy call on President Quirino and Foreign Secretary Elizalde. Then he had lunch with a number of local newspapermen. David Sternberg, who attended the lunch, wrote:

---

[4] *Report to the President of the United States by the Economic Survey Mission to the Philippines* (Washington: Government Printing Office, October 9, 1950). Stevenson had brought with him a useful analysis of the report by Fred Eggan, "The Philippines and the Bell Report," *Human Organization,* Vol. 10, No. 1, Spring, 1951, pp. 16–21.

There was no dearth of popular interest or press coverage for every step of the Governor's itinerary, for, during the recent campaign, he had in the Philippines — perhaps uniquely outside the continental U.S. — a man-in-the-street following. Top stratum Filipino interest in American politics is common enough, since so much of the nation's economic as well as political destiny has been determined by the partisan shifts of American policy, but it was startling to find household servants in Manila — usually unconcerned with even their domestic politics — ready to hazard a guess regarding the Eisenhower-Stevenson contest and prepared to defend their judgment.[5]

That afternoon, after driving around the city, Stevenson spent two hours talking to Ramón Magsaysay, during which, as Albert Ravenholt cryptically stated, "Stevenson was able to learn something of the intense individual and popular dissatisfaction and bitterness that finds its expression in Filipino politics." [6]

Stevenson then spent the evening working on the Look *article. Early the next morning Stevenson flew with Ambassador Spruance to the summer capital of Baguio, nearly five thousand feet above sea level, where they escaped the wet, enervating heat of Manila.* [7]

A large crowd was at the airport when Stevenson's plane landed at Baguio. Most of the people, however, were there to greet Miss Universe of 1953, whose plane arrived a few minutes after Stevenson's. He drew a laugh from the crowd by announcing, as he stepped off his plane, that he was sorry but he was not Miss Universe. [8]

In Baguio the Stevenson party stayed at the embassy residence, but for meals they had to walk about a mile uphill (and back) to Camp

[5] "Stevenson in the Philippines," *New Republic*, April 27, 1953, pp. 10–12.

[6] "Adlai Stevenson and the Philippines," *A Letter to the American Universities Field Staff* (New York: American Universities Field Staff, June 26, 1953), p. 3.

[7] Walter Johnson remained behind to gather information, with the assistance of Albert Ravenholt, from a number of knowledgeable people, including Senator Lorenzo Tañada, independent political leader who had helped persuade Nacionalista chieftains to cooperate in supporting Magsaysay for president; Father Walter Hogan, American Jesuit priest who had been helping build a free, healthy labor movement; Jesus Marcos Roces, secretary to the mayor of Manila — a Nacionalista party leader; Speaker of the House of Representatives Eugenio Perez, a Liberal party leader; David Sternberg of the *Christian Science Monitor;* James Dalton of the Committee for Free Asia; José Lansang, formerly with the *Philippine Herald;* and Robert Hardy of the Mutual Security Agency, who had recently completed a study on how to implement land reform.

[8] This version is drawn from William Attwood's diary written at the time. William McCormick Blair, Jr., has a different version in "A Dazzling Decade," in *As We Knew Adlai: The Stevenson Story by Twenty-two Friends,* edited and with preface by Edward P. Doyle, foreword by Adlai E. Stevenson III (New York: Harper & Row, 1966), p. 238.

John Hay, a U.S. Air Force rest center. "The walks were the best part of the meals, so far as Spruance was concerned," Attwood wrote in his diary. "He's one of those Harry Truman types — up at 5 A.M. for a brisk walk. Puffing up the hill for dinner, he (not puffing) turned to Stevenson and remarked how cool and pleasant it was here, that in Manila our tongues would be hanging out. 'Hanging out?' said Stevenson. 'I've just stepped on mine three times already coming up the hill.'"

Most of that Saturday Stevenson wrote and rewrote the Look article. On Sunday morning he was at it again. Attwood wrote in his diary that Stevenson was "worried that by condensing so much the result will be a superficial reporting job" like what Governor Thomas E. Dewey and others had written about their grand tours.[9] Late that morning Stevenson visited the open-air market, which was teeming with hill people, the men wearing G-strings and carrying big bolo knives and the women smoking cigars, with babies strapped to their backs.

Stevenson remarked that this type of market was much more exciting than the neat supermarkets at home, and he deplored the worldwide standardization of things on the American model. He mused aloud whether it might not have been better if we had left people alone all over the world instead of "trying to export the ways of Main Street."

At noon President Quirino gave a lavish lunch in honor of Stevenson, which was attended by hundreds of Liberal party politicians. Quirino, in introducing Stevenson, said: "We cannot forgo the privilege of hearing one of the most interesting speakers during this — our times." He pointed out that Stevenson was traveling to gather material to make useful observations "regarding life in this region." "But I have the lurking suspicion that his mission will not merely [be] to come and gather data but to learn from the Filipino people how to win an election."

President Quirino praised Stevenson's "admirable and fascinating public career as well as the pattern of public life which he has set for the American people to learn and to emulate." Quirino said that it was unfortunate that Stevenson had "arrived in our midst at this stage of our political development," but added, "I am quite sure he will see through this maze, superficial, partisan political confusion while we are engaged in a local competition to show what element of this country is more earnest in cleaning this country of graft and corruption, and who is more glamorous in this country." He concluded: "But what is more of interest to us is to hear from him some encouraging, inspiring,

---

[9] Thomas E. Dewey, *Journey to the Far Pacific* (Garden City, New York: Doubleday, 1952).

elevating, ennobling talk that has made the American people expect
of him to be one of the greatest American Presidents."
   Stevenson's extemporaneous remarks follow: [10]

Mr. President, Mr. Ambassador, my distinguished friends, and shall I
say, my fellow Democrats: (Laughter)
   I don't know, Mr. President, whether you want those inspiring, elevating, and ennobling thoughts all in one course of speech. (Laughter)
You said that I might have been distracted here. While I have been distracted by the most delicious food and most charming company in my
journey, and I have been deeply touched, as we all have, by the reception which you have accorded us here in the Philippines, your hospitality, your courtesy, and your great good will have left an impression
that will be enduring with me.
   Indeed, when I arrived yesterday, Mr. President, at the Baguio airport, with Ambassador Spruance and my party, there were a great many
people on the field and I thought for a moment that they might have
been there to greet you, Sir, or even the great Miss Universe. But I am
persuaded now they were there for me. (Laughter)
   You know, Mr. President, and Gentlemen and Ladies, that coming
to the Philippines for us is not like going to a foreign country. We feel
when we come here . . . we come to brothers and sisters; we come to
people who share, if not all of our traditions, at least all our objectives
and our aspirations. I am in a way disappointed that I happen to come
here at a time when you are engaged or about to be engaged in a political campaign.
   I think political campaigns do distort somewhat one's impressions of
a country and its preoccupation with its most important affairs. And,
furthermore, having recently had experience with campaigns, my heart
bleeds for all of you. (Laughter) I hope you enjoy the ordeal. You look
fit and healthy. Perhaps you can survive with the same equanimity that
I may say that I do. In fact, had the results of our elections been any
different, Mr. President, I would have been unable to visit the Philippines. So that we find compensation in what appears to be misfortune,
and I found the richest compensation a human being could hope for
in an opportunity to travel in this vast area of the world which is so
[fraught] with the future peace and the security not only of my people
— the United States — but of the whole world.
   What we have seen as we travelled here by way of Japan to tor-

   [10] The full text, as well as Quirino's remarks, were published in the Manila *Times*,
March 30, 1953. The transcribing of the speech was not always accurate. At times
words were missed or garbled. We have corrected such mistakes.

mented, tortured Korea, Formosa, Hongkong, has always been the same — too little land, too few resources, and too many people. And then [here in the Philippines] with an abundance of land, of resources, and a healthy population growing only now and to the full richness of its maturity. It seems to me a most favored, blessed section of the world, and I think that we can take another satisfaction in the Philippines because here is flowering in the Western Pacific, the first great laboratory demonstration of what we feel and know you feel, certain hope for a better world democracy — government by the people, government, if you please, by the consent of the governed — which is something the people have bled and died for for centuries, and you are surrounded by a new tyranny, perhaps the most critical challenge to this tradition of the West that we have seen under the Christian era.

Here in the Philippines is a vast bulwark of the faith that we hold so dear. That my country should have a part in the development of this country is a glorification to every American . . . America asks nothing of anyone, nothing for itself that it could not ask for mankind itself. If we can find the peace, we can find opportunities to develop the economic resources of our world, and find thereby a good life, a better life for many people; that we shall have what we all dream about and pray for — peace in the world.

In my country, while we dispute our elections with vigor — after I am told the manner of the Philippines — while we differ on men and measures, there is little difference between us on objectives. Whether we be Republicans or Democrats, beyond our shores we are the same thing. That, I think, is your view; that, I think, would be the democratic tradition as it evolves in this great experiment in the Philippines, which is under close scrutiny of so much of the world, perhaps more than you who live here realize. There are many problems that you have that I have heard about, many difficult and sometimes almost insoluble problems, but they are as nothing, it seems to me, compared to what surrounds you.

I can think of but one that I shall mention offhand and that is the problem perhaps most difficult of all, because it affects emotions of mankind — the problem of rapprochement with Japan. Here are two complementary economies — one industrial and one basically agriculture; one desperately in need, Japan; and one which is in the very infancy, I dare say, of its enormous and rich development — the Philippines. Surely, there must be ways in which these two countries can help themselves, despite all the bitterness, the anguish and the misery that was left behind by the atrocities perpetrated here not so long ago. And all of this is important to us because these are vast areas to which the

United States must look in its mission eventually, I dare say, not because it wants, but because destiny has assigned the United States an enormous responsibility in the years to come, areas to which we must look for understanding, for common thought. There is more that I should like to say to you, now that the President has so foolishly given me this opportunity to make a speech (Laughter), but because you have been so kind to me, you have been so hospitable, so gracious, I think the least I can do is to be equally charitable with you and say no more. (Applause.)

After Stevenson and Ambassador Spruance had departed, Quirino called a press conference and attacked the U.S. embassy for "meddling in local politics." He expressed his indignation at the dinner the ambassador had given on the evening Stevenson arrived. "Now, why did the American embassy go out of its way to round up all these Nacionalista leaders to meet Stevenson?" he asked. Then he denounced the seating arrangements at the dinner, where Stevenson had sat next to Senator Laurel. "He was quite emotional as he gave details of the dinner," one reporter wrote.[11]

The president then called the reporter's attention to a charge in the Manila papers that morning by Liberal Representative Diosdado Macapagal that the U.S. embassy was interfering in local politics and boosting the candidacy of Ramón Magsaysay. And Quirino added that his office in Manila had released in full an article in Bataan *magazine charging that the U.S. Army and the embassy were pushing for the election of a "man on horseback." [12]*

Albert Ravenholt wrote of this episode: "By questioning Spruance's choice of guests to meet Stevenson, Quirino forced the American Ambassador to publicly reaffirm United States neutrality in the election and thereby scored another point in the President's campaign to prove that the 'paternal republic across the Pacific' is not really opposed to his Liberal administration although his opponents have received much favorable publicity there." [13]

On Monday morning, March 30, after the Look *article was finished, Stevenson returned to Manila. That afternoon, with R. R. Renne as guide, he drove an hour out of Manila to inspect the Los Baños agricultural college. Renne explained the agricultural situation in detail and*

[11] Manila *Times,* March 30, 1953. Actually, the Liberal foreign minister was present at the dinner and two other top Liberals had been invited, accepted, and then failed to appear.

[12] Manila *Times,* March 29, 1953.

[13] "Adlai Stevenson and the Philippines," p. 3.

emphasized that credit for farmers was a particularly pressing problem. At planting time a farmer borrowed rice seeds and at harvest he had to pay back two grains for every one he had borrowed. Moreover, he observed, tenants really had no incentive to produce very much or to be efficient because they knew that no matter how hard they worked they could not buy land.

That evening Stevenson held a press conference with Filipino and foreign newspapermen. When reporters asked for his comments on Quirino's charge that the embassy was interfering in domestic politics, he turned the question aside: "I shan't get involved in local politics about which I know little." He stated that he had been particularly interested in visiting the Philippines, since Filipinos "had a great opportunity to demonstrate the process of free government as an alternative to Communism." He urged, in an answer to one question, a resumption of trade between Japan and the Philippines as beneficial to each.

When asked if he favored negotiating with the Russians, he replied: "We should stand ready at all times to negotiate in good faith." In answer to a complicated question about American public opinion, he jokingly told the reporters that "sometimes the people aren't right — they may have made a mistake in the United States last fall."

After the press conference he dined with Ambassador and Mrs. Spruance and Mr. and Mrs. William Lacy. The ambassador remarked that he had no dealings with the Liberal speaker of the House, Eugenio Perez, because he did not "like crooks." When he met with Quirino, he said, the only praise he could give him was to say that "you are a fine speaker."

Lacy suggested that Quirino's charges against the embassy were precipitated by a letter from President Eisenhower that Spruance had handed Quirino the past Friday when he and Stevenson had made their courtesy call. The letter told Quirino that when he wished to communicate with the United States government he must do it through Spruance and not try to do it through his own ambassador in Washington. Since Quirino knew from the firm tone of Eisenhower's letter that he could not undermine Spruance in Washington, Lacy speculated that Quirino was trying to destory Spruance's effectiveness in the Philippines and possibly force his recall.

Stevenson expressed his concern over the obsessive preoccupation with the game of politics and wondered if this would not have grave effect on the nation's progress. He also said that he almost told the press conference that he would like to see some of the Filipino politicians come to Chicago and give life to the moribund Chicago Democrats.

At the airport that evening before departing for Singapore, Stevenson told reporters that he wished "peace and prosperity to both the Nacio-

*nalista and Liberal parties." In the papers next morning a Liberal con-
gressman observed darkly, "He still put the Nacionalistas first."* [14]

After Stevenson wrote his impressions of the Philippines for Look, *Albert Ravenholt observed: "With the exception of a few minor errors, the
picture he presented was a balanced account of affairs here with which
most informed observers . . . would have been in general agreement.
. . . He dealt accurately with the most immediate problems confronting this country and made several neat criticisms with such skill that no
political faction has been able to use his words to their own advantage.
. . . Wherever they went," he continued, "the Stevenson group revealed
a breadth of intellectual curiosity rare among American VIP visitors to
the Far East. . . . Stevenson and his companions made a far better impression upon Filipinos than most quick visitors from the United States.
The leaders here are alert to good oratory and superior political performance and many of them judge Stevenson a master who somehow reminds them of those firmer and more literate American leaders who
early in the century launched our experiment in these Islands."* [15]

Stevenson wrote of his visit to the Philippines:

BALLOTS AND BULLETS [16]

We stepped out of the airplane in Manila into suffocating heat and
blinding flash bulbs; then came hearty handshakes and American soft
drinks. It was like Chicago in July. And I quickly discovered that a premature political campaign was already in full swing. For me, the pleas-
antest thing about it was being able to view it with impersonal objectivity.

The Filipinos seem obsessed with politics. Although the elections
were seven months away, city people could scarcely talk of anything
else and I was in it before I knew it. Because arrangements already had
been made for me to see President Elpidio Quirino and members of his
Liberal party, our Ambassador, Adm. Raymond Spruance, had invited
a few of the opposition Nationalist leaders to have dinner with us as
soon as we arrived. The Liberals promptly charged the American Ambassador with interference in the election!

For fifty years an American protégé, the Philippines are close to the
hearts of most Americans. To the peoples of Asia, Philippine independence is proof that the United States stands by its promises. Moreover,
this thousand-mile-long archipelago is the southern anchor of a natural

[14] Sternberg, "Stevenson in the Philippines," p. 12.
[15] "Adlai Stevenson and the Philippines," pp. 6–7.
[16] Look, June 2, 1953. The conclusion of this article is reprinted in Chapter
Seven, below.

line of defense on the rim of Asia. So there is no underestimating the importance to us of this troubled republic.

Manila emerged from the war as probably the most devastated capital in the world after Warsaw. The half-submerged hulks of many Japanese ships are still rusting in the harbor, but the city has been largely rebuilt. Meanwhile, the nation has checked the Huk Communist rebellion, taken some encouraging steps toward financial and governmental reform and weathered a major economic crisis (thanks in great part to two billion dollars' worth of U.S. aid for reconstruction, war-damage claims, veterans' pensions and so on).

But if things are better, they are not good. There are squalor and misery behind the facade of fine new buildings, and the average Filipino is 20 to 25 per cent worse off than before the war. The Huks are still active, and their strength and depredations would multiply with deterioration of the army and the economy. (If the economy is still relatively healthy for Asia, it is only because of American expenditures and the duty-free entry of Philippine products into the United States.)

The elections of 1949 were marked with violence, coercion and bribery — and everyone knows it. While President Quirino and his able cabinet have made some notable progress in carrying out the drastic reforms recommended in 1950 by a commission of American experts, there are still ugly reports of corruption; unemployment is high and efficiency low. Nor has any progress been made toward land reform and the release of the small farmer from the landlord, from the Chinese moneylender and from centuries-old systems of land tenure.

Yet this remains a land of promise in East Asia — if only because of its abundant land and still undeveloped natural resources. At the moment, the future is unclear, and this may be the year of decision.

There are many who say that it is "time for a change" (a phrase I have heard before!) and that Ramón Magsaysay, the popular, husky wartime guerrilla leader, will sweep the Liberals out of office — *if the elections are honest.* I talked at length with Magsaysay, an ex-Liberal turned Nationalist. He came with two bodyguards — and with good reason: Politics is rougher here than anything I experienced last fall.

Magsaysay is voluble, ambitious, energetic and worried — worried lest the elections are rigged as they were in 1949.

"Without committing more atrocities than he committed then, President Quirino cannot win," Magsaysay said. "Therefore, he must commit them."

Magsaysay's supporters, seasoned veterans like Sen. José Laurel — who was the Nationalist candidate and victim of the last election — and independent Sen. Lorenzo Tañada, are equally blunt and equally determined "to drive this administration out of office this year, lock, stock and barrel."

Quirino appointed Magsaysay Minister of Defense in 1950. He did a truly great job of reorganizing the army and cleaning up the Huks. His weapons were competence, courage and compassion. He used the army to police the congressional elections in 1951 and they were honest and relatively orderly (only 20 killed!). His unchallenged integrity has won him respect and affection among the common people. But this spring, he resigned from President Quirino's administration, protesting lagging reforms and continuing corruption. Now he is running against his former chief with no holds barred.

Small wonder there is no love lost on Magsaysay in the Quirino camp or that the campaign will outdo in virulence anything the Filipinos have learned from their American tutors in the ways of democracy.

President Quirino, after a lifetime in public service, seems determined to run again. He received me most graciously, both at the Malacañan Palace and together with a large number of his political followers at the summer White House in the mountains near Baguio. An engaging, eloquent political "pro" with a touch of arrogant impatience, he spoke convincingly about his accomplishments and hopes — hydroelectric-power developments in the mountains, shipyards, cement and fertilizer plants, resettlement of surrendered Huks, the opening of new land in Mindanao.

President Quirino lost his wife and two children in the war and the Japanese beheaded the brother of his Foreign Minister, "Mike" Elizalde. However, both emphatically agreed with me on the desirability of friendly relations and commerce between two such complementary economies as Japan's and the Philippines'. As Quirino put it, "God made us neighbors, and we must get on together. It is not possible to transfer the Philippines or Japan to the other side of the globe." (One of the difficulties so far has been the opposition of the Nationalists to ratification of the peace treaty with Japan without agreement on larger and unrealistic reparations payments.)

While President Quirino never mentioned Magsaysay by name, he was at pains to say that he regretted my visit occurred just when the country was preoccupied with politics; but he trusted my "good judgment and perception to see through glamour and words to principles and real problems."

Actually, there are few basic programs or principles dividing the Liberal and Nationalist parties. For years, the theme song of all Philippine political leaders was independence. Now that they have full independence, little new political ammunition has been developed and party conflict centers around men rather than measures, leaders rather than policies.

In the past, the Nationalists have reproached Quirino for his "servile attitude toward America." But today they are demanding outright U.S. intervention to prevent the Liberal party from stealing the election with the help of political police and the constabulary. I suspect Uncle Sam is going to be alternately serenaded and cudgeled in the months ahead in this country, which turns out about two thousand lawyers — all potential politicians — every year.

There is some basis for alarm about a possible repetition of the sorry tactics used in 1949 when Quirino beat Laurel. Already, the President has transferred "responsibility for peace and order" in a large area from the army to the more manageable constabulary.

This is a disturbing sign, and it would be a brutal blow to democratic government in the Orient if the elections in this critical year were crooked. Indeed, there are dark threats of open revolt if the methods of 1949 are used again.

What of the future? Cynics say that the Congress is dominated by vested interests and landlords who finance both parties, and that politicians will continue to procrastinate on land reform and the hard distasteful things that so badly need doing. That may be true, but some important progress has been made under Quirino, and, if Magsaysay is elected, there is reason to believe he means what he says and will earnestly try to do something for the common people. With the counsel of his more experienced friends Laurel and Tañada, Magsaysay could write a bright new chapter in the chronicles of Philippine politics.

On my last day, I escaped from the clamor of Manila and visited the College of Agriculture at Los Baños, where so many Americans were interned by the Japanese during the war. As we entered the tropical campus, an American lady hailed me: "Stand still, Adlai, this is my last film. I was going to use it on water buffalo but I saved it for you." [17] Our Government has put a million dollars into the rebuilding of this once-great institution. Even as we have brought a team from the University of Michigan to help with the acute problem of training needed public administrators, we have also brought agricultural experts from Cornell to help enlarge the student capacity at Los Baños from one to three thousand. In an economy predominantly agricultural, where production must be increased and diversified, there is no more important technical-assistance program in the Philippines.

Can the Filipinos develop an economic and social base to support the democratic political institutions we introduced in the islands? It is by

[17] This incident actually occurred at Angkor, Cambodia. See p. 108, below.

no means certain, but I feel a cautious optimism that this ambitious, self-respecting people can set their political house to rights, tighten their belts and settle down to the long, hard business of developing their great human and natural resources, raising their standard of living and building a stable society. It will take time and patience, for it seems to be easier for us to work with the Filipinos than for them to work with each other. But it can be done.

Seven

Vietnam and Cambodia

APRIL 1 – APRIL 8, 1953

Newsmen, photographers, U.S. Consul General C. F. Baldwin, members of his staff, and several British officials were waiting in the muggy darkness of the Singapore airport at 6 A.M., March 31, when the plane from Manila landed. After an exchange of pleasantries, Stevenson went to the Raffles Hotel to rest.

Except for lunch with Consul General and Mrs. Baldwin, an inspection of the British naval base, and a tour of the Singapore harbor, Stevenson spent the day and evening resting and writing letters and postcards.

To Mrs. Ernest L. Ives [1]

[no date]

I've never felt so far away! We've "done" Japan, Korea, Formosa, Hong Kong, Philippines and now Singapore and I'm about "done" too! Its been fascinating but too fast a pace & of course I have to work every minute day & night literally. I hope you've got to the bottom of your jaw! Have sent for David Bailey [2] to come in to see me tonight. Wish I knew what to buy & had time to shop in the fabulous East — AD.

---

[1] This handwritten postcard is in the Elizabeth Stevenson Ives collection, Illinois State Historical Library. It is postmarked Singapore, April 1, 1953.

[2] Son of Stevenson's second cousin Lady Mildred Bailey. He was an officer in the Royal Navy.

At seven the next morning Stevenson boarded a Cathay Pacific plane for Indochina. During the flight he struggled to catch up with his correspondence.

To Mrs. Edison Dick [3]

April 2, 1953

Japan, Korea, Formosa, Hong Kong, Philippines, a day in Singapore — and now somewhere over the South China Sea en route to Saigon — and the Indo China War. It's just one war after another here! The pace has been too fast and I haven't felt well — to bed last night at 12 (after writing 23 letters of thanks to people along our route) and up this morning at 5 — officials, functions, heat, interviewing, writing, packing, unpacking, and the ubiquitous photographers and newsmen, day after day. Besides, I'm afflicted with a misfortune too embarrassing to mention! I wish I could write you a proper letter. I've spent every moment of spare time trying to do the first of the damn Look pieces and after writing some eight thousand words finally got a superficial newspaper-like thing off from Manila of 4000–5000 [words —] more than their maximum. It's maddening — but it may not be as hard again, trying to squeeze Korea, Japan & Formosa in one tiny piece when I had enough material gathered for a book on each.

I think I'll survive however in spite of sinking spells. The high point for comfort was Hong Kong — an exquisite house to ourselves — 11 servants — the best food of the orient — and a soul stirring view of the placid quiet sea, junks and sampans gliding slowly over the water, tumultuous green islands — it was breathless even leaning against the bamboo curtain, but I hardly got to look at it what with the work. Some day you must see Hong Kong — and Repulse Bay where we stayed. Another lovely interval — writing the damn article — was a mountain top in Baguio in the Phillipines as fine mountain views as I have ever seen — in spite of loin cloth Igorotes. There is so much to say about this fantastic journey that even leaves the "old hands" breathless with our speed and diligence. If it has to be letter for letter — well and good — I surrender! But I can't do much and yours were so informative I should like to earn more of them. Maybe you'll relent! You see they roll out the carpet everywhere and I have to send letters of thanks back as I go etc etc. Now here comes the Australian capt. of this aircraft. O God — if only I could go to sleep, let alone read up on Indo China. The gang's all well. Hope the Dicks are too.

---

[3] This handwritten letter is in the possession of Mrs. Dick.

Four hours after departing from Singapore the plane landed in Saigon. The U.S. ambassador to Vietnam, Laos, and Cambodia, Donald R. Heath, was away and Stevenson was met by Chargé d'Affaires Robert McClintock, who had been on Stevenson's staff when he was chairman of the United States delegation to the Preparatory Commission of the United Nations Organization in London in the fall of 1945. At McClintock's insistence, Stevenson went with him to stay at the ambassador's residence. As William Attwood wrote: "Wherever Stevenson was too hemmed in by officialdom — as in Indochina — Johnson, Bingham and I would see the kind of people who don't get invited to banquets and make notes for him on our conversations; or we'd arrange appointments for him with local reporters, students, businessmen, and opposition leaders." [4]

While Stevenson lunched with McClintock, his aides ate at the Majestic Hotel with Larry Allen of the Associated Press, Henry Lieberman of the New York Times, and John Pickering, former reporter for the Chicago Sun, who was now in charge of the United States Information Service in Saigon. They discussed the friction that existed among the three Associated States of Indochina with their different cultural backgrounds and then talked a good deal about the fighting in the Red River Delta around Hanoi. Lieberman emphasized how strong the opposition in Hanoi was to Chief of State Bao Dai. In the municipal elections the past January an anti–Bao Dai and anti-French city council was elected. They all agreed that the French had been making concessions to Bao Dai's government but doing it much too late to gain any credit for it. In fact, they felt that Bao Dai now had more power than Ho Chi Minh had demanded from the French in 1946.

France in 1887 had established the Federal Government of Indochina consisting of Cochin China, Annam, Tonkin, Cambodia, and Laos. Years before World War II, nationalistic groups had been demanding independence and some wanted a status resembling the British dominions. French-educated and Soviet-trained Ho Chi Minh worked with various nationalistic groups in the broad front of the anticolonial movement. The Japanese occupation of Indochina dealt a severe blow to French prestige and stimulated opposition to Western (white) colonialism. Months before the surrender of Japan, Ho Chi Minh, who had been building a resistance group in southern China, returned to Indochina with a coalition of popular-front political parties known as the Vietminh (a shortened version of the Vietnamese equivalent of Vietnam Independence League). With the Japanese collapse, the Vietminh

---

[4] "Seeing the World with Stevenson," Harper's, November, 1953, p. 57.

moved into Hanoi and proclaimed itself the government with Ho as president. Bao Dai, after he had resigned as emperor of Annam, was made "supreme adviser" to Ho.

The French signed a preliminary agreement with Ho on March 6, 1946, recognizing the "Democratic Republic of Vietnam," which included Annam and Tonkin but not Cochin China, as a free state within the French Union and the Indochinese Federation. That summer Ho and the French carried on detailed negotiations in France. These broke down over such questions as the union of Cochin China with the rest of Vietnam, military relations, and the control of customs and finance. In December, 1946, Ho's forces attacked and almost succeeded in driving the French from the North.

In an attempt to secure the support of nationalists anxious for independence, but who were opposed to Ho's communism, the French negotiated with Bao Dai and recognized him as chief of state of Vietnam in 1949. Cochin China, Annam, and Tonkin were united, and it was agreed that a Vietnamese national army would be created but with the agreement that French Union Forces would defend the country. While the French made a number of concessions, the Vietnamese concessions to the French included privileged economic and cultural status, military bases, customs and monetary union within the Associated States of Indochina, and preference for French advisers and technicians. Moreover, Vietnamese law, in order to be applicable to French nationals resident in Vietnam, had to be promulgated by the French high commissioner. And French and Chinese nationals had to be tried under French law before mixed French-Vietnamese tribunals.

Stevenson and his party on the afternoon of their arrival attended a not-too-informative briefing at the embassy. It was emphasized that there was widespread nationalistic fervor in the Associated States. In Vietnam, it was pointed out, many non-Communists refused to support either Bao Dai's government or the forces of Ho.[5]

The French, Stevenson was told, tried to interpret the 1949 accord most rigidly and the three Indochinese states resented the continuation of French control. The problem for the United States, it was added, was that we wanted the French to continue their military efforts but at the same time we wanted the three states to have self-reliant governments.

The army attaché explained that there was no front in this war as in a classical war. And it was more of a political war than a military

[5] For a discussion of the period 1953–1954, see Melvin Gurtov, *The First Vietnam Crisis* (New York: Columbia University Press, 1966).

one. In the Red River Delta many villages were controlled during the day by French and Vietnamese government forces but in the evenings the Vietminh returned. The French had many troops tied down manning posts, bridges and waterways, while the Vietminh were mobile. He pointed out that when French forces left an area it reverted to the Vietminh. Up to date the French and Bao Dai's government had not developed a political organization to keep villages under their control after the military left.

In response to a question from Stevenson, the army attaché said that the French Union forces numbered some 225,000 from overseas and, in addition, there were 56,000 indigenous Vietnamese. The Vietnamese government had some 94,000 regular forces and 52,000 supplementary ones. Cambodia had about 13,000 and Laos had about 12,000 troops. The operational control of all troops, however, rested with the French.

The Vietminh, he continued, had about 203,000 regional and regular troops. In addition, they had about 110,000 militiamen who fought during the nighttime. The Chinese were supplying the Vietnamese with about 200,000 tons of equipment a month. While the French navy prevented supplies from being landed by water, it was difficult to know whether French bombing of supplies coming through the jungle and mountainous terrain was effective.

The head of the Mutual Security Agency branch (in Vietnam called the Special Technical and Economic Mission) stated that STEM could not place technicians in the Vietnamese government because of French "sensibilities." But in trying to increase rice production, road and bridge construction, relief activities, and combating illiteracy, they worked directly with the governments of the three Associated States. At the moment, with the cooperation of Governor Nguyen Huu Tri, they were building a model village near Hanoi and making it secure against Vietminh raids at night.

The public affairs officer, George Hellyer, noted that the United States Information Service printed posters and leaflets for the Vietnamese and French information services but that neither of them had any concept of a continuing program of psychological warfare. The real problem for the USIS was that many people felt that Ho Chi Minh represented nationalism against French colonialism. The French were so sensitive, he continued, that the USIS could not state in its publications that we believed in independence and illustrate it by the example of the Philippines.

Dinner was at the embassy residence with many French, Vietnamese, and embassy officials present. Although it was difficult to learn much of value, Stevenson had a frank talk with Wilmarth H. Starr, educa-

tional officer of STEM. He emphasized the immense passion of the Vietnamese for independence, and he doubted that after independence they would stay in the French Union. He added that the French in Vietnam were arrogant toward the Vietnamese. Unfortunately, at that moment, the Vietnamese had no real leadership, no cohesion, and no sense of a political polity.

He stated that the leaders of Bao Dai's government treated their own people as arrogantly as the French did. The present elite of Vietnam were cast in the same mold as the French, he added, and behaved like colonial overlords.

French colonial policy, he continued, had been "terrible." They deliberately did not train administrators or technicians and, furthermore, they kept various groups at each other's throats. It was a question of playing not only each of the Associated States off against each other but also groups within each state.

The next morning Stevenson made revisions in his first article for Look *and answered part of his mail.*

To Mrs. Edison Dick [6]

[no date]

I'm low as I am afraid this wretched screed discloses, the pressure is constant, the climate ennervating and I haven't felt well since I left Chicago! But all will be well with me — if you keep me informed & don't expect much in return — as usual!

I can't organize my mind — there is a crowd downstairs — I'm in Saigon now — steaming hot — and am due for another of those God damn ceremonial lunches — with the French High Commissioner "au Palais."

. . . Have no idea yet when I'll get to England. Planning to go to Yugoslavia, Austria and Berlin — the hot spots — and treat France and England very lightly indeed, unless it is for a holiday with the boys or something — or unless *you* had invasion plans.

Just found cable here from Look requesting rewrite of piece — on cables today — because of armistice possibility.[7] I could cry and I think I will!

. . . People really live off fishing here — rice and fish and babies is the scenery in all Asia. Like rice?

[6] This handwritten letter is in the possession of Mrs. Dick.

[7] Although peace talks were in progress, the Korean cease-fire was not signed until July 26, over two months after Stevenson's article appeared.

P.S. Sorry the dear Gov book is such a headache.[8] I'm not the least surprised. Have you seen the "special corres[pondence]." Indeed I wonder if Miss E. [Carol Evans] kept the stuff all separated — there were so many analytical letters. Hasn't WHISTLE STOPPING emerged?[9] I am distressed.

Late that morning Stevenson flew with Barry Bingham and Bill Blair to Dalat to lunch with Bao Dai at his hunting lodge in the hills.[10] Bao Dai expressed strong resentment that the French would not allow the Vietnamese to develop guerrilla forces, and he told Stevenson that he would not wear a military uniform, even though his country was at war, until the Vietnamese had operational control of their own forces.

Meanwhile, Attwood spent several hours in Saigon contending with bureaucratic red tape before he was allowed to cable Stevenson's revision of the Look *article to New York City. He wrote in his diary:*

> Walking around, I wasn't aware of the same friendliness that I sensed in Korea, Hong Kong or even Japan. There seems to be an invisible barrier between whites and natives and their attitude is a blend of vague hostility and indifference. Not only don't people in the native quarter smile at you; they don't even appear to take notice of you. When you speak to them in French there's something sullen about the way they reply — for example, they don't look you in the eye. Maybe I'm imagining things but I don't think so.

Meanwhile, at Stevenson's request, Walter Johnson spent the morning talking to Captain Edward Korn, of the U.S. embassy. Supreme Court Justice William O. Douglas had written to Stevenson recommending that he talk with Korn.

It was a frank and enlightening two hours. Captain Korn stated that many rich Vietnamese were investing their funds in France rather than in their own country and most of them held French citizenship — half of Bao Dai's cabinet, for instance, were French citizens. And the president of the National Council, Nguyen Van Tam, was a French citizen although Korn doubted that Tam was a "stooge" of the French.

---

[8] The proposed volume containing letters Stevenson received after his defeat. See note 31 to Chapter One, above.

[9] Mrs. Dick's reminiscences of the 1952 campaign. See note 31 to Chapter One, above.

[10] For a description of the lunch, see Barry Bingham, "Mistake and Misfortune, Misery, Hunger, Dirt — That's War in Indochina," Louisville *Courier-Journal*, April 26, 1953.

He added, in an understatement, that the French were "not good colonists." They exploited the country and invested back in France much of the money they made from their activities in Vietnam.

He then discussed the Vietnamese nationalists-neutralists. According to his information, all intellectuals, most Catholics, members of the Dai Viet party, and other subsidiary groups were in this category. They wanted tangible signs of independence and a relinquishment of French controls. Although the more logical knew they needed French military aid, they would not cooperate with the Bao Dai government until the French promised independence as soon as the military situation allowed it.

He emphasized that Ngo Dinh Nhu of Saigon was a powerful nationalist leader of the Catholic community. At that moment his brother Ngo Dinh Diem [11] was in exile in the United States, and the third brother, Bishop Ngo Dinh Thuc, lived forty miles from Saigon. At this point, Johnson showed Korn a list of Vietnamese names that Stevenson had brought with him. Korn expressed surprise mixed with admiration that Stevenson had such a list and said, "This is the best list of nationalists-neutralists conceivable. Where did you get it?"

Johnson explained that a Catholic priest — an Asian — had called at Stevenson's office several weeks before he had departed from Chicago. He would not give his name but had told Blair that Stevenson should meet everyone on the list.[12] Korn conjectured that it must have been Father Jacques, who was the representative of the Vietnamese bishops in the United States.

Korn stated that the election of municipal councils the previous January had been "startling." The Catholic groups led by Ngo Dinh Nhu had organized quietly, and in Hanoi an anti-French, anti–Bao Dai council had been elected. Although these councils did not have significant power, Korn added, the elections were an index of public opinion.

[11] In April, 1954, Bao Dai appointed Ngo Dinh Diem premier. At the Geneva Conference, July 21, 1954, the French and the Vietminh agreed to a cease-fire. The French agreed to withdraw from Vietnam, Cambodia, and Laos. A provisional military demarcation line was drawn at the 17th Parallel "to settle military questions with a view to ending hostilities . . . and should not in any way be interpreted as constituting a political or territorial boundary." Free elections were to be held in July, 1956, to unify the country. In October, 1955, Diem held a referendum to decide between Bao Dai and himself. After a nearly unanimous victory, Diem proclaimed the Republic of Vietnam with himself as president. Backed by the United States, Diem refused in 1956 to participate in the elections required by the Geneva Accords. See Neil Sheehan, et al., eds., The Pentagon Papers (New York: Bantam Books, 1971), pp. 21–22.

[12] Before the visit to Vietnam was completed Stevenson's aides were able to talk to about half the persons on the list.

He said that now Ngo Dinh Nhu was working to elect his brother Ngo Dinh Diem to the National Council whenever elections were held.

At this point he stressed that it was incorrect to speak of "the French" in Indochina in monolithic terms. There were some who felt they should get out, but the bureaucrats would not give an inch since they did not want to lose their positions. Also, there were French businessmen who were making great profit from the war and did not want to see it ended. Some French businessmen were selling supplies to the Vietminh, he added, and they had enough power either in Paris or Saigon to get away with it.

He then stated that Ambassador Heath would not transmit this type of information to Washington, nor would he send reports by members of his staff which disagreed with his views. Heath's premise, Korn added, was that the French had to stay, and therefore, the United States should not criticize French actions. The ambassador was fearful that if the American public knew about French mistakes it might turn public opinion against the French. As a result of Heath's attitude, the captain went on, the embassy had almost disregarded the position of the Vietnamese on most matters.[13] Heath's position, Korn remarked, alienated both the Vietnamese who supported Bao Dai and the nationalists-neutralists. The nationalistic fervor of the people could not be denied, he concluded.

As to the military situation, he remarked that the French had more barbed wire in the Red River Delta than we had in Korea, yet in Vietnam it was not a positional war. Furthermore, the French were afraid to train Vietnamese as guerrillas to combat Ho's forces and to conduct real political warfare for fear that the non-Communist guerrillas would turn on the French and drive them out of Indochina. He added that there had been some defections from the French Union forces to the Vietminh, while the French had not been wise in dealing with Vietminh defectors. Instead of training them in psychological warfare and sending them back to their villages, the French kept them in camps or used them for manual labor.

The Vietminh, he said, did not have trouble with guerrillas around them. When they took a town they forced people to attend meetings, used selective rather than mass terror, organized a militia and political

[13] See Donald R. Heath, "France Is Fighting the Good Fight," *Life*, September 21, 1953, wherein Heath objected to charges that France was "half-heartedly fighting a losing war against Communism and simultaneously trying to preserve her domination over a rich colony, a corrupt society fiddling while Indochina burned and American millions misspent in a vain effort to shore up a decadent colonialism."

groups. When they withdrew, they left a structure behind them. The Bao Dai government, however, had no real connection with the people and it could not reach down into the villages. When French Union forces captured a village they built fences and forts but they did not try to organize the people into militia units or political groups. As a result, when they retreated they left no strength behind them.

The French administrators of government, Korn remarked, were efficient but there was widespread corruption among Vietnamese officials. He added that several members of Bao Dai's Council of Ministers had recently invested heavily in France. The nationalists-neutralists knew this and were concerned about finding honest officials to administer the government, when, and if, they came to power. People in Vietnam, he added, said, "Look at Pakistan, India, Burma, the Philippines — these are now free. The British, the Dutch, and the Americans gave up colonies, why doesn't France free us?"

When Johnson reported this conversation later that day, Stevenson asked that an appointment be arranged for him to talk to Korn.

After the conversation with Korn, Attwood and Johnson had lunch with John Pickering and Tran Van An, publisher of the weekly magazine Doi Moi (New Life). An explained that the French resorted to the "subtlety of weakness." Not being a strong power any more (as the Vietnamese well knew), the French resorted to chicanery, bribery, and intrigue among Vietnamese leaders to cling to their privileges. The French, he added, did not even trust their own "stooges" and had laced the Vietnamese government with French advisers at all key levels. As a result, the Vietnamese viewed the government as a French puppet and the Vietminh as a nationalist movement and not as Communist-dominated. He said that since Thailand was the only Asian country to recognize the Associated States of Indochina it was obvious that the French were not fooling anybody in Asia.

An remarked that while a distinction was still being made by the Vietnamese between the French and the Americans, this distinction was diminishing because it was felt that the United States was getting to be a mere accomplice of the French.

Stevenson returned from Dalat that afternoon and, after being briefed by Attwood and Johnson on their interviews during the day, attended a formal dinner given by President Nguyen Van Tam. Attwood and Johnson, however, dined with Ian Fawcett, Reuters correspondent for Indochina. He stated that he had information that Ambassador Heath refused to send reports to Washington critical of the French. He added that many at the U.S. embassy were more French than the French. He said that the Vietnamese army which the French had finally allowed in 1950 could become the hope of the country. When the French army occupied a town, they were viewed as a colonial army, whereas the Vietnamese army were the same color and spoke the same language as the villagers. But the fact that the Vietnamese army had been given no political training hampered their work with the people. He thought that the United States would help its standing with the nationalists-neutralists if it insisted on giving military aid directly to the Vietnamese rather than having it go through the French, since anything that came from the French was suspect. "It's the old colonial story of the people resenting what the colonial power does for them."

Fawcett expressed the hope that when Stevenson wrote about Indochina he would not make statements that American aid was being used efficiently and also that he would emphasize that it required more than bullets to stop Communism. He hoped, too, that Stevenson would not "wave the flag for the French."

The following morning at eight, Stevenson took off from the airport with the French high commissioner and President Tam for the four-hour flight to Hanoi. Henry Lieberman, of the New York Times, and John Pickering joined the group. The plane flew across the bamboo curtain — most of the territory between Hanoi and Saigon was held by the Vietminh. And in the Red River Delta itself the Vietminh were in control of 80 per cent of the territory.

As the plane descended for landing at Hanoi, Stevenson had a fine view of the rich, well-irrigated rice fields of the Red River Delta. En route to the residence of U.S. Consul Paul Sturm, the car stopped and Stevenson prowled through a native market. He visited a school for illiterates set up inside the market with funds from the Mutual Security Agency. A sign in the school read: "Heartfelt Thanks to the U.S.A. for Their Economic Aid."

At lunch Consul Sturm discussed Catholic Bishop Lee Huu Tu, whom Stevenson was to visit the next day. The bishop had once been high in the councils of the Vietminh, but now supported Bao Dai's government. Sturm also discussed Governor Tri, the leader of the Dai Viet party in the North. Tri had accepted the appointment as governor the past November, because he felt he could accomplish more inside the government than as a nationalist-neutralist. He favored building militia in all villages, Sturm added, to have a people's army for their own defense.

Stevenson mentioned to Sturm that President Tam had told him that he favored the election of provincial assemblies and that these in turn should elect a national assembly. Tam added that the Vietnamese government would not give the suffrage to women since they were not ma-

ture enough. Stevenson quipped to Sturm that after what had happened to him the past November, he was tempted to agree.

Late that afternoon Stevenson called on Governor Tri, an articulate advocate of Vietnamese nationalism, who said, in a prepared statement:

> The great utility of village militia to fight the Vietminh is they know the country, they know their own home is at stake so they fight well. The problem is for the people to identify the Vietminh with the Chinese and the Communist International. One year ago you could not say that the people knew that the Chinese were supporting the Vietminh but this knowledge is gradually growing.
>
> Unfortunately, the Vietnamese Government is considered an emanation of the French. The intellectuals of this country are aware we do not have sovereignty. It is necessary for Bao Dai to have authority now and the Vietnamese people should have the power freely to choose the government. Many Vietnamese with wide appeal are on the sidelines, and they are not willing to join in the government until it has real authority.
>
> To weaken the Vietminh it must be understood that this is a contest between the Vietminh and the Vietnam Government for popularity with the people. The struggle is, therefore, more and more a political war. Although more and more people are realizing that their best hope is with Vietnam, the question in their minds is can the Vietnamese protect them from the Vietminh. Until this can be answered satisfactorily, the population is reluctant to come over to our side too much.
>
> The Vietminh organizes all the people. For Vietnam to win, we, too, must get the population mobilized politically, economically and psychologically as well as militarily.
>
> At the present moment, people distrust the Vietnam Government because it does not have any authority from the people. It draws its authority from the 1949 agreement with the French, and its power rests on the French. The Vietminh constantly parades as the truly "National Movement" and points to the French base of the Vietnam Government. We must have a government that does not rest on the French and is not controlled by the French. We must work toward a freely elected, responsible National Assembly.

Governor Tri and Stevenson continued their conversation at dinner. Tri expressed the view that Bao Dai was essential for the future as a symbol to rally Vietnamese nationalism. Consul Sturm said later, however, that he doubted that most nationalists would favor keeping Bao Dai for very long.

The following day Stevenson, Blair and Bingham were escorted by General de Linares on a tour by airplane and jeep of French strong-

points in the delta. After visiting French Union forces and units of the Vietnamese army, they watched officials coping with several thousand refugees from Vietminh territory.

Meanwhile, at Stevenson's request, Attwood and Johnson interviewed four prominent nationalists-neutralists. The vice mayor of Hanoi, Nguyen Duy Quang, insisted that a national assembly was essential to rally support from the public, to furnish an outlet for grievances, and to establish the tradition of rule by law. He said that his group favored a commonwealth status within the French Union comparable to India's position in the British Commonwealth. But, he added, the French probably would move so slowly in making concessions that soon Vietnam would not accept commonwealth status. The vice mayor was critical of Bao Dai's remoteness from the people. Bao Dai, he insisted, could be important as a symbol of national unity, but there had to be an elected national assembly beneath this symbol.

Father Buu Duong, of the Dominican mission in Hanoi, asserted that the fundamental first step was to establish a government acceptable to the people. The present government he viewed as assisting the French to stay in Vietnam. The people, he said, now felt that they had nothing to fight for or defend. If the French continued to work with puppets rather than with those Vietnamese who insisted on being treated as equals, they might find themselves ousted entirely from the country.

Dr. Hoong Co Binh, the third nationalist interviewed, had recently been elected to the Municipal Council. He stated that a rapprochement between nationalist groups and Ho Chi Minh was impossible because of Ho's Moscow ties. But he added that it was meaningless for the government to attack Ho as a Communist since many people still considered him to be a resistance leader. While he felt the national army had to be increased, he warned that unless Bao Dai offered leadership, many soldiers would defect to the Vietminh. He also spoke of the urgent necessity of a national assembly elected directly by the people to give them a stake in their country. He added that the Vietnamese government could not survive unless the French announced a specific date to withdraw.

The final interview that day, before reporting to Stevenson, was with Dr. Phan Huy Quat, who belonged to the same party as Governor Tri. He said that the Vietnamese had a fight against both the French and Ho's Communists. In the struggle against the French, he added, people were not sure that the United States was helping them achieve independence. The United States, he insisted, had to help satisfy the nationalistic aspirations of Vietnam as well as continue to support the struggle against the Communists. He felt that all the so-called fence-sitting neutralists (attentistes) would join the side of the Vietnamese government if the French issued a proclamation — guaranteed by the United States and the United Kingdom — promising independence once the war was over. He also stated that if the Vietminh brought in Chinese in numbers to assist them, this would hurt them with the people since their hatred of the Chinese transcended any ideological bonds.

The next morning, April 5, the Stevenson party drove to visit the model village at Dong Quan that Governor Tri and the Mutual Security Agency had described to Stevenson. En route the group passed village clusters with gutted stone houses and decaying pagodas. Checkpoints and troops were everywhere — French, Moroccan, Senegalese and Vietnamese, looking bedraggled in the rain — and peasants in their conical straw hats and big water buffaloes wallowing in the wet fields. At Dong Quan over an improvised arch was an inscription in Vietnamese, "The people of North Vietnam salute with joy Mr. Stevenson." As Attwood wrote in his diary, "They didn't look very joyful."

Stevenson was then driven to the airport, but his departure was delayed by the heavy military traffic flying troops to Laos to halt an invasion by the Vietminh. He finally reached Siem Reap, Cambodia, after flying three and a half hours across Laos. There he was met by E. Dixie Reese, of the Mutual Security Agency, and was driven to Angkor to visit the impressive ruins of the great palaces and temples built by the once powerful Khmer kings. Stevenson walked through the suffocating heat across a bridge to the main temple, when, as Barry Bingham wrote:

> Suddenly the air was rent by a voice raised in purest Americanese. "Ad-lai, Ad-lai!" it called, following the common mispronunciation of his given name. A large, amiable overheated American lady came steaming up, her camera bumping at her ample bosom. "Ad-lai!" she cried, "I've been saving my last film for a picture of a water buffalo, but I think I'll take you instead!"
>
> Adlai posed, shook her hand warmly and went away chuckling to look at the fantastic wall carvings of the temple. He was still laughing days later at the glory of substituting for a water buffalo.[14]

For two hours Stevenson wandered through Angkor inspecting the intricate carvings, the golden Buddhas peeping out of the jungle, and climbing to the top of several buildings. When several of his aides decided that it was too hot to climb with him, he chided them: "What's the trouble with you fellows? Mrs. Roosevelt climbed this pyramid."

[14] "With Adlai in Asia," in *As We Knew Adlai: The Stevenson Story by Twenty-two Friends,* edited and with preface by Edward P. Doyle, foreword by Adlai E. Stevenson III (New York: Harper & Row, 1966), pp. 196–197.

Since Stevenson had to be in Phnom Penh for dinner and there were no landing lights at the airstrip, he had to leave Angkor two hours after arrival. "We sped back to the airstrip," Attwood wrote in his diary, "wishing we could be leisurely, like other tourists."

The plane landed at Phnom Penh just after nightfall and automobiles and trucks had their headlights on to illuminate the airstrip for the pilot. After a perfect landing in the DC-3, Stevenson had dinner at the fabulous royal palace. King Norodom Sihanouk [15] was away and his father, the regent and former king, presided. The palace was all illuminated and Stevenson had a splendid view of the pagoda-like building with flaring roofs and carved snakes writhing up from every cornice.

During dinner the chief of protocol for the king took immense delight in reminding U.S. Consul Joseph Montlor of the visit of Governor Thomas E. Dewey, during which there was a performance of the Royal Cambodian Balet. "Do you remember," he asked Montlor, who was sadly nodding his head, "that every time one of our lovely dancing girls came out from behind the curtain to dance, Dewey's bodyguard would pull out his revolver from his shoulder holster?"

After dinner Stevenson proceeded to an outdoor pavilion to watch the ballet. "The visual setting is a symphony of yellows," Barry Bingham wrote. "This mystic Buddhist color is used everywhere in the palace. Even the walls are a soft, rich gold, the color of clear honey. The king's dancers perform at night in an open pavilion, lit by flaring torches. Beyond this glowing circle of light is a backdrop of night sky, deeply blue and spangled lightly with stars." [16]

Early the next morning, Mr. and Mrs. Montlor took Stevenson on a tour of the open-air fish and vegetable market in the heart of Phnom Penh. He also visited the royal palace grounds by daylight. Stevenson posed with the royal white elephants — actually they were pinkish-gray — and remarked: "The GOP elephant isn't as tame as those of Cambodia."

Stevenson left the capital of Cambodia in time to lunch in Saigon with Robert McClintock and Captain Korn. The captain covered most of the points that he had discussed with Johnson several days before. He insisted that basic to solving the war was the necessity of winning the support of the people, but the French would be unable to accomplish this until they signed a public statement that they would get out when the military situation was secure. He explained that because the

---

[15] In 1955 he abdicated the throne in favor of his father. He then reverted to his hereditary title of prince and became the premier. When his father died in 1960, the prince assumed the post of Chief of State.

[16] "Asian Panorama, with Dancing Figures," *Virginia Quarterly Review*, Vol. 30, No. 3, Summer, 1954, p. 395.

French had refused to train Vietnamese for top officer positions, the Vietnamese national army lacked experienced leaders. He criticized the French for not dropping paratroopers to cut supply lines from China. When Stevenson said that General de Linares had told him the French did not have sufficient airplanes to do this, Korn remarked that the French had misinformed him.

Stevenson explained that General de Linares planned to drive the Vietminh out of the Red River Delta and thus shut off their supply of rice. Korn replied that even if the French controlled the rice-producing area they could not shut off the supply of rice unless they could get the peasants to work with them.

After this discussion, Stevenson wrote notes of his conversations of the past several days and Attwood and Johnson prepared memoranda for the Look article about Stevenson's visit to the Philippines. Early that evening the embassy held a reception for Stevenson, attended by some four hundred people. Afterward the party walked along the riverfront where, as Attwood wrote in his diary, Stevenson "had a chance to see how the other $9/10$ths live." People were living under the docks in sampans and some were eating on the sidewalk. Stevenson remarked on the futility of expecting people living like rats to vote for freedom and democracy.

At dinner Stevenson was joined by Larry Allen, of the Associated Press, who was most pessimistic about the situation in Vietnam. He told the Governor that 80 per cent of the people preferred Ho Chi Minh to Bao Dai and the French. When Stevenson said that General de Linares had stated that he could win the war in six months if he could get 100 per cent support from the Vietnamese, Allen agreed. But he pointed out that many Vietnamese refused to cooperate, arguing that it was a fight between the French and Ho Chi Minh. He added that the French soldiers he talked to wanted to go home and were saying, "We are fighting America's war." Meanwhile, Allen pointed out, certain French and Vietnamese were getting rich because of the war. It was "a hopeless war," he concluded, "a war without end" unless the Vietnamese people got into it and supported it.

While Stevenson spent the next day writing the first draft of his article on the Philippines, Attwood and Johnson had a lengthy talk with an articulate nationalist-neutralist, Tran Van Tuyen. Mr. Tuyen was the political officer of the Cao Daiist religious sect, a blend of Buddhism, Confucianism and Catholicism. They were headed by a pope, had a regular army of about 17,000, maintained good security against the Vietminh in their area south of Saigon, and although feared by the French, were tolerated by the Vietnamese government.

Tuyen said that a French official had remarked that the Vietnamese government "was nothing but an executive committee to execute French policies." He recommended that a United Nations commission be appointed to supervise the end of French control. The French, he stated, could not convince the people that the Vietminh were their enemy. There could be no real Vietnamese army, he added, as long as French officers controlled it. He praised the way enlisted men in the South Korean army were being trained as officers but said in Vietnam the officers were being drawn from the upper bourgeoisie.

Tuyen added that Vietnam might be willing to stay in the French Union but only as an equal to France. In the current situation, Vietnam was like a child playing in a park under the control of a nursemaid while all the other children of Southeast Asia were playing without a nurse. He was critical of Ambassador Heath for saying that a military solution was possible. "What does he mean by victory? Victory for whom?" Tuyen asked. "Don't Americans realize there are two wars here?" The Vietminh had gained strength, he added, because many people considered them part of the struggle against the French. Then he warned: "The Vietnamese people talk of independence. They do not talk about capitalism versus Communism."

At 6:30 P.M., Stevenson held a short press conference. In reply to a question, he emphasized that the war could not be won unless the people of Vietnam supported it "morally as well as physically." In order to achieve this situation, he added, it was necessary not only to build the Vietnamese army but "the Vietnamese must have independence."

That evening Stevenson found time to answer correspondence.

To Mrs. Edison Dick [17]

April 7, 1953

We're back in Saigon after great adventures in "the North" — Hanoi and the Red River delta where the war is really hot. It's all very strange — hard to understand, harder to explain. The enemy is all around — in front, in back, along side. The French Governor in Cambodia was stabbed to death by a servant — the enemy — in his house the other day. It has been fascinating & elusive — what to do, how to do it. It is a civil war in which both sides are backed from the outside — Viet Minh by Red China, Viet Nam by France and the U.S., but there seems to be little heart for the war among the natives on our side — just why isn't too clear, nationalism, anti French, no understanding of Communism, no leadership by the little Emperor Bao Dai — with whom I spent

[17] This handwritten letter is in the possession of Mrs. Dick.

a long time without a word of thanks to U.S. etc etc. After Hanoi, including a dusty, rugged day at "the front," in the southern sector and many strange, horrible and wonderful sights, we flew in the High Commissioner's private plane over the western mountains, across unpopulated Laos to An[g]kor Vat for a look at the incredible ruins of that forgotten and mysterious civilization — burning hot with the savage jungle threatening all about. A large old gal was waiting at the gates, camera in hand — "I used to live in Danville; I've been waiting for you. I was going to use my last film on a water buffalo, but I've saved it for you!"

In the evening we flew to Phnom Penh — the capital of Cambodia where the Prince Regent — the young King's in Paris writing music — and the "Prime Minister" were waiting to receive me at the throne room in the palace. Later at 10 there was a great banquet followed by a torch light procession thru the grounds and lines of palace guards to an open air pavillion for exquisite Cambodian dancing in the ancient tradition — all that remains of the Khmer empire of Anchar. It was my closest approach to an Arabian night and a forgotten world. . . .

Now we're back in Saigon — after feeding Royal Pink elephants — docile, and hungry like Republicans — paying my respects to the Jade Buddha in the Silver Pagoda etc etc. — and also visiting the fabulous fish market of Phnom Penh. I always visit fish markets. Somehow they fascinate me — and no nonsense about ice or refrigeration in 110°! I must get to work again — but I thought Eddie [Mr. Dick] might be collecting stamps! Love to all the beloved Dicks —

To Mrs. Edwin Winter [18]

[no date]

Dear Ruth —

The most beautiful and fascinating city in the world — Hong Kong — is the verdict of a traveller who feels as tho he had seen them all! and now we're in burning Saigon in the midst of the strangest war in modern history. The enemy is everywhere, in front, behind, alongside — perhaps in the house. Possibly we see here the shape of things to come if there should be a new world war with communism. Love to Eddie [19] & to you —

ADLAI

[18] A friend in Lake Forest, Illinois. This handwritten postcard is in the possession of Mrs. Winter.
[19] Mr. Winter.

Most of the next day, April 8, Stevenson worked on his second article for Look. *His aides lunched with John Pickering, who had been of invaluable assistance. He expressed the hope that Stevenson would emphasize that U.S. aid would not be effective in Vietnam until we insisted that the French grant independence. Moreover, he hoped that it would be noted that our recognition of the Associated States of Indochina had damaged our prestige in Asia since we were thereby recognizing the continuance of French colonialism.*

When Stevenson reached the airport that evening, he observed another example of Vietnamese nonindependence. French police and customs officials were checking the luggage and passports alongside the Vietnamese officials.

Aboard the plane, Stevenson busied himself with reading mail and writing postcards.

To Mrs. Franklin D. Roosevelt [20]

[no date]

Dear Mrs. Roosevelt —

I regret so much that I have been obliged to decline the invitation of the Young Adult Council. Your estimate of what I must do when I get home — if I ever do! — is correct and, besides, I have some sort of legal obligation not to speak much for awhile.[21] I pray that all is well with you. The inquiries about you are constant in this region. It has been a fascinating and exhausting journey.

Cordially —

The Cathay Pacific plane landed in Singapore at 1:45 A.M., April 9. Stevenson was scheduled to leave for Djakarta at 7:00 A.M., but mercifully the plane was delayed and he slept at the Raffles Hotel until late morning.

Stevenson wrote of his visit to Vietnam:

[20] This handwritten postcard is in the Franklin D. Roosevelt Library, Hyde Park, New York.

[21] Mrs. Roosevelt had transmitted an invitation to Stevenson to make a speech to the Young Adult Council. She also had suggested that while he should take active leadership of the Democratic party, he should be careful not to overexpose himself with too many speeches. The "legal obligation" to which he refers is not clear. He perhaps meant that he felt obligated not to make too many speeches before all his articles for *Look* were published. The final article was published in *Look* on September 22, 1953.

BALLOTS AND BULLETS [22]

There was something familiar to me about the political warfare raging in the Philippines; but nothing in my experience had prepared me for the ugly, complicated and seemingly endless shooting war that has been going on in Indochina for nearly seven years.

At a moment when lulling sounds of peace are emanating from Moscow, it is wise to remember that the Reds are still killing our allies in this corner of the world.

Here in the jungles and rice paddies, soldiers of France, French Africa and the famous Foreign Legion — together with their Viet-Namese allies — are battling a native Communist-led force that melts, regroups and fights again, like a quicksilver foe which cannot be crushed.

It's a war that is draining France of blood and treasure: French Union forces have suffered 140,000 casualties since 1946, and nearly half of the French military budget (or three million dollars a day) is earmarked for Indochina. Thus it can be argued that prolongation of the war serves Moscow's interests even better than a victory: In Europe, a weakened France hinders progress toward unity; in Asia, the fighting can be publicized as a "colonial" war waged by the French against Indochinese nationalism. (Properly speaking, French Indochina no longer exists; the three kingdoms of Laos, Cambodia and war-torn Viet-Nam are now called "associated states," whose fledgling governments are only just emerging from French dominion.)

Today, America is footing one third of the bill out here — mostly in supplies and equipment — and we deserve to know more about this war and its importance to the free world: How much longer must it last? Can the Reds be beaten — and at what price? Why have the French failed to achieve victory?

From a look at the map, we can readily see why Indochina must be held. The rice-rich associated states are the strategic gateway to all of Southeast Asia.

If Viet-Nam falls, all of Indochina is doomed; Thailand and Burma would be in mortal danger; Malaya and Indonesia would be exposed and vulnerable. If this vast area of the world, with its 175,000,000 people, its tin, rubber, minerals and oil, is absorbed into the Moscow-Peking empire, the still vaster nations of India and Pakistan would

22 *Look*, June 2, 1953. The beginning of this article is reprinted in Chapter Six, above. Chester Bowles wrote to Stevenson from Essex, Connecticut, June 5, 1953: "I thought that the first two *Look* articles came out very well. Your press has also been generally excellent. I know how concerned you were over the articles, but I honestly feel that you can relax. In my opinion they are the ablest articles which have yet appeared in any magazine of large circulation on the subject of Asia."

quickly lose any freedom of action. All Asia would slide behind the Iron Curtain.

I stayed here a week. After talking with Viet-Namese, French and Americans at Saigon in the relatively pacified south and visiting the reticent Emperor Bao Dai at his rural retreat in the mountains, I flew over Communist-held Central Viet-Nam to Hanoi, near the Chinese border, where the heaviest fighting is now concentrated.

I said this was an ugly, complicated war. It was in Hanoi and the surrounding Red River delta that I began to understand just what our allies — the Viet-Namese and the French — are up against.

At the airport, U.S. transport planes with French pilots were busily airlifting troops to the Laos frontier, where the Communist Viet-Minh were already on the move. With pressure abating in Korea, this could be the first step in a more tempting direction — toward a link-up with Communist dissidents in adjacent Burma and Thailand.

But at the time of writing, the brunt of fighting is still here in the fertile soggy delta as it has been since 1951 — when the late Marshal Jean de Lattre de Tassigny miraculously rallied dispirited French troops, raised a Viet-Namese army, saved Hanoi and began the reconquest of North Viet-Nam.

His work is far from finished. The Franco–Viet-Namese troops have merely infiltrated the delta in this war of "mud and asphalt." They control the roads and principal towns, but the Communist Viet-Minh hold much of the mud — the endless rice paddies and straw-thatched villages. And what they don't hold, they harry with ambushes, mines and raids. At night, none of the roads are safe, for the night belongs to the Viet-Minh. Anywhere, at any time, they may appear in battalion strength.

General de Linares, the big jovial French commander of this northern front, took me to his map room and explained his plan of action — to seal off the Red River delta in the vicinity of Hanoi and the other smaller deltas to the south, deprive the Viet-Minh of rice and drive them back to the mountains.

"But two thirds of my forces are pinned down," he said. "They are guarding highways, bridges, towns and villages. I need more soldiers, more transport planes, greater mobility. We take an area but haven't the troops to prevent the Viet-Minh from seeping back as we move on. There is no front as in Korea, no battle line, seldom any large enemy concentration. They are in front of us, behind us, alongside us. The peasant you will see tomorrow in the rice paddy may be mining the road at night. This is guerrilla warfare. We have all the conventional advantages — aviation, weapons, ports, cities — but they have fluidity.

We must fight the way they do, but only native soldiers can do that. Therefore, Mr. Stevenson, this war is political as well as military."

Early the next morning, in a light French observation plane, we flew from Hanoi south over a sea of young green rice scattered with thatched villages in thickets of bamboo. Of some five thousand villages in the Red River delta, one thousand are "safe," two thousand are controlled by the Viet-Minh and the rest are vulnerable to infiltration. To the south, the mountains appeared — black limestone outcroppings that rise almost vertically out of the flat green floor of the west delta country.

We landed on an airstrip and jounced in jeeps along a "restored" road, through brown villages, along brown canals, past masses of people in brown rags; they are born, live, die and are buried in brown mud and, unlike the Koreans, they didn't smile as we went by.

We stopped at the recently established headquarters of rough and ready General Gilles, who is trying to close one of the three mountain passes into the delta. Tents were strung along the rough spine of dry ground that was a road. We lunched in one with his officers — including only one Viet-Namese — on bread, wine, cheese, bananas, potato chips and cold, emaciated duck; then, with the General at the wheel of the jeep, we bounced south past ruined villages and clusters of troops — black, brown and white.

At intervals, Viet-Nam soldiers were posted along the road with tommy guns, peering out across the rice paddies.

We saw long, ragged, pitiful columns of refugees who had scattered to the hills during the fighting. There must have been three thousand in one group — women, children and old people mostly. Many were blind from trachoma. I have never seen such misery. A Viet-Namese mobile administration unit was in charge. Anti-Communist leaflets in comic-book style were laid out on tables in a small pagoda. Some of the village elders were examining them soberly while the tattered, expressionless women huddled with their myriad hungry children waiting their turn for registration, vaccination and rice.

"We expect at least 15,000 to 20,000," a Viet-Nam officer told me. "There are probably Communist agents among them. We will send officers into their villages and in a few days someone may begin to talk. If there are any strangers about, we may find out in time. It is all very difficult. They are afraid the Viet-Minh may come back. Our job is to reassure them. The only way really is to protect them."

Beyond the last restored bridge, bearded Foreign Legionnaires, many of them German, were digging bunkers and emplacements for automatic weapons on the road embankment as best they could, preparing for a counterattack during the oncoming night. Here, vividly, was one aspect of the French predicament: how to convince those ragged peasants that these Germans, these Frenchmen, Senegalese and Moroccans are fighting for *them* against the Viet-Minh (who are, after all, their own people). In this marshy delta, the Communist enemy isn't dug in as in Korea; but he is dug into the hearts of many natives.

It's a strange war — unlike any in which we Americans have been engaged. But perhaps we see here in remote Tonkin province of remote Viet-Nam the shape of things to come and the pattern of future wars (God forbid!) against communism: fifth columns, infiltration, sabotage, ambush, fluidity — an enemy behind and beside as well as in front. Gov. Nguyen Huu-Tri of North Viet-Nam, a nationalist leader with intelligence and vision, is increasing the village militia from 16 to 40 thousand to give rural areas protection from the guerrillas. At Dong Quan, some 30 miles from Hanoi, a large project is under way, with American aid, to regroup 25 small, isolated villages into a large defensible unit. We went there in a mournful drizzle and were greeted with American flags with 49 stars! (Evidently, Hawaii is doing better in Dong Quan than in Washington.)

It isn't hard to see how the Viet-Minh troops maintain their position against superior firepower and material. A force depending largely on guerrilla tactics, willing to suffer cruelly, sustained by fanaticism, using totalitarian terrorist methods to control willing or unwilling populations, can hold out and fight against far greater forces organized on conventional lines. Moreover, the Viet-Namese people have a simple ideology — nationalism. Dislike, if not hatred, for their erstwhile colonial masters — the French — attracts many to the loudly nationalistic, anti-French Viet-Minh. The passive or active support of millions of Viet-Namese is the Reds' main source of strength. As a captured Viet-Minh manual stated: "In modern war, an army fighting without the support of the people is like a fish fighting on dry land."

Today in Indochina, the French are too often behaving as in the colonial past: occupying the big palaces, commanding the police and the army, censoring the press.

Nationalism is deep and strong in Viet-Nam, as elsewhere in Asia. Nationalist leaders told us that the presence of French officials is especially galling now that neighboring countries like Indonesia, Burma and the Philippines have won their independence. Consequently, substantial numbers of non-Communists are backing the Viet-Minh in the belief they are fighting against the French in a colonial war; or are sitting on the fence, loath to participate in what they consider a puppet government and loath to help the Communists.

Pending a constitution in Viet-Nam, all cabinet ministers are appointed by Bao Dai. Most of them have a record of close association with the French (some even have French wives) and Bao Dai was restored to his throne by the French. So, however patriotic and independent the ministers may be, skepticism among the passionate nationalists is hardly surprising. Actually, Bao Dai has deftly obtained more concessions from the French than even the Communist Ho Chi Minh once . demanded. But Bao Dai, after the manner of Oriental monarchs, has little contact with his people, visits France (where his wife and children live) as often as possible and seems to prefer seclusion and hunting to rallying his people. Of course, the picture is not all somber. I visited one of many popular education classes aimed at reducing adult illiteracy.

The present government, headed by the energetic and engaging Nguyen Van Tam, has produced its first budget and a labor code and established a school of public administration — which is one of the most conspicuous needs of all these new nations so long governed by colonial administrators. And last January, municipal elections were held in all secure areas, the first in Viet-Nam's short history.

Back in Saigon, we heard a lot more about this exhausting conflict, which, as a high Viet-Nam official put it to me, can't be won without the French and can't be won with them. We heard that certain French businessmen are making such exorbitant profits they would rather see the war drag on; that fear of Chinese intervention chills the will to win in Paris and Saigon; that many Viet-Namese are more concerned about the vestiges of French colonialism than the threat of Communist imperialism; that factors of national prestige or future commercial advantages inhibit French officialdom from steps reassuring to Viet-Nam; that the trouble is not so much in Saigon, where the voices of Asia are loud and insistent, but in faraway Paris, with its inconstant governments and African problems.

This much is clear: the French Army has fought gallantly. Its soldiers want to finish the war and get home — as all soldiers do — and I wonder sometimes how long Americans would fight and bleed in similar circumstances.

Finally, it is apparent that forceful measures are long overdue — by both the French and the Viet-Namese — if this is not to be the modern Hundred Years War. I suggest:

1. There should be a prompt and clear-cut declaration of France's intentions about Viet-Nam independence.[23]

[23] In July, 1953, the French government offered to negotiate with the three Associated States for greater independence. New York *Times,* July 6, 24, 1953. The

2. Viet-Nam should make a similar forthright statement about its intentions with respect to France's position.

3. As already planned, the Viet-Nam Army should be built up to meet the Communist guerrillas on their own terms and to replace the French forces as rapidly as possible — just as we have been doing in Korea.

4. Free elections should be held to give substance to Viet-Nam's democratic intentions and start the process of developing responsible leaders.

5. Viet-Nam should commence a land-reform program where needed, to improve the peasants' lot and to balance Viet-Minh promises with Viet-Nam performance.

6. If the U.S. is to bear more and more of the burden, both France and Viet-Nam should welcome greater American participation in policy making.

As General de Linares said, this war is political as well as military. Many Frenchmen I spoke with concede that it can only be won with ideas as well as arms. The best ideas and the best arms of the Viet-Minh are nationalism and anticolonialism. Therefore, the symbols of colonialism should be removed and the symbols of nationalism sharpened. For the old colonial system is dying in Asia and nationalism is a lusty, kicking infant. The outcome in Viet-Nam may decide whether that infant survives or is smothered by the new Communist imperialism.

French fortress of Dien Bien Phu fell to the Vietminh, May 7, 1954. At the Geneva Conference, July, 1954, Vietnam was temporarily partitioned at the 17th Parallel. Ho Chi Minh established the Democratic Republic of Vietnam in the North. The French withdrew from the South, and in October, 1955, Ngo Dinh Diem proclaimed the Republic of Vietnam.

Eight

Indonesia

APRIL 9 – APRIL 13, 1953

O n the KLM plane from Singapore to Djakarta, on April 9, Stevenson worked on his second article for Look. When he landed in
the midafternoon heat of Indonesia, a reporter for Merdeka [1] wrote, he
"fingered his chin, and stroked his bald, shiny head. He tidied up his
dress, and looking at the people who came to welcome him he stepped
from the gangplank, his face all smiles." At the airport restaurant, where
a microphone had been installed, he held a brief press conference.
When a reporter asked him if he had a statement to make, he replied,
"No," and smiled. When asked the purpose of his trip, he answered,
"Education." Was he going to Bali? "No." After a few more questions,
he said, "I give up." "With that," Merdeka reported, "he prevented more
questions from the journalists crowding around him. . . . Stevenson
is an experienced diplomat who knows how to deal with reporters, and
he made the impression that the Democrats had done well in selecting
him for their Presidential candidate." [2]

Ambassador and Mrs. Chester Bowles, who were in Djakarta en route
home after their mission in India, went for a tour of Djakarta with Stevenson.[3] They and their two children joined him for dinner that evening.
"The talk somehow symbolized the crazy pattern of this hectic trip," Attwood wrote in his diary. "Here was Stevenson sitting in Jakarta about

---

[1] Merdeka was a nationalist-oriented paper, critical of the Socialist party. See
Robert C. Bone, Jr., "The Future of Indonesian Political Parties," Far Eastern
Survey, Vol. XXIII, No. 2 (February, 1954), p. 18.
[2] Merdeka, April 18, 1953.
[3] See Chester Bowles, Ambassador's Report (New York: Harper, 1954).

[120]

which he'll be writing two weeks from now, worrying about a piece on the Philippines (where he was two weeks ago, writing about Korea), and talking to Bowles about India, where he will be three weeks and two articles from now."

Bowles told Stevenson that General Eisenhower's remark that "Asians should fight Asians" [4] had had a "devastating impact" in India. He said that while the United States had to have a military policy for Northeast Asia, it had to have an economic policy for the former colonial areas of South and Southeast Asia. While sometimes the two would be in conflict, he insisted that military policy should not always dominate economic policy. He said that he was tired of "blackmail by Asians" who said, "Give us aid or we will go Communist" and suggested that we should extend aid only if governments agreed to tax their people, particularly the large landlords, and adopted a number of reforms, including land reform. If the United States announced this as policy, he thought it would enable us to avoid supporting feudalistic rulers.

He talked at length about India and particularly of the problem of the underemployment of the people. He also said that Secretary of State Dean Acheson had informed him in the summer of 1952 that the Central Intelligence Agency was working with the Nationalist Chinese troops in Northern Burma. Although Bowles said he understood that the CIA was no longer involved, India and other nations of Asia firmly believed that United States influence with the Formosan government was such that we could force the removal of these troops.[5] Bowles then discussed U.S. educational exchanges with India and emphasized his belief that bringing American lecturers to Indian universities was a highly constructive program.

After the Bowleses left, Stevenson worked further on his article for *Look*. At 8 A.M. the following day, Theodore J. Hohenthal, the chargé d'affaires; Robert C. Bone, Jr., the political officer; Harry H. Bell, the economic officer; Eric T. Hagberg, director of *Point Four* — the Technical Cooperation Agency — and John J. Curtis, the public affairs officer, joined Stevenson to discuss Indonesia.

Bone pointed out that the provisional constitution, which established a secular state, had no limit on the term of the president or any provision for him to be elected. To date there had been no elections for the Parliament, and the members of the present Parliament were in effect appointed by the president to represent various groups and re-

[4] New York *Times*, October 3, 1952.

[5] During 1953 and 1954, approximately half of these troops were removed to Formosa. In 1961, more of them were flown to Formosa, but some of them still remain. Frank N. Trager, *Burma from Kingdom to Republic* (New York: Frederic A. Praeger, 1966), p. 116.

gions of the republic. The seventeen-man cabinet, Bone observed, had representatives from nine different parties. Bone predicted when elections were held, the various nationalist parties, including PNI, the major nationalist party, would lose heavily and the Masjumi (Moslem) party would gain control.[6] The PNI was not well organized, he said, whereas the Masjumi party had great strength, inasmuch as ninety per cent of the people were Moslems and the party relied on the village Moslem leaders to help it deliver the vote.

The Indonesian Communist party (the PKI), Stevenson was told, was organizing workers on the rubber and tea plantations, infiltrating the nationalist parties, and gaining strength despite the fact that in 1948, during the civil war with the Dutch, the Communists had revolted against the Republic and in 1951 many of the leaders had been arrested because of a threatened coup d'état.[7] The Socialist party (the PSI), Bone pointed out, was a small elite party of well-trained individuals, which had considerable influence through holding key government positions and through close association with the Masjumi party. The PSI had a difficult time, he added, because it applied logical reasoning to the problems of Indonesia and therefore could not cope with the irrational and emotional elements in the society.

The economic attaché, Harry H. Bell, discussed both the plantation economy, predominantly rubber production and European-controlled, and the native economy of smallholders producing mainly rice. He observed that Java, slightly smaller than Illinois, contained some fifty million people. He described the agrarian problem in terms of excessive interest rates charged by moneylenders, the division of holdings to sons, thus making the holdings smaller and smaller, and low productivity. He pointed out that in 1952 the world price for rubber dropped considerably when the United States stopped its stockpiling. With rubber earning between forty and fifty per cent of their foreign exchange, the drop in revenue necessitated a cut in imports.

Eric Hagberg, head of Point Four, discussed the technical training his agency was performing in agriculture, health, education, and industry. He explained that Indonesian leaders had been highly suspicious of U.S. aid ever since our former ambassador had pushed the Indonesian

---

[6] See Bone, "The Future of Indonesian Political Parties," pp. 17–23. In the elections in 1955, the PNI gained the most votes, Masjumi was second, the Nahdatul Ulama (Moslem Scholars) were third, and the Communist party was fourth. Robert C. Bone, Jr., *Contemporary Southeast Asia* (New York: Random House, 1962), p. 73.

[7] The PKI in 1953 was just coming under the leadership of D. N. Aidid, who rejuvenated it. See Donald Hindley, *The Communist Party of Indonesia, 1951–1963* (Berkeley: University of California Press, 1964).

cabinet into signing an agreement with the Mutual Security program early in 1952, under which, in return for economic assistance, Indonesia agreed to join in the common defense against Communist expansion. In the outcry that followed, the cabinet fell, and the Mutual Security Agency was replaced by the Technical Cooperation Agency, which had no strings attached to it.

Hagberg also explained that nationalistic fervor was forcing Dutch advisers to leave the country and that the Eurasians were consequently in a particularly difficult position. During the struggle for independence from 1945 to 1949, the Eurasians sided with the Dutch. Then in 1949 most of them opted for Dutch citizenship. As a result, they had been ousted from the middle- or lower-range government jobs which they had dominated.

Unlike the British in India and the Americans in the Philippines, it was emphasized, the Dutch had not trained or educated Indonesians. Then suddenly, after their war of independence, Indonesians had to run a government of their own with only a thin layer of trained people. The most important desire of Indonesians now was to maintain an independent foreign policy in order to concentrate on their domestic problems.

After this briefing, Stevenson visited President Sukarno, Prime Minister Wilopo, and Foreign Minister Mukarto. Sukarno talked at length about Irian — West New Guinea — which the Netherlands had not turned over to Indonesia.[8] He insisted that Indonesia must have all of the former East Indies. He also talked at considerable length about the independent foreign policy the United States had pursued after 1783, avoiding a commitment to either Great Britain or France in their struggles for world supremacy. He stated a number of times that of all people on earth, the Americans from their own history should understand Indonesia's desire to remain aloof from the rivalries between the United States and the Soviet Union in order that it could pursue its own internal development. He also expressed in a firm tone his profound antipathy toward the Dutch and charged that individual Dutchmen were fighting in West Java with the outlawed Dar-ul-Islam insurgents.[9]

At a lunch given by Foreign Minister Mukarto, when Mukarto told Stevenson that anti-Dutch feeling would subside in about a decade, Stevenson asked: "By then will you be hating Americans?" "Maybe we will," he replied with a smile. A number of Indonesian officials ex-

[8] After lengthy negotiations, early in 1963, the Netherlands transferred Irian to the United Nations for transferral to Indonesia. Under the agreement, Irian was to hold a plebiscite before the end of 1969 to ascertain whether the people wanted to join Indonesia.

[9] Dar-ul-Islam advocated the establishment of a theocratic Moslem nation.

pressed their hatred of the Japanese for their cruel occupation during World War II, and stated they feared that a remilitarized Japan might try to launch new conquests. Even if it did not, they said their antagonism was so intense that it would be difficult for Japan to get back economically in Indonesia. They also expressed their antagonism for Chiang Kai-shek and Bao Dai. Then, the chief of protocol of the Foreign Ministry stated that one American error was to "impose" aid on Indonesia. "Let us ask for aid if we want it, but don't try to push it at us" was the general consensus.

After lunch, Stevenson went back to writing his second article for Look. Late that afternoon he visited with B. M. Diah, editor of the daily newspaper Merdeka, and Mrs. Diah, editor of the Sunday Minggu Merdeka (she had studied at Columbia University).[10] Two reporters for their publications joined a lengthy conversation. Diah said that the Dar-ul-Islam movement was similar to the extremists in Pakistan who wanted a theocratic state there — "an intolerable government," he added. When Indonesia had free elections, he predicted that the main nationalist party (PNI) and Masjumi party would emerge about equal in power.

He observed that the recent drop in the price of rubber and tin had hurt the Indonesian economy deeply. When Stevenson asked him what Indonesia would do about American synthetic rubber production, Diah said if he were an American he would shut down the factories. Stevenson explained that the reason for these plants was not economic but national defense — and "we could not afford to be caught without rubber."

One of the reporters insisted that Indonesia could remain uncommitted in the power struggle between the United States and the Soviet Union. Even if Communism gained control here, it could not be much worse than the situation already was. But the United States was a rich country, he added, and it would really suffer if Communism took it over.

Stevenson bristled. "Every free country," he declared, "has the most important of all things to lose if the Communists triumph — the liberty of the people. This possession should be particularly precious to those nations that have only recently obtained it after generations of suppression."

When Mr. Diah asked what the United States purpose was in Asia, Stevenson replied: "We want it to be independent." The old threat to Asian independence was colonialism, he added, "now it is Communism." "America doesn't want to run the world," he stated emphatically. Our

[10] For a discussion of the Diahs, see James A. Michener, The Voice of Asia (New York: Random House, 1951).

*present role of leadership was thrust upon us by events, he emphasized.
"Many Americans are opposed to our aiding other parts of the world.
They feel it is too expensive. Such people are a source for a new form
of isolation." He went on to say, "Ignorance about the United States is
one of the most disturbing things I have noticed on this trip." By this
he meant "ignorance of how we live, of the amount of taxes we pay,
of our motives in helping strengthen the free world." "Our help is
disinterested" — except, he added, that we expected that people would
put their own countries in order so that "the seeds of Communism will
not find fertile soil." It would be wonderful someday, once the danger
of war receded, to divert military expenditures to peaceful purposes,
Stevenson observed. Think what we could do with twenty billion dollars
for public works, irrigation, schools and other such things all over the
world.*

*Stevenson then chided his listeners for acting as though American
aid was the most natural thing in the world. The United States, he
added, had not always been rich and powerful. It came into being
through revolution against the dominant power of the world. Its resources were meager then and its friends few.*

*The American people, he explained, made their country with their
own hands. Men went out into the trackless forests with axes over their
shoulders. Women traveled agonizing and dangerous journeys in covered wagons. The pioneers had to fight both nature and human enemies
at once. It was from this struggle that our nation's greatest strength
developed — not our national wealth, but the united determination of
the American people. It was all done by far fewer people, he added,
than lived in Indonesia. The least we could hope for from this new
country, he concluded, was a little of the same will, enterprise and
self-reliance.*[11]

*The listeners were visibly impressed as Stevenson apologized for
making a speech. One of them observed, however, "You had a new
country — we've been here a long time." Stevenson replied that they
seemed too discouraged, that they had great possibilities. "It's a long
pull to achieve what you want. All of our hearts must be attuned to
freedom, independence, and economic security." "If you stay independent in foreign policy," Stevenson added, "it does not bother me as
long as you can maintain your freedom."*

At this point Stevenson returned to the embassy for a reception for

[11] This impromptu talk has been reconstructed from Attwood's and Johnson's
diaries and Barry Bingham's recollection of it. See "East Asians Seem to Have
Made Stevenson Symbol of What They Want America to Be," Louisville *Courier-
Journal*, May 3, 1953.

the diplomatic corps and Indonesian officials. After the reception, he started writing his article on Indochina. Blair remarked to Attwood that the speeches Stevenson had worried most about during the recent campaign invariably turned out to be the best ones. When Attwood reminded Stevenson of this, he replied, "You'd better not count on it this time."

On the following morning, April 11, Stevenson flew to Jogjakarta, the seat of the Republican government during the war of independence from the Dutch. After touring the city, he climbed to the top of the nearby Borobudur, the pyramid-like Buddhist temple built over a thousand years before. When he returned to Djakarta, he worked again on his article for Look.

The following morning, Stevenson called on Sutan Sjahrir, the leader of the Socialist party (PSI), and Dr. Sumitro Djojohadikusumo, the Socialist minister of finance in the current cabinet. They told Stevenson that they hoped for elections by 1954. It then should be easier for the government to govern, instead of procrastinating, since the election would reveal the strength of the contending forces in Indonesia.

They stated that the PSI felt there were serious problems facing the country that had to be solved before anything should be done about Irian. Stevenson remarked that he was baffled at the way Sukarno had talked to him about Irian. Sjahrir, with a trace of a smile, said that the president's training was as a mass leader. He had to have an issue around with which he "can rally the nation. Irian fits this very well."

The various members of the different nationalist parties, Sjahrir added, were molded in the fight against the Dutch. As a result, they were still thinking in terms of the revolution and therefore were unable to apply rational thinking to the present situation. This was the main difference with the PSI, Sjahrir added, since almost all parties in Indonesia were vaguely socialist. He said that the nationalist parties felt that "the PSI is too moderate toward foreigners and too Western in our thinking." The reason they were not antagonistic to foreigners, including the Dutch, was that "we know we must work with them to get our economy on its feet."

Sjahrir added that the Indonesian Communists were working with the nationalist parties against the PSI. The Communists were charging the PSI, he said, with being "agents of Western imperialism." He then emphasized that most people were just too poor to be interested in politics.

Then Dr. Sumitro stated that since Indonesia needed Western capital, "We are more moderate on nationalization than the nationalist parties. To attract Western capital we must stabilize the country, get a better *public administration, and tighten our belts. We say produce more and spend less. But we are having a hard time persuading the cabinet to do this."*

When Stevenson asked Sjahrir what attitudes there were toward the United States, he replied that the nationalist parties and the Communist party were highly suspicious of America but the PSI and the Masjumi party were not. The nationalists and the Communists charged that the United States wanted its allies to move too fast and purely for military reasons. With a wry smile on his face, he added that the PSI was accused as well of pushing too hard to get things done.

Stevenson told them that he had found Indonesia to be a country with great potential. But, he asked, "With your problems, can democracy succeed or do you need a dictatorship?" If democracy could work in Indonesia in view of the huge politically illiterate population and severe economic problems, Stevenson commented, "It can work anywhere."

Sjahrir said that he agreed with the last statement. Then he added: "You must remember we are an extremely tolerant people, we don't like to be bossed. The fact we are an independent-minded people is a great safeguard against dictatorship." [12]

After this conversation Stevenson met with Mohammed Natsir, chairman of the Masjumi party. Stevenson remarked that basic to the success of the revolution was a solution to the vast economic problems. This would be difficult, he added, in view of the low degree of political literacy, and it seemed to him that Indonesian leaders were more concerned with their "personal conflicts than with organizing to lick your problems."

Natsir replied that while only about ten per cent could be called politically literate, the village people had a great hunger for learning and the potential was there for people to gain literacy fast. Moreover, he said that not all their problems were economic. Dar-ul-Islam, for example, was a deeply religious movement and was operating in West Java — the "most mystical part" of Indonesia.

The personal conflict among the political leaders, Natsir explained, was because certain parties had only vague programs. The nationalist parties, particularly the PNI, he said, had not thought out how to use independence. Therefore, they were trying to win popularity with slogans.

Stevenson interjected, "How will you ever get outside capital if you

---

[12] In the year 1960 Sukarno dissolved the Parliament and the following year banned all political opposition. Many leaders, including Sjahrir, were put in jail in January, 1962.

threaten to nationalize property?" Natsir replied that outbursts for nationalization could be checked provided you had a government with a clear-cut economic policy. The Masjumi party, he added, "was not for nationalization just for [the sake of] nationalization." His party wanted the government to issue a policy statement on the extent of nationalization and announce a guarantee to private capital.

Stevenson then said: "With your real economic problems, why do you divert people with the issue of Irian? You need to diversify agriculture, reduce your dependence on rubber and tin, attract foreign capital to relieve unemployment." Natsir agreed that all parties should be united on these objectives. Yet, Stevenson pointed out, Sukarno's sole interest seemed to be Irian. Natsir, ignoring Stevenson's mention of Sukarno, asserted that the election of a parliament would help them attack their economic problems. And he repeated that the PNI tried "to win popularity through slogans."

The Masjumi party, he emphasized, did not favor the creation of a theocratic state. "We feel," he added, "this republic is already closer to Islamic principles than, say, Egypt is." Through education, the Masjumi party was advocating the basic Islamic principles of democracy, social justice, and freedom. He was optimistic, he added, because the people were industrious and were willing to be led.

When Stevenson asked Natsir about his position on foreign policy, he responded, "By not taking sides in world diplomacy, we could best solve our internal problems." The Communists, he said, branded every approach to the West as a step toward losing independence. It was a grave danger, he added, that the Communists were able in this way to use nationalism as a source of strength. "If we do not take sides in the world situation," he continued, "it will give us more strength internally to defeat the Communists. You must remember that the Masjumi party is not only non-Communist, it is anti-Communist."

After this conversation and a drive around Djakarta, Stevenson went back to work on his article for Look. Late that afternoon, Stevenson attended a reception given in his honor by members of the Foreign Affairs Committee of the Parliament. After this affair, Arnold C. Brackman, who had been in Indonesia off and on since 1947 and wrote for the New York Times and the Christian Science Monitor, joined Stevenson for dinner. He explained that the Indonesians' xenophobia was in large part the result of their having won their independence by fighting. They did not feel close to any country, he added, except Burma. They considered the Philippines to be an American puppet, deplored our pro-Japanese policy, shunned Communist China, and resented India because Nehru wanted to lead the rest of Asia.

Stevenson remarked that a congressman at the reception had said that the United States in pushing Japanese rearmament was creating a menace to Indonesia.

Brackman said that the "Indonesians hate paternalism, the same way they hate colonialism, and they look upon Point Four as paternalism." They would much rather receive outside aid through the United Nations, he added.

The best policy for the United States, he suggested, was one of benevolent detachment. Indonesia's present policy was not harmful to the United States, and there was no point in antagonizing the country by trying to force it into an anti-Communist bloc.

Brackman talked about the sultan of Jogjakarta, who had resigned as minister of defense in January. Brackman compared him most favorably with Sukarno and predicted that he would always have a prominent role to play in the country. Sukarno's jealousy of him, as well as the president's desire to undermine the Socialists who were close to the sultan, was behind the sultan's resignation, he added.[13]

Stevenson observed that Sukarno had tried to offer him political blackmail by saying that if the United States would help Indonesia acquire Irian, then Indonesia would have great faith in us. At this point Stevenson remarked how terribly sorry he was that he had to dissipate so much of his energy at official receptions.

After dinner, he went back to writing his article on the Philippines, and Attwood noted in his diary, "By 12:30 Stevenson had finished the Philippines and we went down to the kitchen and celebrated with orange pop."

The next morning, April 13, after saying goodbye to the embassy staff, Stevenson held a crowded press conference. The United States Information Service made a stenographic transcript of it: [14]

Gentlemen and ladies, I want to thank you and your committee for affording me this opportunity to meet with you after my brief visit in Indonesia. I've been very much impressed with what I have seen here. Indonesia has won its independence by revolution and by force. I believe it is the only country in Asia that has done so. It has survived not only that violent experience, but it has likewise survived a Communist rebellion. And all this in a very troubled, anxious and disturbed postwar world.

[13] Stevenson had heard a good deal about the sultan's resignation. For an analysis of the meaning of this affair, see Bone, "The Future of Indonesian Political Parties," pp. 17–18. Vice President Hatta and the sultan were not in Java while Stevenson was there. In 1966, when Sukarno's power was curbed by the military, the sultan became a cabinet member in the new government.

[14] A mimeograph copy is in the possession of Walter Johnson.

There has been great progress here in education, housing — I went yesterday to see the remarkable development in the suburb adjoining Dj[a]karta. There has been great progress in developing a merchant marine and I am told, although I have not had the opportunity to visit the training camps, that the improvement in the armed services, in the air force, the navy and the army is very apparent. All these seem to me important improvements. And in addition there are signs of political stability in this country. I believe that the present cabinet has been in office for more than a year.

All these things in combination convince me that Indonesia has met the difficulties of its infancy and has mastered them. I leave here with the firm conviction that in this ancient civilization with its enormous population, these tremendous resources, both human and natural, that a new country, a force and influence in the world for freedom and for democracy is well on its way. The difficulties are numerous and manifest, largely, it seems to me, economic. Sociologically, I would think there is nothing that couldn't be mastered, couldn't be improved in the course of time. The economic problem, however bad it may appear, and however difficult, likewise with any diversification, some industrialization, and in a more tranquil world, should improve. I think that's perhaps all I have to say and I shall be very glad to attempt to respond to your questions although you must forgive me for what I am afraid will be quickly disclosed as grossest ignorance. Again I thank you all for this privilege and this opportunity to join with you on what I should call, even in Chicago, a warm morning.

I might add one other thing. The information I've received here from various officials of the government and of the other parties about the forthcoming elections is encouraging. It seems to me that a sufficient degree of stability and of political maturity has developed to warrant proceeding now to put into effect all the professions of faith that were a part of the charter of independence, of the program of independence of this great country. And I personally, coming from a practicing democracy, feel that the elections will lay the basis for a more orderly party system and the emergence of political leadership in a formalized way which will serve the country well.

Now are there any questions?

MR. SPRENGERS (*Aneta*): Did the political leaders give you an impression of the political layout in this country?

MR. STEVENSON: Yes, I've talked to the leaders of a number of parties. I think I have some impression of what it is. It's rather complicated. But if you should like for me to tell you about American politics, I think you would conclude that that was complicated too. I think the fact that there is a large number of parties is not a wholesome thing but I think that there again it's something that will break down once elections are held. You'll find out exactly where the majority of public sentiment rests. It will serve the purpose perhaps of contracting, shrinking the number of parties.

MR. HULSBERGEN (NRC): Will you tell us the names of the political leaders you have met?

MR. STEVENSON: Well, I'm not very good on names. I think you'll have to forgive me. It's not easy for us who come from the outside to remember all of the Indonesian names. Perhaps I'm particularly obtuse. The only country I've found that's more difficult is Poland. But anyway, the Moslem party, the Socialist party, the Nationalist party, the President and a number of members of his cabinet and, I think, one or two others.

MR. SUKRISNO (*Antara*): You said the only motive of the United States is giving aid to help free nations become strong enough to withstand communist threats to their independence. But could you explain the economic policy of the U.S.A. in suppressing the price of raw materials which are so vitally important for the economic growth of the under-developed countries.

MR. STEVENSON: The economic policy of the United States in suppressing the price of tin and rubber, is that what you mean? The price of rubber, if I am not mistaken, is made by the British in Malaya, and yet we always seem to get blamed for it. And that's another thing I don't understand. As far as the price of commodities generally is concerned, well I would hope that America could always help the economies of other countries by buying in a high market and selling in a low market. You have to remember that America also has an economics problem. How long the United States indeed can continue to support all of its activities around the world directed to the improvement, the betterment, of the economies of many new nations and many old ones is a matter of the gravest concern for you as well as for us.

MRS. NIELSON (*Copenhagen Daily Politiken*): Do you have any impression of the growing differences between Sumatra, Celebes, and Java?

MR. STEVENSON: Yes, I've heard that mentioned. I haven't attached the greatest importance to it. Maybe you could tell me. Is it a serious thing? Give me your notebook and you talk for a while.

MRS. NEILSON: Well, I just came back from Sumatra, I've been to Sulawesi too and I found it rather acute. I thought maybe you had some information if Sulawesi and Sumatra will be better represented in parliament, in the army and in the air force.

MR. STEVENSON: I think these are the growing pains of a new nation. We had to fight a civil war in the United States to keep our union together because of the separatist feeling of the South at one stage. There are moments now when some of us would like to secede — particularly after elections. But I don't think it's too serious. It's one of the inevitable accompaniments of a country distributed as this is. And I think that's one of the big difficulties Indonesia is going to face, the matter of communications between the central government here in Djakarta and the outlying governments. And you're also, inevitably, going to have to pass through the difficult period of adjustment of state's rights to the federal system. We struggle about it in the United States all the time, even after 150 years — as you've read in our newspapers.

MR. SUKRISNO (*Antara*): Do you expect a change for the good of backward industrialized countries like Indonesia in the U.S. policy? I mean with regard to the U.S. policy of giving aid to the underdeveloped countries. Can we expect the sending of more capital goods from the U.S.A. Until now we have seen here so many luxury cars that are not so vitally important.

MR. STEVENSON: That's your fault, not our fault. And I could lecture you on that. I've already talked to your Finance Minister. It's not our fault that you're spending your money for luxury goods. You should be spending your money for capital goods for the under-developed areas. If you issue export licenses with your limited foreign exchange for luxury goods, and you import Cadillacs instead of farm machinery, that's your fault.

MR. SUKRISNO (*Antara*): But I have been told by our officials that the Indonesian government has asked again and again for capital goods but the United States is now involved in a hard struggle in Korea and so the U.S.A. is lacking ships, lacking transportation, because it is needed for Korea.

MR. STEVENSON: Well, that's true, of course. We're lacking everything in view of the great exertion of this war and the mutual security program all over the world, arms for Europe, and the rest. We can't satisfy everybody's needs at once. And we can't satisfy the taxpayer at all.

MR. HAMZAH (*Aneta*): What will be the relations between America and Indonesia in the future? Will they be strengthened, or not?

MR. STEVENSON: Oh, well I would think strengthened. I hope so. I think we have a common history, a common origin and a great sentimental bond in common which is often more important and enduring than merely commercial relations. I don't know whether I make that clear, but this country achieved its independence and is going through now many of the same struggles that the United States faced when it achieved its independence in the same way. Of course there isn't as much information about Indonesia in the United States as I should like, but I think that will come in time. This is a long way from home, as we say. I would hope and I would certainly expect that our relations would get warmer and warmer.

MR. HAMZAH (*Aneta*): What do you think of the people here in this country?

MR. STEVENSON: I think they're friendly, delightful, charming. I was going to say beautiful. They've been awfully good to me, very courteous, very gay, they smile at you. I think they are also industrious, hard workers. I've driven through the countryside on the way out of Jogjakarta to the Borobudur and so on. I've been out to some villages around Djakarta. They seem to me an industrious people. It's pretty hard for me to work in the middle of the day. I don't know how they do it.

MR. LABALLO (*Indonesia Raya*): You have just told us that the U.S.A. has also its own economic problems. Meanwhile Indonesia has also more difficult economic problems. We would like to see a way out. What do you think about this subject?

MR. STEVENSON: I'm afraid that would take a little longer than a press conference. Furthermore, I'm not an economist. I'm not even a very good politician. I think it's a long pull. I think the basic problem is to develop production in this country. Transmigration of peoples, the development of Sumatra and the adjoining islands, and certainly a greater self-dependence in food. This is condition number one, a gradual industrialization. The tendency of all young peoples, and it's the problem of the United States as well as of Indonesia, is impatience. But you're Asiatics, you're Asians, and Asians somehow manage to endure a long time. And I think you'll conquer the problem of impatience.

MR. LABALLO (*Indonesia Raya*): Why [doesn't] the U.S.A. pay more for tin and rubber?

MR. STEVENSON: We don't pay any more than we have to, I hope. If we do, the American taxpayer ought to put the administration out of office. Evidently everybody out here thinks of themselves and they seldom see it from our point of view. We have the heaviest tax burden in the world in the United States, the heaviest tax burden in the world with the possible exception of Great Britain. Well, you can draw your own conclusions.

MR. SPRENGERS (*Aneta*): Can you answer some questions about world peace?

MR. STEVENSON: Well, you go ahead and I'll say yes or no if I can.

MR. SPRENGERS (*Aneta*): [Question inaudible.]

MR. STEVENSON: As to the new Russian peace moves? Is that your question? I hope that they're sincere. Our experience in the past has been very disillusioning about professions of sincerity and I should feel that we must pursue our same policy, without any changes of developing the strength of the free world, at least those nations who, while they prize peace, prize liberty more. I can hope and pray that we have in front of us an era which will alter the history of the world and that we may find the means of co-existence with communism. But I think that there is no evidence of it whatsoever up to this point. That their peace moves are tactical and strategic rather than sincere, is the question. I hope for the best. Now as for your other question, what was it?

MR. SPRENGERS (*Aneta*): [Question inaudible.] [15]

MR. STEVENSON: Well, I don't know what has happened in Burma. I am going over there to find out. But I certainly wouldn't want troops of any foreign country living on my soil and attacking me.

MR. SUKRISNO (*Antara*): Do you agree that it is possible for a peaceful co-existence between the two world systems? I mean the democratic system and the socialist system. Do you believe in a peaceful co-existence?

MR. STEVENSON: Well, I'm sure it's possible as far as we're concerned. As far as we're concerned it's possible. Is it possible as far as they're concerned?

MR. SUKRISNO (*Antara*): But if there is a hard endeavor . . .

MR. STEVENSON: If you read Lenin and some of the authors of the Russian revolution, you'll conclude it is not possible, that it's world dominion, world revolution, or nothing. I don't know, we have to find

[15] This question dealt with the presence of Nationalist Chinese troops in northern Burma.

out if it is possible. Dostoevsky, in 1868, said that the destiny of holy Russia is the mastery of the whole world.

MR. SUKRISNO: But the writings of the eighteenth century are not applicable to the present time.

MR. STEVENSON: I agree with you.

REPORTER FROM RADIO REPUBLIK INDONESIA: Was your meeting with Chester Bowles in Djakarta arranged for, or was it a coincidence?

MR. STEVENSON: That was arranged. He had to leave India before I got there, so we agreed to meet here. We're old friends. We went to school together, thirty-five years ago. He wanted to tell me about India and I wanted to tell him about the United States. We had a very good meeting place in Djakarta.[16]

MR. LABALLO (*Indonesia Raya*): Do you think a world war will come in ten years?

MR. STEVENSON: No, I don't think so. I don't think we'll have another world war if we remain strong and if we marshal all the strength, and the determination and the will power of the free world. Then they won't dare attack us and we'll not attack them, I can guarantee that.

MR. SPRENGERS (*Aneta*): [Question inaudible.]

MR. STEVENSON: The stock market is already declining — that's a joke in our country. The gentleman over here asked me what, I think he asked me, what the economic effect of the settlement of the war in Korea would be. I told him what the reaction was first. The stock market declined. What I meant by that was that in the United States now we have full employment because of the great exertion in the defense industries. If we no longer have to build weapons and arms, ships, and tanks, and airplanes, and guns and so on and all of the thousands of items, it's assumed that there will be a great decline in the American economy and that we will have perhaps have unemployment, earnings will go down, wages will be affected and the result might be economic recession or depression. Now if you understand, the result of that is the price of securities, of investments, in these industries goes down with the prospect of peace. It does not mean, and this must be understood, that the United States doesn't want a settlement of the war in Korea, because it wants it desperately and has so indicated time and again. We should like to end all the

16 This was, of course, the plain truth. But as Attwood wrote in his diary: "Everyone roared with laughter; they were convinced that the Bowles-Stevenson meeting was part of a secret Democratic party foreign policy maneuver and they just concluded that Stevenson was deftly parrying the question."

places of conflict, all of the conflicts on earth. I hope that's understood. Are there any questions about it? I think one of the most unhappy things that could happen to the world would be economic disaster in the United States. And you can see why.

MR. LABALLO (*Indonesia Raya*): What is your opinion about the advice of John Foster Dulles to stop the Point Four program and help to under-developed countries?

MR. STEVENSON: I didn't know that he made any such proposal.

MR. LABALLO (*Indonesia Raya*): There was a press report this morning.

MR. STEVENSON: Well, that's news to me. I can't comment on it until I know what he said.

MR. SUKRISNO: Mr. Stevenson, may I offer my deepest and heartfelt regret that you were not elected President of the U.S.A.

MR. STEVENSON: Thank you, Sir, thank you. I'm sorry you're not registrated [sic] as a voter in the United States.

MR. SPRENGERS (*Aneta*): Do you think it possible that after the peace in Korea that some, let us say, Chinese soldiers will move over to another place? Are there any means of preventing them from going, for instance, into Indo-China?

MR. STEVENSON: Well, Sir, your guess about communist intentions is just as good as mine. I don't know what they would do.

MR. SPRENGERS (*Aneta*): What I mean is, are there any means to stop them?

MR. STEVENSON: Yes, by strengthening Indo-China so that it wouldn't be profitable.

MR. SPRENGERS: That's the French-American intention?

MR. STEVENSON: That's the Vietnamese intention.

[Question inaudible.]

MR. STEVENSON: They couldn't do it without our help.

MR. SPRENGERS: They couldn't?

MR. STEVENSON: Well, they can in time, just as the Koreans could in time. But they can't now because they haven't the equipment, they haven't the war materials and they haven't the officers, and they haven't a large enough army sufficiently trained. But that's going ahead rapidly. I've just been in Indo-China. The development of the Vietnam army is the most promising in Vietnam. It's coming along.

MR. HULSBERGEN (*Nieuwe Rotterdamsche Courant*): Sir, have you any idea about the Indonesian claim on West Irian?

MR. STEVENSON: I don't really know any too much about it. I've heard some comment about West Irian since I've been here but I should certainly be very loath to comment on a political problem that seems to be as important as that one is, without more understanding of it. I just don't know too much about it.

UNIDENTIFIED REPORTER: What is colonialism in the American sense?

MR. STEVENSON: We're against it. I think the Philippines is the best evidence of our view of colonialism.

UNIDENTIFIED REPORTER: What do you intend to do for Indonesia after leaving this country?

MR. STEVENSON: I'm going to come back and have a vacation sometime. Thank you very much gentlemen.

After the press conference was over, a reporter for Merdeka *wrote: "Stevenson's witty answers often made interviewers burst out laughing. Autograph-hunters rushed and crowded around him. He had given the interviewers exactly one hour. Then he quickly made for the airport in order to continue his trip to other parts of Asia."* [17]
Stevenson wrote of his trip to Indonesia:

FIGHT FOR FREEDOM IN SOUTHEAST ASIA [18]

It takes about two minutes in Indonesia to realize that this nation of some 80 million (no one really knows how many) is still in revolution — skittish as a colt, insecure, wary of outsiders and persuaded that its own problems are the most important in the world.

When we stepped out of the airplane at Djakarta into the troubled suspicious heart of Indonesia — the sixth largest country in the world, stretching in a line of tropical islands across one eighth of the world's surface — reporters at the airport were ready with a barrage of questions:

Why had I come to Indonesia? How long was I going to stay? Which leaders was I going to see? Why was America depressing the prices of tin and rubber?

There are some simple facts about Indonesia that command the respect of Americans and, on balance, are cause for more hope than despair about the future of this steaming, beautiful country, which knows so woefully little about the United States and its motives.

[17] April 18, 1953.
[18] *Look*, June 16, 1953. The rest of this article is reprinted in Chapters Nine and Ten, below.

It is the only nation in Asia which has won its independence by fighting for it. Not only did a handful of young, inexperienced Indonesian leaders organize and win a revolution against the Dutch, but they have beaten down two Communist uprisings, established a government and restored some administrative order to backward, disunited islands scattered along the equator as far as from Maine to California. All this has been done in eight years, on the heels of a cruel and crippling Japanese occupation — and without substantial foreign assistance.

Java — where nearly two thirds of the people live — is still bedeviled with banditry and rebellion among the fanatic Moslems; the economy is precarious and the average annual per capita income is less than fifty dollars. But at least communism is no longer a menace. There is no Communist sympathy among government leaders, and pro-Red sentiment is declining even among the urban unemployed.

As President Achmed Soekarno [19] told me, "We have had to fight the Communists twice. They are no longer a problem." Nor is there fertile ground for communism in the rich volcanic soil of rural Java. For in contrast to other parts of Asia, the Dutch saw to it that farmers, not landlords, owned the land.

Indonesia's basic problems are economic rather than political. They stem from a badly distributed population and low productivity. In crowded Java — the most densely populated area in the world — the marvelously terraced rice paddies even crawl up the sides of the live volcano Merapi, the "flaming mountain," which erupted and killed thousands only 20 years ago. Here, the land problem is one of farm credit and shrinking holdings. Co-operatives are beginning to improve the credit situation, and the government has ambitious plans to resettle millions of farmers in neighboring Sumatra, where there is abundant land. Some 300,000 have already been moved — meanwhile, the population of Java is increasing by 800,000 a year.

Indonesia is rich in rubber, tin, tea, quinine and all manner of tropical products. But since the end of the Korea war boom, the prices of rubber and tin have collapsed (for which the Indonesians blithely blame the United States); tea is in the doldrums and the producing area is overrun with bandits; and quinine has been largely replaced by the new synthetic drugs.

In short, this nation, whose revenue is largely derived from foreign trade, is suffering a severe trade deficit. (In 1938, the Dutch East Indies

---

[19] The President himself spelled his name Sukarno or Soekarno interchangeably. See *Sukarno: An Autobiography as Told to Cindy Adams* (Indianapolis: Bobbs-Merrill, 1965), pp. 26–27.

could buy seven tons of rice for a ton of rubber; in 1952, a ton of rubber brought in only two and a half tons of rice — and Indonesia has to import 400,000 tons each year to feed its rapidly increasing population.) As a result, the realistic young Finance Minister, Dr. Sumitro Djojohadikusumo, is struggling manfully with inflation, rising prices, declining revenues, unbalanced budgets and a legislative assembly with little stomach for austerity and the ugly realities of independence — economic as well as political.

I never saw a wheelbarrow or a shovel in Indonesia, and in this stifling, humid climate, labor productivity and vitality are low at best. Indeed, after walking along one of the great, stagnant, coffee-colored canals which so many city people use for bathtub and toilet, I was not surprised that life expectancy here is about 32 years. I was told, however, that one develops an immunity which makes the canals less lethal than they look, and that the low life expectancy is due chiefly to the high infant-mortality rate.

American technicians are working with Indonesians to improve agriculture, industry, public health and education. But it has been hard to explain to the Indonesians the bewildering shifts from ECA to MSA to TCA. The MSA agreement — which required the Indonesians to join in the common defense against Communist expansion — deeply offended their neutralist sensibilities and resulted in the downfall of the cabinet last year. Our present technical-assistance program is better understood and appreciated, although these proud, sensitive people would prefer assistance through the United Nations.

President Soekarno, with whom I talked in the gleaming white palace of the former Dutch governors, dismissed the MSA "trouble" and spoke emphatically of Indonesia's need for technical assistance. But this forthright, young-looking "father of the revolution" seemed more interested in his country's political problems. He spoke resentfully about the Netherlands' refusal to extradite "Turk" Westerling, the Dutch officer who led an uprising against the government three years ago; and he made it plain he distrusted not only the Dutch but the Chinese — who number two million in Indonesia and whose press takes a generally pro-Communist line.

But most of all, Soekarno wanted to talk about Irian, the western half of New Guinea, which was the only part of the old Dutch East Indies not turned over to Indonesia. The sparsely settled, uncivilized jungle area has no ethnic or cultural link with the Indonesians, but this makes no difference to him. Soekarno wants it for Indonesia because it used to be Dutch — and he means to get it. "The United States should publicly declare that sovereignty over Irian properly belongs to us," he said, implying that America would thereby win the enduring friendship of Indonesia.

I was deeply impressed with this gifted man (as I was by his intimate knowledge of the American Revolution). But at this uneasy stage in Indonesia's adolescence, Irian seems less important than many other pressing problems, and I suspect that it has become a handy political catchword for a president who believes that "a revolution is never finished."

The men who govern Indonesia are young, sincere, eager, industrious — and inexperienced. There is lamentable ignorance about the United States. A newspaper editor brashly told me we paid our soldiers so much that everyone wanted to join the Army. There is mistrust of our motives and power; there is suspicion that we are trying to drive Indonesia into a military alliance, and anxiety about rearming the Japanese (whom the Indonesians dislike even more than they do their former Dutch masters).

Indonesia's leaders are more interested in Tunisian independence than in NATO; more concerned with what goes on in kindred Burma than in London. Defiantly independent, proud of their revolution, these men are touchy about being pushed around or appearing to be anyone's satellite; and they are determined to stay out of the world-wide contest between communism and democracy. But there is little anti-Americanism. They ask questions about America with eager, friendly curiosity. And they talk about their problems with disarming candor and transparent anxiety to find genuine friends and to draw closer to the America which was also born in a revolution against colonialism.

What's ahead for Indonesia politically is hard to predict. There is little political consciousness among a population still largely illiterate. (The nation's 120 daily newspapers have a combined circulation of less than 500,000.) Probably no more than 10,000 people actively "run things." There are 19 parties in the one-chamber parliament, but no elections have yet been held. Cabinets change frequently, and the chief source of political stability seems to be the personal popularity of Soekarno and Vice President Mohammed Hatta.

Indonesia is acutely short of trained administrators, and the few competent people available are all overworked. Yet the number of Dutch administrators employed by the government last year was reduced from 5000 to 2000; and the Dutch military mission which has been reorganizing the armed services is going home this year. The prevailing attitude seems to be: "Get rid of the Dutch even if it ruins us." (Paradoxically, Indonesians will tell you that anti-Dutch feeling is more emotional than real and is rapidly evaporating.)

Elections for a constitutional assembly may be held next year, and this should reveal the strength of the various political parties. I found the Socialist leaders to be the most moderate and realistic in their thinking. But the country is 90 per cent Moslem, and the religious and nationalist parties are by far the strongest.

Indonesia is suffering the growing pains of a new state. It is economically fragile, and emotional slogans will put no one to work. Nor have its leaders realized that only very strong or very weak nations can maintain a truly neutral policy. Indonesia is neither strong nor weak, and it is rich in coveted resources. If the Kremlin launches a trade war and offers to buy rubber and tin at high prices and sell rice at low prices, it will be hard for any Indonesian government to resist starting down the primrose path toward economic and then political vassalage.

Nevertheless, I'm optimistic about the future of these friendly, cheerful people who have achieved nationhood unprepared and in violence, and in a trying and perilous time. They are gradually learning the facts of international life. The hunger for knowledge and education is heartening, and their independent-mindedness is itself a safeguard against dictatorship.

In our impatience for all the free nations to see the common peril in time, we should remember that neutrality long was the historical American position and that Indonesia's present policy is not harmful to us. We should talk straight to the Indonesians, and if we don't like something they do, say so; but we should not lecture them nor press them to accept aid in any form until they ask for it.

It seems to me that our best policy in Indonesia is one of benevolent detachment.

After all, it wasn't so long ago that we Americans were mighty sensitive and suspicious of foreign influence and "foreign entanglements."

Nine

Singapore and Malaya

APRIL 13–APRIL 20, 1953

*A*board the KLM Constellation, returning from Djakarta to Singapore, Stevenson and Attwood revised the second article for Look, and Stevenson found time to write some postcards.

To Margaret Munn [1]

[no date]

Still living but breathing hard — Loved your letters. Bill [Blair] keeps everything under control, including me, how I don't know. We've seen more strange sights and strange people. I must have been neglecting my Nat. Geographic. Now on the way to the jungles of Malaya and another war. Hope all is well with you and Artie.[2]

AES

To Newton N. Minow [3]

[no date]

The floor of this Pagoda is solid silver and there's a fine Jade Budd[h]a.[4] That's all I can remember — except the Cambodian dancing girls! . . .

---

[1] This handwritten postcard is in the possession of Mrs. Munn. It is postmarked Singapore, April 13, 1953.

[2] Stevenson's dog, King Arthur.

[3] This handwritten postcard is in the possession of Mr. Minow. It is postmarked Singapore, April 14, 1953.

[4] The card had a picture of the pagoda in the grounds of the Royal Palace, Phnom Penh, Cambodia. Mr. Minow was administrative assistant to Governor Stevenson in 1952.

Tomorrow the puzzles of Malaya and another war. Hope all goes well with you. Even LaSalle St. in July will look good to me — ADLAI

Stevenson arrived in Singapore at one P.M. on April 13. After lunch he and Attwood completed the final revisions of the Look *article and it was cabled to New York. That evening the Stevenson party dined alone with Malcolm MacDonald, commissioner general for the United Kingdom in Southeast Asia. This impressive, knowledgeable British commissioner general had been stationed in Southeast Asia for the past six years. The encounter produced one of the most fruitful conversations of the entire journey.*

Stevenson reviewed with MacDonald much of the information he had obtained in Indonesia. MacDonald observed that he believed that Sjahrir, Vice President Hatta, and the sultan of Jogjakarta had overcome their immense sensitivity toward the West. In view of the fact that many of the leaders had been in Dutch jails and their relatives had been killed by the Dutch, their views were remarkably restrained. Indonesians were impressed by the way the British had freed India, Pakistan, Ceylon, and allowed Burma to withdraw from the British Commonwealth, MacDonald pointed out.

Five years ago, he added, Indonesian leaders thought the West might frustrate their independence because the West was still "colonial" and the Soviet Union might become their friend. Now, he said, the leaders felt differently, but their followers did not always understand the situation. If Indonesian leaders had to advocate neutralism in order to stay in office, he urged that the United States and the United Kingdom should leave them alone on this issue and not tell them what to do.

The leaders feared, he continued, a revival of militarism in Japan. And they did not understand that they had to adjust to living in the same world with Japan. Except for Sjahrir and the sultan of Jogjakarta, they were terribly introspective, and with the sea all about them they felt they were safe from any Communist threat.

MacDonald discussed the magnetism of Sukarno and the way this "amazing orator" could handle huge crowds of people. Stevenson described the length at which Sukarno had talked to him about Irian and how he had kept urging that the United States put pressure on the Dutch to give it to Indonesia. Stevenson remarked at one point in the conversation, "I told him Vice President Alben Barkley's story about campaigning in Kentucky." Barkley had gone up to an old fellow whom he had helped many times and had said to him, "Hope you're go-

ing to vote for me this time." The old fellow replied that he was not. Barkley said, "Look at all the things I've done for you." The old fellow looked at Barkley and said, "Well, you ain't done nothin' recently." Sukarno, Stevenson said, had exploded with laughter.

MacDonald expressed concern over Sukarno's antagonism for the sultan of Jogjakarta and the way the nationalist parties were trying to attack the Socialist party and remove their members from the army. Mac-Donald remarked that it would be constructive if the Masjumi party won a majority in the parliament. While some in the party favored a theocratic state, he was confident that Natsir did not.

MacDonald then noted the contrast between the situation in Malaya and that in Vietnam.

After long and detailed planning and consultation between the British government, the Malay rulers, and representative groups of the peoples of Malaya, the Federation of Malaya came into existence on February 1, 1948. It comprised the nine Malay states and the two British settlements of Malacca and Penang. The federation was governed by a high commissioner, appointed by London, and an executive council and a legislative council, both appointed by the high commissioner and both predominantly Asian in composition. The nine state governments were headed by the nine Malay rulers, each had a Malay prime minister, a British adviser, and executive and legislative councils. The governments of the two former Straits Settlements were headed by resident commissioners, representing the high commissioner, with both executive and legislative councils.

Singapore, formerly one of the Straits Settlements, had been constituted a Crown Colony in 1946. It was headed by a governor, appointed by London, with an executive council and a partially elected legislative council. Singapore shared with the Federation of Malaya certain common services and technical advisers.[5]

As a result of the obvious British encouragement of self-government and the desire to move toward independence as rapidly as possible, MacDonald observed that, unlike that in Vietnam, the nationalist movement in the Federation of Malaya was working with the British.[6] The Communist terrorist forces that had been waging war since 1948 were approximately ninety-five per cent Chinese, with the hard-core leaders China-born. Not only had they failed to win the support of nationalist

[5] For a discussion of the peoples, resources, history and governmental structure see Norton S. Ginsburg and Chester F. Roberts, Jr., *Malaya*, Human Relations Area Files (Seattle: University of Washington Press, 1958).

[6] The Federation of Malaya achieved independence on August 31, 1957. Singapore received full internal self-government in June, 1959. Singapore and the Federation merged in 1963, but in 1966 Singapore withdrew.

groups but, MacDonald added, they had failed to capture control of the trade unions.[7] *In Indochina, on the other hand, a number of nationalists were in the Vietminh. Moreover, the terrorists in the federation were not numerous — some five thousand armed men — and central control over them was weak compared with Ho Chi Minh's authority.*

The fact, however, that seventy-five per cent of Malaya was covered by a thick jungle had enabled the terrorists to survive and escape capture. They knew the jungle well, he added, since many of them had been guerrillas against the Japanese during the war. After they failed by peaceful means to gain control during the period from 1945 to 1948, they had gone back to the jungle. While they tried to win support by advocating independence and a better standard of living, the British maintained that independence would come soon and, in the meantime, they could better provide the industrialization and agricultural development that would lead to a better standard of living.

The Communist terrorists, he added, were inefficient, made many mistakes that turned the nationalists against them, and were not very sophisticated Communists. The Soviet Union, he remarked, did not give them much support, and he described the terrorists as the "Cinderellas of the Communist world."

He spoke about Thailand, emphasizing the way the military ran the government and the rampant corruption at high levels. He remarked that the prime minister, Marshal Pibul, "was the greatest master of the coup d'état in the world today." MacDonald urged Stevenson to spend as much time as possible with U.S. Ambassador Edwin F. Stanton, who was thoroughly knowledgeable about Thailand. In the case of Burma, he recommended that Stevenson spend time with Prime Minister U Nu and Cabinet Minister U Ba Swe. He observed that Li Mi's Nationalist troops should be removed through Thailand or Indochina to Formosa.

Stevenson reluctantly broke off the conversation, for he had to have sleep before catching an eight A.M. plane for Kuala Lumpur.

Consul General Charles F. Baldwin accompanied Stevenson on April 14 as he flew over mile upon mile of unbroken jungle. As he approached the capital of the Federation of Malaya, he could see the vast tin mines which had led the reigning sultan to move his capital to Kuala Lumpur in the nineteenth century. The day that he arrived, the Malay Mail *explained to its readers:*

[7] Consul General Charles F. Baldwin had given Stevenson an article by Alice W. Shurcliff, "Growth of Democratic Trade-Unions in the Federation of Malaya," *Monthly Labor Review,* September, 1951, of the U.S. Department of Labor's Bureau of Labor Statistics. Stevenson wrote in pencil on the margin of the article: "W. J. — Do we need this — maybe in Chi? Looks pretty good — AES."

Stevenson's visit is in many ways a unique one. Officially, he has no standing whatever, and is only known to the mass of people here as the man who failed to win a particularly important election. And, generally speaking, people are not very interested in failures, however distinguished. But Mr. Stevenson is in a very different category. He is still a power to be reckoned with in United States and world politics.[8]

Stevenson stayed at the residence of General Sir Gerald Templer, high commissioner and director of operations for the Federation of Malaya. Blair and Johnson stayed nearby at the residence of Deputy High Commissioner Sir Donald MacGillivray, while Attwood and Bingham stayed with Hendrik Van Oss, the U.S. consul.

For an hour and a half Templer and MacGillivray talked to Stevenson about the military situation. Templer explained that during the "savage" Japanese occupation, many Chinese had fled to the jungle. The most powerful of the guerrilla armies that were organized was Communist-controlled. The British, before surrendering to the Japanese in 1942, gave guns to the people, and some British went into the jungle to organize and lead them. During the war the British dropped supplies from the air or landed them by submarine. When the Japanese surrendered in 1945, many of their weapons were given to the people. As a result, there was an ample supply of guns available when the Communists fled to the jungle in 1948. And Templer added, "If they have the guts and can shoot straight, they can lay an ambush anywhere at this moment and get more weapons from us."

He estimated there were somewhere between four thousand and six thousand armed terrorists; probably only ten per cent could be called international Communists, but these led all the others. The British, he added, were inflicting heavy casualties on the ten per cent and "they are not replaceable." He said that about forty per cent of the terrorists were really dacoits (bandits). Another forty per cent, he thought, were individuals who had committed crimes and fled from the police. The remaining ten per cent were teenaged boys and girls.

At the present moment, Templer remarked, only about 350 terrorists a month came into contact with British forces. The rest were trying to get enough food to live. If the British could make food control seventy-five per cent efficient, the terrorists would be "finished." He estimated that the food control was now seventy per cent effective. Captured terrorists, he added, were in terrible physical condition.

He then described the jungle and said the only way to get through

8 See Barry Bingham, "East Asians Seem to Have Made Stevenson Symbol of What They Want America to Be," Louisville *Courier-Journal*, May 3, 1953.

it was "on your own flat feet," for the trees were two hundred feet high with thick foliage at the tops. Even on the brightest day it was like a cathedral at night and the undergrowth was "awful and horrible." It was impossible to cultivate under the trees, so that the terrorists had to make clearings in order to grow tapioca. The British spotted the clearings from the air, he said, and then bombed them.

In addition to the terrorists in the jungle, there was an armed work force, living on the fringe of the jungle, that collected food for the terrorists. In addition, there were unarmed supporters — the min-yuen — who tried to collect food and guns and send these into the jungle.

Between 1948 and 1951, Templer observed, the terrorists tried to win the support of the ordinary people but failed because of their violent methods and indiscriminate killing. Since 1951, he added, they had been using selective killing and trying to subvert the ordinary Malays as well as the Chinese.

In order to shut off the food going to the terrorists, the British had resettled some 500,000 Chinese squatters in 509 new villages ringed with barbed wire. The squatters, he added, were "bloody-minded" against the government for this. Since putting them in the new villages, "We have tried to win their hearts by giving them a little land." It was difficult, however, to get land, since the British at the behest of the Malay rulers had set aside reserves for the Malays.

The Malay villages — the kampongs — were not regrouped, he pointed out, and the Malays felt they were being ignored. The terrorists were now trying to appeal to these villagers by saying, "Look what the British did for the Chinese; they didn't do anything for you."

Sir Gerald then talked of the rehabilitation camps for surrendered enemy personnel, where the former terrorists were taught trades. Some of them joined the police or the British troops and went back into the jungle to fight the terrorists or persuade them to surrender.

Templer explained that in pamphlets dropped in the jungle he had given a guarantee in his name that if they would surrender they would not be tried except in exceptional circumstances. Only one person, he said, had been tried since he had made his pledge. This pamphlet had cost him "a great deal of sleep," because some who had surrendered were guilty of murder before they fled into the jungle. But, he added, "I had to give them this pledge to get them out of the jungle."

He also described the detention camps where sympathizers of the terrorists were held. He added that the British were deporting civilian Communists to mainland China. They were being deported in a ship under a Latin American registry, and the agent made arrangements with the Chinese government to accept the deportees.

[147]

Templer then left, and Stevenson talked to Dato Onn Bin Jaafar, a Malay, who was member for home affairs in the federation government and president of the Independence of Malaya party, and Dato E. E. Thuraisingham, a Ceylonese, who was member for education in the federation government.[9] They stated that there was no controversy over independence, since the people knew it would be granted, but that the basic question was one of timing. The gravest problem facing their pluralistic society, they pointed out, was how to get the various ethnic groups in Malaya to feel they were part of a country and had a responsibility to it. A number of Chinese, they added, were not politically conscious so far as Malaya was concerned but were politically conscious toward China, particularly when the Kuomintang controlled it. Chinese schools carefully inculcated love and respect for the motherland. The Chinese Communists, they added, had been trying to infiltrate these schools.

The Chinese in Malaya, they said, fell into three categories: (1) some twenty per cent who had lived there for generations in the old Straits Settlements and Singapore and had become British subjects; (2) the "petty capitalists," Kuomintang Chinese; and (3) the "China Chinese," who did not care who controlled China. The last two groups were the Chinese who opposed being Malayans and objected to national schools replacing communal schools.

The people who came from the Indian subcontinent and Ceylon were quite different, they said, from the Chinese. They always had identified themselves with Malaya, not India.

Stevenson questioned them in detail on how the Malays, Chinese and Indians were to be integrated. It would be a long process, they replied,

---

[9] In the multi-ethnic society of the country, each ethnic group remained almost entirely distinct from the others; each was localized to a considerable extent in different parts of Malaya, and each to varying degrees engaged in specific kinds of activity.

	Federation	Singapore	Total
Malaysians	2,631,000	129,000	2,760,000
Chinese	2,044,000	808,000	2,852,000
Indians and Pakistanis	587,000	76,000	663,000
Europeans	12,000	13,000	25,000
Eurasians	11,000	10,000	21,000
Others	52,000	9,000	61,000
	5,337,000	1,045,000	6,382,000

These figures — an estimate — were supplied to Stevenson by the U.S. consul general.

before the Chinese groups would feel they were Malayan. They described the racial fighting between the Chinese and Malays immediately after the Japanese occupation had ended. Then they warned that there would be chaos if independence came too soon. "I want independence," Dato Onn said, "but I want to be able to keep it."

Economically, the Malays, they pointed out, were at the mercy of the Chinese who controlled trade, banking, and transport. Moreover, Chinese education had been better than Malay education and, as a result, the Chinese were better prepared than the Malays for business. They both favored the abolition of communal schools and the establishment of national schools with English as one of the compulsory languages.

They added that the British were saying, "You had better unite because you are going to be independent." But Dato Thuraisingham pointed out, "For six hundred years our history here has been the isolation of the races." If the British granted independence immediately, they agreed, the "Chinese would buy control from the Malays within fifteen minutes."

Templer returned and joined the discussion at this point and insisted, "You are going to be forced to take independence." The two agreed, but contended that those who did not believe in Malaya should not be permitted the vote. Of the two and a half million Chinese in the federation, about 1,100,000 held federal citizenship and they should vote but not the others. Templer emphasized that it was not a feasible alternative to get rid of the Chinese, and, therefore, they all had to get together.

After lunch, Stevenson conferred with a leading member of the Chinese community, Mr. H. S. Lee, and then talked with military and police officials at their operations headquarters. The officials described the strict rationing system to prevent food from getting into the jungle.

They explained how the terrorists forced many of the 100,000 aborigines living in the jungle to raise food for them. The terrorists told the aborigines that they were fighting the Japanese. The aborigines had been so brutally treated during the occupation that they were delighted to help the terrorists. The British were now building a series of forts, a distance of three or four days' walk into the jungle, and from these forts patrols were searching for terrorists who were controlling the aborigines.

But the military situation was only about twenty-five per cent of the problem, these officials emphasized. The greater task was to better the standard of living and bring coherence and unity among the pluralistic groups in the country.

After this discussion, Stevenson visited the Institute for Medical Re-

search, where important research had been done on typhoid, typhus, and beriberi. He talked with an American Fulbright grantee, Dr. A. J. Walker of Tulane University, who was doing research on malaria.

That evening Sir Gerald Templer held a dinner party in honor of Stevenson. Attwood wrote in his diary, "Templer, brilliant, nervous, unconventional, dominated the talk. He has a way of sidling up, nudging you ferociously and cracking a joke or an oath." Just before dinner, Templer nudged one Stevenson aide and said, "Now, for God's sake, don't quote all I said to you today, because I really let my pants down with you two." One of Sir Gerald's aides observed that he had made a profound impression when he arrived. The Malayans knew he was a strong military personality but they were astonished when he announced that "a people who did not know their history were lost." Then Templer got them to start a national museum and an historical society.

After dinner, Stevenson tried to catch up on his correspondence.

To Mr. and Mrs. Ernest L. Ives [10]

April 14, 1953

Dear Buffy & Ernest —

Staying with General Templer in this boiling capital of Malaya — but in spite of war and worries life goes on in the elegant routine of great British houses. So, except when outdoors, I'm very comfortable in this remote and troubled place.

Have had to work too hard on this journey — we planned too much too quick and the magazine writing — in such superficial and condensed form — irks me no end.

So glad to hear Buffy has weathered her jaw trouble. I don't think it would be kind to the Brookes [11] to be in Belfast at the same time as the Queen — nor good for me with so many Irish in America. I had not understood that they expected me along with the Queen whom I will see in London anyway. So I think I had best cable them that I hope to get there while abroad, but not at that time.

I think now that I will go to Austria & Yugoslavia after Italy — the news value places. Also Germany & very little of France & England this trip. Perhaps at the end there could be a little writing vacation — end of

[10] This handwritten letter is in the Elizabeth Stevenson Ives collection, Illinois State Historical Library.

[11] The Iveses had written that they were to visit the Right Honorable Viscount Brookeborough, prime minister of Northern Ireland, and Stevenson was invited to join them.

July — with you all & Borden in less newsworthy and more comfortable spot.

Now to the jungles!

Love,
AD.

Stevenson headed out of Kuala Lumpur the next morning, riding in General Templer's bulletproof car and escorted by a troop of armored cars — two of them with twin Bren guns. He first visited Petaling Jaya, a new satellite town being constructed to absorb some of the swelling population of the capital. Next he visited a tin dredge belonging to Petaling Tin Ltd., anchored up a diverted river. Great buckets were scooping up the riverbed, and intricate machinery was separating the ore from the mud. "It was a veritable floating factory," Attwood wrote in his diary, "and hotter than hell." Stevenson also toured the processing plant where the ore was refined. While he was there, police and soldiers were on the edge of the jungle, on the dredge — it seemed, in fact, everywhere. Actually, security had so improved in recent months that ordinarily only a few people patrolled while the dredge worked day and night.

The next stop was at a rubber estate where Tamil girls demonstrated how to cut the trees for the liquid to flow into cups. Not to be outdone, Stevenson tried his hand at tapping a tree. He heard complaints about America's synthetic rubber production and falling prices. "Despite the heat Stevenson was striding around, looking attentive and greeting everyone with hearty handshakes and good humor," Attwood remarked in his diary.

After a fiery curry lunch with the manager, MacDonald Bennett, Stevenson visited one of the new villages where twenty-six hundred Chinese had been resettled. It was enclosed in barbed wire and floodlights were turned on at night to prevent anyone from slipping into the village. He visited with a British nurse who had been in Asia for twenty-four years. She said that until the people were put in this village they had never before known medical treatment.

He visited the house of a Chinese farmer, posed for a picture, shook hands, and tweaked the baby's cheek. "He could easily get elected to something out here if he stayed a bit longer," Attwood wrote in his diary.

He next drove with his armored escort to the Sungei Buloh Leper Hospital. After walking through the wards and having tea with the matron, he headed for a Malay kampong. En route, a number of nearly naked aborigines were on the jungle road to greet him. Their chief proceeded to show Stevenson how to use a blowgun and poisoned arrows. When Stevenson was given the blowgun someone urged him to try it. "No," he jokingly replied, "not until I have a Republican in the sights."

An enterprising reporter quickly asked him if he was thinking of bagging a general. "Certainly not," replied Stevenson with a grin, "I have nothing against any generals." [12]

Stevenson left the main road and his heavy escort vehicles behind, to ride in British Land Rovers to reach the kampong several miles in the jungle. When he arrived, the village home guard was drawn up in formation to welcome him. They showed him a huge python they had caught that morning. Stevenson agreed to pose with it provided Attwood took it out of its box. (There was no picture.) When the headman was introduced, Stevenson said to him, "Hello, boss. How's the precinct?" When he left, the kampong appeared to be safely Democratic.

Toward the end of the day the skies darkened and a driving rain drenched the soldiers standing watch with the Bren guns. But, despite the downpour, after the escort delivered him to Kuala Lumpur, Stevenson jumped out of his car and shook hands with every soldier and thanked them for what must have been "a boring day's work for them." "Now, what do you suppose he does that for?" a British officer said to Attwood. "Our chaps will never be able to vote for him." [13]

Early the next morning Stevenson and his aides were flown in two helicopters to a kampong deep in the jungle. After putting on jungle boots, he walked through a jungle trail to a river where he watched a patrol returning from an all-night search for terrorists. He next flew to a jungle clearing that was so small that only one helicopter could go in at a time. After talking to a small patrol composed of British, Commonwealth, and Borneo soldiers, one helicopter, with Attwood, Blair, and Robert Hewitt of the Associated Press, arose from the clearing. A few moments later, Stevenson climbed into the nose of the other helicopter with the pilot, while Bingham, Major-General W. H. Lambert, the British officer in charge of the party, and Johnson climbed into the rear.

Approximately two minutes out of the clearing, the motor of the helicopter began to clang, smoke poured into the cabin, the big propeller began to slow down, and the helicopter started to drop toward the jungle. The pilot and Stevenson spotted an abandoned clearing, and the pilot skillfully maneuvered the disabled aircraft toward it. Suddenly, the helicopter hit the trees and then toppled off and made a smooth

[12] William Attwood, "What Asia Thinks of Adlai," Look, June 6, 1953, p. 71.
[13] Ibid.

landing in an abandoned rice field. Blair, who was watching from the other helicopter, wrote to Carol Evans: "They just made it as the rotors stopped moving — if the engine had stopped a minute earlier, they would have landed in the trees — and I hate to think of what might have happened." [14]

The British general jumped out with his revolver in his hand — the only weapon available. Stevenson climbed down from the nose, stepping into mud up to his knees. He was quite unperturbed, and full of praise for the skill of the pilot, Lieutenant Commander S. H. Suthers.

Meanwhile, the other helicopter flew to a clearing where there were British soldiers, left the rest of the party and flew to rescue Stevenson. Over the radio, British forces were ordered to close in on the rice field. Some fifteen minutes after the crash landing, Stevenson was in the other helicopter flying to Kuala Lumpur.

Waiting at the airport was Sir Gerald Templer, who had been flying in his own helicopter on an inspection tour, when he heard the radio message that Stevenson was down in the jungle. Although he was still visibly alarmed by the accident, he said: "Well, Governor, I hope you don't think I laid that one on."

Before leaving for the airport after lunch, Sir Gerald furnished Stevenson with a confidential memorandum of the cost to the British of the campaign against the terrorists. He stated that if the Malay, Chinese, and Indian politicians would stop talking about racial conflict for ten years, the situation would be immensely improved. The solution for the problem, he reiterated, was national schools.

At the airport, where reporters questioned Stevenson about the crash landing, he observed: "I'm glad nobody reminded me that it was an American helicopter with an American engine."

He mentioned the communal problem and discussed how the American public school system had helped blend many national groups into a coherent society. The struggle against the terrorists, he said, was one of the most difficult he had ever seen. The fact that it was going well was a testimony "to the vigour, courage, and intelligence of the country's leaders." [15]

Stevenson arrived at Singapore in time for dinner. That evening and the next morning he organized his notes on Indonesia and answered correspondence.

[14] This letter, dated April 19, 1953, is in the possession of Miss Evans.
[15] *The Times* (London), April 17, 1953.

To Carol Evans [16]

April 17, 1953

Dear Miss E —

. . . We're back in Singapore for the *4th time* after several days up in Malaya. Yesterday coming back from the Jungle my helicopter gave up with a hideous cough just above the only rice paddy — an old abandoned one — within miles of solid jungle. I don't know how lucky you can be, but I must be exhausting my credit rapidly! Today I'm *resting* in the Am. Counsel's spacious home — with nothing to do except write an article on Indonesia, receive 5 delegations of Chinese, Malayans & students and shake hands with some 500 people at a reception. I think we'll live thru it but don't give odds!

I wish there was some time to write a proper letter to you & Phyllis [17] but just keeping up in the spare moments with the correspondence that accumulates as we travel is about all I can squeeze in — not to mention the pile of postcards that Bill [Blair] hands me to write every day.

I hope things are going alright and please tell Jane that I've seen and entirely approve the correspondence about the letter book.[18] I guess that was a bad idea & we should never have wasted her precious time on it. Margaret Munn has written me a lovely letter from Spfd, but I shall not be able to "do right" by her either.

Love to you all — and home will never look as good to me! I must be getting old — and no thinner either!

A.E.S.

At Stevenson's suggestion, Johnson interviewed S. I. Nadler, of the United States Information Service. He warned against assuming that the overseas Chinese were a monolithic group. In Singapore alone, he said, there were six major groups and some two thousand organizations. He discussed the four Chinese vernacular newspapers and pointed out that the pro–Chiang Kai-shek paper had to be subsidized. The average Chinese in Singapore, he added, definitely was not pro-Chiang. He also analyzed the Chinese belief in their cultural superiority and the strongly anti-white bias existing all over Southeast Asia.

After this meeting Stevenson asked Johnson to interview twelve University of Malaya students drawn from the Malay, Chinese, and Indian communities. A student from a kampong in the federation insisted that color was not the issue. The real problem was to get communication

[16] This handwritten letter is in the possession of Miss Evans.
[17] Phyllis Gustafson, secretary to William McCormick Blair, Jr.
[18] See note 31 to Chapter One, above.

going among the separate groups. They all agreed on the need of ex-panding national schools with English as the primary language. One of the Chinese students stated that Malaya was politically immature and there was no real organization that was noncommunal. If the British pulled out at that moment, he added, "There would be chaos."

When they were asked how their generation differed from the political leaders Stevenson had spoken to in Kuala Lumpur, they replied: "The older men will not listen to us. They call us upstarts. We have broken from the communal web and they have not. The country needs a great expansion of its schools and its higher education in order to pro-duce a growing number of young people who have broken the com-munal web."

Later that afternoon, Stevenson met with six other students from the university. When Stevenson said he thought the British were eager to leave, one student expressed impatience that the British had not set a specific time for independence. He also said young people felt that the achievement of unity among the communal groups, in order to view themselves as Malayans, was not moving fast enough. When the federa-tion had an elective assembly, they all agreed, they did not want pro-portional representation among the groups. The franchise, they insisted, should go only to those people who swore allegiance to Malaya. They stated that achieving an economic balance between Malays and Chinese was far more serious than any racial difference between them.

A little later, twelve leaders of the Kuomintang-oriented Chinese called on Stevenson. The next day one newspaper headlined: "Adlai Ticks Off Pro-Chiang Men." [19] *Their spokesman, Tan Kok Chor, handed Steven-son a lengthy statement, the gist of which was that the United States must aid Chiang to free China of Communism and the United Nations forces must continue to fight in Korea rather than seek a truce.*

Stevenson said: "You want America to shed its life in Korea, the French to do the same in Indochina, and the British do it here. Now tell me, how many Chinese have volunteered to fight in the security forces here or in the police to go after the Chinese Communists in the jungle?"

Immediately there was consternation among the group and they spoke together in Chinese for about five minutes. The answer they agreed upon was: "Indochina is the weakest link. If Indochina falls, then Malaya and Siam will be next. The government here should allow Nationalist troops to join the fight."

Stevenson persisted: "How many of you have volunteered?"

It took them a long time again to agree on an answer. (Blair and

[19] Singapore *Standard*, April 18, 1953.

Johnson estimated that seventy per cent of the total conversation was in Chinese to try to find replies to Stevenson's embarrassing questions.)

Finally, they stated there were twenty thousand Chinese in the police force. Stevenson said: "Well, there are more British than that fighting here and it's not their country. You want the U.S. to fight in Korea. Why don't you fight for your own country here?"

Again there was a lengthy discussion in Chinese. Finally they replied: "You have to be a British subject before you can join the army and you have to speak English. This prevents us from joining."

Stevenson stated: "There are lots of young Chinese who can speak English and are British subjects. Yet only a few of them are fighting. It would be better grace when you ask the United States to fight in Korea, if you people would fight and put up money for the struggle here in Malaya."

They discussed this in Chinese once again and decided to beat a strategic retreat. As they were about to leave they said: "If we can organize our own army, we will fight."

Stevenson replied: "If you really want to organize an army, why don't you go to General Templer and say that you will fight, so the British can get out of here, which they want to do."

Johnson wrote in his diary: "The Governor really handled this magnificently. They went out like crestfallen dogs with their tails between their legs. After they left, Consul General Baldwin said their statement about restrictions on them by the British so they could not fight was a lot of nonsense."

Stevenson was next visited by Dato Sir Cheng-lock Tan, president of the Malayan Chinese Association, and four of its members. Dato Sir Cheng-lock Tan said that some visitors had gained a wrong impression because they had not seen all the groups. "We are here to help you get a balanced view."

Stevenson asked: "When will you have a tranquil state and a viable economy?"

Dato Sir Cheng-lock Tan replied that the British had made a mistake in the constitution of the Federation of Malaya, in that it was based on the idea that Malaya belongs to the Malays. "Thirty years ago," he added, "I pleaded with the English to admit us to the civil service, but it is still closed to the Chinese." (He overstated this, inasmuch as there were Chinese in the civil service, although they were restricted from certain areas of it.) The civil service, he insisted, had to be opened to all Malayans. Each communal group should have proportional representation in the elected parliament, he added.

The suspicion that the Chinese favored making Malaya a province of

China was absolutely wrong, he insisted. "There is simply no proof of this," he said. "The Malays are suspicious of the Chinese because we are prosperous." But, he added, "it is a myth that we own the country." He said: "I don't blame anyone or condemn anyone. We want the Malayan Chinese to be understood. Give the Chinese coolies the same title to farm land as the Malays are given and the coolies will be willing to fight for their land."

With this opening, Stevenson said: "Will you gentlemen please tell me why the Chinese aren't in the armed forces or the police?"

They replied at once without having to discuss their answer in Chinese. They pointed out that until World War II, they had not been encouraged to serve in either. Moreover, the pay was low, and Chinese could earn more in business. But they added, "We realize it is serious that the Chinese don't participate more in the defense of the country. We asked the government to increase the pay but they couldn't afford it." The Malayan Chinese Association, they stated, was trying to explain to Chinese that it was their duty to serve. "We are also willing to have conscription to insure that all peoples serve in the armed forces."

After this meeting, Stevenson held a crowded press conference.

PARTIAL TRANSCRIPT OF STEVENSON PRESS CONFERENCE [20]

First, I'd like to say a few things which may be of interest to you.

I want to express my gratitude to Malcolm MacDonald for his hospitality and courtesy. Also to General Templer. I am most appreciative of the opportunity afforded me to visit military and civilian activities I had only heard about. I was particularly impressed with the:

1. resettlement projects;
2. slum clearance projects;
3. medical research institute;
4. famous leper hospital — one of the finest hospitals I've ever seen.

Also much impressed by

5. agricultural (demonstration) projects;
6. progress of education — national schools and adult education classes;

[20] An employee of the United States Information Service made these notes, but the transcript is not complete as she was not a stenotypist.

7. on the whole [impressed by the] rather more advanced general field of social welfare.

As to Malaya's political future, I of course know very little. I know only what I had heard in advance and what I've gleaned in a few days of rigorous inquiry. I can appreciate Malaya's long national travail and struggle to succeed in the experiment of self-government. My country has been experimenting for 176 years and is still learning. The same stresses and strains are present in Malaya. But with will and strong purpose, this country will succeed in strong, free self-government. As in my country, there are different cultures and backgrounds.

QUESTIONS

Q: Will you comment on [a] possible trusteeship for Formosa?

A: It seems to me that suggestion was first made in 1946 — when the whole question of trusteeships was being discussed all over the world.

Q: But, in view of the recent speculation?

A: I believe this question hinges on the security of the Pacific. It must be examined carefully. But as to Formosa's future, I'm not prepared to say.

Q: What is the military potential of Formosa?

A: There is great military potential in the forces on Formosa. But that's a loose word. It's used by a man whose highest rank in the service has been that of apprentice seaman.

Q: Would you give us your impression of Southeast Asia?

A: The great crisis in the portions of Southeast Asia I've visited seems to be the determination on the part of these people for independence. This, I think, is the most pertinent observation. [Second], intra-trade. This is a great undeveloped power in Asia, which could be developed to make Southeast Asia nations more complementary. As to defenses in the struggle against Communism, there are three actual wars going on — Korea, Indo-China, and Malaya. In all these countries, the effort is to limit communist dominion by armed force. If I go on, I'll soon make a mistake. I'd better stop.

Q: Is Bao Dai['s] government gaining more support from the people of Tonkin?

A: The situation is better in the Red River delta. That's not to say there's still not a job of work to do. I could discuss for any length how the villages fall into the hands of one side, then the other. They go back and forth. But I think the government is gaining confidence. Governor Nguyen Huu Tri of North Vietnam is a man of exceptional intelligence, strong purpose and ideas.

Q: What did you think of Mr. Eisenhower's speech? [21]

A: It was an admirable statement.

Q: Did your observations on Southeast Asia include Japan?

A: Yes. I'm surprised no one has asked about the helicopter accident. But it was just about that important.

Q: Were you hurt?

A: No, but I sank up to my knees in mud — so my trousers were. Landing the craft in that paddy field was a remarkable feat — and I've been in many aircraft accidents.

Q: How serious do you consider the invasion of Laos?

A: Can I talk off the record in Singapore? (A CORRESPONDENT: Yes.) The best judgment on that seemed to be that there was no good reason. Perhaps a food supply line to Thailand; or to widen the fronts of Burma and Thailand to allow for wider deployment of forces and enlarge the war. But I shouldn't be quoted on Laos.

Q: Has any dissatisfaction been expressed in America with the French Commander in Chief, General Raoul Salan?

A: If so, I don't know. I'm not in close contact with Washington, curiously enough.

Q: Did you meet with some University of Malaya students earlier?

A: Yes — charming lads, and mature. Enthusiastic about the future. Might as well have been American students. Right, Walter [Johnson]? Remarkable, really. Wanted all problems settled soon, etc.

Q: Did you meet earlier with Kuomintang leaders?

A: Did I? I don't know. Some Chinese gentlemen presented a memorandum. I asked them what they felt should be done in Korea. They said: keep fighting, there should be no settlement. Then I asked what they were contributing to the fighting here. If communist forces keep fighting in Korea, it seems fitting that an even greater effort should be made in Malaya. This fighting communism is multi-lateral. I never did get an answer. I don't mean to criticize them.

[21] President Eisenhower's speech of April 16, 1953, before the American Society of Newspaper Editors, among other things, called on the Soviet Union to join the United States in "the reduction of the burden of armaments now weighing upon the world." New York *Times*, April 17, 1953.

Q: What did you discuss with Sir Cheng-lock Tan and his group?

A: They asked if there was anything I wanted to ask them.

Q: What is the status of Southeast Asia in the Free World?

A: Perfectly clear. Survival of Southeast Asia is indispensable to the Free World. There is no minimizing the importance of Southeast Asia. It's true there are not too many who know much about it. Is that right? (looking to [U.S. Consul General Charles F.] Baldwin) BALDWIN: Yes, but the consciousness is increasing rapidly. ADLAI: Yes, the soldiers in Korea, for example, have contributed to this increasing awareness.

Q: About intra-regional trade — would it mean any change in American trading policy?

A: I wasn't thinking of that. Japan, a great industrial complex — India, Indonesia, and the Philippines all must be areas where mutually advantageous trade could be developed.

Q: Would British and American trading interests be affected?

A: We Democrats love people. I believe the more developed, the more there is for all of us. This trade wouldn't be at the expense of anyone. Of course, that isn't always the view of the Republicans.

Q: What about Chiang Kai-shek?

A: Oh, I can't go into that.

Two days later Billy Budd wrote [22]:

> The last-but-one defeated Presidential candidate to visit Malaya, Mr. Thomas E. Dewey, created a bad impression so pronounced that the secret of Harry Truman's success was revealed in a blinding flash. His successor, Mr. Adlai Stevenson, has wiped out the belief that defeat at the hands of the great American public corrodes the soul. A more charming man it would be hard to find.
>
> Mr. Stevenson has busted rackets, too, but he must have been very nice about it. Mr. Dewey talked to Malayan pressmen as though he saw in every one a potential Lucky Luciano or Frank Costello. Mr. Stevenson talked to them as if he saw them as potential voters in 1956.
>
> Mr. Dewey could never have said, after a forced landing: "I'm glad nobody reminded me that it was an American engine." He would probably have snapped that Malaya needed American know-how in order to service the thing properly.
>
> Mr. Stevenson has been touring Malaya in the capacity of a

[22] Singapore *Sunday Times,* April 19, 1953.

correspondent for a magazine. So did Mr. Dewey. So did Justice [William O.] Douglas. I have a hunch that Adlai is going to prove a better cub reporter than the other two.

Following the press conference, Mr. and Mrs. Baldwin held a large reception for Stevenson.[23]
During the morning of April 18, Stevenson worked on his article about Indonesia and answered some of his correspondence.

To Arthur M. Schlesinger, Jr.[24]

April 18, 1953

My dear Arthur — Your letter was a joy to us all and you gave us more useful news than we've extracted from the Asian press in a long while, and I am now about to read your piece on psychological warfare.[25] And, speaking of pieces, this journey has been so brutal and the pressures so relentless that I've not even removed your Life draft from the envelope, let alone done anything on it.[26] Whats more it is apparent from our experience thus far that there will be no change, except for the worse, as we progress. My only suggestion is that we try to do something with it when I get back, perhaps connect it somewhat into directions for the Dem. party on the basis of the Rep. record not being afraid to give them credit when credit is due. But then, again, I shudder at the thought of what awaits me when I get back! I don't know, but I'm filled with uneasy distress about putting you to all that trouble in vain. There *must* be some salvage — for the Schlesingers' hungry young mouths!!

I think *I'll* survive, and I'm sure the others will. But we've attempted too much too quick and I am thoroughly discontented with the two superficial condensed articles produced thus far — under most trying

[23] While the rest of the Stevenson group joined the Baldwins for dinner, Johnson spent the evening talking to Mr. and Mrs. S. I. Nadler and Raja Ratnam, editor of the Singapore *Standard*.

Ratnam observed that the pro-Chiang leaders who called on Stevenson were a Chinese group that would not accept that they were Malayans. He stated that before World War II the United States was never included when Southeast Asians criticized the West. Now it was criticized, he said, for supporting such old regimes as Bao Dai, Syngman Rhee, and Chiang Kai-shek. Johnson also explored with him misconceptions of the United States held in this part of Southeast Asia. The Governor had become deeply concerned over such widespread misinformation ever since visiting Japan and, at his request, Johnson gathered as much material as possible for his use.

[24] This handwritten letter is in the Schlesinger papers, John F. Kennedy Library.

[25] "Psychological Warfare: Can It Sell Freedom?" *Reporter*, March 31, 1953.

[26] Mr. Schlesinger cannot recall what this was. Letter to Walter Johnson, October 5, 1967.

circumstances. You'll see what I mean when you read them which I *don't* recommend!

I'll try to see the Paris & Rome people — but not La Luce! [27] Best to Marian [28] —

Hastily,

ADLAI

To Stephen Y. Hord [29]

[no date]

Steve — Thanks for your letter — I'm glad you got your tigers and nothing else.[30] As for me I'm hunting communism, social unrest and problems of all races and sizes — and I've seen a lot of each. Even La Salle St. will look good to me — and if I haven't the answers — well, who the hell has? All the same I'd like a look at Jaipur but Nehru seems to have other ideas for me —

AES

Stevenson took Saturday afternoon off to attend the horse races in Singapore. That evening the colonial secretary of Singapore held a formal dinner party in his honor. Before and after dinner it was impossible for him to carry on a conversation in depth since a British aide de camp would move him to another person every five minutes. In a tone of exasperation, he remarked that "it was like a game of musical chairs." He did, however, have an opportunity to talk to trade union leader Lim Yew Hock. When Stevenson spoke to him of the misconceptions about the United States held by Asians, he mentioned that he had recently been in the United States on an exchange grant and observed that the misconceptions held by Americans about Asia were equally foolish and dangerous.

Stevenson spent all day Sunday working on his article on Indonesia while Attwood did a draft for him on Malaya. During the day Stevenson also wrote the following letter.

[27] Clare Boothe Luce, U.S. ambassador to Italy.
[28] Mrs. Schlesinger.
[29] A Chicago friend and adviser on Stevenson's investments. This handwritten postcard is in the possession of Mr. Hord.
[30] On March 25, 1953, Mr. Hord had described a hunting expedition that he had just been on in India and urged Stevenson to visit Jaipur.

To Mrs. Edison Dick [31]

April 19, 1953

Bless you for that beautiful letter about your visit to Springfield; I wept and laughed late last night — after a great banquet in the great residence of the Governor of Singapore.

. . . There's so much to report it's hopeless — and always those damn articles and my damn deadlines are staring me in the face, goading my perspiring behind and plaguing my addled brain. Do you look cool, collected, poised, self possessed as usual? I knew you should have come along!

I have had a couple of relatively quiet days here in Singapore in a large *air conditioned* bedroom in the large old house of the consul and feel better prepared for the journey which we resume tomorrow — to Thailand, Burma etc. — if only it wasn't for that damn article on Indonesia which I'm supposed to do here and haven't started.

Did you have a good time in Boca Grande [32] — how are the children, Eddie — and you? You always talk of me — and so do I!

And speaking quite unconsciously of *me,* the helicopter accident was really a close call. By a miracle, the great pilot, *Royal Navy!,* got us into the only rice paddy in miles of that black, solid jungle and I stepped out unscathed — up to my knees in dank mud.

But there's no sense in starting — I can't finish even a minor histoire. . . .

P.S. I've seen more strange sights, pathetic, frightening, amusing — like the aborigine in the jungle up in Malaya, fully clothed in his loin cloth, who presented me — surrounded by four armored cars and troops — with a blow gun and 12 poisoned darts. And now how the hell do I get it home? [33]

To Mr. and Mrs. Hermon Dunlap Smith [34]

[no date]

Beloved Smiths —

I've not seen many sunrises — thank God! Its been a weary, fascinat-

[31] This handwritten letter is in the possession of Mrs. Dick.

[32] The island resort on the west coast of Florida where the Dicks spent their winter vacations.

[33] Stevenson enclosed in this letter part of the front page of the Singapore *Standard* of April 18 with four pictures of himself on it. Across the top he scribbled "I've decided the only thing the whole world has in common are photographs and autographs!"

[34] This handwritten postcard is in the possession of Mr. Smith. It is postmarked Singapore, April 20, 1953.

ing journey & we move on to Burma, Thailand, India etc etc tomorrow. I *think* I'll live! but its constant work and little time for sightseeing, shopping or reflection. Evidently we carried all these countries, like the states I *didn't* visit! Home will look better than ever, Desbarats [35] & isolation even better!

ADLAI

At lunch that day Consul General Baldwin expressed the hope that Stevenson would emphasize in his writing the differences between Malaya and Singapore and the rest of Southeast Asia. He said that he had particularly in mind that the communal problem was more acute here. In addition, he explained that the buying of rubber and tin by the United States had a greater impact on the economy here than on any other country in the region. He also felt that most nationalist leaders here, while wanting independence, did not want it to come very soon.

The next afternoon Stevenson left Singapore on a four-hour flight to Bangkok.

He wrote about his visit to Malaya and Singapore:

FIGHT FOR FREEDOM IN SOUTHEAST ASIA [36]

Two days after reaching Singapore, I stood early one morning in the steaming, evil underbrush of the Malayan jungle watching weary young British soldiers wade across a muddy stream, Indian-file, Bren guns held chest-high. They were returning from an ambush in an area where Communist guerrillas were operating. The leader, a big rangy Canadian lieutenant named Roy Bonnie, sloshed up the bank, saluted the officer with me and reported, "No contact, sir; empty bag."

To me he added, pointing to the jungle across the stream, "It's tough. Those guys might be 50 feet away, and you'd never know it until they started shooting."

In Malaya, you are never very far away from the jungle. Thick, dark and tangled, it blankets four fifths of the peninsula — down to the very edge of the great port of Singapore, crossroads of the Orient. And the

[35] The Smiths' summer camp, which Stevenson visited frequently. Mr. Smith has written of "the lovely country of rocky islands and blue water at Desbarats, in Ontario, near the Canadian Sault." "Politics and R & R," in *As We Knew Adlai: The Stevenson Story by Twenty-two Friends,* edited and with preface by Edward P. Doyle, foreword by Adlai E. Stevenson III (New York: Harper & Row, 1966), p. 38.

[36] *Look,* June 16, 1953. The rest of this article is reprinted in Chapter Eight, above, and Chapter Ten, below.

jungle is the best ally of the Communist-led terrorists who have been waging a cruel hit-and-run war against British rule for the past five years.

This is the third war I have seen in the past month, but the first where I heard no gunfire. The fighting here is the silent, stealthy kind that Daniel Boone would have understood. From their jungle lairs, the terrorists prey on both soldiers and civilians — on Malays, Chinese and Indians as well as Europeans. And the problem confronting the security forces under British command is to track down, one by one, 5000 needles in a gigantic haystack.

I visited an area where 1000 soldiers and police had just spent five months liquidating 50 terrorists; I inspected a newly arrived unit — Baker Company of the Royal West Kent Regiment — whose principal mission was destroying an enemy force of 15. In most wars, victories are measured in scores, hundreds or thousands of enemy killed or captured. In Malaya, a half dozen killed, captured or surrendered is a major triumph.

It's a long, grinding, costly war, but unlike the heart-breaking struggle in Indochina, the end is in sight. The terrorists are being whittled down, and their losses cannot be replaced. Since last year, the number of "incidents" has been steadily decreasing, and more and more guerrillas are surrendering.

Who are these people? They are 90 per cent Chinese who came to Malaya in recent years. Of the rank and file, some are criminals, some professional bandits; others are educated, idealistic young people. But the hard core and the leadership are fanatical Communists who fought the Japanese. Their goal is a Communist state in Malaya (which produces a third of the world's rubber and tin and commands one of the world's main highways). For five years since their postwar effort to seize control narrowly failed, they have ambushed and murdered thousands, derailed trains, slashed countless acres of rubber trees and plundered rice, medicine and money from helpless squatter villages scattered along the jungle walls.

If Malaya is finally pacified, much of the credit will belong to Britain's brisk, wiry, energetic High Commissioner, Gen. Sir Gerald Templer, who arrived early in 1952 (after his predecessor had been ambushed and shot). With an "it-can-be-done" spirit, he has stiffened up soldiers and civilians alike. At his headquarters in Kuala Lumpur, a bustling, modern city of a quarter million surrounded by great tin mines, vast rubber estates and jungle, General Templer and his devoted, competent staff showed me why, in his words, "we've got the beggars on the run at last."

I saw troops in the field, tin mines, rubber plantations, a leper hospital, Malay kampongs, slum-clearance projects and "new villages." On a little-traveled road, I met Malay aborigines wearing "home-guard" brassards (and little else!) who presented me with a blowgun and quiver of arrows. I even survived a masterful forced landing when our helicopter's engine stalled on the way back from the jungle "front." I comforted my embarrassed British hosts by reminding them that the engine was American.

Everything I saw and heard seemed to justify General Templer's salty optimism. The strategy of the British is to starve the enemy out of the jungle, and their four-pronged tactics are decimating the terrorist ranks at the rate of about 70 a month:

1. Food supplies are being gradually choked off by resettling isolated villages into new defensible communities protected by wire fence and armed militia. No fewer than 510,000 people have been moved into 509 new villages in one of the greatest mass movements of modern times.

2. Constant, aggressive patrolling keeps the jungle-weary terrorists on the move. Loudspeakers in airplanes promise them clemency if they come out and surrender, death if they don't.

3. Home-guard units are being built up, so that today the Malays, Indians — and, to a lesser extent, the Chinese — are actively participating in the pacification campaign. Since the terrorists are largely Chinese, they have been unable to identify themselves — as in other Asian countries — with legitimate nationalist movements.

4. Rehabilitation centers — to which captured terrorists and suspects are sent from detention camps — are solving the problem of making useful citizens out of Communist sympathizers. In the centers, they are taught trades, as well as reading and writing; after six months, all but a handful are released. Of the last thousand "graduates," there have been only nine cases of relapse, and in many instances, grateful alumni return to the centers for annual reunions.

Of course, no one pretends that the emergency is over — or is likely to be for a long time to come. In one day while I was there, terrorists murdered five civilians in an ambush near Ipoh, looted a village in Kelantan State and attacked a plantation manager in Johore. It's still not safe to travel through much of the countryside without an armed escort; and, as a British police officer told me, "Only the opportunists and the fair-weather Commies are surrendering; the hard core have to be captured or killed and the women are the toughest of all."

Nevertheless, progress has been so good that General Templer and his staff now devote most of their thinking to Malaya's post-emergency future. Better aware of the imperatives of Asian nationalism than some of the old-school British colonialists, they are in full sympathy with Britain's declaration of self-government for Malaya.

The only question in the minds of men like Templer and the wise Malcolm MacDonald, Commissioner General for Southeast Asia, is one of timing: How soon after the fighting stops should British rule come to an end?

MacDonald put it this way: "Asia is trying to do in years what we did in generations. This is inevitable, but it creates appalling difficulties."

In Malaya, the difficulty is illustrated by the population statistics. Of the 6,500,000 people who live on the Malayan Peninsula — including the crown colony of Singapore — nearly 3,000,000 are Chinese and 700,000 are Indians: The Malays are a minority in their own country, and there is no counterpart here for the great melting-pot experiment of American democracy. The Chinese community is clannish and tightly knit; it has its own schools, secret societies, guilds and cultural organizations. Incredibly industrious and frugal, the Chinese dominate Malaya's commercial and financial life. The great majority are politically indifferent. Business comes first, and so does China, where many still have family ties. Last year, an estimated million dollars in remittances went to Red China each month.

In the north, I was surprised to see how relatively few Chinese were serving in the security forces. Later, in Singapore, a delegation of Chinese leaders called on me and frankly deplored the peace rumors in Korea; they wanted United Nations troops to keep on fighting the Communists. I asked them how they reconciled the clamor for battle against the Reds in China — by others — with the meager effort of the Chinese against the terrorists in Malaya. The answer was: poor army pay, traditional Chinese aversion to soldiering and the prewar preference given to Malays in the armed services.

While things are changing now, most of the Chinese still do not identify themselves with the country in which they make their living (and many make millions). This problem exists throughout Southeast Asia. But it is most acute in Malaya, where the Chinese are politically weak and economically strong, the Malays politically strong and economically weak. The Malays fear Chinese economic domination; the Chinese resent unequal treatment and Malay political domination. The Indians, although most of them are laborers, include some of the most politically sophisticated and patriotic Malayans.

Until the great mass of the Malayan Chinese think of themselves as citizens of Malaya *first* and members of separate communities *second*, independence may be a bloody blessing in this divided nation where the Moslem Malays won't eat in the homes of the pork-loving Chinese. As a Malay political leader told me, "There will be chaos if independence comes too soon. I want independence, but only when we are capable of it."

The immediate hope for orderly independence lies in a delicate balancing of the racial groups. But the only real hope lies in a common education for the young, with English as a common language. Our own experience has shown that our public schools were largely responsible for integrating immigrants of diverse national origins into a cohesive American society. If the British sincerely want to prepare Malaya for independence — and I believe they do — they will hasten the process of breaking down the Chinese wall that divides Malaya's peoples. General Templer crisply put it this way: "When children kick each other's shins on a common playground, they get along together when they grow up."

One of his aides remarked ruefully (and rightly) that Britain will be accused of colonialism so long as it continues to govern Malaya. This can't be helped. For the moment, no one should question the need for the British to remain here until the jungle war is won and a plausible basis for independent self-government has been found.

Britain's postwar policies in India and Burma have been sound and progressive; I believe the free world can trust the British to be just as sensible and sincere about Malaya.

Ten

Thailand and Burma

APRIL 20–APRIL 28, 1953

At six P.M. on April 20, Stevenson was met at the Bangkok airport by representatives of the government of Thailand, Ambassador Edwin F. Stanton[1] and members of his staff, and reporters and photographers.

Stevenson was driven some twenty miles to Bangkok through a countryside with rice fields almost everywhere and now and then an elaborate Buddhist temple rising out of the landscape. The Thai government insisted on being host, putting the Stevenson group up at a guesthouse. When Stevenson had protested by cable from Singapore to the American ambassador that he was traveling as a private citizen and wished to stay at a hotel, the ambassador had replied that the invitation could not be refused "under any circumstances." As Attwood wrote in his diary, "Stevenson doesn't want to make a fuss. As it turned out he should have."

Stevenson had planned to have the evening free since he was still writing about Indonesia for his Look article. But at the airport, the head of the U.S. Economic Assistance Administration invited him to dinner and assured him that just his group would be present for a quick and informal dinner. When Stevenson arrived for dinner there were some sixty people awaiting him! "I thought Stevenson would blow his stack (he should have)," Attwood noted in his diary, "but instead he went through the ordeal of handshaking and time consuming small talk."

[1] See Stanton's book, *Brief Authority: Excursions of a Common Man in an Uncommon World* (New York: Harper, 1956).

*After dinner Stevenson returned to the guesthouse, which had no
fans and no screens on the windows. While the rest of Stevenson's party
tried to sleep, he worked on his article for* Look. *In the stifling heat,
he stripped to his shorts. By the time he retired to a sleepless night, he
was covered with mosquito bites. (The next day he acquired a supply
of DDT.) Johnson dictated in his diary, "The only difficulty was that
the guest house was practically on top of a railroad track and the railroad station was just down the road, so that between the railroad trains
all night and the barking of dogs when the railroad trains weren't moving, and the mosquitoes, we had an impossible night." Attwood wrote
in his diary, "I fell asleep about 2:45. At 5:30 the sun came streaming
in and woke us and I began packing my things to go to the hotel."*

*Somehow before he had retired, Stevenson, as Attwood wrote in his
diary, "finished Indonesia during last night's torment, and I took it with
me to the hotel in the morning. . . . I edited the piece at the hotel
(mostly reorganizing and cutting — the bones were in it this time)."*

*In the morning Stevenson met with a Thai who held an important
government post. Unlike the old days, he explained, when the country
had one authoritarian king, now it had "ten kings, all of whom are
above the law."* [2]

*The Thai official explained to Stevenson that the members of the
military clique in power were making large sums of money. The Thai
people had a phrase,* mai pen rai, *which meant, he added, "It does not
matter." The people were easygoing and tolerant. But, he stated, despite this the people were getting restless. Taxes were increasing and
he wondered how long the people would put up with the situation when
the government did so little in the way of public improvements and
education for the tax money received.*

[2] The absolute monarchy was overthrown on June 24, 1932, by young liberals
and military officers, including Pibul Songgram (also spelled Phibun Songkhram),
and a constitutional government was established. Pibul became premier in 1938
and commander-in-chief of the army. He was in power during most of the Japanese
occupation but resigned in 1944 as Japanese fortunes were waning. In 1945,
civilians led by Pridi Phanamyong assumed control. Two years later army officers
staged a *coup d'état* and Marshal Pibul Songgram became premier again. "The
militarists have been most brazen in their reliance on autocratic methods," Walter F.
Vella wrote. "They have controlled Thai government for eleven of the fourteen
years since 1938, and during these years they have ruled by force. The absolutism
of the monarchy based on tradition and respect has been converted by the militarists into an absolutism based on arms. The historical and religious appeals of the
monarchy have been replaced by nationalistic and militaristic appeals." *The Impact
of the West on Government in Thailand,* University of California Publications in
Political Science, Vol. 4, No. 3 (Berkeley: University of California Press, 1955),
p. 397.

After this conversation, Stevenson made a formal call on the foreign minister and then went to the embassy, where Ambassador Edwin F. Stanton discussed Premier Pibul Songgram's military oligarchy. While it was now firmly in control, there was a constant jockeying for position, primarily between General Phao Sriyanon, director general of the police, and Field Marshal Sarit Thanarat, deputy commander-in-chief of the army. The Thais, the ambassador added, were saying that the premier was "riding two tigers." The two tigers, he remarked, "could fly at each other's throats at any time." [3]

The ambassador noted that about twenty per cent of the population (three million) were Chinese. Chinese Communists were trying to infiltrate the Chinese-language newspapers, Chinese schools, and Chinese trade guilds. In November, 1952, Stanton added, the Thai government passed an anti-Communist law and jailed many Chinese and Thai Communists.

The ambassador called northeast Thailand — the poorest section of the country — a serious problem for the government. There were between forty thousand and sixty thousand Vietnamese living there and most of them were pro-Vietminh. The Thai government, he added, was watching developments on its border with concern and was cooperating with the British to stop Malayan terrorists from entering Thailand to recuperate. Thailand, he pointed out, had been permitting supplies to go to Li Mi's Nationalist troops in the Shan states of Burma, but the premier had recently agreed to assist in the evacuation of these troops.

At this point Stevenson remarked that the foreign minister, Prince Wan, had talked to him about the autonomous Thai government which the Chinese had established in Yunnan province to appeal to Thai people inside and outside Thailand. Stanton observed that the Pan-Thai movement had strong appeal. It was based on the ethnic and historic connection between the Thai of Thailand and the Thai-speaking peoples in Laos, the Shan states of Burma, and Yunnan province. When Premier Pibul was in power earlier, in 1939, Stanton pointed out, he had changed the name of the country from Siam — a non-Thai geographic word — to Thailand, "the land of the Thai." [4]

The ambassador said that not only Pibul, but Premier Pridi, while he had been in power from 1945 to 1947, had encouraged the Pan-Thai movement. Pridi was now in exile, Stanton added; no one was positive, but he might be in China.

[3] In October, 1958, Sarit seized power by a *coup d'état.*
[4] The name Siam was reinstated in 1945, but on May 11, 1949, again under Pibul Songgram, the name was once more officially changed to Thailand.

There was a brief discussion of the Mutual Security Agency's activities to increase rice production, to eradicate malaria, and to support elementary and vocational education.

The head of the United States military assistance advisory group noted that some people might wonder why the United States should help Thailand, since the country had a favorable balance of trade. But he remarked: "If we don't help those who are friendly to us, then where are we?"

When the colonel finished discussing the training of Thai troops, Ambassador Stanton returned to the subject of the government. He shook his head and said, "The government here is pretty bad on corruption." People were complaining about it, and according to the ambassador, the premier himself was talking about remedying the situation. Pibul had overthrown the Pridi government in 1947 on the charge that "it had become so corrupt." And the ambassador added, "The present clique is reaching much the same stage."

The Stevenson party went on to a lengthy lunch with Premier Pibul Songgram in his exquisite marble palace. It was at this lunch that Stevenson met General Phao and General Sarit. He asked the premier whether he was concerned with Vietminh activity in Laos. Marshal Pibul replied that he was watching it "most carefully." The French ambassador had just told him, however, that the French could control the situation. He then talked a bit about the Thai state that had been set up in China and of the Thai peoples living outside of Thailand.

After lunch Stevenson, Bingham and Blair visited the shop where Princeton University graduate James Thompson had revived the silk-making industry of Thailand. Attwood finished a draft of the Malaya article for Look.

At Stevenson's suggestion, Johnson talked to William Cummings of the Food and Agricultural Organization of the United Nations. He emphasized that while Thailand was a rice-exporting nation, nevertheless the yield per acre was low. But, since the country was not overpopulated at the moment, there was a sufficiency of rice. There were so many "squeezes" and bribes along the way to the marketing of rice that the farmer received very little return for his labor. Cummings said the ruling clique took a "squeeze" of fifteen dollars per ton on all rice exported. The country would be ahead if this money went into roads and schools, but it went into the pockets of the clique. The clique also put its members on the boards of directors of banks and business firms involved in the importing business. Bribery and corruption was at the breaking point, he said, and the situation resembled China under Chiang Kai-shek's Nationalists.

Johnson next interviewed Alexander MacDonald, editor of the Bang-kok Post.[5] *He, too, talked of the widespread corruption among the ruling clique. Bribery had a long tradition in Thailand, he remarked, "but not on the scale of the present moment." It was not only intellectuals who were sickened by it; knowledge of it was spreading to the public. "The public could, as a result," he said, "throw its support to the Commu-nists." It was distressing, he continued, that American aid bulwarked the clique in power. There was need for the United States to put "pres-sure on the clique to stop the squeeze."*

On his return to the guesthouse, Johnson briefed Stevenson on these two conversations. Just before dinner that evening, Stevenson drew the foreign minister out about corruption in government. Prince Wan ex-plained that it was not considered unethical in Thailand for a govern-ment minister to award contracts to companies he owned. At this point dinner was announced, and the conversation could not be pursued.

After dinner Prince Wan toasted Stevenson with a graceful tribute to the United States. He pointed out that missionaries were the first Amer-icans to come to the country and that they had established the first printing press and newspaper and had opened schools and hospitals. He cited the number of Thai students who had studied in the United States and then expressed his country's gratitude for the economic and military aid received since World War II.

Stevenson thanked him for having spoken so movingly of the help received from American missionaries and from the United States gov-ernment. He added that he was "deeply gratified" by Prince Wan's words of appreciation since he had found all too few Asian countries that were grateful for U.S. assistance. He thanked the foreign minister for the cordial hospitality and remarked that if he stayed too long in Thailand, "I would not get home at all."

After these two toasts the dinner party was entertained with an hour of exquisite Siamese dancing.

The following day Attwood wrote in his diary: "Stevenson punished himself some more by rising at 5 to visit the floating markets. . . . He has a passion for markets — I don't think he's missed one in any country we've been to. But 5 A.M. is going too far."

Barry Bingham wrote:

> Early morning on Bangkok's canals is a world in itself.
> We were on the river in a launch by 6 o'clock. The operator of the boat warmed up his engine with an acetylene torch, an old but quite successful method.

[5] See MacDonald's *Bangkok Editor* (New York: Macmillan, 1949).

As we swung out into the current, the sky was a pale primrose-yellow and very clear. Etched in black against the horizon were the fanciful shapes of a dozen pagodas.

Tallest of all was the Temple of The Dawn, as delicate as black lace against the pale sky.

Soon the first rays of the sun began picking up the rich blues, greens and yellows of the porcelain flowers that encrust the temple walls in a wild fantasy of color.

We swung into a canal perhaps 25 feet wide. Of Bangkok's more than a million people, two-thirds live on the water and virtually in it. The city is a sprawling network of canals.

Generations of Bangkok people are born, live and die on sampans — frail little boats, with only an awning for cover, a tiny charcoal brazier for fire, and a single lamp for light.

Others by the hundreds of thousands live in loosely constructed wooden houses that seem to spill right out into the canals. The living quarters are open to the water for air and light. As we slid along in our launch, we felt we were invading the living room–bedroom-kitchen privacy of the citizens of Bangkok.

Not a one of them seemed to mind.

Some late sleepers were still stretched out on the straw mats over bare boards that serve them for beds. Dogs were padding home, jaded and knowing-looking, from their all-night maraudings. Bantam roosters crowed. Ducks waddled toward the water. The whole canal world sprang into life.

We barely had room to scrape along between boats. Many were the lightest of skiffs, rowed by women or children on early errands. Others were heavy-bellied scows full of charcoal, so deep in the water that their gunwales were awash. Myriads of other tiny craft were hurrying to the floating market, stacked with fresh vegetables, duck eggs, fruits both familiar and as strange as those Christina Rossetti describes in "Goblin Market."

In the midst of all this commercial activity, family life flourishes.

Each member of the household steps off his miniature porch and into the canal for a morning bath. They soap themselves vigorously. Many wash their hair, and all brush their teeth in the brown canal water, blissfully unaware of the theory of germs.

The women and girls are very modest. They walk into the water in the Thai equivalent of sarongs, and do their washing most discreetly. Many are remarkably pretty, small-boned and delicately made.

The Thais are a race of slender, erect people. A young girl with a basket of watercress on her head moves as gracefully as one of the palace dancers in her pagoda-shaped crown of gold and jewels.

The community bathing hour is a cheerful affair. The youngest baby in the family is usually dipped into the water by the father,

with responsive gurgles of delight. The older children, from 3 on up, swim around in the canals like baby seals, their bodies sleek and shining in the water. Some float on a stray coconut or a bamboo log, laughing and singing.

Through the welter of canal life, Buddhist monks thread their way in canoes. All are dressed in robes of brilliant yellow. Each carries a brass cooking vessel, which he holds out for offerings of food from the faithful. The boat dwellers and the occupants of the canal-bank shanties hand out bowls of rice. The monks empty them gravely into their jars and pass on. They have taken a vow of absolute poverty. . . .[6]

After breakfast, Stevenson visited the royal palace and the temple of the Emerald Buddha. As he posed for photographs beside one of the carved demons, he remarked: "It's not a demon, it's just a Republican."

Late morning and early afternoon he rode in a motor launch up the Chao Phraya River and visited a number of rural villages. When he returned, he visited a snake farm to watch the extraction of venom from the snakes.[7] Amidst all the day's activities he wrote a number of postcards.

To Margaret Munn [8]

[no date]

Dear Margaret —

Thanks for your wonderful letter and all the news. I'm glad you reminded me to write Vin Dallman.[9] We inspected this incredible collection of incredible temples this morning & then took a boat trip on the river where thousands live their lives afloat in little boats. Its a strange world out here and I often wonder if Americans know how

[6] "Thailand," Louisville *Courier-Journal*, May 10, 1953.

[7] While Stevenson was at the snake farm, Johnson interviewed Lauriston Sharp, professor of anthropology at Cornell University, who was doing research on a Fulbright grant. He remarked that Thailand was an amorphous society even in the villages. Village people did not know what a committee was and did not know how to organize a protest or a petition to the government. The Thai elite, he added, dismissed the peasants by saying they had food to eat. But, Sharp said, "They overlook the fact that the peasants now want bicycles, watches and many other things. The revolution of rising expectations is on in Thailand." See Lauriston Sharp, "Peasants and Politics in Thailand," *Far Eastern Survey*, XIX (September 13, 1950), pp. 157–161.

[8] This handwritten postcard is in the possession of Mrs. Munn. It bears a Washington postmark of April 29, 1953, and thus must have been sent to the United States by diplomatic pouch.

[9] V. Y. Dallman, editor of the *Illinois State Register*, Springfield, Illinois.

fortunate they are. Next its Burma & then the super heat of India — if anything worse than Bangkok is possible! Bless you — affectionately —

AES

That evening Ambassador and Mrs. Stanton held a large reception and dinner in honor of Stevenson. A member of the Dutch embassy told him that the military clique was really blackmailing the United States. "You Americans are in a tough spot," he said. "You feel you have to aid them; this is understandable, but the question is whether the Thais will stand up to the Chinese if they come through Indochina. After all, the Japanese came through Indochina and the Thais didn't stand up."

At breakfast the next morning, Stevenson visited with Archie Mac-Kenzie, a member of the British embassy, whom he had met during the 1946 and 1947 meetings of the United Nations Assembly. Stevenson remarked that the people of Thailand were "tremendously attractive, but what I see beneath the surface is very disturbing." MacKenzie agreed and said that if the prosperity bubble should break, there would be serious internal strife. He stated that Premier Pibul had sent troops to Korea in order to insure help later if Thailand needed it. If the Chinese attacked, MacKenzie added, Thailand would fold as it had done when the Japanese had invaded the country.

The breakfast conversation was disrupted by a phone call announcing that the BOAC Comet was leaving for Rangoon earlier than expected. Stevenson rushed to the airport and had only the briefest time to talk to reporters. He said: "I do not see any evidence of sincerity or peaceful intentions in the Communists' activities in Southeast Asia. Since the truce negotiations began in Korea, Laos has been invaded and I think Thailand is the objective because Thailand has the rice. I hope the Thai Government and all the people appreciate fully the importance of the Laos invasion and move in the direction of Thailand." [10]

One hour after he departed from Bangkok on April 23, Stevenson landed at Rangoon, where "a crowd of Burmese officials and well-wishers awaited him, and Stevenson campaign buttons were much in evidence," Dr. Maung Maung wrote in the New Republic. *"The Burmese as a race are great gamblers, but when they laid their bets four to one on Stevenson as favorite during the Presidential elections, it was not an expression of their gambling spirit merely. They hoped he would win. The ebb and flow of the election campaigns, fully covered by the*

[10] New York *Times*, April 24, 1953.

Dining in Kyoto, Japan.
William Attwood and Walter Johnson are at the left.

Meeting with Chiang Kai-shek in Taiwan.

Writing notes on a plane en route to Singapore.

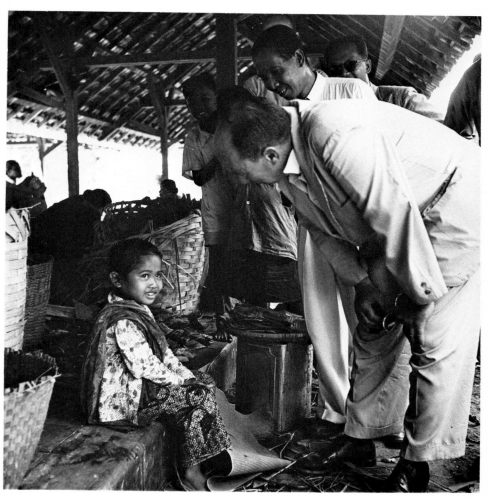

Visiting a market in Djakarta, Indonesia.

*Watching the tapping of a rubber tree
on a Malaysian plantation.*

*Shoeless pilgrimage to a temple
in Rangoon, Burma.*

Boarding a shikara *on the way to Shalimar Garden, Kashmir.*

Lunch with Sheikh Abdullah in Kashmir.

*Prime Minister Nehru receiving Stevenson
in New Delhi, May 5, 1953.*

Dining with King Ibn Saud in Riyadh, Saudi Arabia.

Rangoon press, were closely watched by the Burmese and Adlai Stevenson soon became a household name." [11]

Maung Maung pointed out that the period Stevenson arrived was an embarrassing one for Americans in Burma since *weapons and documents captured from Li Mi's Nationalist troops in the Shan state "proved that American private enterprise was involved. . . . Late in March, the Burma army captured, in an engagement with the Chinese, three white men, dead, later identified to be Americans.*" As a result, relations between Burmese and Americans were "*rather cool,*" Maung Maung observed. "*Into this atmosphere Adlai Stevenson arrived, and the Burmese forgot that they were supposed to be on formal terms with Americans when they gave him a sincerely joyous welcome. Stevenson dispelled the moods. His visit at that delicate time was as fortunate for American-Burmese friendship as that of any other American of equal stature might well have been ill chosen.*"

"*The week in Rangoon was Stevenson Week,*" Maung Maung added. "*. . . Stevenson campaign buttons were worn at parties and Adlai remarked that it was a little too early to start campaigning again.*" [12]

Stevenson and Blair stayed at the president's residence in Rangoon. Although they had cabled from Bangkok their preference for a hotel, the embassy had insisted that the president's hospitality could not be refused. As it turned out, they could not have had a more pleasant experience. Blair wrote on April 27 to Carol Evans and Phyllis Gustafson: "*The Gov. and I have been roughing it here with the President for the past four days — very comfortable cottage with about 182 rooms — also a tennis court (grass) where we have had our first exercise since we took off — except for an occasional swim.*"

Shortly after his arrival, Stevenson lunched with the president, Dr. Ba U. The president discussed the problem created by General Li Mi's Nationalist troops and was critical of Thailand for allowing equipment and men from Taiwan to cross its territory to augment Li Mi's forces.

[11] "Burma — The Bets Will Be on Stevenson," *New Republic,* June 8, 1953, p. 10.

[12] Ibid., p. 11. Several years later Stevenson read the typescript of Stuart Gerry Brown's *Conscience in Politics: Adlai E. Stevenson in the 1950's* (Syracuse: Syracuse University Press, 1961). In Chapter 2, p. 24, Brown wrote: "During the greater part of 1953 he had been abroad on a world tour. As an unofficial roving ambassador for his party and as a representative statesman of his country." After the word "country," Stevenson wrote in an asterisk. At the bottom of the page, he wrote in pencil: "With a wider following, and even greater respect abroad than at home. (Often said that AES 'carried' every country in the world except the U.S.)" The manuscript is in the Stuart Gerry Brown papers, Syracuse University Library.

After lunch Stevenson attended a not-too-perceptive briefing at the embassy. It was pointed out that although the leaders of the governing party — the Anti-Fascist People's Freedom League — were Marxist in their economic beliefs, they decidedly were not Communists. Ever since independence in 1948, the government had been fighting simultaneous rebellions by two distinct Communist groups, the White Flag and the Red Flag Communists; the People's Volunteer Organization; and many Karens — one of the minorities in the Union of Burma — who wished a Karenistan separate from Burma.

The military attaché observed that the insurrections might all have been suppressed by now except that the Burmese army had had to be diverted to fight General Li Mi's army. Although the Nationalist troops had been a nuisance since 1949, it was not until 1952 that they had expanded their forces and begun to loot villages and murder civilians. The attaché added that Burmese leaders feared that the presence of Nationalist troops on their soil might provide an excuse for Communist China to invade the country.

The military attaché concluded that if trouble arose between the Burmese civilian authorities and the military leaders, the army would support General Ne Win. The ambassador said, however, that there was no evidence of a threatened coup d'état.[13]

The economic attaché described the destruction caused by World War II and by the various insurrections since 1948. Transportation had been hampered particularly by the insurrections, and Burma was still not exporting as much rice as it had in 1939. He discussed the excessive interest rates charged by moneylenders and added that the law limiting their charges had not yet been enforced, nor had the Land National-ization Act of 1948, designed to put an end to landlordism, as yet been implemented.[14]

He pointed out that the Burmese tended to equate colonialism with capitalism. It was not clear how much foreign capital would be welcomed, he said, since the government had not decided what part of the economy was to be nationalized and what would remain in the private sector.

The labor attaché remarked that the Communists controlled only

[13] General Ne Win staged a *coup d'état* nearly ten years later on March 2, 1962. He set aside the constitution, abolished both chambers of Parliament, and placed U Nu and other leaders under arrest. Between October, 1956, and April, 1960, General Ne Win had headed a "caretaker" civilian government. U Nu had returned as prime minister as a result of elections in February, 1960.

[14] The law was implemented after 1954. See Frank N. Trager, *Burma from Kingdom to Republic: A Historical and Political Analysis* (New York: Praeger, 1966), p. 152.

about one thousand out of seventy thousand union members. The rest were independent or controlled by the socialists. The socialists, he added, were winning out over the Communists for control of the unions. While the country had compulsory arbitration, he said, the unions were completely dependent on the government.

Frank N. Trager, director of the Technical Cooperation Administration, noted that on March 17 the Burmese government had announced that the program had to be terminated as of June 30, 1953. He explained that the Burmese were dismayed at their inability, and the inability of U.S. ambassadors in Burma, to persuade Washington to put pressure on Chiang Kai-shek to remove Li Mi's troops from Burma. He described TCA's work in rebuilding the harbor of Rangoon, its work in public health, technical training, and projects to increase agricultural production.

Ambassador William J. Sebald summarized the situation by saying that Burma had a hypersensitive, nationalistic government that insisted on being uncommitted in world politics. The leaders, while impetuous, had valid reasons many times for what they did. The canceling of the TCA agreement was a case in point, he said. The government was being accused by its opponent of remaining quiet about Li Mi's troops because of the "hush money" from the TCA. Prime Minister U Nu had told him that it was the most difficult decision he had had to make, but that it was essential if the government was not to fall.

The ambassador added that "the typhoon will blow out against the U.S." and this government should be supported. The Burmese, he predicted, would ask for aid later.[15]

After a private dinner with the president, Stevenson spent the evening finishing the article on Malaya for Look. *At Stevenson's suggestion, Johnson interviewed James Ward, labor attaché, and Lewis M. Purnell, political attaché, both of whom had been in Burma several years and had established firm contacts with many Burmese. They pointed out how the socialists in the Anti-Fascist People's Freedom League had been able to out-organize the Communists in the trade unions, from a standpoint of both tactics and Marxian dialectics. They discussed the two factions within the governing party — U Nu and his followers with a heavy overtone of Buddhism, nationalism, and anticolonialism and the socialist wing headed by U Kyaw Nyein, acting foreign minister, and U Ba Swe, minister of defense.*

They explained how much Marshal Tito was respected by the Burmese government not only for his role as a guerrilla leader during

---

[15] Some assistance was renewed in 1956. Ibid., pp. 322–325.

World War II but for his break with the Soviet Union in 1948 and his subsequent independent path between the U.S.S.R. and the U.S.

The following morning, April 24, Stevenson placed a wreath at the tomb of Bogyoke Aung San, who had been assassinated in July, 1947, along with eight other independence leaders.[16] He then visited the Shwedagon pagoda, where he struck the gong as the Burmese did to invite all hearers to rejoice that a good deed had been done.

With Ambassador Sebald he then called on Prime Minister U Nu and, a little later, on the acting foreign minister, U Kyaw Nyein.

After lunch that day Stevenson met with Thakin Tin, minister for land nationalization and head of the All-Burma Peasants' Organization. The minister discussed absentee landlords but emphasized that the major agrarian problem was excessive rates charged by moneylenders. To counteract this, he said, the government was experimenting slowly with cooperative banks. He also explained the plans for implementing the Land Nationalization Act of 1948. There would be three types of landholding — cooperatives, collectives, and state tenants. He pointed out that the 1948 constitution stated: "The state is the ultimate owner of all lands." Land nationalization, as they envisaged it, he added, was only the beginning of a total reorganization of rural life. Stevenson asked how they were going to finance land nationalization since they had announced compensation for the land nationalized. He also remarked that he did not understand why the government wanted to nationalize land already owned by small farmers. (Stevenson did not feel that he received a clear answer to either question.)

Later that afternoon, Stevenson played tennis — two sets of doubles — despite the heat. He was honored at a dinner that evening given by the president. The guests included General Ne Win, Minister of Defense U Ba Swe, and U Thant, secretary of the Ministry of Information (who later became Secretary-General of the United Nations after the death of Dag Hammarskjöld in 1961). After the dinner there was an evening of Burmese dancing.

The following morning Stevenson visited an agricultural demonstration center as well as a rehabilitation center for insurgents who had surrendered. At 10:30 A.M., as Johnson dictated in his diary, "the Governor went to the USIS library to say hello to all the members of the American Embassy staff and their wives, whom we hadn't already met. I might say parenthetically that here, like in almost all other countries that we've been to, not only are the nationals of the country pro-

---

[16] He led Burma to complete independence through a peaceful, anticolonial revolution. He was only thirty-two at his death. "A hero in Burmese eyes, he had the qualities of great leadership that Burma sorely needed and needs." Ibid., p. 89.

Stevenson, but the Embassy staffs are overwhelmingly so. And here the Ambassador or somebody set most of the formal occasions up as purely stag affairs, so the wives of the American Embassy officials were just raising holy hell when we arrived. The Ambassador had to unbend a little bit and ask the Governor if he would come to this USIS library to chat with the female American population. The Governor made a three- or four-minute talk and then went around and shook hands with everybody, so that seems to have eased the social crisis of Rangoon."

After this meeting Stevenson had lunch with the president and spent the afternoon writing about Thailand for Look.[17] At Stevenson's suggestion, Johnson talked with the knowledgeable J. S. Furnivall, who had served in Burma as a member of the Indian Civil Service for nearly half a century. (After 1948, he was so respected that he was the only Englishman asked to remain as adviser to the newly independent government.)

Stevenson was particularly interested in Furnivall's view that the British had ignored the human resources of Burma and that this had led to political instability.[18] Furnivall explained that before independence the British believed that everyone would prosper if business and industry were built up in underdeveloped countries. In Burma, however, Indians, Chinese and Europeans had gained control of business, while the Burmese had not. In fact, he stated, the British largely ignored the Burmese. Little of the wealth from business and industry reached the masses, yet at the same time the factory system broke down the old social structure, and unrest and frustration followed. For any economic aid program to be successful, he insisted, it had to reach the masses and capture their imagination.

He also discussed the scarcity of trained people. Not until 1923 and 1924 did the British allow Burmese in the Indian civil service. Moreover, the less important Burma civil service was heavily dominated by Eurasians and Burmese were relegated to the lowest grades of service. When independence came, he remarked, there were practically no high-level Burmese bureaucrats. As a result, he added, it was "a miracle" that the government had done as well as it had and had made so few mistakes.

He remarked that the people hungered for an education. He had been

[17] Stevenson wanted to do two separate articles on Thailand and Burma. This would have been an article in addition to those contracted for. Look cabled back a refusal and Stevenson had to condense his visit to the two countries into 1,000 words.

[18] See, for instance, J. S. Furnivall, *Colonial Policy and Practice: A Comparative Study of Burma and Netherlands Indies* (Cambridge: Cambridge University Press, 1948).

recommending to the government that it concentrate on village schools. From the standpoint of achieving a unified country, education had a great role to play. He emphasized that there was a pressing need for government administrators who understood the villages of Burma. With the exception of Thakin Tin, minister for land nationalization, few of the present leaders, he said, had ever known the village life of the country. The insurrections, he added, were in one sense a "blessing." The government had had to spend so much time fighting the rebels that they could not implement all the 1948 laws immediately. As a result, as the leaders had gained experience they had modified some of the laws and improved them.

During the afternoon Attwood interviewed several Burmese journalists, including the editor of the Nation, Ed Lawyone. They were curious as to the purpose of Stevenson's visit and finally accepted the explanation that he was seeking to educate himself about Asia and the Middle East.

The following day, April 26, a columnist in the Sunday Nation wrote: "Mr. Stevenson has come with a big reputation. Though beaten very badly by General Eisenhower . . . Mr. Stevenson was not disgraced. . . . Why did people say that it would be a close election, in spite of the fact that General Eisenhower was a world-character and the American who had led the Americans and the Allies to victory in the last war? Because Mr. Stevenson had showed during his Presidential campaign that he really was a clever man — in fact, a very clever man. All the intelligentsia in America rose in a body and acclaimed him." The columnist added: "As a clever man, Mr. Stevenson will, I hope, be able to assess the situation in Burma better than Judge Douglas.[19] It is a very complex situation, no doubt, but it is for clever men to be able correctly to assess complex situations."

Ambassador Sebald held a buffet supper in Stevenson's honor, Saturday, April 25. Stevenson talked at considerable length with Prime Minister U Nu about the Buddhist revival in the country. U Ba Swe had declined the ambassador's suggestion that he sit at the same table with U Nu, and instead sat at a table with a Stevenson aide. He discussed the fighting against Li Mi's Nationalist troops. U Ba Swe also talked about the diversity of peoples in the Union of Burma, but thought there was no long-range problem except with the Karens. Many Karens, he added, were "sick and tired" of their insurgents and desired a settlement.

The next morning Stevenson and Blair left Rangoon by airplane to

[19] See William O. Douglas, *North from Malaya: Adventures on Five Fronts* (Garden City, N.Y.: Doubleday, 1953).

visit Mandalay while the rest of his party interviewed different people in the capital. Johnson had a lengthy discussion with Dr. Ba Maw, an early nationalist leader who had been chief minister (1937–1939) under the limited constitutional government granted by the British, and chief of state during the Japanese occupation. After independence, he had led a non-Communist opposition to the Anti-Fascist People's party.

He spoke warmly of his Filipino friend Senator José Laurel, and stated that American experience in the Philippines had been a misleading experience for the United States in its relations with Asia. Instead of taking over an Asian nation with a well-developed culture, the United States had replaced a different Western culture which had dominated the Philippines for three hundred years. Therefore, the United States had had no useful experience in the Philippines that would help it in working with strong Asian cultures.

Another misleading experience in Asia, he asserted, stemmed from America's missionary activities. Instead of working with the various Asian cultures, American missionaries emphasized the moral superiority of Christianity and created, in the United States, a false picture of Asians as corrupt, decadent, and heathen. Then he noted, "I didn't like a single sentence in Dewey's book about Asia." [20] *Americans contended, he added, that the most important thing in the world was to be anti-Communist, and this leads them into the trap of thinking that most Asian nationalist movements are Communist. U.S. propaganda, he insisted, did not realize that most Asian nationalists are non-Communist, not anti-Communist, but assumed that people were either Communists or anti-Communists.*

Asians, he stated, could not support the West in the present struggle with the Soviet Union because they had been dominated by the West for too long, and if an Asian did speak out for us, "this Asian is either a liar or he is out to get something from you." In Burma, he claimed, "When we want to please the United States, we let U Nu speak; when we want to please China, we let U Ba Swe speak; when we do not want to please either, we let U Kyaw Nyein speak."

To Asians, he stated, both the Soviet and Western systems had strong points. It had to be remembered that Marxist economic theory appealed to a former colonial, exploited people. But, at the same time, "We know that Americans are far more decent than the Russians — thus you can see why we are torn between the two systems."

He expressed concern that China would try to absorb Burma. The peoples in the hill country were restless. Some had joined Li Mi's

[20] Thomas E. Dewey, *Journey to the Far Pacific* (Garden City, N.Y.: Doubleday, 1952).

Nationalist troops, while agents from China were working to convert others to Communism, he remarked. The Vietminh move into Laos, he said, could be extremely dangerous for Burma.

Dr. Ba Maw then stated that Burmese were frightened by the "ominous" figures of John Foster Dulles, Senator Joseph McCarthy and Senator Pat McCarran. On the other hand, Stevenson had "made a great name in Asia" during the campaign. His "intellectual qualities appealed to us" and he demonstrated a sophisticated mind that did not reduce all issues to pro-Communism or anti-Communism.

Later that day, through the assistance of James Ward and Lewis M. Purnell, Johnson met with two members of the non-rebel Karen opposition to the government. They explained that a "great fire for independence burns in the hearts of the Karens." They described the section of the Union of Burma which they felt should be independent. But to accomplish this the Karens required leadership and organization, both of which were lacking.

When Stevenson returned from Mandalay, the acting foreign minister, U Kyaw Nyein, gave a reception in his honor. When he arrived, the Yugoslav ambassador and some Burmese officials were discussing a news report that Senator McCarthy had just "forced" the U.S. Information Agency to investigate the writings of Mrs. Franklin D. Roosevelt and Adlai E. Stevenson "for any Communist leanings." "How do you Americans think you can ever be a world leader if you act this way?" one person inquired. Stevenson expressed his contempt for McCarthy but cautioned that the senator should not be confused with the whole country.

The acting foreign minister remarked: "I look on Senator McCarthy as conducting a Spanish Inquisition." He added, however, that he expected American foreign policy to remain "moderate" because of the influence of the Democrats in the United States Senate.

After the reception Stevenson returned to the president's house to finish his article for Look. At Stevenson's suggestion, Johnson talked to Jimmy Setuya, one of the "Thirty Heroes" who had helped organize the Burma Independence Army, which cooperated with the Japanese in driving the British out of Burma. (During the Japanese occupation, when Setuya — also known as Thakin Aung Than or Bo SetYa — began to organize against the Japanese, Dr. Ba Maw sent him to Japan as a military attaché to save him from imprisonment. In 1947 he was a member of the Burmese delegation that went to London to work out the agreement on independence. In 1953 Setuya was treasurer of the Trade Union Congress of Burma.)

Setuya charged that U Nu was building support for himself through the Buddhist priests ("pongyis"). He urged that Stevenson not make the mistake that Justice William O. Douglas had made. U Nu, he said, had persuaded Douglas that the Buddhist revival in Burma was a great anti-Communist force. Setuya insisted that this was not so. He and other socialists, through organizing trade unions and working with peasant organizations, were the powerful anti-Communist force in Burma.

He denounced the United States for supporting Chiang Kai-shek, "You have taken the side of Chiang against Burma and the rest of Southeast Asia." It was ironic, he added, that Americans considered the Vietminh move into Laos as an act of aggression but "do not regard General Li Mi's Nationalist troops in Burma as an act of aggression." These troops, he said, were raiding Burmese villages and raping Burmese women. At the same time that the United States offered Burma economic aid, he stated, we were "offering us fire in the other hand" by your support of Chiang.

He then stated that Burma was watching developments in Yugoslavia most clearly, particularly the decentralization of the economy that was taking place. "Yugoslavia impressed us by standing up to the Russians," he added, "yet we know it is not a stooge of the United States and the capitalist powers. We look upon Yugoslavia as like us — in neither camp." The Yugoslavs declared, "We accept American aid. We are not afraid of it. If the Americans step over a given line, we will throw out the aid."

At 5:30 the next morning, April 27, Stevenson went to the Shwedagon pagoda to join thousands of Burmese who were celebrating the day of Buddha's birth. "That morning visit escaped the newsmen," Dr. Maung Maung wrote, "but when the news leaked out and reached the people it pleased them." [21]

The remainder of the morning Stevenson devoted to writing his article for Look.

At noon the Trade Union Congress of Burma gave a luncheon for Stevenson. (Embassy officials explained that when they had informed Defense Minister U Ba Swe, who was also president of the TUCB, that Stevenson had cabled that he wanted to meet with him, the defense minister had replied that the TUCB wished to honor Stevenson with a luncheon. The embassy officials remarked that this was the first time that Burmese labor leaders had so honored any American.) Some twenty-one trade union leaders were present. Stevenson sat between U Ba Swe and the acting foreign minister, U Kyaw Nyein. Behind

[21] "Burma — The Bets Will Be on Stevenson," p. 11.

them on the wall was a red flag with a hammer and sickle and a star with a picture of a peacock on it — the Burmese socialists' flag.

U Ba Swe and U Kyaw Nyein explained to Stevenson that despite their anger over the fact that the leaders of Thailand were permitting supplies and men to reach General Li Mi's forces, Burma was anxious to improve relations. They were particularly eager, they added, to reach defense and economic agreements with Thailand. They also discussed with Stevenson the government's plans to rehabilitate captured insurrectionists. They described in considerable detail how they, as socialists, had out-organized the Communists and won control of the trade union movement.

After lunch Stevenson met privately with U Ba Swe, U Kyaw Nyein, and General Ne Win. They asked him if he could help Burma obtain military equipment from the United States at a reduced rate. They added that since Burma had canceled the economic aid agreement, they were fearful that the United States might be unwilling to sell military equipment at a price they could afford. Stevenson suggested that they send a representative to the United States immediately, and he added that he would support the request.[22]

Later that afternoon Stevenson visited the University of Rangoon, where he talked to a group of twelve students. Johnson's record of the dialogue reads:

> 1. Suppose you were an Asian. What would you think therefore of Eisenhower's statement that "Asians should fight Asians"?
> The Governor replied that we believe in fighting for principles; we believe in the struggle for freedom and it is not a question of Asians fight[ing] Asians, it is a question of all people of good will who believe in freedom struggling to make sure that freedom is not lost.
> 2. Do you believe that respect for the sovereignty and independence of each nation is the key to world peace?
> The Governor answered, naturally, absolutely.
> 3. What are your frank opinions of the third force idea founded by the Asian Socialists?
> The Governor said, it is up to each country to decide where its best interest resides. No one else should impose his views on that country, but he said, I must warn you that historically only the very strong or the very weak have been able to be neutral.
> 4. He was asked his opinion on the KMT [Kuomintang] troops in Burma.
> He said, from what I know they are the most unwelcome guests

[22] When Stevenson saw President Eisenhower and Secretary of State John Foster Dulles on his return, he recommended the proposal to them.

that have ever been in Burma. He said, I think they will get out, I think they will be disarmed. I expect them to be withdrawn via Thailand to Formosa. He said, I think this will be over before too much longer. He said, I would like to see evidence of American weapons if they are being used by the KMT. He told the students he had asked the Defense Minister of Burma if they had captured any American weapons and the Defense Minister said they had not.

5. Why should the United States aid Chiang Kai-shek?

The Governor said that any country like the United States should help another to improve the health, agriculture, education, and the roads of a country. And, he said, this was the largest per cent of the U.S. aid which had gone to Formosa.

6. He was asked the question, are not Germany and Japan monsters?

The Governor replied, we do not think that we should suppress people; we will have to take our chance.

7. Why don't you recognize Communist China?

He replied, we will not recognize China until China stops being an aggressive nation.

8. He was asked, isn't the Vietminh liberating Indo-China?

He replied, liberating from whom? And by whom? What makes you think China and the Vietminh are liberating Indo-China? He said, you people were willing to fight the British and needed the Japanese to get in here, then when you got totalitarian Japan you immediately realized how much happier you had been with the British, and most of them nodded agreement on this point. Then he said, in Indo-China lots of people feel that they want to fight the French, but, the Governor said, I hope that they will learn that the Vietminh is as great a danger to them as you learned that totalitarian Japan was to you.

After the discussion with the students, Stevenson held a press conference that was taken down in shorthand by a secretary of the United States Information Service:

Q: What is your personal reaction to Burma's complaint in the UN regarding the KMT [Kuomintang] invasion? [23]

[23] Burma had requested the United Nations to condemn the Chinese Nationalist government in Taiwan as aggressors in Burma. The Seventh General Assembly adopted a Mexican-Lebanese-Argentine-Chilean resolution condemning "the presence of these forces in Burma" and endorsed the "good offices of certain member states" designed to remove the forces. Before the resolution was adopted, the United States had belatedly offered to help solve the problem. The U.S. and Thailand, meeting separately with Burma and Taiwan, arranged the voluntary repatriation of the troops. A token evacuation began in August, 1953. In 1954, about

A: I heartily agree with the decision of the UN and the resolution that was adopted by it calling upon those troops to withdraw and all nations to cooperate to that end. Furthermore, I hope that this will bring about an early solution to this problem by the voluntary and peaceful withdrawal of those troops after they have been disarmed.

Q: What is your opinion on the peace moves made by the new Soviet government?

A: I hope it is sincere. But it looks very much to me that, stalemated in Korea and Europe, the Communist axis is increasing pressure in Southeast Asia. I refer to the invasion of Laos, another country invaded by the Communists. The best evidence of the sincerity of the Russian peace efforts will be the discontinuance of the rebellion in Vietnam, withdrawal of the forces they have supported in Laos, peace in Malaya, and Russian acquiescence in the disarmament proposal — providing international inspection of armaments.[24]

Q: From what you have seen in Southeast Asia, what are the chances of combating Communism?

A: I think they are very good. Within the last five years the Communists started a civil war in Vietnam, a violent insurrection in the Philippines, violent rebellions in Burma, Malaya, and Indonesia, and in not one of these countries have they succeeded. So I think the prospects are good, were it not for this thrust into Laos. In other words, I think Southeast Asia has stood up to the pressure very well.

Q: Am I correct in assuming that the invasion of Laos by Vietminh is directed against French colonialism?

A: I don't know. It is directed against the sovereignty of Laos.

Q: . . . With the connivance of Laotian people?

A: I don't know.

Q: Laotian and Cambodians are not satisfied with the French.

A: I don't think anyone is satisfied with colonialism. These countries

seven thousand to eight thousand persons (soldiers and families) were removed. Taiwan "disavowed" those who remained. In 1961, another evacuation occurred, but after this evacuation, the Burmese estimated that only about eight hundred remained. Trager, *Burma from Kingdom to Republic*, pp. 321, 429. On April 23, 1953, while Stevenson was in Rangoon, the Trade Union Congress of Burma denounced the United States for not supporting the Burmese resolution condemning Taiwan by name as the aggressor. See the *New Times of Burma*, April 24, 1953; the *Nation*, April 24, 1953.

24 On April 16, 1953, President Eisenhower had proposed universal disarmament, international control of atomic energy, and the universal prohibition of atomic weapons under a United Nations system of inspection. New York *Times*, April 17, 1953.

have all been promised their independence after the end of hostilities in Vietnam. They have a huge measure of self-government now. They can't win their war without French officers because they do not have enough officers of their own. The Vietnamese army is growing rapidly and it will soon have its own officers. There are Vietnamese training in the United States right now.

Q: How long?

A: I should imagine they will be able to carry the brunt of the fight next year. The Vietnamese forces, both military and police, outnumber French Union forces.

Q: How much do you subscribe to the "resurrection" of Chiang Kai-shek?

A: I think the improvement of the quality in government and public administration in Formosa is very remarkable. It is a demonstration of what could have been done in the past on the mainland of China and I am glad to see that some of it is brought about by American engineers — public health [activities] that reduced incidence of child mortality greatly last year; primary school education; building of roads and bridges; hydroelectric plants in the mountains and rural rehabilitation; land redistribution; improved seeds; great[er] production. All these things are fine examples of what can be done, what could have been done. I think all this is very encouraging. Beyond that to the military potential, I don't know. When asked that once before, I replied that my only experience in military strategy is that I was an apprentice seaman in the U.S. Navy.

Q: We think Chiang Kai-shek is trying to build himself to be the big anti-Communist leader in Asia. There are many anti-Communist leaders here. Should not America try to recognize the anti-Communist activities of each leader and each area?

A: I think it does.

Q: . . . Rather than just Chiang Kai-shek?

A: I think your conclusion is a *non sequitur*. I think the United States government does recognize others: the Huk rebellion in the Philippines, two Communist rebellions in Indonesia, the efforts they have made in Malaya to restore order, likewise in Burma, the extraordinary accomplishments of the government to fight five simultaneous rebellions including a Communist uprising. These are not only recognized but widely applauded.

Q: Do you think America is betting on the wrong horse in aiding the Chiang Kai-shek government?

A: He's the only horse on Formosa, isn't he? I think the security of Formosa is very important to the defenses in the Pacific.

Q: Is it true that American aid is a form of surplus goods and is given to ward off an economic crisis?

A: No, you are quite wrong about that. About surplus — there is a terrible shortage that you will find everywhere. Every country is looking to America: Europe (both Eastern and Western), North Africa, the Middle East, and Asia, and we don't have enough. As far as the depression is concerned, I think it will be a lot better for the world if the American military budget could be cut twenty billion dollars a year and a portion of that put into direct technical assistance to countries that need it, because military goods is a wasting asset.

Q: Will America let Chiang Kai-shek down if Mao Tse-tung becomes a Tito?

A: I didn't bring my crystal ball.

Q: Would you advise an increase in TCA aid or similar aid to the underdeveloped countries?

A: I think that the great obstacle to further assistance in the technical development of the world is the tremendous portion of the budget for the military in the United States and I think it is true everywhere in the world, especially in Europe. This gets a priority. If the emergency subsided and it could be converted into technical or other assistance, that would be a very good thing.

Q: From what you have seen of the aid programs in this part of the world, do you think they are worthwhile?

A: They have been conspicuously successful. I have talked about Formosa. The story in the Philippines is rather elaborate. It has been very successful and very expensive. Manila was the second-worst destroyed city in the world next to Warsaw — perhaps Mandalay — but the rehabilitation job which has been done and the work going on in the same fields have been successful. It still has a long way to go. In Indonesia we have done a lot in the same fields, and in the interesting field of encouraging small industries. For example, I visited a blacksmith shop which employed two people. They were using American tools to make horseshoes. There are many cases where we have supplied the tools and the government supplies the industries. We have set up people in business, in trades that are needed to help with the rehabilitation. The Ambassador knows better than I do. That is to the good. I know something of what's been done in Thailand. The same general overall pattern which is producing results. There is still a long way to go. I have seen examples where we have been of assistance in Burma. That's all I can say without going into the subject of Korea, which is too big.

Q: So, in your opinion you think it is worthwhile?

A: Yes. We will have to learn to live with it. The progress should be taken objectively, over a long period of time. They have been too ambitious at first. I think it would be better to rationalize a bit.

Q: Do you agree to UN trusteeship of Formosa?

A: Is that being discussed? I am afraid that I can't comment on that. I have no views on that.

Q: Do you believe East and West Germany can be united?

A: Do you mean immediately? I don't believe so without Soviet acquiescence and I don't believe that would be forthcoming. I would hope so. Of course they can be united physically and they want to unite but whether politically it is possible at this time, I don't know.

Q: ECA was started by [the] Truman administration and you are one of the important personages — I mean Democratic leaders. Burma has given notice to terminate it, and I want to know your feelings on it.

A: That's Burma's option — to terminate it.

Q: Is it so that in America politics are mixed up with crime?

A: You will find that in some cities — not national or state politics, but mostly cities. Gamblers [politicians?] take rake-offs for gambling but it is minute.

Q: Are not nearly all American politicians corrupt — on the payroll of racketeers? The Kefauver Committee had to conduct an inquiry into the lives of gangsters.[25]

A: We are troubled by lawless elements: gangsters, etc. You have dacoits in this country.

Q: But not to the extent of being on the payroll.

A: You might find a handful of people in the whole country who might be on the payroll — it is mostly in the cities and then on a ward level. They have influence with the city councils. If that is all our trouble, we could handle that.

[25] Senator Estes Kefauver headed the Senate Special Committee to Investigate Organized Crime in Interstate Commerce. The hearings in 1950 exposed embarrassing connections between criminals and Democratic city machines, particularly in New York and Chicago. See Eric F. Goldman, *The Crucial Decade: America, 1945–1955* (New York: Alfred A. Knopf, 1956), pp. 190–198.

Q: I have read comments that [Senator Joseph] McCarthy is investigating your writings, along with Mrs. Roosevelt.

A: I shall be very much flattered to ever be identified with that great and good lady, Mrs. Roosevelt.[26]

Q: Do you think there is a chance of settlement in Korea?

A: Yes. I think there is a chance of an armistice.

Q: Not just an armistice, but lasting peace?

A: I would have to answer yes. If you said on what terms, I would be in trouble. Yes.

Q: Do you think Chiang Kai-shek has enough military force to launch an attack?

A: As I said before, I am not a military strategist.

At dinner at the president's house after the press conference, the president and Stevenson descended the staircase arm in arm to join the guests in the lounge. The Burmese present broke out in applause as Stevenson entered the room wearing the Burmese skirt (longyi), the Burmese hat (gaung baung), and the Burmese jacket (co-eingyi).

Immediately after dinner he retired and arose early on April 28 to catch a seven A.M. plane to Calcutta.

Stevenson wrote about his visits to Thailand and Burma:

FIGHT FOR FREEDOM IN SOUTHEAST ASIA [27]

To the north of Malaya lie Thailand and Burma, both rich in rice, both devoutly Buddhist and both in trouble. As I write this brief synopsis of my visits to Bangkok and Rangoon, the Communist thrust into Laos imperils Thailand's borders, and refugee Chinese Nationalist troops imperil Burma's security and sovereignty.

What are the Communists' objectives in Laos? Some say they are exploiting the anti-French nationalism in Laos and Cambodia to seize these weakly defended countries and thus encircle Viet-Nam. Because the Laotians and Cambodians are Thais,[28] the Communists could then

[26] Some reporters apparently expected Stevenson to lash out at President Eisenhower, Secretary of State Dulles, and Senator McCarthy. The *Nation* (Rangoon) wrote after the press conference: "The impression he [Stevenson] leaves in Rangoon is one of a careful, calculating lawyer rather than of a shrewd observer or warmhearted writer." William Attwood, "Seeing the World with Stevenson: Twenty Questions and Their Answers," *Harper's*, November, 1953, p. 60.

[27] *Look*, June 16, 1953. The rest of this article is reprinted in Chapters Eight and Nine, above.

[28] Stevenson was in error here. The Cambodians are not a Thai people.

make bad medicine next door in Thailand with the old Thai dream of "that happy day when all of the Thai peoples are united." Besides, there are many believers in the anti-French propaganda among the large Viet-Namese population in northern Thailand, and no one knows just how strong the Red organization is among the 3,000,000 Chinese in Thailand.

In short, there is good reason for placid Thailand to be worried.

Burma, too, is worried, not so much because of Communists without as anti-Communists within. Gen. Li Mi's Chinese army of four or five thousand men took refuge in mountainous northeast Burma when Chiang Kai-shek's Nationalists melted before the Reds in 1949. Last fall, these forces, enlarged somehow to more than 10,000, suddenly began striking out at the Burmese — looting villages, murdering civilians and allegedly aiding rebellious tribesmen (including Communist rebels).

The Burmese assert that these troops are supplied from Formosa directly, or via Thailand. And they blame the United States for not cracking down on Chiang, whom they consider an American puppet. In March, the Burmese government formally renounced further U.S. technical assistance (which Burma needs and wants), just to silence critics who called the aid hush money to make Burma keep still about Li Mi's army.

Burma and Thailand have never been very good neighbors, and they differ in many ways.

Burma is a young, rough-and-ready nation; on the other hand, Thailand, though surrounded for a century by French and British colonies, managed to preserve its independence. Thanks to its rice surplus, even the plentiful poor have enough to eat. So there has never been much cause for unrest — either political or economic.

Unlike neutralist Burma, Thailand has unequivocally cast its lot with the West and was one of the first to send troops to Korea. Its government, an absolute monarchy until 20 years ago, is now an easy-going police state operated by the politically conscious upper crust; in lieu of elections, there are bloodless military *coups d'etat*. Of late, Prime Minister Pibul Songgram, a man of force and character, has made good progress, with U.S. assistance, in strengthening the army and improving education, health and agriculture.

But avaricious, ambitious officials still shamelessly use public positions for self-enrichment. (In official Bangkok, they talk laughingly about the "ice-cold war" between the rival politicians who control the Coca-Cola and Pepsi-Cola concessions.) And there is evidence that the peasants in the rice paddies, and the colorful canal folk, are beginning to talk critically about politics and politicians for the first time.

I heard more positive expressions of appreciation for American assistance in Thailand than anywhere else. But many wonder how effectively the Thais would resist invasion. They have not been hardened by revolution, nor did they suffer like their neighbors during the Japanese occupation. Fortunately, their aversion to the Chinese may stiffen their will to resist anything introduced from China, especially communism.

If there is any doubt about Thailand's fighting spirit, there is none about Burma's. The Burmese will take on anyone who threatens their newly won independence. For the past five years, Burma's army has been battling five separate and simultaneous insurrections (two of them Communist), in addition to Gen. Li Mi's Chinese freebooters. At the same time, the government has had to grapple with staggering economic and social problems, massive war damage, poverty, illiteracy, disease and a shortage of trained administrators and technicians. But Burma has been winning its battles one by one. Were it not for the Chinese irregulars, the new nation would at long last be pacified today — no wonder the Burmese are exasperated!

The President, Dr. Ba U, an accomplished elder statesman, and the young leaders of this young nation reminded me of the men who govern Indonesia. Hospitable, forthright, prejudiced, sensitive and nationalistic, they are determined to create their own way of life in their favored land, independent of all "big brothers," be they capitalist or Communist.

The Prime Minister, U Nu, a gentle, deeply spiritual man of 44, and his even younger associates (mostly in their thirties) have one thing in common — their early Marxist connections. Why, then, is Burma emphatically non-Communist? Simply because the Burmese have matured; they know that communism is international and means the loss of their precious independence and sovereignty. While they deplore with simple candor America's "identification with reactionary forces" and reject capitalism with the summary confidence of those who have learned all about free enterprise from Marx, they are equally determined to avoid the snares of international communism.

Their alternative is a co-operative Socialist state, practicing strict neutrality in foreign affairs. But their students who go abroad for training invariably choose the West, not China or Russia.

As in Indonesia, I sensed some feeling that America is more concerned with fighting communism than promoting democracy, and Burma's great, basic good will is tinged with the suspicion that we are trying to buy allies with dollars.

We should not press our aid or advice; and candor and straight talk won't hurt us or the earnest, uncertain young men who are building nations out here. We cannot hope, nor should we try, to remake this distant and different world in our image.

But we can be patient with its peoples' misunderstanding and misinformation, and we can show them a sincere heart and a concern for their independence as well as our security.

I should like to talk more about this vast, churning, tropical area and about Thailand and Burma in particular. For history is being made in Southeast Asia, and its significance to America and the free world is growing daily. Let's not forget that Communists have tried to shoot their way to power in Indochina, Burma, the Philippines, Malaya and Indonesia. Nowhere have they succeeded. Meanwhile, the revolution in Southeast Asia, the struggle for independence — independence from Communist imperialism as much as from Western imperialism — is succeeding. For this revolution in Asia is not just anti-Western — it is pro-Asian.

But the Communists have not given up by any means. Even as the Kremlin, stalemated in Europe and Korea, proclaims its thirst for peace, the Communists are stabbing toward the rice basket of Southeast Asia with redoubled violence.

Eleven

India

APRIL 28–MAY 14, 1953

*S*tevenson's introduction to India came at 10:30 A.M., April 28, when
the plane from Rangoon landed at the sweltering metropolis of Calcutta. There he found an extraordinary number of reporters waiting to
question him.

Stevenson protested that he would have to withhold his comments
on India until the end of the trip. He did, however, in response to a
question about Southeast Asia, describe the Vietminh invasion of Laos
as "a major invasion of an independent country." One Indian reporter
wrote: "India did not expect Stevenson, of all Americans, to describe
Laos as 'an independent country' — India, even today, is more aroused
by the presence of retreating colonialism than by the danger of ad-
vancing Communism." [1]

At noon Stevenson talked at considerable length to Dr. B. C. Roy,
the knowledgeable chief minister of the state of West Bengal. Dr. Roy
described India's first general election the year before when Prime Minister Nehru's Congress party had won firm control of the Parliament.[2]
But principally he discussed the partition, at the time of independence
in 1947, of Bengal between India (West Bengal) and Pakistan (East
Bengal). The partition, he insisted, had created havoc. West Bengal had
the jute and silk mills, while East Bengal raised the raw materials.

[1] Kirshnalal Shridharani, "Stevenson Charms and Disappoints Delhi," *New Republic,* June 1, 1953, p. 11.
[2] For a discussion of the election, see Hugh Tinker, *India and Pakistan: A Political Analysis* (New York: Frederick A. Praeger, 1962), pp. 52–56.

Since partition, it had been impossible, he added, to work out an agreement. As a result West Bengal was now raising jute — taking land away from needed food cultivation — and East Bengal had built jute mills.

Dr. Roy observed that there were about twelve million Hindus and about twenty-five million Moslems in East Bengal at the time of partition.[3] In all, he estimated, three million Hindus had fled to West Bengal, and at the moment, there were something like twenty-one million Hindus in West Bengal and four million Moslems. There had been considerable bloodshed in 1947 between the two groups and there still were some skirmishes along the border. "We are always faced with apprehension," he stated.

He expressed his concern over the fanaticism of the Moslem religious leaders — the mullahs — who insisted on strict adherence to the Koran. It was fitted, he said, for the desert area and the seventh century that had produced it, not for urban living in the present century. There are limits, he added, "to how much you can keep to the Koran."

Early that afternoon, Stevenson visited the Calcutta offices of the Damodar Valley Corporation. The chairman of the board of directors, S. N. Mozumdar, described the vast project (of the Tennessee Valley Authority type) that they were constructing in the Damodar Valley, northeast of Calcutta. He showed Stevenson a map with a system of dams to prevent destructive floods, irrigate a million acres of land, produce 400,000 kilowatts of power, and encourage a complex of steel mills and related factories.[4]

After this glimpse into the brighter future for India, Stevenson saw some of the grim facts of India's present when he visited Calcutta's main railroad station. Barry Bingham wrote:

> . . . The whole station is occupied by refugees, half-naked and living like animals on the floor of a vast smoky shed.
>
> Here we saw dying men, already rigid as corpses, stretched on the bare stones while women fanned the fetid air around them.
>
> In one corner cowered a dog, a symbol of all the human misery around him. One leg had been severed by a train, and the raw stump ran with blood. With a terrible dumb patience the dog stood waiting for death. No Hindu could destroy him to end his pain, for their religion forbids the taking of any animal's life.[5]

[3] For a discussion of the 1947 partition, see Sir Percival Griffiths, *Modern India* (New York: Frederick A. Praeger, 1965), pp. 97–102.

[4] A number of Americans from the TVA were involved in the Damodar Valley project. See *The Journals of David E. Lilienthal*, Vol. III, *Venturesome Years: 1950–1955* (New York: Harper & Row, 1966), pp. 106, 111, 113, for a discussion by the former chairman of the TVA of his visit to the project in 1951.

[5] "There's Trouble in Eden," Louisville *Courier-Journal*, May 17, 1953.

Stevenson told his aides the next day that he had not been able to sleep all night, since he could not get this scene out of his mind.

From the railroad station Stevenson went to call on the governor of the state of West Bengal, Dr. H. C. Mookerjee. Stevenson asked why nothing was being done about these refugees. Dr. Mookerjee explained that the government had settled them on farm land but after a short while they had poured into Calcutta. "We cannot help them because if we did it might encourage more to leave the land and come to Calcutta," he said.

He discussed the bloodshed between Hindus and Moslems following the partitioning of the country. But he asked, "If we Hindus are really so bad, why is it we have so many Moslems still living in India?" He pointed to the fact that while there were two Moslems in Nehru's cabinet, there were no non-Moslems in the Pakistani government.

He then told Stevenson that Chinese Communists were active among the hill people along the Tibetan border. "We are fearful," he said, "that the Communists will build a fifth column there and then spread their influence throughout India." He expressed his gratitude for United States economic assistance and remarked: "If you help strengthen us, it will help stave off the Communist threat."

Stevenson had his party up early the next morning to fly to the Damodar Valley. In heat of 110 degrees Stevenson climbed up and down the earthen dams and watched bulldozers, tractors, and human manpower remaking the valley. He was intrigued with the way rocks were being loaded into trucks: he remarked that after seeing "the way women worked in Asia," he had decided "women at home don't work enough. Look at those gallant gentlemen putting rocks on women's heads and then letting the women carry them to the trucks."

After lunch the airplane flew him from the new India of economic development to the holy city of Benares, where Stevenson saw one aspect of India's long past. When he arrived at the Green Hotel, the manager had tea ready. But Stevenson told him: "I am an impetuous tourist. I don't want tea. I want to see the people and the temples." After depositing his suitcases, he visited Sarnath, where Buddha preached his first sermon and won his first converts. After climbing through the ruins of temples destroyed by the Moslem invasion of the twelfth century, Stevenson went into the heart of Benares to visit the Hindu holy places. There were crowds of people pushing and shoving to enter the various temples. Old people seemed to be everywhere. To die in Benares was to go straight to heaven, so Hindus were borne to the city in thousands to await death.

When Stevenson reached the Ganges, a full moon was sparkling on the river. By the water's edge were the burning ghats, public pyres where corpses were burned. After watching the pilgrims bathing in the river and boatloads of pilgrims passing by, Stevenson decided the party should go for a ride on the river. But by now, it was nine P.M. The Stevenson party had been in the relentless heat of Benares for three hours. All of his aides were exhausted. After one complained that he did not have his chief's "chronic stamina," Stevenson agreed that it was time to return to the hotel for dinner.

Barry Bingham wrote of that night in Benares:

> We were sharing a room in a small hotel. When we went to bed we found ourselves almost smothered under mosquito netting, with no breath of air coming through the staring windows. Each of us tossed and turned in his bed for a while, remembering the burning ghats we had seen that day loaded with corpses, remembering, too, the wrecks of humanity we had seen creeping through the streets, people who had come to die in the holy city by the Ganges.
>
> After a while we gave up and began to talk. We talked all night, until a pale light came to herald another burning day. An hour later Adlai was up, apparently rested and ready to continue the inexorable schedule.[6]

At six A.M. Stevenson left the hotel to go for a boat ride on the Ganges. He watched thousands of people bathing in the river, countless other thousands walking along the banks of the river going from one temple to another. From his boat he could see bodies burning on the pyres and mourners scattering ashes in the river. He mused aloud that Benares was the old India — the India that "the new India had to overcome to carry out its plans."

After he left the river, Stevenson walked some more through the crowded streets to see several temples by daylight. Then he boarded the airplane to visit the Taj Mahal at Agra. "The perfect time to see the Taj is by moonlight," Barry Bingham wrote. "We saw it at noon on a day of 106 degree heat. The light was harsh and glaring, the air was filled with a brown film of dust. Even in such circumstances, the noble symmetry of this monument to a dead queen's beauty stood out sharp and pure as a note in music." [7]

Stevenson was full of admiration for the majesty of the exterior. But he was most impressed by the simple beauty of the interior with its

---

[6] "With Adlai in Asia," in *As We Knew Adlai: The Stevenson Story by Twenty-two Friends,* edited and with preface by Edward P. Doyle, foreword by Adlai E. Stevenson III (New York: Harper & Row, 1966), p. 196.

[7] "There's Trouble in Eden."

flowers in mosaic patterns. After a two-hour visit, Stevenson reluctantly left the Taj to fly to New Delhi.

A host of Indian officials, Ambassador George Allen, and crowds of reporters welcomed Stevenson to the capital of India. He answered a few questions posed by the reporters, but explained that he would answer their questions more fully at a press conference at the close of his visit. The reporters were audibly unhappy when he announced that he would make no speeches while in India.

A reporter for the Statesman (*New Delhi*) observed that Stevenson's remarks on arriving "were so different from the banalities usually uttered by visiting celebrities that we were not disappointed. Even in his trivialia, he has the qualities of wit and sanity we came to expect from him in his election speeches. . . . It would be an occasion to remember if Mr. Stevenson could be prevailed upon to make at least one public speech during his short stay in the capital. He would, I am certain, be astonished at the warmth of the welcome he would receive." [8]

That evening New York Times *correspondent Robert Trumbull and Mrs. Trumbull joined Stevenson for a brief talk. Trumbull described troubled Kashmir, to which Stevenson was flying the next morning for a rest.*

At the time of the partition in 1947, the state of Jammu and Kashmir had approximately four million people. Over three million Moslems and most of the Hindus lived in Jammu. The ruler of Jammu and Kashmir, Sir Hari Singh, was a high-caste Hindu. In October, 1947, Moslem tribesmen from the Northwest Frontier invaded Kashmir and allied themselves with their coreligionists against the maharajah and the Hindu ruling class. The maharajah appealed to India for help. He was told that no aid would be given unless Kashmir acceded to India. On October 26, 1947, the maharajah did so, and Indian troops were flown in and soon controlled three-fourths of Kashmir. Soldiers of the Pakistan army entered to assist the Azad (Free) Kashmir army. A cease-fire was arranged on January 1, 1949. India then referred the question to the Security Council of the United Nations. The UN appointed a commission and arbitrators to find a solution. India gave conditional consent to the holding of a plebiscite but refused to accept the actual plans for conducting it. In 1956 Prime Minister Jawaharlal Nehru stated that the idea of a plebiscite was out of date and recommended partition on the basis of the existing cease-fire line. Pakistan rejected the proposal. It recommended the withdrawal of all Indian and Pakistani troops from Kashmir and the stationing of United Nations forces there as a preliminary to a plebiscite. Fighting broke out in Kashmir across

[8] May 1, 1953.

the cease-fire line in August and September, 1965, and also across the international boundary between India and Pakistan. After three weeks India and Pakistan yielded to pressure from the United Nations and agreed to a cease-fire. India continued to refuse the Pakistani demand for a plebiscite in Kashmir.[9]

Trumbull told Stevenson that the only hope he could see for Kashmir was partition but he did not foresee this occurring. He added that India would never allow a plebiscite if they thought the results would favor Pakistan.

The next morning, May 1, Stevenson was up at 6:30 and left the airport on an Indian National Airlines DC–3. The plane flew over the brown, sun-baked earth to Jammu. It was 107 degrees in the shade, and there was no shade. Finally, the plane took off and soon it flew through a pass in the mountains. To the west were snow-covered peaks reaching to 16,000 feet and to the east, along the Chinese-Tibetan border, were mountains 20,000 feet and higher. When the plane landed in Kashmir the temperature was a gentle 75 degrees.

Stevenson was met by a representative of Sheikh Mohammed Abdullah, the chief minister of the state of Jammu and Kashmir, and Mr. Butt, a Kashmiri who owned the houseboats the Stevenson party was to live on. There were fields of wild white iris and groves of almond trees along the road to the houseboats. When Stevenson arrived there were five houseboats strung along the bank of the lake. Pansies, iris, and roses were growing in landscaped gardens.

After lunch and a nap, Stevenson and Mr. Butt went for a ride in a shikara, a light gondola-type boat canopied with white curtains and equipped with scarlet cushions covered with delicate Kashmir embroidery. Mr. Butt described to Stevenson how much Sheikh Abdullah was loved by the people. He explained that Abdullah had started in 1931 to organize against the dictatorial maharajah. The people trusted Abdullah so much, Mr. Butt stated, that they would join India or Pakistan depending on his decision. Mr. Butt added that while he had great sympathy for his "Moslem brothers" in Pakistan, he could not forget the way the Moslem tribesmen invaded Kashmir in 1947, pillaging and raping.

After a fine Kashmiri dinner on the houseboat, Stevenson slept under blankets for the first time since Korea.

The next morning he made a brief courtesy call on the chief minister, and then shopped at the Kashmiri Emporium. He and his aides then joined Sheikh Abdullah for lunch.

Abdullah described how the maharajah had jailed him for "sedition"

[9] Griffiths, Modern India, pp. 171–179.

in 1946. When the Moslem tribesmen invaded, the maharajah fled, and
Abdullah was released from jail and organized an emergency government. His government, he explained, saw to it that Moslems and
Hindus did not attack each other as they had done in so much of India.
He emphasized that he was "noncommunal" in his attitudes. "I am a
Moslem myself, but Pakistan wants to go back to the Middle Ages. I
want progress for my people." India, he added, was more progressive
than Pakistan. Both Gandhi and Nehru fought for a secular state and
"we must have a secular state based on progress and freedom, not on
religion," Abdullah stated.

The chief minister talked a bit about the school-building program his
government had launched and he also described the land reforms to
break up the old landed estates.

After lunch Stevenson visited a camp of Kazaks who had fled from
Chinese Turkestan and walked for two years across the desert and the
Himalayan mountains to reach the Vale of Kashmir. Only 350 survived
out of over 20,000 who had started the trek. Following a brief conversation, interpreted by a Harvard-trained anthropologist, M. J. Clark,
the Kazaks folk-danced for the party. The rest of that day Stevenson
spent in a leisurely manner aboard the houseboats.

Early the following morning three Kazaks arrived to repay the visit.
After breakfast Stevenson was paddled in a shikara across the lake to
Shalimar Garden with its pattern of flowers, waterfalls, and fountains.
As he strolled through the garden, Stevenson remarked that he knew of
no other place in the world where one could find the combinations
present in Kashmir: "Forty-five minutes by air from where it is a
hundred and ten degrees; magnificent mountain ranges rising to over
twenty thousand feet; and people with a different cultural and physical
background from what you find just over the mountains in Jammu and
in other parts of India."

During the rest of the day, Stevenson answered the heavy volume of
mail that had been awaiting him in New Delhi.

To James Reston [10]

[no date]

Dear Scotty —

(1) Someone sent me your review of my speeches and I am moved &
grateful for your charity — and jealous of that graceful penetrating pen
of yours.[11]

[10] This handwritten postcard is in the possession of Mr. Reston.
[11] In his review of *Major Campaign Speeches of Adlai E. Stevenson, 1952,*
Mr. Reston said among other things, "He is first and foremost a philosopher and a

[202]

(2) We were all delighted with the news of your "elevation." [12] I even heard myself humming "Hail to the Orange." Its a big, miserable world, but not quite as unhealthy minded as I had expected.

To Mr. and Mrs. Ronald Tree [13]

[no date]

I didn't ride in this [14] but I was photographed with the royal elephants in Siam — a *pink* variety that [Senator] McCarthy should investigate at once! Its been a fabulous and weary journey. At the moment we are in retreat from the heat, languishing on a house-boat in the Vale of Kashmir — which is as lovely as represented — except, *No* pale hands beside beside the Shalimar. The dream ends this afternoon when we plunge back into the inferno of India.

Love
ADLAI

To Mr. and Mrs. Richard Bentley [15]

[no date]

My dear Bentleys —

It's as good as represented. We retreated from the heat to the vale of Kashmir to mend body & mind after 6 weeks in steaming South Asia. It's a cool heaven but the enchantment ends today and we plunge back into the inferno of India. With that new digestive apparatus [16] you'll be already for Asia — and God knows you need the best in that line! It's been a fascinating journey & home never looked as good!

ADLAI

To Mr. and Mrs. Edison Dick [17]

[no date]

Jane's wonderful reports of Inside U.S.A. and Illinois remind me that; there *is* an Ill. & U.S.A. For the last 3 days I haven't cared, however,

---

writer. . . . He appealed more to the best in our national character, and made fewer concessions to self-interest and greed than most Presidential candidates of our time." *New York Times Book Review*, April 19, 1953.

[12] Mr. Reston had just become chief correspondent of the Washington bureau of the New York *Times*.

[13] This handwritten postcard is in the possession of Mr. and Mrs. Tree.

[14] The picture on the card was a long, ornate boat with about fifty rowers.

[15] Mr. Bentley was the Chicago attorney who had represented Stevenson in his divorce proceedings in 1949. This handwritten postcard with a picture of Kashmir is in the possession of Mr. Bentley.

[16] He had just had an intestinal operation.

[17] This handwritten postcard is in the possession of Mrs. Dick.

because we're languishing in the enchanted vale of Kashmir recuperating and mending body and mind after the frenzy and hideous heat of the past 6 weeks in SE Asia. This afternoon we plunge back into the Indian frying pan — and on and on. Bill [Blair] is fine and says I am, why I don't know. Love to all.

On the last day of the visit to Kashmir, Sheikh Abdullah invited Stevenson to lunch with him and members of the cabinet before flying back to New Delhi.[18] The chief minister talked a good deal about their land reform program. Landlords were left with sufficient land to support their families and the remainder was distributed to the tenants. The tenants were not required to pay for the land nor were the landlords reimbursed. Beginning with days of Moghul rule, Abdullah explained, the rulers had given land to their favorites and the tillers thus lost control of it and had to work as tenants.

Stevenson asked him why there had been so little communal trouble once the Moslem tribesmen's invasion had been checked. Abdullah replied: "We told the people that communalism could not solve the land problem or the food problem. . . . We focused the people's view on the economic problem and took their minds away from the religious differences between Moslems, Sikhs, and Hindus." Moreover, he added, the people of Kashmir were all Aryans, spoke the same language, and had the same customs.

Abdullah then discussed the options open to Kashmir. One was to join Pakistan, which he rejected because he did not approve of a country run on religious principles. Another possibility was for Kashmir to join India as a state. The third was to have an autonomous state with India in charge only of defense and foreign affairs. He did not indicate to Stevenson that he preferred the third course to the second.[19]

After Abdullah had described the alternatives facing Kashmir, Stevenson, who had made no comments on the conversation up to this point, told Abdullah and the others that he was disturbed at the way

[18] Walter Johnson was present during the conversation and recorded it in his diary.

[19] In 1951, Abdullah had made the same points to David E. Lilienthal. *Venturesome Years: 1950–1955*, p. 98. Stevenson did not know when he visited Kashmir that some Indian leaders believed that Mrs. Loy Henderson, the wife of the former U.S. ambassador to India, had encouraged Abdullah to make Kashmir an independent state. Nor did Stevenson know that the same Indian leaders believed that agents of the Central Intelligence Agency had encouraged Abdullah to make Kashmir independent. Interview, Governor B. K. Nehru with Walter Johnson, April 4, 1969. Governor Nehru stated that he had no doubt that Stevenson was "innocent" about the activities of Mrs. Henderson and the C.I.A. agents.

Asians distrusted American motives. Abdullah rejoined that perhaps "this is because of your allies," citing U.S. support of the colonial nations France and Britain. "Americans," he continued, "must understand the aspirations of Asia. . . . You must not be so strongly anti-Communist that certain people can blackmail you. . . . Chiang Kai-shek in China did this to you. He blackmailed you in the name of being anti-Communist and the Chinese people didn't get your aid. . . . Don't depend on the old colonial powers to give you views of Asia."

Stevenson agreed that Americans had a great deal to learn about Asia but he expressed concern whether we had "the patience to learn" or would just say "the devil with it."

One member of the cabinet remarked that Americans were too impatient. They had been isolationists so long that they did not understand the complexities of Asia. Americans cannot fight Communists just with guns, he added, Americans must also win the hearts and minds of people.

Stevenson interjected: "I made a lot of speeches on that in my campaign."

"I know," the cabinet minister replied, "I am just repeating your own viewpoint." When Stevenson seemed startled by this remark, the cabinet minister explained that they had read his speeches in the New York *Times* every day during the campaign.

Abdullah added that Asians believed that the French wanted to stay on in Indochina. The United States must announce it wanted freedom for Indochina. In fact, "You should produce an Atlantic Charter for Asia. Until you do, you lack the promise which Russia holds out to people and the tragedy is that many people don't know Russia doesn't live up to its promises."

Abdullah then denounced the British and doubted that they would leave Malaya. "We know that the United States has no ulterior motives, but colonial powers play on you to get money on an anti-Communist approach."

Stevenson replied most firmly that the United States did not want to run Asia. Instead, "We want to help you get a better standard of living."

Abdullah then criticized the United States for being rigid about negotiations with the Russians. "Your Excellency," Stevenson replied, "you must realize that in negotiating with the Russians, which I have done for several years in the United Nations, they knock down any proposal you put up. Then they come up with a ridiculous proposal and then announce to the world that because the United States will not accept it, the United States is not interested in compromise. I nearly *lost my mind for three years negotiating with the Russians, so I went into American politics." Then he concluded, "We simply have to treat the Russians the same way in negotiations in terms of rigidity at the start, the way they treat us, or else we can accomplish nothing."*

At this point, Stevenson received word from the airport that the plane could not depart since the mountain pass was blocked with clouds. He turned to Abdullah and said that he should rent a car and drive over the mountains to Jammu. Abdullah pointed out that it was an eleven- to fifteen-hour drive and most of it would be at night on a difficult, tortuous road.

When he returned to the houseboats, the head servant clapped his hands in glee, and the owner, Mr. Butt, ran out of one of the houseboats and announced that he had been praying to Allah all morning that Mr. Stevenson would not be able to leave. Stevenson said to him, "But haven't you rented the houseboat to someone else?" Mr. Butt replied, "If I have, I can make arrangements so you can stay here. It is an honor to have 'Your Honor' here."

Stevenson, realizing that the situation was beyond his control, went for a walk to a nearby village.

When he returned, he answered more of his correspondence. Attwood wrote in his diary: "Stevenson was restless about being stuck here and intends to get a car and drive to Jammu tomorrow if the pass is still blocked."

To Carol Evans [20]

May 4, 1953

Dear Carol —

You shame me. But please don't marry a South American or I'll have to move there too.[21] I loved your letter and all the little news. Tomorrow in Delhi I hope to get off a multiple letter to the boys about their summer plans which have me a little baffled. I'll send you a copy — when I get hold of one of those girls in the Embassy whom I'm told want to volunteer their evening services (stenographic!) to their hero.

As for the hero — he's still gaining weight in spite of heat and incessant travel. I seem to travel, however, from one oriental palace and one appalling banquet to another. But I'm not oblivious to the miseries and poverty of the "common people" and when the security police that shadow us permit I drag my protesting companions to the streets and

[20] This handwritten letter is in the possession of Miss Evans.

[21] Miss Evans wrote Stevenson on April 21, 1953, that everyone she talked to seemed to have received a card from him except her. (She had not yet received his letter to her of April 17 from Singapore.) Jokingly she wrote that she had decided to get married and go to South America.

markets. Actually the work load, the interviewing, functions, conferences, writing and ghastly load of pursuing corres. has kept me working every available instant — and I'm having little rest or "vacation" out of it all. But the past 3 days have been heaven — in spite of 46 letters of thanks and postcards and I regret that etc! We're in the vale of Kashmir on a luxurious houseboat (luxury is a wholly relative term in these parts) and we've recovered our health and sanity a bit. We were to fly back to Delhi and the ghastly heat this afternoon — after a long luncheon with Sheik Abdullah — the head of Kashmir — but the plane didn't take off due to hostile weather over the pass out of the Himalayas. So we have another night here — and you have a letter! The "boys" are playing hilarious bridge beside me and mumbling hopes that the weather won't clear and we'll be marooned here beside the Shalimar. As for me, I can't wait to get back to the heat and the journey thru South India!

Its been a great adventure, but perhaps we undertook too much. I don't know. If we live thru it I'll have no regrets — and a head full of confusing thoughts and recollections. As it is I can hardly recall what happened in which country — and never let me say again that the world has shrunk — its altogether too large for my taste.

I hope the checks and my funds are holding out. I get a little homesick now and then, but not very! All the same this pilgrimage should satisfy my wanderlust for a long time to come. Give Phyllis [Gustafson] my best and report when you have a chance on any Springfield gossip. Have you heard, by the way, that Artie sneaks into the Mansion yard early each morning to filch the fine bones set out for that non-wandering proper Republican Great Dane? [22] I hope you found the [Richard Paul] Graebels, Margaret [Munn] and Frances [23] well. Dick would have made a perfect member of this travelling circus and might have helped me keep the boys in order.

I don't know what I'm writing — almost no light, as if that made any difference — and now to bed for my last cool night for weeks and weeks to come.

Yrs
AES

p.s. Give Jane [Dick] my love and thanks for helping out. Bill [Blair] miraculously keeps his health and equilibrium in spite of difficulties & crises beyond belief.

[22] The Chicago *Sun-Times*, May 24, 1953, described King Arthur's daily visits in Springfield, including a ten A.M. stroll by the executive mansion.
[23] Mrs. Frances Ruys, a secretary at the executive mansion during Stevenson's administration.

To Arthur M. Schlesinger, Jr.[24]

[no date]

I thought you might like the portrait of the Rep. administration in search of a new foreign policy.[25] We were delighted with your letter & the analysis of recent Soviet behavior — it puts in better words with more cogent reasons what I have been saying to the Asiatics as we move wearily from country to country. At the moment we're happily marooned by weather in Kashmir! But tomorrow we lift our packs.

AES

After breakfast the next morning, May 5, the pass was clear and the plane was soon flying into the heat of Jammu and Amritsar. When it landed at Delhi, Stevenson stepped out to be greeted by a crowd of Indian and American officials. This arrival at the capital of India was considered by Indian authorities to be the beginning of his "unofficial, official" visit. The government put him up at the president's palace. Delhi's Hindustan Times *said: "As the defeated Presidential candidate he has no official standing in his own country comparable, for instance, to the Leader of the Opposition in Britain, but that he is of Presidential timber has earned for him high regard both at home and abroad so that his views command weight accordingly."* [26]

Stevenson was driven from the airport to meet with Prime Minister Jawaharlal Nehru. Nehru described his six-day trip through a drought-stricken area of India. His mission on such trips, he explained, was to try to educate the people to their responsibilities as citizens in a representative government. Although he described the dust as terrible, he said that he found these trips far more exhilarating than staying in Delhi. When he mentioned that he had made as many as twenty speeches a day, Stevenson asked: "How do you have time to write them?" Nehru threw up his hands and said, "I never write my speeches. I don't have time."

Nehru mentioned that the princely states, which had not been a part of the British Indian government, had been merged into the Indian government in 1947 without any serious problems. The government treated the maharajahs, he added, most generously with a yearly grant

[24] This handwritten postcard is in the Schlesinger papers, John F. Kennedy Library.
[25] The picture on the card was a Buddha contemplating his navel.
[26] Quoted in Shridharani, "Stevenson Charms and Disappoints Delhi," p. 11.

of funds. It might be too generous, he remarked, but it had helped India surmount what otherwise could have been a difficult problem.

Stevenson and Nehru talked briefly about the visit to Kashmir. Nehru stated firmly that India was building a secular state, while in Pakistan Allah was the source of all power. As he left, Nehru clasped Stevenson's hand and with feeling said, "I have looked forward to meeting you for a long, long time." [27]

Stevenson had lunch with Ambassador Allen and some of his staff, including Frazier Wilkins and John Loftus. There was a discussion of the political and economic situation in India and all agreed that a basic question was what would happen to India after Nehru.[28]

That afternoon Stevenson had a lengthy session with the members of India's Planning Commission, including C. D. Deshmukh, the minister of finance, and V. T. Krishnamchari, deputy chairman of the commission. Deshmukh described their five-year plan (in its third year at this point) for economic growth and the percentage of funds they were putting into power projects, irrigation, transportation, agriculture, industrialization, and education. He also discussed the need for foreign investment to carry out the plan. He remarked that India preferred long-term loans from other countries rather than gifts. In the case of the United States, he said, they wanted surpluses like wheat and could repay over a long-term basis.

Stevenson and the ambassador argued with him at this point and said perhaps we should not talk of U.S. surpluses. Instead we should talk in terms of the fact that the U.S. should assist India for "good given reasons." The minister of finance replied, "That's up to you to say, not for us to say why you want to loan us money."

Later that afternoon Stevenson called on the president, Dr. Rajenda Prasad. He discussed in detail the rioting and killing at the time of partition, and observed that the Congress party had reluctantly agreed to partition since the British would not leave until the Congress party and the Moslem League agreed on a plan. He then talked of the some forty million Moslems still living in India and the steps the government had taken to prevent communal troubles. After this meeting, Stevenson called on Vice President Sarvepalli Radhakrishnan.

That evening Stevenson and Barry Bingham dined alone with Nehru. Bingham wrote:

[27] Actually, this was not their first meeting. "The Governor, a few years before in Chicago, had reduced a crowd, including himself and Nehru, to helpless laughter by asking the crowd to remain seated 'until the Prime Minister passes out.'" William McCormick Blair, Jr., "A Dazzling Decade," in *As We Knew Adlai*, p. 238. See also *The Papers of Adlai E. Stevenson*, Vol. III, pp. 181–182.

[28] Nehru died May 27, 1964.

The play of intellect between Stevenson and Nehru was fascinating to observe. Adlai was of course noted for his command of English. Nehru, who was said by Gandhi to have dreamed in English, showed the same delicate grasp of the nuances of the language.

Those two men, from opposite ends of the world, talked as though they had enjoyed an intellectual friendship for decades. Each spoke lucidly and with candor. They were not talking at each other for effect, but striving to communicate ideas as though they had been storing up thoughts for years for this particular occasion.

At one point they fell to talking about the rigors of political campaigning in America. To my surprise, Nehru expressed a positive joy in contact with multitudes of people. Whenever he grew stale and restless from the grind of administrative work, he said, he found that the best tonic was to go out among crowds and refresh himself from their inexhaustible enthusiasm.

Stevenson nodded in complete understanding. Here were two men, both considered almost too civilized for the sweaty business of politics, acknowledging the same feeling of satisfaction in communion with swarms of eager people along the highways and in town squares.[29]

After dinner with Nehru, Stevenson wrote the following letter.

To Mrs. Edison Dick [30]

May 5, 1953

. . . What a day! I'm back in Delhi after our lyric interlude beside the Shalimar in the vale of Kashmir and find your Jakarta and subsequent report from the home front — together with the evidence that the graphic arts people did justice to "Whistle Stopping" and the "client" [31] — shameful word for Katherine Mansfield Dick! [32] Thanks — and thanks again!

Our return from the enchanted vale was delayed by weather overnight and I arrived at 1 — in time to lunch with the new Ambassador and his staff, call on the Prime Minister, the President, the Vice President, visit Old Delhi, see the Mosque and the Red Fort and dine alone

---

29 "With Adlai in Asia," in *As We Knew Adlai*, pp. 195–196.

30 This handwritten letter is in the possession of Mrs. Dick.

31 Mrs. Dick's book on her experiences in the 1952 presidential campaign, *Whistle Stopping with Adlai*, was selected by the American Society of Graphic Arts as one of the fifty best books (for format) of 1953. In the award she was referred to as the "client."

32 Mrs. Dick admired and owned a collection of the writings of Katherine Mansfield.

with Nehru — 2½ hrs of talk — and what talk! Surely here *is* a remarkable man — and then I think of [Senator Joseph] McCarthy, [Senator Styles] Bridges, [Senator John] Bricker — and even some Democrats! And now it's 11 and I am back in my room in the utterly fantastic Residence the British built for their Viceroys — air conditioned, a bed 10 feet wide, literally, silver fittings, chandeliers, Roman bath tub. Ho Hum I wonder how I made do in that Executive Mansion so long!

Tomorrow we are off at 7 AM to visit a village project and the next day we leave for Madras and south India for several days, returning here before going on to Pakistan.

God, it's late and I'm tired, and here's Bill [Blair] with 50 more letters! Au revoir — forgive this scrawl but I had to let you know where I was staying!! . . .

The next morning Stevenson, Ambassador Allen, and Horace Holmes, of the Point Four program, drove out of Delhi some eighty-five miles to visit the community village project at Nilokheri. Stevenson was taken first to a squalid village where no development had been undertaken. After that he visited the community project where new plows were turning up the sun-baked earth, wells were being dug, and small industries were being developed. About noon, after he had been tramping in the 110-degree sun for over two hours, he saw a rustic cot in a farmhouse and confessed to the farmer that he wished he had time for a nap on it.

At noon he sat down to an extremely heavy lunch on a stifling day. Horace Holmes discussed the pressing needs for land reform to give the farmer security, a greater return to farmers for their labors, and credit at reasonable rates of interest.

The drive back to New Delhi was so hot that the windows in the automobiles were kept closed (the automobiles were not air-conditioned) since the outside air was more stifling than the air inside.

When he reached the embassy, Stevenson talked with John Loftus and Frazier Wilkins. Wilkins said that he explained Nehru's emphasis on a neutral foreign policy because India was so close to China and, secondly, he wanted to concentrate on solving India's economic problems. According to Wilkins, Nehru had told Ambassador Chester Bowles that he knew China was "dangerously aggressive," but he would not say this publicly since he did not want to be drawn into the East-West conflict.

Stevenson mentioned that the previous evening he had attempted to get Nehru to talk about China and the Vietminh move into Laos, but

Nehru had simply replied that it was unthinkable to him the Chinese would precipitate a world war, because of the great internal tasks facing the country.

Stevenson reported that Nehru also felt China wanted to get its troops out of Korea because China did not want to become more indebted to the Soviet Union. While they had not gained anything from the conflict, Nehru thought that China had entered the fighting because it gave them an appeal to unite China and demand that all the people work together, and furthermore, that they had entered when they did because they considered the crossing of the 38th parallel by United States troops a threat to their security.

Stevenson added that Nehru put great faith in a split between China and Russia and had stated: "It is inconceivable to me that Mao Tse-tung will accept the position of being a satellite." Furthermore, Nehru said that he did not think the Chinese Communists had sinister ambitions in Southeast Asia.

Nehru then told Stevenson that the Indian Communists were under firm control. Mr. Wilkins agreed with this and said that Nehru had been "absolutely ruthless" toward domestic Communists. The Indian Communists, Wilkins continued, were working through certain state governments and were waiting for distintegration to take place in India.

Both Wilkins and Loftus warned that if the economic situation deteriorated and food shortages continued, communal difficulties could develop, and communal troubles, they warned, could lead to fanaticism. Kashmir could explode at any time. Nehru alone held the country together, they insisted.

Stevenson said that Nehru had told him that he had to hold the Congress party together, try and stir officials to get reforms, and, at the same time, administer the government. Since land reform was the province of the state governments, all he could do "was to prod the states into action." When Stevenson asked Nehru about young leaders who might be emerging, Nehru shook his head and said, "Yes, we must bring up such leaders for the future."

Stevenson went on to say that Vice President Radhakrishnan had spoken not only of the need for land reform but equally of the need for educational reform. Higher education, he pointed out, trained students in the liberal arts but not in engineering, business administration, and other vocational subjects. Most university graduates wanted to enter government service, but the government could not absorb them. India was training, he concluded, "too many useless people."

After the discussion at the embassy, the ambassador held a recep-

tion in Stevenson's honor. Later that evening he had time to dictate several letters.

To Adlai, Borden, and John Fell Stevenson

May 7, 1953

Dear Boys:

I am in New Delhi after a few days in the beautiful vale of Kashmir, and find Borden's cable and John Fell's letter. I assume by this time that you have received the new itinerary from Miss [Carol] Evans. If not, here it is: Egypt May 27–June 1; Lebanon (Beirut), June 1–3; Syria, June 3–4; Jordan, June 5–6; Israel, June 7–11; Cypress, June 11–14; Istanbul, June 15–18; Athens, June 18–20; Rome, June 21–27; Belgrade, June 27–July 2.

I have made no plans beyond the travel to Yugoslavia, but from there will probably go to Austria and then to Germany, Paris, London and home in time to see Adlai before he goes to the West Coast.[33] Just when that is, I don't know, but obviously it would be difficult to get home at the earliest before the first of August with this schedule.

I have just sent a cable to Borden, suggesting that he meet me in Israel, on the assumption that he is still planning to go to England in time for the Coronation with Aunt Mary Spears or Aunt Betty.[34] If not, he could travel about with his friends or join the Ives' until I arrive in Israel. I will write Borden again as promptly as possible just where I will be, but he would have little trouble finding me and can always communicate to any of these places care of the American Embassy. . . . I trust Borden has also made arrangements or has some idea what he will do in Europe after I leave for home around the end of July.

About John Fell, I shall merely express my disappointment about his French, and the word I have from Mr. Shirk [35] is that he seems more interested in cars than his work. However, I know he will try as hard as he can. I am not sure he should come abroad because he gives me no information about what he plans to do except to travel with me for the short time I will be there. Have any arrangements been made about living with a French family through the Experiment for International Living? Or is he planning to stay with his friend Ames [36] in London? At

[33] Adlai III had been commissioned a second lieutenant in the United States Marine Corps on September 20, 1952. He was scheduled to report to the West Coast for assignment to Korea about the end of July.

[34] Mrs. Ralph Hines of New York, Ellen Stevenson's sister.

[35] Allan F. Sherk, a history teacher and John Fell's housemaster at Milton Academy.

[36] John S. Ames III, later John Fell's roommate at Harvard University, whose father was with the U.S. embassy in London.

this distance I am a little bewildered. However, if his mother has carefully considered the situation and all are agreed that he should come, I suppose he should meet us in Rome between June 21 and 27. I am not sure that I want to take him to Yugoslavia in view of travel and other difficulties there, but he could travel about Italy with the Ives', and perhaps meet me in Vienna July 3 or thereabouts.

I do not know what the boys are doing about passports, visas and so forth, but I am sure they could get some help from Dorothy Fosdick.[37] I think it imperative that both Borden and John Fell call Aunt Buffy in Southern Pines to coordinate their plans with her. If John Fell should decide not to come, I remind him that I will be in Libertyville from about the first of August and he could go off with me to Desbarats or somewhere for a holiday — which I will sorely need if I survive this appalling journey!

Both the boys should bring grey flannels, jackets, and Borden at least should have evening clothes, white dinner jacket, if he wants to go with me to some of the interminable parties that seem to be strewn in my path. Little else is needed besides shirts and strong shoes for a lot of walking. If we go off for a holiday, a rough pair of pants, sport shirt and bathing trunks will be needed.

I apologize for this disorderly letter which I am writing in great haste, with the difficult schedule I seem to have all the time.

I was delighted to hear from Aunt Buffy, about her triumphant journey through North Carolina, and that the news from Tim [Ives] is good. I am also so glad to hear that Adlai has found so many friends in Louisville [38] and seems to be prospering. My journey is fascinating and exhausting. I dined with Nehru alone and talked with him for a couple of hours, and so it goes from place to place. We leave in the morning for South India and the heat is shocking. All day today we have been inspecting a village project so many miles from Delhi, a most interesting trip in spite of the ghastly heat. Now I must be off to the inevitable reception at the Embassy, and I apologize for this hasty and disorderly letter. Love to you all and I look forward impatiently to seeing you in another month.

John Fell need have no worry about "seeing things." If anything, he would see too much!

[37] Daughter of the famous preacher Harry Emerson Fosdick and a good friend of Stevenson. She was then with the Department of State, Washington, D.C.
[38] Adlai III became engaged to Nancy Anderson, daughter of Mr. and Mrs. Warwick Anderson, of Louisville, Kentucky, in September, 1954.

To Estes Kefauver

May 7, 1953

Dear Estes:

Thanks so much for your letter of April 18 and the enclosure. I shall try to see the gentleman [39] if and when I get to Germany. In my present state of exhaustion, I have some misgivings as to whether I will get out of India!

It has been a fascinating and profitable journey, and I have seen and learned much, but I shall be more than ready for home if it ever ends!

I hope all goes well with you and I wish I had more news of the Senate and the Democratic Party. I'm afraid somebody will have to listen long and patiently to a recital of my tiresome adventures when I get home.

With warmest regards,

Cordially yours,

While in New Delhi, Stevenson received a letter from Mrs. John Currie, of Great Barrington, Massachusetts. [40] *Mrs. Currie wrote: "You think your name is strange. Mine is Bethia. . . . Thanks to your honored grandfather you have at least the comfort of knowing that there are other Adlai's. I have yet to meet another Bethia. I derive some consolation from the thought that I may be the last." She also mentioned that her husband had just told her that he intended to sue Stevenson for alienation of affections "if he manages to make it back here without tripping over that 6 foot blowpipe and fracturing his parang." She added she was enclosing a check for $9.61. She had wanted to send him $10.00 for a limited edition of* Major Campaign Speeches of Adlai E. Stevenson, *but her husband had said, "Do him a* real *favor, wait until the book is remaindered next month at the corner drug store for 39 cents and send him the difference. He can apply it to the Democratic National Committee debt or use it to help defray freight charges on that damned blowpipe."*

---

[39] Not known to whom Stevenson refers.

[40] Stevenson did not know Mrs. Currie or her husband at this time. Mrs. Currie later worked for Stevenson's nomination for President in 1956.

To Mrs. John Currie [41]

[no date]

My dear <u>Bethia</u> L.S. <u>Currie</u> —

Oh you poor, wretched unfortunate. I weep for a Bethia — or is that perspiration! But why don't we form a club for name malcontents? All Americans think of organizing something — especially malcontents — so why don't we? With that Bethia you are clearly entitled to the Presidency and Adlai will modestly accept the Vice Presidency — on your acclamation. Besides I've learned to accept philosophically something less than the top, and perhaps you haven't been exposed to such rude indignities. What's more the National Association of Dissatisfied Monikers (sp?) (*You* might be able to improve that title) has a balance in the treasury of $9.61 — which will make it easy to attract a good Executive Secretary. There are a lot of Indians with distressing names that will apply — particularly if there is even a visitor's visa in it. And think of the potential political power in such another group of malcontents — with enormous branches in all of Asia!

Well I could go on and on — and usually do, particularly to such suffering and kindred mortals as *Bethias* married to *Johns*. But enough — you have the idea and the misfortune. Meanwhile I am depositing your gracious and inspiring check — to all except the publishers of my book — in the fund for fractured Democratic parangs!

Yrs.

On May 7 Stevenson, Blair and Bingham left New Delhi for a visit to Madras, Trivandrum, and Bombay. [42]

En route to Madras, he wrote the following letter:

To Mrs. Edison Dick [43]

May 7, 1953

Somehow I can't seem to find time, strength or talent to properly compensate you for your good letters on the state of the Union. I was interrupted and will be again presently when this airplane lands in Hyderabad and I have to go thru the inevitable formalities and press

[41] This handwritten letter is in the possession of Mrs. Currie. It was written on the stationery of the president's residence, New Delhi. The envelope was postmarked Washington, D.C., May 16, 1953. It apparently was sent by embassy pouch to the Department of State and posted in Washington.

[42] The description of this trip is based on notes kept by Barry Bingham, a copy of which is in the possession of Walter Johnson.

[43] This handwritten letter is in the possession of Mrs. Dick.

conference — even autographs again. We're en route to Madras across the endless red, grey, brown barren expanse of India, over the myriad villages and ruins of cities and civilizations that have long since had their hour and passed away — even as this one will which they and we too are struggling so desperately to strengthen.

All India looks pretty much alike to me, physically, at least so far, and all of it trembles in this pitiless sun! Now Hyderabad — it will be at least 110°. . . .

It was 112! And now Madras is next. Flying over Hyderabad the Indian pilot pointed out the Nizam's palaces — including the one "where he keeps the veemens!" . . .

How are you doing with the second draft of the Perils of Publicity? [44] Could it be that my vision of your daily struggle with the most killing prose of the century is inaccurate?

I wish I could think of something really interesting to say in a few lines and the balance of this page, but I'm full of so much of such a variety that there's no starting, let alone stopping — but where was it that the two elderly Am[erican] tourist gals stopped me to proudly announce that they, or one of them, knew Mrs. Dick of Chicago. I think it was the airport in Srinigar, and I think I kissed her!

My shopping has been scandalous — with no time & no patience or imagination or list of presents or taste — I've charged into a few stores and seized the first thing in sight, much to the discomfiture and bewilderment of Bill [Blair], who by the way, maintains his equilibrium and performs mammoth feats of management of this circus every day. What a man he is. Poor Attwood has been perpetually ill & Johnson not too well. We've left both behind in Delhi and Bingham and Blair were against it [45] — but the old man came to see and by God he's going to see!! I don't know what the children's plans are but cabled Borden yesterday. Unless he has something worth while to do I'm not sure JF [John Fell] should come.

In Madras, Stevenson had a lengthy conversation with C. R. Rajago-palachari, chief minister of the state and a powerful leader of the Congress party.[46] *The chief minister told Stevenson that the future of India hung on "hope, if not faith and charity." In the struggle for independence, he said, the aspirations of the various language groups in the country were exploited to achieve national sentiment against*

[44] See note 30 to Chapter One.
[45] The trip to South India.
[46] He was the first Indian to be governor general of India. Before Nehru's death he left the Congress party.

Great Britain. The Congress party had promised the major language groups that state boundaries would be drawn along linguistic lines. Now, he added, there was a growing demand that this be implemented and "the Indian Communists are exploiting the issue."

Political consciousness developed in India, he told Stevenson, mainly as hatred of foreign rule, but it had not yet progressed to a strong sense of civic duty and responsibility. Since the great religions of India all shared the teaching of service, unselfishness, and detachment, he concluded, religious faith could be harnessed for the benefit of a good society.

In Trivandrum, Stevenson talked to A. J. John, chief minister of the state of Travancore-Cochin,[47] *and P. G. Menon, minister of finance and industries. They discussed the overpopulation of the Malabar Coast and the widespread unemployment. Young people and intellectuals were frustrated, they remarked, and in a ready mood to listen to Communist appeals.*

Stevenson also talked to K. P. N. Pillai, speaker of the unicameral legislature of the state. (As a Socialist, he had received Congress party backing for election as speaker.) He stated that the only real issue between the Socialists and the Congress party was over land reform. His party wanted immediate action, but the Congress party leaders were advocating gradualism since funds were not available to provide compensation to the owners. He also criticized the central government in Delhi for failing to understand the severe economic problems of **Travancore-Cochin** *and for locating various types of factories elsewhere instead of in the state.*

After Stevenson called on the mayor of Trivandrum, the mayor introduced him to a large crowd that had gathered to greet him. When the mayor welcomed him on behalf of the common people of Travancore-Cochin, Stevenson answered laughingly: "We of the Democratic party also speak for the common people back home, and I have great pleasure in making all you good people of Trivandrum honorary members of the Democratic party." A reporter present wrote: "At this the crowd roared with enthusiasm and laughter." The local Communist party leader was overheard saying: "Dash it all! First we have [Ambassador] Bowles to contend with; then Mrs. Roosevelt had to come here — now we have Stevenson. And they're all so dashed human and attractive that it undoes months of propaganda on our part." [48]

[47] When the Indian states were reorganized, Travencore-Cochin became part of what is now Kerala.

[48] Oliver Pirie, "Sir, You Are in Solid Democratic Territory!" *New Republic,* June 15, 1953, p. 10. "Oliver Pirie represents five journalists who followed Stevenson

In the evening, colorful scenes from the epic dance-drama Ramajana *were performed for Stevenson.*

According to Oliver Pirie, word of Stevenson's informality and good humor spread through the city. As a result, "Wherever he went huge crowds watched him with wide eyes." [49]

While on the Malabar Coast, Stevenson had one day for rest, sight-seeing, swimming, and writing postcards to old friends.

To Mr. and Mrs. Ivan Elliott [50]

[no date]

My dear Elliotts —

It has been a fabulous journey and I'm as tired as I was during the campaign. But we carried all of Asia! I hope things are well with you and the boys. I still yearn for Springfield and all our troubles — even after swimming this afternoon in the Arabian sea on the Malabar coast of S W India — much to the astonishment of the Moslem fishermen!

Yrs

ADLAI

To the Reverend and Mrs. Richard Paul Graebel [51]

[no date]

My conclusions so far? 1. The world is too big. 2. Everybody wants to eat and sleep a little every day. 3. I sympathize with all of 'em. I want a glass of cold milk! At the moment I am on the Malabar coast of S.W. India — beautiful, impoverished and hot — and the largest Christian and communist population in India. St. Thomas passed this way and the missionaries in the second century. But I must stop!

ADLAI

In Bombay, Stevenson had a long talk with Morarji Desai, chief minister of Bombay State. [52] *Desai spoke most forcefully against the creation of linguistic states, remarking that there were four languages in Bombay State alone. He discussed the critical food shortages in*

in his Indian travels and whose collective efforts and separate reports are combined in this article." Ibid.

[49] Ibid., p. 11.

[50] Mr. Elliott was attorney general of Illinois during Stevenson's governorship. This handwritten postcard is in the possession of Mr. Elliott.

[51] This handwritten postcard is in the possession of Mr. Graebel.

[52] Nehru later made Desai minister of finance in the central government. Under Mrs. Indira Gandhi, he became deputy prime minister.

Bombay, the state government's rationing of food and the role of state-owned stores in the disaster areas selling food at cost. He spoke of plans for increased industrialization and described how his government had banned cows from roaming the streets. The government built stables in an underdeveloped area and sent all the cows there. It was now the largest dairy center in Asia, Desai observed. He explained that there had been serious religious objection to the banishing of cows from streets, but he said that he had convinced ardent Hindus that it was necessary.

Stevenson also spent considerable time with Frank Moraes, editor of the Times of India.[53] Moraes remarked that while the success of the five-year plan for economic development was important, it had to be realized that the impact of it on the average citizen would be slow, for while China had reorganized its economic system through force and violence, India could not proceed that way. There had to be a revolution through persuasion — the price of a democratic form of government. He also talked of the need of cultivating a "dirty-hands mentality" among Indian leaders. Educated people, he explained, were not willing to soil their hands with manual labor.

On May 12, Stevenson left Bombay for Delhi.[54] A columnist in the Times of India observed: "Mr. Stevenson, touring India, continues to leave behind a trail of happy phrases. . . . The underlying earnestness and humility of the man gives his utterances a natural nobility." [55]

Soon after Stevenson returned to Delhi on May 12, he met with two leading members of the Socialist party, Mr. and Mrs. Acharya J. B. Kripalani. They discussed the need of redistributing the land and the

[53] Moraes later wrote that Stevenson's "quick lively mind and nimble wit had impressed those who had encountered him" in India in 1953. *Yonder One World: A Study of Asia and the West* (New York: Macmillan, 1958), p. 187.

[54] While Stevenson, Blair and Bingham were in South India, Attwood and/or Johnson interviewed a number of people, including Lakshmi Jain of the Indian Cooperative Union; D. R. Mankekar, editor of the Delhi edition of the *Times of India;* Dr. S. P. Mookerjee, head of the Hindu Jan Sangh party; Harin Shah, editor of the *Indian Worker,* the paper of the Indian National Trade Union Congress; C. G. K. Reddy, a Socialist member of the Council of State — the upper house of Parliament; Hiren Mukerjee, a leading Communist member of the House of the People — the lower house of Parliament; Selig Harrison of the Associated Press; Henry Sokolove, Jack Curran and Wesley Adams, members of the embassy staff; Donald L. Ensminger, director of the Ford Foundation program in India; Prem Bhatia, correspondent for the *Statesman* (New Delhi), New York architect Albert Mayer, adviser to the state government of Uttar Pradesh on planning village community projects; Madam Vijayalakshmi Pandit, Nehru's sister and president of the United Nations Assembly, 1953–1954; Dr. V. K. R. V. Rao, director of the School of Economics, Delhi University; and Y. K. Puri of the Pakistan desk of the Indian Foreign Office.

[55] Quoted in Shridharani, "Stevenson Charms and Disappoints Delhi," p. 11.

ending of landlordism. Mr. Kripalani, who had been close to Gandhi and once had been a highly respected member of the Congress party, emphasized that the fundamental difference between the Congress party and the Socialists was over industrialization. The Socialists favored, he said, a decentralized industry while the Congress wanted centralization of control. He then complained that the Congress party talked about overcoming poverty and ending corruption in government but "it does not act." They both stated they favored nationalization of banks, insurance companies, oil, and coal. Stevenson interjected, "You will never get needed foreign capital on those terms."

After this discussion, Stevenson visited the Parliament building and had tea with some hundred members of the legislature. Dinner that evening was at the prime minister's home with some forty people present. After dinner Nehru, Stevenson, Ambassador Allen, and several cabinet ministers withdrew for an hour of conversation.

Ambassador Allen wrote:

. . . When we entered the room Nehru motioned to Adlai to sit at one end of the long sofa and me to the other end. He sat between. In front of the sofa was a low coffee-type table on which a copy of the *New Statesman* was lying open, ostentatiously so, it seemed to me. Soon after we sat down, Nehru picked up the magazine (the *New Statesman* was his favorite periodical) and, turning to Adlai, commented that he had just seen a further evidence that Winston Churchill was the greatest master of the English language alive today. He pointed to a quotation in an article he had been reading, and read the quote to the group. It was an eloquent plea for peace and quoted the number of school buildings, hospitals, orphanages, etc. which could be built for the cost of one modern battleship. He dropped the magazine back on the table with something of a flourish, commenting again that Churchill was matchless in phraseology.

I thought I recognized the quote as he read it but did not wish to interrupt the flow of conversation and waited until Nehru was turned fullface toward Adlai before putting on my glasses and picking up the magazine to examine the quote closer. At the end of the quote was an asterisk, and the footnote at the bottom of the page stated that it was a quote from President Eisenhower's inaugural address delivered on January 20. The situation was rather awkward for me because I knew that Nehru considered the Republican victory in the recent elections as something of a catastrophe for India. Moreover, while he had not met Eisenhower personally, he was predisposed to dislike him, partly because he had been elected on the Republican ticket but chiefly because he was a military man.

I did not believe, nevertheless, that I could let Nehru's attribution of Ike's phraseology to Churchill go unnoticed. After a few minutes, when Adlai was talking with [Minister of Defense] Ayanger, I handed the magazine to Nehru and asked him to read the small print in the footnote. He fished for his glasses, with some indication of petulance, and read it. He looked back at the quotation and then again at the footnote to make certain that it referred to the quote he had read. After this careful scanning he tossed the magazine on the table and said with obvious annoyance, "Well, I'm dashed! I took it for granted that it was Churchill."

Adlai was still talking to the other Ministers and was not aware of what was going on. I made no further mention of it until we had left the Prime Minister's residence. Adlai got a good laugh out of it. . . .[56]

At 8:30 the next morning Stevenson placed a wreath at Gandhi's tomb. A few minutes later he met with the entire staff of the embassy. In introducing him, Ambassador Allen said: "If the 360 million Indians had been able to vote in our last election, there wouldn't have been any doubt of the outcome. Sir, you are in solid Democratic territory." Stevenson responded: "The ambassador's remarks have confirmed the impression that I should have run for office here, but I am loath to report that nobody in India suggested that."

After his brief talk, Stevenson went off to tour the Red Fort built by the Moghul emperors. He also visited the Pusa Agricultural Institute and the National Physical Laboratory. That afternoon he had a meeting with Ragavan Pillai, the secretary general of the Ministry of External Affairs. Stevenson told him that there were three issues that disturbed Americans: one was Kashmir; the second was the question of water distribution between Pakistan and India; and the third was the neutralist foreign policy of India.

The minister replied that only the prime ministers of the two countries could solve the Kashmiri question. He added that legally the maharajah had acceded to India, and, as a result, Pakistan had no right to have any troops there at all. Prior to a plebiscite, the minister stated, India insisted that Pakistan must withdraw her troops.

He stated that there was no real issue over water since there was plenty for both countries. The fundamental problem, he added, in relations with Pakistan was that fanatic exponents of Islam had too much power in that country. He expressed the belief that the new Pakistani prime minister, Mohammed Ali, wanted to settle the outstanding problems.

[56] Letter to Walter Johnson, July 7, 1967.

When he began to discuss India's foreign policy, Stevenson said, "I argued a long while with the prime minister that neutralism was the wrong word to describe your foreign policy. You feel that you do not want to be caught in the East-West power conflict." Stevenson added that India was "not neutral, you are uncommitted."

The minister replied, "You are absolutely right. We want time to tackle our own economic problems. But if the conflict comes, there is no doubt that we are anti-Soviet." He pointed out that India had practically no trade with China or the Soviet Union but cautioned: "Remember that Indians are sensitive and they resent infringements on their sovereignty and they do not like pressure to have them say we will not trade with China or the Soviet Union at all."

Stevenson replied, "I understand your feeling on this matter and perhaps the United States has been too quick to shout at others on this issue."

The minister said India was irritated with the United States on a number of issues. "We feel that you support colonialism in Indochina." And, he charged, the British were suppressing the rights of Indians in that part of Africa under their control. "We feel, of course, that you are responsible indirectly since you support Great Britain." He closed the discussion by observing: "Ambassador Bowles brought a great spirit here to India."

After this meeting, Stevenson attended a debate in the House of the People as to the respective powers of the House and the Council of States. Following the debate, he held a crowded press conference.[57]

Gentlemen and ladies:

I ask leave, if I might, to say just a few words in advance of your questions. I would like to take this opportunity to express in the presence of all of you my profound gratitude to the Prime Minister and to the Indian Government for all of the courtesies and the hospitality that they have extended to me during my brief visit to India.

Never before have I, nor do I expect anyone else has, enjoyed such graciousness, and such thoughtfulness and such anxiety to make my journey so easy, convenient and comfortable as the Indian Government has made mine, and I am deeply grateful.

I should also like to say that in the limited time that I have been

[57] The United States Information Service transcribed the press conference. A mimeograph copy is in the possession of Walter Johnson. Robert Trumbull wrote a lengthy dispatch about the press conference. See the New York *Times,* May 14, 1953.

here I have been able to travel across a good deal of India, from Calcutta to Delhi, from Kashmir to Travancore-Cochin. Although I haven't been able to see by any means as much as we would have liked to see, we have seen enough, I think, to be very much impressed with the effort that India is making to take full advantage of its opportunities to make real the independence and the hopes for peace and prosperity which it has earned and deserves. I have had some occasion to see some of the tangible aspects of the Five Year Plan. While I don't minimize the difficulties that India confronts for want of money, because of its enormous population, etc., on the whole I think that the progress is impressive and I for one have been very much gratified by what I have found here. I shall not elaborate on that and if you have any questions that you wish to ask me I suggest that we proceed now.

Q: Would you say how far the U.S. foreign policy is bipartisan?

A: I'm afraid I can't. I have been away from the United States since the first of March; that was only a short while after the inauguration of the new Administration, and I don't know what consultative committees have been appointed, if any, and I am really afraid I am not competent to answer that question accurately. I am sure that there is an anxiety on the part of the new Administration to establish bipartisanship in the conduct of our foreign affairs. To what extent it has implemented that desire and by what means, I don't know.

Q: You are reported as saying that the Vietminh attack on Laos was aggression against an independent nation.[58] Are you correctly reported and do you believe that the people of Laos are free?

A: Perhaps I should have said that "as a result of some agreements which were reached in Paris, the States of Indochina have some measure of independence and more contemplated for the future." Something like that. I don't know how to elaborate it.

Q: Do you think that some kind of proclamation by France that she will transfer full power as soon as possible after the cessation of hostilities would help in mobilizing resistance to the Communist attack?

A: Yes. I do feel that that would be helpful and I have so written in an article that has been or will be published in the United States.[59] I wrote it some six weeks or two months ago. I think it would be very desirable if the French would clarify the situation, and make a statement amplifying their intended position for the future. I hope they will do that.

[58] Stevenson had made this statement in Calcutta.
[59] Probably a reference to "Ballots and Bullets," *Look,* June 2, 1953.

Q: It is reported that you had two meetings with Sheikh Abdullah.

A: I had three. (Laughter) I had lunch with him twice and I had a separate conference.

Q: In the press only two were reported.

A: Maybe that is because the first two followed in such rapid succession. There was only time for me to go and spend some of my hard earned money buying shawls of Kashmir, etc. . . . (laughter).

Q: Will you tell us something of what transpired between you and Sheikh Abdullah? [60]

A: I am not an old politician but I am old enough for that one. No, sir. I don't mean to be evasive, I merely mean to say that when talking to the responsible Chief of State I have always followed the practice that he should quote himself. We discussed the Kashmir question.[61]

Q: In what direction do you think the solution to the Kashmir problem lies?

A: I would be very bold indeed if I thought I had found a solution to the Kashmir question, and I haven't. But I think step number one would be consultations and conferences between the Chiefs of State of India and Pakistan directly, Prime Minister Nehru and Prime Minister Ali. I think discussions should be in a spirit of goodwill and

[60] This question was asked by a Pakistani reporter.

[61] In August, 1953, Abdullah was arrested and jailed. Prime Minister Nehru stated that this was necessary in "the interest of the peace of the state, which was threatened in various ways." Abdullah's successor, Bakshi Ghulam Mohammed, accused "interested foreign powers" of having encouraged Abdullah to talk in terms of creating an independent state.

Soon it was charged that Stevenson had conspired with Abdullah. One writer asserted, "It seems that Delhi concurrence in the *coup d'etat* was made possible by an accidental tactlessness of Adlai Stevenson, who said on his arrival in Kashmir that he had come purely as a tourist and then spent virtually his whole time closeted with Sheikh Abdullah talking about independence."

When Stevenson heard about these charges, he cabled a message to Ambassador George V. Allen on August 15, 1953, for transmittal to the Indian government:

"I neither had nor expressed any views in my discussions with Sheik Abdullah, which were my first in Indian Kashmir. I recall perfectly his partiality for India and his casual suggestion that independent status might be an alternative solution. I am not sure on this point, but I believe he was referring to all except Azad Kashmir (one section of the state).

"I also believe I conveyed my impressions of his attitude to Prime Minister Nehru, who asked me if I had seen Abdullah. I could not have given Abdullah even unconscious encouragement re independence, which did not seem to me realistic and made little impression. I was listening, not talking, and was most interested at that time in why the United Nations plebiscite did not go forward."

For newspaper accounts, see *Manchester Guardian Weekly,* September 3, 1953; Robert Trumbull, New York *Times,* August 30, 1953, Section 4, p. 5; Taya Zinkin, Manchester *Guardian,* September 22, 1953.

general anxiety to resolve this issue and I think that it presents nothing that is insoluble and that it could be resolved. I should hope also that such a meeting might result in a declaration of some kind that this is a soluble problem between neighbors who are destined to live here for centuries to come side by side, and that if they join in a common resolution they will resolve all of their difficulties present and future without recourse to war.

Q: To clarify your statement: do you think there should be a joint declaration of the two governments that under no circumstances they would resort to war.

A: I don't know whether it is joint or several . . . ??? I said I thought step number one would be [interrupted].

Q: Yes, but what is step number two?

A: I don't know, sir. If I did I don't know if I could answer it in any brief space of time at a press conference. I don't know too much about it. I have tried to educate myself but I don't feel at liberty to draw any conclusions now.

Q: Have you any comment to make on the statement by [Prime Minister Clement] Attlee that there is an element in America that does not want peace in America?

A: If there is such an element I don't know about it. I have never encountered it and I don't know where it lives. I would like to get the address.

Q: He said elements.

A: They have never come to my attention. It may be. I didn't read what Mr. Attlee said but it may be that he was not saying that there are elements who don't want peace but that there are those who fear that peace might result in economic depression in the U.S. I'm not sure, but wasn't it probably the latter? I just can't believe that there is anyone in the United States who doesn't want peace in Korea. Wait. There might be people who would feel, and I am speaking of the Chinese community, that it would be better to go on fighting in Korea. I don't know what Mr. Attlee meant but I can assure you that the great majority of the American people that I have had contact with are most eager and hopeful for peace in Korea.

Q: He said that there was a strong influence of the Chiang Kai-shek element in America. [Question not clearly understood.] [Repeated]

A: There may be. I haven't had any intimate traffic with them.

Q: He also advocated that there should be spokesmen from other countries represented in these discussions at Panmunjom. What is your reaction?

A: Well, I don't know why there shouldn't be others. Have others asked to be included? I think that there was an agreement that was reached some two years ago at the time of the initiation of the first armistice talks that the UN would be represented by the US and that North Korea and China would be represented by North Korea. If it should be modified, I have no objection.

Q: Do you now feel in retrospect that you did not play up Korea enough in your election campaign?

A: Are you asking me do I think I made a mistake? (Laughter) Is this a confessional? On the assumption that the press are not present I would say that probably I made a mistake from the point of view of winning the election. From the point of view of my own satisfaction as to how it should be won, I did not make a mistake.[62]

Q: Do you think that the changes in the military high command in the United States are the effect of the change of policy, or that they might involve a change of policy.

A: I think that it came about by virtue of the approaching retirement or expiration of the period of appointment of the existing Chiefs of Staff. I believe that perhaps someone here could inform me — when does General [Omar] Bradley's term expire? In the summer sometime? I do not think it was made for the purpose of making any change of policy. As to whether or not it does foretell a change in policy, I can't answer that. I don't see any reason why it should, from what little I know of General [Alfred] Gruenther and [Matthew B.] Ridgway. I can't say to you that it bears any indication of any alteration.

Q: Why is it that America is such a misunderstood country abroad?

[62] Stevenson wrote in his introduction to the volume of his 1952 campaign speeches: "In early August I decided, if elected, to make a quick journey to Japan, Korea and India 'to see for myself,' meet the people with whom I would have to deal, and to give the best possible evidence of our profound concern for the Orient. We kept the plan secret, fearful that it might be construed as a political gesture. This may have been a mistake, and while I cannot approve the General's speech or the misleading use that was made of it, I think he did the right thing to go out there and that we will all benefit from his first-hand information. I only wish that time and circumstances had permitted him to travel farther." *Major Campaign Speeches of Adlai E. Stevenson, 1952* (New York: Random House, 1953), p. xxvii.

A: At the end of this press conference *I* had hoped to conduct a press conference at which I was going to ask *you* that question. I am sorry to say I can't contribute any useful information in response to your question. I do know that that is often the case and I deplore it. I think it probably springs in part from a whole lot of acts, but you should know better than I what they are. You look at us from the outside; I see us from within. I think one of the things is the fact that we are uninhibited in public debate and in the conduct of our public affairs and there is a price you have to pay for freedom of speech. I might say freedom sometimes ad nauseam. Perhaps that is one thing. Another thing I suspect is the impression that has grown up around the world that all the United States is interested in — largely because it falls to our lot — not a lot we asked for or enjoy — that we become in effect the restorer and defender of the balance of power in the world; a role which was fulfilled in a large measure for a hundred years by Great Britain. In undertaking this responsible and difficult task, we necessarily had to take the initiative in a lot of things and have made mistakes. Therefore we have to suffer the consequences. Perhaps also we have not always put our best foot forward in expressing the deeper purity of our motives which has sometimes been obscured by the expediency of our motives. I hope I am not being too ambiguous. Now you make ready to answer the questions I have to ask you.

Q: How far is Senator McCarthy and his activities supported by the American public in general?

A: This is an awkward question to ask me. Now if his activities relate to hunting out subversives, disloyal people and that sort of thing to which he has not contributed perceptibly although he has talked incontinently, I would think he is widely supported. Not McCarthy as an individual, but the objective, because we have found as every nation does I suppose at one time or another, that there have been disloyal persons in our government and in responsible positions. In that respect, I suppose — I am trying to speak very objectively about this matter — he has the support of a great many people. When it comes to his means, guilt by association, irresponsible accusations and methods of that kind, I don't believe he has any widespread support in the United States. The only reason that he appears to do so is that the ends that he purports to have in view are approved. Now I might say, off the record, that that is a triumph of gentleness, tolerance, Christianity, Hinduism, or whatever you want to call it. (Laughter)

Q: What are your reactions to Mr. Churchill's proposal for a Big Power Conference? [63]

A: I can only say here what I have said before on many occasions and that is that I think we should always keep the door open, and wide, for consultation and negotiation with a view to the peaceful resolution of the conflicts that divide and torment the world. Therefore, I view the suggestion favorably. In other words, I would agree with him but I would have to say this at the same time, and I daresay he would too, although I haven't read his statement: that the world should not anticipate that such a Four Power conference would necessarily result in the solution of anything. I should hate to see such conferences take place and if they failed then there would be a great depression, further aggravation of the state of mind — hysterical tension in the world. In other words, if we could have such conferences, and I favor them, and approach them without any high hopes that they would yield high consequences, I would say fine.

Q: What is your interpretation of India's independent foreign policy? Is it neutral?

A: Well, my impression of it is not so much neutrality in the sense of indifference in a conflict between — using my own words — tyranny and freedom or tolerance and intolerance. I don't believe it is that. I think it is more noninvolvement — an anxiety to keep free from involvement in any conflict that besets the world, either hot or cold. Perhaps that is a wholly inadequate explanation but I've come to think more about it since I have been here and I think it is rather noninvolvement than neutrality.[64]

Q: Tell us a little more elaborately what are the things by which you were impressed.

A: I was impressed by the effort to improve in both simple and uncomplicated ways the way of living in the villages, and I was also very much impressed by the Damodar Valley Project which I went up and saw when I was in Calcutta. I have been impressed with the effort to increase agricultural production by irrigation projects, by improved seeds, by improved machinery or farm implements, the

[63] On May 11, 1953, British Prime Minister Sir Winston Churchill proposed before the House of Commons a four-power conference to meet with the Soviet Union to relieve world tensions. He withdrew his proposal on November 4, 1953, after failing to persuade the major powers to meet.

[64] Krishnalal Shridharani wrote: "Stevenson did an unusual thing for an American. He became one of the very few Americans to interpret India's foreign policy as India would like it to be interpreted." "Stevenson Charms and Disappoints Delhi," p. 11.

extension work, as we call it in my country, in the way of building up education at the village level in the field of agriculture, public health, sanitation, education and all the improved amenities that have been brought about or at least are contemplated. I don't know whether that is an adequate answer.

Q: Regarding the community projects — do you think the money was well worth being spent?

A: Yes, I do. I think it is well worth being spent. Money is only well worth spent in relation to alternative choices for the expenditure. It is a question of establishing priorities. From what little I have been able to discover about the Indian economy money is scarce, therefore expenditure must be directed where it will serve the greatest good. I would think that in order to maintain enthusiasm and hope that one of the most important things to do was to bring concrete evidence of improvement to the villages and in that respect I think this is an important expenditure. Whether it can be justified with the need for industrialization I don't feel at liberty to express an opinion.

Q: You gave an interpretation of India's foreign policy which I think would be accepted. But would you like to comment on (a) the intrinsic worth and (b) the practicability of this policy of noninvolvement?

A: I think you will have to forgive me for declining to answer that question. I think India must make its own foreign policy and certainly any suggestion from me would be highly gratuitous.

Q: Do you think that the Korean question can be solved independently of the Communist aggression in Vietnam and other countries?

A: I do.

Q: In order to have a truce in Korea, do you think we must resolve all problems of Communism vs. Democracy? [not verbatim]

A: No. I think you can settle Korea as a separate item.

Q: Then how do you link Vietnam with Korea?

A: Who's linking them?

Q: When you said that the American role was to restore the balance of power. Doesn't it remind you of the British role in the 19th century when Britain checked all other powers in Europe and expanded her colonies to the largest political extent?

A: I just got through saying that that was the role that the British had fulfilled trying to keep one power from getting too powerful. I think that is very much the situation we find ourselves in now, that that is the role that has fallen unhappily to the United States. It certainly isn't agreeable to the United States.

Q: Would you say Communism can co-exist with the democratic ideal?

A: As an ideology, yes, as an instrument for world domination, no.

Q: Do you mean a Communist state can get along with a non-Communist state?

A: Yes. That is, if one is not aggressive, if it doesn't purport to suppress freedom, if it doesn't try to make everybody else feel and think alike. It all depends on who is in charge of the state.

Q: Do you favor the policy of containment or new policy?

A: I wish that word containment had never been used. I believe in stopping the expansion of Soviet power at the expense of free and independent states.

Q: There are certain countries in Asia for whom China happens to be a natural market. Is it appreciated by the U.S. that when it advocates a policy of blockade of China that policy will not be popular with certain Asian countries?

A: Oh, indeed. Yes, indeed. I might point out to you that a major natural market for Japan is North China. The Japanese economy only survives nowadays by virtue of American spending in Japan for off-shore procurement for the troops and other purposes incidental to the occupation and to the Korean war. I think, I am not sure, that I have the figures exactly but in the last calendar year the Japanese budget would have been unbalanced by some $756 million had it not been for American expenditures. So that it is obviously a great expense to us in Japan and will be probably for some time to come and also to the Japanese people and to their economy that they are not trading with China. We are fully aware of that.

Q: Do you think that U.S. recognition of the Peking Government should follow immediately after achievement of the armistice in Korea?

A: I do not. That can only be determined in view of the circumstances at that time. That it could follow immediately seems doubtful.

Q: (asked by Stevenson): I wish the gentlemen would now tell me why it is the U.S. seems to be misunderstood so often.

A: McCarthy and his activities is one reason.

Q: After the second world war the U.S. spent a great deal of money putting life back into Western Europe. Do you find that any of the Western countries are today grateful to the United States for that help?

A: I think that they are. Far more than the press of many of them would seem to indicate. I am on my way to Europe. Perhaps I could answer that question better after I have been there. I have had contact and correspondence with many of these countries.

Q: Would you say that there is a large element in your country desirous of friendship with India? Has it increased?

A: I would say it was almost unanimous. I don't know of anybody, and I am speaking consciously and consider[e]dly, I don't know of anybody who doesn't have the warmest feeling towards India. There have been, of course, misunderstandings about this subject of neutralism and so on but the people in America have an overwhelming desire for peace. I think that has been eloquently evidenced by these large expenditures in Western Europe that we have just made to restore the equilibrium and happy conditions of life to the countries ravaged by the late war. There is, in addition, the evidence of the fight in Korea. We don't believe in our country that appeasement pays. We have learned an enduring lesson from Munich. These tremendous sums and this huge casualty list have been incurred with the virtually unanimous approval of the American people. This is evidence of their desire for peace. We also have, I believe you will agree, a long history of anticolonialism. Whatever may appear to you, I would ask you to take into account the fact that the United States was the first country in the modern world to gain its independence from foreign domination. I should think the story of what we did in the Philippines is equal evidence of our view about colonialism. In addition to that, I think that two American representatives were asked to leave this country by Great Britain because of our feeling on freedom for India.[65] These are only some of the things I could cite that indicate, I think, the view of the American people about the freedom and independence of the colonial peoples who are competent, ready and able to govern themselves, as is the case in India. My lord, I'm making a speech!

Q: In this country some people believe that America is underwriting colonialism.

A: That is another reason for the misunderstanding. I wish you would all help us with that. It is not an American opinion.

Q: If you and your party can do something to make us believe that is so, that would be very nice.

A: We may have to wait four years.

[65] The editors are unable to discover whom Stevenson refers to.

After the press conference, Ambassador Allen held a large reception. At eight the next morning, Stevenson left the Delhi airport for Karachi. One reporter wrote: "He stood as a splendid example of an intelligent, responsible American leadership . . . a leader greatly respected and admired. . . . Throughout India he added to the stature of the United States." [66]

Stevenson wrote of his visit to India:

WILL INDIA TURN COMMUNIST? [67]

Whatever the temperature, India is "hot" in every sense of the word. After China, this is the world's most populous country, the world's most powerful "neutral" and the greatest influence in free Asia. China, struggling for rebirth, has gone Communist. Which way will India go? The answer to this question may well decide the destiny of Asia and hold the key to peace in our time.

At the broiling airport in Calcutta, the reporters told me I'd picked the hottest time of year to visit India. But it was now or never to satisfy a lifelong ambition to see this ancient land. And somehow we staggered through that shattering heat from Calcutta to the Khyber Pass and from the Himalayas to the southern tip of the great subcontinent. There were brief moments of relief: When we flew over the Banihal Pass from Jammu into the beautiful Vale of Kashmir, the temperature dropped from 115 to 70 in half an hour!

Never have I heard and seen so much in two weeks — including Hindu businessmen prostrate before their deity, Ganesa. He has the head of an elephant, and I thought of home and the GOP!

I came to vast India expecting contrasts, and I found them: sacred cattle lying in the shade of modern office buildings; tribesmen with bows and arrows against a background of belching steel furnaces; women carrying stones on their heads alongside giant Diesel tractors; mud villages and palaces; camel caravans and truck convoys; green fields and blazing deserts; illiteracy and scholarship; hunger and plenty; poverty and pomp.

[66] Pirie, "Sir, You Are in Solid Democratic Territory!" p. 12.

[67] *Look*, July 14, 1953. The remainder of this article is reprinted in Chapter Twelve, below. Chester Bowles, the former U.S. ambassador to India and Nepal from 1951 to 1953 (and later to India, 1963–1969), wrote Stevenson on July 10, 1953: "I thought your Look article on India and Pakistan was really outstanding." George V. Allen, who was U.S. ambassador during Stevenson's visit to India, wrote: "Proof of his wisdom and judgment could not be more clearly demonstrated because his views on India are even more impressive 14 years later, during which almost every impression he gained . . . have been borne out." Letter to Walter Johnson, July 7, 1967.

And I also came to the new India filled with curiosity and questions: *What sort of man is Prime Minister Jawaharlal Nehru? Is he a shrewd statesman or an incomprehensible mystic? Is he really neutral or indifferent in our struggle against Communist imperialism?*

Why do Indian leaders sometimes talk as though the United States were as great a threat to peace and freedom as Soviet Russia? Are American aims misunderstood, and why?

Can impoverished, crowded, illiterate India build a stable, democratic state — and what can or should we do to help?

Why isn't the bitter Kashmir controversy with Pakistan settled amicably and quickly if India really wants a peaceful world so badly? And, finally — what will happen after Nehru?

Well, it wasn't long before the troubles and uncertainties I found in the rest of Asia began to shrivel in the churning caldron of India's 360 million people and myriad problems, projects, religious castes, languages and diversities.

Let's begin with Pandit Nehru, "the spiritual successor of Gandhi." For this small, frail, intense aristocrat embodies the moral force, the political cement and the intellectual leadership of the new India. The masses which are India believe in him; the middle classes which make up the government follow him; the West looks to him for understanding; the nations of Asia and Africa whose aspirations are unfulfilled turn to him for support, and even the Communist bloc has not given up hope of persuading him.

The first time I talked to this complicated, cultivated man, he had just returned from a week of grueling travel through a famine area during an India "heat wave" — 200 miles a day over bad roads, with ten to twenty stops for speeches and inspections. But that was nothing to his campaign tour last year, when he traveled 26,000 miles in 46 days and made 305 speeches to 30 million people (without benefit of TV!). How does he do it? "The people exhilarate me," he said simply.

I had several talks with this sensitive and heavily burdened man, who is not only the leader and spokesman of the majority Congress party, but also Prime Minister, Foreign Minister and Defense Minister. He is the mediator of all parliamentary and party controversies, the executive head of a huge governmental structure, the final arbiter of all domestic policies and the author and executor of India's foreign policy.

Perhaps the most perplexing and dangerous question India faces is: Who and what after Nehru? Most of the leaders of India who fought the long battle for independence from the British are aging and weary. And one has the feeling that the Congress party as a whole is losing its revolutionary momentum and zeal. Little new inspirational leadership is emerging. I asked Nehru himself about this, and, with a troubled look, he said, "Yes, we must give more attention to that."

I asked him, too, about India's so-called "neutral" position between communism and democracy. "Our policy," he said, "is non-involvement. In any conflict between freedom and tyranny, India will not be neutral." And then he added emphatically: "Mere anti-Communist talk will attract no one in Asia." By which he meant that the textbook case for communism — social and economic equality, land reform, industrialization, an end to corruption and exploitation — are the very goals of the Asian revolution. Thus the advertised objectives of communism have great appeal to the impoverished Asian masses, who know nothing of its brutal realities.

I also asked Nehru about his statement lauding Stalin as a man of peace at the time of his death, which shocked me and so many Americans. He explained that he meant Stalin had kept peace in Russia and the Communist party. (A better explanation might be that Nehru spoke impetuously without considering the effect of his words.)

As to Korea, Nehru agrees that U.N. intervention was right, but feels that it was a great mistake to cross the 38th parallel and agitate China's fear of invasion or injury. And he thinks that China will never yield to Moscow's yoke and, properly handled, will take a progressively independent position. Because of China's monstrous internal problems (not unlike India's), he discounts the danger of Chinese aggression in Southeast Asia. I think I detected a sort of fraternal sentimentality about China, which adopted Buddhism from India and, like India, was long exploited by Europeans.

We talked of colonialism, of Indochina, North Africa and South Africa and of Russia, too. It is not easy to set down my impressions in a few simple words. Nehru admires Communist accomplishments in developing backward countries with little outside aid — the same problem he faces in India. But he detests intolerance and violence. Means are as important to Nehru as ends; and he and his associates, like the old sage Chakravarti Rajagopalachari of Madras, have dealt firmly and effectively with Communist violence in India.

The more America presses India to join the anti-Communist front, the more I suspect that Nehru and, for that matter, most Indian leaders will balk. What perhaps we have not fully realized is that the proud new nations of Asia may perversely prefer suicide to even a suspicion of the Western domination and dictation which they have been fighting for so long. Like Indonesia and Burma, for example, I suspect India would prefer to go without aid and risk the consequences, rather than accept aid with a political price tag attached. In India, colonialism and racialism are vivid memories, and always associated with the West. (For instance, most Indians regard colonial France as the villain in Indochina, rather than the new Communist imperialism.)

The leading newspaper publisher of south India [68] said to me: "India will save the world from communism because of the deep religious faith of the Hindus, which is the direct antithesis of communism's denial of God." And there are religious depths in Nehru, the man of action who is also Gandhi's heir. He believes in tolerance, nonviolence and individual freedom of action. Peaceful coexistence between men and nations is the Gandhian gospel, and I suspect that Nehru, though a little impatient with the distractions of foreign affairs, rather fancies the role of a noninvolved peacemaker. Besides, Russia and China are India's northern neighbors.

Also, most Indians know little of totalitarian ruthlessness.[69] They have known only one enemy — the civilized British. Passive resistance — such as lying down in front of a British tank — used to land you in jail. They don't realize that a Soviet tank would probably just keep rolling.

I cannot wholly explain the paradoxes and contradictions in Nehru, who so often seems to temper his judgments of India's totalitarian neighbors to the north and criticize his country's real friends in the West. But it is clear that he is essentially a liberal in the best Western sense, that India has a democratic constitution laying great emphasis on individual rights, and that Nehru is going to build the new India by voluntary democratic means or perish in the effort.

Perhaps we can better understand India if we remember our own long tradition of isolation, neutrality and preoccupation with our own affairs. India's internal problems are appalling, and, unless they are solved, speculation about India's and Nehru's attitude toward the external Communist threat is simply a waste of time.

There are pockets of communism all over India. I visited one in the far south — the state of Travancore-Cochin, on the tropical Malabar coast. (It was here that St. Thomas and many Christian missionaries are said to have come in the first and second centuries, and the area is sprinkled with Catholic and Protestant missions and colleges.) This state has the highest degree of literacy in all India, the greatest popu-

---

[68] The editors have been unable to discover whom Stevenson refers to.

[69] Krishnalal Shridharani wrote: "The liberals were disappointed to hear from *his* mouth the familiar phrasing of all issues in terms of the conflict with Communism. . . . The belief in Delhi's official circles that Democrats, though alert to the Communist danger, were less 'hysterical' than Republicans was somewhat shaken." "Stevenson Charms and Disappoints Delhi," p. 11.

lation density (up to 2500 per square mile along the coast) — and the most Christians and Communists. (The latter seemed confused by my visit in the south: One newspaper said I was a stalking horse for Secretary of State John Foster Dulles; another declared I was being gagged by the State Department.)[70]

Why do the advocates of communism flourish in this lush and lovely area? Because they exploit discontent: The coconut-matting industry is depressed, many are out of work, and families of ten or fifteen are trying to scrape a living off a single acre.

The main source of Communist organization here, as elsewhere, is found among the "educated unemployed" — young men who struggled hard for an education and now can't find employment suitable to intellectuals. They find an outlet for their resentment in Communist denunciation of everybody and everything.

Government leaders — especially the renowned philosopher Vice-President [Sir] Sarvepalli Radhakrishnan — are fully aware that there is too much classical education in the old British tradition. India needs agriculturists, engineers, scientists and technicians, and efforts are being made to change the educational emphasis.

The "untouchables" — low-caste Hindus — are also easy game for the Communists, and I suspect it will take many years, especially in the country, to uproot the ancient caste system, which regards manual labor as degrading.

At least, our journey along the lovely Travancore-Cochin coast ended on a light note. My companions and I all turned up at the airport wearing blue seersucker suits, and an admiring official congratulated us on what he thought was "the summer uniform of the American Democratic party."

If the root causes of communism have yet to be eradicated in India, Nehru and the Congress party have been more successful in their efforts to create a secular state free of intolerance and religious strife. It has been only six years since the ghastly Hindu-Moslem massacres (when millions were slaughtered), and the scars and bloodstains are not easily erased. But India's 40 million Moslems now live in comparative safety, and it looks as though the secular state is firmly established.

Also encouraging is the progress of the $4.3 billion five-year plan for economic development, which was launched two years ago. For the

[70] On May 10, 1953, *Crossroads* denounced him as a tool of Wall Street and John Foster Dulles. The paper asserted: "The bad reactions produced by Eisenhower's original blustering to make Asians fight Asians are sought to be wiped out by the palpable Christian platitudes that Stevenson will dole out." *Blitz*, May 10, 1953, stated that he had been "gagged" by Ambassador Allen and forbidden to give public speeches or hold a press conference.

building of a strong, viable democracy depends on the speed and success with which India meets the wants of masses of people who, naturally enough, think more with their stomachs than with their heads. Many were persuaded that independence would usher in Utopia.

This is the revolution of rising expectations that I have found everywhere in Asia. And if the new leaders of free Asia don't make good their promises, the Communists are sure to exploit the resulting disillusionment.

Because India spends $500 million annually on food imports, the first pressing objective of the five-year plan is to increase food production by improving methods, incentives, roads, health, education, irrigation, reclamation and equipment.

The second is industrialization. Already, the production of cloth, cement, sugar and coal has exceeded the targets. I visited the great Damodar Valley project northwest of Calcutta, modeled on the TVA. Here, huge dams are rising for power and irrigation; a large fertilizer plant has been constructed; steel capacity is being trebled.

And this is but one of several large power, irrigation and industrial developments that are calculated to end India's chronic food deficiency, provide more consumer goods and more jobs for India's 60 to 100 million unemployed or underemployed.

In the villages, improvement has started on a small but rapidly expanding scale. "Village leaders" are being trained, with American help, in 30 centers all over India. Their problems are manifold: A different fodder crop may be better — but what if it is not suitable for thatch? Green manure is good for the soil — but you can't turn it under with a primitive plow. Certainly, the mud huts should have chimneys to remove the smoke — but then the precious fuel, dried dung, will burn too fast.

It takes patience and persistence, and, with 600,000 villages, the task of rural rehabilitation is enormous. Old habits and ways of doing things are tenacious in India. As one village leader said to me, "Our job is psychological. We must help the villagers to want what they should want, and then help them to discover that they can do it for themselves."

I visited villages before and after "the treatment." It works. The people are more responsive to change than I had expected. But what will happen when the trained village leaders are transferred to other communities and the initial enthusiasm dies down? That is still an unanswered and anxious question.

The five-year plan will not work any quick miracles. Even if India gets the remaining half billion dollars she must have from abroad to finance this huge and realistic undertaking, and even if it succeeds in full, it will raise per capita average income only from about $52 to $58 a year. India's population is increasing by five million a year, and it will take nearly two decades before living standards can be materially improved. As Dr. V. K. R. V. Rao, director of the Delhi School of Economics, said, "Economic development involves, not only toil and sweat, but also tears and abstinence for many years to come."

Russia accomplished her transformation by ruthless exploitation of the people. Red China is doing the same. But in India, Nehru and his government are trying to carry out their revolution by consent, not coercion. They are banking heavily on the five-year plan, on gradual improvement and on a growing national consciousness and a sense of civic responsibility to replace the anti-British dynamic of the independence struggle.

The great contest in Asia is between the totalitarian and the democratic approach to the development of backward areas. We can be thankful that India has chosen the voluntary way — which is also the hard way. Fortunately, India's present leaders and top civil servants are British-educated and imbued with the ideals of a free society. The next ten years will tell whether these ideals are a permanent part of the new India, or whether this great nation will turn to stronger, quicker, harsher methods of economic improvement — to the peril of India, Asia and the world.

Thus it seems to me far more important for India to strengthen her fledgling democracy than to proclaim her allegiance to "our side" in foreign affairs. For a healthy democracy, even in a "neutralist" India, will be a stronger bulwark against communism in Asia than a shaky, uncertain state — no matter how loudly pro-American or anti-Communist its leaders speak.

And I say again that these proud Asian peoples cannot be browbeaten, bribed or cajoled. And we can win no friends merely by shouting anti-Communist slogans. For skeptics are best won over by the positive aspects of democracy.

And there is still much skepticism about America. Indians think we are too bellicose and have lost our democratic bearings. They tend to equate the Communist treason trials, for example, with the methods used in some congressional investigations. Recently, I read this in the conservative *Times of India:* "To Indians, the United States, founded because of the need of man to worship as he desired, to speak as he thought fit, to enjoy liberty, had always seemed the natural home of all civil rights. They hear today that the intellectual atmosphere is often vitiated by persecution and fear, even in academic surroundings, while those responsible for such conditions sit in high places and receive respect."

Chester Bowles, our former ambassador to India, did pioneer work in personally dispelling Indian misconceptions about America. His able successor, George Allen, I'm confident, will carry on in the same way. There is no more important job for an American in India today.

What are India's chances? I have listed some of the positive factors — among which are great undeveloped resources. On the negative side, I found other, disturbing elements:

1. India is far from united. Twelve major languages are each spoken by more than 10 million people, and there is strong pressure, abetted by the Communists, further to divide the nation into linguistic states.

2. The Communists, though numbering no more than 50,000 party members, are well organized, energetic and quick to capitalize on popular dissatisfaction.

3. Land reform is a reality on paper, but lagging in practice.

4. Skilled managerial personnel and capital for industrial development are lacking, and slow progress may create impatience with democratic means.

But we should also bear in mind that the totalitarian successes were achieved in countries with no such democratic traditions or leadership as India has.

On balance, I think the prospects for a free India are good. But I wish I had found an answer to the question of what will happen after Nehru. In America, we believe that there is no such thing as an indispensable man. Perhaps that is true in India, too, but the fact remains that there is no younger man in sight with an "all India" appeal to give this vast country the firm, confident direction she so badly needs.

Of one thing I'm sure: Regardless of the strange, petty, unreasonable (indeed, sometimes irresponsible) attitudes and judgments of Indians — including Pandit Nehru himself — this country will never go the authoritarian way and abandon the human values of democracy so long as he is in power.

Twelve

Pakistan

MAY 14–MAY 24, 1953

W hen the Indian National Airlines plane landed at Karachi, representatives of the Pakistan government and members of the
American embassy, including Chargé d'Affaires John Emmerson, were
waiting to welcome Stevenson to Pakistan.

Stevenson and Blair stayed at the residence of Governor General
Ghulam Mohammed, while the rest of the group were at the Metropole
Hotel. Except for tea with the governor general, Stevenson spent the
afternoon planning his article on India. Dinner that evening was with
the governor general, Prime Minister Mohammed Ali and members of
the cabinet.

Early next morning Stevenson attended one of the best embassy
briefings that he had on his trip. John Emmerson described the weak-
nesses of the country: (1) It was a "geographical monstrosity" based
on religion, with West and East Pakistan separated by India; (2) the
economy had to depend on cotton and jute for its cash crops; (3) there
was an acute shortage of trained personnel, since the Hindus had left
at the time of partition; (4) there was an acute language problem, with
Urdu the language of West Pakistan and Bengali the language of East
Pakistan; and (5) the country was split between those who wanted
Pakistan to be an Islamic state, but a progressive one, and the many
religious leaders, the mullahs, who demanded the strict application of
Islamic principles in the running of state affairs.

At the same time, Emmerson observed, religion was a strength in
that it was the unifying force in the nation. Among other strengths, he

remarked, were (1) the determination to survive; (2) great potential resources in agriculture to be developed; (3) the human resources of 75 million people; and (4) Pakistan's orientation toward the West. He added that the progressive elements in Pakistan looked to Turkey as a model.

There was a discussion prompted by Stevenson's question about the change in government just a month before. It was explained that the previous prime minister had given in to the mullahs on the constitution that was being drafted for the nation. The mullahs had insisted that a board of not more than five persons "well-versed in Islamic laws" be appointed to advise the head of state about any laws repugnant to the Koran. Then the mullahs had started to agitate against Foreign Minister Sir Zafrulla Khan and other moderates. Rioting broke out in Lahore, but Prime Minister Khwaja Nazimuddin did nothing. Civil servants and the defense secretary, Major General Iskander Mirza, pressed the governor general for action. Martial law was proclaimed, the army restored order in Lahore, and the prime minister was dismissed from office.[1]

At this point, Stevenson remarked that the previous evening A. K. Brohi, the minister of law, had told him that the cabinet was not going to accept the draft of the constitution that had been influenced by the mullahs.

Members of the embassy staff also discussed the Kashmir question and the division of water between India and Pakistan. Stevenson asked particularly for details about the Indus River system. It was explained that the rivers of the system originated in India but most of the canals were in Pakistan. Crop failures in Pakistan in 1952 had led to charges that India was cutting off water at planting time. One member of the embassy staff observed that "it is not what is happening or what's happened but what people believe, and the Pakistanis believe they are near starvation in certain areas because of India, and of course they would rather fight than starve." He then added that the World Bank was working on the Indus River problem.[2] There was general agreement that until Kashmir and the water question were solved the two countries could not have close relations.

After the briefing, Stevenson spoke to the entire embassy staff. He

[1] For a discussion of the constitution that was adopted in 1956 and the military *coup d'état* that made General Ayub Khan the president of Pakistan in 1958, see Hugh Tinker, *India and Pakistan: A Political Analysis* (New York: Frederick A. Praeger, 1962), pp. 80–85.

[2] David E. Lilienthal discusses his recommendations as a consultant to the World Bank in *The Journals of David E. Lilienthal*, Vol. III, *Venturesome Years: 1950–1955* (New York: Harper & Row, 1966), pp. 86–87, 199, 232, 235, 311.

praised their devotion under great stress and strain, particularly in view of the way the Department of State and the Foreign Service were being attacked by Senator Joseph McCarthy.[3]

Stevenson then made a courtesy call on the prime minister. Following that visit he had a lengthy discussion with Sir Zafrulla Khan. Stevenson began the conversation by observing that the question of a theocratic versus a secular state was perplexing to Americans. Sir Zafrulla talked at length and with force: "You must remember Islam governs everyday life more than any other religion does. The Koran lays down certain principles and the Prophet illustrated these in his own lifetime. . . . Islam is a way of life and our institutions should reflect Islamic ideals. That is all we mean when we say we want an Islamic state." *He then observed:* "The chief difficulty Westerners have in understanding an Islamic state is they do not realize that Islam is a complete way of life in which there is no priesthood. Every individual — and this is much like the Quakers — has the fullest right to understand, study, and interpret Islam as set forth in the Koran and the way the Prophet illustrated Islamic principles in his own life. During the last four centuries while Islam was in a decline, self-constituted priests, or mullahs, pronounced themselves as the true enunciators of Islam. There is no place in true Islam for such a priesthood."

Sir Zafrulla remarked that since partition in 1947 some mullahs had demanded the power to set forth the meaning of "true Islam." What they really wanted, he added, was power. People who were versed in Islam could serve in Parliament if they could get elected, he argued, and thus there was no need of a board of mullahs to decide whether a law passed by Parliament offended Islamic principles.

At this point Stevenson said: "You believe, like the late Ali Jinnah,[4] in a secular state devoted to Islamic principles. This other group believes in a state that is controlled by a board, or somebody, who tells everybody what Islam is." *Sir Zafrulla replied that that was a succinct summary, but it should be remembered, he added, that* "we see no difference between secular and theocratic because we consider Islam to be a total way of life."

He then read some Islamic principles, set forth by the Pakistan Constituent Assembly in 1949, which were to be the basis of the new constitution:

[3] Richard H. Rovere, *Senator Joe McCarthy* (New York: Harcourt, Brace, 1959), pp. 189ff.

[4] Mohammed Ali Jinnah, the architect of Pakistan and its first governor general (1947–1948).

(1) The principles of democracy, freedom, equality, tolerance and social justice as enunciated by Islam shall be fully observed;

(2) adequate provisions shall be made for the minorities freely to profess and practice their religions and develop their cultures;

(3) wherein shall be guaranteed fundamental rights including equality of status of opportunity and before law, social, economic and political justice, and freedom of thought, expression, belief, faith, worship and association, subject to law and public morality.

Since the majority of Parliament would always be Moslem, there would be no danger to Islamic principles, he continued. If the mullahs prevailed here, he added, that would be "retrogression."

Sir Zafrulla then said: "Governor, I agree with your statement in New Delhi about Kashmir." Stevenson, he went on, was right that what mattered was not what India or Pakistan desired but what the people in Kashmir wished. India, however, "cannot win a plebiscite and knows it," he stated.

After this conversation Stevenson and his party had lunch with the governor general, the prime minister and several other officials. During the afternoon he rested. In the evening John Emmerson gave a reception in Stevenson's honor followed by a dinner with some of the embassy staff.

Stevenson had received a cable that day announcing that a long-playing record titled Adlai Stevenson Speaks *had been issued and he was asked: "What makes campaign oration live?" He replied on a postcard: "Forgive my Hindu modesty, but I have no idea."* [5]

He had also learned that day that photographer William M. Gallagher of the Flint, Michigan, Journal *had won a Pulitzer prize with his 1952 campaign picture showing a hole in one of Stevenson's shoes. Stevenson wrote him on a postcard:*

To William M. Gallagher [6]

[no date]

I hear you won with a hole in one. Congratulations and very best wishes from a distant traveler.

Stevenson had also received that day a lengthy letter from Mrs. Dick containing clippings about political developments in the United States.

[5] New York *Times*, May 31, 1953.
[6] This handwritten postcard is in the possession of Mr. Gallagher.

To Mrs. Edison Dick [7]

May 15, 1953

Thanks for the clippings, the charming little fishes and the more charming BIG letter. But imagine writing me in that wide-eyed excited vein of innocence about your political dexterity and triumph in the LWV! [8] As though *I* didn't know what a subtle, wise and adroit pol you really are. Anyway, I was enchanted to read this engaging effort to recapture your amateur standing and, soaked with Hindu and Moslem indoctrination, I say that of course you prevailed because you had faith in truth and justice and you were right. And the Hindus are right, and so are the Moslems, and of course the Buddhists and all the rest are wrong — at least that's what they all confidentially tell me.

I'm getting a little groggy and if I don't get out of this religious zone we're traveling thru and this heat I'll be a little groggy too or a little yogi, maybe. So we're going to the N[orth] W[est] Frontier and the mountains, and then to the cool green spaces of the Arabian desert to see Ibn Saud!

It's 1 AM again. Stood for 2½ hours at a reception this evening, shaking hands, then a dinner, then home to my immodest lodgings in another palace to struggle with my ghastly mail and chaotic brief case. Who the woman is that wrote these letters I don't know. There may be something in the file, but I have no recollection of her or ever writing her. What do you recommend? She's evidently highly educated and unbalanced — and why do I attract so many of that kind when all I like is the wholesome, sober, steady type. . . .[9]

The next day Stevenson talked to the minister of finance and economic affairs and to the civil servants in charge of the ministries of industries, foreign affairs, commerce, defense, and food. After these conversations he walked among the wretched shacks in Karachi and spoke to some of the Moslem refugees from India.

At a press conference in the afternoon, he made a brief opening statement describing the bitter disputes that had occurred in the past between Canada and the United States over the boundary between the

[7] This handwritten letter is in the possession of Mrs. Dick.

[8] Mrs. Dick had persuaded the League of Women Voters to include on its agenda a study of the activities of the Illinois Department of Public Welfare.

[9] There are several bulky file folders in the Stevenson papers at Princeton University Library containing many handwritten letters from women. Someone has written "Eccentric Correspondence" on these folders.

two countries. He described how, during the past century, the two countries had solved their disputes peacefully. As he finished, he was immediately asked whether India or Pakistan was right in the dispute over Kashmir. He dodged the question by replying that the plans for an early meeting between Prime Minister Mohammed Ali and Prime Minister Jawaharlal Nehru he regarded as "one of the most reassuring and satisfying developments" in international affairs recently.

When he was asked for his view of Prime Minister Winston Churchill's proposal a week earlier that the great powers meet in a conference, Stevenson replied, "I always have been in favor of keeping the door open for discussion" but added, "I would like to see some evidence of a Communist change of heart."

One reporter asked whether the United States should demand air bases and other military cooperation in return for economic assistance. Stevenson replied by expressing the hope that the United States would have the voluntary cooperation of Asians "quite independent of any aid we may give them." He also remarked that certain Asian nations, which were recently under the weight of colonialism, needed American assistance more quickly than others for their internal development.

There was the inevitable question about Senator McCarthy's attacks on the Department of State and the Information Agency which Stevenson characterized as an "unfortunate capitalization of people's fears." [10]

After the press conference Stevenson met with the minister of food, Khan Abdul Qaiyum Kham, who discussed the short-range and long-term plans for irrigation to make Pakistan a food surplus area in wheat and rice. He emphasized that Pakistan wanted the same distribution of water flowing from Kashmir and other mountainous areas that had existed before partition. He charged that India had "held off water" and as a result some areas "have become barren." He also explained the need of wheat from the United States to avert famine. (The wheat was shipped a few months later.)

After this discussion, the prime minister gave a dinner in Stevenson's honor.

At seven A.M. the next morning Stevenson left Karachi in the embassy plane for Lahore.[11] He was accompanied by M. A. Hamid, chief engineer of Pakistan's irrigation system. The DC–3 flew low over the countryside while Mr. Hamid described the river and canal system to Stevenson.

On arrival at Lahore, he was driven to the home of Governor Amin-

[10] *Dawn* (Karachi), May 17, 1953.

[11] Barry Bingham had to leave the group at this point to return to his post at the Louisville *Courier-Journal*. Attwood remained in Karachi for a day and rejoined the group at Rawalpindi.

ud-Din, where he was to stay. The governor took Stevenson on a tour of his palatial residence and lovely gardens of a transplanted England, and Stevenson remarked that he agreed with Ring Lardner's statement: "The best is good enough for me."

Amin-ud-Din described how the city of Lahore had doubled its population since 1947 and how Pakistan's population was growing at the rate of a million people a year. "Where the standard of living is low," he commented, "procreation seems to be the only recreation." He stated that Pakistan had to do something to curb its population growth, but, he added, Moslems resisted birth control. He remarked that the common man in South Asia had never had a "real bellyful of food." The land could not support the population, he continued, and as a result both Pakistan and India had to industrialize.

After lunch Stevenson retired to his room to write postcards. Suddenly he called, "Bill, Walter!" They hurried into his room to find him counting his money. He looked at Blair accusingly and said: "I started this trip with a thousand dollars and now all I have left is seven hundred. Where did it go?" Blair patiently reminded him of the presents he had bought in Hong Kong, Bangkok, and Kashmir. Then Blair said: "If you've only spent three hundred dollars for all those gifts, I must have used some of my money to pay for your gifts." Stevenson looked startled, put his bills back in his wallet, and said no more about money during the remainder of the trip.

That afternoon he went sightseeing. He visited the Shalimar Gardens and then walked through the narrow streets of the old walled city with its bazaars, spicy smells, and teeming people. He said: "This is what I prefer; I could walk all day in these crowded streets." One of the Pakistani officials who was with him remarked to one of Stevenson's aides that he thought Stevenson was "insane to want to rub shoulders with the masses." Stevenson took particular delight in seeing the Zam Zam gun — the great brass cannon, cast in the seventeenth century — on which Rudyard Kipling's Kim played "king of the castle." Stevenson with relish quoted from his childhood reading of Kim's adventures.

Early in the evening Consul General Ernest Fisk held a reception for Stevenson to meet members of his staff and American Fulbright grantees who were teaching in Lahore. At dinner with Governor Amin-ud-Din that evening, Stevenson heard about the three months of martial law in the city (it had been lifted the day before he arrived). The governor described how the government had "smashed" the mullahs. "We are not going to allow those fellows to take us back into the tenth century," he said.

After a six A.M. breakfast the next day Stevenson flew to Peshawar in

*the Northwest Frontier Province. As he approached the airport he
could see the mountains of the Hindu Kush and Afghanistan in the distance. Automobiles were waiting at the airport to drive Stevenson
through the Khyber Pass to the Afghan border. When he reached the
village of Jamrud at the entrance to the pass, an honor guard of frontier
scouts was waiting to welcome him. In addition, a number of tribal
leaders had come in from the mountains to greet him. They placed
garland after garland of flowers around his neck. Then he was presented
with a pair of the highly decorated sandals worn by bridegrooms,
which he attempted to put on (though they were far too small), ex-
plaining to the chieftains that he was available. Next he was given a
revolver stamped "Made in England." (It was explained to him later
that the tribesmen made them and put that stamp on in order to sell
them at a higher price.) Finally, he was presented with a shoulder bag
of the kind the tribesmen used to carry their food and ammunition.*

*For about twenty minutes the tribesmen kept him encircled, and, as
he later said to his aides, "They gave me the works on Kashmir." They
explained that the only reason they had withdrawn from Kashmir five
years before was that they expected a settlement. The United States,
they insisted, should boycott India until it agreed to a plebiscite.*

*After the chieftains had finished talking to him, Stevenson drove into
the Khyber Pass. As the road wound through the mountains he saw
many forts, watchtowers, and sentry boxes that the British had used to
keep the Pathan tribesmen under control.*

*The Pakistani political agent for the area explained to Stevenson that
as recently as 1930 tribesmen had raided the city of Peshawar and that
until partition in 1947 it had not been safe for outsiders to travel
through the pass.*

*After seeing the frontier of Afghanistan, he had lunch with a
Pakistani regiment at the village of Landi Kotal. When he returned to
Peshawar, Stevenson walked around the old fort and spent an hour
examining the goods for sale in the bazaars.*

*At dinner that evening Stevenson sat next to Field Marshal Mo-
hammed Ayub Khan (who later became president of Pakistan, in 1958)
and across from the chief justice of the Northwest Frontier Province,
Sheikh Mohammad Shaffi. The chief justice was insistent that the
United States should force India to agree to a United Nations plebiscite
on Kashmir. He was unstoppable and undistractable throughout the
evening.*

*Early the next morning Stevenson flew to Rawalpindi to have break-
fast with the chief of staff of the Pakistani army, General Nasir Ali.*

He then took Stevenson to visit an armored unit in training and to see the military hospital.

Following this visit to the headquarters of the army, Stevenson met with three separate groups of leaders from Azad Kashmir (the Pakistani-controlled area). The first group urged him to visit Azad Kashmir, inasmuch as he had been to Srinagar. Stevenson explained that he was happy to learn about Kashmir but they had to understand that he had no influence over the issue. The spokesman for the group stated that they wanted a plebiscite immediately, and added that the plebiscite would be fairer if all troops were removed beforehand. At least, they argued, India should reduce the number of its troops.

Stevenson explained to them that India objected to the Azad Kashmir troops because they were not part of the regular Pakistani army. They replied that they were willing to disband and disarm in order to secure a plebiscite.

The spokesman of the second group told Stevenson that Pakistan needed no troops to maintain internal security in Azad Kashmir. India did need troops in its part of Kashmir, however. But he said the big question was whether India really wanted a plebiscite at all. If a plebiscite was held immediately, he predicted, Pakistan would win overwhelmingly.

The third group was led by a mullah who had fled from Srinagar during the fighting. He too insisted that Pakistan would win a plebiscite. He charged that Sheikh Abdullah's government contained Communists and these individuals favored an independent Kashmir. He rejected this idea and said nobody really desired it.

That afternoon Stevenson had planned to fly over Gilgit Province, Swat, and other mountainous areas, but heavy clouds blocked the passes. With two hours free in the schedule, Stevenson said to Johnson: "Walter, let the two of us visit Alexander's village. The rest are all tired and they can stay here and have a nap."

After a twenty-two-mile drive they reached the village of Taxila. They visited the remains of the old city and in the museum saw many Greek artifacts and Buddhas sculptured in Greek style. All during the tour Stevenson, with animation in his voice, described the historical and archaeological significance of what they were seeing.

On their return to Rawalpindi, Stevenson, Leon Poullada from the consulate in Lahore, and Johnson climbed in one car, and Blair, Attwood and a secretary on leave from the embassy in Karachi, Miss Bernita Alice Snyder, rode in a second car. It took four hours to drive the sixty miles to Nathia Gali. Much of the way the road clung to the side of the mountains. Rain had washed the gravel away and the turns, with precipitous drops, were extremely slippery. Halfway between the town of Murree and Nathia Gali the cars stopped at a cluster of four houses in order that the drivers could break their fast. (Stevenson traveled in the Moslem countries during the month of Ramadan, when Moslems eat and drink nothing from sunup to sundown.)

The policeman in charge of the little village asked Mr. Poullada in Urdu if the members of the party were Americans. He then said, "I have seen the sahib's picture." He pronounced a name that sounded like "Stevenson" and said, "He's head of the Democratic party and was General Eisenhower's opponent." Stevenson clasped the man's hand and observed to his aides, "I have carried this precinct, all right."

The last twelve miles of the drive were in darkness and dense fog. At one point Stevenson noticed that the other car was not behind him. The elevation was now 8500 feet and Stevenson felt the cold, particularly since he was still wearing a seersucker suit from the hot plains of Rawalpindi. Stevenson announced that he "wasn't going to sit in the car and shiver." He started off down the road in pitch darkness, slipping in the mud. Attwood wrote in his diary: "The car Blair and I and Miss Snyder were in skidded and damn near went off the road. While we tugged and heaved at it, Stevenson came charging down the road in the dark. He thought we had gone over the edge. So he lent a hand and we got the car moving again."

Finally the Stevenson party reached the summer home of the governor of the Northwest Frontier Province. During the next day Stevenson sorted out his notes on India and Pakistan in preparation for writing his article for Look.

He dined that evening with Governor K. Shahabuddin and the chief minister of the Northwest Frontier Province, A. Rashid Khan. Governor Shahabuddin explained that Pakistan was most anxious for a plebiscite in Kashmir supervised by forces from the United Nations. Nehru, he charged, wanted a settlement only on his terms. He added that if the United Nations did not solve the Kashmiri question, it would become as weak as the League of Nations.

During the four days in Nathia Gali, Stevenson spent many hours writing and rewriting his article on India and Pakistan for Look. As Miss Snyder typed draft after draft, his aides edited the material. Blair wrote to Miss Carol Evans, May 22, 1953: "At the moment we are resting in what must be the most isolated spot in the world — 9,000 feet high in the Himalayas with not a soul within 40 miles. The Gov. loves it and is getting a lot of work done." [12]

[12] This handwritten letter is in the possession of Miss Evans.

At six A.M. *on Sunday, May 24, Stevenson drove down the winding road to Rawalpindi and immediately flew to Karachi. Aboard the plane Stevenson caught up on his correspondence.*

To Mrs. Edison Dick [13]

[no date]

Bless you for all those enthralling letters — I've eaten them — mostly boiled or broiled in this incredible heat. Everywhere we've been from the Phillipines onward — we managed to be there at "the very worst time of the year."

. . . It's impossible to write on this absurd plane that seems to bound from one rising hot air column to another.

I wrote the boys a letter yesterday . . . copy to Miss Evans, Buffy [Ives] and Ellen [Stevenson], about Europe and joining me. I'm bewildered but I think Borden would be O.K. and would get something out of it if he joined me in Israel about June 7. From Rome I'm going to Yugoslavia & don't want to take John Fell — I think but am not sure, but if he comes he could stay with the Ives & join me later in Vienna I suppose. We might have a month together and I suppose it's worth it but I would feel better if I thought he had something good to do after I come home the end of July — a French family. . . .

It's hellish hard to manage from this distance & all communication with Ellen has ceased as you know. Divorce is hell. . . .

. . . May not write you for long time. Terrible schedule ahead & Bill [Blair] insists that I write some 300 *political* postcards. Thus far I have done *none* of this!

The prime minister had an excellent lunch waiting for Stevenson at the airport. Stevenson had planned ahead of time to stay at the airport, since Secretary of State John Foster Dulles was in Karachi conferring with Pakistani officials and he did not want to intrude.

At 3:15 P.M. *Stevenson boarded a KLM Constellation for Dhahran, Saudi Arabia. He wrote of his visit to Pakistan:*

WILL INDIA TURN COMMUNIST? [14]

Besides camels, the first things you see in the capital of Pakistan are the endless acres of mud shacks where thousands of the Moslem

[13] This handwritten letter is in the possession of Mrs. Dick.

[14] *Look*, July 14, 1953, pp. 42–44. Stevenson's account of his visits to both India and Pakistan appeared in this article. See Chapter Eleven, above.

refugees from India still dwell six years after bloody partition. Refugees have swelled dry, dusty Karachi's population from 300,000 to 1,200,000 since 1947, and they constitute but one of the troubles of this Islamic state. For Pakistan is a geographic monstrosity — the handiwork of religious passion, rather than geography, language or economics.

Karachi is on the Arabian Sea at the southern extremity of West Pakistan, which stretches 1500 miles north and includes some 35 million people. A thousand miles eastward, on the other side of India, is East Pakistan, carved out of Bengal, with 40 million people. In the east, the people speak Bengali; in the west, Urdu. There are few natural resources, little industry, and the economy rests on cotton in the dry west and jute in the wet east. Partition separated the jute-producing areas from the mills. And, instead of working things out together, Pakistan has built mills on her side of the heavily guarded border and India has gone in heavily for raising jute. (Concentration on this nonedible crop may have contributed to the great famine of 1951, when the U.S. loaned India $190 million's worth of wheat.)

The new Pakistan government is strong at the top — its leaders are young, competent and dedicated. But most of the Hindus, who fared better in the crack British Indian civil service and were also accountants, bankers, traders and technicians in pre-partition Pakistan, have fled to India. So the new state is sorely in need of trained personnel to staff the ranks of government and business.

But Pakistan has far more pressing difficulties. Last year, jute and cotton prices collapsed when the Korean war boom subsided, and the country's foreign exchange earnings dropped 50 per cent. After two years of drought and crop failures, Pakistan had to import 800,000 tons of wheat in 1952 — and 1953 looks even worse.

Food shortages have created want and unrest among the impoverished masses. Drastic economy measures and rigid foreign exchange controls mean business stagnation. Extremist mullahs — Moslem religious teachers — have fanned discontent for political ends. This spring, there were riots and violence, partly sectarian, partly in protest against living conditions.

Acting swiftly, Governor General Ghulam Mohammed dismissed Prime Minister Al-Haj Khwaja Nazimuddin and installed forthright and vigorous Mohammed Ali, former ambassador in Washington. A forward-looking, modern-minded administration has taken over. Order has been restored by the army, albeit on an uneasy base of widespread discontent. The new government has asked the United States for a loan or grant of a million tons of wheat to stabilize prices and tide the country over the food crisis.

I trust that we will be generous in Pakistan's present crisis. With normal rainfall and irrigation development, food production will recover. There is an invigorating spirit in Pakistan and no indecision about communism; like her hardy Moslem cousin, Turkey, Pakistan is decisively oriented toward the free world. But I think we should insist that the proceeds of our wheat aid be used for agricultural development and not for some premature industrial project.

Even assuming that Pakistan solves her economic problems, there remain two big question marks — her relations with India and the danger of religious fanaticism in a "Moslem state," which Pakistan proclaims herself to be.

Ever since partition, Pakistan and India have glared at each other over their long twin borders. Visas are required by both countries, passenger trains stop at the frontiers, trade has withered. With all her difficulties, Pakistan, like India, maintains an army — and a very good one — larger than Britain needed for all of undivided India. The air is poisoned with suspicion and mistrust. Pakistanis firmly believe that India's leaders have never accepted the fact of partition, that India is aggravating their refugee problem by driving out more Moslems and trying to starve them by diverting water from the rivers and irrigation canals that flow from India into Pakistan.

To all of these charges, India has answers and countercharges. Actually, just three major issues divide these two inextricably involved neighbors: Kashmir, the canal and river waters and the settlement of refugee claims. The last one can be worked out in time, and experts from the World Bank are studying the water question. With good will on both sides, I believe the two nations can also settle the future of the great mountainous state of Kashmir, which the U.N. has been struggling with since India and Pakistan agreed to cease fighting over it five years ago.

The Kashmir dispute is long and complicated. I heard about it from Sheikh Abdullah, a Moslem and the popular leader of the large portion of Kashmir now occupied by Indian forces. I heard about it from three of the leaders of Azad Kashmir, the territory on the Pakistan side of the U.N. cease-fire line. I heard about it from Prime Minister Nehru of India and Prime Minister Ali of Pakistan, from dozens of other leaders in both countries.

I cannot in this brief article relate all the charges of conspiracy and bad faith that have been poured into my ears. The short of it is, in my judgment, that Pakistan is eager to settle the question promptly by a plebiscite. But India seems to be prolonging the present situation with her troops occupying most of the country, partly, I suspect, because time works to her advantage and partly for more worthy reasons. Nehru does not want religious strife to flare up again. For, if trouble should break out between the three million Moslems and the one million Hindus in Kashmir, it could spread to India, with ghastly consequences.

Since most of the Hindus are concentrated in the southern part of Kashmir bordering on India, it would seem to me that a regional plebiscite might be the best solution of a dispute that must be settled fairly and promptly if the relations of these two countries, so important to the peace and security of the world, are to improve. And, personally, it irks me to see the costly armies these countries maintain — in part, at least, against each other — while the American taxpayer contributes to both.

Happily, India-Pakistan relations are improving. Mohammed Ali's first act as Prime Minister was a friendly gesture to India. Nehru responded in the same vein, and, as I write this, they are about to meet face to face. Mohammed Ali's government has also given assuring evidence of its determination that Pakistan is to be a modern state based on Islamic moral principles but not dominated by obsolete Mohammedan orthodoxy.

If these faraway squabbles seem pretty remote to us Americans, we should remember that they involve almost three times as many people as live in the United States. Let us pray that reasonable men, acting in good faith and in a spirit of give and take, can resolve their differences — for the sake of their own countries, Asia and the world.

Before leaving Pakistan for the Near East, I drove up the Khyber Pass to the Afghan border. Beyond rose the white wall of the Hindu Kush mountain range. I thought of the exploits of Alexander's Greeks, of Tamerlane, Genghis Khan and Baber and all the conquerors and martial hosts that had passed through Khyber to the plains of India from time out of mind. The rocky pass was cool, quiet and peaceful now. At least, I thought it was peaceful until a group of bearded tribal chieftains, with cartridge belts and rifles slung over their shoulders, ceremoniously presented me with a fine revolver — homemade!

For nearly three months now, I have been traveling through Asia — this vast area of old civilizations and new nations where totalitarianism and free institutions are freely compared to determine which method can give its miserable millions a better way of life. China has succumbed by force of arms and Indochina is in peril. The rest of Asia is free, but fluid.

For a long time, the peace and destiny of the world were decided by the balance of power in Europe. Now, a new factor has emerged.

What happens in free Asia can upset the balance of power and of principle in the world.

Fortunately, its present leaders hate tyranny and dictation. They fought and suffered for freedom and independence. They believe, passionately for the most part, in representative institutions; and many still look to revolutionary, democratic America for inspiration and encouragement.

But their countries are poor and backward. Their peoples know little of democracy and the blessings of human freedom, but they want to eat every day — and they mean to do it.

The next few years will tell whether these leaders can make democracy work in this great new area of decision — Asia.

Thirteen

Saudi Arabia

MAY 24 – MAY 27, 1953

O n Sunday evening, May 24, after a four-hour flight from Karachi,
the KLM plane landed at Dhahran on the east coast of Saudi
Arabia. When Stevenson stepped off the plane he was met by his old
friend Ambassador Raymond Hare and some two hundred employees
of the Arabian-American Oil Company (Aramco).

He was driven to an Aramco air-conditioned guesthouse near a field
where a night baseball game was in progress. At dinner Ambassador
Hare remarked that Saudi Arabia had been out of the stream of history
for centuries until oil was discovered there in the 1930's. It was not until
1948, he added, that oil began to produce great revenues. Fred Davies,
vice president of Aramco, commented that the company had paid the
Saudi Arabian government about 175 million dollars in royalties in 1952.

Ambassador Hare observed that in Saudi Arabia the king was an
absolute monarch who ruled by decree and was responsible for up-
holding the religious law of Islam. There was no written constitution,
insofar as the rights of the subjects and the form of administration were
concerned. The king, Ambassador Hare added, was advised by counselors of his own choosing. His two sons, Crown Prince Saud and Prince
Faisal, were the viceroys general of the Nejd and Hejaz, respectively.
The viceroyalties were divided into amirates, each headed by an amir
or governor.

The ambassador said that he had just flown to Dhahran from Jidda,
the principal port city of western Saudi Arabia where the foreign
missions were located. While the Saudi Arabian ministries of foreign

affairs, finance, defense, and others were in Jidda, they had to go to the royal capital of Riyadh for decisions.

The ambassador remarked that King Ibn Saud had "great political sense" but that he had "little feel for economics." When it was a desert economy this was not a particular handicap. The ambassador also mentioned that the boundaries between Saudi Arabia and such states as the Aden Protectorate, the Sultanate of Muscat and Oman and the Trucial Coast had never been defined. This had not caused trouble, he added, until the discovery of oil. He warned Stevenson that the king would probably discuss this question when they met.

The ambassador also warned Stevenson that the Saudi Arabians felt strong emotions over the issue of Israel. But, he said, "They don't talk much about it to you because they are not immediately bordering on Israel." He then remarked that Saudi Arabia was determined to prevent Iraq, Jordan, and Syria from forming "a greater Syria." And, he added, King Ibn Saud did not like the destruction of the monarchy in Egypt the year before and its replacement by a republic.

The next morning Mr. Davies and other Aramco officials briefed Stevenson about their operations. They had a concession of 400 thousand square miles and were producing about 900 thousand barrels of crude oil a day. Mr. Davies remarked that their relations with the government were quite satisfactory and that Aramco had pioneered by agreeing to a fifty per cent division of the profits. They described to Stevenson the technical training program they conducted for their approximately 25,000 Arab employees. As a result, a middle class — something new for Saudi Arabia — was being created.

Mr. Davies pointed out that Aramco drilled many water wells and then the government installed pumps. This to the Bedouins meant much more than oil, he remarked, for these new wells had made it possible for the nomads to go further out into the desert with their camels. But, he commented, it was difficult to teach the people to conserve water. Around the royal city of Riyadh, he said, they really "mined" the water and were lowering the water table at a rapid rate.

Mr. Davies also described how Aramco, at the Saudi Arabian government's request and expense, had built docks, highways, and a 350-mile railroad from Dammam on the east coast to Riyadh. With trucks and the railroad, new products were being introduced and altering the society. Frozen foods were now becoming available and cement was being used instead of adobe for houses.

Late that morning, at the invitation of the king, Stevenson, Ambassador Hare, Blair and Johnson were flown to Riyadh in the DC-3 airplane that President Franklin D. Roosevelt had presented to Ibn Saud at their meeting in February, 1945, when Roosevelt was en route home from the Yalta Conference.[1]

When the plane landed at this oasis city surrounded by what seemed an interminable desert, Stevenson was greeted by Sheikh Yusuf Yasin, the deputy foreign minister. While exchanging pleasantries, through an interpreter, in the air-conditioned room of the tiny airport terminal, Stevenson praised the lovely Oriental rugs on the floor. Ambassador Hare whispered: "Adlai, you'll regret that remark before the day is over."

As he drove in an air-conditioned Cadillac to the walled city, camel caravans were plodding alongside the paved highway en route to the city from the desert. After driving through the gate to the city, Stevenson and his group were taken to a mud-brick guest palace. At this point, Stevenson told the deputy foreign minister that he was looking forward to seeing Prince Faisal, the foreign minister, with whom he had worked at the founding of the United Nations at the San Francisco Conference in 1945.[2] *Then Stevenson added that he thought the Saudi Arabians should ban Americans from visiting Riyadh since Secretary of State John Foster Dulles had just been here, and now he and his party were impinging on their hospitality.*

The deputy foreign minister replied: "No, it is our privilege. We want to talk over our respective views. We want and need America's friendship. But we don't know how you feel about needing our friendship."

Stevenson answered: "Friendship must be bilateral, and we are interested in your friendship. This friendship is much beyond just the question of oil."[3]

The deputy foreign minister replied: "It's important that the United States understand our desires. We know you love freedom and support freedom-loving people. That is why we like you. But there are difficulties in American-Arabian relations. Through explanation maybe the United States will understand our aims better."

Stevenson answered: "The United States is proud of the cordial relations it has with Saudi Arabia. We know there are difficulties in the Middle East, but we bespeak your patience just as you want patience from us. In a country as large as the United States, there are many streams of opinion. This is the price and the penalty of freedom. The

[1] William Attwood had flown on ahead to Cairo to make arrangements for Stevenson's visit to Egypt.

[2] Prince Faisal was second in line to the throne. When his father died later in 1953, Prince Saud became king. In November, 1964, however, Faisal forced his abdication and became king.

[3] The ambassador had warned Stevenson on the flight from Dhahran to Riyadh that the Saudis would try to get him to support their demand for the oasis of Buraimi, where there was the possibility that oil would be found. See note 5, below.

problem of democracy is to channel these streams, but most countries do not understand our problems." He paused and added: "Often a foolish statement by an American is interpreted overseas as being the point of view of all of America, but the deputy foreign minister, I am sure, knows, there are foolish statements frequently that do not represent the American people."

When Stevenson commented that there were few places in the world that had attracted so much curiosity in the United States as Saudi Arabia, the deputy foreign minister said: "Spiritually and materialistically we have a basis of friendship, and this was cemented when President Roosevelt met with King Ibn Saud."

Stevenson replied: "You must remember that King Ibn Saud is almost as much a figure in the United States as he is here. We are concerned for his health and pray that he will live long and flourish."

After the deputy foreign minister thanked him for his statement, Stevenson remarked that he wanted to see the people of Riyadh. Although Stevenson preferred to walk, he was put in a Cadillac and driven through streets just wide enough for the automobile, provided pedestrians stepped into doorways.

After a few minutes, Stevenson tapped the shoulder of the chauffeur. When the car stopped, Stevenson got out and started walking. The Saudi official in charge was so taken aback that he did not have time to protest. At one point, Stevenson came to a public kitchen where rice and lamb were being cooked for children and he lingered there to talk to the children, who seemed delighted at the intrusion.

Later that afternoon Stevenson and his party had an audience with the king. Ibn Saud, whose health had recently deteriorated, was sitting in a wheelchair at one end of the room and along the walls his personal bodyguards were squatting on the floor clasping either curved swords or long rifles. Although the king's voice was nearly inaudible, his hands were most expressive and his strong face and shoulders indicated what a towering figure he had been.[4]

When Stevenson, through an interpreter, told the king how famous he was in the United States, Ibn Saud smiled and nodded. The two exchanged pleasantries about the close relations between their respective countries. Then the king talked for fifteen minutes about the Arab concept of a friend: "A friend is one who tells you when you are wrong and who supports you when you are right." As he talked he grew more animated and gestured with his powerful hands. Then he turned

---

[4] In 1902 Ibn Saud captured Riyadh. During the next twenty-five years the legendary old warrior, by force of arms, created his kingdom from the mosaic of warring tribes who inhabited the peninsula. In September, 1932, he was proclaimed king of the Kingdom of Saudi Arabia. He died five months after Stevenson's visit.

from Stevenson to Ambassador Hare and spoke specifically to him about Buraimi.[5]

Following the audience with the king, Stevenson and his group spent over an hour with Prince Faisal, the deputy foreign minister, and several other officials. One of the officials attacked British and French imperialism, but Stevenson remarked that the world had made considerable progress on that question since the close of World War II.

All the Saudis insisted that the United States should help North Africa and the protectorates of southern Arabia gain their independence from the French and the British. When Stevenson urged patience, they warned that there "might not be too much time left." Stevenson insisted that while imperialism was shrinking, Communism was growing. They emphasized that the Islamic religion was strongly opposed to Communism. But they stated: "We cannot see that imperialism is shrinking in the Middle East."

At this point one official — a refugee from Palestine — said: "And don't forget the cancer that you have placed in our hearts." Stevenson replied, "Cancer?" (He knew full well that this referred to Israel. It was the only time in the lengthy conversation that the subject was raised.) Another official shifted the conversation back to the British, charging that the United States did not know what the British were doing in the Middle East.

After Stevenson returned to his residence, Ambassador Hare said, "One has to keep in mind that the world revolves for Saudi Arabia around the dispute over Buraimi," and anti-British sentiment had increased as a result. Stevenson remarked that all over people wanted the United States to support them on such issues as Buraimi and that "if we don't, they get disillusioned about us. I feel that we should urge patience to them."

The ambassador observed that the Saudi Arabians were trying to use the United States to get at the British in the immediate dispute. But it should be kept in mind that there were powerful anti-imperialistic feelings throughout the Middle East. President Woodrow Wilson's Fourteen Points, and particularly his call for the self-determination of

[5] At the time, the areas of the Arabian coast that had let oil concessions to the British-dominated Iraq Petroleum Company and the Saudi Arabian government, which had let its oil concessions to the American-owned Arabian-American Petroleum Company, were in dispute over the title to this isolated desert oasis, thought to be rich in petroleum. Although the boundaries had never been defined, Ibn Saud had sent a governor there a year before. Since two sheikdoms under British protection also claimed the oasis, British troops were sent to surround the oasis. Ibn Saud felt that the United States was not supporting him in his quarrel with the British.

peoples, had stimulated "a great clarion cry in the Middle East against imperialism."

Stevenson and his party then joined the king, Crown Prince Saud, Prince Faisal, and a number of his other sons for dinner. The table was set on a balcony from which Stevenson could see the moon sparkling on the desert. The table was laden with twenty whole roasted lambs (from the nose to the tail), lamb chops, rice, eggs, squab, macaroni, and frozen peas. Behind each guest stood a servant with a sharp knife to slice the lamb. Since the king was in frail health, there was a minimum of conversation. After about half an hour, the king was wheeled out and Stevenson followed, leaving the table still covered with the sumptuous feast to be eaten by younger members of the family and by servants.

On another balcony Stevenson was served spiced coffee. He tasted his but did not drink it all. When the servant took the cup to fill it for the next person, he dumped what was left on a lovely Oriental rug, much to Stevenson's dismay. Another servant sprayed perfume on his hands and still another carried a charcoal brazier so that he could breathe the smoke.

After the king was wheeled away, Stevenson departed for his residence. Soon there was a phone call from the crown prince inviting him to a midnight supper at his palace some four miles out of town in the desert. Over the entrance to the palace grounds were blue and white neon signs in Arabic: "Long Live the King," "Long Live the Crown Prince."

Prince Saud took Stevenson for a walk through a beautiful garden of flowers and bushes imported from all over the world. A substantial wall shut off another garden and swimming pool for his wives and mistresses from where Stevenson was walking. The crown prince, however, showed him their grounds as well, but no women were in sight. (Saudi Arabian women — except for slaves — were in purdah and when out in public wore the heaviest of veils with a mere slit for their eyes.)

During the conversation in the garden, Prince Saud stated that British troops had to be removed from the Suez Canal Zone. He then said that Israel was a "threat to the stability of the whole Middle East" and would try to invade the other countries. "Anyone who supports our enemy, Israel," he added, "is our enemy as well."

Prince Saud then insisted that the Arab refugees who had fled Palestine during the Israeli-Arab war (1948–1949) must be allowed to return to their old homes in Israel. The Arab countries, he remarked, did not want them in their countries. He added: "If outside help to Israel *were stopped, we could solve the problem of Israel." When Stevenson asked what he meant by that statement, Saud replied: "If Israel does not take back the refugees voluntarily, we will force them to take them back."*

After a few more remarks that the Jews were the aggressors in the Middle East, the crown prince expressed his displeasure that the United States had not supported Saudi Arabia over the oasis of Buraimi. At this point several of the crown prince's sons joined the party. One prince said to Stevenson: "I was in the States during the campaign. You're the greatest orator of the twentieth century." Stevenson thanked him, remarking that had he won the election he would not have been able to visit Saudi Arabia.

Crown Prince Saud changed the subject from American politics and observed that the population of Saudi Arabia was fifteen million. (That morning the deputy foreign minister had said that the population of Riyadh was one million. Ambassador Hare, however, had pointed out that there never had been a census. He thought there were between two and a half to five million people in the country and about 80,000 in Riyadh.)

When Stevenson returned to his residence, he was met by a representative of the king, who presented him with a curved Arabian sword and a gold case made from hammered British sovereigns. Stevenson thanked the official and then turned to an aide and whispered rather weakly, "It's pretty, isn't it?"

Further comment was interrupted by two servants who staggered into the room carrying a huge Oriental rug. As they unrolled the rug across the floor, Stevenson's eyes grew larger and larger in complete disbelief at what he was seeing. When he realized that the rug was to be presented to him, he turned to the ambassador and in a plaintive tone whispered, "Can't I refuse this and thank them very much?" The ambassador shook his head and said, "You'll have to take it and get it out of the country, because the king will know if you don't." (The rug was shipped from Dhahran to Stevenson's home at Libertyville.)

Stevenson thereupon made a speech expressing gratitude to the king for his hospitality and his generosity. Servants then appeared with Arab gowns, replete with gold bands for the headdress, for Stevenson and his party. In addition, his aides were presented with Swiss watches. After Stevenson made another speech of thanks, he retired exhausted from his most unusual experiences in the heart of Arabia.

En route to the airport the next morning, Stevenson said to the ambassador: "I should keep my big mouth from wagging. When I got to the airport yesterday I needed something to say and I saw those rugs. Now look what's happened to me!"

On his return to Dhahran, Stevenson spent most of the afternoon answering his correspondence with the help of a secretary from Aramco.

To Mrs. Edison Dick [6]

May 26, 1953

So much has happened, is happening and will happen, that I can repay your precious letter to Karachi in poor coin. How you succeed in condensing so much information in so few words is an art I haven't acquired.

We concluded our visit to Pakistan with four days on top of a 9,000 foot mountain in the Himalayas visiting the Governor of the Northwest Frontier and then we suddenly dropped from that frigid altitude to Karachi and thence to the deserts of Saudi Arabia in one day. Last night we dined under the stars in Riyadh with King Ibn Saud and his court and somehow made do with 20 whole roast sheep and some 64 other dishes, although they tell me I could see only a few of them from where I sat. Two Arabs stood behind me waving filthy towels to drive away the flies. But you know the Stevenson appetite.

The "indisposition" in southern India was a hasty excuse to get out of a couple of receptions and formal speeches, and I hope no greater offenses are going to mar my path to Nirvana.

From this strange land, with its curious contrasts between the 12th and 20th centuries — with the former still ahead — we travel on to Egypt. I have had a disconcerting foretaste of the abrupt end of my honeymoon through Asia. To say that the Arabs are discontented would be a diplomatic understatement.

As to the Perils of Publicity,[7] I haven't and shall have no opportunity to look at it in this desperate travel and work. I do hope I can do a little about it when I get home — if I ever do!

I was delighted to hear that Adlai turned up. It looks now as though I would not be back before early August which means I would probably have to go to California to see him before he leaves for Korea. I am hoping to find Borden in Cairo and John Fell somewhere along the route later on. What an adventure for all of us! What a pity that they have to travel in this mad way with me. I am thinking a

---

[6] The original of this typewritten letter is in the possession of Mrs. Dick.
[7] See note 30 to Chapter One, above.

little of staying on after the last article is concluded to have a holiday with them somewhere in Europe, depending on Adlai's plans.

And now I must try to catch up with the pursuing mail — after telling you nothing about our adventures in strange lands among strange people. Dearest love to all of the Dicks.

To Stephen A. Mitchell [8]

May 26, 1953

Dear Steve:

So many thanks for your letter of May 11 and the enclosures about the 1954 convention plan.[9] Even if you are obliged to drop the idea in view of the extensive opposition, the very fact that it was discussed is, I think, wholesome evidence of lively party spirit and interest.

I am still alive, breathing, and unfortunately, eating altogether too well. However, I shall have much to report after witnessing at first hand some of the appalling complexities of this vast world but I have no answers and I am loath, therefore, to do much speaking for some time after I get back. We have travelled with such rapidity and our impressions have registered so rapidly that it is hard to find and keep an overall perspective. I hope I can find one at all — let alone keep it! We were delighted to read in the paper about your journey south and I am heartened indeed by several communications from around the country indicating respect and confidence in your leadership.[10] It must have been a very trying period and I am still hoping for the best with regard to relations with our friend in New York.[11]

Last night we dined under the stars with Ibn Saud on 20 whole roast sheep!

My best to you, Clayton,[12] Hi,[13] and your "colleagues" — as we itinerant diplomats say.

Yours,

ADLAI

[8] Chairman of the Democratic National Committee. The original is in the papers of S. A. Mitchell, the Harry S. Truman Library.

[9] Mr. Mitchell had proposed that the Democratic party hold a national convention in 1954. The idea was dropped later.

[10] Mr. Mitchell had recently traveled extensively in the South to rebuild party strength.

[11] Dwight Palmer, treasurer of the Democratic National Committee. According to Mitchell, Palmer wanted to replace him as national chairman. Letter to Carol Evans, September 14, 1967.

[12] Clayton Fritchey, deputy chairman of the Democratic National Committee.

[13] Hyman B. (Hy) Raskin, deputy chairman of the Democratic National Committee.

Later that afternoon Stevenson received a visit from Dr. Husni Khalifa, managing editor of the Egyptian News Agency in Cairo, who was visiting Dhahran as a guest of Aramco. He was lavish in his praise of Aramco's training program for Saudi Arabians. Then he asserted that the British had persuaded Secretary of State Dulles that the Egyptians only wanted to destroy the military base in the Suez area. He said this was not true: "Egypt wants to maintain the base as a bastion of freedom, but we hate the British and we cannot join any joint defense of the Suez with the British." [14] Dr. Khalifa recommended that the United States sponsor an Arab defense pact, but he said: "We don't want the British or the French in it because they will continue to exploit the Arab world, whereas we know the United States doesn't want to exploit the Arabs." [15] Stevenson replied: "The United States has long favored regional pacts. If the Arab countries will not support an extension of the North Atlantic Treaty Organization, then apparently a regional pact is the only one that will work."

According to Dr. Khalifa, the British asserted that the Egyptians could not maintain the Suez base. "We haven't enough technicians and we are willing to employ technicians, including the English, but we must command the base." He added that the British were proposing to withdraw their troops but insisted on leaving ten thousand tech-

[14] After Britain invaded Egypt in 1882, it promised a total of 66 times to evacuate the country before it finally did so in 1954. From the Egyptian point of view, Britain was the enemy. On October 13, 1951, the United States, France, the United Kingdom and Turkey presented proposals inviting the Egyptian government to become a founding member of a proposed Allied Command, by which it would grant facilities, use of ports and airfields, and the establishment of a headquarters on Egyptian territory. The United Kingdom, the proposals stated, would be prepared to agree to the supersession of the Anglo-Egyptian Treaty of 1936 (whereby the British were entrusted with the defense of the canal) and would be willing to withdraw from Egypt such British forces as were not allocated to the Middle East Command by agreement between Egypt and the other parties concerned. On October 15, 1951, the Egyptian government rejected the proposals and the Egyptian Parliament unanimously voted abrogation of the 1936 Anglo-Egyptian Treaty. Great Britain declared Egypt's step illegal and reinforced her garrison in the canal zone. George Lenczowski, *The Middle East in World Affairs* (Ithaca: Cornell University Press, 1952), pp. 329–337.

[15] William R. Polk has written: "The 19th century witnessed the steady incursions of the Western powers into the Arab world. By the end of World War I virtually the entire area was under the control of European powers. . . . The Syrians, who were conquered by the French, bitterly hated the French and tended to look to Britain for some relief; while the Egyptians, who were conquered by Britain, fought the British and tended to think of the French as friends." *What the Arabs Think* (New York: Foreign Policy Association Headline Series, No. 96, 1952), p. 33. See also William R. Polk, *The United States and the Arab World* (Cambridge: Harvard University Press, 1965), for a perceptive discussion of such things as Arab nationalism, Palestine, and the Arabs' quest for identity and dignity.

nicians to operate the base. "This means," Khalifa continued, "that no Egyptians can be employed in these posts." He concluded by telling Stevenson that the United States had to be "strict with the British."

Stevenson replied: "Imperialism is withering around the world. You have able new leaders.[16] Although you may detest the past we all must learn to live together. In Asia, where I have just been, the leaders are so preoccupied with the past that they let hatred of their past colonial experience cloud their vision. As a result, they are still fighting the past instead of channeling the dynamic of their revolution into building a new economy."

Dr. Khalifa observed that in Egypt the Naguib revolution was "tackling the economic problem." The standard of living "had been dreadful under the king. We had two hundred families running our society, but now we are making progress." He stated, however, "Our main problem is the British occupation right now, and we must get rid of it. As long as they are there they can interfere in our politics. You got rid of them by revolution." He added: "Unless we get rid of them the ground will be fertile for Communism. The Communists identify themselves with nationalism and their slogans have an appeal to the illiterate masses. We must fight for our freedom. We cannot remain as cattle." He concluded with the observation that Naguib's government would be overthrown if it did not protest the British occupation. The Moslem Brotherhood, he remarked, was already criticizing Naguib for being too lenient toward the British.[17]

The next morning Stevenson went on a tour of carpentry and machine shops where Aramco trained Saudi Arabian workers. He also visited a general school where Aramco taught reading and writing, typing and shorthand. In the afternoon he toured Aramco's medical center. As a result of Aramco's free medical care for its employees and their families, Stevenson was told, there was a growing demand from the people that the government establish hospitals in the country.

He spent most of the afternoon talking with professional linguists and sociologists who were employed by Aramco to study the movement of tribes within the country, economic conditions, and the development of public opinion. They explained that what Aramco was doing in

[16] On July 23, 1952, General Mohammed Naguib and other army officers seized the government, exiled King Farouk, arrested most of the top officials, instituted a land reform program, and abolished the title *pasha* (lord).

[17] The anti-Western Moslem Brotherhood had been founded in 1929. After a series of terrorist acts, including the killing of the Cairo chief of police, the Egyptian government outlawed the movement in December, 1948. It was permitted to resume its activities in 1951. For a discussion of the movement see James Heyworth-Dunne, *Religious and Political Trends in Moslem Egypt* (Washington: published by the author, 1950).

elementary and technical education and in medicine was known through-out the country. They emphasized that the bulk of the population was migratory, moving around the country for water, and during the dry season, the Bedouins flocked to Aramco installations where there were wells. The past year, they added, as many as fifteen thousand camels had been concentrated at one of their stations. The desert, they re-marked, was now quite safe for the Aramco people and there practically was no such thing as brigandage.

When Stevenson asked them about the institution of slavery, they replied that it was dying out. The government had agreed to allow no more importation of slaves from Africa and there was a growing ten-dency to manumit slaves, although some white women were still being brought in from the Mediterranean coast as concubines to the royal family and to some of the governors.

They stated that the concept of rising expectations on the part of the public was still far behind the rest of the Middle East but it was on the increase. Today, they pointed out, there was much more protest than ten years ago if the government misused its funds. When they ex-plained that there was no political opposition in the country, Stevenson observed that "this was a hell of a place for politicians."

After dinner that evening, Stevenson boarded a KLM Constellation for Egypt. He wrote about his visit to Saudi Arabia:

NO PEACE FOR ISRAEL [18]

The long-slumbering Middle East is wide awake today — shaking off its colonial shackles and smoldering with anger. This can't be said too often or too emphatically at home, where we tend to focus our attention on Europe and the Far East.

I traveled for three unforgettable weeks through this turbulent half-way world between Asia and the West: from the oil-rich desert kingdom of Saudi Arabia to an Egypt in revolution; from Lebanon, Syria and Jordan with their camps of sullen, seething Arab refugees to holy Jerusalem, now torn asunder by barbed wire and bitterness. And there, across a desolated strip of no man's land, I stepped into the stony, strug-gling pioneer State of Israel, where gunfire still crackles almost nightly along uncertain frontiers.

But the story of these three weeks properly begins in Arabia, the heart-land and spiritual home of a Moslem community that stretches from Casablanca to the South Pacific.

[18] *Look,* August 11, 1953. The rest of this article is reprinted in Chapters Fourteen through Sixteen, below.

My first glimpse of the Arab world was this up-to-date American oil city [Dhahran, Saudi Arabia] sprawling over treeless sand and stone. Here, under a pitiless sun, the Arabian American Oil Company is developing the fabulous oil resources of King Ibn Saud's immense domain that includes the most sacred shrines of Islam in the "forbidden" cities of Mecca and Medina.

Dhahran is a transplanted fragment of enlightened industrial statesmanship. Along with modern technology, the company has introduced schools, vocational training, hospitals and modern housing for its 25,000 employees, many of them long-haired Bedouins who had never seen an automobile or an airplane until they came — sometimes a thousand miles — to work for Aramco. Now, roads are probing the desert; camel caravans are disappearing; corn flakes compete with dates; enterprising Arabians are starting contracting firms, traveling abroad, asking questions. A middle class is rising from the sands of feudal Arabia. "Oil has telescoped a thousand years into twenty" and thrust even this last corner of the old Arab world into the twentieth century.

From Dhahran, we flew over the hot sands to Riyadh, the desert-ringed capital where the great Ibn Saud, aging but still a towering, majestic figure, holds court in a mud-brick palace with air-conditioned bedrooms, surrounded by camels and Cadillacs, swimming pools and drought-stricken nomads. His hospitality is legendary: When I absent-mindedly admired an Oriental rug, he promptly presented it to me! Then, flanked by retainers with great ornamental swords, cartridge belts and rifles, we sat down to dinner under the stars with his ministers, the crown prince and some of the King's 36 other sons. (No statistics on daughters are available.)

The table was heaped with dishes of the East and West and 20 whole roast sheep reclining on mountains of rice. It was Ramadan, the Moslem month of fasting from dawn to sunset, and King Ibn Saud, nibbling cracked wheat, assured me that every morsel of the fabulous feast would vanish the moment we surrendered the table to his numberless servants and the poor.

Afterwards came the water basins and towels, rose water, spiced coffee, perfume and incense to sweeten the hands and beards; but neither tobacco, alcohol nor ladies were visible in that orthodox Moslem court where the new and the old collide.

I wanted to talk about the problems of the Middle East and the impact of Western ways on Saudi Arabia. But at the moment, the chief concern and main topic of conversation was the oasis of Baremi,[19]

---

[19] Stevenson preferred this spelling to the more usual Buraimi. "The transcription

lying somewhere along the kingdom's undefined southeastern border. In the past — before the discovery of oil — frontiers meant little to the nomads of the Arabian peninsula. But today, Ibn Saud claims Baremi; and so do two adjoining sheikdoms under British protection.

The King is mighty angry with the British and insistent on American support. I thought about all our global headaches from Berlin to Korea, and I honestly told him I didn't know where we stood on Baremi!

or transliteration from Arabic is always an open question." Raymond Hare to Walter Johnson, July 13, 1967.

Fourteen

Egypt

MAY 28 – JUNE 2, 1953

E^{*n route from Dhahran to Cairo on the evening of May 27, the KLM}
Constellation landed at Baghdad. During the hour layover Stevenson was permitted to leave the airport and he wandered through the old
bazaar examining the variety of goods and food for sale. He remarked
how thoroughly he enjoyed "these off moments on the trip."*

At one A.M. *the plane landed in Cairo, where Stevenson was welcomed by a sizable crowd, including Foreign Minister Mahmoud Fawzi
and G. Lewis Jones, deputy chief of mission at the U.S. embassy. After
a night's sleep and breakfast, Stevenson met with Mr. Jones. He explained that Prime Minister Mohammed Naguib had cleaned up corruption and had started a program of land reform. Now the Egyptian
government, he continued, wanted to build a huge dam at Aswan on
the Nile to increase the irrigated land of the country by one-third. But,
he added, the leaders were obsessed with the British base in the Suez
and this issue cut across all others.[1] He explained that the British were
willing to evacuate their troops but wanted British technicians to
manage the installations. Egypt insisted, however, that it must manage
the base stretching alongside the Suez Canal for over a hundred miles
as a matter of principle and sovereignty.*

*After this discussion, Stevenson called on the foreign minister. Mr.
Fawzi remarked that the Middle East was a weak area and that the
free world could not afford to leave it that way. Stevenson observed
that the leaders where he had just been in Asia wanted to carry on eco-*

[1] See note 14 to Chapter Thirteen, above.

nomic development by consent and not by totalitarian methods of coercion. Economic development by the democratic process, he continued, would be slower, and he wondered if it would prove fast enough in view of the problem. Then he remarked that the great problem in the Middle East was economic. "Issues like the base in the Suez and Israel are divergencies to take your mind from the basic problem. How, therefore, can you focus on your top priority — economic development?"

The foreign minister replied that Egypt did not want to use coercion to bring about economic growth or coercion to solve other problems. "But you must remember that we have had British occupation here for seventy years and we feel that this is coercing us." [2] *If the British remained, he added, Egypt would be a weak ally and maybe hostile to the Western nations. In the present situation, he continued, "We definitely cannot join in an agreement on an overall defense pact, but when we get the British out of the Suez then we are free to do it as equals."* [3]

Mr. Fawzi remarked that Egypt would utilize British technicians to maintain the Suez base, but the British were insisting that they had to manage the equipment and control its utilization from London. He stated: "The British technicians must be employees of Egypt. It will be all right with us if the instructions are issued from London, but they must go through Egyptian officials before they reach the technicians. And we feel we should increase the number of Egyptian technicians as quickly as possible."

He added that the man in the street "may feel that we are being too moderate on this, but we are trying to act as leaders and if we can reach this agreement we will try to persuade the people that this is a

[2] From this and other conversations, Stevenson realized the intensity of Egyptian nationalism. In 1953, the British had 80,000 troops in the Suez base, a force approximately twice the size of the Egyptian army. It was only a two-hour taxi drive from the base to Cairo, and the British had demonstrated their willingness in the past to use force at any time the Egyptian government had shown an unwonted spirited independence. The U.S. government's attempt to persuade the Egyptians to "buy" some new form of designation for the base as a part of the protection against Soviet encroachment simply labeled the United States as the successors of British imperialism.

[3] In January, 1955, Iraq joined a defense alliance with Turkey, the Baghdad Pact. Britain, Pakistan, and Iran subsequently joined the alliance — the Middle East Treaty Organization. Egypt saw this as an attempt by Britain to reestablish elsewhere in the Arab world a military position after it had withdrawn from the Suez base in July, 1954. (Withdrawal was not completed until 1956.) It was also viewed as an attempt to isolate Egypt from the other Arab states. As a countermove, Egypt and Syria signed a mutual defense treaty, the Damascus Pact, in March, 1955. See Charles F. Gallagher, "The United Arab Republic Today, Part 1: The Liberation of Egypt," American University Field Staff *Reports Service*, January 8, 1960.

wise agreement." Mr. Fawzi then insisted that a solution to the Suez question was the key to solving many other situations. "Even Israel," he suggested, "may be easier to solve because to solve the Suez will help to gain the goodwill of the Arab world and of Moslems everywhere for the West."

Stevenson replied: "What you say is fair, and I think inevitable, but Britain will withdraw ,her soldiers. This is dramatic progress. Therefore, is the last issue of technical management, which is still a management problem, a wise one for Egypt to assume at the present moment?" The foreign minister answered that they were willing to have a mixed commission of Egyptian and British to decide what technicians were needed. Stevenson then raised the possibility of an international organization to run the installations until Egyptian technicians were trained.

Fawzi replied that this was a reasonable suggestion, but "You must remember this whole question in terms of our background. Our background requires that we must find a formula that does not violate the sovereignty of Egypt. Our people want quick action." He added: "During the two world wars Egypt was not the keeper of the door in its own house. We have been the bearers of wood and the diggers of ditches for colonial powers.[4] We have not been the masters in our own country."

When Stevenson left the conference with the foreign minister, he remarked that he was "immensely impressed" with Fawzi's rational approach to difficult problems.

Stevenson next spent an hour alone with the prime minister, General Mohammed Naguib. When Stevenson left the conference, General Naguib walked with him to a waiting automobile. Reporters swarmed around the two, but all Stevenson would say was: "He gave me a good cup of coffee."

Stevenson reported to his aides that Naguib suspected that the British did not really want to leave Egypt. If this happened, the prime minister warned that he "could not control the people." Some Communists, he said, were creating incidents in the troubled situation and he was going to have to take counter steps very quickly. Stevenson explained that he had suggested the appointment of a commission to make an inventory of the managerial talent needed to operate the base.

[4] David Landes, *Bankers and Pashas: International Finance and Economic Imperialism in Egypt* (Cambridge: Harvard University Press, 1958), documents the way in which the Egyptians, who were indeed the diggers, lost control not only of the canal itself, but also of virtually their entire economy by their own greed and stupidity and by the incredibly sharp practices of the European banking community. By the time of Stevenson's visit to Egypt, the canal itself was the symbol of European rapacity and greed as well as the weakness and ineffectiveness of the Egyptians.

Later that afternoon Stevenson visited the embassy for a briefing. Deputy Chief of Mission G. Lewis Jones stressed that Egyptian public opinion had been anti-British for years and that the present generation of leaders was raised in that atmosphere. He pointed out that the leaders of the Revolutionary Command Council, headed by Colonel Gamal Abdel Nasser, had stirred the public by talking about guerrilla warfare and blood flowing. Three weeks earlier, however, when the situation was explosive, Nasser and the others had stopped talking about military action against the British. He speculated that they realized they would not stand a chance in such fighting. An attack by Egypt also would have made it possible for the British to occupy Cairo and Alexandria. Moreover, the Egyptian troops around Gaza could not have been supplied and Israel would have been able to inflict a serious defeat.

Jones then observed that none of the military leaders who had taken control of the government a year ago were from wealthy Egyptian families. They were all middle class in background and products of British military training. The Revolutionary Command Council, he added, had picked Naguib as prime minister to be a "front man" for them. It was doubtful that he could take a decision against the rest of the members of the council. Colonel Nasser, he thought, was the man who produced the ideas for the council.

Stevenson remarked that General Naguib had told him that his reforms had created enmity for his regime among the rich. At the same time, he told Stevenson, the Communists and the British were stirring discontent among the masses. The only thing that could unite the wealthy and the masses was their hatred for the British. Jones commented that Naguib was "absolutely right." If the rich and the masses felt that Naguib was "soft on the British, they might be able to oust him." If the British did leave, he added, "The politicians will have to find a new issue."

Randall S. Williams, Jr., counsellor of embassy for economic affairs, described the economic plight of Egypt as grim. It was basically a one-crop country with 80 per cent of the arable land devoted to cotton. Unfortunately, the price of cotton had dropped disastrously and Egypt's foreign exchange was extremely low. He noted that the population had been 12 million in 1932 and now had reached 21 million. Population was increasing two per cent a year. Prospects for ameliorating poverty, he stated, centered in water. The new dam that was being proposed would increase the acreage by one-third and it would double the yield of another million acres already in use.

Following this conversation, Stevenson visited with General Sir

Brian Robertson, the principal British negotiator on the Suez base question, who was returning to London to attend the coronation of Queen Elizabeth. Stevenson opened the conversation by saying that both Naguib and Fawzi desired to negotiate and neither had sounded as intemperate as he had expected. He added that he had suggested the creation of a commission to examine the complexities of operating the base.

Sir Brian said that all the clamor about the British was largely to divert attention from Egypt's real problems. He reiterated the British position of willingness to withdraw all troops so long as British technicians were left to keep the base in first-class condition in case war came. He stated that the Naguib government was committed to the use of force unless the issue was resolved. He added that if the British did not achieve a settlement with Naguib, any successor government would be less reasonable to work with. He insisted that certain jobs had to be held by British subjects. If this proved unacceptable to the Egyptians, he said, it would be better to close down the base altogether despite the peril to the North Atlantic Treaty Organization and the Middle East.

The British wanted to be sure, he continued, that if war came they could reenter the base. "Our concern would be lessened," he added, "if the United States showed she had a lively interest in seeing that the agreement would be adhered to if war came." Stevenson pointed out to him that General Naguib had expressed opposition to the United States underwriting any Anglo-Egyptian agreement. It would just mean "taking on a new enemy," Naguib had asserted. As the discussion ended, Stevenson said that it was his impression that both sides were not so far apart as each thought. He expressed the belief that a formula of words could be found to satisfy Egypt's sovereignty and Britain's concern with maintaining a usable base.

Early that evening G. Lewis Jones held a large reception for Stevenson to meet the diplomatic community and a number of prominent Egyptians. There was time, however, for a brief uninterrupted talk with William Lakeland, political officer at the U.S. embassy. He placed heavy emphasis on the powerful nationalistic feelings of the members of the Revolutionary Command Council. He said that these young officers blamed the British for not training the Egyptian army well enough, under the 1936 Anglo-Egyptian treaty, to fight Israel more effectively in 1948–1949. Then he described the members of the Revolutionary Command Council as middle-class individuals who wanted to raise the standard of living through orderly change. He added that the

Moslem Brotherhood was powerful and that it might be able to take over the country.[5]

Later that evening, after an already arduous day, the embassy persuaded Stevenson to attend the commencement exercises at the American University of Cairo. When he arrived he was astonished to see his name in the printed program as an honored guest. (Obviously, the embassy had committed him to attend without seeking his approval.)

Early the next morning, he called on Ambassador Jefferson Caffery. The ambassador said that the British in Egypt and Naguib wanted to settle the issue of the base. He stated, however, that a number of Conservative party leaders in London were blocking a settlement assuming that Naguib would then fall and the British would be able to negotiate better with a new government. The ambassador said such thinking was absolutely wrong. If Naguib fell, the new government would be dominated by either the extreme right or the extreme left.

After this conversation, Stevenson, Blair, and Borden Stevenson, who had just arrived from the United States, flew to Luxor to see the ancient monuments.[6]

On Stevenson's return from Luxor on May 30, he lunched with the British ambassador. The ambassador told Stevenson that the Egyptians were not capable of running the base. The base, he insisted, would deteriorate under their control and be of no use in an emergency. Furthermore, he said, if the Egyptians gained control of the base, the British had no faith that instructions from London would be transmitted by the Egyptians to the technicians.

After lunch, Stevenson met with Colonel Gamal Abdel Nasser, Major Abdel Hakim Amer, and Wing Commander Abdel Latif Baghdady. They described how their grandfathers and their fathers had talked constantly of the British occupation of Egypt. In view of the violently anti-British sentiment among the people, they stated, the base was really of little use to the British. They expressed their opposition to talk of the base being "a base for the free world," since it sounded like just another name for continuing the British occupation.

They too said they were willing to have London send instructions to British technicians in the base, provided the instructions were transmitted through the Egyptian government. Otherwise, Egyptian sovereignty was not complete. Colonel Nasser made it clear that they wanted

[5] In October, 1954, the Moslem Brotherhood attempted to assassinate Colonel Nasser. He arrested several thousand members of the brotherhood and two were executed.

[6] Attwood and Johnson remained in Cairo to interview a number of people, including Egyptian educators and foreign correspondents.

to maintain the base and build the Middle East "into a bastion of freedom." He added: "The British say, however, if they pull out there will be a vacuum here. We reply, there is a vacuum here right now, as long as the British are in that base, because the Arab countries, Egypt included, will do nothing in the way of organizing a defense scheme until the British leave."

Colonel Nasser emphasized that the Communists were particularly active at that moment and were telling the people that the Western nations were imperialistic while the Russians were anticolonial. As he started to describe the internal opposition to the Naguib government, Stevenson said: "You underestimate your own strength with the people. Since you took power last July you have worked miracles. You have ousted the king and the old regime. You have gotten from the British the Sudan agreement.[7] As far as the Suez is concerned, you have a British pledge that they will withdraw all their troops. Remember, just as you have a public opinion to worry about in Egypt, the British have a public opinion at home. Do not push them so far that the whole question becomes unsolvable." He observed: "If I owned the United States Steel Corporation, I would still have to hire the present management to run it. You have to do the same thing in the base." The three representatives of the Revolutionary Command Council continued to insist, however, that any instructions from London had to be transmitted through Egyptian officials. "Otherwise the public will not accept the agreement," they stated.

That evening Ambassador and Mrs. Caffery gave a formal dinner in Stevenson's honor. Among those present were General Naguib and Foreign Minister Fawzi. After dinner, Stevenson, Caffery, Naguib, and Fawzi withdrew for a talk. According to Stevenson, Naguib was not as insistent as Colonel Nasser had been that instructions from London to the technicians at the base had to be transmitted through the Egyptian government.

After breakfast the next morning, Stevenson visited the National Museum to see the jewelry, sculptures, and other artifacts that had been found in the tomb of King Tutankhamen. Then the group visited a number of farm villages to see how some of the fifteen million fellaheen (peasants) lived. Attwood wrote in his diary: "We scurried from village

---

[7] In 1898, British and Egyptian troops won control of the Sudan. The following year a joint British-Egyptian government was established. But, in fact, Egyptian participation in the Anglo-Egyptian Sudan was nominal. In 1921, the British ended even the nominal aspects of Egyptian control. In 1953, the "joint" domination was terminated. An international commission was created to assist the Sudan in a transition to self-government. On January 1, 1956, Britain and Egypt recognized the independence of the Sudan.

to village in a blinding cloud of dust." Very depressing to Stevenson were the thousands upon thousands of flies in the streets and inside the houses. Even more depressing, however, was to see flies all over the eyes, noses, and mouths of little children. He was told that five out of every ten children born alive died before the age of five.

That afternoon he visited the tombs and pyramids of the old city of Memphis south of Cairo. "We staggered around the desert in the most scorching heat and finally ducked into a cool tomb called the tomb of Ti where we looked at walls covered with drawings and inscriptions," Attwood wrote in his diary. Finally, Stevenson broke away and was driven to Gizeh for the traditional camel trip around the pyramids and the Sphinx.

The next morning Stevenson was flown in a British airplane up and down the length of the military base in the Suez Canal Zone. The plane landed at British headquarters near the Great Bitter Lake. At lunch with General Sir Cameron Nicholson, Air Chief Marshal Arthur Sanders and several other officers, Sanders told Stevenson that he was the first leading American — civilian or military — to visit the base to see how extensive it actually was. They all expressed concern that the base would deteriorate if left in Egyptian hands. But they all agreed that the base would not be very useful if the Egyptian population was hostile to a continued British presence.

Stevenson explained to them his understanding of the Egyptian position that London could control the technicians who would remain after troops were evacuated as long as the instructions were transmitted through the Egyptian government. They seemed pleased to have this information, since discussions between the two countries had been suspended early in May.

They expressed concern that fanatics not under Naguib's control might create incidents that could lead to an outbreak of fighting. They all made it clear that they considered Naguib's government the best in terms of reasonable men with whom to negotiate. It was pointed out that the Suez Canal Company would be most unhappy if the British evacuated the base, since they feared that the Egyptians might then nationalize the canal.[8]

On his return to Cairo, Stevenson had a conference with Dr. Hussein Kamel Selim, dean of the School of Commerce and Business of Fouad I University. Stevenson told Selim that neither the British nor the Egyptians, in his opinion, completely understood each other's position with

---

[8] On June 13, 1956, the British withdrew their last troops from the canal zone, leaving full responsibility for the defense of the canal to Egypt. Egyptian President Gamal Abdel Nasser nationalized the canal on July 26, 1956, precipitating an international crisis.

clarity and neither seemed quite to understand how far the other side would go in negotiations, and he explained to the dean his understanding of what this was.

Selim replied that he did not think General Naguib understood that the British were willing to go as far as Stevenson had outlined. He thought that it would be helpful, in the situation, if the British would state publicly that instructions to the technicians would be transmitted through the Naguib government. He also agreed that a joint commission to study the maintenance of the base was an acceptable idea.

Stevenson suggested that both sides should get down to fundamentals and be reasonable on the question of management or control. He said that it was possible that some Egyptians in the negotiations did not understand English well enough to grasp technical details. The dean said that he thought this was an important point.

When the conversation was finished, Stevenson went up to the roof of the Semiramis Hotel, where he was staying, to attend a dinner given in his honor by General Naguib and the members of the Revolutionary Command Council. Stevenson sat with General Naguib, Colonel Nasser, Foreign Minister Fawzi, and Ambassador Caffery. They discussed again the respective positions of the two countries on the Suez base and Stevenson reiterated the points he had made earlier to Dean Selim.

Before retiring that evening, Stevenson found time to write his sister:

To Mrs. Ernest L. Ives [9]

June 1, 1953

Dear Buff:

Forgive the haste. It's dreadfully late but I want to get this off . . . before we leave early in the morning.

1. Arrive Rome June 28 — Reservations for my party, including Borden, are being made by Pan American at either the Hassler or Excelsior Hotel.

2. Lv. Rome for Venice by air July 6 — and on to Vienna by train that night.

3. Vienna for 2 days, then Germany for 5 and arrive Paris night of 15th.

4. Bill [Blair] says he has made air & hotel res. for you & Ernest & John Fell from Rome on. If you don't want them, you can cancel of course at any time. Perhaps you will want to join us in Venice — per-

[9] This letter is in the Elizabeth Stevenson Ives collection, Illinois State Historical Library.

haps staying there with John Fell while I'm rushing around Vienna & rejoin in Germany. We can see. In Rome I'll have to write a piece which means I'll have to lock up somewhere for 3 or 4 days but I'll find somebody to show the boys around.

I think I'm going to live thru this trip but sometimes wonder! Spent today in Canal Zone on the British base and tonight talking with Neguibe [Naguib] for 3 hrs!

Love,

AD.

Bordie O.K. Doubt if its worth your while to come to Athens. I'll be there only a day & a half I think — interviewing — but do as you wish.

The next morning, June 2, Stevenson held a brief press conference. The questions mainly concerned the Suez base and whether he had a solution to the issue. He refused to propose or endorse any solution but he did repeat several times that he felt the two nations were closer to an understanding than either realized. When Stevenson and his party reached the airport to depart for Beirut, General Naguib, Foreign Minister Fawzi, and a number of other officials were there to see him off. Photographers insisted that Stevenson wave to the group from the boarding platform. As he did he told Naguib: "General, I'm not running for office in Egypt." Naguib waved back and replied: "We all like you. That's why they want your picture."

Stevenson wrote about his visit to Egypt:

NO PEACE FOR ISRAEL [10]

But the anti-British feeling was worse in Egypt — eclipsing, in Cairo, even the bitterness about Israel that permeates every Arab country. Two burning issues kindle the passions of the Middle East — the great British military base along the Suez Canal and Israel's lusty little beachhead in a hostile Moslem world. Both are overcharged with emotion and both threaten stability and progress in the whole Middle East. And there is no overestimating the importance of this area. Look at the map, consider the oil, think of the 40 million Arabs and the world's vast Moslem community.

Emerging only now from sleepy centuries and independent for the first time in modern history, the Arab nations face the same staggering social, economic and political problems as the new Asia: ignorance,

[10] *Look*, August 11, 1953. This excerpt is a continuation of the portion reprinted at the end of Chapter Thirteen, above, and continues in Chapters Fifteen and Sixteen, below.

poverty, disease, feudalism, instability. These are the *real* problems, but "imperialism" and "injustice" are the universal preoccupations. Out here, communism is remote and for tomorrow; Suez and Israel are next door and for today. So I am glad Secretary of State John Foster Dulles took time out this spring to look at the Middle East for himself.

In Egypt, I saw the ancient monuments and dreamed by moonlight in the Temple of Karnak, which must surely be "the biggest thing in ruins." I recommend it to anyone suffering from self-importance. I visited the Sphinx on camelback (with protests from the camel), inspected the vast British canal-zone base and jeeped along dusty country roads of the fertile, overcrowded Nile Valley, where 20 million people live off six million acres of land and half the national income goes to 1.5 per cent of the population. I saw poverty and squalor in primitive, fly-infested villages. But all I *heard* was Suez, Suez, Suez. I heard about it from Gen. Mohammed Naguib, the modest, genial, soft-spoken leader of the so-called Revolutionary Committee that seized power a year ago, kicked out King Farouk and scattered the ruling clique of pashas and corrupt politicians — probably forever. I heard about it from Col. Abdel Nasser and some of the other young, inexperienced but dedicated army officers who make up the committee; from the wise and sophisticated Foreign Minister, Mahmoud Fawzi, and from many other Egyptians in and out of public life.

The men who run Egypt nowadays are not military dictators in the classic mold. They impressed me as sincere, realistic men with no illusions about the enormity of the task of setting Egypt's old house in order. They don't pretend to know how to solve all of Egypt's grim social and economic problems, but at least they know the people's needs.

Decency and selflessness, vigorous land reforms, relentless attacks on corruption, economic-control measures, political house cleaning and social improvement have won Naguib widespread public support and have given Egypt a new sense of national pride, purpose and hope.

But will the present healthy and hopeful movement evolve into something enduring — or will it degenerate into another dictatorship?

Although military bases exist on friendly foreign soil throughout the world, in Egypt the press and politicians compete in inflammatory denunciation of imperialism and the British base. And Naguib and his associates believe that no Egyptian government can survive unless this last vestige of the long British occupation is ended. He put it to me this way: "We don't propose to be doormen in our own house any longer." And he illustrated Egypt's insistence on complete and immediate control of the base with the Arab story of a man who gave his house away but kept one nail for himself. Now and then, the man would drop in to examine and polish his nail. Finally, he hung a dead cat on it — and the occupants moved out.

Naguib says, "We don't want a single British nail in our house." But at the same time, he and every responsible Egyptian I talked to conceded the imperative importance of this great base and of its proper maintenance for the defense not only of the Suez Canal and of the whole Middle East but of Egypt itself.

I also discussed the problem with the British in Cairo and the commanders at the base itself, where airfields, hospitals, supply depots and workshops line the canal for more than one hundred miles. The British insist, not unreasonably, that only trained British technicians can keep the base and its costly British-made equipment in combat-ready condition, at least for the present. They are prepared to withdraw their troops and turn the security of the base over to the Egyptian army — but not the management and operation of their vast installations.

Stripped of the excessive polemics, the situation adds up to this: This great base, perhaps the largest in the world, is a vital link in the free world's defenses.

The Egyptians say that the base on their soil is an intolerable violation of sovereignty and that Britain must evacuate lock, stock and barrel and let Egypt run it with British help and evidently at British and U.S. expense.

The British agree that as a besieged fortress in a hostile Egypt, the base would be useless. But they point out that it would also be useless unless efficiently maintained, and they question Egypt's present state of political stability and technical proficiency for the job. And they raise further questions about the right of re-entry with military forces in an emergency.

The sad thing is that both sides are right (though I think the Egyptians underestimate the skills needed to keep the base in operation). And a logical man would probably say that if the base is indispensable to the international defense structure, the proper solution is internationalization.

It seems to me that the area of real dispute between Egypt and Britain about who "controls," "manages" and "operates" the base — and how — is in reality so narrow that an accommodation could be found consistent both with Egyptian sovereignty and with efficient maintenance.

The root of the trouble is lack of confidence and more public heat than light. The long background of occupation, frustration and mutual distrust — abetted by decades of political fireworks — makes it hard for

Egyptians and Britons to sit down together and talk reasonably and trustingly. Perhaps a third party could assist. Our able ambassador, Jefferson Caffery, was certainly helpful in the Anglo-Egyptian dispute over the Sudan. But so far, Egypt has rejected three-party talks.

One thing is certain: In Egypt, an agreement on Suez takes precedence over regional-defense discussions or peace with Israel — even over pressing internal problems. And the survival of General Naguib's relatively temperate and certainly honest government — the best Egypt has had in decades — may well depend on a satisfactory settlement with Britain. Waiting in the wings are political extremists ready to exploit anything that looks like weakness or appeasement.

Fortunately, Egypt's responsible leaders are far more reasonable in private than their public utterances would indicate. The British, too, are anxious for an early settlement with this government. So the will exists; and with temperance and reason — perhaps help — a way can be found.

Fifteen

Lebanon, Syria, Jordan

JUNE 2 – JUNE 7, 1953

When the plane of the Middle East Airways landed at Beirut after a flight out over the Mediterranean to avoid Israel, Stevenson was met by a welcoming committee which included Halim Bey Abu Izzedine, chief of protocol of the Lebanese government, and U.S. Ambassador Harold B. Minor. The reporters present pressed Stevenson for his views on the British military base in the Suez. He expressed confidence that Egypt and Britain would find an early solution to the dispute over Suez "consistent with Egypt's undisputable sovereignty and the main necessities concerning the base."

After this brief statement, Stevenson went to the embassy for a briefing. Ambassador Minor pointed out that American educators and missionaries had been active in Lebanon for over a hundred years. The establishment of such institutions as the American University of Beirut (1866) had built goodwill for the United States. The emigration of Lebanese to the United States had been another factor contributing to good relations between the two countries. The ambassador remarked that there were as many Lebanese in North and South America as there were in Lebanon. (The population in 1953 was some 1¼ million, not including 120,000 refugees from Palestine.) He also stated that the activities of American oil companies in the Middle East, with their fifty-fifty profit-sharing plan, had strengthened goodwill toward the United States.

But, the ambassador continued, this goodwill had been dissipated by United States support of Israel. Arabs, he added, viewed Israel as an

"American creation." The Arab world also was violently anticolonial and felt that the United States supported the British in Egypt and the French in North Africa.[1]

The ambassador warned that if the United States did not respond to the demand of the Arabs for safety against Israel, the entire area might turn against the United States. He contended that the national interest of the United States required a policy that did not prefer Israel but stood for equal treatment for all and a preference for none.

The ambassador observed that all the Arab states (except the Kingdom of Jordan) favored the internationalization of Jerusalem. He added that the Arabs wanted the 1948 partition line,[2] but he thought that somewhere between the partition line and the present boundaries might be acceptable to the Arabs. He also emphasized that the Arab states upheld the right of the over 800,000 refugees, who had fled from Israel during the fighting, to return to their homes. For those who did not return, the Arabs demanded compensation for bank balances and property left behind.

Mr. Minor expressed the fear that violence would break out unless there was a settlement of the refugee problem and agreement on redrawing the boundaries, and unless Jerusalem, or at least the Holy Places, were internationalized. He reemphasized that the United States should stop favoring Israel. United States policy, he contended, was a "prisoner of the Zionists." The United States, he added, had not made Israel live up to the various UN resolutions. The first step the United States should take, he thought, was to support the internationalization of Jerusalem.

Stevenson observed that the ambassador apparently treated the question of Jerusalem apart from the boundary question. The ambassador

[1] Following World War I, Lebanon and Syria had become French mandates. In 1943 independence was granted, but French troops did not leave until after the war.

[2] On November 29, 1947, the United Nations General Assembly recommended the partition of Palestine into an Arab state and a Jewish state, together with the internationalization of Jerusalem. On May 14, 1948, the British officially terminated their mandate over Palestine. The Jewish state of Israel was proclaimed that day and President Harry S. Truman extended de facto recognition. Soon afterward Arab armies entered Palestine. Between January and July, 1949, the UN mediator, Dr. Ralph Bunche, helped to conclude armistice agreements. In the fighting Israel had extended its control into areas that the 1948 UN partition plan had allocated to the new Arab state. The armistice agreements basically maintained the territorial disposition resulting from the war operations. Israel contended that by invading Israel on May 15, 1948, the Arabs had invalidated the partition resolution and therefore the Arab states had no claims under it. Israel and the Kingdom of Jordan rejected UN resolutions for the internationalization of Jerusalem, and the city was divided between the two countries. See George Lenczowski, The Middle East in World Affairs (Ithaca: Cornell University Press, 1952), pp. 279–288.

replied that probably all that was needed was a little rectification of boundaries, recognition of the abstract right of refugees to return, and compensation to the refugees who did not.

To a question from Stevenson about the lack of unity among the Arab states, the ambassador agreed that it was difficult for them to work together and extremely difficult for American diplomats to work with Arab leaders. He reminded Stevenson that the Arabs were still smarting from the humiliation of being defeated by "tiny" Israel. (At the beginning of the war in 1948 there had been some 640,000 Jews in Palestine.) "The emotionalism on the street against Israel," he observed, "was terrific." The terrorists and fanatics at large in the Arab world made it unhealthy, he added, for leaders to be conciliatory toward Israel. (In 1951 King Abdullah of Jordan had been assassinated while working on an agreement with Israel.)

The political officer, Armin H. Meyer, remarked that Lebanon was not nearly as fanatical as other Arab states. Literacy was higher here — probably as many as seventy per cent were literate. From ancient times Lebanon had been an important commercial trading center for the entire area. The role of traditional middlemen of international trade had given the Lebanese a different outlook from the people in the countries surrounding them. Meyer also remarked that another important factor was that Lebanon was a country of religious minorities. Approximately fifty per cent were Christians. The largest number of these were Maronite Christians [3] and the others mainly were Greek Orthodox, Roman Catholics and Protestants. The Moslems, slightly less than a majority of the country, were divided into Shiia Moslems, Sunni Moslems and the Druses, a sect that had broken off from Islam in the eleventh century. There were about 5,000 Jews, he added. The religious mixture in the country contributed, he concluded, to moderation.

The economic officer, James C. Lobenstine, said that the diversified economy of Lebanon — one-fourteenth the size of Illinois — was an important factor contributing to stability. The tourist industry, the export of citrus, apples, and textiles, and the importance of Beirut as a trading and financial center brought the country the highest standard of living in the Arab world, though this standard was still low compared to that of Western nations, he remarked, and there was considerable underemployment among the fifty per cent of the population engaged in agriculture.

After the briefing, Stevenson and Johnson went to the American Uni-

[3] The Maronite Christians originally split from the Roman Catholic Church and then reunited with it. But they still have some distinct rites and have a distinct community history in Lebanon.

versity of Beirut to talk to some twenty members of the faculty, both Arab and American. They told Stevenson that the United States had taken a too active role in helping Israel. The Arabs, they insisted, would never feel secure as long as outside aid supported Israel. Reasonable Arabs knew that Israel should not be driven into the sea, but it was essential, they felt, that the three UN resolutions — calling for Jerusalem to be internationalized, boundaries rectified, and the refugees repatriated — be implemented.

Stevenson expressed doubt that all three objectives could be achieved. They immediately responded that Israel should stop welcoming immigrants and instead take back some refugees. Stevenson then asked them about the minimum terms acceptable to the Arab world. They replied that the three UN resolutions were already a compromise and they could not compromise any further. Stevenson reminded them that they could not "turn back the clock of history." To enforce the three resolutions might require U.S. soldiers, he added, and the United States did not want to do that.

They insisted that the United States had to choose between the Arabs and the Israelis. The implementation of the three resolutions was necessary to win the support of the Arabs. They objected to Stevenson's position that it was unrealistic to insist on all three resolutions. He replied: "You cannot abolish Israel. How can you get all three? If the Arabs want everything, I want to know." They answered: "Yes, they do. This is basic and all Arabs feel this way." Stevenson said: "I'm puzzled as to what Arab opinion is. In Egypt the most important issue is Suez. In Saudi Arabia it's Buraimi. They are not as concerned as you are on this issue."

They replied that Arabs were only asking for a minimum when they demanded the implementation of the three resolutions. One of the Americans present said that Arabs feared that Israel would commit aggression. A former Palestinian remarked that if Israel grew too strong it would expand and the Arabs might be annihilated. He spoke eloquently as he stated that the West had to take steps to prevent Israel from expanding. Another teacher pointed out that the Arabs were not afraid of the Communists or the Soviet Union since they had had no direct contact with Russia. But they had had direct contact with Israel.

When the meeting ended, one of the American teachers told Stevenson that when Arabs were in a group they tended to adopt an extreme position. Privately, however, they admitted that they would accept less than their demands. This teacher added that he doubted that most of the refugees wanted to return to Israel. Compensation for their property, he said, should be obtained.

After this conversation, Stevenson had a talk with James Bell and David Richardson of Time Incorporated. The conversation centered mainly on the problem of the refugees who were living in wretched camps and multiplying at the rate of 25,000 a year. The reporters felt that a half-million of them could be resettled in Syria and Iraq, to the advantage of both countries. The Arab states contended, however, that to do so would abandon the principle that the refugees had the right to return to Palestine. It was pointed out that the leaders in the Arab states feared the power and influence of the refugees if they were allowed to become citizens of the countries where they now were living.

The next morning Stevenson had breakfast with three leading Lebanese Socialists: Kamal Djumblatt, Clovis Maksoud, and Nassim Majdalami. They emphasized that Lebanon was leading an Arab renaissance. "We are unstable, restless, and we are on the move," they said. "The masses must be given work, bread, education, and social security." Djumblatt added that many people felt that Russia had been stimulating social reform but "we don't want to be like Russia; we want social justice and freedom in a democratic framework."

He then remarked: "We want to be treated by the West as something more than elements of military strategy. We may be underdeveloped economically but we are not underdeveloped in our culture and in our religion." He added: "You cannot separate Lebanon from the rest of the Middle East. We are the brains, Egypt is the heart, and the Iraqis are the politicians and the Prussians of the Middle East."

When Stevenson queried Djumblatt about the willingness of Arab leaders — many of whom were large landlords — to allow social reform, he replied: "The dynamics for revolution are here in the Middle East. The only question is what direction it will follow — Communist or social democratic." The socialists, he stated, were the main foe of the Communists. Some intellectuals, he said, had become extreme rightist nationalists while some, out of frustration over the plight of the masses, had become Communists.

All three agreed that "most intellectuals here believe that the West, either directly or indirectly, backs the status quo. You are so concerned with strategic problems that you talk of anti-Communism all the time. Because of your fear of Communism you back whatever government you find in power, like [Generalissimo Francisco] Franco in Spain, regardless of whether it is reactionary, fascist, or progressive." They added that it was important for Americans "not to talk so much anti-Communism and instead talk in terms of positive social reform. If you did that, the Communists would crumble all over the Arab world."

Stevenson replied that there were great diversities in American pub-

lic opinion. For tactical reasons, he explained, some leaders who favored economic aid programs justified them as contributing to stopping Communism in order to get Congress to adopt them.

Mr. Djumblatt replied, "We want the United States to understand the complexities of our society and our problems and we don't want you to get completely preoccupied by your anti-Communist attitudes." He then explained that one reason the Arabs were skeptical of the West was that in World War I the West promised them independence and instead they were placed under League of Nations mandates. After World War II the West "gave us the canker of Israel." He added: "We want the United States to have the same ideals in its foreign policy as it had in its own revolutionary concepts of freedom and progress. . . . The United States should champion freedom for all peoples and not compromise with British and French colonialism."

After this conversation Stevenson, Johnson and Ambassador Minor called on Foreign Minister George B. Hakim. He remarked that leadership was weak in the Arab world and had to be demagogic occasionally in order to compete with the demagogues who tried to mislead the people. The great force in the Arab world, he added, was nationalism: "Anything that touches on national pride and sovereignty affects the masses and the leaders had to be careful or they would lose power if they objected to this nationalist upsurge."

As to Israel, he observed, "The leaders are crippled and they do not dare to compromise. If they did they would be charged with treason."

The foreign minister then suggested that the United States impose a solution and this would "help take the leaders off a hook." The solution, he continued, would have to take into account: (1) The refugee problem. The refugees should have the abstract right to go back and be free to leave again if they did not like the changed conditions in Israel. Actually, he added, the refugees could be a great strength where they now were, but "you have to be careful about saying these things in public." Those refugees who did not return had to be compensated for their property and this money should be used to resettle them. (2) Jerusalem should be internationalized. (3) The boundaries should be roughly those of the partition plan before the fighting started in 1948.

He then stated: "We have no illusion about Zionist objectives." The way they were building up their population, he continued, made him fear they would expand their country. "We want a firm guarantee against Israeli expansion. If we have this, we won't worry about our demands that Israeli immigration be limited."

After this conversation, Stevenson and Johnson called on President

Camille Chamoun, with whom Stevenson had worked at the United Nations from 1945 to 1947. The president observed that the Arabs had been friendly to the United States until the creation of Israel. "Israel is an American baby. We are bitter toward the United States, but it is not a deep hatred," he stated. It was essential, he added, for the United States to impose a solution on the situation. "What are you prepared to do?" he asked. Before Stevenson could respond, the president said that the United States should help obtain a solution of the Suez base. Secondly, the United States should extend financial aid to the Arabs. But most of all, there was Israel. If the Arabs received fifty per cent of what they wanted on boundary rectification, this would allow some of the refugees to settle in the new Arab area created. "If the United States can do the above, the past will be forgotten," he remarked.

The president then said that the internationalization of Jerusalem was less important than the question of the boundaries and the problem of the refugees. He repeated that fifty per cent of the territory allocated to the Arabs by the United Nations resolution in 1947 would be satisfactory. "It doesn't mean much territory," he observed, "but it will help ease the whole issue and would be a good gesture, coming from the United States, and it could absorb some refugees. It's your baby and you must find a solution."

At this point, Stevenson emphasized that the Arab leaders had to work toward a solution to the question of Israel as well as the United States. The president agreed but stated that Lebanon could not influence the other Arabs unless the United States first took corrective action along the approach that he had already mentioned.

Following this conversation, the Beirut Alumni of the American University gave a luncheon in Stevenson's honor. The presiding officer, Habib Abi Chahda, a member of Parliament, in introducing Stevenson remarked that he was "reluctant to speak before one of the great orators of the world. I want you to know we welcome you most sincerely." He then praised the contribution of the American University of Beirut to the Arab world and emphasized that it was an Arab institution as well as an American one. As he looked at Stevenson he said: "We want the Arabs to be understood by the United States. We have suffered because we are not understood. We want you as a man of authority to help us explain the Arab world." Just before concluding his introduction, Mr. Chahda read some excerpts from Stevenson's 1952 campaign speeches, including his speech accepting the Democratic nomination.

Stevenson in his impromptu remarks said: "I enjoyed hearing my own speeches again." He thanked Mr. Chahda for calling him a great orator *and observed: "Flattery is all right as long as you don't inhale it, and I don't intend to inhale it." "I came," he continued, "to learn about your historic country and about your problems."*

He expressed his pleasure at the words of praise for the American University of Beirut. He added that he did "not want to talk, however, about the Arab world but of the free world. We all want to build on tolerance and consent and not on totalitarianism. Democracy was difficult to achieve but only through non-coercion can freedom be achieved."

He then observed that "Lebanon could be the bridge between the West and the Middle East and could help solve the problems of the Middle East through good spirit and determination." He closed by observing: "The great authority that the chairman attributed to me ended last November. But we all have our consciences and thus we have authority in that sense. I hope that I can use mine to end the misunderstandings with you. We are not only interested in you for strategic reasons but because you people want, just as Americans do, a better life, security and a serenity of spirit." [4]

After the lunch Stevenson visited a camp of Palestinian refugees with some United Nations officials.

When he returned, he had a lengthy conversation with William Eddy, who had grown up in the Middle East, had been a professor of English at Dartmouth College, and now was an adviser to the Arabian-American Oil Company. Eddy talked first about Saudi Arabia and remarked that the king was unaware of the amount of money "the group of wolves around him" were stealing. The issue of Buraimi, he said, was not very important. "The way the king talked to you of this issue shows he has lost his grip. They have many more serious problems, including graft."

Eddy then said that British prestige was "slipping badly" in the Middle East. The United States, he continued, "has to establish an independent position from the British. . . . We must find out what is the mutual interest of the United States and the Arabs without doing it through the British."

Eddy remarked that the Arabs knew they could not destroy Israel, but they feared Israel's expansion. "If Israel takes many more people, they will have to expand. The Zionist movement could be abandoned if all the Jews wanted was the present state of Israel. They want to expand, however, from the Nile to the Tigris and Euphrates rivers."

Eddy then declared: "I urge the United Nations to internationalize

---

[4] Attwood wrote in his diary that Stevenson "always amazes me with his ability to plunge into an improvised sentence way out past uncharted clauses and somehow to make his way back grammatically to the period or semicolon."

Jerusalem at once. What you have there now is aggression by Israel against the United Nations." As to the refugees, he recommended that jobs be given them to help develop areas in North Syria, along the Jordan, and in parts of Iraq. After they developed these areas, he thought, they would settle there permanently.

Some of the territory now occupied by Israel, Eddy stated, had to be returned to the Arabs for psychological reasons.

Dinner that evening was given by President and Mrs. Chamoun in Stevenson's honor. After dinner when the ladies withdrew, including Mrs. William Attwood, who had joined the group in Egypt, Stevenson had a hilarious time telling stories about American politics. "Stevenson was in fine form," Attwood wrote in his diary, "and had Chamoun and all his cabinet ministers roaring at his jokes — unlike the Asians, who never quite got his political gags, the French-educated Lebanese were a most appreciative audience." [5] *Stevenson said later: "I enjoyed them. After you cut through the façade, they are like a bunch of back-room politicians at home."*

After an early breakfast the next morning, June 4, the Stevenson party drove up over the mountains and down into the green Bekaa valley. President Chamoun and Stevenson laid the cornerstone of a dairy barn. This joint Lebanese–Point Four project when completed was to be a modern livestock and experimental demonstration farm.

From there the Stevenson party drove to the Graeco-Roman temple site at Baalbeck. When he reached the ruins, Stevenson took Johnson aside and said: "Let the guide take the rest of the party and you and I go by ourselves." He then explained the meaning of the great columns standing amidst the ruins. His knowledge of the various ruins he had visited already on the trip had been impressive, and finally, Johnson turned to him and said, "Look, Adlai, where did you learn all this?"

With a twinkle in his eyes, he replied, "You've heard of the University of Chicago?"

When Johnson nodded, he said, "Well, you've heard of James Breasted?" [6]

Johnson replied, "Yes. Unfortunately, he was no longer at the university when I joined the faculty."

Stevenson then said, "It comes as no surprise to you, Walter, that I was sort of bored by the law?"

[5] Attwood added in his diary: "At this point it's quite obvious to everyone to see that Stevenson is bearing up far better than any of us. He seems to have found his second wind in Egypt."

[6] James H. Breasted (1865–1935), professor of Egyptology and Oriental history at the University of Chicago, director of archaeological expeditions to Egypt and Mesopotamia, and author of many books on ancient civilizations.

Johnson said, "No, that's no surprise to me."

"Well," Stevenson added, "I used to sneak out of my office down-town and come out to the university and listen to Breasted's lectures on the Middle East and Asia."

Johnson looked at Stevenson and said, "And you never forgot a damn thing he ever said to you, either, did you?"

He paused for a moment and then remarked: "I guess I didn't."

After a picnic lunch amidst the ruins, the Stevenson party drove to the Syrian border, where they were met by Syrian officials and repre-sentatives of the embassy. When Stevenson arrived at Damascus an hour later, he went to the president's home to sign the official guest book. Then he went to the embassy for a briefing by Ambassador James S. Moose, Jr., and members of his staff.

It was pointed out that although under the constitution of 1950 Syria was a parliamentary republic, in November, 1951, the chief of staff, General Adib Shishakli, had seized control of the government. He had dissolved parliament and the political parties except for his Arab Lib-eration Movement. The ambassador explained that Shishakli had am-bitious plans for the economic development of this predominantly agricultural society. Work was already under way to develop Syria's only important harbor at Latakia into a major port. There were plans to expand highways in northeastern Syria, to link the city of Aleppo by railroad to Latakia, and to develop dams for irrigation and hydroelectric power in the Yarmuk and Euphrates rivers.

The ambassador pointed out that Syria, which had fought repeated engagements against the French and had been forced to live, during most of the period between the two world wars, under martial rule by the French, was extremely sensitive about its sovereignty. It was strongly anticolonial and viewed Israel as the latest example of "West-ern imperialism." As a result, there was bitterness toward the United States. And there was a "psychosis of fear" about Israel.

It was contended that Israel had to take back some of the refugees, agree to some boundary revision and the internationalization of Jeru-salem. If Israel would take such steps, it was argued, General Shishakli would be in a stronger position to "deal with his own people." He was under attack, it was added, for being "too pro-Western."

Following the briefing, Stevenson called on General Shishakli. He stated that the recent visit of Secretary of State John Foster Dulles and now Stevenson's visit were extremely pleasing to him since "they showed the increasing interest of Americans in Middle Eastern activities." He next remarked: "We want to restore confidence in the United States. In the past we knew you were for liberty and we wanted the United States to take a [League of Nations] mandate here in 1919, but unfortunately you put your ocean between yourselves and the rest of us and let the Europeans run the area. Then the French exploited us and tried to divide group against group."

When asked for his recommendations on current problems, the general began by saying that it was "horrible" the way Israel had driven people from their homes. The refugee camps were miserable and the "people there have no hope." (There were some 80,000 refugees in Syria, while — not counting the refugees — Syria had a population of over 3½ million.) The United States had to do "something positive" about the refugees, he stated. "I do not think the United States should help us throw Israel into the sea. Israel is here to stay. I know some refugees don't want to go back and those who don't should be compensated so they can start again. There should be revisions of boundaries to allow some of them to go back. Furthermore, Jerusalem should be internationalized. If these are done, good feeling can be restored and fear between Israel and Arabs will be weakened."

He expressed to Stevenson his apprehension that Israel desired to expand from the Nile to the Euphrates. "The United States," he insisted, "should see that its aid to Israel and to the Arabs was not used by them to fight each other." He then discussed his plans for economic development. He remarked that Syria had refused technical assistance under the Point Four program, because what it wanted were long-term loans for self-liquidating projects. He concluded: "Your aid would help people to feel that you are not alone helping Israel and, if you do this, it will help to reduce fear."

That evening General Shishakli gave a dinner in Stevenson's honor. He talked further about Israel in much the same words he had used in the afternoon. When Stevenson queried him about the Arabs' willingness to end their economic boycott of Israel, the general made it clear that he favored its continuation.

The next morning a group of Americans involved in business and missionary activities in Syria called on Stevenson. They plied him with questions about the United States and Asia and, as Attwood wrote in his diary, "of course he obliged in his customary gracious way." Finally, Stevenson switched the conversation to Syria and Israel. In answer to a question from Stevenson, they said that Syria could and should resettle some of the refugees. All of them agreed that the right of repatriation, compensation for property, boundary rectification, and the internationalization of Jerusalem were prerequisite to a settlement with Israel. But as Stevenson put it to them: "Do we have any assurance that the Arabs will then lift their blockade of Israel? In other words, have they offered *any quid for the quo?"* The group could give no satisfactory answer to the question.

After this meeting, Stevenson visited a refugee camp, the Ommayad Mosque in Damascus, and the National Museum where he saw artifacts from Syria's richly historic past.

Early that afternoon (June 5), Attwood chartered a seven-seater biplane of rather ancient design to fly the party to Amman, the capital of Jordan. During the hour flight the plane flew so low that Stevenson could see the parched landscape, needing irrigation to become productive.

At Amman Stevenson stayed with Ambassador Joseph C. Green. They spent the afternoon looking at old mosaics; then Stevenson dined with him that evening. The ambassador described at length the refugee population of some 460,000 Palestinian Arabs (before 1948 there had been some 810,000 people in Jordan). He also described the British subsidy to the Jordanian government — approximately one-half the budget — for the Arab Legion and limited economic development.

After breakfast the next morning, Stevenson and the ambassador called on Lieutenant-General John Bagot Glubb, commander of the Arab Legion, who had spent most of his life in the Near East. They talked a bit about the Arab past before discussing the current situation. The general observed that he believed the Israelis were committing incidents on their side of the border, blaming them on Jordan, and then using them as a pretext to cross the Jordanian border and retaliate.

After this brief talk Stevenson signed the official guest book at the palace (eighteen-year-old King Hussein was not in Amman during the visit), and paid courtesy calls on the prime minister and the foreign minister.

Later that morning Stevenson and his party, accompanied by Ambassador Green, left Amman by automobile with an armed escort of Arab Legionnaires for Jerusalem. En route Stevenson visited a camp of refugees at Jericho. Attwood wrote in his diary: ". . . a vast conglomeration of mud huts where some 90,000 people are existing and rotting of idleness . . . We talked to some, who spoke just as they had two years ago [when Attwood had last visited the camp]; we want to go home to Palestine. It's a pitiful sight. But there was no evidence of hostility toward us as Americans and the kids, as everywhere, were cheerful."

Stevenson lunched in Jericho and then drove to the Dead Sea through the barren terrain known in the Bible as "the abomination of desolation."

Near Bethlehem, Stevenson stopped and walked along the demarcation line — *barbed wire* — *in two villages where farmers' fields had been separated from their houses by the cease-fire line. When he reached the Church of the Nativity in Bethlehem, he was immediately surrounded by a crowd of officials and Orthodox priests, who escorted him through the church.*

Early in the evening Stevenson reached the American Colony Hotel in Jerusalem. He dined that evening with U.S. Consul General S. Roger Tyler and Mrs. Tyler, General William Riley, head of military observers, United Nations Palestine Commission, and Anwar Nusibeh, former minister of defense in the government of Jordan.

Nusibeh insisted that the absurd boundaries that Stevenson had just seen, which separated the land from where the farmer lived, had to be rectified. If these boundaries were rectified, it would reduce the amount of compensation.

When Stevenson asked about the possibility of internationalizing Jerusalem, General Riley remarked that he favored it but did not see how it would work in view of the hatred between the Arabs and the Israelis.

On the following morning, Sunday, June 7, a beautiful sunny day, Stevenson and his party visited the Garden of Gethsemane, peaceful and lovely with hollyhocks, nasturtiums, petunias, geraniums, and morning glories in bloom. Escorted by an Arab scholar, he then walked to the Dome of the Rock — the Mosque of Omar. From there he walked to the Wailing Wall and then along the Via Dolorosa to the Church of the Holy Sepulcher.

Later that morning, with United Nations personnel as escorts, he was driven through the Mandelbaum Gate and 'across the no-man's-land that separated Israeli Jerusalem from Jordanian Jerusalem.

Stevenson wrote of his visit to Lebanon, Syria and Jordan:

NO PEACE FOR ISRAEL [7]

In Lebanon, Syria and Jordan, the refrain changes from Suez and sovereignty to Israel and "justice for the Arabs." Communism and Russia are far away, but the 800,000 Arab refugees from Israel are on the doorstep; and America, which "planted and nourishes this cancer in our body," is the villain of the plot.

As in Egypt, the Arab leaders seem to be often the prisoners rather than the leaders of public opinion they themselves helped create, and

[7] *Look*, August 11, 1953. Other extracts from this article are reprinted in Chapters Thirteen and Fourteen, above, and Chapter Sixteen, below.

are more realistic and reasonable in private than in public. They have finally accepted the fact that Israel is here to stay. But their bitterness is profound. They believe that the new State of Israel was created only at American insistence and survives only with American money. Still smarting from their failure to crush Israel in the 1948 war, they are quick to blame the U.S. and the Zionists for their woes, and American prestige and popularity — once so high — have fallen to a low estate.

What exactly do the Arabs want?

They want the refugees to have the right either to go back to their homes in Israel or to receive compensation for their property.

They want the boundaries of Israel contracted to the dimensions originally fixed by the United Nations partition plan of 1947.

They want (with some dissent in Jordan) Jerusalem internationalized in accordance with the U.N. resolution.

In addition, Jordan wants an outlet to the sea or port facilities in Israel, and General Naguib resents the fact that Israel severs the land communications of the Arab-Moslem world for the first time in history.

We will hear more about all these demands before peace and neighborliness replace hatred and violence in the Holy Land.

Meanwhile, the thousands of displaced, homeless Palestinian Arabs have been rotting for five years in wretched, sprawling camps in Jordan, Egypt, Lebanon and Syria — supported at a subsistence level by the United Nations (the U.S. pays 70 per cent of the cost). In Jordan alone, some 530,000 refugees constitute nearly half the country's population.

Why isn't something permanent done about them? Some say the Arab states have little real compassion, no place to put them and no money. It is true that Egypt, Lebanon and Jordan are awfully crowded; but Syria and Iraq are underpopulated, and, with some land reclamation, the refugees now multiplying at the rate of 25,000 a year could become a strength instead of a burden.

The best reason for inaction, I suspect, is that to settle the refugees permanently would prejudice the Arab case for repatriation to their former homes in Israel. In the camps I visited, the refugees told me they wanted to "go home," although I am sure they little appreciate the new conditions and environment they would find in Jewish Israel.

It does little good to examine the background of this tragedy. In Israel, they say the Arabs fled voluntarily when the fighting started in 1948, expecting to return in a few days after the Jews had been crushed. The Arabs say they were driven out in panic by the Jews and point accusingly to Deir Yassin — the village where 250 Arabs, including women and children, were massacred by Jewish terrorists in April, 1948.[8]

Wherever the responsibility lies, the embattled Jews were not crushed. On the contrary, in the 1948 fighting, they almost doubled the area of Palestine assigned to them by the U.N. partition plan and drove to the center of Jerusalem. The armistice lines were drawn along the battle front, with the result that you find villages chopped in two, Arab farmers with their land in Israel and their homes in Jordan — even houses and outhouses separated — and Jerusalem itself divided by a wide swath of no man's land that marks the boundary between the old city in Jordan and the new city in Israel. I stood with Arab peasants and looked across the barbed wire to their neglected fields and orchards on the other side; I stood on a balcony in old Jerusalem with an Arab lawyer pointing to his house in Israel — which he hadn't been able to visit in five years. And a few hundred yards away, Jews gaze wistfully at the wrecked "Jewish quarter" of the old city, their Wailing Wall and their sacred places — now inaccessible in Jordan.

The results of such unnatural boundaries are continual border incidents: hardly a week goes by without gunfire and casualties. Jews and Arabs blame each other. Jordan authorities admitted to me that refugees often sneak across the line, but insist that the major incidents bear the marks of deliberate instigation. Why? "Because," they replied, "if the Jews appear to be in mortal danger, they get bigger contributions from America." If not besieged, Israel is certainly blockaded by her Arab neighbors. For years, no oil has flowed from Iraq through the pipeline to Israel's refinery at Haifa. With vast quantities of oil at her back door, Israel imports fuel from Venezuela. No food or raw materials move from the Middle East to nourish the people and limping industries of Israel. Tourists with an Israel visa on their passports can't enter the Arab states. There is no mail or telegraph service between Israel and her neighbors. Armies are too big and too expensive. Everyone suffers.

I talked to most of the leaders of the Arab states, including an old friend, Camille Chamoun, the alert, handsome Christian president of tiny Lebanon, a country stripped of its cedars but not of its culture that belongs to both East and West; and General Adeeb Shishekly [Adib Shishakli], Syria's chief of state, a rugged, friendly, blunt man who quite frankly wants U.S. arms and money more than technical assistance for his development projects. In Jordan, largely dependent on British aid, the story was the same.

[8] See Lenczowski, *The Middle East in World Affairs,* p. 287, for a discussion of this.

Everywhere, there is fear of Israeli expansion and suspicion that Jewish immigration is encouraged to make expansion necessary; everywhere, there is a sense of Arab brotherhood in the face of common peril; and everywhere, I heard polite but barbed references to Zionist influence in America, to U.S. partiality for Israel and to our responsibility for wrongs done the Arabs.

On the other side, I have also heard it said the Arabs are skulking in their tents waiting for the right moment to pounce upon the Jews and drive them into the sea, even as Saladin drove the Crusaders out of Palestine 800 years ago. Personally, I detected no such dark designs but a genuine fear that the Jews will always covet *all* of Palestine.

From Amman and the land of Moab, we drove down long, rocky gorges, where pink oleanders etched the creek beds, and out into the arid wasteland of the Jordan Valley and the Dead Sea — "the abomination of desolation." And hereafter these Biblical words will have a new and vivid meaning for me. For 90,000 refugees are now strewn along the naked foothills of Judea west of the blessed river. Beside them lies Jericho, the oldest existing town on earth; behind them, the valley of John the Baptist, and on the heights above — Jerusalem.

My last day in the Arab world, a Sunday, I wandered about Bethlehem and Old Jerusalem through the imperishable scenes enlivened by names that never die. Standing in the dim hush of the "earth's most sacred spot," in the Church of the Nativity, surrounded by priests of all faiths and Arab dignitaries, someone made a little speech about mercy, justice and Jesus, ending on a rising note about justice for the Arabs!

In Jerusalem, walking from the Mosque of Omar and the site of the sacred Hebrew temples, down past the Wailing Wall, deserted now, and up the busy bazaar that is the Via Dolorosa to the Holy Sepulcher, I was burdened with the overtones of hate in the city, sacred to Christianity, Judaism and Islam. Moments of reverence were interrupted by scenes of war damage and descriptions of atrocities: Outside the Damascus Gate, I was reminded that 23 Arabs were killed there in April by gunfire from the roof of a nearby convent — in Israel.

There, by the gate where Saul strode off toward Damascus, I wondered for a moment who speaks for Christianity in Jerusalem, which has seen so much of piety, heard so much of truth, known so little of peace. And I thought, too, about how much in common have the Arabs, Jews and Christians who have shared the Sacred City for so long; how their common inspiration — faith in one God — sprang from these same rocky hills and deserts; how Jews and Arabs lived together here in harmony for 1300 years; and how the great concepts that unite us converge within the walls of Old Jerusalem. Surely here, one would think, we could settle our differences in the face of peril to our common faith in God. Instead, ill will is growing like the weeds that sprout amongst the rubble of Jerusalem's no man's land.

Sixteen

Israel

JUNE 7–JUNE 11, 1953

*S*tevenson was welcomed to Israel on Sunday, June 7, by front-page
stories in the Israeli press. Ha'aretz wrote:

> Mr. Stevenson cannot help notice during his stay, that in Israel
> no less than in other countries, he is held in the highest esteem
> for his public appearances in American public life.

Davar, *in its lead story, stated:*

> The guest will be received in our state with feelings of friend-
> ship, as one of the distinguished representatives of a friendly na-
> tion, as a public figure of stature in his country and abroad, as an
> old friend and as a man of deep insight.

Ma'ariv *announced:*

> It was a great achievement that 27 million should have voted for
> a man who became presidential candidate almost against his will,
> on the mere strength of his record and his brilliant election speeches.
> . . . Mr. Stevenson comes to Israel as a private citizen, without any
> authority except the esteem due anybody whose greatness does not
> depend on his office or a regime, but on personal merit.

*Soon after arrival, Stevenson attended a small reception given by Gen-
eral and Mrs. S. Roger Tyler. Among those present were Francis Rus-*

sell, chargé d'affaires *of the embassy; Teddy Kollek, an aide to Prime Minister David Ben-Gurion; and Gershon Agron, editor of the Jerusalem Post. In addition, his old friend David L. Cohn, who had drafted speeches for him during the 1952 campaign, joined the reception and then traveled with Stevenson in Israel.*

Cohn wrote of his meeting with Stevenson in Jerusalem:

> Drifting around the halcyon shores of the Mediterranean where men sit in coffee houses and women are dancing girls — an admirable society we might well imitate — I ran into a man named Adlai Stevenson — I had last seen him in Springfield — shortly after the election, a rather lonely figure in his eighteenth century rationality and tweed suit.

Cohn added that what he found in Jerusalem

> was the once crisp Stevenson slightly wilted, and the once bright glance gone glassy-eyed though but midway in his penance [the trip]. He had been "briefed" within an inch of his life. . . . The poor man, besides, had heard everybody's troubles; the one commodity that everywhere is in oversupply. . . . The candidate had also shaken thousands of hands. But since none of them would ever mark a Democratic ballot, he was like the lad who pursued a maiden and clasped a reed. Nor was this the end of his agony. With but one digestive tract to give to his country, he had given it at dozens of official dinners.[1]

Later that afternoon Stevenson visited the Hadassah Hospital and the Hebrew University. After this sightseeing, he and Francis Russell called on President Yitzhak Ben-Zvi, who told Stevenson that the main problem Israel had been facing was absorbing some 700,000 people who had entered the country since independence. He emphasized that Israel needed help to absorb the remaining Jews in Europe and the Moslem world. "We want more to come to build the country," he added.

Stevenson and Russell then called on the sixty-seven-year-old Prime Minister David Ben-Gurion.[2] He welcomed Stevenson by saying:

---

[1] "Adlai Seemed Wilted Midway in Tour," Washington *Post,* July 12, 1953.

[2] Ben-Gurion immigrated to Palestine in 1906. He was exiled for his Zionist activities and lived in the United States from 1915 to 1918. He returned to Palestine in 1920 and organized the Histadrut — the General Federation of Jewish Labor in Israel. After 1935 he was the head of the Jewish Agency, whose aim was the resettlement of Jews in Israel. As the leader of the Maipai party (Socialist-Labor) he became prime minister in 1948.

"*You captured the imagination of the world by your eloquence and your sincerity. America made a mistake in the election.*"

He proceeded to inform Stevenson that "*internally we have three aims. Each is difficult, almost impossible, but we hope to accomplish them. We want to save the Jews in Eastern Europe and in the Oriental areas because they are condemned to degradation and extinction. Second, we must rebuild the desert. Modern science can cultivate it. Our devotion is so great, we can do it. Third, we must build a civilization based on our Bible but in the context of modern civilization. It has to be done and therefore we believe it can be done.*"

He then stated that there were no circumstances that prevented good relations with their Arab neighbors, provided all were interested in the welfare of the people. He explained that he had told Secretary of State John Foster Dulles on his recent visit that the United States should help the Arabs to achieve a better life. "*However,*" he added, "*not all the Arab leaders are interested in building a better life.*"

What was needed throughout the Near East, he continued, was "*economic development, education, and social welfare. But do all the Arab leaders believe in these? Some just want to fight us or fight the British. If they try this, as they did once, it will be tragic.*"

The prime minister then stated that in 1947 his people had been willing to accept the United Nations' decision (creating a Jewish state and an Arab state and internationalizing Jerusalem) even though they did not like it. But, he declared, the "*Arabs wanted to exterminate us.*" At this point he interjected that he did not know what John Foster Dulles meant in his recent speech that Israel should look upon itself as part of the Near East.[3]

Ben-Gurion noted that while the Israelis intended to have their own language and civilization, Israel was willing to cooperate with others. "*If the national interest means the welfare of the people, we can see no conflict between us and the Arabs.*" But he insisted that it would not be in the interest of peace or the Arab people for the United States to arm the present Arab governments. He doubted, he said, that these

---

[3] On his return from his trip to the Middle East, Pakistan, and India, Secretary of State Dulles delivered a policy address. The portion Ben-Gurion referred to read: "Israel should become part of the Near East Community and cease to look upon itself, or be looked upon by others, as alien to this community. This is possible. To achieve it will require concessions on the part of both sides. But the gains to both will far outweigh the concessions required to win those gains." Department of State *Bulletin*, June 15, 1953, Vol. 28, 1953, No. 729, p. 834.

For a discussion of U.S. policy following the Dulles visit, see William R. Polk, *The United States and the Arab World* (Cambridge: Harvard University Press, 1965), pp. 265–266.

countries were ready or capable of fighting for freedom in the world since they did not have freedom in their own countries. To arm the Arabs might mean they would fight Israel. "We, however," he stated, "will fight for freedom in the world because Jews cannot exist under totalitarianism whether it be the Hitler or the Stalin type. Unfortunately, our neighbors do not feel this way."

If a world war came, the Arabs would not fight for democracy, the prime minister observed. "You must look for those who will fight for freedom — and we will. Even if we lose we will go down fighting." If, however, the world could expect peace, then the United States should assist economic development, education, and health in the Arab world, since "Providence made you the leader and you can do it." The Arab states needed liberal regimes and the United States could help achieve this. If you could do this "America would be making a great contribution," he added.

Ben-Gurion then stated that Israel was ready for peace at any time — tomorrow or in ten years — they could be patient. But to secure peace, he said, they would not give up Jerusalem or other territory. The Arabs had plenty of waste areas they had not settled and thus did not need more land. "We know how Christians feel about Jerusalem, but that does not mean that we have to give it up," he continued. "We are willing to have the United Nations supervise the Holy Places, but most of these are on the Arab side." Jerusalem, he insisted, was "Jewish-made some three thousand years ago. There is no reason — human, religious or spiritual — why we should not retain it. It can only be taken away over our dead bodies. This is the seat of our government and there can be no other place for a government of a Jewish state."

Stevenson reminded him that he had said that Israel had once accepted the November, 1947, United Nations resolution for the internationalization of Jerusalem. The prime minister answered: "A war of extermination was started and the United Nations didn't really help us nor did the United Nations prevent the Arabs from trying to destroy Jerusalem. . . . We had to fight and die for our state. The old city is holy to us but we don't intend to take it away from Jordan. History decided that this side of Jerusalem should be ours. We do not feel that the UN resolution is morally binding on us because the UN did nothing to save us. Their resolutions ceased to exist when we were attacked and the UN didn't help us."

Stevenson, probing for some area of possible conciliation with the Arab states, inquired about the prime minister's position on the repatriation of refugees or compensation for them. Ben-Gurion replied: "We are willing to compensate all who left property here. They didn't leave by any of our doing. They fled before Israel was established — why, I do not know. We are surrounded by four hostile states who refuse to make peace. To bring back the refugees would mean the destruction of Israel." He then stated: *"It's best to settle these people in the Arab states — Iraq and Syria need people. Just as we can settle two million more people here, they can settle the Arab refugees and we will compensate the refugees."*

When Stevenson asked where the money would come from for this compensation, the prime minister answered that he did not know.

Stevenson then asked about rectification of the boundaries. Ben-Gurion replied that if there could be peace, Israel was willing to adjust the divisions that took place within a town or a farm. *"We can make exchanges on the absurd boundaries,"* he concluded.

Stevenson next asked how Israel could absorb two million more people. *"The Arabs,"* he pointed out, *"feel that it means you will have to expand."* Ben-Gurion replied: *"We cannot absorb these people overnight, but in ten years we can do it — particularly in the Negev desert."* He added: *"The Arabs shouldn't fear us. There are forty million of them. We have no design on them. We are willing to guarantee frontiers if they make peace."*

He then returned to the subject of the refugees and said it was *"not in the national interest of the Arab states to have them come back. They can live among their own people and not live among Jews. The same reason that impels us to bring Jews here should motivate the Arab states to welcome refugees unless they don't really want to have peace with us."*

Stevenson remarked that as he saw the situation, the first way to break the deadlock was to solve the refugee problem. *"If Israel would take some, it might help,"* he suggested. *"The only reason they want to resettle Arabs here,"* Ben-Gurion replied, *"is to destroy us through subversion. If they don't want them to come back, it is a step toward peace."*

After this frank conversation, Stevenson and his party had dinner with Mr. and Mrs. Ben-Gurion, Foreign Minister Moshe Sharett, and Gershon Agron.

When Stevenson mentioned that General John Bagot Glubb and the Jordanians wanted to avoid the sort of border incidents that had been occurring, the prime minister observed that Israel did too. *"If you will tell them through your embassy, we are ready to meet with them."* (*Francis Russell, from the embassy, was present at the dinner.*) The remainder of the conversation dealt with the problem of adjusting the immigrants to Israel. The prime minister remarked that the flow was now down to 1,000 a month. Unity was being achieved, he said, because Hebrew was insisted upon as the common language. Moreover, the public schools and army service for all — both men and women — provided a common experience.

After dinner about fifty people (including the members of the cabinet) came to meet Stevenson. The prime minister arranged it so that five or six persons at a time sat around Stevenson and talked with him.

At nine the next morning, the Stevenson party, accompanied by Francis Russell, Reuven Shiloah of the Foreign Office, plainclothes policemen, photographers and reporters, drove in a five-car convoy to Tel Aviv. First stop en route was to a kibbutz — Maaleh Hahamisha. Stevenson visited a kindergarten where the photographers took pictures of him with one of the children on his lap. "I don't see why we don't spend the morning here," Stevenson said in a plaintive voice, but he was soon off to visit a peach orchard. Next he visited the Eddie Cantor Youth Aliyah village project. One of the girls said to him in Hebrew: "Like all the children in the world, we have read and heard much about you. But unlike the others, we have the honor of meeting you in person. Welcome, dear Mr. Stevenson."

After this was translated, he replied: "I have heard much more about you than I have heard about many other children in the world. I'm glad to see you so strong and healthy." "And tell her," he added, indicating the girl who had welcomed him, "if she doesn't look out she'll end up in politics." When everybody laughed at this, he sat down to eat oranges with the students. He sat next to a volunteer helper from Chicago. When she told him that she had been there for two and a half years, Stevenson quipped: "You mean to say that I lost a vote because of you?" "I'm ready to go back to the States every four years to vote for you," she assured him.

The convoy soon was under way to visit the Weizmann Institute in Rehovat. Stevenson talked to the scientists present about their research to make the Negev desert productive and their exploration for oil. When two of them explained that they had voted for him the past fall, Stevenson remarked wryly: "I didn't know so many of my supporters had left the country."

Stevenson then called on Mrs. Weizmann and told her that he had first met her late husband (the first president of Israel) in London in 1944. Mrs. Weizmann told him: "I've read the highlights of your speeches. They are wonderful. My husband would have loved them." With Mrs. Weizmann accompanying him, Stevenson then laid a wreath on the late president's grave.[4]

As Stevenson approached Tel Aviv, motorcycle policemen joined the convoy and escorted it through the city with sirens blaring, much to his irritation. When he asked Reuven Shiloah if the sirens couldn't be turned off, Shiloah shook his head and said it was orders from "B.G."

Once he was in Tel Aviv, the embassy staff gave a restful beach picnic in Stevenson's honor.

Later that afternoon, Stevenson and Francis Russell met with Foreign Minister Moshe Sharett.[5]

Sharett opened the discussion by saying: "I know that the refugees prey on your mind — it does on ours. It is the main stumbling block to peace. We are ready to share our part of the responsibility but we are not being given the opportunity. We will discuss it separately from the overall peace, but we will discuss it only with the United Nations and pay compensation to an international fund for refugee development."

He added that Israel by now had released one million pounds sterling to compensate Arabs for their bank deposits. He explained: "We feel free to revert to our earlier position that compensation must be part of a total peace. After all, this money is going to people living in enemy countries, and some of our people don't like the fact that we have paid the million pounds." He also commented: "The way our people grumble makes our ancestors' complaints against Moses seem mild."

He pointed out that repatriation would not mean that the refugees would go back to their old homes and farms, since these were now occupied. Thus they would have to be resettled. "We cannot afford it economically, psychologically, or racially."

He made it clear that the Arabs who stayed in Israel were in quite a different category from those who fled. If the refugees were brought back, they would be viewed as newcomers by the Jews who had arrived since 1948. Moreover, the Jews "who fled Arab countries would resent seeing these Arabs brought back." The refugees must see their future, he added, in terms of resettlement in Arab countries.

The foreign minister then expressed his opposition to Secretary of State John Foster Dulles's statement that some refugees should re-

[4] Dahn Ben Amotz, "Adlai Stevenson Takes the Countryside in His Stride," Jerusalem *Post,* June 11, 1953.

[5] Sharett immigrated to Palestine in 1906. In 1933 he became a leader of the Jewish Agency. Eventually he became its spokesman at international discussions concerning the future of Palestine and was an important influence in the Zionists' success at the United Nations in achieving the political establishment of Israel.

turn.[6] As long as people talked of repatriation, the mood and spirit of the refugees was against being settled in Arab countries, he insisted. The phrase "some refugees," he argued, was "assumed by all refugees to mean them." He next explained most carefully that "by no repatriation, we mean the problem cannot be solved by it." This did not mean, however, that Israel was opposed to having some return to join their families and, in fact, this was happening. He remarked that oil-rich Kuwait and Saudi Arabia should lend money to Syria, Jordan, and Egypt to assist them in resettling the refugees.

Sharett next observed that had the November, 1947, resolutions of the United Nations been implemented, Israel would have accepted the situation even though it would have placed Israel in a precarious position. But the Arabs refused the proposals and forced war on Israel. "The Arab leaders told the Arab population to leave so that they would not be in the way of their military operations. We placarded the country telling the Arabs not to leave," he commented.

At this point in his monologue, he suddenly mentioned that they had had a special cabinet session that day and had arrested some Jewish terrorists. Stevenson interjected: "Mr. Foreign Minister, General Glubb told me in Amman that you would have to do this." Sharett paused and then avoided further discussion of Glubb's charge that Jewish terrorists were committing atrocities and blaming them on Jordanians by commenting: "I take Glubb with a grain of salt."

Sharett then talked about boundaries and agreed that Israel was prepared "to make adjustments in the context of a general peace settlement." He knew, he said, that Egypt wanted a transit area across Israeli territory to the Arab states. Israel would not cede the Southern Negev or give up its foothold in the Red Sea (at Elath) but was willing to grant a right-of-way to Egypt with international guarantees. He added that Israel had secretly offered to discuss this with Egypt. In the case of Jordan, he stated, the natural boundary was the Jordan River, but Israel was willing to compromise on that. (Jordan gained the area from Jerusalem to the Jordan River when no new Arab state was created in 1948.) "The trouble," he insisted, "is the Arab states want it

[6] In his speech Dulles stated: "Closely huddled around Israel are most of the over 800,000 Arab refugees, who fled from Palestine as the Israelis took over. They mostly exist in makeshift camps, with few facilities either for health, work, or recreation. Within these camps the inmates rot away, spiritually and physically. Even the Grim Reaper offers no solution, for as the older die, infants are born to inherit their parents' bitter fate. Some of these refugees could be settled in the area presently controlled by Israel. Most, however, could more readily be integrated into the lives of the neighboring Arab countries. This, however, awaits on irrigation projects, which will permit more soil to be cultivated." Department of State *Bulletin*, June 15, 1953, Vol. 28, 1953, No. 729, p. 832.

both ways. They are full of complaints but won't join in a general peace setlement."

When Stevenson queried him about Jerusalem, Sharett stated that Israel was willing to have an international authority to supervise the Holy Places. He was emphatic, however, that Israel was against an international government for the city.

He concluded this lengthy meeting by insisting that it was up to the Arabs to start the negotiations. Israel was willing, he added, to give Jordan free port facilities but not a corridor from the port to that country. (Until the 1948–1949 war Haifa had been an important port used by the kingdom of Transjordan.)

But, Sharett stated, Israel could not do this or give free port facilities to Iraq as long as the Arabs continued to boycott her. The boycott hurt Israel in that meat had to be imported from Argentina, oil from Venezuela and cotton from the United States; it hurt the tourist trade for both sides, and it prevented water development on a cooperative basis.

After this conversation, the Stevenson party had dinner with Mr. and Mrs. Sharett. A few others, including Teddy Kollek and Leo Kohn of the Foreign Office, joined the party after dinner. They plied Stevenson with questions about whether there would be a cease-fire in Korea, questions that he was unable to answer with any definitiveness, since he was not in touch with the Eisenhower Administration. (The truce was signed July 27.)

Sharett remarked that he believed that the Russians were altering their course in foreign policy since Stalin's blustering and intimidation had failed. He also said that internally he thought there would be more freedom of speech for intellectuals and differences within the Communist party would be tolerated and debated.

There was some discussion about the merits of life on a kibbutz and whether it was a good idea to separate the children from their mothers all day long. Stevenson argued that it was not. The Israelis insisted that the children saw their mothers just as much as they did in the United States, "where all bourgeois families turn their children over to nurses and governesses." Stevenson's protest that most middle-class families could not afford nurses and governesses fell on deaf ears.

The following morning Stevenson attended a briefing at the embassy. There was considerable discussion, as a result of his questions, of the difficult economic situation facing Israel. The country had been facing an adverse balance of trade of about 300 million dollars a year. Up to date, it was pointed out, twenty to twenty-five per cent of the deficit was met by funds from international Jewry and fifty per cent more came from the United States government and individual citizens. The remainder was met by Israel out of her current funds. For three years the United States government had provided funds to save Israel from defaulting on its overseas debt. Reparations of a billion dollars that were soon to be paid by the West German government, it was stated, would ease the situation somewhat.

The economic attaché, Owen Jones, observed that Israel produced only thirty per cent of its food needs and that industry was not producing at full capacity, partly because of shortages of foreign exchange to buy raw materials. He added, however, that although the country was poor in natural resources, Israel had a highly trained, able population. Thirty per cent of the million and a half population was of the professional or managerial class. Even if the Arab boycott was lifted, it was pointed out, Israel would have to depend on funds from world Jewry. Mr. Jones then described the powerful inflationary forces at work and the steps being taken by the Israeli government to keep the situation under control.

Defense expenditures, it was pointed out, took thirty per cent of the budget. Morale in the army was described as excellent. The army, Stevenson was told, was a significant factor in integrating and educating the new immigrants (700,000 in the preceding five years).

The political attaché, Milton Fried, described the seventeen parties in the previous election, but he talked principally about Ben-Gurion's Maipai party, the General Zionist party (in 1953 these two parties made up the coalition government), the Orthodox religious parties, and the Mapam party.

Francis Russell closed the briefing by stating that border incidents were acute at that moment. Jordan was not strict enough in preventing people from crossing into Israel, but the Israelis, he stated, were too ruthless toward many harmless people who crossed the border to visit relatives or harvest their land at night. Both Britain and the U.S., he added, had informed Israel that they were opposed to these reprisals.

When Stevenson asked for his view of the possibility of internationalizing Jerusalem, Russell reminded him that the night before, Dr. Leo Kohn, of the Foreign Office, had stated: "Israel without Jerusalem is Zionism without Zion." On this question, Russell observed, with both the Jews and the Arabs, one was involved with attitudes formed over many centuries.

When Stevenson left the embassy, a sizable crowd had gathered to see him. The crowd broke into applause and he made a few remarks before joining Mr. and Mrs. Russell for a picnic on the beach. That evening the Israeli-American Friendship League held a reception in his honor.

Attwood wrote in his diary: "Copies of the June 16 Look with [Senator] McCarthy on the cover had arrived and I showed them to our group. The consensus was that the cover packed a wallop but that the article was rather weasel-worded. However, as Stevenson said later, 'I'll probably weasel around when I write about Israel.' (Thinking of the Zionist reaction at home)." [7]

The following morning, June 10, Stevenson, his son Borden, Blair, and David L. Cohn flew south to the Israeli port of Elath on the Gulf of Aqaba and from there drove into the Negev desert. After this tour they flew to Haifa in the north of Israel.[8]

After an interview with him, the Haifa correspondent of the Manchester Guardian wrote that on his visit Stevenson had been trying in his mind to work out the solutions to two sets of problems:

> The first are those urgent, grating, everyday matters that make headlines and keep nervous foreign attaches working overtime — the British versus the Egyptians, the Arabs versus Israel. The second, closer to Mr. Stevenson's way of thinking, are those questions deeper, more remote, and more important in the long run, which deal with freedom, with human hopes, and development.[9]

The Stevenson group spent the evening at the Meggido Hotel overlooking the sea. During dinner, David L. Cohn "briefed us on the alarming extent of thought control and political intimidation that exists in Texas today. He said that oil men like [H. L.] Hunt are ready and eager to back [Senator] McCarthy as a leader of a Neo-Fascist movement," Attwood wrote in his diary. "I remarked to Stevenson that maybe we ought to hurry home and do something about it, to which

---

[7] Attwood wrote later: "As it turned out, he didn't weasel, and he didn't pull his punches. It annoyed a lot of Zionists and Arabs, but the article was a solid piece of objective reporting." "Seeing the World with Stevenson," *Harper's*, November, 1953, p. 59.

[8] Meanwhile, Mr. and Mrs. Attwood drove to Haifa, and Johnson remained behind in Tel Aviv and Jerusalem to interview at Stevenson's request a number of people, including Reuven Shiloah of the Foreign Office; Shimon Bejerano, an industrialist and a member of the General Zionist party; Vinhas Lavon, minister without portfolio in the cabinet; Mr. and Mrs. Gershon Agron of the Jerusalem *Post;* David Horowitz, under secretary of the treasury and about to become the next governor of the Central Bank of Israel; Dr. Leo Kohn of the Foreign Office; two officials of Histadrut, the General Federation of Jewish Workers; and Dr. Giova Yoseftal, who was in charge of handling immigrants on their arrival.

[9] "Mr. Stevenson's Visit to the Middle East," *Manchester Guardian Weekly*, June 25, 1953.

he replied jokingly that perhaps it would be safer not to go home at all if Look is willing to support us indefinitely."

The following morning Stevenson had breakfast with the mayor of Haifa, Aba Hushi, and U.S. Consul Wilbur Chase. At 8:30 he and his group drove to Nazareth and the Sea of Galilee. David L. Cohn wrote of this trip:

> A handicap of the Middle East is that its people have always lacked the refining influence of the D.A.R. Hence for three thousand years they have been ready to fight at the drop of a dogma, making this a tough area to handle from Herod Antipas, 33 B.C., to John Foster Dulles, 1953 A.D.
>
> Here where vanished civilizations lie layer upon layer like wedges of a prize-winning cake, Stevenson lunched one day on the Lake of Tiberias. Antiquity watching from the Galilean hills, perhaps he profited more from that moment than from his briefings. For a local man once wrote that where there is no vision the people perish; a good thing to know even at the cost of one's digestion.[10]

Late that afternoon Stevenson returned to Tel Aviv where he held a brief press conference. He said in a prepared statement:

> What is most conspicuous in my mind is the anxiety within the Arab states as well as in Israel, for peace — for normal relations. I am frank to say that the feeling on both sides is very deep. One finds on the Arab side a profound fear of Israel's future expansion. One finds here profound misgivings about the purposes and the intentions of the Arab states. The greatest trouble of all, it seems to me, is psychological. Indeed, I might say pathological. The removal of these basic fears and tension is certainly the greatest challenge to statesmanship in this area of the world.

In response to a question from a reporter as to what he recommended to ease the tension between Israel and the Arabs, Stevenson replied that tension could be "alleviated by direct communication between the chiefs of state and by an exchange of assurances." He then stated: "The United States should offer its good offices to bring about this objective, which is so manifestly desirable." [11]

At dinner that evening, Francis Russell told Stevenson that when Secretary of State Dulles had been in Israel in May, Dulles had asked Ben-Gurion to aid him and President Eisenhower in keeping U.S. Jews from becoming hysterical if the Eisenhower Administration attempted to work out a peace with the Arabs. Dulles added that otherwise, "we

10 "Adlai Seemed Wilted Midway in Tour."
11 The New York *Times*, June 12, 1953, published part of the press conference.

will wipe out our interest in this area." This statement, Russell told Stevenson, apparently had frightened the Israeli leaders more than Dulles's speech when he returned home.[12]

At nine P.M., Stevenson and Russell went to say goodbye to the prime minister. Teddy Kollek rode with them and ventured that Ben-Gurion might have sounded extreme to Stevenson the other day about the refugees, rectifying boundaries, and the internationalization of Jerusalem. But Kollek insisted, "He is not really that extreme. He was upset by Dulles's speech."

At the prime minister's home, he and Stevenson discussed what the Bible said about the places that Stevenson had just visited. Then Stevenson asked Ben-Gurion how Israel could afford its high standard of living. He replied that Israel could not afford it, but he explained that his generation of immigrants "had decided they could not live like Arabs. They had to have soap and a book." But, in view of the pressing need of investments in industry and agriculture, the prime minister said, "We must reduce the standard of living and we will do it."

Stevenson next asked how Israel would close the gap in its balance of payments. Ben-Gurion replied that it would be extremely difficult to do, although "we can do it in ten years, but we will need outside help during that period."

Then Stevenson wondered again how Israel could absorb two million more immigrants. Ben-Gurion said: "I know that that has been worrying you. However, we can do it in ten years. The experts told us that we could not live here with more than 600,000 people and now we have 1,700,000 people. One cannot trust the judgment of experts. We will do it. More people will have to go out on the land and become farmers. Forty years ago we went out on the land and we worked the land and we learned. The new immigrants will have to do it as well. Of course, we have to rely on the good will of world Jewry in order to be able to accomplish this." [13]

[12] Dana Adams Schmidt wrote in the New York *Times,* June 29, 1953: "Probably no people in the world are so sensitive as the Israelis to what people of other countries, especially Americans, think about their country. . . . Almost every word written abroad about Israel is studied here with dismay or delight. Lately the dismay has predominated. The advent of a Republican Administration in the United States, with a new emphasis on winning the friendship of the Arabs, has made some Israelis realize that the world's concept of Israel is changing. . . . Leading Israelis were disappointed with the objective coolness they detected in Adlai E. Stevenson during his visit this month. 'He was too bipartisan for us,' one official remarked glumly after the departure of the defeated 1952 Democratic Presidential candidate."

[13] For developments in Israel since 1953, see Terence Prittie, *Israel: Miracle in the Desert* (New York: Frederick A. Praeger, 1967).

Following this conversation, while Stevenson stuffed his papers into his bulging briefcase and packed his suitcases, Blair wrote to Carol Evans: "I'm afraid that I have let you down lately but we have been moving at a terrific pace since Nathia Gali and are still going strong. As a matter of fact, we have been touring all of Israel since 6 A.M. this morning and it is now midnight — and we take off for Cyprus at 2 A.M.!!!" [14]

Stevenson wrote about his visit to Israel:

NO PEACE FOR ISRAEL [15]

A moment later, I was saying goodbye to the Arab governor of the Old City and passing through the wreckage and barbed wire at the Mandelbaum Gate into New Jerusalem and Israel.

As you come into Israel by the back door after long months of travel in the East, the first impact is the abrupt change in living standards — no one is barefoot, no one is dressed in rags. Then you notice the modern European aspect of New Jerusalem, the bustling crowds, the new construction. For the Jews are moving their capital to Jerusalem in spite of the talk of internationalization and in spite of the city's division and location, because, as one said to me, "Jerusalem has a meaning for Jews which no Gentile can understand."

In the next few days, I traveled through Israel from Elath, on the ill-favored shores of the Red Sea, to the mount overlooking the Sea of Galilee where Jesus said, "Blessed are the peacemakers. . . . Do good to them that hate you." And I crossed the Valley of Esdralon where my namesake, Adlai, was a shepherd of King David. It looked more peaceful than politics — or the Middle East.

Much has been written about the modern miracles wrought by Israel, and I will not repeat what others have reported about the camps for new immigrants, the new villages, collective farms, housing, schools and factories. These achievements exceeded my expectations, and I concluded that more human and material progress is concentrated in tiny Israel than in the rest of the Middle East put together. Rather let me report what may be less familiar — that Israel's road is as rocky as its soil.

Imports exceed exports five to one. Last year, Israel earned only about 20 per cent of the foreign currency she spent. The balance came from

---

[14] This handwritten letter, dated June 11, 1953, is in the possession of Miss Evans.
[15] *Look*, August 11, 1953. This is the concluding portion of the article, which also described the visits to other Middle Eastern countries. These portions are reprinted in Chapters Thirteen, Fourteen, and Fifteen, above.

investments, loans and gifts from abroad, mostly from American Jews and the U.S. Government. Almost three fourths of last year's budget came from abroad. Nearly a third of Israel's foreign debt matures within a year. Productivity is low, costs high, resources meager, industry slowing down for want of foreign exchange for raw materials. And Israel is only about 30 per cent self-sufficient in food. In spite of more than a billion dollars of gifts, loans and investments from abroad in the past five years, Israel is still further from paying her own way than any other nation. As one official said to me, "Flushed with a victory that had looked so doubtful, we thought we could have everything all at once — unlimited immigration and assimilation, rapid industrialization, agricultural development, social security, high wages and living standards and a big army. We were wrong."

Is Israel doing anything about her present plight? She certainly is. Inflation has been checked; real wages came down 10 or 15 per cent in the last year; supply now exceeds purchasing power and the inflated living standard is declining — as it must before it can go up. With increasing unemployment, there is a great drive to raise agricultural output by diverting more people to the land. And I believe that Israel, possessed of great resources of intelligence and ingenuity and with a record of so many difficulties already mastered, has both the courage and the leadership to take the distasteful steps necessary to earn more and spend less foreign exchange.

Two other factors will ease the situation: Net immigration is down from more than 25,000 a month last year to 900. And Germany has agreed to pay "moral reparations" to Israel in the form of $750 million worth of goods over the next 12 years.

But, as an official said, "We have only a slight margin, if any, for error." At best, Israel will need generous friends for a long time.

More food can be wrested from the soil, but Israel lacks both water and farmers. Water exploration is being pushed with some success, but large irrigation projects would involve her hostile neighbors, Syria and Jordan. Only 15 per cent of the population are in agriculture; the bulk of the 700,000 immigrants (from 48 countries) who arrived since 1948 are urban professional people, shopkeepers, artisans and traders with little taste for farming. The result is that you see too much neglected land, too many machines and sprinklers imported from abroad and too little manual labor in the manner of the Arabs and Asians. This would be understandable if Israel had plenty of money and a shortage of manpower. But the reverse is true; and the resistance to working on the land will continue to be a problem until another generation is trained.

What would it mean to Israel's economy if the Arab blockade of

Israel were lifted? The estimates vary from $15 million to $70 million a year. Whatever it is, with cheaper food and materials, living and production costs would go down and the competitive position of Israel's industries would improve. But peace is prerequisite to ending the blockade — and the prospects look no brighter on this side of the border.

Prime Minister David Ben-Gurion, an energetic, friendly, stubborn fighter who has seen his Zionist dream come true, said to me, "We want to live in friendly co-operation with our Arab neighbors. Our aim is peace." Then I asked him about the Arab demands. He minced no words — nor did Moshe Sharett, the confident, articulate Foreign Minister: "Jerusalem will be internationalized — over our dead bodies. Repatriation? We won't accept a single Arab."

Foreigners sometimes wonder why Israel insists on making her capital Jerusalem — a half-city in a narrow salient. Ben-Gurion explained it in these words: "We are ready to accept divided Jerusalem as it is and we have no objection to international supervision of the holy places. But Israel without Jerusalem is like Zionism without Zion."

As to the boundary changes demanded by the Arabs, the Israeli position is this: "We took no territory from any Arab state in the war; we have no border dispute with Lebanon; we will discuss and settle the small strip Syria claims; we will give Egypt a passage across our southern extremity, with guarantees; we will meet Jordan's port requirements, and we almost reached an agreement with Jordan last year to correct the present frontier absurdities. But to go back to the lines originally fixed by the U.N. — never!"

Sharett put it this way: "The Arabs could have accepted the U.N. boundaries, but they didn't. They forced us to fight for our lives. They can't have it both ways. Our territory was increased by war — and only war can alter it."

The Arab refugees? The Israelis made it plain where they stood. About 160,000 Arabs who didn't flee during the fighting are still living in Israel, and a few thousand more are being admitted to reunite families. Any more, it is said, would create a security risk and an acute assimilation problem. I suspect any large number of returned refugees certainly would not leave much more room for the 2.5 million Jews still behind the Iron Curtain, who, Ben-Gurion says, would be welcomed.

Sharett preferred to talk about resettlement rather than repatriation of the Arab refugees: "If Israel with its small area and limited resources could within a few years absorb 700,000 destitute newcomers — 250,000 of them Jews from Arab lands — it is evident that the bigger and better-endowed Arab countries could find homes for the same number of their kinsmen, if only the will existed."

Israel does, however, recognize an obligation to compensate the Arab refugees for the property they left behind. The Israelis don't know where they will get the money, but, as Ben-Gurion often says, "It can be done because it has to be done."

When do they propose to do something about indemnification? Only as part of an over-all peace settlement. But the Israelis have now agreed to release to the refugees a portion of their $7 million in bank deposits which Israel has frozen for the past five years.

The Arab states fear Jewish aggression. Likewise, the Israelis fear that any arms the U.S. gives the Arabs will be used to attack Israel rather than to defend the Middle East. So again, as in Egypt, it is obvious that a regional defense organization must await the solution of problems that have higher local priority in this part of the world than defense against Soviet imperialism.

As in so many other countries I have visited during this long journey, I was both exhilarated and depressed by what I found in Israel — exhilarated by what has been accomplished by the pride of the ordinary people (like the taxi driver who boasted about what "we Jews" are doing to irrigate the Negev Desert) and by the vision in Israel of a better future for all of the Middle East.

And I was depressed by the gulf that separates Israel from the Arab world and by the bleak facts of her economic life. Regardless of world politics and the importance of unity and strength in the great strategic vacuum of the Middle East, the good will of her neighbors is as vital to Israel's survival in the long run as aid from abroad is today. Israel's many friends in America should remember that good relations between Jews and Arabs are the only alternative to endless contributions of money to a permanently beleaguered fortress surrounded by embittered neighbors.

And "peace" is not just a word in a treaty which, signed today, means friendly relations tomorrow. Real, enduring peace is a state of mind which will only stem from mutual confidence and a community of interests between Jews and Arabs. This may take a long time. But the first and urgent step is to settle the four outstanding disputes — over boundaries, Jerusalem, compensation and repatriation.

My own feeling is that insistence on any *major* alteration of Israel's boundaries is unrealistic.

As to Jerusalem, it is hard to see how a city divided against itself can stand, let alone flourish; and certainly *all* the faiths are concerned.

The refugees constitute the hardest problem, and it is crying tragically for settlement. Indemnification for their property is no more than fair and just. As to repatriation, I doubt that any substantial number of Arab refugees would care to live as Israeli citizens under conditions and in an environment quite different from what they remember; and especially if opportunities were opened to them to resettle with help and hope among their kinfolk in Arab countries.

Finally and most emphatically, the Arab states must be made to feel that America's friendship for Israel does not mean we are "anti-Arab" or esteem them the less. But this will take far more than words.

At the outset of this article, I said that the Middle East is smoldering with anger. Yes, and with nationalism, pride, mistrust and intemperance too. Demagoguery and inflamed public passions make reasonable, effective leadership difficult on both sides. Conciliation and compromise in the public interest invite charges of appeasement and treachery, even the risk of assassination — as the late King Abdullah of Jordan found out.

Perhaps it is too much to expect that solutions will be worked out — as they should have been long ago — by the Arabs and the Jews sitting down together. But they might welcome reasonable solutions imposed by outsiders willing to be damned by both sides.

If this sounds like tough talk, I recall the pleading words of a sad-eyed old Mohammedan *caid:* "Two sick men need a doctor." He said it in Nazareth.

Seventeen

Cyprus and Turkey

JUNE 12–JUNE 22, 1953

W hen *Stevenson stepped out of the airplane at Nicosia, Cyprus, at 3:15 A.M., he was greeted by U.S. Consul Joseph Wagner. Attwood wrote in his diary:*

Stevenson began automatically asking him questions about the island's population, economy and politics and so on. Finally I reminded him that this was the *one* place we've been to on this trip where he didn't have to know a damn thing or write a line about it. He seemed kind of punchy, as though he weren't quite sure just where he was in the world or where we were going next.[1] He is often like this and curiously enough it is part of his charm; for example shaking hands eagerly with people he has already met and not offending them by doing so. I have also noted his frequent bewildered enthusiasm and engaging spontaneity. I remember when he met Sim [Mrs. Attwood] for the first time in Cairo; for the first half minute he had no idea who I was introducing him to and gave her the quick smile and hearty handshake; then when he realized who she was he suddenly patted her cheek and explained, "Why bless you my dear — we've been chasing you for 15,000 miles."

Stevenson and his party were driven over the hills to Kyrenia, on the coast, where the manager of the Dome Hotel, a former Princeton stu-

[1] Stevenson had told Johnson the day before that he felt just as he had felt the last week of the 1952 campaign. When Johnson asked what that meant, he replied, "Numb, numb all over."

dent, was waiting to greet them. Stevenson spent most of the restful days at Kyrenia writing his article on the Middle East for Look.

Four days later, after Stevenson had completed his first draft in longhand and Mrs. Attwood had typed it, Attwood wrote in his diary:

> I began editing in earnest after breakfast and felt obliged to do an almost complete rewrite of the lead and first few pages. As a writer Stevenson has lyrical flashes and uses words refreshingly but his style is not adapted to the technique of reporting. I suspect he is more successful in dealing with ideas, abstract ones especially, than with facts. Bill [Blair] tells me that he wrote his acceptance speech entirely by himself and that was certainly a fine piece of prose; but a soaring, inspiring speech and a hard-hitting down-to-earth article are two different things.

Stevenson interrupted his writing one day to pay a courtesy call on the British governor of Cyprus and to dine aboard the British cruiser H.M.S. Bermuda, *anchored off Kyrenia. One day he took three hours away from his desk to hike amidst the spectacular ruins of the old Crusader castle, St. Hilarion. It was on this visit that he talked about the type of book that he wanted to write as a result of the trip. He emphasized that he did not want to write a travelogue but a book that raised philosophical and general questions. He was interested in discussing, he explained, such things as: "Are people more stirred by hunger or by religious and emotional issues?" "What is the importance of anticolonial and anti-Western feeling?" "What form of government is most suited to the nations of the underdeveloped world?" "What attitudes do these nations have toward the United States?"*

The troubles that were soon to befall this beautiful island crowded in on Stevenson during his visit. Every day he received lengthy telegrams from Greek-Cypriots urging him to help free the "enslaved" people of Cyprus from the British so that Cyprus could join Greece.[2] Only a few telegrams came from Turkish-Cypriots opposing union with Greece. Blair wrote his parents on June 14: "We have been here for two days now and it is exactly what we had hoped for — a nice, quiet hotel

---

[2] Approximately 80 per cent of the Cypriots were of Greek origin and 20 per cent were of Turkish origin. The Turks had acquired the island from the Venetians. In 1878 Turkey turned the island over to the British as a protectorate. The British annexed the island in November, 1914, after declaring war on Turkey. In August, 1960, the British granted Cyprus its independence. Under the agreement, the president was elected by and from the ethnic Greek community and the vice president from and by the ethnic Turkish community. Archbishop Makarios was elected president in 1960. Fighting between the Greek-Cypriots and the Turkish-Cypriots broke out in December, 1963, and a United Nations peace force had to establish an uneasy truce the next year.

on the water — good swimming, delicious food, no engagements, or appointments as long as I can hold off the local politicians who are agitating for union with Greece." (Blair succeeded, except for a call from the mayor of Kyrenia.)

On the last day in Cyprus, before boarding a plane for Turkey, Stevenson called on Archbishop Makarios of the Greek Orthodox Church. For nearly twenty minutes they discussed the history of the island and the various invasions it had suffered. The archbishop described how the Church had kept the Greek people on the island united despite the foreign occupations. The hardest time, he said, was during the Crusaders' domination when they tried to make the Greeks Roman Catholics.

The archbishop, who was the leader of the movement for union with Greece, told Stevenson: "We are Greeks and always have been. We were a Greek city-state before the many invasions. We feel that our national aspirations must be fulfilled. As head of the Church I am also head of the nationalist movement."

He noted that the Greek-Cypriots had petitioned the British governor to no avail. While he knew that Cyprus was an important British military base, he argued that it would be a better military base for the free world if the people were contented politically. "We now feel," he concluded, "that we must petition the United Nations for simple justice. We know that our petition will be used by the Communists, but nevertheless we feel that we must move on the issue."

During the discussion Stevenson made no statement in reply to the archbishop's appeal for union with Greece.

As he left, photographers took pictures of the two men. A little later, at the airport, reporters besieged him. He was asked whether the British needed Cyprus as a military base. Stevenson replied that he had been writing an article during his stay and had not had time to look into this question nor into the political situation. He added that he had had a "wonderful time on this charming island" and wanted to return.

Another reporter persisted and asked for Stevenson's view of "the desires of the people for union with Greece." Stevenson simply repeated that he had been too busy working on his own affairs to inquire into the situation. Next he was asked why the American people "didn't support the right of self-determination." He replied that Woodrow Wilson had set forth the self-determination of peoples as a policy of the United States and that it remained as a policy.

Stevenson boarded a Cyprus Airways plane at 1:45 P.M. and landed at Ankara some two hours later, where he was met by Ambassador George McGhee, William Roundtree and others of the embassy staff.

Stevenson spent several hours before dinner rewriting his article on the Middle East for Look. At dinner with Ambassador and Mrs. Mc-Ghee, the ambasador talked knowledgeably about Turkish history and developments since United States aid had started under the Truman Doctrine. The admission of Turkey into the North Atlantic Treaty Organization [3] was significant, he remarked, in that it was the first time in centuries that Turks had been accepted as Europeans.[4] No criticism of Ataturk, the founder of the republic, was allowed. Under Ataturk and his successor, Ismet Inonu, the republican form of government only thinly veiled the autocratic leadership of the country. Then in 1946 President Inonu allowed the formation of political parties and four years later his Republican party had been defeated by the new Democratic party. The ambassador remarked that Inonu deserved great credit for allowing the opposition to take control.

Ambassador McGhee spoke in optimistic terms about Turkey's economic situation. It had now become a wheat-exporting nation, cotton production was expanding, and prospecting for oil was under way. The

[3] Greece and Turkey joined the North Atlantic Treaty Organization in March, 1952. In February, 1953, Yugoslavia, Greece, and Turkey signed a treaty of friendship (Treaty of Ankara). In August, 1954, this treaty was supplemented by a military alliance (Bled Alliance).

[4] In the aftermath of Turkey's defeat in World War I, a group of young military officers under the leadership of Mustafa Kemal Ataturk reconstructed Turkey. Joseph C. Grew, the American ambassador to Turkey in 1930, wrote in his diary: "Modern Turkey . . . is working out a problem which never before has been attempted in so short a space of time. Realizing that in the exacting demands of modern competition, parity with European nations could only be achieved through the adoption of western civilization and western culture, the new Turkish Republic has thrown off the retarding trammels of orientalism as practiced under the regimes of Abdul Hamid and his predecessors. The Sultanate and the Caliphate have been abolished, and with them has gone, too, the old-time fez which was symbolic of the unprogressive past. The Government has separated itself from Islam; the old Moslem schools, where the youth of the country spent its formative years chanting the Koran and were largely hindered from acquiring a western education, have been suppressed; the women have been unveiled and will, according to present indications, eventually receive the vote; polygamy has been abolished and western codes of civil, criminal and commercial law have been adapted to the Turkish needs; the Latin alphabet has supplanted the old Arabic script — and all this has been done not as a process of slow development, but in the very few years that have elapsed since the Republic was founded. One by one the old branches, dead and rotting, have been chopped off, almost overnight, from the central tree-trunk where the sap is healthy and capable of contributing to new and healthy growth. This amazing revolution is due to a keen and forceful nationalistic spirit, much of the same intensity as that which inspired our own country in 1776, but it is due in greatest measure to one man, the father of this country, Mustafa Kemal who, having driven the foreign invaders from this land, set about to cure 'The Sick Man of Europe' and to make him permanently well and strong." *Turbulent Era: A Diplomatic Record of Forty Years, 1904–1945,* edited by Walter Johnson (Boston: Houghton Mifflin, 1952), Vol. II, pp. 707–708.

gross national product had risen twenty-five per cent in the past three years and while annual income was still low ($175), it had been $150 just three years before. He described the American aid program under the Truman Doctrine — about $300,000,000 a year — and particularly the road-building that had been accomplished.

The ambassador observed that Turkey was an absolutely reliable ally as a result of the coincidence that the Soviet Union was a common enemy. Historically the Turks had fought the Russians many times. He stated that it was said that "the reason the Turks hate Communism is because it's Russian-made."

Later in the evening Stevenson and the ambassador attended a reception that the Turkish government gave in honor of the visiting prime minister of Greece, Marshal Papagos. The next morning Stevenson worked again on his draft of his article for Look.

Ambassador and Mrs. McGhee gave a luncheon in Stevenson's honor where he was introduced to some thirty Turkish leaders. After lunch he talked to embassy officers about the work of the Mutual Security Agency. There was a discussion of the assistance given to expand wheat and cotton production, to build roads, and to improve port facilities. It was pointed out that under Ataturk the government had taken control of mining concessions and had run them as state enterprises. The Democratic party, however, was now reducing state activity in mining and encouraging investment by foreign capital.

"The Turks have a boom psychology," Stevenson was told. "They are not afraid of tomorrow. They are sure they can carry out their plans. They feel they are a great people. They have the resources and with our aid they are developing those resources."

Later in the afternoon Stevenson called on Prime Minister Adnan Menderes [5] *and Foreign Minister Fuad Koprulu. The prime minister thanked Stevenson for visiting Turkey and expressed his regrets that the presence of the Greek prime minister in Ankara made it impossible to have talks as long as they wished. When Stevenson praised the economic developments of recent years, the prime minister launched into a detailed account of the increased production in sectors of the economy and said, "American aid has been very significant to our progress."*

Then Stevenson asked them to discuss the Middle East and Israel with him. The foreign minister responded: "If the Arabs are left to themselves, there will be no solution to this issue. If the refugee issue can be settled, however, you may be able to bring a compromise be-

[5] In 1959, military leaders overthrew the Menderes government. He was executed shortly after the coup.

tween the Arabs and the Jews. The Arabs need to have guarantees against Israeli expansion." He closed with the comment: "The United States and the West are too favorable to Israel and more impartiality is needed."

Stevenson remarked, "Some Arab leaders speak much wilder in public than in private." The foreign minister replied, "This is because there are no real leaders in the Arab countries. A real leader sometimes must do things the masses don't always like, but for the long run it is better for the people that the leaders actually do these things."

At this point the prime minister said, "There is a Turkish proverb: 'A man is the slave of what he says and the master of what he doesn't say.'"

The foreign minister said in a scornful tone: "Look at the Arab world. There's Saudi Arabia. It has no government at all. It keeps going on the basis of the king and oil. Look at Egypt. It was looted by Farouk and the Pashas. Five per cent of the people have owned the country. Now General Naguib is only a façade and the Revolutionary Committee is divided from extreme right to extreme left. Look at Jordan. It's a completely artificial country. It's a tribal society. It doesn't have any government. And little Lebanon — just a few wealthy families rule."

As the foreign minister reached Syria, he gestured with his hands and said: "Coup d'état after coup d'état. Of all the Arab countries, Iraq is the most stable. It is more like a government but they are divided, too, into Sunni and Shii Moslems and have minorities of Kurds, Turks, and Iranians." He threw up his hands and said: "This is the Arab world."

"Don't misunderstand," he added. "We always are friendly with them, but now they bear us a grudge because they say we are too close to the West and they objected to our joining NATO. We must, however, strengthen the Arabs to check subversives there. But, no matter how much America arms the Arabs, they won't be as good as three Turkish divisions."

The prime minister remarked that the Arabs "have the idea of Oriental bargaining. Whatever they get from you, they think they have been cheated. They exaggerate their own importance and they think they are essential. There is no unity among the Arabs despite the existence of the Arab League. The Arabs have the illusion that the Eisenhower Administration will be kinder toward them. This should be dispelled." He closed with the suggestion that if funds could be provided, Syria and Iraq might be able to absorb the refugees.

Immediately after this conference, Stevenson called on President Celal Bayar. Stevenson said later that the president had told him that

Turkey was willing to join the United States, the United Kingdom, and France in guaranteeing the boundaries between Israel and the Arabs. He was also told: "If any Communists appear in Turkey, we arrest them. If I suggested a law to the Grand National Assembly to hang all Communists, it would pass."

After this meeting, Stevenson hurried to the railroad station to say goodbye to Ambassador and Mrs. McGhee, who were returning to Washington. Then he spent the evening revising his article for Look. *He completed it at three A.M.*

The following morning after breakfast, Stevenson met with an editor of an Istanbul newspaper. The remainder of the morning he spent visiting Turkish military installations with General W. P. Shepard of the American military advisory mission.

That afternoon, with the assistance of a secretary at the embassy, he tried to catch up with his correspondence.

To Arthur M. Schlesinger, Jr.[6]

June 19, 1953

My dear Arthur:

Your letters are a delight and give us briefly and delightfully more information about the state of the Union than we glean from all the press — including *Time* and *Newsweek!*

The journey progresses and I am getting impatient and weary. I had no idea there were so many troubles in the world, and the "Communist menace" seems to be about the least in most of the countries we have passed through. It is hard to get them off of their local problems, grievances and nationalism and on to the major things. But Turkey is pleasantly uncomplicated!

I hardly know what to say about Mrs. Bruce's [7] invitation to stay with them in Paris. By that time I will have two boys with me and also probably the Ives tagging along, together with Bill Blair. In many ways I should love to do it but I think perhaps I better "stick with the gang."

If you conclude that I ought to have something potent to say on the domestic scene when I arrive in New York please send it along. Meanwhile I have followed the policy of not commenting on domestic

[6] The original is in the Schlesinger papers, John F. Kennedy Library. The postscript is handwritten.

[7] David K. E. Bruce served in 1953 as special U.S. observer at the Interim Committee of the European Defense Community, and as special American representative to the European High Authority for Coal and Steel.

affairs, particularly critically, during my journey and I *think* it has been wise.

Love to Marian,[8] and don't lose your typewriter!

Yours,

ADLAI

P.S. Isn't the time coming when we should launch an all out attack on McCarthyism, repression etc? It recurs in press conferences in Asia constantly. Also the new dispensation in the State Dept. is having ugly effects.[9]

AES

To Stephen A. Mitchell [10]

June 19, 1953

Dear Steve:

So many thanks for your wonderfully informative letter of May 28th. But that schedule of your journey sounds as bad as mine, and I pray that you are not as tired.[11]

I am not sure that I shall be able to take advantage of Cardinal Stritch's letter [12] but I have written him a courteous acknowledgement

---

[8] Mrs. Schlesinger.

[9] Senator Joseph McCarthy's attacks on the United States Information Agency led Secretary of State Dulles to issue a directive in February, 1953, that "no material by any Communists, fellow-travelers, et cetera, will be used under any circumstances." In March, Dulles had ordered the removal from United States Information Service libraries of books by those "who obviously follow the Communist line or participate in Communist front organizations" and the withdrawal of any magazine containing "material detrimental to the U.S. objectives." Frightened officials overseas removed even books and magazines that never appeared on lists drafted later in Washington. In addition, Dulles retired career diplomats John Carter Vincent and John Paton Davies, not because of lack of loyalty but on the ground that they had become too burdensome for him to carry in his relations with right-wing Republicans in Congress. Dulles also appointed Scott McLeod to head the security-loyalty program in the Department of State. As a result of all these actions, there was a frightening drop in morale visible in the embassies Stevenson had visited. On January 17, 1954, five distinguished retired career diplomats — Norman Armour, Robert Woods Bliss, Joseph C. Grew, William Phillips, and G. Howland Shaw — published a letter in the New York *Times* warning that the foreign service was being destroyed and conformity was being forced on officials. See Walter Johnson, *1600 Pennsylvania Avenue: Presidents and the People since 1929* (Boston: Little, Brown, 1963), pp. 290–291, 297–298.

[10] The original is in the papers of Stephen A. Mitchell, Harry S. Truman Library. The postscript is handwritten.

[11] Mr. Mitchell had described a twelve-day speaking schedule that he had just made to twelve states.

[12] Mr. Mitchell had informed Stevenson that Cardinal Stritch of Chicago had written to the pope to arrange an interview when Stevenson reached Rome.

and have also asked him to notify the Vatican that I should like to see the Pope * if it is at all possible — but not Clare Luce! [13]

Although I do not have it at hand, I think you also wrote me about a mass meeting in Chicago in mid-September. I should think that might be alright if you are confident that the Party can make some money out of it. I expect to get back in early August, more dead than alive, and will probably take to the woods after a few days in Chicago and a look at the horrible accumulation there. Perhaps any announcement or final plans could be deferred until I get home. If not, try to keep things as tentative as possible. Meanwhile I am declining all the speaking requests that pursue me as our journey advances.[14]

Yours,

P.S. I have suggested to George McGhee that he talk to you after he gets back. You will remember him as our Ambassador to Turkey and formerly Assistant Secretary of State — an excellent man and a *genuine* Texas Democrat. I think he could be very useful down there but he will probably prefer to live in Washington and could be helpful on program planning and international affairs. Also he is *very* well off and I have talked to him about the financial situation. At all events, be sure to give him an accurate picture.

* A letter since received from Rome reports that it has been arranged.

To Mrs. Ernest L. Ives [15]

June 19, 1953

Dear Buffy —

Now find we don't get to Rome until June 30 from Athens — just as you leave. Hope we cross before you get away. If not will pick up John Fell at Grand Hotel.

Will have to write another of these damn pieces in Italy — finished last one at 3 AM today! — and may hide out somewhere on Sorrento peninsula. Not sure whether you want to rush thru Austria and Germany at our pace or would rather take John Fell for more leisurely trip along Rhine or something — or stay in Austria — Vienna, Salzburg ? ? — while I'm rushing thru my everlasting interviews and work.

[13] Stevenson finally did see Ambassador Luce, but he declined her invitation to honor him with a lunch or dinner.

[14] Mr. Mitchell had written that he hoped Stevenson would not make any speaking engagements that might conflict with Democratic party affairs.

[15] This handwritten letter is in the Elizabeth Stevenson Ives collection, Illinois State Historical Library.

Have been able to give Borden little time, but he's enjoying and profiting from trip I'm sure.

Love,
AD.

P.S. Our plane from Athens arrives Rome on BEA line about 2 PM. If you have left leave message with John Fell.

To Joseph C. Green [16]

June 19, 1953

Dear Joe:

I was delighted to see you again and shall always be grateful to you and Mrs. Green for your extraordinary courtesy and hospitality. I feel as though it must have been an ungrateful imposition to impose on your time with such intemperance as well as your hospitality — but I enjoyed and profited from every minute of it!

Borden is back in shape again and both of us appreciate so much all you did for him. You were more than good to us and my heart and thoughts are very much with you.

With warmest regards and the utmost gratitude, *to you & dear Mrs. Green*, I am

Sincerely yours,

P.S. And my regards to Suzanne! [17]

Early in the evening of June 19, Stevenson called on former President Ismet Inonu, who told him that Turkey's most serious problem was Russia. "We alone had to protest" Russian demands in 1945 for control of the Dardanelles. "But it is now a great step that the Russian situation is a world problem," he added. He recommended that West Germany be brought into NATO to help check Russian expansion.

The economic situation in Turkey, he said, was the most pressing problem after relations with Russia. "We used to be like the Arab countries. You have just been there and you know what I mean. We used to be semi-medieval but in the last twenty-five years we have transformed our society." But, he remarked, Turkey's defense effort had been far too heavy for the economy to bear since 1939 and had impaired investment in education, health, and other social measures.

[16] The original is in the possession of Mr. Green. The P.S. and the words "to you & *dear Mrs. Green*" were added by hand.
[17] The Greens' daughter.

He praised United States aid for road-building and the improvement of agricultural production. He spoke of the need of increased industrial production and said that his party had warned the Democrats that Turkey was importing more than it was exporting. Turkey had to import goods from abroad just for productive enterprises and not to meet consumer demands, he explained.

When Stevenson asked him about the two-party system in the country, the former president remarked that he had assumed a heavy responsibility in 1946 in deciding that Turkey was ready for democracy. He added that his party had no desire to return to the one-party system. Stevenson asked him if he felt Turkey could have carried out its remarkable transformation from semi-medievalism to the twentieth century without one-party rule, and Inonu stated, "Absolutely not."

Stevenson then asked whether the Arab countries could solve their economic and social problems with democratic institutions. "Not at all," he replied immediately. "The Turks had to have one party and firm leadership to get it done. You must keep in mind that the Arabs have had no experience in government. . . . They have no idea of the crises a nation must go through before it really becomes a nation."

After breakfast the next morning, Stevenson and his party left Ankara for Istanbul and the Park Hotel overlooking the Bosporus. Aboard the plane he caught up on correspondence.

To Mrs. Edison Dick [18]

[no date]

. . . Today is the 20th of June — Isn't that the longest day in the year?

. . . The last weeks have been hot and violent — from Pakistan to Turkey — thru the Moslem world. Even our "rest" at Cyprus for me was worse than Barbados — I had to write an article and hardly got outdoors.

Borden joined up at Cairo and is enjoying it all, I think. . . .

I haven't been able to read the Perils of Pub.[19] yet — It's hard I know for you to understand why I have so little time. Just think of the campaign — it's about the same — *all* the time, except for the strain of creative work & speaking, and I get so I dream on my feet about being on my back with my eyes closed and not a single foreigner or problem in sight — for just fifteen minutes!!

---

[18] This handwritten letter is in the possession of Mrs. Dick. It is postmarked June 20, 1953.

[19] See note 30 to Chapter One, above.

But I'm sure it's wonderful and just right (the article) and I've not the slightest idea what to do about it next!

Bill [Blair] is well but tired too, indeed we're all okay — even Attwood now that his charming wife has joined us. I pray all is well with you — I've had no word for weeks and weeks — or does it just seem that way!

We're tired of mutton and rice & I yearn for fish — but after ages in the desert the seas are just ahead. . . .

At the hotel! — I find your *"fat"* letter . . . and how glad I am to hear from you again!! . . .

I plan to take some time with the boys at the end, but Borden may want to travel with friends. . . . Besides I want to get back to see Adlai off and his sailing plans are indefinite now I gather.

I must run now to "a luncheon" — so hurry and get ready with your best diplomatic talk and perpetual charm — curiosity, wisdom and — oh God! . . .

Stevenson lunched that day with Mr. and Mrs. Arthur Cable, old friends of Blair; Consul General Robert MacAttee; and Miss Betty Carp of the consulate. Stevenson endeared himself to Miss Carp by saying to her after he was introduced: "Why, this is the famous Betty Carp." [20]

Following lunch, he visited a fourth-century Byzantine church which experts from Dumbarton Oaks were in the process of restoring. He then toured the Blue Mosque and St. Sofia. Early that evening Stevenson was guest of honor at a reception at the consulate.

The Stevenson party dined alone that evening and discussed a statement by an embassy official that the USIS library at Ankara had removed Dashiell Hammett's mystery stories The Thin Man *and* The Maltese Falcon *from the shelves.* The Canterbury Tales, *with illustrations by Rockwell Kent, had also been removed. Attwood wrote in his diary:*

> Talk centered on McCarthyism, with Johnson, Blair, and I urging
> Stevenson to take advantage of this issue when he gets home. It

[20] Miss Carp had lived most of her life in Turkey and was on the staff of the U.S. consulate general in Istanbul. When Ambassador Joseph C. Grew arrived in Turkey in 1927, in describing his staff he wrote: ". . . and by no means last or least Miss Betty Carp. Carpie is known throughout the Foreign Service — whether for her inimitable letters or her sunny personality or merely her extraordinary ability and efficiency in getting things done, I know not, but the name of Betty Carp is respected and admired." *Turbulent Era: A Diplomatic Record of Forty Years, 1904–1945,* Vol. II, p. 716.

seems to us that this world tour has given him a good opportunity to approach McCarthyism from a new angle, namely, the crippling effect it has had on our foreign service, our propaganda effort and our relations with our allies. Stevenson confessed that he had been genuinely shocked by what he has seen abroad and heard from home.

The next morning Stevenson visited briefly with two Yugoslav correspondents, who asked him about his schedule when he reached their country. The rest of the morning and most of the afternoon he and his group spent in the consul general's launch, going down the Bosporus to the Sea of Marmara and then back up the Bosporus and into the Black Sea.

In the evening, Stevenson talked over developments in the United States with Mrs. India Edwards, of the Democratic National Committee, who had just arrived in Istanbul. He also had time to attend to correspondence.

To Mrs. James Mulroy [21]

[no date]

Dear Helen —

East of the Bosphorus the women do the work and the men the politicking — and they are *older* civilizations! We hear alarming tales about things at home — and for that matter alarming tales about things everywhere. Moreover everyone wants to eat every day in Asia which will be hard to arrange —

Yrs,

The next morning, June 22, Stevenson held a brief press conference. When asked to comment on his visit to Turkey, he said that the emergence of Turkey as a strong, self-reliant, democratic state was "one of the wonders of modern history." He was asked also to comment on South Korean President Syngman Rhee's order releasing anti-Communist North Korean prisoners who did not want to be repatriated. (This action had nearly disrupted the truce talks.) He replied: "I hope and pray President Rhee has not lost his mind." He added that he could understand the depth of Rhee's feelings, but that "today cool heads and sound minds" were needed in the world.

[21] This handwritten postcard is in the possession of Mrs. James Huntington Patton, whose late husband, James Mulroy, was Governor Stevenson's executive secretary during part of his administration in Springfield. It is postmarked June 22, 1953.

After the press conference, Stevenson called on Fahrettin Kerim Gokay, the governor-mayor of Istanbul. Stevenson, noting that the governor was a world-renowned psychologist, added, "I gather this is the best training for politics." The governor replied, "It helps."

Stevenson then asked him to explain the difference between the two major political parties. The governor observed that each of them followed Ataturk's main policies. Both were in agreement on foreign policy; the main difference was in economic policy. The Democrats favored more private enterprise and fewer state-owned activities. They had had to retain a number of state-owned enterprises, however, since there was a shortage of private capital to take them over. The Democrats, he concluded, placed greater emphasis than the Republicans on mechanizing agriculture and raising the standard of living of the peasants.

Following this meeting, the Stevenson party drove to the airport and boarded a plane for Yugoslavia.

Stevenson wrote about his visit to Turkey:

THE WEST BUILDS A BALKAN BARRIER [22]

I entered Europe through the back door — across the Bosporus at Istanbul and into the long-feuding Balkans, now severed by the Iron Curtain. First in Turkey, then in Greece and Yugoslavia, I met the leaders of some of our newest and scrappiest allies. I talked at length with that commanding and controversial figure, Marshal Tito; in Athens, I saw another stern soldier, Marshal Papagos, and lunched with King Paul and young Queen Frederika; and in Ankara, the tough, fearless Turks told me how these neighbor nations, who were still glaring at each other five years ago, managed to cast aside old grudges and join hands in a pact against Soviet aggression.

Everywhere, I was impressed by the hard-headed realism of the leaders and invigorated by the spirit of the people. There are no illusions in this corner of the world about the nature of the enemy, no neutralism and no speculation about the pros and cons of resistance. Differences aplenty distinguish royalist Greece from republican Turkey, and both from Yugoslavia, still experimenting with her native brand of communism. But they all have put our liberal aid to good use, and they all have stout hearts. For that, we Americans can be thankful.

[22] *Look*, August 25, 1953. Other portions of this article are reprinted in Chapters Eighteen and Nineteen, below.

Of all our allies, the Turks were the first to send troops to Korea, and at a time when it looked as though the Reds would drive our outnumbered forces into the sea.

On the day the Turkish government announced its decision to contribute a brigade of 5000 men to the United Nations command, one of Istanbul's leading papers published a cartoon showing a female Uncle Sam about to be ravished by a brutal North Korean. Charging to the rescue in the nick of time was a husky Turkish soldier. The cartoon expressed what the Turks felt then and what they feel today: that they are the world's best fighting men and America's most dependable ally.

After three years, the Turks' thirst for battle has not been quenched. While I was in Ankara, the fourth replacement brigade was about to embark for the Far East, and a contest was being held among the Turkish Army's cooks for the privilege of sailing with the brigade. American officers told me that the barbed wire surrounding the staging area at the port of embarkation was not to stop soldiers from going AWOL but to prevent other soldiers from sneaking in and going to Korea.

Probably the Turks' chief regret about Korea is that they were not able to fight Russians directly. I have not seen a country where dislike and distrust of the Russians and their ways were more universal and deep-rooted. In Turkey, this feeling has only a secondary connection with Communist aggression; mostly, it is an ancient hatred of the Turks' Muscovite neighbors (they still derisively call the Russians *moskofs*), with whom they have been fighting off and on for centuries. You hear it said that the reason they dislike communism so much is because it is Russian.

My guess is that the Turks will be the last people in the world to be lulled to sleep by the Kremlin's current peace policy. The Turks remember well that, in 1945, Stalin put in a claim to Turkish territory in the east and demanded the right to share in the "defense" of the Dardanelles, the strait from the Black Sea out into the Aegean. At that time, Russia and the Western nations were friendly, victorious allies and Turkey a weak and isolated neutral, only two decades removed from the slothful medievalism of the Ottoman Empire. Yet the Turks never flinched; they mobilized their sturdy but ill-equipped army and told the Russians where to get off.

Turkey's defiant spirit is a striking and refreshing contrast for anyone coming from the uncertain, troubled lands of Asia and the Middle East. This spirit is also one of the few things that have survived the mighty transformation wrought in Turkey in the past 30 years.

I last visited Turkey in the 1920's, when the transformation was just beginning.[23] Shorn of her empire after World War I, this nation, which had been wallowing for so long in a theocratic medieval past, was led at a gallop into the 20th century by Kemal Ataturk. This rough, hard-living, dedicated man swept away the symbols of the past, abolished polygamy and the musty caliphate and forced the Turks to adopt Western dress, Western legal codes and the Latin alphabet. When he died in 1938, Turkey was well on the way to becoming a vigorous, modern-minded state.

Today, the process is still going on, spurred by $1,250,000,000 worth of U.S. aid, mostly military since 1947, and by a healthy two-party liberal democracy — in many ways similar to our own.

In Ankara, the Democrats are in office. I spoke with leaders of both parties and was impressed by their candor, common sense and complete harmony on questions of foreign policy. Many of them were educated at Robert College, the old American college at Istanbul. The Democratic party leaders — President Celal Bayar, Prime Minister Adnan Menderes and Foreign Minister Fuad Koprulu — are strong, confident men, warmly appreciative of American aid and pleased with Turkey's progress and defense capabilities. Impatient with their Arab neighbors to the south, they feel that the only possible Middle East defense organization at the present time is a grouping of Turkey, the U.S., Britain and France, which the Arabs could join later. The Turks would join in a regional guarantee of nonaggression if it would help to allay suspicion and tension in the Middle East.

These leaders came to power in 1950 when the Democratic party, which emerged as a protest against one-party dictatorship, swept the nation's first completely free election and ousted Ataturk's own Republican People's party that had ruled Turkey for nearly 30 years. Their victory surprised everyone, including the Democrats themselves, as it was hard to believe that a dictatorship would allow itself to be voted out of office, especially in a country with no democratic tradition. That it did is a tribute to Ataturk's heirs and especially to his friend and comrade in arms, former President Ismet Inonu.

I had a long talk with Inonu, now aging and deaf but still the alert and vigorous leader of the Republican opposition. He told me that dictatorship and state capitalism were essential at first to Turkey's modernization, that the great reforms would have been impossible otherwise, but that democracy was always Ataturk's ultimate goal.

"By 1950, our people were ready," he said, "and now the goal has

[23] In 1926 he had visited Turkey and after great difficulties he secured a visa in Istanbul to enter the Soviet Union. See *The Papers of Adlai E. Stevenson*, Vol. I, pp. 167–169.

been reached." He attributed the Democrats' triumph to "time for a change" feeling and efficient grass-roots organization. He was confident that the two-party system would endure in Turkey.

About the only discernible difference between the parties is that the Democrats seem to stand for less "statism" and a freer economy, and greater tolerance in press and political expression. Extremist sentiment is negligible. The outlawed Communists are weak and the right-wing religious groups are divided and impotent. As President Bayar said, "We have no political problems in Turkey." I wonder how many presidents can say as much and mean it!

I found Turkey's economic prospects were just as bright. Unlike so many countries, Turkey is not cursed by overpopulation. In fact, with more land development, the country could accommodate twice its present population of 21,000,000. Giant strides have been made since the Truman Doctrine brought American aid and advice to threatened Turkey in 1947. Wheat production has doubled (Turkey imported wheat three years ago and now plans to export 2,000,000 tons in 1953); cotton production has trebled; highway mileage has risen from 6000 (mostly mule tracks) to 16,000 miles of all-weather roads; port facilities have increased tenfold — from 25,000 to 250,000 tons a month. Turkey has become the world's fourth largest exporter of cereals, average per capita income is up from $150 to $175 a year, and the gross national product has risen 30 per cent.

At the same time, the Turks are earmarking 40 per cent of their budget for the armed forces — more than any other NATO country, they say.

And Turkey's U.S.-trained and -equipped army is the West's only reliable bulwark in the Middle East. The Turks are even talking about a bridge over the Bosporus to link Europe and Asia!

I could go on adding facts and figures to buttress what was repeatedly confirmed by Americans serving in our various economic and military missions — that "Turkey is one place where every American dollar is well spent." But it is only fair to say that signs of strain are developing, and Turkey is having trouble matching her heavy imports with exports.

A leading Turkish editor said to me, "A new stream of life has come to Turkey from American co-operation." Perhaps the best thing about this bright spot on the globe is that, as Inonu said, "you Americans don't have to explain your aims or justify your policies to us." Like ourselves, Turks have no illusions about what ails the world. Long isolated and ignored by the West, the Turks today are proud to be partners in NATO (though I suspect they are sometimes scornful of their less sturdy, more sophisticated allies). With the signing last winter of the Balkan pact with Greece and Yugoslavia, Turkey has cemented new friendships and now no longer faces Russia alone across the Black Sea and the Caucasus.

The week before I reached Ankara, the Russians declared they were renouncing their 1945 claims on the straits and Turkey's eastern territories. To the Turks, this gesture proves that the policy of standing fast has paid off. Everyone I talked with was pleased that Russia had "chosen the wisest course" and was becoming more conciliatory. But they made it plain that nothing the Kremlin can do will ever drive a wedge between Turkey and its new friends in the West.

"Friendship with Russia," said an editorial in the newspaper *Milliyet*, "must be something like that of the ancient knights who visited their neighbors clad in armor." Thanks to the United States, the Turkish knights have a lot of armor and they take very good care of it.

Eighteen

Yugoslavia

JUNE 22–JUNE 27, 1953

*E*n *route from Istanbul to Belgrade, the plane landed at Salonika,
Greece, where some hundred Greek officials, newspapermen, and
Mr. and Mrs. Charles House of the American Farm School were waiting
to greet Stevenson. Mr. House, wrapped in a Class of '09 Princeton banner, thoughtfully had a supply of fresh Farm School milk — by far the
finest milk the weary travelers had had since Honolulu. After an exchange of pleasantries and the signing of autographs, the plane left for
Yugoslavia.*

*When Stevenson stepped off the plane in Belgrade late that after-
noon, he was greeted by a sizable number of Yugoslav officials, headed
by Vice President Milovan Djilas, representatives of the press, including
Jack Raymond of the New York* Times *and Helen Fisher of the United
Press, and representatives of the American embassy. Stevenson made
only a few brief remarks to the reporters. He was critical, as he had
been in Istanbul, of President Syngman Rhee's action in freeing the
prisoners of war as possibly jeopardizing the current negotiations for
a truce. He added:* "Our objective and our hope is still a strong, free
and independent, united Korea, but it has to await the conclusion of
peace and further negotiations." *When asked how he justified American
aid to Communist Yugoslavia, he replied,* "The need to resist Soviet
aggression is sufficient justification for American aid to Communist
Yugoslavia."

*After depositing his suitcases at the Majestic Hotel, Stevenson and
members of his party walked along a main boulevard near the hotel.*

He was quickly stopped by a girl who asked for an autograph. Then, as he was peering into a store window, a man tapped Johnson on the shoulder, pointed, and asked, "Stevenson?" He and others gathered to watch Stevenson as he inspected store after store.

That evening Stevenson and his party dined with Chargé d'Affaires Woodruff Wallner, Mrs. Wallner, and Turner C. Cameron, Jr., political attaché at the embassy. Wallner said that the death of Stalin had been the biggest event in Yugoslavia since the country had broken away from the Soviet Union in 1948. Yugoslav leaders were convinced, he remarked, that Stalin's death marked an important turning point in Soviet history. Among other things, they were concerned that the Russians would now be able to persuade the West that they were non-aggressive. If they succeeded, where would Yugoslavia stand in terms of further economic and military aid from the United States?

Wallner emphasized that the Yugoslavs were extremely nationalistic. As a result, Tito's decision to break with the Soviet Union had strengthened him with the non-Communists in Yugoslavia. Mr. Wallner stressed that President Tito and the four vice presidents [1] who ran the country were a closely knit group undivided by any ideological differences.

Wallner described U.S. military and economic aid to Yugoslavia and told Stevenson that "it has been quite an effort to justify this expenditure in a Communist country with members of Congress." He said he had been appalled when he heard that Roy Cohn and G. David Schine of Senator Joseph McCarthy's staff were coming to Yugoslavia to investigate the United States Information Service. He decided to take the offensive with them. When they arrived in Belgrade, he said, "Boys, you are now in the fightingest anti-Soviet country in Europe." They had seemed impressed by this, he added, and did not cause much trouble during their visit.

At the embassy briefing the next morning, Stevenson was told that Yugoslavia was moving away from the Soviet economic system and experimenting with new forms of socialism. They regarded the Russians as deviationists while they were true to the socialist ideal. It was explained that forced delivery by the peasants of certain crops

[1] Eduard Kardelj, Aleksandar Rankovic, Mosa Pijade, and Milovan Djilas. In 1955, Djilas was convicted of conspiring against the government and received a suspended sentence. The next year, after the Soviet Union crushed an uprising in Hungary, Djilas published an article in an American weekly, the *New Leader*, stating the revolt had raised the question of the "replacement of the Communist system itself by a new social system." He was sent to prison where he wrote *The New Class*, a strong attack on Communist regimes that was smuggled out and published in New York. He was paroled in 1961. But in 1962 he went back to prison for publishing a book, *Conversations with Stalin*. He was released by Tito in 1967. Rankovic was removed from office in 1966.

had been abandoned and the government was now allowing some collective farms to be decollectivized. The government had also started to decentralize control of the economy, and workers' councils now had managerial responsibility for the factories or stores where they worked.

The economic attaché, James S. Killen, pointed out that prior to the June, 1948, break with the Soviet Union almost all the trade of Yugoslavia was with the Soviets or the satellite countries. When this trade was canceled, the Yugoslavs had to do without capital goods from these countries. The World Bank had extended them a loan in 1951 and the United States, France, and the United Kingdom had agreed on an aid program that same year. Three years of serious drought beginning in 1950 had added to Yugoslavia's difficulties. Killen predicted, when Stevenson inquired about Yugoslavia's increasing trade with Western nations, that adjusting to this trade would continue to bring changes in the economy that Yugoslavia's leaders could not foresee.

The army attaché described the U.S. military aid program designed to help the country build a modern army. He estimated that twenty per cent of the gross national product went to the military. He added that the Yugoslavs were superb soldiers and could hold their own against any attack from the satellite countries. He also pointed out that to reduce traditional antagonism among the various nationalities in the country, the Yugoslavs maintained the same ratio of Croats, Serbs, Slovenes, and Macedonians in each army unit, where they worked together instead of fighting each other as in the past.

After the briefing Stevenson talked alone with Vice President Edward Kardelj and Vice President Djilas, and to Secretary of State for Foreign Affairs Koca Popovic. Kardelj gave a lunch that day in the Governor's honor. Among those present were Djilas, Popovic, Dr. Alex Bebler, under secretary of state for foreign affairs, and Svetozar Vukmanovic, chairman of the Economic Council.

There was an excellent exchange of views during the luncheon, interspersed with many humorous remarks. Djilas at one point said that the proof Yugoslavia was a great country was that "the planners couldn't kill it." When everyone burst into laughter, Stevenson said, "I'm delighted to see you have a sense of humor in Yugoslavia." Alex Bebler replied, "That's why we had to break with the Russians — they have none."

Djilas, in proposing a toast, emphasized that Stevenson had made a great impression on Yugoslavia during his campaign. Stevenson responded by expressing the hope that "happy relations between the United States and Yugoslavia have only begun. I feel we need a new nomenclature in the world to get along better — the words Communism, socialism, democracy, have all been so badly misused. Instead of talking about Communism, socialism, and democracy, let us drink to friendship and mutual interests."

At midafternoon, Stevenson broke up the lunch by remarking, "This is a socialist country and everybody is supposed to work. We must not impose on these chiefs of state any longer."

During the remainder of the afternoon, Stevenson drove around Belgrade, visited a rural village, and stopped off at a beach on the river. The crowds there immediately swarmed around him. As he talked to some of the swimmers through an interpreter, amateur photographers were active with their cameras.

On his return to the hotel, he interviewed Jack Raymond of the New York Times, Helen Fisher of the United Press, and several other American reporters about developments in Yugoslavia. When Stevenson asked about current Soviet-Yugoslav relations, Raymond replied that Tito had recently said they could never again trust the Russians one hundred per cent and had urged the satellite countries to follow Yugoslavia's independent course. One reporter added that the Yugoslavs referred to the Russians as "primitive despots."

After this discussion, Stevenson went to a reception in his honor attended by foreign diplomats, Yugoslavs, and Americans. When the reception ended, Stevenson and his party were the guests of Koca Popovic at a performance of Yugoslav folk dancing.

The next morning, Stevenson spent an hour alone talking to Svetozar Vukmanovic about the economic situation in the country. When this conversation was completed, Stevenson and his party boarded the Yugoslav air force plane which President Tito had provided to fly them around the country. Aboard the plane, Stevenson remarked that in his conversations with the Yugoslav leaders during the previous twenty-four hours each had expressed deep concern over one particular point: what United States policy would be if the Soviet Union relinquished its control of the satellite nations. They asked, "Would the United States then try to put back into power the old regimes of monarchists and landlords?" Stevenson said that the Yugoslavs were fearful of this because they wanted to influence the satellites to adopt their system of government. The leaders also expressed their concern over the way Radio Free Europe used the upper middle class and rich émigrés, who had fled Yugoslavia and the satellites at the close of World War II, to broadcast to these countries.

The airplane reached Zagreb in time for lunch with the president of the Croatian Republic, Dr. Vladimir Bakaric. After lunch with the president and a number of other officials, Stevenson drove around

Zagreb and visited a museum. Then he drove to a village where he talked with the assistance of an interpreter to several farmers about crop conditions that year.

Later that afternoon the plane took off for Pula on the Adriatic coast. Then a group of officials drove Stevenson and his party to a Yugoslav naval launch which took them across the mile-wide strait to President Tito's island retreat of Brioni.[2] No one was allowed on the island without Tito's permission. After the Stevenson party reached the guest hotel, Attwood wrote in his diary: "Tired as he was, Stevenson promptly took off on foot for a hike around the island. He has reached the point where he is unable to relax or even sit still (Blair says he was the same during the campaign) and just has to keep moving."

The following day the Stevenson party had lunch with President Tito, drove around the island with him, and then Stevenson and Tito spent several hours alone in discussion. One Yugoslav wrote:

> In spite of the private nature of the visit and the unofficial character of the conversations that were held there was in their meeting a special value which should be underlined: it was the first meeting between Tito and an American statesman of Mr. Stevenson's stature, the first meeting between two men who represent the best in their respective nations. And that is not insignificant.[3]

The same writer stated that it was fortunate that Stevenson's visit followed quickly on the trip that Secretary of State John Foster Dulles had recently made. Unlike Dulles's official visit, he remarked, Stevenson's was "unofficial and his relationship to the people he met and to the events he witnessed was, consequently, more direct and more flexible. We feel that his conclusions and his experiences are therefore apt to be more valuable and could have a more profound effect upon the public opinion of his countrymen than those of Mr. Dulles."

The day after Stevenson's talk with Tito, Attwood wrote in his diary that there were "no interviews, no typing, no pictures, no legwork, no airports." Stevenson visited the ancient city of Dubrovnik to tour the old fortress, the churches, the squares and the crooked streets. At noon a launch took him down the coast to a cove where he swam in the Adriatic and lunched at a little tavern near the beach. "Nobody talked politics," Attwood wrote in his diary, "and for once Stevenson was content to relax and not ask questions."

[2] Johnson had to leave the trip at Zagreb to return to teaching. The account of the remainder of the trip is based on William Attwood's diary.

[3] D. J. Jerkovic, "Stevenson — Rome and Belgrade," *New Republic*, July 27, 1953, p. 15.

The next day, June 27, the Yugoslav army plane flew Stevenson and his group to Skopje, the capital of the Republic of Macedonia. After a tour of the bazaars, Stevenson lunched with the president of Macedonia and other local officials. When he returned to the airport to depart for Athens, he told the Yugoslav officials and reporters who crowded around him to say goodbye, "I leave you admiring all that you have done and all that you are now doing. I am proud that my country is contributing to the strength and vitality of Yugoslavia."
One Yugoslav wrote:

> No one answered him; there was no need. For during his entire stay he must certainly have become convinced that there is in Yugoslavia a great deal of good will, friendship and respect for his country. He undoubtedly understood that here confidence in American democracy equalled the hopes which the entire world places in the United States.[4]

Stevenson wrote about his visit to Yugoslavia:

THE WEST BUILDS A BALKAN BARRIER [5]

If the Soviet nightmare is fresh and vivid in Greece and the lusty Turks have no use for their old Muscovite enemy, you haven't heard anything of bitterness and mistrust of Russia until you go to Communist Yugoslavia, where the people danced in the streets of Belgrade the day Stalin died.

Marshal (and now President) Tito told me the East Berlin riots were "the most significant event since the war." Then he hastily added, "Next to our break with Russia in 1948." (I remarked that 1948 was also important because it was the year I entered politics and was elected Governor of Illinois. So he gallantly proposed a toast to "the great year 1948!")

The importance of the 1948 break should never be underestimated. When Tito shook off Moscow's shackles and turned to the West, the whole nation rejoiced and still does. And on that act of defiance, seeds of courage and discontent were planted behind the Iron Curtain — seeds that have sprouted in East Germany, in Czechoslovakia and who knows where else.

"Nationalism," said Tito, "is a mighty influence in the world, and the satellites were once free and independent. The events in East

[4] Ibid.

[5] *Look*, August 25, 1953. Other portions of this article are reprinted in Chapter Seventeen, above, and Chapter Nineteen, below.

Germany showed the depth of the resentment of Russian oppression. The workers themselves revolted. They would have borne their burdens in a free Democratic Socialist state, but they knew they were exploited by Russia, which takes but doesn't give."

Just as "state capitalist bureaucratic despotism" is the way Yugoslavia's leaders describe the Soviet Union, so "democratic socialism" seems to be their approved description of Yugoslavia today.

I heard it said over and over again by the bright, tough young men who fought with Tito in the mountains against the Nazis and who now run the country under his fearsome eye. But I found they were still a long way from the political democracy of Greece and Turkey, let alone the U.S.

Belgrade looked more prosperous than I had expected, but still austere by Western European standards. Goods are plentiful but prices are high. You see trolley buses but few automobiles.

I talked to most of the leaders of "Democratic Socialist" Yugoslavia before going to see President Tito on his private island retreat at Brioni off the Adriatic Coast. They are young, as in so many of the other "new" nations I visited in Asia, energetic, self-confident, cheerful and very friendly. Nearly all veterans of the savage partisan fighting against the Germans, they stuck together in defying the almighty Kremlin in 1948. At lunch one day, I sensed a high-spirited fraternity that reminded me of a college classmates' reunion.

There may be trying times ahead for Yugoslavia, but the self-confidence of its leaders springs from what they have already accomplished in restoring their war-ravaged nation. Almost 2,000,000 Yugoslavs — one out of every nine — were killed and as many more scarred by war wounds and the brutalities of concentration camps. Aside from human resources, the war also took a heavy toll of livestock, vineyards, orchards and farm buildings; railroad trackage in half the country was torn up; 3,500,000 people were homeless, and 40 per cent of the mines, factories and power plants were out of commission or destroyed.

Reconstruction and recovery were barely under way — thanks, in large part, to UNRRA emergency relief — when Yugoslavia seceded from the Soviet empire and cut herself off from her chief source of trade and capital goods needed to implement an ambitious five-year plan of industrial development. Short of goods and food, Yugoslavia turned West for friends and help. She found them. Since 1948, the U.S. has given Yugoslavia more than $350,000,000, in addition to military aid. Britain, France and other NATO countries have also come to the rescue during the crippling crop failures of 1950 and 1952.

Meanwhile, exposed to attack from three neighboring Soviet satellites, Yugoslavia's fragile economy has been strained with her heavy defense effort. Last year, Yugoslavia probably spent more of her resources for defense than any country this side of the Iron Curtain, including the United States. But, like her Greek and Turkish partners, Yugoslavia has something impressive to show for her effort and our help — 300,000 superb soldiers, backed by trained reserves. Our military-aid mission was at first received with suspicion, but the barriers are crumbling and, today, relations are relaxed and cordial. Vestiges of Soviet influence in the army are disappearing: Yugoslav officers now go to Western Europe and the U.S. for training; uniforms are being changed from the Russian to the British style, and, significantly, political commissars in army units were abolished in June.

Soviet practices are gradually being altered in other fields as well. Until recently, peasants were compelled to deliver certain quotas of their produce to the state at low fixed prices. Now the system of compulsory deliveries has been reversed, and farmers can sell their produce on the open market, where prices depend on supply and demand. Food rationing has been abandoned and incentive taxation introduced to encourage increased agricultural production and marketing. Also in the Moscow pattern, Tito's regime introduced collective farming. But in spite of all the incentives — liberal credit, tractors and fertilizer — collectivization was never popular with the individualistic peasants and never affected more than 25 per cent of the land. So, last March the government permitted the collectives to "decollectivize," and soon only six or seven per cent of the arable land will be farmed on a collective basis mostly in areas better adapted to large-scale agricultural methods.

It may be that this reversal was the price that the nation's practical-minded leaders were willing to pay for more contented peasants, who comprise 70 per cent of the population and who have never been conspicuously enthusiastic about the regime.

On the industrial front, there has been an even more drastic redefinition of communism to stimulate competition and increase production. Until last year, ministries in Belgrade made every decision for industry — where to buy raw materials, where to sell and at what prices, how much to produce, what tax rates and wage scales to pay. Now the pendulum has swung to the other extreme, and "workers' councils" have full managerial responsibility for the factories, stores and enterprises in which they work. The councils can decide what to do with the profits, if any. They may expand plant facilities, build housing or even declare a wage bonus.

All these fundamental steps away from Soviet practice appear to be leading toward an economy more and more dependent upon supply and demand and at least limited competition. The functions of the state have been reduced to policy planning, over-all direction and supervision, with the result that there are a lot of vacant offices in the once top-heavy bureaucracy of "communism," a word you now seldom hear in Yugoslavia.

But the nation's leaders do not consider decentralization and "debureaucratization" and their radical Western-tinged deviations from the Moscow gospel to be deviations from the Communist idea. On the contrary, the breakup of the collectives was hailed as a step toward true socialism. Russia, they assert, is the traitor while they are the protectors of the revolution and are building democratic socialism and a true Marxist society.

I talked to Milovan Djilas, the tall, outspoken vice-president of the Executive Committee and the leading theoretician of the regime, who assured me that, in another generation, the whole world would be Socialist. I talked to the big, jovial, tousled chairman of the Economic Council, Svetozar Vukmanovic. They both condemned regimentation and force, the "gray life" in Russia, and joked about their former comrades: "Stalin liquidated kulaks, also production." Like all Yugoslav leaders, they were expressively grateful for our aid.

Speaking of the new industrial reforms, Vukmanovic said, "There were no incentives to efficiency and economy in the old system. Now the workers fix their wages, and their profits depend on their production, sales, thrift and efficiency. So you see, Mr. Stevenson, we have a free capitalist competition, minus the capitalism."

I talked with Tito's close associate in war and peace, Eduard Kardelj, secretary general to the Federal Executive Committee and "number two" in the Yugoslav hierarchy. A smallish, bespectacled, good-humored man of 45, the scholarly Kardelj is wise to the ways of his former friends and mentors in the Kremlin. He was pleased that Russia had just proposed to exchange ambassadors with Yugoslavia after five years of cold contempt.

"When we rebelled against Russian domination," he said, "many thought we were right, but few thought we could win. But we have. And while we welcome the Soviet proposal, we have no illusions."

There are people at home who suspect that Yugoslavia has either secretly conspired with Russia all along or will inevitably return to the Moscow fold. Nothing I heard in Yugoslavia supports this view. Kardelj, for example, believes that Russia "has reversed Stalinism," both to strengthen the regime within the Soviet empire and to divide and soothe the West. But while he recommends negotiation, to contradict Soviet propaganda that the West is plotting war, he warns solemnly against any retreat in our defense effort, "for the policy of strength and resistance is what has unmasked the Russians' weakness and made necessary their present change of tactics."

I went to Tito's heavily guarded summer residence at Brioni. I was driven to Tito's villa in an open carriage through a beautiful park strewn with Roman ruins and the shuttered homes of the island's former Italian occupants. I detected none of the austere simplicity our more radical brethren attribute to classless communism.

I found Tito trim, tanned and immaculately dressed, and much younger-looking than his 61 years. His manner is stern, his speech crisp and concise, his gestures brusque and forceful. But there is an easy mirth behind his cold, pale blue eyes. He struck me as a confident, strong-willed man with a [sic] few self-doubts — one who knows his power and enjoys it. We talked first of Yugoslavia's evolving economic system. When he told me that the new policy of decentralizing industrial management recognized the incentives of better wages and living standards, I replied that he sounded like an American capitalist. When I agreed that the state had a responsibility for the well being of the people, he said I talked like a Yugoslav Socialist!

What about communism? "Communism," he said, "when all people will be well off, is for much later — a distant goal." What about Russia? He replied with characteristic assurance that the Soviet system was not Communist at all but "autocratic state capitalism."

Tito is personally acquainted with all the men who now rule Russia and said they are flexible realists who have concluded that "Stalin's strong-arm methods have failed at home and abroad." So long as Stalin was alive, said Tito, they could not change the policy, for Stalin was "an autocrat" who would brook no opposition.

"A kind of Peter the Great," I suggested. Said Tito, "Not Peter the Great — Ivan the Terrible!"

With Stalin out of the way, Tito thinks that the Kremlin's new leaders are adjusting their policy to cope with rapidly growing unrest within the Soviet empire and to reduce tensions abroad. So he believes there is a good prospect for a period of peace in Europe while Russia attempts to stall our growing strength, to block the integration of Germany with the West and to woo the masses of Asia.

But he made it clear that a change of *tactics* must not be mistaken for a change of *objectives*. Reassuring peace gestures, he said, have not changed Russia's basic expansionist designs. The signal of a real change of heart will come from within, "when force and violence are replaced by consent and co-operation, when the brutal autocracy of the police state is replaced by democratic socialism." Until that happens, Tito says, we must assume that the "state capitalist despotism" will press ahead to bend more and more people to its will. And even then, "the Russians can never be trusted 100 per cent."

Nevertheless, Tito favors four-power talks with Russia, if only to manifest our desire for peace and "to feel their pulse," but thinks any relaxation of our defense effort would be "foolish."

I asked him what he thought of the incessant Soviet charges that America is imperialistic. "No country can be imperialistic," he replied, "when it gives more than it takes." He added that he believed Yugoslavia would no longer need U.S. aid after two years.

When I asked Tito if he was planning to visit the United States, he replied with a smile, "I would like to very much, but I don't suppose McCarthy would let me in!"

Before I left Yugoslavia, a newspaperman asked me how I would describe the regime. Was it Communist, Socialist, collectivist, syndicalist or a combination of several with an admixture of capitalism? I don't know what it is. Certainly, it is a long way from our ideas of democracy and free enterprise, but it is a lot better than the rigid Soviet-style regimentation of a few years ago. And it seemed to me that Yugoslavia's leaders are coming around to the view that more consent and less force are better and safer. Maybe the Russians are too.

Nor are the changes in Yugoslavia confined to politics and economics. On my last day there, in ancient Dubrovnik, I heard even officials using the traditional response to a greeting: "Thanks to God, I am well." Until not very long ago, that phrase was forbidden in a rigidly Communist Yugoslavia.

Nineteen

Greece

JUNE 27–JUNE 30, 1953

W hen Stevenson stepped off the airplane in Athens, the sizable crowd waiting for him broke into applause. Attwood wrote in his diary, "The Yugoslav Ambassador was on hand, too, looking worried and obviously wondering what Stevenson was going to say after his visit there. When asked about conditions in Yugoslavia, however, Stevenson replied 'excellent' and the Ambassador looked much relieved."

Stevenson and his party went to the home of Ambassador John Peurifoy for dinner. The ambassador mentioned to Stevenson that he was soon to be transferred to Guatemala. (His Democratic party preference was well known and as Assistant Secretary of State in charge of security, March 17, 1947, to April 21, 1949, he had clashed with right-wing Republicans who had charged there were Communists in the Department.) Peurifoy asked Stevenson, however, not to mention his transfer. "It's the sort of news that would further depress the already shaky morale of career officers locally," Attwood noted in his diary.

At dinner the hope was expressed that Prime Minister Papagos would institute social and economic reforms. His government had been paring the overstaffed bureaucracy and the currency had been devalued to stimulate exports. There was also a discussion of Queen Frederika's too-active interest in politics and her intrigues to rule as well as reign.

After dinner, when Stevenson saw the Acropolis shimmering in the bright moonlight, he insisted on climbing up to it and wandering among the ruins. The next morning after breakfast, he returned to visit the Acropolis by daylight. Then he and his son Borden had lunch with the king and queen. *Later that day the ambassador gave a huge reception, followed by a small dinner party where Stevenson was able to discuss the situation in the country with the Greeks who were present.*

The next morning Stevenson and Blair called on some of the leaders of the opposition, including two former prime ministers, Sophocles Venizelos and General Nicholas Plastiras. Stevenson was struck by the fact, he later told Attwood, that these opposition leaders had no alternative programs to those of Prime Minister Papagos. Plastiras remarked to Stevenson that he "wished Papagos well" but was confident that he would fail unless more attention was paid to improving the welfare of the masses. Following these conversations, Stevenson attended a briefing at the embassy and then took a trip to the countryside with the ambassador.[1]

When Stevenson returned, he visited with Mrs. Franklin D. Roosevelt, who had arrived that day in Athens en route to Yugoslavia to interview President Tito. Stevenson and Mrs. Roosevelt met privately and talked principally about the political situation at home.

Before dinner that evening Stevenson and Attwood interviewed Mario Modiano, correspondent of The Times *of London. Modiano suggested a few questions that Stevenson might ask the prime minister the following day, including what the government was doing to compensate the workers for the rise in prices that had accompanied the devaluation of the currency. Modiano pointed out that there was a growing sentiment in the country that Greece was maintaining too large an army and bearing too heavy a load for defense compared to its partners in the North Atlantic Treaty Organization, and that the country would be strengthened if part of the forty per cent of the budget that went to the armed forces were spent instead on improving the living standards of the people.*

After this conversation, Stevenson dined in his room and spent the evening writing his article on the visit to Yugoslavia. He did have time, however, to attend to correspondence.

To Mr. and Mrs. Edison Dick[2]

[no date]

See — we're on our way home! Outside my window guns are firing a salute for the King on his "name day," and five thousand people are drinking coffee in Constitutional Square, each one convincing the other

[1] Since the inexorable deadline for another *Look* article was approaching, Stevenson asked Attwood to do a first draft dealing with Turkey. As a result, Attwood did not attend the above meetings.

[2] This handwritten postcard is in the possession of Mrs. Dick. The picture on the front is of a great expanse of desert, with a small camel train crossing it.

that he should be Prime Minister of Greece. Thanks for your letters and all the news from Dicks and home. Both still seem too far away, but we're making progress in spite of hazards and enchantments — and surprises. Mrs. FDR arrived this afternoon!

The Stevenson party rose early the next morning, June 30, to pack for the trip to Rome.[3] Meanwhile Stevenson had an interview with Prime Minister Papagos before hurrying to the airport to board the plane.

Stevenson wrote of his visit to Greece:

THE WEST BUILDS A BALKAN BARRIER [4]

Greek fortitude, backed by American money and advice, has made this gallant little country another one of the stronger military links in a Western defense system that stretches from the Caucasus to the Arctic. This was my most striking impression of an all-too-brief visit to the country that cradled Western civilization and has suffered so cruelly at the hands of its enemies in our own troubled time.

Like Turkey, long her traditional foe, Greece is a fighting nation and a rugged, reliable ally. Think of the record of the past 13 years: Invaded by Mussolini's legions in 1940, Greece astounded the world by routing the Italian Fascists so decisively that the Germans had to come in and take over the war. Nazi panzers finally crushed Greece in 1941. In nearly four years of brutal occupation, 700,000 Greeks, one tenth of the population, died of starvation, disease or in partisan fighting against the enemy.

After liberation, the Kremlin decided that ragged, impoverished Greece should be an easy prey. Red rebels, supplied from the north, plunged the weary nation into bloody civil war. By 1947, close to 600,000 homeless refugees were streaming down from rebel-held territory and Communist guerrillas were a few miles from Athens. Then came President Truman's announcement that the U.S. would under-

[3] As Stevenson had intended from the outset, the Western European part of his world tour was much condensed. He had never been in Asia before but had been a frequent traveler to Europe before 1939 and was more familiar with European conditions. In 1943–1944 he had been on a special mission to liberated Italy, he was on the State Department's staff at the San Francisco Conference, he headed the American delegation to the United Nations Preparatory Commission in London in 1945–1946 and attended the 1946 and 1947 sessions of the United Nations Assembly.

[4] *Look,* August 25, 1953. Other portions of this article are reprinted in Chapters Seventeen and Eighteen, above.

write the economy and security of both Greece and Turkey. With that bold and historic decision, the Eastern Mediterranean was secured and the tide began at last to turn against Moscow.

As as American, I am proud that we had the vision to act decisively in that moment of crisis; as a Democrat, I am proud that this turning point will be remembered as the Truman Doctrine. I doubt that we have made any better investments in security or humanity.

Since the war, we have spent about $2 billion — half of it in military aid — to save Greece from economic collapse and Communist engulfment. I found more gratitude there for what we had done than in any country I have visited on this long journey. Three Prime Ministers, past and present, echoed the same sentiment: "We owe our freedom and rehabilitation to the United States; because our danger was greatest, our gratitude is greatest."

Greeks have seen the bitter reality of invasion, Communist and Nazi, and they will not soon forget what they saw: ruined villages, kidnapped children, senseless massacres and worse. When Soviet imperialism struck in Korea, the Greeks responded, like Turkey, by sending troops from this cold-war front to the hotter one in Asia.

My short stay in Greece was so busy that I found time off only to climb up the imperishable Acropolis, but not to visit the Delphic Oracle (where I had hoped to ask some unimportant questions about politics and some important ones about the World Series).

I talked with the erect, strong-willed, unsmiling old soldier Marshal Papagos, the Prime Minister and leader of the so-called Greek Rally, as well as with his associates and members of the opposition parties. I heard the American side of the story from our effective Ambassador, John Peurifoy, and his staff. I spoke with countless Greeks and Americans in and out of public life. Finally, I lunched with King Paul and his energetic, attractive young Queen at their summer palace at Tatoi. They are visiting the U.S. in October. Queen Frederika asked me for a date for a chocolate soda at an American drug store.

Due to the election laws, the new government has 80 per cent of the seats in Parliament, although it polled but 49 per cent of the vote last fall. Hence, it is stable and strong, which is what Greece badly needed. The country was running France a close second for instability. The government, in spite of unpopular measures, is respected largely because of the personal prestige of Marshal Papagos, the nation's outstanding military hero and a newcomer to politics.

He impressed me as a man of authority, integrity and courage — qualities which have often been lacking in the nation's intrigue-ridden political life.

"We must save drastically and develop our resources," I was told by both the Prime Minister and his dynamic, ambitious chief assistant, Spyros Markezinis. They know full well they cannot count on American aid to support their desperately poor country much longer. Marshal Papagos added, "I am not interested in forming a political party. I do what I think necessary, however hard and unpopular. I don't care about being pleasant; I want to be useful."

His government seems to be moving in both directions — unpleasant and useful. It has devalued the inflated currency to move the tobacco and raisin crops, has sharply cut the use of government automobiles and telephones and is whittling down the overstaffed bureaucracy and tightening up tax collections. Even the salaries of deputies have been cut. A balanced budget is in sight, and, for a few months, Greece has had — miracle of miracles — a favorable balance of trade.

But food prices are going up, unemployment is serious and the challenge of better living standards in a country with one acre per capita of arable land and limited resources to develop (and limited means to develop them) is formidable indeed.

Marshal Papagos also has to cope with the delicate problem of a royal family that takes a too active interest in politics. One hears that the lively Queen Frederika, already the nation's first social worker as well as first lady, would like to rule as well as reign.

Opposition leaders like Sophocles Venizelos of the Liberal party and beloved old Gen. Nicholas Plastiras of the left-of-center Progressives feel that the government savors too much of the right and the "economic oligarchy" and that more attention must be paid to the welfare of the masses and salaried people if the Kremlin's new "popular front" appeal is not to make inroads on long-suffering Greece.

But there is no conflict on foreign policy: as in Turkey, the various political leaders reflect the will of the Greek people to participate fully and loyally in the Western defense system. A young American who was traveling in the remote mountain villages of the north soon after Greece was admitted to NATO told me that everywhere he found the peasants touchingly proud and enthusiastic about belonging to this community of free nations. Again, I was reminded of what I saw and heard in Turkey.

But Greece faces two as yet unanswered questions. First, can the nation's postwar recovery continue if U.S. aid stops altogether as expected in 1955? Already, we are disengaging. Military assistance is still substantial, but our economic contribution has shrunk from $280,000,000 in 1951–52 to $20,000,000 in 1953–54. Will Greece's meager economy make the grade? She faces a much harder struggle than Turkey, for

Greece is like a convalescent patient who has had a long illness and a narrow escape. I doubt that we can tell ahead of time whether she can do without medical care and not suffer a crippling relapse.

The second riddle confronting Greece is whether to reduce a proportionately large army (ten divisions) that eats up 40 per cent of her budget, and to devote some of this revenue to strengthening the economy. Stern Marshal Papagos says, "The Army is a tremendous burden, but national security has first priority. We won't reduce by one man as long as present conditions prevail." There is fast-growing sentiment in the country, however, that Greece is doing more than her share in the NATO team, more than other nations with much larger populations and far higher standards of living.

Aside from the economy's desperate need for more internal revenue, some revision may be necessary, if only because it will cost the U.S. plenty to sustain the austere Greek Army at its present level. And revision may also be possible because the new Balkan pact should enable Greece to withdraw forces from the long Yugoslav border and to concentrate them on the shorter fronts facing Soviet Bulgaria and Albania. Similarly, Turkey and Yugoslavia are expected soon to redeploy troops facing Greece and to reinforce their frontiers along the Iron Curtain. Marshal Papagos, by the way, made it clear to me that he would welcome Yugoslavia into NATO because "all countries who want to be free should form a great coalition," and he greatly deplores the ill will between Yugoslavia and Italy. Italy, too, is essential to Balkan strength.

But the problems that perplex Greece are minor in comparison with the chaos and misery of only six years ago. A civil war was raging; refugees cluttered the country; the economy was all but wrecked. From the point of view of the free world, this was one of the softest spots in Europe: democracy was fighting a desperate holding action on the southern tip of the Balkans.

Today, the free Balkans are solid and strong. Greece and Turkey are ready to give a good account of themselves against any aggression. Thanks to Marshal Tito of Yugoslavia, the West has driven a bridgehead into Eastern Europe. Where, a few years ago, it looked as though all were lost in the Eastern Mediterranean, the Soviet leaders now face a mighty threat to the left flank of armies headed for the Atlantic.

I said I was invigorated by what I found in Turkey. I can say the same for Greece.

I left for Yugoslavia eager to meet the man responsible for one of the Kremlin's most telling defeats in this long cold war.[5]

[5] This sentence is inaccurate, since Stevenson visited Yugoslavia before Greece.

Twenty

Italy, Austria, West Germany, and France

JUNE 30–JULY 22, 1953

O n the plane from Athens to Rome, the British ambassador to
Greece sat down beside Stevenson and said that "on instructions
from my government" he had just read his book Major Campaign
Speeches, 1952. Stevenson laughingly remarked that if the ambassador
had been working for the U.S. government these days, his instructions
might well have been not to read it.

When the plane landed in Rome, Stevenson's seventeen-year-old son
John Fell was waiting to join him for the remainder of the trip. Attwood
wrote in his diary, "Stevenson insisted on driving into Rome via the old
Appian Way so as not to miss any ruins. In fact we made three other
stops in the city before reaching the hotel just to look at a few of the
more spectacular Roman relics."

On arrival at the Hassler Hotel, Attwood wrote, "Stevenson seemed
tired and harassed, especially since there was a stack of about 90 letters
waiting for him and for the first time admitted that the trip was exhausting and not as much fun as he had expected." An American correspondent, Frank Gervasi, commented: "Stevenson was over-traveled
and over-worked." [1]

Soon after arrival Stevenson went to the embassy to talk to the
political and economic attachés. (Ambassador Clare Boothe Luce was
in Florence. Stevenson was told that she was "piqued" at his refusing
her dinner party invitation as well as her Fourth of July reception.)

[1] D. J. Jerkovic, "Stevenson — Rome and Belgrade," New Republic, July 27,
1953, p. 14.

[353]

The political attaché said that the outstanding fact of the year in Italy was that Palmiro Togliatti's Communist party and Pietro Nenni's left-wing Socialist party had increased their vote four per cent over the 1948 election. As a result of the Monarchist party gaining votes as well, Prime Minister Alcide de Gasperi's Christian Democratic party was without a majority. At the present moment, it was pointed out, de Gasperi was trying to form a coalition government with Giuseppe Saragat's Social Democrats, the Liberal and Republican parties. Saragat, however, was trying to persuade de Gasperi to include Nenni's left-wing Socialists as a means of splitting this party away from their Communist allies. (De Gasperi later rejected this suggestion.)

Among the factors that had weakened de Gasperi in the election, Stevenson was told, was that he had been in power for seven years and the "time for a change" factor had been against him. Moreover, Nenni's decision to run a ticket independent of the Communist party had attracted a number of anticlerical but non-Communist protest votes. Furthermore, the economic progress of recent years had been insufficient to convince the majority of voters that they had much more to gain from de Gasperi since unemployment was increasing and the average per capita annual income was still only $300.

Stevenson then observed that he had last seen Italy in December, 1943, and January, 1944, when he had headed a U.S. mission to survey the problems of reconstructing the war-devastated Italian economy.[2] From Palermo to Naples and nearly up to Cassino he had seen mangled cities and towns, broken bridges, destroyed roads, and a harassed, hopeless, hungry people.

The economic attaché then described how the economic goals under the Marshall Plan had largely been achieved. But, it was pointed out to Stevenson, there nevertheless were still two million unemployed out of a labor force of twenty million and Italy still had an unfavorable balance of trade with the United States. Without extraordinary U.S. aid, Italy's balance of payments would be short some 325 million dollars every year. U.S. tariffs, particularly on agricultural goods, Stevenson was told, hurt the Italian economy.

After the briefing, Stevenson dined and spent the evening with his two sons. The next morning he spent over an hour talking alone to Prime Minister de Gasperi at his summer villa. Back in Rome, Attwood arranged for Stevenson to have lunch with Stanley Swinton of the Associated Press, Edmund Stevens of the Christian Science Monitor,

[2] See *The Papers of Adlai E. Stevenson,* Vol. II, pp. 163–205, for Stevenson's diary of the mission and the gist of the report. The report in full is *Report of FEA Survey Mission to Italy,* Adlai E. Stevenson to Leo Crowley, Administrator, FEA and Laughlin Currie, Deputy Administrator, FEA, February 5, 1944 (mimeographed).

Claire Sterling of the Reporter, *and Frank Gervasi, formerly of* Collier's *magazine. These knowledgeable correspondents told Stevenson that the recent election was a healthy reaction against "a well-meaning but do-nothing government" which had coasted on American aid and had failed to "implement a program of social and agricultural reform." They also emphasized that anticlericalism was another important factor in the elections. They stated that the Vatican was moving to the right and that the United States by supporting the Christian Democrats so strongly had become "irretrievably identified with the Catholic Church." They felt that this American "all-out support" of the Christian Democrats had prevented the emergence of a strong anti-Communist left that might have severely weakened the Communist party and Nenni's Socialists.*

The reporters described to Stevenson how American prestige was now at an "all-time low" in Italy as the result of the feeling that positive leadership was lacking in Washington and that McCarthyism was "riding high." Gervasi remarked that the pro-American de Gasperi party was on the defensive in the election because "America doesn't stand for anything any more." He added, "In 1945 they expected Garibaldi from us. They would have settled for Jefferson. But all they are getting now is Hoover."

Throughout the lunch Stevenson mainly listened until the reporters queried him about McCarthyism. He attempted to explain it in terms of a basic American "immaturity." He remarked: "The combination of prophet, pundit, and politician is almost irresistible to people who view the world in simple clear-cut terms and who are bewildered by the magnitude of the problems and events swirling around them."

During the luncheon several Italian newsreel photographers kept asking permission to take pictures of Stevenson at the table. Their request was refused. As Stevenson was leaving the dining room, an Italian who identified himself as an artist and a great admirer said he wished to present him with one of his paintings. Not wishing to hurt the man's feelings, Stevenson followed him to another room, where the Italian presented him with a framed oil painting while the newsreel men suddenly materialized and took their pictures. (Stevenson later found out that the pseudo artist was a member of the camera crew who had bought the painting from the restaurant.)

Later that afternoon Stevenson made a courtesy call on Ambassador Luce and then spent the remainder of the day working on his article about Yugoslavia.

The next morning he spent an hour with Pope Pius XII, and then had a conference with Frank Gervasi. Gervasi wrote later:

Inevitably one mentally draws parallels between the late Wendell Willkie's wartime global whirl and the Governor's tour, and sees the contrasts in the two men. The Stevenson I knew in Rome and Positano had none of the hearty showmanship and all-around out-wardness of the Willkie I met in the Middle East in the late summer of 1942. Willkie could stir you, he could make a stone figure move. Stevenson, however, can persuade. This is a time for persuaders.[3]

Stevenson had a lengthy lunch with the enlightened industrialist Adriano Olivetti, during which he questioned Olivetti about the economic situation in Italy. Afterwards he had a meeting with the Christian Democratic finance minister.[4] Later that day Giuseppe Saragat, the leader of the Democratic Socialists, called on Stevenson, and Attwood served as interpreter.

Saragat told Stevenson that the central problem in Italy was the danger of Communism, which drew its strength from continuing social and economic injustice. The only way to weaken Communism, he stated, was to have a government with a left-wing orientation. This was why he was trying to persuade de Gasperi to include the Nenni Socialists in his new government; such a step, he contended, would win them away from Communist party control.[5] During the campaign Nenni had stated that he was willing to work loyally in a democratic coalition. Therefore, Saragat said to Stevenson, "The moment is propitious to call on him to make good his promises or to unmask them as insincere."

The alternative to this attempt, Saragat continued, was a continuation of the ineffectual coalition of parties of the center to which he belonged. He warned that another four years of the "same status quo policy" and the extremists of the right or left would take over. The Christian Democrats, he stated, were paralyzed by a faction within the party dominated by Italy's economic oligarchy opposed to any reforms. "Italy's tragedy," Saragat said, "is that the country has no democratic tradition and its ruling classes have no social conscience." The prime minister himself, Saragat remarked, had "risen above the prejudices of his class but on the question of making approaches to Nenni he is hamstrung by direct orders from the United States and the Vatican not to lean to the left." No democracy in Western Europe could long survive, he observed, "without a strong admixture of socialism."

[3] "Stevenson — Rome and Belgrade," p. 15.

[4] Attwood did not attend these two meetings since he was writing the first draft of the article on the visit to Greece.

[5] The Communist party and the Nenni Socialists later fell out, and the Nenni Socialists were included in the government coalition in 1963.

When Stevenson asked Saragat about anti-American feeling in Italy, he replied that it was growing partly because Italians as poor people felt "a vague hostility, or at least a lack of affinity, towards rich America." Furthermore, the average Italian had little opportunity to learn about the real America. "If a Hollywood actor arrives in Rome he gets banner headlines," Saragat remarked, "but if John Dewey dies there is not a line in the press."

Another obstacle to mutual understanding, he continued, "is that American envoys to Italy mix almost exclusively with Roman aristocrats who represent absolutely nothing. The best thing for Italo-American relations at the present," he added, "would be for Washington to send intelligent, inquisitive representatives to Italy rather than political appointees no matter how winsome."

When Saragat again discussed his strategy concerning Nenni, Stevenson observed that in his own experience, "It is wiser to work for your ideals within the framework of your own party than to seek precarious alliances with people on the outside." Saragat replied that politics in America were not the same as in Italy and that an approach to Nenni was the only alternative either to the status quo or to a swing towards the extreme right.

A few days later one reporter interpreted Stevenson's concluding remarks at his press conference as directed at Saragat:

> Like everyone else, I hope that Italy will continue to be confident and responsible, because the condition of a better life is peace and security — less expenditures for guns and more for the people. Government indecision, confusion and impatience is a hazard in Italy as it is elsewhere in the democratic world.
>
> Everyone cannot win in a free political election, as I have good reason to know. But in these days of peril, I hope opposition elements do not play into the hands of those who detest the free way of life, who detest government by consent of the governed.[6]

The next morning, July 3, at 7:10, the Stevenson party caught the train to Naples. Two cars were waiting at Naples to drive them along the winding coastal road to Positano, where their hotel had a spectacular view of the Mediterranean. Stevenson had decided two days before that he could never complete his next article for Look if he stayed in Rome. Blair wrote Carol Evans on July 2: "Rome is the worst yet as far as mail, requests for appointments, etc. are concerned. In fact, it's a campaign all over again."

[6] "Stevenson — Rome and Belgrade," p. 14.

The remainder of that day and most of the next two days, Stevenson wrote his article on the visit to Yugoslavia and rewrote Attwood's draft of the article dealing with the visits to Turkey and Greece.

On July 6, Stevenson and his group drove to Naples and took the train back to Rome. All the way to Rome, Stevenson continued to rewrite his article for Look. *Later that afternoon at a press conference, he described the physical reconstruction of Italy since he had last visited the country as a "spectacular recovery of an indomitable people."* [7]

He also told the reporters: "The world shows evidence of increasing stability. Communist efforts, including armed insurrections, have failed. The free world has stood firm. We are reaping a harvest of patience, firmness and sacrifice. Yugoslavia has shaken off the Soviet shackles, and recently in Berlin and in Czechoslovakia the Iron Curtain has shown signs of strain."

In response to a question about Yugoslavia, he said that he had found Marshal Tito "very healthy and vigorous" and it was his impression that Yugoslavia "is oriented to the West and will stay that way."

When a reporter asked him for his opinion on the future of Germany, he stated that he favored the inclusion of "West Germany and ultimately a unified Germany in the Western community and defense plans because that is where Germany properly belongs."

He observed that the recent rioting in Berlin in June and unrest among the Soviet satellites were "perhaps as significant as anything that has happened since the war. My guess is that these developments are exceedingly contagious, but I would not be so bold as to prophesy what they will lead to."

Asked if he agreed with Mrs. Franklin D. Roosevelt's remark in Athens that Senator McCarthy was doing the United States "a great deal of harm abroad," he responded: "Mrs. Roosevelt must have traveled in some of the same places to which I have been. I have expressed myself before on this subject, and I may say more after I return to the United States." [8]

The following day, July 7, Stevenson and his party took an early plane to Venice to sightsee and then continued on to Vienna. On the

[7] Frank Gervasi wrote: "Here was a new note. Italians have heard more criticism than praise from American politicians, big and little, lately, certainly since November, 1952. . . . Too often and too blatantly American politicos — as distinct from honest, earnest public servants — have stressed the sacrifices of American taxpayers and their constituents' collective largesse in making possible European reconstruction, ignoring both the obvious advantage that accrued to the American economy from European economic recovery and the contribution made to recovery by the Europeans themselves." Ibid., p. 14.

[8] New York *Herald Tribune,* July 8, 1953.

morning of July 8, Stevenson called on Austrian Chancellor Julius Raab, Vice Chancellor Adolf Schärf and Foreign Minister Karl J. Gruber, and explored with them the difficulties that were preventing a final peace settlement.[9] *He then had lunch with them and a number of the other leaders of the Austrian government. Later that afternoon the embassy held a reception in his honor at the Bristol Hotel, "where he was promptly surrounded by a worshipful crowd of admirers, including what appeared to be the entire female secretarial section," Attwood wrote in his diary. "Somebody who didn't know I was with the party said he understood that Stevenson was accompanied by some ghost writer from Look, so I thanked him for the compliment but pointed out that this doesn't quite describe my duties."*

That evening Stevenson and his party attended an operetta as the guests of Ambassador Llewellyn Thompson and Mrs. Thompson. Then they dined with the Thompsons, and Stevenson and the ambassador discussed developments in the Soviet Union and the satellites since Stalin's death. Meanwhile, Mrs. Thompson described to Attwood the serious drop in morale in the Department of State since John Foster Dulles had become secretary of state.

The next morning Stevenson had a lengthy conversation with Bernard MacGuigan, press officer at the embassy. MacGuigan explained that he had submitted his resignation since there was no longer much satisfaction in government service under the Eisenhower administration. He also described the April visit to Vienna of Roy Cohn and G. David Schine, of Senator McCarthy's staff, and the "disastrous" impact this had on American prestige. He also discussed the February 19 directive from the Information Agency to overseas libraries that "no material by any Communists, fellow-travelers, et cetera, will be used under any circumstances."[10] *No one had ever explained what an "et cetera" was and there was much confusion as to what books and magazines should remain on library shelves, MacGuigan remarked.*

Stevenson lunched with several embassy officials and then devoted part of the afternoon to answering his correspondence.

[9] At the close of World War II Austria was considered a liberated, rather than a defeated, country. In April, 1945, Austria was granted her own government. The country, however, was subject to four-power occupation and her sovereignty was restricted. The Soviet Union blocked a peace treaty until May, 1955. Occupation troops were withdrawn in October, 1955. Austria had to agree to maintain a neutral position between the East and the West.

[10] That day in Washington, Dulles approved a new directive which essentially returned to the policy followed prior to February 19. For a discussion of this episode see Walter Johnson, *1600 Pennsylvania Avenue: Presidents and the People since 1929* (Boston: Little, Brown, 1960), pp. 290–291.

To Barry Bingham [11]

July 9, 1953

Dear Barry:

Thanks for your as always engaging letter. I am so glad Adlai acquitted himself well and you were good to think of writing me about it.[12]

The caravan proceeds with ever increasing fury and frenzy but the Atlantic draws nearer, thank god.

I handled the delicate matter in Rome by courtesy — I hope! — declining all invitations and paying a brief and casual call at the Embassy. She [13] seemed to me an agitated, frightened and much chastened lady.

You should not have mentioned Chatham [Massachusetts] and an empty beach. In my depleted state it gives me nightmares — of the right kind! I may conclude to stay in Europe for a week or ten days of rest after the work is over. If not I will have to do something when I get home but probably nearer Chicago. In all events I hope I can keep it as an alternative.

Love to Mary,[14]

Yours,
ADLAI

During its centennial celebration in 1952, Chesterton, Indiana, gave Dwight D. Eisenhower and Adlai E. Stevenson each $\frac{1}{26}$ *square inch of land. Jack L. Goodfriend, an insurance man in Chicago, read that the two gentlemen were in arrears in paying their taxes. He sent a check for $6.00 to Chesterton. Stevenson first heard about it in Greece.*[15]

To Jack L. Goodfriend

July 9, 1953

Dear Mr. Goodfriend:

You fed me and saved me from the mortification of tax delinquency. I should have bought you a bottle of Greek wine. With many thanks,

Sincerely,

[11] The original is in the Adlai E. Stevenson collection, Illinois State Historical Library.

[12] Adlai Stevenson III had made a visit to Louisville.

[13] Clare Boothe Luce.

[14] Mrs. Bingham.

[15] See the Chicago *Sun-Times,* August 7, 1953.

To Chester L. Stemp [16]

July 9, 1953

Dear Mr. Stemp:

I was tempted to fly home at once to examine my estate but then I had word of the taxes, which rapidly computed represented 180,000 drachmas (Greek currency).

It sounded too big so I settled for a dinner and a bottle of wine.

Now comes word that Mr. Goodfriend has befriended me and I have lot, dinner and a good friend.

Sincerely,

Later that afternoon Stevenson talked to Russell Hill, head of the Vienna news bureau of Radio Free Europe. Stevenson made a brief statement for Radio Free Europe expressing American solidarity with the oppressed peoples of Eastern Europe and praised the courage of the workers in East Berlin who had rebelled against Soviet exploitation on June 17.

After the broadcast he attended another reception at the U.S. embassy, where he talked with John MacCormac of the New York Times. *The next morning MacCormac and Stevenson continued the conversation. They discussed the news they had just heard that Lavrenti P. Beria, chief of the Soviet secret police, had been arrested and executed. MacCormac also described the potential for further economic growth in Austria and then mentioned the damage that McCarthyism was doing to American foreign relations.*

At a subsequent press conference, Stevenson made a remark that was well appreciated when he announced that he was happy he was not in politics in Russia today. He then limited himself in his replies to questions about his reactions to the removal of Beria by observing that the standard Soviet procedure in dealing with internal matters was to find a scapegoat. (The Tass and Pravda *correspondents present asked no questions.) In reply to questions about Senator McCarthy, he said he had expressed himself before on that subject, "and I may say more after I return to the United States."*

Shortly after the press conference on July 10, the Stevenson party flew to West Berlin, where Mayor Ernst Reuter and a large group of officials, along with more cameramen than he had seen since Tokyo, were waiting to welcome him. After an exchange of greetings, the Stevenson group was driven to the Hotel Kempinski, where Stevenson's

[16] A Chesterton official. See the Chicago *Daily News*, August 6, 1953.

brother-in-law, Ernest L. Ives, a retired foreign service officer, joined the group for the remainder of the trip.

The next morning Stevenson attended a briefing at the office of the United States High Commission. Then Mayor Reuter and the city council gave a luncheon in his honor, attended by leading German and Allied officials. Stevenson later told Attwood that while he and the mayor were talking alone, Reuter asked him to deliver a personal message when he saw President Eisenhower in Washington. Reuter explained that he knew Eisenhower well and respected him but could not understand what had happened to the man. He wanted Stevenson to tell Ike that "American prestige has been injured almost beyond repair in Europe during the past few months." And he hoped that Eisenhower would do something about it — and McCarthy — while there was still time. "McCarthy," Reuter added, "has done more to hurt America abroad in eight months than Soviet propaganda did in eight years."

After Mayor Reuter delivered a gracious toast to him, Stevenson arose and remarked that he wished a man like the mayor would come to the United States and educate "some of our immature politicians." He then said:

I pray for the day when Germans will rise again in freedom and unity.

From what I have seen it seems that West Berlin is winning its struggle against the devastation of war.

I salute the indomitable spirit of an indomitable people. I salute also your courageous brothers across the line in East Berlin.

There, too, the flame of resistance to tyranny burns ever bright.

Even now, we see further evidence that a great people will not forever remain the docile vassals of tyranny.

From the Rathaus the Stevenson party entered two automobiles, one with an American flag on the fender, and drove into the Soviet sector of Berlin. They drove down Unter den Linden to the bunker where Hitler had died. Stevenson clambered over the broken concrete and Attwood and Blair took pictures. When they walked back to their cars, they were surrounded by a squad of East German soldiers. The Stevenson party got into their cars but one soldier with a Russian submachine gun stuck his head in the window and said, "You move, and we shoot." (In relating the incident later, Stevenson said, "You know, curiously, I didn't move.")

Cecil B. Lyon, Berlin director for the U.S. High Commission and Major Edwin Lumpkin, U.S. Army escort officer, who had accompanied

Stevenson, demanded that the soldiers go and return with some Russians. The Germans insisted instead that the Americans accompany them to headquarters. Lyon refused. Finally, the Germans agreed to send a messenger to the Soviet embassy. For about twenty minutes Stevenson and his party strolled around while the soldiers kept them covered. Then a motorcyclist arrived with a message that they were to be released on condition that all film was surrendered.

Attwood wrote in his diary: "I was quite pleased about the detention because nothing else could have brought home so vividly to Stevenson the reality of the city's division or so effectively dramatized the existence of the Iron Curtain (which was only two hundred yards away from where we stood). Although within sight of people in the West sector we were completely at the mercy of the Communist tommy-gunners. Stevenson agreed that it had been 'an advantageous experience.'"

After Blair and Attwood surrendered their film, the party drove to the Russian War Memorial. En route, Stevenson wanted to visit several department stores, but Lyon dissuaded him. While Stevenson was walking around the memorial, Donald Doane of the Associated Press arrived to take some pictures of him. When Doane heard the story of the detention, he took off for West Berlin and his typewriter.[17]

Stevenson's party drove back to West Berlin without further incident and then toured that section of the divided city. Attwood wrote in his diary that Mrs. Attwood and he "left the party at that point, and went out to buy Stevenson a new briefcase as his is beginning to look like the soles of his shoes during the campaign."

Stevenson dined that evening with the British, French, and American commanders of the Allied forces in West Berlin. Although there was considerable speculation as to the reasons behind Beria's fall from grace in the Soviet Union, Attwood noted that "no one had anything fresh to say."

The following morning Stevenson went to visit some refugees from the East German uprising of June 17, and listened to their experiences. On his return he held a crowded press conference. When he was asked to comment on President Eisenhower's policy of going slow on a four-power conference with the Russians, he said:

Delay might clarify the situation. I've always believed it is desirable to keep the doors open to negotiations and consultation. These are doors to peace. When they are shut, the alternative is more serious.

---

[17] The Chicago *Daily News,* July 11, 1953, carried his report on its front page.

But I wouldn't attempt to say this is the moment for a conference. There might be a reaction — if it didn't turn out successfully — that would be unfortunate.

The next move is Russia's anyhow. We've had no reply to the western nations' note to Moscow last September on free elections as the basis for Germany's reunification. I hope Germany will be reunited and that its orientation will be toward the west, where its friends are.

He said to a question about the fall of Beria, "I don't think the elimination of Beria is necessarily a case that calls for rejoicing in the world. Obviously something is very wrong when two members of the triumvirate in Moscow eliminate the third."

Stevenson's "irrepressible smile broke out," a reporter for the Associated Press wrote, when he was asked if Beria had been responsible for the Soviet Union's recent "soft policy." "I don't know," he replied. "He never took me into his confidence." [18] *He added, "I'm very happy that if I'm to be in politics, it's in the United States and not the Soviet Union."*

Asked for his comments on his detention the day before, he replied:

It was a rather important experience for two reasons. . . . One of the police informed me that taking photographs was not permitted in the United States. Having lived there 53 years without knowing this I was grateful for the information.

The second reason the experience was important to me was that it gave meaning to the term, Iron Curtain. A few hundred yards away, there was West Berlin — no Iron Curtain, no restrictions, no threatening with tommy guns.

Although he declined to discuss Senator McCarthy until he returned home, Stevenson said, "I'm distressed by the injury to American respect and prestige that I've observed all the way from Tokyo to Berlin as a result of recent developments."

Stevenson grimaced when a reporter asked if he thought the last presidential election would have turned out differently if it had been held in 1953. "You couldn't mention anything to me that is more distasteful than an election," he said. "But I'm sure we'd have done awfully well — outside the United States." [19]

[18] Chicago *Sun-Times*, July 13, 1953.
[19] While Stevenson was in Germany, Arthur Krock wrote: "As Adlai E. Stevenson draws near home to complete his world-girdling journey his host of supporters for the Democratic renomination in 1956 can point to an impressive record thus far of

Following the press conference, he had lunch with Cecil B. Lyon and other members of the American staff in Berlin. Later that day he interviewed Walter Sullivan of the New York Times; *Joseph Wechsberg, who was writing an article for the* New Yorker *on the June 17 uprising; James O'Donnell of the* Saturday Evening Post; *and Gordon Ewing, deputy director of RIAS, the United States radio station in Berlin. There was general agreement that the June 17 uprising was the kind of revolution envisaged by Karl Marx. The two conditions for a revolutionary situation existed, namely, intolerably oppressed workers and weakness and confusion among the German Communist leadership. Although the revolt, Stevenson was told, started as a protest against the economic situation, it rapidly gained momentum and became political and emotional. For several hours the workers actually had control of East Germany's major cities until Russian tanks and troops came to the assistance of East German soldiers.*

At dinner several of these reporters discussed with Stevenson the dismissal of Theodore Kaghan, public affairs officer in Berlin, by the United States Information Agency after he had been attacked by Senator McCarthy. Attwood wrote in his diary:

> It seems that both Mayor Reuter of Berlin and ex-Chancellor Figl of Austria wrote letters to Washington in support of Kaghan, stating that he was an ardent anti-Communist and so on. Now many Germans are kidding us about these letters, recalling that right after the war many lesser Nazis invariably could produce character references from some Jew or Socialist they had befriended during the war in order to get a clearance from the U.S. authorities. The Germans find it amusing that they are now in the position of giving these kind of letters to Americans.

Early the next morning, July 13, the Stevenson party flew to Cologne, where embassy cars were waiting to drive them to Bonn. Stevenson and Ernest L. Ives had lunch with U.S. High Commissioner James Bryant Conant. Later that afternoon the German government gave a reception in Stevenson's honor.

thoughtful and penetrating accounts of global conditions that the best reporters could envy. They can point also to expressions of a political philosophy in the best American 'liberal' tradition that have helped to restore the admirable meaning of this abused word. Moreover, the Democratic candidate of 1952 has made none of the errors of judgment and behavior into which a man could easily fall in such difficult circumstances as, for example, the incident last week in the Soviet sector of Berlin.

"Stevenson will return to the United States with increased stature as a national figure and added equipment for the practice of international affairs — barring some implausible and grave mistake on his part in the meantime." New York *Times,* July 14, 1953.

That evening Attwood arranged for Stevenson to talk to David Nichol of the Chicago Daily News *and William Long of the Associated Press, both of whom had been in Germany for years.*

The next day Stevenson called on leaders of the Christian Democratic Union and the Social Democratic party. Following these conversations, he took a short boat trip on the Rhine and then held a crowded press conference. He told over one hundred reporters present that he was amazed at West Germany's economic recovery, which he called "little short of phenomenal." Asked about the prospects for a meeting of the Big Four, he repeated much of what he had said in Berlin and added that the Soviet Union "could demonstrate the seriousness of its intention to negotiate peaceful settlements by agreeing to the reunification of Korea, Austria and Germany."

"The reunification of Germany," he said, "would contribute greatly to stability and peace, and everything should be done to bring this about. Western European unity," he added, "is as important for the German people as for the other Western European people."

In response to a question, he denied that the sole objective of the United States in pushing a European Defense Community "was to build military strength. The United States is not engaged in a power struggle, but it is resisting aggression and Soviet imperialism."

Asked if he thought President Eisenhower "had stood up adequately to McCarthy on current issues of freedom," Stevenson said he had "no comment for the present."

Asked to comment on McCarthy's recent activities, he went a bit further than he had at Berlin when he replied: "I have been distressed by what I observed in the 4½ months of my travels in the loss of American prestige and respect abroad as a result of activities there. I will have more to say about this when I return to the United States." [20]

Before attending a reception given in his honor by embassy officials, Stevenson tried to catch up on his correspondence.

To Mrs. Edison Dick [21]

July 14, 1953

The pace never slackens. Indeed, it seems to be gathering momentum as we draw nearer to the Atlantic. Borden drove off from Rome with college friends, and I shipped John Fell to Buffie [Ives] in Switzerland, while I traveled through Austria and Germany. I will meet him again

[20] The New York *Times*, July 15, 1953, summarized the press conference.
[21] This handwritten letter is in the possession of Mrs. Dick.

in Paris for a week there, followed by a week in London with two of those damnable articles to write.

I hardly know what to do, I am so eager to get home and unpacked. . . .

I suppose you are right about staying over here for a bit. We will see. Salzburg is a possibility with the Stanley Woodwards,[22] but Libertyville looks better than anything I have seen yet. . . .

Love to you all. I envy your journey to the Kelloggs.[23] No, I take that back. I don't envy anybody a *journey!*

After a reception and dinner, Stevenson and his party boarded the overnight train to Paris.

When the train arrived in Paris, Stevenson obligingly posed with the engineer for photographers.

"Tired as he obviously was by his travels, Stevenson's good humor and wit never deserted him. This aspect of his character was much commented on in the French press," Blair Clark wrote. "He even got away with the crack [at the railroad station] that he had dared not come back to France since 1945 because he was afraid he might be asked to form a government — this when French morale was just recovering from a record-breaking governmental crisis." [24]

At the Hotel George V, Stevenson and Blair went through a new load of correspondence and requests for appointments. The four telephones in their suite rang incessantly, and they soon left the hotel to attend a briefing at the embassy. "Paris has been unbelievably hectic," Blair wrote to Carol Evans on July 22, 1953.

After the briefing, Stevenson visited the headquarters of SHAPE to lunch with Allied military leaders. Following lunch, he paid a courtesy call on French President Vincent Auriol. Later that day the Committee on Cultural Freedom held a reception in his honor where he talked, among others, to novelist James T. Farrell.

When Stevenson returned to the hotel, Mrs. Ernest L. Ives, his cousin Lady Mildred Bailey [25] *and his son John Fell had just arrived from*

22 Mr. Woodward, treasurer of the Democratic National Committee (1953–1955), had been U.S. ambassador to Canada, 1950–1952. Stevenson was unable to visit him in Salzburg.

23 Mr. and Mrs. John P. Kellogg, Libertyville neighbors of Stevenson, who had a summer home near Vancouver, British Columbia.

24 "Stevenson in Paris — On the Way Home," *New Republic*, August 3, 1953, p. 5.

25 Lady Mildred Bailey before her marriage was Mildred Bromwell. Her grandmother was a sister of Stevenson's paternal grandmother; thus she was his second cousin.

Switzerland. Stevenson took them to the Eiffel Tower and to a quiet family supper.

The next day was as crowded as any he had had on his trip. He had breakfast with René Mayer [26] *and later called on Premier Joseph Laniel for what he afterward felt was an unproductive talk. A luncheon arranged by Attwood, however, was highly productive. Among those present were Pierre Mendès-France, who had nearly become premier in the cabinet crisis a month earlier; Pierre Lazareff, publisher of France-Soir; Hervé Mille, director of France-Soir; J. J. Servan-Schreiber, editor of L'Express; Maurice Schuman, under secretary for foreign affairs; and General Corniglion-Molinier, minister of state.*

The conversation ranged over a variety of subjects. Although there were sharp disagreements on most points, there was general agreement that Indochina was basic to all of France's problems. Stevenson was told that France could not carry the burdens of full participation in Western European defense, continuation of the war in Vietnam, and economic improvement at home. The problem was to decide which one of the three had to be set aside.

Mendès-France stated that the burden of Indochina was the one that should be jettisoned. [27] *Stevenson disagreed and explained that Southeast Asia was one of the prime Soviet targets. The French had to remain in Indochina, he added, but to win the war they had to win over the people and make good their promises of full independence.* [28]

The question of McCarthyism arose inevitably. Stevenson in summing up the discussion observed that it was unfortunate that "we Americans seemed to be losing confidence in ourselves at the very moment when the Soviet Empire is showing signs of internal weakness and when Europe seems to be trying to go its own way independent of American leadership. For this is the moment," he concluded, "when a united free world should be ready with a dynamic policy to exploit the possibilities inherent in the fluid situation behind the Iron Curtain."

Following the lunch, Stevenson visited the offices of the special representative in Europe of the Mutual Security Agency. As he walked across the courtyard the employees leaned out the windows and applauded.

---

[26] René Mayer had served in a number of cabinets since 1944 and in 1955 became chairman of the High Authority of the European Coal and Steel Community, which had been launched in August, 1952.

[27] Mendès-France later became premier during the 1954 Geneva Conference at which France agreed to withdraw from Indochina.

[28] "If Stevenson held fast to the opinion that Indo-China must under no circumstances be lost, he was aware of the exhausting nature of the war. He was perhaps not quite as familiar with the effects of this drain on France's posture in Europe. If this was a gap in his knowledge, he had it filled by Mendès-France." Clark, "Stevenson in Paris — On the Way Home," p. 5.

With son Borden and Mrs. William Attwood
en route to the pyramids, south of Cairo.

Greeting Arab children in a village outside of Cairo.

Visiting Arab refugees, Lebanon.

On the Jordan side of the Israeli border.

A talk with Israeli prime minister David Ben-Gurion.

Inspecting a youth housing project in Israel.

Even the interpreter enjoyed what Stevenson said to President Tito.

With President Tito on his island retreat at Brioni. Others in the picture include an interpreter, Borden Stevenson, and Mr. and Mrs. William Attwood.

Surrounded by young Yugoslavs in Belgrade.

With Queen Elizabeth at Goodwood racecourse in Sussex, England.

As he approached the doorway they gave him a confetti-tossing ovation. He smiled, waved, and told them he "would spare them a speech." After this visit he returned to the hotel to meet with former Premier Antoine Pinay.

In response to a question from Stevenson, Pinay stated that "stability and confidence" were the key elements necessary to solve France's problems. He was optimistic, he said, about "the prospects of achieving them." He remarked that every cabinet crisis hastened the day when France would have a government that governed. Every premier in recent months, he added, "has managed to get more power from the Assembly than the last. Within a few more months a premier will find himself with sufficient authority to reform the constitution."

When Stevenson asked him about the extent of anti-American sentiment in France, Pinay remarked that it had grown recently. He attributed it partly to an "apparent pro-German policy" in Washington and partly to McCarthyism. There was the feeling, he continued, that the Republicans did not understand and were not sympathetic to French problems.

Pinay discussed French concern over a rearmed Germany and said that as a result the National Assembly was reluctant to ratify the treaty creating the European Defense Community. He also stated that public opinion in France was finally aware that creeping inflation was neither inevitable nor an act of God but could be controlled by their elected representatives. He prided himself, he told Stevenson, on having convinced the French people of this when he was premier. But he had not had time, he said, to restore confidence in the government to the point that the bulk of "sterile capital" was poured into productive channels.[29]

Following this conversation Mr. and Mrs. Attwood had a number of correspondents to their home for drinks and dinner with Stevenson. Among those present were Walter Kerr *and* Don Cook *of the New York* Herald Tribune, Theodore White *of the* Reporter, Robert Kleimen *of* U.S. News & World Report, William Stoneman *of the Chicago* Daily News, Michel Gordey *of* France-Soir, Preston Grover *of the Associated* Press, *and* Robert Yoakum *of the World Veterans Federation.*

Although there was disagreement among these veteran reporters

---

[29] Paul Ghali wrote from Paris to the Chicago *Daily News*, July 29, 1953: "To the average French politician, Adlai E. Stevenson is President Dwight D. Eisenhower's secret emissary rather than his defeated political opponent. . . . It is almost impossible to convince the French that Stevenson will not go straight to the White House when he lands in the States to give the President a full report and his personal suggestions. It is even more impossible to make them believe that the suggestions of his Democratic rival will not have considerable weight with the President."

about the many events in Europe, there was agreement that the problem of Germany continued to dominate everything else. The European Defense Community was not popular, they agreed, "because of the feeling that even this much German rearmament is unnecessary and partly because it is thought to be unworkable." Everyone was in agreement that the goal of a European federation was generally acceptable and even popular when not linked with German rearmament.

The reporters thought that it was quite probable that Soviet imperialism was assuming a new and less military form. Michel Gordey said that he believed it likely that the new form of Soviet imperialism would be outwardly peaceful and would aim at economic penetration and exploitation of political opportunities in the more backward areas. The question was raised, "Is the United States ready psychologically and economically to cope with a nonmilitary Soviet offensive?"

Attwood wrote in his diary:

> Throughout the discussion Stevenson acted like a moderator trying to extract the hard facts from the general free for all. Finally the assembled group raised the question of McCarthyism and Stevenson, after making it plain how he felt personally, said that his hope was that sooner or later the conservative Republicans would declare war on the guy. For he feels that McCarthyism is bigger than the partisan issue and realizes that if liberal democrats like himself launch the attack — as he probably will — it may only help solidify the Republicans who still feel they can use McCarthy for their own ends. Stevenson confessed that he wished he were somebody like Jim Duff,[30] a tough hard-bitten Republican; if he were he could go out around the country and call McCarthy "a lying son of a bitch" who is the Kremlin's best friend in America (which wouldn't be hard to prove) and a real agent provocateur. In other words, defeat McCarthy with his own weapons. It has been obvious on this trip through Europe that Europeans tend to equate McCarthyism with Fascism — and Stevenson, I think, is not sure that they may not be right, especially if the Republicans don't act soon. He admitted that he can't explain the President's inaction on this matter but said that if he is doing it for political reasons then the menace of McCarthy is very great indeed.

The discussion broke up after midnight. Stevenson probably wrote the following letter when he returned to the hotel.

---

[30] James H. Duff, Republican senator from Pennsylvania.

To Mrs. Edison Dick [31]

[no date]

I'm so weary. I've never felt this way before. . . .

I want to come home so bad and be left alone — and talk and talk and talk — quietly, on my back instead of my bottom. . . .

I want to get in grass again — oh the hot delicious swoon of the midsummer noon, when the year is brought to prime by the bees in the thyme. Do you have any thyme?

P.S. 1 A.M. — as usual.

The next morning Stevenson had a lengthy talk with Jean Monnet, chairman of the European Coal and Steel Community. He discussed the activities of the Coal and Steel Community and predicted that even the French Socialists would vote for the European Defense Community provided it was linked to a political federation.

After this talk, Stevenson and Attwood drove to the home of Mr. and Mrs. David K. E. Bruce in Versailles to spend the weekend writing the next article for Look.[32] Stevenson spent the remainder of that day and the next, Attwood wrote in his diary, "going over his and my notes and groaning about the complexity of Europe's problems." Attwood wrote on July 19, "He started writing late last night, and our assembly line went into action this morning. I knocked out a short introduction, which he accepted, and began editing the copy, mostly, at the outset for length."

At noon Mr. and Mrs. Ernest L. Ives and Senator and Mrs. J. W. Fulbright drove out from Paris for lunch. Fulbright and Stevenson had a talk alone about Washington politics. When they left, Stevenson went back to work on the article. Later he and Attwood called on General Alfred Gruenther, supreme commander of NATO forces. Gruenther mentioned that he was deeply disturbed over charges in the United States that Frenchmen did not pay their taxes. He pointed out that the French not only paid taxes but the burden was proportionately heavier than in the United States, although the burden fell on those who could least afford to pay.

He remarked that in a sense Paris was France's worst advertisement

---

[31] This handwritten letter is in the possession of Mrs. Dick.

[32] Mr. Bruce was U.S. special representative to the High Authority of the European Coal and Steel Community. The Bruces remained in Paris so that Stevenson could be secluded. Mrs. Attwood served as cook and typist. Stevenson wrote Attwood, October 6, 1953, "Tell my beloved Sim I haven't had a proper lunch since we left Versailles, or an equivalent hostess."

because of its apparent opulence, high prices, and luxury. He added that he wished visiting Americans were compelled — before they came to Paris — to spend at least a week in the provinces, where they could see how the people really lived.

He described his difficulties in trying to "hammer sense" into some congressmen who at recent hearings in Washington opposed further aid to France because "France is Communist."

On his return to the Bruces' eighteenth-century château, Stevenson talked to three young Frenchmen who represented left-of-center youth groups. They spoke of the need of fighting Communism in France by giving people faith in a better future. The youth were especially cynical, they explained, "because they no longer see France as a land of opportunity." They pointed out that the economy was not growing and society was even more stratified than before the war. They emphasized that the large Communist vote in France was mostly "a protest vote against conditions which never seem to improve and against discredited governments which accomplish little except stay in office and live off U.S. aid." All three told him that the best thing for French politicians would be to deprive them "of this unending postwar source of dollars which has enabled them to duck having to come to grips with social and economic problems."

They illustrated the difference in attitude toward Communists in their country and in the United States by pointing out that in France "nearly everyone has a friend who votes Communist — therefore it's hard to think of them as sinister, dangerous fifth columnists."

After the three had left Stevenson and Attwood had dinner and went back to work on the Look *article. All the next day they worked uninterruptedly, with Mrs. Attwood typing and retyping drafts. Over a drink before dinner they discussed President Eisenhower. Stevenson told Attwood that he did not know Eisenhower "very well." Attwood wrote in his diary, "Stevenson seems to have warm admiration for Ike's decent impulses but little respect for his intellectual capacity."*

The next day, July 21, Stevenson continued to work on the article until late afternoon, when they returned to Paris. Attwood wrote in his diary, "Back at the George V, all was confusion — the phones ringing, the Ives packing, people coming in and out." After a drink with Mr. and Mrs. Bruce, Stevenson returned to work on the article. Mrs. Attwood told her husband that writing these articles reminded her "of childbirth, only these take longer, and happen more frequently." Stevenson stayed up until three A.M. working on the article.

When Attwood arrived at the hotel the next morning to cable the finished article to New York, Stevenson was deep in conversation with

Pierre Mendès-France. Again Mendès-France insisted that the Indochina war was an almost insupportable burden for France. He disagreed with Stevenson's contention that holding Indochina was essential to the strategy of the free world.

Blair Clark wrote, "Stevenson's words on this subject, both in public and private, were not popular with those who held this view." Clark also wrote:

> Adlai Stevenson's one week visit to Paris convinced the most skeptical Frenchmen that the advance billing was justified. They expected charm, wit and intellect. They were looking for a man of spirit and sympathy. In the course of his stay here he demonstrated that he had these qualities and that he was that sort of man.
>
> If there was any exception to the general and hearty approbation for Stevenson in France, it existed precisely in those political quarters which expected the most from him, the moderate left.[33]

After his conversation with Mendès-France, Stevenson held a large press conference. He told the reporters that his world trip had been "fascinating, fatiguing and fattening."

"Stevenson characteristically issued no blasts or pronunciamentos during his journey of self-education," Blair Clark wrote. "The one newsmaking exception in Paris was on the subject of McCarthyism." When asked about its effect on America's relations abroad, Stevenson stayed silent "for a good half minute and then made a carefully phrased attack on 'this current infirmity, whose effects' he said, had contributed to the 'perceptible decline of American prestige and leadership abroad.' " [34]

In response to most of the questions, he repeated what he had just written in his article for Look.[35] *After the press conference on July 22, Stevenson, John Fell Stevenson, Mr. and Mrs. Ernest L. Ives, and William McCormick Blair, Jr., boarded a plane for London.*

Stevenson wrote about Western Europe:

ADLAI STEVENSON ANSWERS FIVE QUESTIONS ABOUT EUROPE [36]

Like a spring freshet after a long freeze, Western Europe is bubbling and struggling with new ideas and new forces in this seventh summer

[33] "Stevenson in Paris — On the Way Home," p. 5.
[34] Ibid.
[35] *U.S. News & World Report*, July 31, 1953, published the stenographic transcript of the press conference. It is not reprinted here, since the *Look* article develops his answers more thoroughly.
[36] *Look*, September 8, 1953.

of the cold war. The ice of misery, devastation and helplessness is thawing. Convulsions in the Soviet empire coincide with a rising tide of European assertiveness and an ebbing tide of American influence. Change is in the air.

In the short time I spent in Western Europe, East Germany was rocked by revolt, Lavrenti Beria was eliminated in Russia, France and Italy grappled with political crises, and our own government decided to wind up the foreign-aid program. Events, not always of our own making, were hurrying history; which way, few could predict.

From Italy, reborn since my last visit in the muddy, bloody winter of 1943, I went to Vienna, the Western world's best listening post in Central Europe; then to Berlin, springing out of its ruins, for a closer look at both sides of the Iron Curtain; to Bonn and West Germany, and finally to Paris, where political refinement and controversy are an intricate art and where I envied the thousands of Americans who were there just to see the sights and have a good time in this loveliest of cities.

Even more than Asia and the Middle East, Europe is floundering in a multitude of problems and ringing with discordant voices. And I cannot hope in this brief space to report all I heard and felt and saw. But I can at least try to round up some conclusions and answer in broad strokes some questions which recur in every conversation — questions which deeply concern this convalescing continent and which directly affect every American who pays taxes, gets drafted or prays for peace.

First, some conclusions: Paradoxically, there seems to be far more fear of communism in our powerful and prosperous United States than in Europe — where your neighbor often votes Communist and Soviet legions are just over the horizon. But don't mistake this attitude for indifference or ignorance. The stoic Europeans have no use for Soviet tyranny. They have suffered from tyranny and war more acutely than we Americans. But the European seems to me to be sick of fear. And he is painfully bewildered by the repression and confusion now creeping across the United States, which for seven years has been exhorting and helping him to stand firm and fearless. The book-burning burlesque didn't amuse him. It was too reminiscent of the Nazis and Fascists.[37]

I was also impressed by the rebirth of a self-assertive nationalism in

[37] He is referring to the European reaction to Senator McCarthy's investigation of the United States Information Agency, the trip of Roy Cohn and G. David Schine to Europe to investigate the United States Information Service's libraries, and the removal of some books and magazines from these libraries as well as the actual burning of a few of the books.

Western Europe. I saw this powerful elemental force at work in the new nations of Asia, and it is natural, I suppose, that proud and convalescent Europe should begin to assert itself. But I was surprised to discover that it is not uncommon for politicians to accuse opponents of being too subservient to the United States.

Europe's growing independence should not be confused with anti-Americanism or even neutralism. Both exist, to be sure, but you have a feeling that this pride and patriotism are not just negative factors but symptoms of more robust national health. At all events, this new nationalism can be neither ignored nor discounted. And if the roles were reversed, we Americans would be acting much the same way and denouncing every sign of "foreign" interference or influence. Indeed, we do anyway!

One of the by-products of that trend is parliamentary weakness and indecisive majorities for the governments with whom we have successfully worked in the past few years. The postwar constitutions in France and Italy, for example, seem to have been drafted in fear of a strong executive, and the resulting constitutional weakness has been aggravated by bolder opposition to government policies, as the sobering and unifying fear of communism recedes. The familiar "time for a change" spirit is growing.

Another characteristic of the new Europe which is not fully understood at home is the limited scope of private enterprise and free competition, as we understand these phrases. A scarcity economy of limited production, high prices and low wages still prevails for the most part. And the extent of state enterprise, even under the most conservative governments, surprises many Americans, especially those concerned about "creeping socialism" in the U.S.

The explanation, of course, is that government investment was the only practical means of economic recovery after the war when private capital fled from uncertainty or was insufficient.

Socialism in Europe in one form or another is here to stay. Consider Italy. The recovery has been phenomenal: Inflation has been contained, the currency is stable, production is way above prewar, and the dreadful ravages have been repaired. Yet two million Italians are chronically unemployed, the disparity between rich and poor is still enormous, and, in June, nearly 40 per cent of the electorate voted for some kind of socialism. It is freely predicted that, without a more effective program of social betterment, extremism will wreck the present shaky center government.

In Austria, where U.S. aid has helped create an industrial base that did not exist before, production is up a third over prewar, food is plentiful, and there is little extreme wealth or poverty. But half of industry is nationalized, and the violently anti-Communist Socialists polled the largest popular vote in February.

In West Berlin, rising like the phoenix from grim miles of rubble, the municipal government is headed by a Socialist — hearty and vigorous Mayor Ernst Reuter. And in West Germany, the Socialists expect to score gains in the September elections and confidently predict that they will take over the government when Germany is unified.

Whatever the political future of Germany, one thing is certain: In the historic June [17, 1953] uprising, the workers of East Germany (and I talked with many who escaped to West Berlin) were rebelling against foreign Soviet exploitation and their Communist puppet rulers. It was a nationalist German revolt and not an endorsement of the Adenauer government, European federation or U.S. policy — and if we interpret it that way, we may be sadly disillusioned.

As for France, let me just cite the report of a group of Catholic bishops who recently investigated the causes of social unrest in this rich but mismanaged country. They pointed out that workers' wages are proportionately lower than before the war (even though national income has gone up), that the workers have always had to use force to improve their lot and that most are convinced they are the victims of organized injustice. If Americans knew how French industrial and white-collar workers live we would not be surprised that so many vote Communist in protest against a continuing struggle to make ends meet.

I state all these generalizations about Western Europe, not because they are original observations of mine, but because it is well for us Americans to understand what is happening this summer when the familiar pattern of the long cold war seems to be changing. For important decisions affecting our relations with Europe and the Russians are in the offing: the fate of the European army, the unification and future orientation of Germany, European political federation, the Indochina war and the Austrian peace treaty — to mention only a few urgent problems whose solution will bear heavily on the shape of things to come.

Impatience and irritation are often spawned by ignorance or misunderstanding; and the intricacies of European politics are hard enough for an American to understand and evaluate abroad, let alone at home. Nationalism, pride, socialism, ancient grudges and a variety of philosophical attitudes will condition much of Europe's thinking about these decisions. The cold war is not over. Good relations with our European allies are still vital to our mutual security. They will be cultivated neither by dollars nor by dictation — but only by understanding and patience.

Western Europe gave me the impression that I had just seen a man rising from a sick bed, flexing his muscles and arguing with the doctor. I was glad that the patient was feeling so much better.

Now for some of the recurring questions you hear about Western Europe:

1. Who is winning the cold war?

The cold war began to turn our way a long time ago in Europe. The milestones along the road to the great explosion in East Germany were the Truman Doctrine, to rescue Greece and Turkey; the Marshall Plan, to help Europe get on its feet and stem the rising tide of communism; Tito's defection, which cracked the unity of the Soviet bloc; and the Berlin airlift, which frustrated Russia's plan to plug this hole in the Iron Curtain. The North Atlantic Treaty, the decision to resist aggression in Korea, the organization of NATO and the concept of a European army followed in quick succession in clear evidence of the free world's determination to stand together and to fight together if need be.

Meanwhile, there were shuddering sounds of atomic development in the United States, coupled with a gigantic rearmament program superimposed on a vigorous domestic economy that showed no signs of collapse (as the Soviet theorists confidently predicted). And in Europe, the striking force of internal Communist movements waned with economic recovery; while less-heralded signs of cohesion began to emerge, like the Schuman Plan to pool coal and steel resources in Western Europe.

During all this time, Stalin never relaxed the pressure on the Soviet empire. The last shred of independence was torn away from Czechoslovakia and the last drop of sweat was systematically squeezed from the satellites, for the greater glory of their masters in Moscow. (In Berlin, the difference in living conditions between the Soviet and Allied sectors is plain for all to see, as I did in spite of a trigger-nervous Red police.)

Finally came the workers' revolt in East Berlin, which quickly spread to the major centers of East Germany. The long-accumulating head of steam burst before Stalin's successors could ease the pressure. As this is written, a new government has been installed in Hungary to reverse the Stalinist program, and reports of trouble elsewhere filter into Western Europe from beyond the barbed wire that stretches from the Baltic to the Black Sea.

Yes, the cold war is going well, maybe too well for the fortitude of many who ache from strain and austerity. But not once did I talk with a responsible public figure who discounted the difficulties and dangers still in the path to peace (and I talked with scores — from His Holiness Pope Pius XII to President Vincent Auriol of France). Amid the sober rejoicing about the enemy's confusion, I detected another note of agreement that I had heard before in the capitals of Asia: apprehension that American policy is too preoccupied with military factors and too inflexible to cope with the Kremlin's changing tactics — and just at a time when Russia seeks to divide the free world and to exploit misgivings about American "militarism."

So I came away comforted by the favorable progress of the cold war in Europe; and I also came away mindful that the Western alliance is not a rubber stamp but a team and that no one member can hope to call all the signals or carry the ball on every play.

2. Has U.S. aid served the purpose for which it was intended — and can Europe now get along without it?

This question is in part answered by the economic progress since the advent of the Marshall Plan: The recovery, the reconstruction and the vitality both startle and exhilarate anyone like myself who last saw Europe during the war, broken and bleeding, hungry and shivering. What has happened in West Germany under Konrad Adenauer and in Italy under Alcide de Gasperi, for example, is spectacular. It would be foolish to say that every dollar has been wisely spent in Europe, and the progress is uneven. Problems of trade, markets, unemployment, housing, dollar shortages and low living standards still plague many countries. But there is little real misery, and you see plenty of new factories, buildings, power plants, automobiles, bridges — and crowded parks and cafes.

But if U.S. aid has largely accomplished its purpose, there are difficulties ahead. The "dollar gap" has not been eliminated. Markets must be found for the great workshop of Europe. I heard more concern about this than about further aid. Pressure will increase for more East-West trade, especially if we raise our own tariffs. Western Europe must sell its goods somewhere, and its economists and businessmen are sometimes a little baffled when we preach freer trade to them from behind our own tariff barriers.

With the exception of France, Western Europe has about reached the point where it can get along without further U.S. economic aid. The dollar crutch is already being removed very rapidly. And it *should* be removed whenever aid only postpones the day of necessary reckoning. In France, the end of all U.S. aid may be premature, but it might even compel reforms that no government has so far been able to make and survive: The currency is unstable, restrictive practices throttle competition, the tax burden falls unfairly on the poorer classes, and the constitution must be amended to stabilize governments and give them a chance to rule effectively.

But economic aid must be distinguished from military aid. While the former has just about served its purpose and the defensive strength of Europe has been vastly increased, further military assistance will be needed for some time if we expect NATO to live up to expectations. For example, if we cut military aid to Indochina, France will have to either reduce her military budget for Europe or get out of Indochina. And if the German army ever comes into being, we can expect a demand for weapons from the Germans.

In conclusion, I would say that American aid has accomplished its purpose and that most of Western Europe, at least, is about ready to stand on its own feet; but military aid is a different matter.

3. Have Soviet intentions changed since Stalin's death?

Well, all I can say is that there is plenty of guessing in Europe — and it is all *guessing*, just as it is at home.

Certainly, there have been few incidents in Europe, since the storming of the Bastille, like the East Berlin uprising. This was the kind of revolution envisaged by Karl Marx himself, when embattled and embittered workers rise to strike down their oppressors. But it happened in a Communist workers' paradise!

The many symptoms of unrest, plus the fall of Beria, leave little doubt that there is plenty of trouble in the Soviet empire; and, in the opinion of the people I talked to, the screws will be loosened a bit inside the empire to ease the pressure that exploded in East Berlin.

I met no one who saw for certain the possibility of secure coexistence with Russia and Red China. And there was general agreement that: 1. Soviet attack on Western Europe is unlikely at present because the Russians know that aggression now means World War III. 2. The Soviets will make a great effort to divide the free world and shatter the Atlantic alliance. 3. They want to prevent the creation of a strong and prosperous Western Europe and will do almost anything short of war to block Germany's integration with the West.

In Berlin, I was also assured by the Germans that, after the June rebellion, East Germany would be a constant headache for the Russians and that the German Communists had lost what little prestige they had.

A former French Premier summarized his views with a fable of La Fontaine's about Boreas, the God of the North Wind, and Phoebus, the

Sun God. "Phoebus Malenkov," he said, "will melt with warmth the European army which Boreas Stalin's chilling wind made necessary."

4. What is the matter with France?

This is a question which many Americans ask and which some answer with thoughtless, insensitive remarks like: "France is decadent," "Frenchmen won't work," and "Confidentially, the French are Communists at heart."

It would take more space and information than I have to analyze properly America's oldest ally, but I do know that none of these mischievous generalities will help us hammer out an intelligent policy in Europe.

It is true that nearly five million Frenchmen still vote Communist on election day. But even the party claims only 800,000 members, its official press is shriveling up, and its leaders are lucky if they can muster 25,000 of the faithful at a mass meeting in Paris. Their big vote is less pro-Communist than anti-government. Voting Communist was the only way of registering a protest when all other parties were identified with the government — and masses of Frenchmen have plenty to complain about. Besides, protesting is a favorite pastime in France, where individual freedom is as cherished as good cooking.

This is not to say that real Communist influence is negligible, especially in the labor movement; but the danger of France's "going Communist" is long since past.

There are other current myths about France, including the one that the French don't pay taxes. Actually, the tax burden in France is about 34 per cent of the gross national product and much greater than in the United States. But the collection system is inefficient, cheating is commonplace, and the heaviest load falls on those who can least afford it.

Twice in a generation, France has been a battlefield. In the last war, the destruction of physical and human resources by the Nazis during four years of occupation have left scars that are not easily erased. And somewhere deep down, I suspect, is the wounded pride of a people who for centuries were a mighty influence in the world and who now know that day has passed.

But the core of the French problem is that the nation can't support an exhausting war in Indochina and a large defense establishment in Europe and make the needed economic recovery effort at home all at the same time — even with U.S. aid.

The result is a mounting demand to pull out of Indochina, where many Frenchmen still see the fighting as a colonial war for vested interests and not as a struggle against Communist imperialism in a vital area of the world.[38] Mistakes have been made in Indochina (and I wrote critically of them myself not long ago),[39] but they are being corrected. The impatience and weariness with this long, costly, faraway war were my most disturbing observations in Paris. For Indochina must be held.

There are other disturbing things about France: the chronic political infirmity which must be cured; the cynicism of young people who see no future in a static social structure and unexpanding economy; and, finally, the conflict of fear and fact about Germany.

As it is, hard-pressed France has to maintain a growing army, navy and air force; Germany does not — let alone fight a major war. The average Frenchman knows full well that resurgent Germany should be contributing to the common defense — but rearmed Germany makes him uneasy; he also knows that if the Germans must be rearmed, it would be best to merge all forces in a European army — but he hates to surrender sovereignty over his own forces (and especially in an organization which might in time be dominated by a larger, stronger Germany).

Therefore, about the only thing the French agree upon is to postpone action on the European Defense Community until after talks with Russia. And if the Russians, realizing they can't sovietize the Germans, propose a unified, disarmed and neutral Germany — with free elections — a lot of influential Frenchmen will say "amen." And so would most Germans, who want unification above all. (Mayor Reuter of West Berlin told me, "Unification is worth twenty German divisions.") But it is difficult for me to believe that Germany would ever voluntarily relinquish control of her own destiny.

Whatever happens, I suspect the French will want the British and American forces to stay on the Continent (despite the fact that an American master sergeant is better paid than a French general). And so will the Germans want that.[40]

This rambling essay about the French started with the question

[38] The French agreed to withdraw from Vietnam in 1954. At the Geneva Conference in the summer of 1954, a provisional military demarcation line at the Seventeenth parallel was established. General elections were to be held in 1956. These never took place.

[39] "Ballots and Bullets," *Look*, June 2, 1953.

[40] In 1954, Secretary of State John Foster Dulles warned the French that unless they agreed to a rearmed Germany within a European Defense Community, the United States would make an "agonizing reappraisal" of the policy toward Europe. The French, however, refused to ratify the EDC treaty. Then, under the leadership of Anthony Eden, a weaker Western European Union was formed. West Germany (the Federal Republic of Germany) was granted full sovereignty, allowed to rearm, and invited to join NATO. To calm French fears of Germany, both the United States and the United Kingdom agreed to keep troops on the Continent.

"What is the matter with France?" Most of France's troubles are psychological, moral and political. Perhaps I should have answered the question in one phrase: "Not much that forceful, effective and progressive leadership can't cure." And the prolonged cabinet crisis this spring will have served a useful purpose if reform and political coherence are the consequences.

5. What are the prospects for European unity?

It is easy to see things in unhappy perspective from Paris. The sharp decline in our normal position of leadership, combined with the Russian peace offensive, has critically weakened the Atlantic alliance. Winston Churchill's eagerness for a settlement with the Russians fell on receptive ears in Europe. Meanwhile, de Gasperi's government suffered a defeat,[41] thanks in part to our blunders; Robert Schuman has disappeared from the French political scene,[42] at least temporarily; and Adenauer's position in Germany is uncertain.[43] It was these three men who together gave impetus to the cause of European unity.

As it looks now, the European Defense Community is in trouble and, with it, the high hopes of greater integration. But is that the way things really are?

Somehow, the perspective doesn't seem so gloomy where this is being written, in the verdant, vigorous French countryside.

For there is more fussing and fuming about EDC among politicians

---

[41] On July 29, only a few weeks after Stevenson's visit to Italy, Alcide de Gasperi became the first postwar Italian premier to be voted out of office. While he was closely aligned with the West on NATO, EDC and other cold war issues, a major reason for his downfall was the U.S. position on Trieste. Italy and Yugoslavia both claim this commercially important area, which is inhabited mainly by Italians. To help de Gasperi win the 1948 election at the expense of the Communists, the U.S. pledged to see Trieste returned to Italy. However, by 1953, Tito had broken from Stalin and the U.S., seeing a chance to weaken Eastern European Communism, had begun to give military aid to Yugoslavia and to soften its position on returning Trieste to Italy. In the election, it worked to his disadvantage that de Gasperi, despite his close ties with the West, could not arrange a settlement favorable to Italy of this highly emotional issue.

[42] Schuman, the foremost French advocate of European integration and principal author of the European Coal and Steel Community, had been foreign minister in the Pinay government that resigned on December 23, 1952. The cabinet put together by René Mayer following a two-week cabinet crisis contained a number of Gaullists and other nationalist-minded members, and this, together with Mayer's own shift away from European integration, resulted in Schuman's exclusion from the government.

[43] Chancellor Konrad Adenauer was strongly in favor of a united Europe, but was opposed by the German Social Democrats, who favored reunification of Germany first. Many observers feared this conflict would lose Adenauer popular support. Later in September, however, his Christian Democratic Union party was returned to office in what was regarded as a mandate for his European policies.

than among people. Most Europeans know, or will readily understand, that the ultimate integration of Europe is important, indeed imperative, to end discord among themselves and to meet the economic, political and military challenge from the East. In a world polarized between Russia, on the one hand, and the United States and the British Commonwealth, on the other, the nations of continental Europe have little importance separately; but, in combination, this mighty reservoir of people, skills, industry and culture could become one of the world's great powers.

Already, a genuinely international community is managing the coal and steel resources of Western Europe. Headed by Jean Monnet, a Frenchman, this community has a parliament, an executive and a court of appeal. So far as coal and steel are concerned, French, West Germany, Italy, Belgium, the Netherlands and Luxembourg have given up their sovereign power of decision over tariffs, quotas, subsidies and so on to a common authority. This is not merely *cooperation* between sovereign nations but a real federal institution — for the first time in the history of Europe.

The coal-steel pool was a French conception; so is the European Defense Community, for a single army under one command. EDC has the vigorous backing of the United States and has been approved in principle by most of Western Europe's leaders. But some soldiers, like Field Marshal Lord Montgomery, are skeptical; the French are uncertain, as I have pointed out; the Communists are dead against it, of course; and the powerful German Socialists oppose it (largely because Adenauer is for it).

So I repeat: EDC is in trouble. But one reason for that, I think, is that it has been presented too often as an end in itself rather than as one more step in the progressive federation of Europe — which has already moved on from the coal and steel community to consideration of a draft constitution for a political community of the six nations of Western Europe and open to all others to join.

When we recall that, even with a common language and common heritage and after a war against a common enemy, it took us Americans fifteen years to advance from the Continental Congress to the Constitution, the postwar progress in a Europe of differing languages and ancient animosities is the more remarkable. And I think we must forgive Europeans for being a little irked by American impatience and exhortations to hurry up, in view of the fact that we are so vehemently jealous of our own sovereignty and that, in seven years, we have not made much progress in integrating even our own Army, Navy and Air Force.

[383]

People in Europe want something new. The concept of a federated Europe, of forging a mighty new force for peace in a world that seems divided between two hostile giants, is a change so vast that few yet comprehend it. I trust that we will. For there is great hope for us all in a reborn Europe.

Europe has come a long way quickly. And if, just now, McCarthyism and fear have tarnished the symbolism of "the land of the free and the home of the brave" for Europeans, they still don't forget *goodness,* greatness and mercy.

De Gasperi for over seven trying years the Prime Minister of Italy, said to me as I left him: "Remember one thing above all, Mr. Stevenson. Without America, there would be nothing in Europe today."

Twenty-one

London

JULY 22 – AUGUST 5, 1953

tevenson did not visit London with the intention of writing an article about the British. Instead, he wanted to discuss his impressions of Asia, the Middle East, and Europe with British leaders. In addition, he wanted to renew friendships he had made over the years and particularly those formed when he had been the head of the American delegation to the Preparatory Commission of the United Nations in London in the fall of 1945.

The first afternoon that he was in London, he rented a pair of striped pants, a cutaway coat, and a gray topper to attend Queen Elizabeth's final Buckingham Palace garden party of the year. "I didn't think she'd know who I was," he said later. "But the first thing she asked was when I had left on my round-the-world-trip. She likes to travel, and was looking forward to her own royal tour next winter."

When he talked to the Duke of Edinburgh, he recalled:

> I told the Duke I sympathized with him about the hardships of public life because I knew something of public life and meeting so many people in my own country.
>
> "But we don't have to run for public office, Mr. Stevenson," he said.
>
> I thought that was pretty good. I told him it still must be hard on him as it was on us. I was tempted to say also that he didn't have to worry about losing his job.[1]

[1] Chicago *Sun-Times*, July 24, 1953.

Stevenson spent his first weekend in Britain as the guest of Lord Salisbury, the acting foreign secretary (Anthony Eden was in the United States). While he was at Hatfield House, the historic home of the Cecil family, the Sunday newspapers published reviews of the British edition of his Major Campaign Speeches, 1952. *Sir Harold Nicolson wrote: "Much as I like Ike, I should assuredly have voted for Stevenson, together with 27,000,000 of the very best Americans."* [2] *The British Broadcasting Corporation produced a special program of the "Speeches of Adlai Stevenson." The commentator described them as the "only really interesting and responsible political speeches the world has heard since the end of the war . . . Stevenson is as near the true center of world political power in his ideas as it is possible to be. His speeches are a great contribution to modern political thinking."* [3]

On his return to London, Geoffrey Crowther of the Economist *gave a dinner in his honor. Leo Rosten, who was present, told William Attwood the next day that apparently Stevenson had not been properly briefed on the "top-level brains that Crowther had assembled, and talked to them about Asia and the world as though they were the Lions Club of Topeka — a lot of ABC stuff." Attwood wrote, "It seems the total impression he made was disappointing."*

On July 28 Stevenson met reporters at what was described as "probably the biggest such conference we have seen in London since the war." [4]

The correspondent for Reuters described the opening of the press conference:

> Adlai Stevenson was treated today to a 10-minute harangue delivered in pure brogue on the heartburning question of Irish reunification.
>
> The ex-Presidential candidate, tanned and natty, had just finished his opening remarks at a press conference. Then a reporter jumped to his feet and began what turned out to be a speech on the reuniting of Ulster with Eire.
>
> The confident smile on Stevenson's face faded and changed from puzzlement to resignation. As the reporter went on, filling his remarks with phrases concerning "the privileges of the smaller nations" and "your party's election promises," Stevenson settled himself in a chair and with slow deliberation lit a cigaret.

[2] *Observer,* July 26, 1953.

[3] By November, 1953, the British edition of the speeches had sold 50,000 copies. "This is considered phenomenal," Ernie Hill wrote in the Chicago *Daily News,* November 5, 1953.

[4] "Last Stop London: Stevenson Heads for Home," *New Republic,* August 24, 1953, p. 5.

Finally, there was a momentary pause and Stevenson, leaping to his feet, asked, "What is the question, please?"

The reporter began all over again.

He referred to representative John Fogarty's (Dem. R.I.) resolution at the beginning of the new Congressional session for Ireland's reunification.

"Are you aware, Sir," the newsman shouted, "that the resolution has the signatures of 91 states?"

"Did you say 'States,' Sir?" Stevenson asked. "I know many things have happened since I've been away, but I hadn't realized . . ." Laughter drowned the rest.

"I have been put down by others, Sir," the reporter continued in injured tone, ". . . by Gen. Bradley and President Eisenhower."

"So have I, Sir," Stevenson retorted.

The repartee came to an end when the reporter asked Stevenson if he was prepared to support the unification of Ireland. Stevenson said, "Whatever personal views I might have, I don't feel free to present them here." [5]

After this exchange, Stevenson was asked whether he was in favor of admitting Red China to the UN. He replied: "If you mean now — most emphatically not. Until I am more certain of the future purposes of Red China I would not feel there was any occasion for suddenly smiling on Red China and embracing her to the bosom of free nations whose objective is peace, on the morrow of a war in which my country suffered 144,000 casualties in trying to protect security."

Asked to comment on Soviet policy, Stevenson observed that there was an "almost pathetic desire" to exploit opportunities of an agreement with the Soviet Union. "But the impression that something has changed basically in the nature of Russian imperialism and international Communism is both alarming and dangerous," he stated.

One reporter asked him, "Have you anything complimentary you can say about Senator McCarthy?" Stevenson replied loudly, "Nothing." Then he added, "Except that he has the great good fortune to live in a beautiful state which adjoins mine." [6]

[5] A copy of this Reuters wire dispatch is in the possession of Walter Johnson.

[6] New York *Times,* July 29, 1953. The other questions at the press conference followed the pattern of a television interview the next day. Since this was recorded verbatim, it is printed in the following pages. Stevenson's views on China and the Soviet Union "disillusioned many of his hero worshippers here," Joseph Newman wrote from London in the Chicago *Sun-Times,* July 29, 1953. Reuters from Moscow reported that *Izvestia* called Stevenson a mouthpiece for the White House. Chicago *Tribune,* August 6, 1953. The New *Statesman and Nation* (London) wrote that "he should never have become the darling of American progressives" and added that "the trouble about Mr. Stevenson is that although he would have made a better Republican President than General Eisenhower, he was

Following this press conference, he met with a group of American correspondents for an off-the-record discussion. After Stevenson talked about some of the impressions he had as a result of his trip, they discussed the British viewpoint on the recognition of Communist China. The British, they explained, believed that the United States was too inflexible about this and the admission of China to the United Nations. The basic difference was, they added, that the United States regarded recognition as approval of the regime while the British regarded it as a convenience and attached no implication of approval to it.

The following day Stevenson attended a briefing at the American embassy and then he drove to Chequers to have lunch with Prime Minister Winston Churchill. Following the lengthy luncheon, Stevenson hurried back to London to attend an English-Speaking Union reception in his honor. He told the people present that the prime minister had reminded him that his mother was an American and that one of his ancestors had been an officer in General George Washington's army. The prime minister, Stevenson said, had asked him to offer his good wishes to the English-Speaking Union and had added, "I too am an English-Speaking Union."

Stevenson remarked that he had been told that Anglo-American relations were strained. "Why do we get so excited if a Senator abuses Britain or if an English member of Parliament should criticize America? Perhaps," he added, "it is because we are so closely and intimately related that we expect special understanding." [7]

That evening he faced a television panel of British editors. The moderator of the program was William Clark of the Observer.[8]

CLARK: Good evening. This is a very special occasion for us. We're all very glad to welcome Mr. Stevenson here as, not merely another famous American political figure — he's something more than that: he is someone whom we heard or we read all last autumn and we felt that a lot of what he was saying to the American people, made a good deal of sense to the British people. He managed to put, I felt, into words and sometimes into jokes, a good deal of the common sense about politics that is the common heritage of both Britain and America. So, Governor Stevenson, now that you're here, amongst

---

selected as a Democrat." William Attwood, "Seeing the World with Stevenson: Twenty Questions and Their Answers," *Harper's*, November, 1953, p. 61.

[7] A copy of this Reuters wire dispatch is in the possession of Walter Johnson.

[8] The British Broadcasting Corporation prepared this transcript from a telediphone recording. R. T. Curran, special assistant to the director of the United States Information Agency, obtained this copy from the BBC for this volume.

the British people, I wonder if you would like to say something direct to the British people, since we've so far only heard you from a distance.

STEVENSON: Thank you Mr. Clark and I should like to very much. First, I should like to express my thanks to you sir for your kind introduction. I have said once during that campaign to which you referred that perhaps flattery — a little flattery — is all right if you don't inhale. I feel that way, and, I should like to take this occasion — a happy occasion for me indeed to be invited here to B.B.C. to express my profound — my heartfelt thanks and gratitude to countless Britons who were good enough to give me heart and encouragement in my political endeavours in the United States, and who wrote me following the election and expressed their regret. I have met many of them here — many who have been good enough to write me and ask to come to see me, I have not been able to meet. I thank them all — I thank them from the bottom of a very full heart. I sometimes think, Mr. Clark, that maybe I ran for office in the wrong country . . . LAUGHTER.

Be that as it may, I shall leave — I shall leave Britain in a few days confident that the discrimination of the electorate here is very good indeed. And I should like also to say that for the last five months, I have been travelling incessantly around the world, I have not been in my country, and therefore I shall not be when subjected to the interrogation that lies in front of me here this evening, perhaps as current with American affairs as I should be.

I think many of us in my country want something in the way of a more visual familiarity with the problems that bedevil our world at the mid point of the twentieth century and I took this opportunity — an opportunity I have not had before — to take — to take a long journey. I've travelled throughout the Far East, through the south — through east Asia, through south Asia, through the Middle East and I'm now going home by way of Europe, and it's fitting in a way, it seems to me, that I should be leaving for America from England, from Britain; which after all knows so much about the world and has had so much to do with the civilisation in which we live. Our place — America's place in the world I've never minimised. I, for one, have felt that both — that we had a great responsibility in the war and that we had also a great responsibility in the peace: responsibility albeit which was very distasteful to many Americans who have lived for a long time in — behind their vast oceans, and secluded on their rich continent. Not too conscious of the anxieties and the troubles and the torments of the world beyond. Now we're very much in it because overnight our position has changed from that — as in the first war of a debtor nation to a creditor nation. It has changed in this war from the periphery of the centre of gravity to perhaps the centre of gravity in world affairs.

This is a burden which came abruptly with little preparation for many of us. I felt therefore that it was desirable to go and see for myself, and there's nothing like seeing. I've been richly rewarded by this journey. It's been difficult to be sure, and it's been tiring; I said in Paris the other day when they asked me about my trip that it had been fascinating, fatiguing and also fattening . . . LAUGHTER . . . I'm embarrassed particularly about the fattening, because I shall get very little sympathy at home, when I go back, I suspect.

People have asked me what I am — what is a Democrat in America? It's not easy for me to describe that, and certainly not in the time that's available to me here this evening. We Democrats — at least as I see it — at least my convictions are — that we are truly liberals, that we believe in freedom of thought; in freedom of speech; freedom to trade; freedom to succeed and freedom to fail. But we also acknowledge the fact that in this modern, complex society, the man on the assembly line — or the farmer on the tractor — isn't the master of his own destiny. He neither controls the markets in which he sells his eggs, nor does he control the destiny of his firm. Therefore the State has obligations too, and it's the reconciliation of these obligations of Government, with the freedom — the total freedom of peoples — that constitutes the problem of our times, and the political dispute of our age.

CLARK: Well thank you very much. . . .

STEVENSON: I should like to say one other word and that's to express my earnest hope for the very prompt recovery of your indomitable Prime Minister, Sir Winston Churchill[9] and your Foreign Secretary, Mr. Anthony Eden,[10] who has recently returned. I count them both my friends, and I know that for the sake of Britain, and of all of us, that their early restoration to health and to the proper and full time devotion of their talents and their ability to the public service will be the service of us all.

[9] Churchill had been ordered by his physicians on June 27, 1953, to rest because of strain and fatigue caused by overwork.

[10] Eden had undergone medical treatment at the London Clinic for an intestinal ailment. He left the hospital on May 19, 1953, for a convalescence at Churchill's official country residence, Chequers.

CLARK: Well thank you very much Mr. Stevenson, I'm sorry I interrupted you . . .

STEVENSON: Well I was just trying to take time so that they wouldn't have — that much less time to question me . . . (LAUGHTER)

. . . We saw the point sir.

CLARK: I would like to introduce the people who are going to ask the questions and I hope you'll feel you're amongst friends — we're going to try and make the questions tough so that you will feel at home. Sitting on my left is Malcolm Muggeridge whom you probably knew as 'THE DAILY TELEGRAPH' correspondent in Washington, and who is now the Editor of 'PUNCH.' And beyond him is Aylmer Vallance, the deputy-Editor of 'THE NEW STATESMAN AND NATION' and to ask the first question is the Foreign Editor of 'THE FINANCIAL TIMES,' Andrew Shonfield.

SHONFIELD: Well I wondered Mr. Stevenson if we could begin on Korea, partly because you've been there, but equally important because there's a truce there and it's a truce with a time limit, and what I'm wondering, with the threat of war breaking out again, I'm wondering what you think we can do on our side to prevent the fighting from breaking out — on our side?

STEVENSON: On our side — well, I think we've got to approach the negotiations that will follow the ninety-day interval for the stay — for the return of the prisoners, with an open mind, and we have to realise that perhaps the definition of negotiation is give and take. That we mustn't approach it from the point of view that there has to be unconditional surrender, and I for one shall hope and pray that out of it may emerge something in the nature of a lasting and enduring settlement of our infinite difficulties in Asia.

SHONFIELD: What about the give in the give and take? What do you envisage us giving, assuming that we get some indication of decent behaviour — reasonable behaviour from the other side? What sort of things can we give, or do you think we can give?

STEVENSON: Well, it's very hard for me to say. I must confess to you at the outset that I have not either been able to nor have I been — followed the detailed negotiations that have led up to this truce . . . I've been travelling very rapidly in areas where I have not had access to full information. But what I mean by giving is that if we take any arbitrary inflexible position which doesn't take into account — other — the considerations of the — of our adversary at the table, perhaps we will not take full advantage of the chances that we may have. We could give, I suppose, in the last analysis — and you must understand the American position on this and I don't know that this is the time to elaborate it.

SHONFIELD: Do.

STEVENSON: . . . Problems of recognition — I mean admission to the United Nations with respect to China, and I wish all the British who hear me — who are watching this programme now — would remember this; that America has contributed not only vast treasure — billions of dollars — to the war in Korea, but that it has also suffered a hundred and forty thousand casualties, and that this has touched almost every home in our country directly — or indirectly. It is small wonder then, it seems to me, that we take a very dim view indeed of the idea that now that the fighting is over, and that the truce has come, that we should promptly embrace the enemy when we have fought so desperately for so long — and for what purpose? For any purpose of ours — for the advantage or benefit of the United States? Not at all. But to fulfill our obligations under the Charter of the United States [Nations], and for the first time in all history to establish the proposition that the system of collective security — to which we are all pledged — can work.

VALLANCE: But Governor Stevenson, I don't think any of us here underestimate the great part which America has played in the Korean war. What's worrying us a little is your statement that you are not at any — at all disposed at the moment to consider the admission of China to the United Nations, and also worried by the apparent reluctance of the Administration in Washington to consider any relaxation of the present embargo on trade with China. Do you see, you said yourself that Korea can't be settled in Korea, from which I take it you meant that the ultimate settlement must be part of a wider easing of tension all over the Far East . . .

STEVENSON: Well I would say that the masters are in Peiping or in Moscow . . .

VALLANCE: Quite . . .

STEVENSON: They're not the North Korean Army.

VALLANCE: Exactly, yes. Well now quite; if we are not going to have a conference confined merely to perpetuating the partition of Korea, as an interim settlement, mustn't we look to some wider d'entente [détente] — some wider agreement which would have as one of its main points, the inclusion of China in the United Nations?

STEVENSON: Yes, and I should very much hope that China would give evidence now of her anxiety to fulfill the obligations of a member of the United Nations, which is that it will not seek recourse to war, but will resolve its disputes by a peaceful negotiation, and I remind you sir, if I may, that China at this moment is supporting an aggressive war against the integrity of a — of a — of the State of Vietnam and also of Laos.

VALLANCE: Well would you — would you not suggest that that war too might be settled by negotiation?

STEVENSON: I would hope very much that if China felt disposed — and that would be the best evidence . . .

VALLANCE: Quite . . .

STEVENSON: . . . of her anxiety to fulfill her — the obligations of a member . . .

VALLANCE: Quite . . .

STEVENSON: . . . of the United Nations.

VALLANCE: In other words, you aren't at all rigid about the idea of a general Far Eastern settlement?

STEVENSON: Oh no . . .

VALLANCE: No?

STEVENSON: No, what I was trying to ask for was some understanding in Britain, and in all of Europe for that matter, about America's attitude with respect to Red China — following this war.

VALLANCE: I quite see, yes.

MUGGERIDGE: Mr. Stevenson, there's one remark that you were reported as having made in Paris, which interested me very much. You said that you thought that American prestige had greatly declined, and I wondered whether you felt that that applied to other areas than France or even Western Europe, and what you thought was the explanation of it.

STEVENSON: Mr. Muggeridge, it's not easy to condense it in a few words, but there's an accumulation of things, some of which were avoidable, some perhaps not avoidable, that have contributed to that. In the first place, I think that many people — due to what we call McCarthyism, the sense of repression and fear, that has slipped over the United States — are very apprehensive that the United States has lost confidence in itself, and this is one of the most calamitous things that could happen . . .

MUGGERIDGE: And not true?

STEVENSON: I don't think it's true in the least . . .

MUGGERIDGE: Nor do I.

STEVENSON: Secondly, I think we have to face the fact that the United States has contributed vast sums of money to binding up the wounds; to restoring the rest of the world to a condition of health following the war. I think this was a great thing to do. I think it was a magnanimous and generous thing to do. But inevitably it has caused a feeling that one has for his creditor. I think it's unimportant and that it can be forgotten. Then there's also the fact that contributes to this feeling that as these countries emerge from the conditions that they found themselves in following the war and they are healthier and begin to flex their biceps, if I can put it that way, they get more self-assertive and nationalism and independence — declaration of independence from Washington, if you please — is forthcoming. Now all these things contribute and — to what appears to be a decline in American prestige.

MUGGERIDGE: But you don't think it's a real decline, you think it's an appearance rather than a real decline?

STEVENSON: No, I think it's a real one, and I don't think it's a wholly bad thing, because so many of them have been dependent on us and this dependence is now coming to an end. Some of it is bad; some of it is good; on balance, I don't think it's too serious.

CLARK: But Mr. Stevenson, do you think that in fact American aid is coming to an end — should be coming to an end, or ought it to continue for some time to come? And if it doesn't, what is going to be put in its place to produce dollars in the world? (LAUGHTER)

STEVENSON: Have you any little questions you'd like to ask me? (LAUGHTER)

. . . a sixty-four billion dollar question . . .

STEVENSON: That's a sixty-four billion dollar question. Well I think that there are very few countries in the world who want aid if they can support themselves. Pride, self-respect and so on, is just as characteristic of nations as it is of individuals. And I think therefore that all of these countries are glad to dispense with aid the minute they can stand on their own feet. And that's what we want them to do. Most emphatically. It's been a terrible burden for the American taxpayer. Our burden is perhaps second only to Britain's in these past years. Now, what happens? Most of these countries are restored to a relative degree of economic health. I would hope very much that while we can discontinue and/or sharply reduce it and most of the countries want us to reduce, terminate indeed our foreign economic assistance — economic assistance from the United States — it will be impossible for some time to wholly discontinue military assistance. We must distinguish between economic assistance and military assistance. Military assistance, I daresay will go on; economic assistance I suspect, is very rapidly coming to an end. I would hope that this time, in contrast to the way we handled Lend-Lease, it won't be an arbitrary cut-off, for everybody, everywhere, at the same moment. But that it can be tapered and adjusted in the manner which is calculated to result in the least possible strain on the economies emerging from this outside aid to utter self-discipline.

CLARK: But Mr. Stevenson, there was the point that Lend-Lease, quite properly, had to be followed by something else which was aid. I agree with you entirely — I think we all do — that we want to end aid as soon as we can. The question — and it is, I know, the biggest and most difficult question is — what do you think the chances are of that being followed by some method of trading relations coming into being, which will make dollars available in the world? Because if they're not, then there will have to be an economic system that excludes America.

STEVENSON: Well you're asking me whether or not I think that the United States is going to relax its trade restrictions in order to enlarge its own markets for foreign goods?

CLARK: Yes.

STEVENSON: I am not a prophet. It would be very difficult for me to foretell what's going to happen. I can say, however, that there is a large body of opinion in my country that recognises the fact that we can't expect America — foreign countries to buy American goods unless they can also sell their goods; that they must have some means of paying, and that we too, like Britain, like Germany, like Japan, and all the other great trading nations, are going to have to find markets for our goods, because we have developed our plant for war purposes, to a point where our productivity now is almost incalculable, therefore I for one, would hope very much that we could approach the day when we could relax on bilateral negotiated bases, our trade restrictions in the United States and enlarge our market.

SHONFIELD: I wonder, Governor Stevenson, if we could come back to this general problem of East-West relations, which is what concerns us very much at the moment. I mean one of the reasons for the decline of American prestige, I think, is that people suspect that the

minimum conditions that America — the present American Government would regard as necessary from the Communists, would be
very much greater before they entered into negotiation than the
European countries would. Now, what I would like to know is, what
you would regard concretely as the minimum conditions for giving,
say, China, a seat in the United Nations?

STEVENSON: The minimum conditions — it would be impossible for me
to answer that question, and I would be a very brave itinerant politician indeed, if I presumed to lay down . . .

SHONFIELD: M-mm . . . we know you are . . .

STEVENSON: . . . what these conditions would be. But I can readily see
how any major contribution to peace in the world would be very
warmly received in the United States — as it would in Britain — and
everywhere else for that matter. And if, if China were to help with
the reunification of Korea — the creation of a viable economic state
there and a natural state; if it were to help us settle — end the war
in Indo-China — permit Vietnam to emerge as a free and independent state; if it were to do some of these things, it would contribute
measurably to our sense of security around the world. We would
have an entirely different attitude.

SHONFIELD: A small point there, Governor Stevenson. Do you see the
war in Indo-China as entirely a Chinese affair? I mean there is a
view that that war is at least — to the extent of half or more — a
local phenomenon conducted by local Communists. If you're really
demanding of China that they shall put a stop to that, you're demanding a very great deal, aren't you?

STEVENSON: Well I don't want to be misunderstood. Yes the war in
Vietnam is a — in Indo-China as we call it, is a civil war, it's a rebellion. It is, however, supported, as we well know by arms, muni-
tions, assistance from China, and that without these it would have a
hard time. It would have a hard time — the Vietminh, sustaining
their operations. Now it's only to that extent that I meant that China
was involved.

CLARK: Governor, I want to take us off from the Far East, if I may for
a moment, and jump into Europe, just very briefly, you were there
for quite a little time. Tell me, do you see any signs of relaxation
there of the cold war, and do you think that a four-Power meeting
with Russia is really likely to bring about any sort of a European
settlement?

STEVENSON: Well I can only report what's been told me, by many statesmen as I've travelled around Europe, and that is that — yes, it's quite apparent now that there is a — a softer wind is blowing from the steppes of Russia and from Moscow. And that we are now in the — either in or the presence of a — what's called a peace offensive, or it's — one's about to terminate, but certainly the gestures that have already been made; the proposal for the relax — for the relinquishment of the claims against Turkey — its Eastern Provinces; special rights in the Dardanelles; exchange of Ambassadors with Yugoslavia; et cetera, et cetera . . . All of these things give evidence of the fact that — that at least momentarily, the Russians have a different view of things in the West. And I think this has come about due to the fact that they knew quite well that the pressures, particularly in the satellite countries had built up to a very dangerous point which finally exploded in East Berlin. Also, that they had failed in the West. I believe our policy post-war has succeeded.

MUGGERIDGE: Mr. Stevenson, the only vice that I acquired, living in America as a correspondent, was an interest in American politics.

STEVENSON: Well you always bring vices to America, you British . . . (LAUGHTER)

MUGGERIDGE: That's the only one that I either brought or acquired there, and therefore I cannot resist asking you whether it is your present intention to offer yourself as a Presidential — or to accept a Presidential nomination in the next Presidential Election, which I think is in 1956?

CLARK: It's an interesting question Sir.

STEVENSON: If the last question was a sixty-four billion dollar question, this is — the mark is somewhat higher on this . . .

MUGGERIDGE: Yes, that's what I thought.

STEVENSON: And Mr. Muggeridge, I'm obliged to say to you that if I could answer your question, which I can't — I wouldn't . . . (LAUGHTER)

CLARK: Fair enough. I'd just like to ask you the other part of this question — a rather easier one if I may say so — priced down to a few billion dollars — what use has this trip been to you and what are you going to do about it when you get back home?

STEVENSON: It's a fair question. I sometimes wonder what use it has been to me, aside from the fact that I've had a most interesting experience. I think it's been this use that — as I tried to say at the outset, that many of us, particularly in my country, could well do with a broader view of the world, and a more intimate experience and familiarity, visually, if you please — and by smell as well — with those areas of the world which are not too familiar to us. I for one have profited enormously from having travelled myself and seen for myself, Asia, the Far East, and the Middle East. I count this an invaluable experience.

CLARK: What are you going to do with it?

STEVENSON: As to what I'm going to do with it. What does one do with education? What do you do with any larger understanding? Or with any greater perception; and perhaps that's a presumptuous thing for me to say, maybe I have no larger understanding, maybe I have no greater perception. I sometimes doubt if I do; I've gotten, after travelling through twenty-six countries, I sometimes wonder who it was said what and in what country . . . But anyway, on the whole I think it's been a most useful experience and I shall always be grateful that I had it.

VALLANCE: I wonder, Governor, if I might put a gloss on Malcolm Muggeridge's question, and put it this way. Supposing, as we all hope, that you are the next President of the United States . . .

STEVENSON: Thank you, sir . . .

VALLANCE: Would you . . .

STEVENSON: I don't hope it, I'm sorry . . .

VALLANCE: Ah well, some of us hope it, I'm sure all of us really do, you pretend not to . . . On that assumption, could we take it that you would try and meet the other half of the world half-way in the sense, if there is, as you say, a softer wind — a warmer wind blowing from Moscow, I hope you wouldn't take that as a sign of weakness to be exploited, in order to perpetuate the cold war and try and win a tactical advantage that way. But would see what you could do to get an agreement — to get a relaxation of this appalling tension by at least meeting halfway any friendly gesture the Russians made. Would that be your line sir?

STEVENSON: Well Mr. Vallance, I've expressed my convictions on this score many times, and that is that I believe emphatically that we must never close the door to the conference room; that we must negotiate; we must explore every possible avenue to peace, which is the heart's desire of every human being . . . I think behind, as well as in front of the Iron Curtain, and that our obligation — the United States, because of its peculiar position, is perhaps almost more conspicuous than that of other countries, in that regard. I would hope that our attitude would never become inflexible, because the policy of unconditional surrender is — falls on very unwelcome ears among many of our allies — many of our friends — who are closer to the danger and suffer more acutely from the tension.

CLARK: Muggeridge, I think.

MUGGERIDGE: Well, I — there's one question that I've been wanting to ask you all the time, and have been induced to keep to the last, and it's a purely human question. But I came — that last time I saw you — you might remember — was in your delightful house in Springfield, Illinois and it was just after the Republican Convention, and Mr. Eisenhower had just been nominated and you were going through all the period of pressure to accept the Democratic nomination. And at that time, you were very certain that you wouldn't accede to this pressure. And I, as a pure outsider, had very strongly the feeling that you would. Anyway, you did in the end.

STEVENSON: You're a better diagnostician than I am . . .

MUGGERIDGE: No, it was purely because of an outsider, sir — one could see that it was bound to happen. Now then, what I would like to know is — it did happen, and you've done your trip round the world. Do you regret it? Do you wish you hadn't?

STEVENSON: No, sir. I'm deeply grateful for the opportunity that befell me. I didn't seek it, and I didn't want it. But once it was asked — it was presented to me, I felt it was the duty — and I still do — of any American in good health to assume that momentous responsibility and we have no greater one in my country and I count myself richly rewarded, not only because of the encouragement and help of many friends, and the millions who voted for me, but because of the opportunity it gave me to see at first hand, more of my country — to enjoy an experience that comes to few, in the way of intimate contact with the might, the majesty, the simple dignity of the American people.

CLARK: Well, Governor, thank you very much indeed for that — particularly for these last remarks which touched us all, I think.[11] That's all we've got time for tonight. Thank you very much indeed, for coming here and answering our questions, and we hope we'll have an opportunity again some day, in the next four years and thereafter.

[11] William Attwood, who was in the studio, wrote: "As he wound up one eloquent, ad-lib reply with a reference to 'the might, the majesty, and the simple dignity of the American people,' the studio audience burst into applause. Later he said he felt so tired he hardly knew what he was saying. 'Was it really all right?'" "Seeing the World with Stevenson: Twenty Questions and Their Answers," p. 58.

STEVENSON: Thank you, it's been a great privilege to be with you to-night. I'm deeply grateful to all of you for your courtesies.

The following day, Stevenson and Attwood, who had just rejoined the group after a brief vacation with his family in France, left London to stay at the home of Mr. and Mrs. Herbert Agar in Sussex. Before leaving London, Stevenson had received the news of the death of Senator Robert Taft. He told reporters that all America would mourn his death: "Senator Taft enjoyed all the inducements to a safe and tranquil life. Instead, he followed in his father's footsteps and chose the toil and peril of public life to serve his country as he saw fit. I hope his example will be followed by many Americans." [12]

The Agars arranged for Stevenson to go with them to the races being held at nearby Goodwood. There, Stevenson, saying only that he had to "go somewhere," left his party in response to a summons from Queen Elizabeth, who had learned that he was present, and made his way alone to the royal box, where he had tea with the queen.

During the four days at the home of the Agars, Stevenson and Attwood completed the concluding article for Look.

Attwood wrote in his diary on July 31: "We went to work. Stevenson started shuffling through my outline and a pile of notes, including all his previous articles. Meanwhile I wrote a 1000 word lead, which he thought was okay. That got him off the ground, and by nightfall he was putting words on paper."

That day Stevenson received the news that his son Adlai — an officer in the Marine Corps — was about to be sent to Korea. He phoned Adlai in California and proposed flying there to say goodbye, but Adlai III dissuaded him from doing this.

At one point, a London newspaper phoned Herbert Agar to inquire about what Stevenson was doing. The reply was, "Resting, writing and playing croquet." Stevenson told Attwood that Agar should have told them softball or tennis — "Croquet won't sound so good in the Midwest."

Attwood then wrote in his diary: "Later, at dinner, Stevenson indicated that the British atmosphere is infectious — at least so far as he is concerned. When asked how he liked the port, he replied, 'jolly good.' Later when asked if he'd have another glass, he said, 'rather!' " Attwood added: "We'd better get him home pretty soon before he starts playing cricket and tucking a handkerchief in his sleeve."

One day playwright Robert E. Sherwood joined Stevenson and Agar for lunch. They discussed his future plans and the Governor told his old

[12] Chicago *Tribune*, August 1, 1953.

*friends that he rather dreaded getting back into the political arena —
with all of the effort it implied. Sherwood advised him not to worry
about it and just return home and "be himself."*

By August 3, Stevenson had completed the second draft of his Look
*article. When Agar read it and liked it, "Stevenson cheered up a bit,"
Attwood wrote in his diary. But Stevenson stayed up late that evening
rewriting the article.*

While he was at the Agars', the Sunday Times *remarked:*

> Despite his vivacity and wit, there is a curious loneliness about
> Adlai Stevenson. Perhaps the true liberal is doomed to be lonely in
> politics, hardly hearing his own voice amid the din of extremism,
> and dogged by his own doubts amid the clatter of confident asser-
> tion.[13]

The British correspondent for the New Republic *wrote:*

> Stevenson came up to England's expectations. We should have
> welcomed perhaps a little more than we got of his wit, which ca-
> vorts so happily along the line where British and American humor
> meet. We could have done with more of his wisdom than questions
> and answers permit . . . We liked his personality. We liked his
> way of thought.[14]

*When Stevenson returned to London for a day he found time to an-
swer some of his correspondence.*

To Mrs. Edison Dick [15]

August 5, 1953

How has it been in England? Precisely like the campaign, but we are
off now, the last article finished, the last engagement met, the last "few
words" uttered, and tons of mail unanswered! John Fell and Bill [Blair]
and I leave for the south of France in the early morning and the Ives
go to Lady Astor for a few days before sailing home.

I am not quite sure where we will stay, but the address will be c/o
the American Consul, Nice. We will fly back on August 19th to New
York and directly on to Chicago on a plane leaving New York around
noon on August 20. I think I will go direct to the country — and unpack,
thank God! Some people may want to come out to Chicago to "brief"

[13] *Sunday Times* (London), August 2, 1953.
[14] "Last Stop London: Stevenson Heads for Home," *New Republic*, August 24,
1953, p. 5.
[15] The original is in the possession of Mrs. Dick.

me over the weekend and I would appreciate it if you could alert
Beatrice [16] against the possibility that there will be two or three for Saturday night of that week. Perhaps she ought also to sign up someone
to help her . . . from Friday through Monday. I am afraid this is all a
little vague because I am *too,* and it is difficult to foretell precisely what
my needs will be! I think the following week I shall try to go up to Desbarats or somewhere for a fortnight of rest and reflection possibly taking
along Miss Evans and the accumulation of office work. And, of course,
any Dicks would contribute to both rest, reflection — and recreation!

I am assuming that the Fields have left for Hawaii and that the house
is vacant.[17] After Labour Day I shall have to make some arrangements
with them, I suppose, for my permanent occupancy.

I escaped from the London frenzy for a few days in the country with
the Agars to write my last piece. It was wholly delightful but coincided
with a festival week and the house was full of guests and commotion,
but somehow I contrived to get the wretched thing written. . . .

Need I add to this confused letter that I am utterly confused myself,
but some days in the sun should smooth a disordered mind — I hope.
I trust all is well with you and shall make no effort to reply in detail to
your last letters at this time, in view of the pile which is in front of me
which I should dispose of or live in harassment during my holiday in
France.

P.S. I was tempted to go shooting-and fishing- in Scotland but the
weather is so unreliable, and I also wanted to do a little more with John
Fell's French if I could. Hence the Riviera instead of my beloved Britain.

*During his last day in London (August 5) Stevenson had a series of
appointments, including one with historian Arnold Toynbee. Before
Stevenson left the Dorchester Hotel to board a plane for the Riviera,
Attwood wrote in his diary: "He started talking about the possibility of
making a swing around Africa next winter. Talk about chronic stamina.
. . . It was a great trip. Never again."*

Stevenson wrote in his final article for Look *about his world tour:*

THE WORLD I SAW [18]

This is the last of these reports of a long and strenuous journey. In five
months, I traveled many thousands of miles through 30 friendly, hos-

16 Mrs. Frank Holland, his housekeeper at the Libertyville farm.
17 Mr. and Mrs. Marshall Field IV had rented Stevenson's Libertyville house.
18 *Look,* September 22, 1953.

pitable countries by ship, plane, train, automobile, jeep, helicopter and motor boat — even by camel. I slept (or tried to sleep) in 68 different beds, good, bad and indifferent, in many temperatures — mostly hot; and I dined on far more than 57 varieties of food — mostly good (I remember somewhere describing this trip as fascinating, fatiguing — and fattening!).

I have been asked how this journey compared with last year's Presidential campaign. The answer is: Just as exhausting — but I didn't encounter as much opposition.

Nearly a billion people live in the lands I visited. I call them a billion neighbors because, like ourselves, they live in what we call "the free world."

A billion is a lot of people; and it's a figure we Americans, who sometimes think of ourselves as bigger, stronger and more self-sufficient than we really are, would do well to remember. For example, consider Pakistan and Indonesia — two countries that don't often appear in our headlines; together, they come close to outnumbering us Americans. And in the struggles of today and tomorrow, *people* are more important than assembly lines — or atom bombs.

The word "neighbors" is important too. We don't always agree with our friends and allies about how we should cope with the dangers and difficulties that beset us all. But, despite our differences, let us not forget that our basic interests are as closely bound as those of people living on the same block who borrow each other's lawn mowers and send their kids to the same school.

What each of us does — and particularly we Americans, because we are the richest family on the block — affects us all. In moments of impatience and irritation, and we all have them, the phrase "go it alone" has its charms; but it is as pernicious as it is impractical.

It was a long, crowded trip — so long that I have never felt so homesick for Illinois, for my little farm, my friends and my *own* neighbors. Many things have happened since I left San Francisco on March 2: The Communists invaded Laos; political crises have shaken France and Italy; Senator McCarthy has stamped to the center of the American stage before a bewildered world; Stalin died and there have followed violent unrest in the satellites, purges in Russia and conciliatory Soviet gestures toward the West. Finally, the Communist high command has agreed to a truce in Korea.

My impressions of what I have seen, heard and felt are still disordered. But before trying to sort them out, I want to state some general conclusions whose validity has been deeply impressed upon me everywhere.

The first is this: Russia's intentions are unchanged — despite Stalin's death and signs of domestic convulsions and a "softer" Kremlin policy, the Russian objective is still a Communist world. (But while there is no convincing sign that Russia is yet ready for peaceful coexistence — for "live and let live" — there is universal hope and desire to explore every possibility of settlement by conference and negotiation.)

What has taken place in these last eventful months is a change in Soviet tactics — in means rather than ends. Stalin's methods have not paid off. Soviet pressure did not paralyze the free world but, rather, forged its unity and rearmed America. So the Communists have pulled out of the Korean war, at least temporarily — as they previously called off the Berlin blockade and the Greek civil war when we dug in our heels.

In a word, the patience, unity and strength of the non-Communist world under American leadership have forced the Russians to try a new tack.

What now? Until there is positive evidence of a change of heart, I think we can expect more subtle, more challenging, more *divisive* tactics — always with the same goal of world domination. We can expect Communists to encourage and exploit every sign of weakness, distrust, misunderstanding or jealousy between us and our neighbors; they will probe the soft spots in the free nations and tempt the backward areas — the colonial states and the new nations of Asia — with both economic and emotional lures. And they will try to invade with trade.

So I feel that this is no time to relax. And precisely because people everywhere are weary of continual tension, the period ahead is as perilous as any since the end of World War II. Peace is more secure, yes. The chances of another major war within the next ten years are diminishing every day. But with the Soviet threat less obvious and less naked — can we maintain the teamwork that was cemented in the shadow of aggression?

My second conclusion is that the free world — the non-Communist world — is far from being a happy team. Already, it is rent with conflicts and ill will: India and Pakistan are at odds over Kashmir; bitterness divides Israel from her Arab neighbors; Trieste poisons relations between Yugoslavia and Italy; France is fearful of renascent Germany; Burma is angry about the Chinese Nationalist forces on her soil; Britain and Egypt are quarreling over the Suez base; the Greeks are demanding Cyprus and the Indonesians West Borneo; and the French are getting tired of the bloody, costly war in Indochina which imperils all Southeast Asia. Each of these offers opportunities to the Kremlin to fish in troubled waters.

Finally, I have been distressed by America's declining prestige and influence. The causes are many: Proud countries are sensitive about dependence on U.S. aid; there is widespread feeling that we are impetuous, inflexible and dedicated to the extermination of communism; and that we have confused a military policy with a foreign policy. Republican campaign talk of "liberating" Eastern Europe last fall sounded too much like saber rattling.

Telling our allies to make greater defense efforts "or else" has disturbed *them,* not our enemies. The phenomena of McCarthyism (which has become a new word in the world's dictionary) and of fear and repression in mighty America were subjects that came up in every press conference from Tokyo to London. (One of Western Europe's most responsible and respected leaders told me that McCarthyism had done America more harm in eight months than Soviet propaganda had done in eight years.) Inquisitions, amateur sleuths traveling around Europe, purges of libraries, purges in the State Department and embassies, invasion of the President's executive domain — all these things have conspired to blur the shining image of a big, strong, free and fearless America.

And foreigners are confused by Washington's warnings of continuing peril coinciding with cuts in defense expenditures; by indignation over East-West trade coinciding with cuts in aid to friendly nations and legislation to increase our tariff barriers (defeated, happily, thanks to Democratic votes). People asked me why we were so surprised and upset by President Rhee's actions after all the recent Republican oratory about "victory" and driving to the Yalu.

But far more serious than confusion about U.S. policy is the widespread impression that our country is scared and losing confidence in itself just when things are going better and cracks are appearing in the Iron Curtain.

To summarize: There is no reliable evidence yet that Russia is ready to abandon her goal of world domination; the non-Communist world is by no means a harmonious household and includes every variety of attitude; there is a growing sentiment in Europe and Asia for meeting the Russians "half way" (half way to what the Europeans and Asians don't exactly know) and, finally, faith in American leadership is shaken as confidence declines in America's self-confidence.

Asia

Asia is in revolution. Our friends — and all the Asians are our friends except Red China — welcome our help and cooperation but not dictation nor interference.

The Russians are likely to make their biggest effort in Asia. For here is the greatest reservoir of human and physical resources — and the greatest poverty and ignorance. The Communist appeal is to elemental wants and feelings — land, bread, peace, nationalism and anticolonialism. The tragedy of Indochina, now our biggest headache, was France's earlier failure to consider these aspirations and passions.

Incessant anti-Communist talk makes little impression on people who have not seen communism in brutal practice. The ideological struggle is meaningless to most, but Communist promises of a better break for the common people sound good to the poor — and the white man from the West is still a suspicious symbol of the old order. Many influential Asian intellectuals are theoretical Marxists who know little of the blunt facts of contemporary international life. What they do know is feudalism, militarism and colonialism. Winning their confidence is a great unfinished task.

(I remember the Marxist students in Rangoon who triumphantly pointed out that our Federal expenditures for education were only a tiny fraction of our military spending — triumphantly, that is, until I explained that education in the U.S. was largely supported by the states and private endowments, not the Federal government.)

Asia's mind, for the most part, is open. Democracy and communism are freely compared, often from a basis of little understanding of either. There is much to be done in Asia to demonstrate that the free way of life has more to offer the common man and that communism is a new imperial despotism. And we must recapture the word "peace" from the Reds because people in Asia (as everywhere else) are sick and tired of war. The West is at a disadvantage because of the Communists' shameless contempt for truth; and because the Iron Curtain makes comparison difficult.

I concluded that, while we can give them needed help and counsel, the long, slow job of Asian enlightenment must be done by Asians. (To this end, I think, our student and teacher exchange programs are highly effective.)

Yet Asia on the whole was encouraging. Communist efforts to seize power by violence have been thwarted, and Asia's present leaders are dedicated to democratic principles and struggling to develop parliamentary systems on a very thin base of political consciousness, and effective governments with a paucity of trained administrators.

And in China — overpopulated, poor and without the vast, undeveloped resources of Soviet Russia — the Communists, though solidly installed, face monstrous problems. Industrialization and increased food production will require goods and machinery from the West. That's why many experts I talked to conclude that China wants peace and trade above all, even though, like Russia, she will continue to press for sympathetic Communist states around her borders; and few will predict just where China's investment in the Indochina war will cease.

Our allies are hungry for trade with China too, and they feel that normal commercial relations will reduce China's dependence on Russia and ease the pressure toward the rice, rubber and tin of Southeast Asia.

We will shortly hear more about all this, for some kind of Western policy on China must be worked out, now that the Korean fighting has ceased. Views among the allies are far apart now; but if China wants unrestricted trade, admission to the U.N., diplomatic recognition and Formosa, and if we want a unified Korea, peace in Indochina and a separate status for Formosa, there is at least a broad base for negotiation.

In these critical negotiations, keeping a united front on our side of the table will not be the least of our difficulties; we shall also have to develop flexibility and balance on questions involving the Pacific — where we have fought and bled so much for peace, justice and security.

One last word about Japan — now striving to graft a peaceful, democratic system onto autocratic, expansionist roots. (Someone told me that 80 different Japanese words have been used to attempt to convey the idea of "democracy.") Because of her large industrial plant and skilled, hard-working population, Japan can be a mighty dike against the tide of Asian communism. For that very reason, this overpopulated, highly civilized and beautiful land is bound to be wooed by the Reds.

Like Germany and Britain, Japan cannot live without trade. The hostility generated by Japanese occupation in Southeast Asia and the drive toward economic self-sufficiency in the new nations are big obstacles to redeveloping markets in that area; so is British, German, Dutch and American competition. Therefore, trade with China and Russia attracts the practical Japanese, who know that, since the war, only American dollars have sustained Japan's balance of payments.

We Americans face many hard questions in the Orient — the Indochina war, what to do about Red China, the ideological battleground of India (where a third of these billion neighbors live) and, finally, Japan. I have a strong feeling that it will take a long time and a mighty cataclysm for communism to engulf the energetic, wary and resourceful Japanese.

Middle East

The Middle East, the bridge between Europe, Asia and Africa and the repository of fabulous oil resources, is a vast region of deserts, fertile valleys, poor people, old civilizations and new nations. Strong men and personal governments are the rule, but genuine democracy and representative institutions are the avowed goals. Some states are poor, others rich (and getting richer) from their oil. Iran staggers from crisis to crisis. Ancient Egypt is starting afresh and throwing off the last vestige of foreign influence. In other states, the Arabs glare sullenly at the unwelcome newcomer in their midst — lusty little Israel, a monument to humanitarianism and indomitable faith in Jewish destiny.

There is a power vacuum in the Middle East which cannot be filled until passions cool, fears subside and these problems are resolved one by one. The problems here are not insoluble. Communism is less a problem than economic and political maturity. The Suez dispute *can* be settled. The Jews and Arabs *can* find at least a *modus vivendi* — as they must in their own self-interest. We can help, and in doing so, we don't have to play favorites: Being proud of our part in creating the Jewish home state doesn't mean disrespect or less concern for the Arabs.

With much land to be reclaimed and resources to be developed, one thinks of the possibilities of creating a pool of capital from the excess resources of the oil-rich states for development projects among their needier brethren. And the vision of happier disposition of the 800,000 wretched Arab refugees from Israel, now huddled in their squalid camps, is something which haunts a traveler long after he passes out of the dry, dusty Middle East through the hardy Balkans into green, fertile Western Europe.

But procrastination and pious words will accomplish nothing in the Middle East. What we need out here is a policy — and the resolution to carry it out.

Western Europe

I recently wrote of the spectacular recovery of Europe, thanks to hard work and American aid, and of the frustrating indecision that afflicts the Continent just when things look better and great decisions must be made. In France, nothing is as permanent as impermanence, and now Italy, too, has taken the path of political instability. In Austria, people talk impatiently of a peace treaty at almost any price. In Germany, the idea of quick unification has become an obsession.

Everywhere, there are impatience, anxiety and an almost pathetic eagerness to "settle things" — somehow; everywhere, that is, except in tough, sober Britain, where heads are cool.

The British would like to sound out the Russians, but they expect no miracles and won't be stampeded into paying too high a price for anything. Britain seems to want the European Defense Community and political integration of the Continent as much as we do. She desperately wants "trade, not aid" — freer world trade, wider markets, a more liberal U.S. commercial policy. The British pray for prosperity in the United States because the effects of recession would be multiplied many times over in Britain.

But what they want most of all is to be considered an equal and not a junior partner or satellite of the United States.

As I see it, the immediate problems facing us in Europe are the future of Germany and how to keep the French fighting in Indochina. Five months ago, I wrote that the riddle of Indochina was that the war could be won neither *with* the French nor *without* them. Today, with clearer guarantees of independence for Viet-Nam and more aggressive military tactics, the prospects are much brighter. But, in Paris, there is a growing desire to cut the intolerable cost of Indochina — to pull out or settle, as we did in Korea. Influential Frenchmen, like Pierre Mendès-France (who narrowly missed becoming Premier in June), told me that France can no longer afford to bear her share of the NATO defense burden, to fight communism with social reform at home and also to fight the Indochina war — all at once. One must be sacrificed; and the French contend that Indochina is not as important as European defense or internal economic improvement in the struggle against communism.

Indeed, I found an alarming indifference to the Indochina war throughout Europe, except among the British, who are also engaged in a long, weary war of attrition in the jungles of neighboring Malaya. And I suspect that, as colonial empires shrink, Europe's horizons will too, and that more and more of the responsibility for defending Asia and the Pacific will fall to America.

But there is no indifference to the urgent problem of Germany — the breeding ground of two world wars which have plunged Europe into its present plight. The problem can be stated as the dilemma of European unification *or* the reunification of Germany.

The great hope for strength, for balancing Russia's power and for peace on the Continent is a united Western Europe. But a united Europe without its strongest member, Germany, would be a fragile thing indeed. And that is precisely why Russia will do her best to prevent German integration with Western Europe. The bait may be reunification of East and West Germany, which all Germans are loudly demanding, in exchange for neutralization of Germany and renunciation of European unity.

But such a solution would be a disastrous price for Germany and Europe to pay for "peace in our time." For Europe, with its old rivalries, would thereby lose its best chance for strength and security. Internal communism would remain a menace; so would the rebirth of aggressive nationalism in an isolated Germany.

But Germany is just one of the many thorny questions confronting us in the world, one of the many that offer Russia opportunities to drive wedges between us and our allies. For, in Korea, we have vindicated collective security for the first time in history, and no greater disaster could befall us than that the free nations should fall apart and lower their guard on the eve of victory in the long, cold struggle. That is why I said at the outset that our perils are not past and the future will call for all the statesmanship and vision we can summon. We must bend every effort to build strength through unity, mutual assistance and mutual confidence. It will get harder as the immediate danger lessens.

And now let me conclude this report and also this long, eventful journey with some random gleanings from my notebooks about the world in general:

1. I think we have been on the right track, by and large, since we grasped Russia's aggressive postwar intentions. The policy of resistance and assistance has succeeded. The non-Communist world is stronger, safer, more self-reliant. There have been no Communist victories for a long while, and the strain of the cold war is beginning to show through the Iron Curtain. The danger of World War III is receding. Stalin's death, the sequels and the rebellions in the "people's paradise" are ushering in a new era of cold peace.

2. This is not the time to wobble, but it is likewise no time for arrogance and inflexibility. We owe it to ourselves and to our anxious, weary friends to disclose Russian intentions *if* we can; to confer, negotiate and accommodate *when* we can; to reduce tensions and restore hope *where* we can. We may have to eat a lot of intemperate, witless words and modify some rigid attitudes. I pray that we will be big enough, wise enough, strong enough to do these things.

3. I have noticed repeatedly on this journey the politicians' habit of saying extreme things and taking extreme positions to arouse the multitude and get the better of an opponent. It is easy to get out on a limb with cheers but hard to get back without jeers of "appeasement," "compromise," "retreat." It is the same at home. But passion must never be the master of reason nor narrow consistency the master of wider wisdom.

4. I doubt very much if peace and security will ever come out of one

grand world-wide peace conference. We will have to make progress bit by bit, item by item, place by place. We can define and agree with our allies and friends on common aims, minimal conditions and methods, and negotiate partial solutions in the framework of such common policy. The process may be slow and frustrating; but the stakes are epic in this transition from the world we know to a world we don't know.

5. Looking back across endless months and miles and candid conversations, I sometimes feel that mutual misunderstanding is our greatest handicap and hazard. Ugly illusions about the United States are all too prevalent, but there is also a touching, moving admiration and wonder about big, brash, magnanimous America that talks tough and insensitively but sends money and friendly, earnest people everywhere to help. The suspicion of the strong, the envy of the rich are diluted with an almost pathetic hope that America of the Declaration of Independence and the Bill of Rights won't confirm suspicions of emotional, economic and moral irresponsibility.

And our illusions about the rest of the world are just as serious: that we have a monopoly of energy, know-how, culture and morality; that other people live and think as we do — or should. But if an illiterate Burmese peasant has an excuse not to understand America better, we Americans, with all the means of communication at our disposal, have none. So I am convinced that we must know more about our world to live up to the leadership that has been thrust upon us by circumstances.

6. Many of the world's troubles are not due just to Russia or communism. They would be with us in any event because we live in an era of revolution — the revolution of rising expectations. In Asia, the masses now count for something. Tomorrow, they will count for more. And, for better or for worse, the future belongs to those who understand the hopes and fears of masses in ferment. The new nations want independence, including the inalienable right to make their own mistakes. The people want respect — and something to eat every day. And they want something better for their children.

These things, then, America must face squarely and promptly:

FIRST: *Our leadership and influence have sagged. Fear is contagious, and if we appear to distrust ourselves and our ideals, we can't expect others to trust us.*

SECOND: *Germany is imperative to the West.*

THIRD: *Red China is a reality that cannot be wished away; Formosa must be a bastion of peace and security in the Pacific.*

FOURTH: *Trade is life itself for the great industrial nations, and their well-being is our security.*

FIFTH: *Southeast Asia's security hinges on war in Indochina.*

SIXTH: *The crisis of our times is moral as well as material, and the spirit of man is stronger and hungrier than the body.*

This journey has been a glorious adventure for me. I have seen many strange sights, much of ugliness, more of beauty. I wish more Americans could have the opportunity to wander inquisitively across this vast globe, where change is relentless and peace is a prayer.

One of my last stops was Chequers — an ancient country house surrounded by the rolling fields, great oaks and beech trees of England. There, I met an imperishable figure of our time, Sir Winston Churchill. In accents tinged with emotion, he told me why he had proposed a conference with the new men in the Kremlin. He wanted to talk with them, he said, about the wicked futility of war, "because I must in good conscience make sure, if I can, that nothing is overlooked heedlessly."

I don't recommend a working trip around the world to anyone who likes to keep cool, sleep in the mornings or take Sundays off. But I strongly recommend it to anyone who thinks the world's problems are simple and that we can solve them all.

Twenty-two

Report to the Nation

When the concluding article for Look was completed, Stevenson went with John Fell Stevenson and William McCormick Blair, Jr., to Nice for a vacation on the Riviera. After this, Stevenson flew to New York.

As he neared home, American newspapers were replete with speculation on Stevenson's political future. Thomas L. Stokes wrote:

> It was apparent during the 1952 campaign that Adlai Stevenson was a rather special sort of candidate for president. Since then it has, if anything, become even more apparent despite defeat and in defeat.
>
> In proof of this now is the anticipation among Democrats, almost atwitter it is, of his return home in a few weeks from his world travels.[1]

Cabell Phillips wrote:

> Mr. Stevenson's return is expected again to turn the spotlight on the most glamorous political figure the Democrats have produced since the early Presidential years of Franklin D. Roosevelt. The former Illinois Governor's talent for combining humility with sophistication and for preserving his stature in the midst of defeat has caused him to be acclaimed a political "natural."
>
> His five month tour of virtually every major capital in the free world, his talks with national leaders of all shades of political faith

[1] Chicago *Sun-Times*, July 22, 1953.

and his observations in Look magazine on the turmoil and the misery he has witnessed have added to his prestige.[2]

When Stevenson's plane landed at New York City on the morning of August 20, he was met by a group of leading Democrats, including Averell Harriman, Wilson Wyatt, and Richard H. Balch, chairman of the New York State Democratic Committee. In a brief statement before television newsreel cameras, he expressed the hope that the way would be found in the months ahead to hold together the "grand alliance of the free people of the world. No one else but the United States can do it."

At the Biltmore Hotel, at a press conference arranged by the Democratic State Committee, he read a prepared statement to a roomful of 250 reporters and cameramen:

I have been away from the United States for almost six months and I am glad to be home again, and to see old friends and familiar sights — and to unpack, at last.

This is not going to be a report on my long journey. I will have something more to say in a speech from Chicago on Sept. 15, and probably still more to say after that.

But you have honored me with your presence here this morning on my return and I will make a few brief observations on how the world through which I have traveled looks to me and how we look to it.

I have traveled tens of thousands of miles by airplane, train, boat, automobile — even camel — through some thirty countries from Japan to Britain, and I have talked with everyone, from cobblers to kings. It has not been a vacation, but a hard and remorseless though very gratifying journey. I wish all Americans could have the same experience. It would be a good thing for them and for the world, too.

Everywhere I was greeted with the utmost courtesy, hospitality and friendliness, and I was repeatedly amazed by the eagerness and candor with which people talked to me.

For this unfailing courtesy and frankness and for such gracious hospitality in so many countries, I want, first of all, to express my gratitude from a full heart.

And I should like to take this occasion, too, to thank the Administration in Washington and many Ambassadors and American officials along the way for the courtesy and helpfulness which eased and simplified a long, complicated and closely timed itinerary.

I for one am proud of the Americans representing us abroad and of

[2] New York *Times*, August 2, 1953.

the good will and respect they enjoy in their stations. And I often thought in distant places of what we at home owe in gratitude to many of our fellow citizens who serve their country abroad with fidelity and devotion, often in the most trying circumstances. I hope prompt and decisive steps will be taken to restore the self-confidence and initiative of our foreign service which have been sadly undermined of late from home.

Many people have asked me why I undertook this extensive and trying journey. I took it for my own education because this is the first opportunity I have ever had to travel through Asia and the Middle East, and because we live in an interdependent world with a multitude of neighbors of all kinds. We want to live in peace and security. In order to do so we have fought in two world wars, and to this end our postwar foreign policy has been directed. There is no substitute for seeing with you own eyes and hearing with your own ears. I wanted to see and hear for myself. And what I have seen and heard is both encouraging and sobering.

As long as totalitarian regimes rule such powerful nations as Russia and China; as long as the decision of war or peace rests with inscrutable men, we cannot be complacent. But there are grounds for hope. The policy of building the economic and military strength of the non-Communist world has worked well.

Communist insurrections in the Philippines, Indonesia and Burma have been crushed. The terrorists in Malaya are losing ground. South Korea has been liberated by an historic combined resolve to punish aggression and preserve the peace. The spread of communism has been arrested; signs of strain and defiance are evident, and cracks are opening in the Iron Curtain, notably in East Germany.

Since Stalin's death, it appears that Russia has changed its tactics and begun a cautious retreat. But there is as yet no certain evidence that the long-term objective of world domination has changed.

The recovery of Europe from the war has been phenomenal and has been widely reported in the American press. But governments everywhere, the old and the new, are struggling with hard economic and social problems and none is turning to force, coercion or totalitarian methods for their solution.

In short, we have been winning the cold war step by step, which is the best tribute to the success of our post-war policies of assistance and resistance and to the power of free people working together with resolution, fortitude and faith. In consequence the danger of world war has diminished, at least for the present. But this is no time to relax or lower our guard.

Given this central success you might expect that the free nations would be more calm, more sure, more determined and united than ever. But that is not the case. There are many tensions: Kashmir, Suez, Arab unrest, Trieste, and Indo-China, to mention a few. There is neutralism in Asia, political instability in France and Italy; the future of Germany and the political and military unification of Europe are still uncertain.

If there is strength in unity there is weakness in disunity, and one thing is certain, the Communists will exploit every possibility of dividing America and her allies. Historically allies have often fallen apart after wars and after the common danger has subsided, and what has happened in war can happen in cold war.

This as I see it is one of the greatest hazards in a world in ferment divided between the totalitarian peoples, the free peoples and the uncommitted peoples. Everyone does not share our views of communism and its menace. Many who have lived in thralldom or insecurity for centuries do not share in the same degree America's alarm. Nor do they think that we are endowed with all the wisdom, power and morality in the world.

While there is much misunderstanding *in* America, there is as much or more misunderstanding *of* America.

Just now, unhappily, our prestige and moral influence have declined, together with faith in our judgment and our leadership. But don't misunderstand me, please. In its broad outlines, the image of magnanimous America still stands out, clear and radiant. And the gratitude for what we have done and tried to do to assist far-flung peoples in everything from rearmament to agriculture is both touching and comforting.

But in detail the reflection of America is blurred and distorted. There is an impression that we are inflexible and erratic; that faith in cooperation is being replaced by belief in unilateral action — a readiness to go it alone. It is hard for them to reconcile our view of the danger with a cut in our defense build-up. There is an impression that "trade not aid" is becoming no aid and no trade.

Book-burning, purges and invasions of executive responsibility have obscured the bright image of America; and when we give the impression that we are scared and freedom of speech and freedom of expression are on the defensive in the United States, we put the United States on the defensive.

But I doubt if anything has been lost that cannot be regained. President Eisenhower's Administration faces many acute problems in the foreign field — in Korea (where we pray the fighting has stopped for keeps), in Indo-China, China, Germany, world trade, etc. While abroad

I have never criticized the Administration's handling of our foreign affairs; rather I have sought to explain American attitudes and positions when I had to and as best I could.

But let me say that holding together the grand alliance of the free, is in my judgment, the most important and difficult task our Government faces, for unilateralism is just the new face of isolationism, and it spells disaster.

In conclusion, let me add that while I have not been able to follow events here closely during my absence, I do know that the Democratic minority in the Congress has made a record of which I for one am proud and thankful, and for which the President should be even more thankful. This has been opposition at its best.

As for myself, my plans are not definite. I have a living to make and a lot of things I want to do, including some reading and some plain, ordinary, quiet living, which has eluded me for the past thirteen years, and especially the past thirteen months.

I want to do everything I can to keep our country free and strong; a land to which all people in the world can look in the future, as in the past, with respect, confidence, and, if I may say so, with love.

After Stevenson had finished his statement, he was asked whether he regarded himself as the Democratic party's leader. He replied: "The only way I know how to answer is: I want to do whatever I can to further the best interests of my country, as I see them, and also of my party. By best serving the country's interest, I will best serve the party's. If that is leadership, make the most of it."

Asked about friction between the United States and Britain over international problems, he responded that it was natural that there would be some misunderstandings but that the unity and common purpose of these two nations were the most important elements of stability in the world today. He added: "We both believe in diversity but the things that bind us together, from our common poetry to our nursery rhymes and the language of our prayers, are far more important than elocution and protestations of good will. There is nothing fundamentally wrong with the relations between Britain and the United States, and I hope and trust and pray that there won't be."

Observing an exchange of words between a cameraman and a reporter over who was interfering with whose attempts to record the interview properly, he grinned and said, "I see there is tension here as well as abroad."

*Stevenson pointed out that he had been questioned abroad more
often about McCarthyism than any other subject. "I attempted," he
said, "to answer these questions in two ways: I said I felt it was mag-
nified out of its proper proportion and I would have more to say about
it when I returned home."* [3]

*Following the press conference, Stevenson was the guest at a recep-
tion and luncheon given by the Democratic State Committee. Later
that afternoon he flew home to Chicago to be welcomed by a group of
some two hundred of his supporters. He told the reporters, "I don't
know whether I am going to run in 1956, and if I did I wouldn't tell
you." He remarked that he thought Democratic chances of capturing
Congress in 1954 were excellent. "I think the Democratic party in Congress has given the country an example of the best in loyal opposition,"
he added. As he got in his car to drive to Libertyville, he told the press,
"There is one thing I can report with certainty. On the lips of everyone
in all the vast regions of this tremendous earth, there is a prayer for
peace."* [4]

*During the next few days he rested at his country home on the
banks of the Des Plaines River near Libertyville. Richard H. Rovere,
who visited him there, wrote that Stevenson was "sorting out his impressions of America and the world and turning over and over in his
mind the question of what, precisely, a man in his unique and not altogether enviable position ought to do."*

*Rovere added that the impressions friends "get is not that of a man
whose body craves repose — well tanned and perhaps a trifle plumper
than before, he looks, actually, in better trim now than during the
campaign — but that of a man who feels that he has crowded too much
experience into too short a time.*

*"What he needs now and is getting is time for assimilation — and
also for catching up, by reading and conversation — on the experience
he has missed through being away. There are large gaps in his knowledge of recent goings on in the United States, and a good part of his
time is spent in closing them. And he will go on doing that as long as
possible."* [5]

Stevenson spent part of his time answering correspondence:

[3] New York *Times*, August 21, 1953. The *Times* wrote in an editorial: "It is not
on record that during all those crowded months where he was subject to the
temptation to rash and impetuous speech at every turn, he ever said a thing that
did not help his country, or anything that could embarrass the Eisenhower Administration. This was an achievement, not of an adroit politician, but of an understanding mind and heart."

[4] Chicago *Sun-Times*, August 21, 1953.

[5] "Adlai Stevenson of Libertyville, Illinois," *New York Times Magazine*,
September 13, 1953, p. 9.

To Mr. and Mrs. Hermon Dunlap Smith [6]

August 23, 1953

Dear Dutch and Ellen:

I am back at last — thank God! — and in the process of organizing my chaos. The weather is beautiful and so is the Libertyville place and John Fell is with me. Hence, I am tempted to stay here, resting and working quietly, with no more travel. But if the telephone situation and the interruptions get too bad I may telephone you for permission to come up for a taste of that delicious Desbarats and my beloved Smiths. But you will understand that I should like to stay here and enjoy the rarity of living at home, if I can swing it, and also see something of John Fell and get caught up in a leisurely way with my accumulated troubles.

. . . I dread getting back into the old speech routine, but interest in the September 15 affair may stimulate my torpid spirit as time goes on. For the moment all I seem to want to do is to look at the trees and fields with half shut eyes.

Love to you both and the dear Haights. [7]

Yours,
ADLAI

To Ernest L. Ives

August 23, 1953

Dear Ernest:

I believe you have a list of my bills you have paid which were forwarded to you by Miss Evans in March through May. They aggregate $4,567.53. Included was the personal property taxes on the oil royalties retained in the Kansas farm in the amount of $13.30, for which Buffie is liable for half. Accordingly, I have deducted one-half, or $6.65, and enclose my check to you for $4,560.88.

If I have made any miscalculation and am further in your debt, please let me know. I am ever so grateful for helping me out while I was away.

Yours,
ADLAI

P.S. And I'm sure I owe you & Buff money from abro[a]d, looking after John Fell etc. Please let me know how much. I'm trying to get my neglected affairs in order. [8]

[6] The original is in the possession of Mr. Smith.
[7] Mr. and Mrs. John Haight. Mrs. Haight was the Smiths' oldest daughter, Deborah.
[8] The postscript is handwritten.

To Lloyd K. Garrison

August 23, 1953

Dear Lloyd:

I am distressed that my passage through New York left so little time to talk with you and Ellen.[9] There will be another opportunity soon, I trust. Meanwhile, Miss Evans reminds me that we have had no statement from you for all of your rescue work in my new career as a writer, a career which I suspect will be short lived![10]

Please get me off your cuff, and don't spare the horses (rather a nice metaphor!). I am languishing on my place in Libertyville and enjoying the tranquil view. How long it will last I don't know, but I should prefer to stay here rather than go to Canada, if possible.

Hastily yours,

ADLAI

Joseph C. Green, U.S. ambassador to Jordan at the time of Stevenson's visit to that country, wrote that to his bitter disappointment he was being relieved of his post.

To Joseph C. Green [11]

August 23, 1953

My dear Joe:

I am just back after my long journey and find your letter of July 20. I am grieved by the news but I can hardly say I am surprised in view of the many similar, if less noteworthy, incidents, which I encountered during my travels. I took occasion, as you may have noticed on my arrival in New York, to say something about the demoralization in our foreign services. As you well know, it is bad, and I can imagine how you must feel, especially in view of the Secretary's long personal acquaintance.

Please give my affectionate regards to Mrs. Green and my thanks once more for rescuing Borden in his first experience with that dread disease.[12] He has often spoken of your kindness. As for me, I shall long

[9] Mrs. Garrison.

[10] Mr. Garrison was serving as Stevenson's literary agent. See *The Papers of Adlai E. Stevenson*, Vol. IV, pp. 218, 238–239, 349.

[11] The original is in the Adlai E. Stevenson collection, Illinois State Historical Library.

[12] Dysentery.

remember the world's foremost authority on the Bible and the holy places, and a grand companion.

Sincerely yours,

ADLAI

To Margaret Munn [13]

August 24, 1953

Dear Margaret:

I have written Mrs. Conway [14] as per the enclosed copy. I would rather not ask the Adjutant General [15] to fly Artie [16] up here unless the plane is coming for some other reason and they could load him aboard, in which case I could meet him at Glenview or wherever they land, I suppose. It might be better if you knew of someone who was driving to Chicago who wouldn't mind putting him in the back seat. I could pick him up in town when they arrived. If nothing turns up promptly don't worry about it. I can always get him later on when I come to Bloomington, although that would not be until after the 15th of September.

Yours,

AES

To Mrs. E. F. Conway

August 24, 1953

Dear Mrs. Conway:

I am back from my long journey now and living on my place in the country north of Chicago. Also, I have one of my boys with me and another one will be here before long. We pine for Artie, as you can understand, and I have asked Margaret Munn to help me arrange to have him brought up here in the near future.

Meanwhile, I wanted you to know how grateful I am for taking such good care of him, and I am sure you will forgive and understand a "father's" anxiety to reunite his family.

With warm good wishes to you and your son, I am

Cordially yours,

[13] The original is in the possession of Mrs. Munn.

[14] Mrs. E. F. Conway, who lived on South Fourth Street in Springfield, a few blocks from the mansion, had often cared for the Governor's dog on his habitual rambles, and cared for him while Stevenson was abroad.

[15] Major General Leo M. Boyle.

[16] Stevenson's dalmatian, King Arthur.

P.S. If you have incurred any expenses I should, of course, be glad to reimburse you.

While in Bonn, Germany, Stevenson had talked about his political philosophy with Robert K. Woetzel, an American studying at Oriel College, Oxford, England. Mr. Woetzel wrote Stevenson on August 10, 1953, expressing his concern over the conflict between goals and actual policies in politics and asking Stevenson about the threat of Mc-Carthy to American idealism.

To Robert K. Woetzel

August 25, 1953

My dear Mr. Woetzel:

Thank you so much for your kind letter which I find on my return to America.

I can appreciate some of your misgivings, but I hope you have realized that the world is always disordered and that there will always be contradictions of one's ethics and idealism. The important thing is to appreciate that things are never as one would have them and at the same time never to despair that it is worth while trying to make them better.

As for McCarthyism, of course challenges of this kind are recurrent. Actually I understand he has been losing ground of late, due in large measure to his attack on the Protestant clergy.[17] But if it is not Mc-Carthy, something or someone else arises another time to offend our faith, and he is far from dead, I suspect. The threat of fascism is always present and it may be on the increase just now. Whether it is dangerous I hardly know. My point is that you must not be upset or diverted from any chosen path by these anxieties and disillusionments because they are "here for keeps."

I am afraid this letter is not very helpful; and I enjoyed my brief glimpse of you.

With all best wishes, I am

Sincerely yours,

[17] Senator McCarthy had hired Joseph B. Matthews in June, 1953, to be staff director of his Senate subcommittee. His approval by the Senate became highly controversial when an article appeared in the July issue of the *American Mercury* in which Matthews charged the Protestant clergy with aiding the Communist movement in the United States. Matthews resigned on July 9, after White House and congressional opposition forced McCarthy to withdraw his appointment.

While in Paris, Stevenson had had a conversation with his old friend Archibald S. Alexander, Democratic National Committeeman from New Jersey, about American politics and his own future. When he returned, Mr. Alexander wrote a lengthy letter on August 28, 1953, analyzing the situation in the Democratic party. He concluded: "As you seem to me, you have absorbed and believe in most of the best that has shown itself in our political history since before the Civil War. With this background you have combined deep and patient humility, the courage of your convictions and the ability to express them in a manner second to none of your contemporaries; you avoid the extremes which only lead to counter-extremes, and yet you decline to return to the past or to accept the present as good enough for the future. . . . There is no acceptable substitute for you as the leader of the party in the immediate future [and] as the next candidate of the party for the Presidency."

To Archibald S. Alexander

August 31, 1953

Dear Archie:

I have read with much interest and a full heart your letter of August 28. I hope we *can* get together for a talk some time in the fall, and I shall make it my business to do so if I am in your vicinity. I think the letter is splendid, but I wish I had more enthusiasm for assuming the crushing burdens of constant talk and travel — "leadership," if that is what it is. I still feel that the South can be reconciled bit by bit as disillusionment with the new administration increases, and I am not in the least downhearted, but, of course, we face basic divergencies just as the Republicans do which may be with us for a long while.

As for myself, I plan to spend the autumn quietly, or as much so as possible, recuperating from a long siege of incessant pressure, and writing a little, perhaps a book, and speaking only for the National Committee at fund-raising affairs. There seems to be no other way to discriminate between the literally hundreds of requests. Then I shall have to think about a job, perhaps the law, commencing next year. As to more distant political goals, I genuinely don't know. Certainly I want to continue active and helpful if I can, but I don't enjoy being constantly pictured in the role of a scheming and ambitious candidate eager to run again, which I am not.

With affectionate regards to you and your wife, I am

Yours,

To Mr. and Mrs. O. J. Keller [18]

August 31, 1953

Dear Kellers:

Bless you for that welcoming wire. But I am glad you were *not* at the airport. I should have been very self-conscious about the passionate caress I propose to deliver to Mrs. Keller! I am told I will see you on the 14th or 15th or both.

Affectionately,

ADLAI

Before Stevenson's departure, President Eisenhower had asked to have the highlights of the trip on his return. On August 24, 1953, the President wrote to remind Stevenson of this request.

To Dwight D. Eisenhower

August 31, 1953

My dear Mr. President:

Thank you so much for your kind letter. While I am afraid I have little to report of value, I should, of course, be delighted to call on you at your convenience after your return to Washington. If Mr. Stephens [19] will be good enough to call me in Chicago at DEarborn 2-3122 I shall be at your command.[20]

Respectfully yours,

To Margaret Munn [21]

September 1, 1953

Dear Margaret:

Artie arrived via Larry Irvin [22] and seems to remember the old place and his master. I am delighted, of course, and I only hope we can make

[18] Personal friends in Springfield, Illinois. Mr. Keller was with station WTAX in Springfield.

[19] Thomas Stephens, President Eisenhower's appointments secretary.

[20] Stevenson was disappointed, when they met at the White House on October 1, 1953, by the brevity of his conversation with the President before they joined others for lunch. He did, however, have a longer conversation with the Secretary of State.

[21] The original is in the possession of Mrs. Munn.

[22] Lawrence Irvin, Stevenson's assistant during his governorship. Mr. Irvin recalls that on seeing Stevenson, Artie ran to his master and jumped up on him in a display of affection. In his characteristic self-depreciating way, Stevenson remarked, "Well, I guess he does remember me after all."

life agreeable to him, and enough so that he will want to stick around. Meanwhile, the heat has taken care of it.

It was wonderful to see you again and we shall have to have another foregathering of the beloved clan one of these days. Heartfelt thanks for looking after my interests on all fronts, including the canine.

Yours,
AES

John Kenneth Galbraith, professor of economics at Harvard University, had been an active drafter of speeches during the 1952 campaign. On August 25, 1953, Galbraith wrote Stevenson welcoming him home and adding: "Our misfortunes of last autumn were a great boon to scholarship. There are no calls from Washington; the hills hereabouts are full of professors busy on books or at least contemplating deeply the errors of the New Team. We are probably entering a great period in American science and letters. I am happy to think that my own labors of last fall may have been in some way responsible."

To John Kenneth Galbraith

September 5, 1953

Dear Ken:

Thanks for your note. When my too brief holiday in France was disturbed to return home I was deep in Galbraith, having virtually wrenched the book [23] out of Bill Benton's [24] hands. Now I am stalled again what with the load awaiting me here. But my education will be resumed when I can find my copy somewhere in my "mess."

I had not thought of our contribution as being to the higher learning, but if it is true the campaign was a success. The trouble is now how to do something about the lower learning.

I hope we can meet soon.

Yours,

By the time Stevenson had reached Rome late in June, Stephen A. Mitchell, with Stevenson's concurrence, had organized a meeting of the Democratic National Committee for Chicago in September and a non-partisan group of Chicago citizens headed by Laird Bell had reserved the Opera House for Stevenson to speak on his experiences.

[23] *American Capitalism: The Concept of Countervailing Power* (Boston: Houghton Mifflin, 1952).
[24] Democratic Senator William Benton of Connecticut.

On September 14, 1953, Stevenson delivered one of the speeches at the Democratic party's fund-raising dinner in Chicago. During the day he met with many party leaders, including former President Harry S. Truman, to discuss the future course of the party.

The following evening at the Chicago Opera House, he delivered his report to the nation:

TRAVELER'S REPORT [25]

For six months I have traveled across this vast and troubled world, for tens of thousands of miles — which were just as exhausting as the campaign, but I didn't encounter as much opposition! My mind is filled with recollections of people I talked with from Syngman Rhee and the Emperor of Japan, to Pope Pius and Queen Elizabeth; of the sights I've seen, moving and beautiful, sordid and sickening; of the rugged front in ravaged Korea where, pray God, the strife has stopped for keeps; of the ugly war in the wet, green rice paddies of Indo-China where Communism, masquerading as nationalism, imperils the whole of southeast Asia; and of millions of refugees huddled in squalid camps and hovels stretching from Korea across Asia to western Europe — remnants of many more victims of the wars, revolutions, intolerance and savagery that have cursed our time on earth.

A trip like mine is a sobering experience. It is more than a privilege, it is a responsibility to be an American in this world. It isn't one world; it's more like three worlds — the allied world, the Communist world, and the uncommitted world. Almost a billion people live along the route I took in 1953. Most of them live in Asia and most of the so-called uncommitted peoples live in Asia. They don't belong to the white minority of the human race, and tragically many of them are poor, undernourished, and illiterate.

Asia is in revolution. Civilizations are very old, but political independence is very young. In the new states the economies are shaky, public administration is weak; and they are hungry and poor, sensitive and proud. Nationalism is rampant. And the West, identified with the hated colonialism, is suspect. Utterly preoccupied with their own overwhelming problems, they see little of the world conflict and don't appreciate America's global responsibilities. They know from experience a lot about feudalism, landlords, money lenders, and oppressors, and the theories of Karl Marx sound pretty good to many of them, who know surprisingly little about the ugly realities of Communism in practice.

[25] The text is from *What I Think* (New York: Harper, 1954), pp. 193–199.

Nor is there the perception one would expect of the menace of international Communism as a new imperialism.

There is little tradition of democracy in these new states, but independence, won at long last, is a passion, which partly accounts in some quarters for their opaque view of Communist China where to many Asians it appears that the foreigners have been thrown out and the ignominy of centuries erased by Asians. There is reverent admiration for the ideas of the American Revolution, the Bill of Rights, and the great utterances of human freedom. But they think they see contradictions in waves of conformity and fear here at home, and hypocrisy in our alliances with the colonial powers and professed devotion to freedom and self-determination.

The ideological conflict in the world doesn't mean much to the masses. Anti-Communist preaching wins few hearts. They want to know what we are for, not just what we are against. And in nations like India, Indonesia, and Burma they don't accept the thesis that everyone has to choose sides, that they have to be for us or against us. Nor do I believe that we should press alliances on unwilling allies. After all, we had a long record of neutrality and non-involvement ourselves, and the important thing is that such nations keep their independence and don't join the hostile coalition.

But in spite of all their doubts and difficulties I was impressed by the devotion of the leaders of Asia to the democratic idea of government by consent rather than force, and by the decisive manner in which so many of the new countries of Asia have dealt with violent Communist insurrections and conspiracies. Their revolutions have not produced Utopia and they are struggling with infinite difficulties to raise living standards and satisfy the rising tide of expectations. They want rice and respect, and they want to believe in wondrous America that sends friendly, earnest people to help them, and that believes in them, and the aspirations of all God's children for peace, dignity, and freedom.

We are on the eve of great decisions in Asia. Korea is the first step. Personally I have been skeptical of Red China's intentions, but when we search for settlements we have to *search*, and when we negotiate we have to have something to negotiate *with* as well as *for*. Many of our friends think China wants peace and trade above all, as they themselves do. With so much at stake in Asia — the unification of Korea, Formosa, peace and security in Indo-China — it would seem to me that we owe it to ourselves as well as to our friends at least to find out, if we can, what Communist China's ultimate intentions are.

If I may risk a prophecy, the hostile world is going to pay more and more attention to Asia, especially huge, uncommitted India. And I suspect that as Europe's Eastern empires shrink, there will be left to us more of the burden of defense and of helping to guide the great forces which great changes have unleashed in Asia.

The Middle East is largely a power and defense vacuum, except for doughty little Israel and tough, strong Turkey. Peace is imperative in the Middle East — peace between the Arab states and Israel, which is engaged in an historic effort to provide refuge and new hope to oppressed people.

In Europe, the recovery since the war is spectacular. In western Germany it looks ironically as though the vanquished were better off than the victors. In France the progress has not kept pace; there is grave social unrest and political frustration which can be remedied and will be, pray Heaven, by heroic measures. Among Frenchmen the conviction is growing that France can no longer maintain the defense effort in Europe, fight Communism in Indo-China with weapons and at home with larger social and economic expenditures, all at the same time. We should bear in mind that many Frenchmen vote Communist not from conviction, but in protest. Hence the increasing clamor to get out of Indo-China altogether and spend more on housing, industrial development, and social betterment at home.

The most urgent problem in Europe today is, of course, Germany: how to channel its developing strength and resources into paths that will benefit both Europe and the world, how to resolve the age-old rivalries of France and Germany, and how to satisfy the intense German desire for reunification, whetted by the gallant workers' revolt of June, 1953, in the Soviet Zone, which exhilarated the whole free world.

In short, the difficulties are many and the hazards great everywhere. But things are better. There is hope in the air, born of America's postwar policy of assistance and resistance, of growing strength and self-confidence, and of Stalin's death followed by shifting winds from Moscow, truce in Korea, rebellion in eastern Europe, troubles behind the iron curtain.

But the world is weary; there is universal anxiety and impatience to ease the tensions, to explore every possibility of settlements by conference and negotiation. The Soviet will exploit discord in our ranks at every opportunity in order to divide and enfeeble the grand alliance of the free. There is uncertainty abroad about America and our objective. Is our objective to discover through negotiation ways to relax tensions, or is it intensification of the cold war; is it coexistence or extermination of Communist power?

Some of the misunderstandings may seem incredible to us, but it is well to try to see ourselves as others see us. Many think we are intemperate, inflexible, and frightened. And people who have lived in insecurity for centuries don't understand how there can be insecurity and fear in America which has never been bombed or lived in thralldom. Also, like ourselves, proud nations resent any real or suspected interference in their domestic affairs. Nor can they reconcile our exhortations about the peril with deep cuts in our defense budget. And everywhere people think they recognize the dominant mood of America in what is called "McCarthyism," now a world-wide word. Inquisitions, purges, book-burning, repression, and fear have obscured the bright vision of the land of the free and the home of the brave.

Most of our friends want and need trade, not aid. There is an uneasy feeling that the United States is showing signs of economic nationalism, of a drift toward no trade and no aid. But our friends must trade to live, and not many are going to go hungry, I suspect, to prove to us just how anti-Communist they are.

Just as there are many misconceptions about us, we have many illusions about others, and one of them is that irritations, doubts, and disagreements are symbols of ingratitude or anti-Americanism. Some hostile feeling is inevitable, particularly in occupied areas, but I found surprisingly little. Misgivings about our wisdom, unity, and clear purpose, yes, but also widespread admiration and gratitude for our faith and fortitude, and prayerful hopes for the sobriety, good judgment, and moral vitality of American leadership. At my journey's end Winston Churchill said to me with emotion: "America has saved the world."

Our foreign assistance programs have succeeded, especially in Europe. They have cost us dearly, but I bless the day when President Truman went to the aid of Greece and Turkey and commenced the Marshall Plan. Stronger, more self-reliant, our friends are feeling more independent of Washington, and are talking back to us now, which seems to me a healthy sign.

I think we are winning the cold war step by step. The spread of Communism has been arrested. And while Moscow has military potency, the Communist idea has diminishing appeal, at least in Europe.

But though the imminent danger has receded, this is no time to wobble or lower our guards, not with the hydrogen bomb and no certain evidence that the seductive music from Moscow reflects any basic change in the Soviet design of world dominion. And it is no time for arrogance, petulance, or inflexibility either.

If I am not mistaken, holding our allies together is going to be an ever-harder job which will tax mightily our patience, resolve, and statesmanship. For we can't "go it alone." Unilateralism is but the new face of isolationalism and it spells disaster.

Looking to the future, it seemed to me clearer than ever that the economic, military, and political integration of Europe is the best hope for balancing Soviet power and for enabling the states of Europe to exercise a powerful, positive, and peaceful influence in the modern world. We have already invested years of effort and encouragement and billions of dollars toward this bold and imaginative end.

We must surmount a thicket of difficulty; we must bring the discussion back to the level where once again it challenges the imagination and the hopes of all Europe.

We must now think afresh; and, I believe, in terms of a European system of durable assurances of non-aggression — for Russia, as well as for France, Germany and the rest of us. But whatever commitments we make to our European allies to buttress such assurances we must be prepared to make on a long-term basis. For there is anxiety lest the shaping of our policy may be slipping from the respected hands of President Eisenhower into the hands of men less concerned with strengthening our alliances abroad than with appeasing our isolationists at home.

And at this moment a new fact confers a grim and pressing urgency on the international situation — the hydrogen bomb. For some years efforts toward the limitation and control of armaments have been stalemated. Once more, I think, we should fix our sights high, as we did in 1947, and resume the initiative in re-exploring the possibility of disarmament. The alternative to safety through an effective plan for arms limitation is safety through more massive military spending and more frightening weapons development.

As it is, we seem now to be taking the initiative in unilateral disarmament. We've tried that before, and I am as opposed to unilateralism in our disarmament policy as I am in our foreign policy.

In the past, new initiatives have had little impact on the Kremlin. I do not know that they would have any more today. But conditions have changed. The Soviet threat has aroused the massed military power of the free peoples. Russia learned in Korea that the West has the will to meet force with force. The death of Stalin and revolt in the satellites altered the situation inside the Soviet Union.

In these circumstances we should press forward — not under any foolish illusion that one grand conference would yield security, but rather with realistic recognition that the foundations of stability must be laid, stone by stone, with patient persistence. We owe it to ourselves and our anxious, weary friends to expose Communist intentions if we can; to confer when we can; to reduce tensions and restore hope where we can. The door to the conference room is the door to peace. Let it never be said that America was reluctant to enter.

Under our Constitution, foreign policy is the responsibility of the Executive. The Democrats in Congress have shown that they are eager to help the President carry out an effective foreign policy, restore the leadership of America, and give fresh inspiration and confidence to the great alliance which is indispensable to our security. If it brings the President great personal success we will all rejoice, because the nation and the free world will be the beneficiaries.

And, finally, we must bear in mind that the world's troubles do not all spring from aggressive Communism. Many of them would be here anyway, and always will be. The quest for peace and tranquillity isn't a day's work, it is everlasting. We will have to learn to think of the responsibility of leadership not as a passing annoyance but as a status in an interdependent world that we Americans, Democrats and Republicans alike, must live in, trade in, work in, and pray for, in the accents of mercy, justice, and faith in a power greater than ours or any man's.

We may be approaching the end of the first phase of this era — stopping the spread and influence of Communism. Will strength and perseverance prevail in the second phase and the great threat wither? We haven't the resources to remedy all the ills of man. And we can't remake the world in our image and likeness. But we have erected here in the United States man's happiest home. Respect for our own principles and the courage to live by them, at home and abroad, will be a potent force in the world, and, in the long run, our greatest contribution to a world in which peace is a prayer.

Twenty-three

Call to Greatness

S hortly after his return from his trip, Stevenson discussed, with Cass Canfield and John Fischer of Harper & Brothers, the possibility of his writing a book. He had already agreed to deliver the Godkin lectures at Harvard University. In these lectures he intended to present his general conclusions on the world situation. Canfield and Fischer urged him to write a more lengthy book than the lectures. Walter Johnson, who was present, volunteered to write a first draft, expanding the articles in Look and doing a section describing "How Others See America" and "How America Sees Others." These two sections, it was proposed, would precede his general conclusions.

At one point in the conversation Stevenson rubbed his brow in a characteristic gesture and remarked, "I cannot make up my mind on this. I'm Hamlet, you know." Finally it was left that Johnson would do a first draft of the two sections with the editorial assistance of John Fischer and Miss Marguerite Hoyle of Harper's.

Johnson presented this draft to Stevenson in the spring of 1954 when the latter was recuperating from an operation.[1] He asked, "How long will it take me to turn this manuscript into my own style?" Johnson replied, "Six weeks." He said, "I haven't got six weeks. I leave soon to speak in Alaska for the Democrats and I intend to spend the next few months campaigning to elect Democrats to Congress."

He therefore decided that the Godkin lectures alone would comprise the book. They were delivered at Harvard University in March,

[1] See The Papers of Adlai E. Stevenson, Vol. IV, pp. 349ff.

1954. Harper & Brothers published Call to Greatness *in 1954, and Atheneum issued a paperback edition in 1962.*[2]

Foreword

At Harvard University in March of 1954 I talked to the students and faculty about the troubled world in which we live. My purpose was to sketch the genesis and set in some crude historical perspective the world scene of that time, and then to attempt to defrost a tiny segment of the opaque window through which we see others and others see us — and to do it briefly — having listened to many lectures myself!

The following introductory remarks to the audience at Harvard on the evening of March 17, 1954, describe the circumstances of the writing of these lectures.

"More than a year ago in a light-hearted, careless moment I accepted your invitation to give the Godkin lectures this year. I have been regretting it acutely of late — while trying to prepare something for you and at the same time keep abreast of my other work, my mail, my visitors, the telephone, the newspapers — and the Republicans! Moreover, I fear that I have spent more time wondering nervously why I undertook to do these lectures than in doing them. My conclusion, in case you are interested in the rise and fall of political meteors, is that after the election of 1952, with gracious and intoxicating applause ringing in my ears from many centres of learning, my lecturing at Harvard did not seem as absurd to me as it does now, and as it shortly will to you, I fear.

"Confronted, surrounded indeed, as I am here in Cambridge tonight by more highly educated fellow citizens than I have ever faced, and inadequately prepared, I am uncomfortably reminded of the abiding truth of those classic words that never occurred to Horace: 'Via ovicipitum dura est,' or for the benefit of the engineers among you: 'The way of the egghead is hard.'[3]

"At first, I thought I would talk to you about state government in our scheme of things — a subject which I had a rare opportunity to learn something about as one who was elected Governor of a great state without any prior political experience. It was also a subject entirely consistent with the terms of the gift creating this, the Godkin lectureship: 'On the Essentials of Free Government and the Duties of the Citizen.'

[2] The lectures are reprinted here with the special permission of Cass Canfield, of Harper & Row, and Alfred A. Knopf, Jr., of Atheneum. The text is taken from the Atheneum edition.

[3] For the origin of this epigram, see *The Papers of Adlai E. Stevenson*, Vol. IV, p. 305.

But instead of talking about state government, which I do know something about, I am going to talk about the troubled age we live in, which many of you know a great deal more about.

"So I have compounded the indiscretion of speaking here at all with an imprudent choice of subject. But in spite of the fact that world affairs fill your press, your journals and forums, I concluded to talk about the same thing because it seems to me that the historic drama of the twentieth century in which we are inextricably involved dwarfs in immensity all our other concerns, and places in new perspective 'the essentials of free government and the duties of the citizen.'"

Thereupon, and for three successive evenings, I belaboured the gracious audience as hereafter set forth. Now more than eight years have passed and I am afraid the swift currents of these times may have washed away the significance of many of my words. But I have made no revisions in the text to bring it up to date.

ADLAI E. STEVENSON

New York
1962

Ordeal of the Mid-Century

Great movements and forces, springing from deep wells, have converged at this mid-century point, and I suspect we have barely begun to comprehend what has happened and why. In the foreground is the mortal contest with world communism, which is apparent, if the means of dealing with it are not always apparent. But in the background are the opaque, moving forms and shadows of a world revolution, of which communism is more the scavenger than the inspiration; a world in transition from an age with which we are familiar to an age shrouded in mist. We Americans have to deal with both the foreground and the background of this troubled, anxious age.

It is easy to state our ends, our goals, but it is hard to fit them to our means. Every day, for example, politicians, of which there are plenty, swear eternal devotion to the ends of peace and security. They always remind me of the elder Holmes' apostrophe to a katydid: "Thou say'st an undisputed thing in such a solemn way." And every day statesmen, of which there are few, must struggle with limited means to achieve these unlimited ends, both in fact and in understanding. For the nation's purposes always exceed its means, and it is finding a balance between means and ends that is the heart of foreign policy and that makes it such a speculative, uncertain business.

We thought and hoped we had found it. After all the struggle and sacrifice of two world wars to fence in the mad dogs and preserve peace and security, we thought the reward was calm and the enjoyment of the fruits of our exertions. History seems to record such intervals of confidence, security, dignity as the fitting conclusion of great exertion — the Augustan Age of Rome, the France of the Grand Monarch, and Victoria's England. But whether serenity was the interest on past or current investments, such gentle grace has not been our lot in the twentieth century. Instead the first and second planetary wars have helped to make of this half century the most barbaric interval of the Christian era, branded with the restoration of slavery and torture, the destruction of whole cities and the extermination of tens of millions of our fellow men, far more indeed than in the past thousand years.

History has not stood still for us. Instead it has moved faster than ever before, and with the development of the H-bomb and the ferment of revolution spreading from Asia to Africa, history's dizzy pace shows no signs of moderating.

So now, at mid-century, we talk about the land hunger of the Indian peasant and read of Communists in Guatemala and terrorists in Kenya as though they were all citizens of Illinois. It is the same abroad. For those who can read and the many more who can listen, our words and deeds in Washington are as significant in Delhi, Moscow and Jakarta as they are in Boston, but they are not as well understood.

There was a time, and it was only yesterday, when the United States could and did stand aloof. In the days of our national youth Washington warned against "entangling alliances," John Adams spoke of that "system of neutrality and impartiality" which was to serve us long and well, and Jefferson enumerated among our blessings that we were "kindly separated by nature and a wide ocean from the exterminating havoc of one quarter of the globe." But those days are gone forever. They ended when the First World War began just forty years ago. The youngest Republic is now the oldest, and if life begins at forty, the circumstances of middle age are nonetheless hard and in many ways disappointing.

Once we were weak and stood apart; now we are powerful and permanently involved. Once we were uncommitted and the New World was called upon to redress the balance of the Old; now we are committed and the job of maintaining the balance is at once less glamorous and more importunate than an occasional call to tip the scales. The world at our mid-century is, as someone has said, like a drum — strike it anywhere and it resounds everywhere. The problems of peoples whom we scarcely knew existed, unless we read the *National Geographic,* now resound in our ears and sap our strength, and also our patience. And those distant peoples have suddenly become aware that they too are not masters of their own destiny; that their future, their history, is inseparable from ours. The boundless main is no longer the safeguard of our remove but the measure of our employ.

The world has endured violent and unprecedented dislocations in this past half century of technological, political and social revolution. For us the shock has been severe and in great depth. Conditioned as we have been for a hundred years to the growth, enrichment and development of a continent in security behind our ocean barriers, for most Americans a successful foreign policy would be one which did not involve us in foreign affairs. The ideal is total isolation. But the reality is total and permanent involvement with all mankind.

For many of us our new dimensions are still incomprehensible. For many the idea that we are no longer wholly dependent on ourselves but also on masses of Europeans, Africans, Asians and Latin Americans is not only distasteful but incredible. And for everyone confrontation everywhere by the implacable hostility of the Communist conspiracy is exasperating and frightening. The bright expectations of the moment of victory, of V–E Day and V–J Day, have faded into bitter, bewildering disillusion.

Doubtless this cluster of frustrations and disappointments arising from a complex of causes accounts for the dangerously diverting tendency to adopt the simple explanations of wantonness, stupidity or treachery for our predicament. But of course the roots of our difficulties are not in the actions, wise or unwise, of any individual, nor their explanation in such simplicities. Our difficulties are the price of our blessings — the power and pivotal position of our country between East and West in an interval of profound global convulsion.

The fact is that the West is besieged in body and mind; and burning books, abusing scapegoats, assailing straw men — or even Democrats! — will not lift the siege. We cannot insure the security of the Republic by insuring the insecurity of its intelligence. Nor can we cope with our difficulties successfully in absolutes of right or wrong, black or white, or by exploiting the public appetite for simple solutions and prompt and inexpensive results.

To begin let me review some of the major developments that have contributed to the extraordinary drama of our century and to our infinite difficulties and anxieties, because I believe that there is more real security for Americans in understanding than in H-bombs.

I am not a historian, but I doubt if anyone will dispute the incomparably dramatic qualities of the twentieth century. It began with the horse-and-buggy Victorian security of an orderly world in nice balance. Now at mid-century what do we see? In fifty years, distance has been obliterated by a technological revolution that has brought all mankind cheek to jowl, and that has released the creative and obliterative power of the atom. The Golden Age is outside the door but inside all is anxiety and turmoil. Political revolution has shattered the map and created many new fragments of sovereignty. National independence and democracy have scored spectacular victories and suffered shocking defeats. The center of gravity, the power and influence, in world affairs, after moving slowly west from the Tigris and Euphrates valleys, the Fertile Crescent of the Near East, to Egypt, Greece, Rome, Paris and London, has suddenly split and jumped westward clear across the Atlantic to the Western Hemisphere and Washington, and eastward clear across Europe to Moscow on the doorstep of Asia. Two new colossi, the United States and the Soviet Union, have suddenly emerged. Ideas, on which the West has had an export monopoly for centuries, are now also flowing out of the East and colliding everywhere with our Western ideas.

America's rise to world power in the past fifty years is one of the great realities of this epoch. The final conquest of our rich, protected continent; our sudden change from a debtor to a creditor position; and, finally, our emergence from the war physically unscathed as the mightiest military and industrial power and the richest nation on a shattered globe — all this is familiar. But we should also bear in mind something even more important than these physical facts, namely, that our political institutions have matured around the idea of popular consent as the only valid basis of government and of political power. This heretical notion that government derives its just powers from the consent of the governed, we have come to take for granted as the only tolerable way of organized living.

These historically recent concepts of authority springing from the people, of consent, of republicanism, of democracy and human freedom, have had great vogue in the Western World of late and stirred the imaginations and aspirations of people everywhere. Woodrow Wilson talked of "making the world safe for democracy," and of "self-determination." New democracies sprouted out of the ashes of imperial Germany and Austria-Hungary after the first war, and the revolutionary Western ideas of government by consent, of individual dignity and freedom, have had massive impact throughout the world. But it is also well to recall that even some of our native-born Western brethren, notably the Italians under Mussolini and the Germans under Hitler, lapsed into tyranny and violence to solve their problems. And it is well to recall, too, that the Western ideas which we have so long taken for granted have not been universally accepted and are now brutally beleaguered.

At the same time that the United States was spreading across this continent and Europeans, English, Scotch and Irish were flowing to us and into the new empires beyond the seas, the Muscovite Russians were pressing outward in all directions — to the Arctic, to the Baltic, to the Black Sea and eastward to the Pacific. They even crossed the straits to Alaska and down the coast of California. It was their presence on the then distant Pacific coast which prompted President Monroe to issue his famous doctrine; and it was only a long lifetime ago, 85 years, that a reluctant Congress finally agreed to put up some $7 million to purchase Alaska and get the Russians out of this hemisphere. "Seward's Folly," it was called, and there appears to have been little concern in America at that time for the implications of Russia's rapid growth. (In fact, some historians suggest that the Czar's envoy even had to bribe members of Congress to get the appropriation bill passed. Evidently Russian subversion is nothing new!)

But there were some who foresaw Russia's might and a collision with the United States as each filled out a continent, developed its resources, and rose to intercontinental power. In 1865 Lord Palmerston wrote: "As to Russia, she will in due time become a power almost as great as the old Roman Empire."

That acute observer, Alexis de Tocqueville, the Frenchman, as early as 1835, writes of America and Russia:

> The principal instrument of the former is freedom, of the latter slavery. Their points of departure are different, they follow different paths. Nonetheless, each of them seems intended through some secret design of Providence to hold in its hands the destinies of half the world.

And our own Henry Adams at the turn of the century reflected apprehensively and prophetically lest "the vast force of inertia known as China was to be united with the huge bulk of Russia in a single mass which no amount of new force could henceforth deflect."

So we have not been without warning of a collision with Russian imperialism that has come to many Americans all the same as a rude, incomprehensible shock, and that is not explained but only aggravated by communism.

One aspect of Czarist Russian expansion, coinciding in time with ours, is worth noting because it doubtless contributes to the Russian attitude today as it did yesterday and will tomorrow. In the vast areas encompassed by the Russian state there is a lack of natural defenses. Anxiety about the security of its borders is hardly surprising in view of

Russia's geography and a history of five invasions from the West since 1610, not to mention the defeat in the East in the Russo-Japanese War. While Russia has lived in a state of insecurity for centuries and was invaded and devastated by Hitler's armies as recently as 1941, it is only now with the development of the long-range bomber and the guided missile that the United States is experiencing for the first time the sensation of vulnerability.

Also the Russian state which commenced and grew from a centralized absolutism did not follow the Western pattern and evolve from autocracy to democracy. Instead the Bolshevik conspiracy that quickly smothered the beginnings of government by consent and captured the democratic revolution of 1917 was but a new expression of absolutism. So Russia remains a fortress of ever more inscrutable, centralized and ruthless despotism. And, as George Kennan has pointed out, "the pursuit of unlimited authority domestically" has compelled the Soviet state to develop what Stalin called "the organs of suppression" to a degree hitherto unknown. Soviet control has, therefore, never been submitted to the test of popular consent because no one fears conspiracy as much as a conspirator.

This, again, is the exact antithesis of the American experience. Here the idea of government, power and policy based on consent has evolved through successive stages of expanding public participation in the processes of popular government; the slaves have been emancipated and enfranchised; property qualifications for voting have been all but abolished; the suffrage has been extended to women; and now we are seriously considering reducing the voting age to eighteen and enfranchising the District of Columbia. Meanwhile we devote more and more effort and money to enlarge participation in public affairs and in the electoral process. Nonpartisan "get out the vote" campaigns are commonplace and we have political action and education groups of all kinds.

In Russia, on the contrary, even the tentative, experimental compromises with absolutism after the rebellion of 1905 have been replaced by the Soviets' reliance on force, thought control, compulsory conformity and the one-party system.

A third difference in the evolution and attitude of Russia and America also deserves mention. Starting east of the Alleghenies the United States rapidly consolidated its continental territory by acquiring large areas by purchase — Florida, the Louisiana Purchase and the Gadsden Purchase. We also fought what looked to some like a war of aggression in Mexico. (Lincoln is reputed to have remarked that the Mexican War reminded him of the Illinois farmer who said: "I ain't greedy 'bout land.

I only want what jines mine.") We even experimented with imperialism in Puerto Rico and the Philippines, and promptly salved an uneasy conscience by pouring vast sums into them, not for exploitation but improvement, and then by giving or offering them independence. And it must be added that since the war we have obtained the right to maintain armed forces in West Germany and Japan, traditional threats to Russia, and have built air bases encircling the Soviet Union from Greenland to Saudi Arabia. While these are defensive steps we must expect charges of imperialism from the Communists and not be surprised or indignant if even friendly countries are anxiously mindful that what is defensive can also be offensive.

Yet, aside from the consolidation of the continental land mass at the expense of the aboriginal Indians or by purchase and more recent defensive precautions, the United States has, I think it fair to say, disclosed little expansionist tendency. In fact, both in preaching and practicing the doctrine of self-determination and independence, the sincerity and vigor of our anti-imperialism have been discomforting to some of our colonial allies and embarrassed our relations with our brethren in the democratic faith.

Meanwhile Russia has been consolidating her vast continental land mass, one sixth of the earth's surface, and, in the process, gobbling up all manner of peoples linguistically and ethnically unrelated. For generations Russia has been warring with the Turks and pressing relentlessly but vainly toward the Dardanelles and the Mediterranean. Latterly, however, the Soviet Union has swallowed up her Baltic neighbors Lithuania, Latvia, and Estonia, and recovered territories in the Ukraine and White Russia wrenched away from the Muscovite Czars by the West in the thirteenth and fourteenth centuries. And since the war, of course, the Soviet Union has occupied and subjugated all of Eastern Europe from the Baltic to the Black Sea and recovered rights and real estate in Asia lost in the Russo-Japanese War.

To the great force of this centrifugal outward thrust which is rooted in the distant past of a messianic "Holy Russia" the modern Russians have added a new and potent weapon of imperialism. Communism is the enemy of all antecedent and different systems, and its votaries insist that its destiny is universal triumph over all other systems. Its fundamental philosophical conflict with democracy and the Western humanist tradition is familiar. Repetition would only serve to point out how communism has further accentuated the profound differences between Russia and the United States, politically, geographically, historically and philosophically, differences which long preceded the advent of communism.

So, born in violence and nurtured in fear, despotism and relentless expansion, Russia, already armed with the military weapons of the West, is now armed with this still more dangerous weapon of imperialist aggression. Communism "originated as a product of uneasy Western consciences," to use Dr. Arnold Toynbee's words, and now these Western weapons in Russian hands have been turned against us. Thus at the mid-point of this incredible century the West faces the most serious challenge of modern history.

In addition to the emergence of the United States and the Soviet Union as the major centers of power, with other nations polarized around them or trying to keep out of either magnetic field of attraction — trying to keep neutral — this new and uncomfortable position of the West constitutes one of the dramatic developments of our times, a development it is not easy for us to comprehend because it is so new for us. But it is not new historically. The West was besieged in the early Middle Ages for about 300 years by the Arabs from the south. Then the Mongol flood from the east swept all the way to the Carpathian slopes. Later the Ottoman Turks overran southern Europe and pressed up the Danube valley for three centuries.

But since the Turks fell back from the walls of Vienna in 1683, Europe has not been on the defensive. Indeed for more than 250 years the West has been on the offensive, a posture we have long taken for granted. First came the Crusades, then the voyages of discovery more than 400 years ago, followed by the missionaries, the conquerors, the traders and the colonizers. Europeans seized and occupied the great Western hemisphere, they divided up much of Africa and many Africans were shipped to America as slaves. In the crowded lands of Asia they will remind you that Europeans occupied the vacant areas like Australia and New Zealand; that the Dutch empire in the East Indies stretched across 3,000 miles of Asia; that Britain's Asian empire numbered a quarter of all mankind; and that during the past century everyone punched profitable holes in the soft seaward side of China. Also, as we have seen, Russia has been invaded five times by Western armies since 1610. Moreover, Western aggression was not confined to distant lands and other peoples. Westerners even aggressed against one another. Since the Napoleonic Wars, Germany has attacked its neighbors three times and precipitated much of the misery as well as the power imbalance and dislocation which now afflict the world. In short, it was Western failures that first introduced modern totalitarianism, Fascism and Nazism, to the West; and it was Western jealousy and disunity that opened Europe's door to the Soviet Union for the first time.

From even such a quick review of Western expansion and aggression we should not be surprised and hurt that most of the non-Western majority of the world finds the West guilty of aggression as charged in the Communist indictment, or that on history's long record the West may look as untrustworthy to the Russians as they do to us. And we must likewise expect that some sensitive Asians will view our outrage over Communist aggressions as a little hypocritical. Nor should it be hard for us to understand why so much of the illiterate population of Indo-China has found it so hard to believe that their long-time colonial masters, the French, are fighting Indo-Chinese for Indo-China's independence.

But the chapter of Western offense and ascendancy ended abruptly with the last war at the mid-century point and the community of Western nations and Western ideas, wherever they have taken root, is now beset more perilously than it ever was before by Arabs, Mongols or Turks — more perilously beset because of the technological revolution of this century and because of the new ideological weapon of communism, which we know is effectively used to exploit grievance, discontent, poverty, nationalism and racism everywhere, and especially among the uncommitted or neutral peoples whose allegiance could tip the scales of power decisively.

The technological revolution, another phenomenon of this strange era, has made our geographies obsolete and also many of our concepts of power and warfare. As the Western United States opened up a hundred years ago, county seats were located roughly in the center of the county so as to be no more than a day's journey by horse from the county limits. Now in the air age the whole United States is no larger than a county fifty years ago or indeed, no larger than a Greek state 500 years before Christ. You can get to Washington in a day's journey from anywhere. Oceans and continents have shriveled, and even wars, as in Korea, are conducted thousands of miles from the combatants' home bases. We are all standing shoulder to shoulder — with a hydrogen bomb ticking in our pockets.

In the past we have seen the small Greek city-states submerged in the Roman Empire, the medieval city-states enveloped by the European nation-states, and the nation-states grow larger and stronger under the whip of technological development. Where political unity and hence effective power have lagged behind the procession, the result has usually been subjugation and disaster for the laggards. During the period of Western ascendancy and rapid technological development from horse to steam, to electricity and internal combustion, and all the related military developments, we have seen the number of separate sovereignties shrink and the power bases in the world get fewer and bigger. The

German principalities united; Austria-Hungary gathered separate entities under a single scepter; Italy united, tardily. Even today the sun never sets on Britain's Commonwealth and overseas empire. Preserving a balance between these larger, fewer units of power has been the principal function of diplomacy since Napoleon.

Now, with the destruction of the two wars, the collapse of empire, and the development of jet propulsion and the new weapons, the great nations of Western Europe have shrunk in stature, and power, real and relative, has further concentrated in the superstates of Russia and the United States. But at the same time a large number of separate independent states have emerged from the ashes of empire, mostly in Asia, where the new rulers of China, the Eastern partner of the new Moscow-Peiping axis, are probably dreaming the old dreams of empire like their Soviet colleagues.

Let us look for a moment at this sudden redistribution of sovereignty which is a further remarkable development of the twentieth century and which has nothing to do with communism. In a generation more than 40 million Egyptians and Arabs, some six states, have attained independence. In a few years 570 million Indians, Pakistanis, Ceylonese, Burmese, Indonesians, Israelis, Filipinos and South Koreans, eight more nations, have attained their sovereignty and stepped onto the world's stage. Twenty-five million more Vietnamese, Laotians and Cambodians are in transition. In all some seventeen sovereignties, more than 635 million people, are free and independent of foreign masters or are on the way. And now all Africa is restive in the twilight of colonialism and the dawn of universal independence. Freedom, in short, has served to divide its followers and multiplied the parties, flags, tariffs, currencies, armies, ambitions and voices that bedevil the world.

In Eastern Europe the process has been reversed. Ten states from the Baltic to the Black Sea — about 85 million people — have lost their independence and been enveloped by force in the Soviet power complex. And China, too, the largest country and culture of all, has gone Communist and has spread the siege of the new imperialism to the borders of all Asia. To the more than 8½ million square miles and 200 million inhabitants of the Soviet Union, 4 million square miles of China and 450 million Chinese have been added to the Communist domain. And we could also add Tibet and North Korea to fill out the enormous land base of Communist power that now extends from central Europe to southeast Asia, from Prague to Canton, from the Baltic Sea to the South China Sea.

On balance, therefore, there has been both an unparalleled growth and an unparalleled decline of national freedom in this century. But what of individual freedom and democratic government? What reinforcements or losses have all this new freedom and the transformed map brought to the beleaguered West's concept of popular consent as man's only tolerable way of life?

In Europe the gains have been substantial. Our adversaries in the last war, Italy and Western Germany, have repudiated their Fascist and Nazi antidemocratic heresies. Greece, formerly a dictatorship, is democratic again, and the only vestiges of the authoritarianism of the 1930's are Spain, Portugal and Yugoslavia. In the Near East, Israel is a genuine and vital democracy, and the triumph of the democratic constitutional spirit in Turkey is one of the miracles of our age. Elsewhere in the Near East democratic mechanisms command universal lip service and increasing genuine experimentation. In Latin America the struggle goes on, even if the progress is uneven. While only a few of the countries can be called truly democratic, their institutions and the hopes of their people reflect democratic aspirations.

But in Asia the advance in the direction of popular government is spectacular in fact and the more so because there was so little of democratic tradition. India, Pakistan and Ceylon — almost 450 million people — have joined the democratic ranks in the last few years. Burma, another former British domain, after many rebellions and troubles, is also on the way to greater stability and democratic government. Colonialism and the exploitation of subject peoples have always been repugnant to Americans and they are now. But while British imperialism has many sins on its conscience, we should not deprecate its many virtues, one of which is British education in the democratic tradition, or its many achievements, one of which is the successful preparation of colonial peoples for democratic self-government.

In addition to these former British areas, the Philippines is a going democratic concern in which the government changed leadership last year in a peaceful and honest election. Indonesia, with little preparation for self-government and many difficulties, also has hopes of building on a democratic foundation. And in Japan the old authoritarian system has given way to something still in transition but resembling much more a modern constitutional democracy.

If a box score was possible we might balance the loss of the 470 millions of China and North Korea with the addition of the 635 million to democracy's ranks among the Asian countries I have mentioned. And if our definition of "democracy" was even more elastic we might add another 58 million in South Korea, Formosa and Indo-China, raising our total of reinforcements to almost 700 million.

But numbers are misleading and the really important question is whether these nations, new or old, can preserve their newly-won political independence. There will be no chance for government by consent, for democracy and individual freedom, if the fragile newcomers or enfeebled older members of the family of independent nations fall victim by force or guile to the siege of the new Communist imperialism. More and weaker nations do not make for greater strength and resistance. If the lesson of history is that only the strong can be free and the weak must unite or perish, then it is well to remember, as I have said, that the postwar development is disunity, fragmentation of the map and the subdivision of power. Blood brothers have even divided the Indian continent into a Hindu India and a Moslem Pakistan to the misfortune of both. And both have within them dangerous seeds of further subdivision.

I have tried to suggest some of the dramatic changes of this century that lie behind and beneath the present: the sudden rise to world power of the United States and the Soviet Union from totally different origins, national experiences and basic principles; the technological and political revolutions that have shrunk the world and multiplied the number of states that have a voice in our destiny; and the defensive posture of the West for the first time in 250 years.

We may have been slow to appreciate these massive changes of the twentieth century and their full impact may yet be imperfectly perceived. But the events immediately following the last war are fresh and clear. In China, with the defeat of Japan, Mao Tse-tung exploited the wartime confusion and weakness and the inadequacy of Chiang Kai-shek's government and the Kuomintang party; the military initiative quickly passed to the Communist peasant army, and in a few short years the vastly larger Nationalist forces melted like the snows and all China was a Communist state. The re-creation of China as a great power has come to pass after more than a century of impotence, but under quite different management than we intended.

In Europe the Russian armies advanced on the heels of the retreating Germans into Eastern Europe, from the Baltic to the Black Sea, and settled down to stay, yes, and to attempt to press on to the Eastern Mediterranean and the Czars' long-time goal. Western Europe and Britain were enfeebled, exhausted and impoverished by the gigantic exertion of two wars in rapid succession. The Communists, who had been so active in the resistance movements in the occupied areas, were well organized, aggressive and ready. They moved quickly into positions of influence and power in the countries that had been occupied by the Nazis. We forget that the Vice Premier of liberated France in 1947 was a Communist.[4]

And here in the United States, comforted by our assumed monopoly of atomic weapons and reassured by excessive reliance on the infant United Nations, we quickly demobilized and reverted to the ways of peace and of our past. But the illusion of security and normalcy was short-lived. And we were soon confronted with the fact that our problems had not been resolved by the defeat of Germany and Japan. Instead new vacuums of power had created new difficulties. Russia's cynical violation of its agreements in Eastern Europe and its pressure on Greece and Turkey posed new threats to security. The concept of great power harmony underlying the United Nations proved an illusion. In short, it became apparent that Russian power could no longer be balanced, or Russian expansion contained, without the active participation and leadership of the United States. There was no longer anyone to do the job for us.

Sixty years ago Lord Bryce wrote of America:

> Safe from attack, safe even from menace, she hears from afar the warring cries of European nations and faiths. For the present at least — it may not always be so — America sails upon a summer sea.

Well, it was no longer so.

Never before, I dare say, have a government and a people had to learn so much so quickly. That we did face the realities decisively and in time may have changed the course of history.

The year 1846 was one of decision for the United States — the decision to fill out its continental position and thereby to become a great power in the world.

The year 1947 was another year of decision for the United States — the decision to shoulder the burdens of a great power in the world.

I suppose the historians will pay increasing attention to 1947. In that year, after two years of futile peace negotiations with the Russians, General George Marshall, as our new Secretary of State, faced the fact that negotiation without power was futile and that the United States and its allies were almost powerless. Since the war the United States Army in Europe had dropped from 3,500,000 to two divisions with no more than six ready battalions in reserve at home. The British and the French, with large overseas commitments, were similarly enfeebled,

---

[4] Maurice Thorez.

while the Russians had forty combat divisions in Europe and a hundred in reserve. Moreover, the economic deterioration was, if anything, worse. Even food was desperately short. Bread rations in France and Italy fell to half a pound a day that autumn.

Confronted with implacable malice, the menacing preponderance of Soviet strength, and the futility of further negotiation from manifest weakness, the warborn alliance with the USSR ended in 1947, and the East and the West divided in open recognition of a state of enmity that still persists. And it was in that year that the United States took the bold initiative with a series of steps designed to save Greece and Turkey and, by restoring economic health and political stability to Europe, to enable the allies to negotiate from strength instead of weakness. The steps initiated in 1947 are within the fresh memory of all of us:

Aid to Greece and Turkey, sorely beset by Soviet threats and Communist guerrillas.

Announcement by President Truman of the policy of assistance to peoples threatened internally or externally and prepared to resist.

The Marshall proposal to arrest the economic anemia and vulnerability and restore the health and strength of Western Europe.

The first steps toward the re-establishment of Germany as an asset instead of a burden on the defensive strength of the West.

The Inter-American Treaty of Reciprocal Assistance, our first permanent alliance, which foreshadowed the North Atlantic Treaty and similar alliances in the Pacific.

(And it was also back in 1947 that the loyalty review system in Federal employment was instituted in response to emerging evidence of subversion.)

These first positive steps to organize and sustain resistance to the spread of communism have been rapidly followed by many others: our successful resistance to the Berlin blockade, the establishment of the Federal Republic of Germany, the defense mobilization, the world-wide economic and military assistance programs, the North Atlantic Treaty Organization, the European Defense Community proposal, the system of Pacific treaties, the bloody war in Korea, aid to Indo-China, and so forth. Together they constitute a mighty and global effort to contain aggression, redress the balance of power, counter Communist penetration, and build the free world's moral, economic and military vitality to the end that the weak and strong can be independent; can live in peace and each work out its own way of life.

How are we getting along with this appalling undertaking? Out of a job — thanks to the voters — I went to see for myself. Starting from San Francisco in March, 1953, with four companions I traveled for six months around the edges of the Communist empire through Asia, the Middle East and Western Europe. I talked to the Emperor of Japan, the Queen of England, the Pope and to all the kings, presidents and prime ministers along my route. And I also talked to countless diplomats, politicians, journalists, students, soldiers, peasants, porters, and multitudes of new and warmhearted friends. Everywhere I encountered an eagerness to talk and a candor of expression among officials that touched and astonished me — and has heavily taxed my discretion. And often the hospitality made me wonder if my hosts were confused and thought I had been elected President in 1952!

It was a sobering experience. For it is more than a privilege; it is a responsibility to be an American in this changing world. It isn't one world; it is more like three worlds — the Communist world, the allied world and the uncommitted world. By the Communist rulers we are feared and hated; feared possibly more than we fear them; hated because we have frustrated their designs, and hated as only totalitarian orthodoxy hates defiant nonconformity. The allied world looks to us for aid, understanding and sober leadership in building the structure of defense, economic order and well-being, and strengthening the grand coalition, on which the security of all of us depends. The uncommitted world, nervous, argumentative, insecure, preoccupied with difficulties and grievances, wants to remain aloof but looks to us, furtively and suspiciously perhaps, for understanding and friendship.

I came back exhilarated by the successes since the United States in 1947 faced the realities of a sick, tottering world and the Soviet Union's aggressive purposes. The Eastern Mediterranean has been saved. Prostrate Europe has risen from its sick bed and its defenses have been restored. Violent Communist insurrections have failed in the Philippines, Indonesia, Burma and Malaya. The Republic of Korea has been successfully defended. For the first time in history collective security has been made to work in a savage test. The newly independent states are still intact, and since the *coup d'état* in Czechoslovakia, the Soviet Union has not added an inch of territory to its domain.

But I also came back oppressed with the infinity of troubles, large and small, which afflict the world. In most of them the United States is concerned, be it the price of rubber, which is so vital to Indonesia's economy; or the Anglo-Egyptian dispute over the Suez base, which is so vital to Middle East defense; or the interminable war in the steaming rice paddies of Indo-China, which is a gate to all Southeast Asia; or neutralism in India, which is the prime Communist target; or world trade, which is obviously indispensable to the workshop nations like

Japan, Germany and Britain, and less obviously, but hardly less indispensable, to the producers of raw materials.

One could go on and on reciting the headaches that plague every continent, every corner and every country of the globe — and always the United States. In the state of Travancore-Cochin on the Malabar coast of India, which has the highest percentage of literacy, the highest percentage of Christians and the highest percentage of Communists in all India, the worried leaders told me that owing to the collapse of the market for coco mats in the United States unemployment in that local industry had increased Communist sympathy. In the Khyber Pass the tribal chieftains solemnly insisted that the United States must see that justice was done to Pakistan in Kashmir. In Cyprus I was deluged with pleas for United States support for union with Greece. And so it went right around the world.

Just being an American nowadays is not always comfortable. In the sensitive new areas some will denounce American aid as imperialism; but if it is not forthcoming we are denounced for indifference or discrimination. And sometimes if we stand correctly aloof from the local political scene we are accused of supporting reaction and the status quo. But if we don't keep our hands off and indicate some preference for policies or politicians then we are denounced for interfering. We are damned if we do and damned if we don't — at least now and then.

And there is much misunderstanding and many misconceptions about us, just as one of our major hazards is the strange and distorted pictures we have of others. The neutrals don't fully understand our impatience with neutrality in view of our own long history of neutrality and non-involvement. Nor do all our friends, who share our view about communism, share our views about Communists. I recall the anti-Communist Catholic youth delegation that called on me in France and left a friend outside in their car because he was a Communist. And peoples who have lived for centuries in perpetual insecurity among predatory neighbors don't understand how there can be such insecurity and fear in America, which has never even been bombed, let alone occupied by an enemy. "McCarthyism," conformity and demagoguery are equated with the Communist and Fascist methods they know and despise. And, of course, there are misconceptions about our militarism, materialism and bottomless wealth; and suspicion that we are less concerned with helping others than helping ourselves. In some quarters there is a feeling that the United States is impulsive, reckless and unreliable, that we are embittered and divided at home, and that domestic political influences may carry more weight in our decisions than America's partners do.

In many places there is little understanding of the burden of suffering and expense Americans have borne in recent years in the common cause, or of the social reforms in this country during the past twenty years. Too often the impression is of a rich, reactionary unreconstructed nineteenth century country. Ignorance, propaganda and our own behavior discolor and distort the vision of America.

The list of misconceptions, diligently cultivated by Communist propaganda and often confirmed by our loud, arrogant voices, is long. While the misunderstanding is often irritating it is not incomprehensible, and on the whole it is more than balanced by admiration and gratitude for our faith and fortitude and for our persistence in a monumental effort embracing everything from money, men and machines for defense to malaria control and education of large numbers of students. Here again the illustrations of an awareness of the sincerity of our motives and the magnitude of the effort could be multiplied.

But enough of these familiar facts of mass information and misinformation about one another in this era of mass communication. I came back persuaded that America would stand or fall not just by the tangibles, but by the intangibles of American power and character. And one of them is the effect of words, utterances, language on ourselves and on others.

As Americans we are accustomed to political bad manners and billingsgate. After a century and a half we have developed some immunity to vilification, abuse and misrepresentation in our domestic public dialogue. If not an ornament to the American tradition it is at least a part of it, and we have learned somehow to give it a rough evaluation and get along surprisingly well in spite of deceit, demagoguery and verbal violence. While rough-and-tumble American political manners have been an interesting curiosity to foreigners for generations, they have had little effect on the rest of the world.

But now the situation has changed with the change in America's position in the world. Everyone is listening attentively to what we say but without even our imperfect capacity to evaluate its significance. The voice of America is not just the government radio but the angry words, defiant proclamations and oratorical attitudes of American politicians and leaders. They may be talking to the folks back home for votes or effect, but what they say echoes and re-echoes around the world. And I can personally testify that what they say is often greeted in deadly seriousness as a reflection of America.

The opinions of America are formed from the composite of the voices of America, official and unofficial, true and false. Listening to the hot words, the wild accusations, the bad history, the policy contradictions and plain nonsense on our daily menu dished up for domestic consumption, it is small wonder that the image of America is not always distinct or that the bright vision of the land of the free and the home of the brave is sometimes obscure. We do not realize what injury heedless words and bad manners can do us abroad when the world is all on the same wave length and everyone is listening. To see ourselves as others see us, we must hear ourselves as others hear us. For, in the words of the Apostle: "if the trumpet give an uncertain sound, who shall prepare himself to the battle?"

But there is still another danger in loud, loose tongues. We not only confuse and mislead foreigners but we can mislead and deceive ourselves; we can become the victims of our own propaganda, especially in times of tension and impatience. When passions run high they can also run away. I recall the engaging remark of the French revolutionary who ran to the window muttering: "The mob is in the street. I must see which way they are going, for I am their leader."

Unaccustomed as we are to moderate speech, our petulance, temper or partisanship can have its effect on us as well as the foreigner, especially when it is cloaked in the garments of righteousness and impatience with any solutions that do not promise quick returns. We must be on our guard against the danger to our own people, as well as to our friends, of confusing pronouncements with reality and proclamations with policy. For these are ingredients of extremist opinion. And in these days when moderation and reason are so often equated with appeasement or even disloyalty, we must be careful lest unreason and extremism not only frighten and alienate our friends and fan the flames of neutralism in the world but also mislead the American people.

Looking back to the clamor about the unpopular Jay Treaty in 1795 and John Adams' courageous resistance of the loud demands for war with France a few years later, our history reveals many instances where aroused and articulate public opinion has made wise executive policy more difficult. There is no doubt, for example, that the Kellogg-Briand Pact, now a monument to illusion, was a creation of the force of unrealistic opinion rather than official judgment. And there is little doubt that hostile public opinion delayed repeal of the Neutrality Act and other desirable steps between the outbreak of the last war in 1939 and the attack on Pearl Harbor in 1941.

More recently Korea may have some value as an illustration of what I mean. We intervened there not to unite Korea by force but to resist the Communist attempt to unite Korea by force. When in the fall of

1951 we had repelled the invasion and driven the crumbling North Korean army beyond the 38th parallel, the Indian government warned us of the danger of further advances. A few wise counselors in our own government also anticipated the Chinese reaction if we approached the Yalu River. China's intervention and two years of war may well have been the price for rejecting that advice. How much did the pressure of vocal, articulate public opinion influence the decision? I don't know. But I do know that in our system public opinion is our sovereign; its temperance or caprice is the Republic's shield or hazard. It is easier to light fires than to extinguish them, and passion and extremism are dangerous leaders.

If public opinion is our sovereign in this people's government, then the enlightenment and maturity of our public opinion about this troubled world pose vast difficulties for us in competition with dictators uninhibited by the public's myriad voices, wise and foolish, thoughtful and heedless.

The culmination of the ordeal of the twentieth century, then, is a world in which power has concentrated more closely and, conversely, the weakness of disunion has been spread more widely by nationalism and independence. And this world is sharply divided. It has fallen to America's lot to organize and lead that portion of the world which adheres to the principle of consent in the ordering of human affairs against its first attack in several hundred years. It is an assignment we undertook not by choice but by necessity and without prior experience. The burden is without historical parallel and so is the danger, and so is our response. The first phase is ending. The outward thrust of aggression in Europe has been arrested. And now we shall have to address ourselves to Asia, to perpetual siege and to the unending tasks of greatness. For the quest for peace and security is not a day's or a decade's work. For us it may be everlasting.

Edmund Burke said that "We can never walk surely but by being sensible of our blindness." As we enter the second half of this century of crisis, the next but probably not the last era of decision between consent and compulsion, a consciousness of the limits of our wisdom is our best companion because it is the root of responsibility. And freedom is the reward of responsibility. We will have to learn to think of our responsibilities not as a passing annoyance but as a status in an interdependent world that we Americans must live in, work in and pray for in the accents of humility and faith in a power greater than ours, our enemies' or any man's.

Perpetual Peril

I have attempted to uncover some of the roots and origins of the difficulties and perils of this troubled age, and some of the steps that have been taken to set things right. We have looked backward a bit to the near and distant past. Now let us look for a moment at the fresher events of yesterday and today; let us take a little inventory of the present.

The tense scene at mid-century seems to me to be dominated by two immense facts. The first is the revolution of rising expectations and the new political independence of masses of awakening peoples. From West Africa to Indonesia millions of human beings are now emerging from foreign domination and fiercely demanding relief from hunger, pestilence and oppression. The second is the constant overhanging threat of aggressive communism to national independence and to our concepts of political freedom and individualism which we have taken for granted for so long.

Our attention in America and the attention of the Western World has been largely focused on the second of these facts — the Communist challenge and, more narrowly, on Russia. But the attention of the peoples in revolution has not. Preoccupied with their own ferment and anti-Western revolutionary tradition, they have not measured the Communist threat to their tender independence in our dimensions of time and magnitude.

The postwar behavior of the Soviet Union has outraged and angered us in the West — in part, I suppose, because of the illusory hopes built up during the warborn alliance and because of our own idealistic and moralistic dogmas of international behavior. Nations — especially recent allies — are supposed to leave one another alone, to live and let live. It was in defense of this simple, sensible and moral principle of international conduct that, in association with Russia, we administered a terrible licking to Germany and Japan. Yet to our shocked surprise, almost before we had ceased to fight and denounce our common enemies, the Nazis and the "Japs," the treacherous Russian bear, our comrade in arms, rose up to bite the hand that fed it, to prey upon the enfeebled victims of war, to try to subjugate friend and foe alike by a noxious design of conquest through coercion or subversion.

Perhaps we had no right to be surprised. Some of the farthest-seeing men who had studied the Russians at close hand — men like George Kennan and Averell Harriman — had cautioned us against these illusions. Others among us raised warning flags very early. I, myself, if I may insert an immodest self-quotation, said in March of 1946 to an audience in Chicago that "We must forsake any hope that [the Soviet Union] is going to lie still and lick her awful wounds. She's not. . . . She intends to advance her aims, many of them objectives of the Czars, to the utmost." Nevertheless, justified or not, surprised we were, and our surprise became outrage, horror, and fear, as the Kremlin's dread design of world dominion became more naked and more grasping, as blow after blow of the iron fist smashed at liberty in Europe, in the Middle East, in Asia.

Today there can be no more surprises about the nature of Communist imperialism, about its cynical ambitions, about its use of every means from military aggression to Trojan horse tactics of fifth columns and internal subversion in every country in the world. But today, it seems to me, we are overinclined to let outrage and fear — bad masters — influence our response to events consistently conforming with this ruthless, implacable pattern; and we have certainly let the exploiters of fear and moral indignation reach dangerous heights of public influence in our country.

Today, furthermore, we have become so fascinated by the evil conspiracy directed from Moscow that we tend to overlook the massive problems that stare down on us elsewhere. By no means all of our troubles are due to communism or Russia, and we must take care not to oversimplify or underestimate the complexity and dimensions of our responsibility by attributing all the difficulties of the present to communism and to failure to solve the Communist threat. We were overborne and almost drowned by the torrent of wishful thinking after the war — what D. W. Brogan has termed "the illusion of American omnipotence." We have not yet recovered our sanity or balance from the shock of dismay that China didn't turn out as we expected, that friends became enemies and enemies friends, and that our power and influence to arrange things according to our own liking turned out to be limited. There may be further surprises and disappointments, and they are the more likely if we do not understand the limits of our own strength and if our preoccupation with the Communist menace is too exclusive. For, after all, communism is not the only cause even of the Russian problem. On the record of history, an industrialized Russia would very likely be expansionist if Czars instead of commissars sat in the Kremlin; and as for Asia and Africa, inexorable changes would be taking place there if Marx's *Kapital* was a forgotten book in the dusty recesses of our libraries.

The fact is that even if Russia did not exist, even if Karl Marx had never been born and if there were no Communist parties or sympathizers, a multitude of problems would still bedevil the world. I shall mention only some of them. In Europe, thanks to American assistance, economic recovery from the war has been spectacular; but, now that economic aid is ending, Europeans are anxiously seeking the expanding foreign trade that must support them in the future. In the Near East, insurgent nationalism has resulted in the eviction of the British from Iran, the dispute with Egypt over the great military base that stretches for 100 miles along the Suez Canal, and the cold bitterness of Arab-Israel relations that seem no better five years after the armistice in their shooting war. In Asia, Japan has lost its empire, its sources of raw materials and also many of its nearby markets owing in part to bitter memories of wartime occupation as well as the passion for economic self-sufficiency in formerly dependent areas. In Malaya, fighting the Communist terrorists in the jungles is not Britain's only task. There is also the riddle of how to prepare the country for independence and self-government when there are as many Chinese as Malays. Indonesia is demanding Irian, the western portion of New Guinea; India and Pakistan after five years have not yet agreed on even the method of settlement of the long standing and dangerous dispute about the future allegiance of the great province of Kashmir.

And looming over all these immediate points of friction and danger is the massive fact of the suddenly unchained aspirations of hundreds of millions of people in the Near East, Asia and Africa. Independence and self-government have come to most of these people in a recent blinding rush. They have not yet solved the tremendous problems of poverty, illiteracy, administrative inexperience, economic underdevelopment, political instability and decaying feudalism. Restless millions live barely above the starvation line, and, fast as they increase their output of food, their populations are growing faster with the spectacular success of disease control and public health programs.

Is it any wonder that much of the non-Communist world is more preoccupied with its own affairs than with the menace of international communism? Is it any wonder that, conscious as its leaders are of Soviet expansion in Europe and the Communist conquest of China, they are also mindful of their hard-won independence from their former colonial masters and that large fragments of the world are still under the domination of what they regard as Western imperialism?

We will be hearing about nationalism, a Western product, for a long time to come and in more places than Indo-China. The explosive forces of nationalism, anticolonialism and independence, which we in America, the first modern product of anticolonial revolution, should understand very well, were not invented by communism. But communism will aggravate them, and exploit them, and gain by them, whenever and wherever it can. And we in the United States will have to learn to expect such exploitation of natural forces to which slogans like "massive retaliation" are no answer and nuclear intimidation no solution.

In short the Western message of independence has reverberated around the world — with results sometimes disconcerting to us of the West. And so has the message of Western technology — the message of a technology which has shattered time and distance and released sources of energy beyond our comprehension — the message which means unmistakably that poverty, hunger, disease and servitude are not the immutable destiny of the long-suffering two-thirds of the human race who are largely colored. This revolution of rising expectations, this awareness that there can be relief and improvement, this insistence that science and engineering must have the answers, and quickly, is a product not of communism but of our own industrial revolution and material progress.

In the underdeveloped areas the people know about the great contrast in productivity between their non-industrialized nations and the Western nations, especially the fabulous United States. They are mostly illiterate, they read no newspapers, they hear no radios, but the word has traveled, they have heard, they know. And they too want to industrialize, to use their raw materials for their own enjoyment, and to create jobs for the many unemployed or underemployed in their overcrowded, static, agrarian societies. They want to change a world which has not changed for centuries; and they want to make up for lost time.

Is it any wonder that from their standpoint, and to some of them, the end looks more important than the means? Is it any wonder that they are impressed by Russia's dramatic — and well-dramatized — achievements in industrialization and by the highly colored stories that are coming out of China? Can they win Operation Bootstrap by democratic, voluntary methods, or is force the only answer? This is the underlying issue in a large area of the world. It is the most important issue of our time and it is not an easy issue to solve, even in more fortunate regions, let alone in the heat, the teeming pressures and the urgency of an Asian capital. And, needless to say, it is not an issue that will be resolved merely by anti-Communist pronouncements or by nervous exclusive emphasis on military defense.

For the Communist conspiracy is eagerly trying to cash in on all these tensions and troubles, be it the poverty of a factory worker in Turin, anticolonialism in North Africa, political instability in the Middle East, a peasant's credulity in Indo-China or his land hunger in Iran. Communism everywhere seeks to ally itself with this vast revolution as its friend and convert it to its ends. And this is a threat at least as great as the long, red shadow of the military might of the Soviet Union with which we are more familiar.

These, then, are the two elements in our present situation which pose our greatest problems — the menace of Communist aggression in all its forms, and the revolution of rising expectations. And let it be said to our credit that by and large our national policies these last years have been well directed toward meeting exactly these problems. The Marshall Plan and the Point Four program, the military assistance measures and the battle for Korea, these great endeavors of our foreign policy have been attempts to grapple with the real, the actual problems before us.

And now what is our position? After seven years of ceaseless effort, enormous expenditures, burdensome taxes and the loss of many lives, where are we?

I think it can be said, briefly and soberly, that we have survived the major crisis, that an unsteady equilibrium has been established in Europe and, if Indo-China is saved, in Asia as well, but that no settlement or security is in sight and we are now settling down for a long endurance contest. If such an estimate of the present situation is cold comfort, I think we Americans can find great satisfaction in reflecting on what the situation might be had we not made and sustained this great exertion.

And failure would have been so easy. It is little short of a miracle of politics and diplomacy that we have successfully resolved the constant dilemma between the requirements — in military effort, money, political maturity and fortitude — that flow from being the only power strong enough to organize and lead a great coalition of nations, and the costs — economic, political and psychological — of meeting those requirements. This achievement has exacted its price, not only in money and resources, but in interior strain and spiritual anxiety. Yet the fact that it has been sustained so long is heartening evidence, it seems to me, of democracy's will to survive — above all, of democracy's ability to compete with totalitarianism, not just in war but in the more complex tasks of cold war, when we must rely on co-operation and persuasion where the enemy can employ coercion and command.

We have come a long way, but I suspect we also have a longer way to go. Through the conquest of China, communism is striking for dominance in the Far East. There is a truce but no peace in sight in Korea; Communist armies are attacking harder and harder in Indo-China, and Communist parties are fishing in all the troubled waters of Asia. Europe is divided, and the Berlin Conference left no doubt that

Russia intends to maintain its military and political line in Europe, and will exploit every crack in Western unity. It is a reasonable assumption that the Geneva Conference will reveal the same objectives in Asia. In Latin America Communist pressure has been evident in British Guiana and in Guatemala near the Panama Canal. Anticolonialism in Africa is a fertile field for Communist agitation for change. There are even some Communists in North America who seem to command a disproportionate amount of our attention.

In contrast to our behavior after the First World War the United States has made the decision that it cannot retreat into isolation and let the rest of the world slip under the Iron Curtain bit by bit, drawing the cord of strangulation around our own necks tighter and tighter as it goes. So the United States, as the only power great enough to organize and lead the resistance, must be committed to the struggle as long as it lasts. Most of the great sieges of history have lasted a long while. The Greeks and Romans spread their dominion and culture across the known world for almost a thousand years, and the Greek language of the New Testament was understood from the Malabar coast of India to Marseilles. Then Islam, armed with a creed and a passion for reform, rose from the Arabian desert and for almost another thousand years gradually spread out and around the heartland of Christian Europe all the way to the plains of India on the East and to the Atlantic on the West. Even to this day the Moslem religion is dominant in distant Indonesia and deep into Africa and the same written Arabic can be read by Moslems from Morocco to Iran. The Western expansion which followed, with its conquest of the seas and its encirclement of Islam, has been of much shorter duration. And now in our time its course has been reversed, not alone by external enemies, but also by our own internal disunion and by our own Western contributions to world revolution through nationalism and technology.

It would be foolish to suggest that the present expansion of communism is another great historical movement with the durable qualities of its predecessors. On the contrary, it has no basic moral, spiritual or cultural content. Marxian materialism is in fact a cruel denial of humanity's hunger of the heart and spirit; the police state is a brutal rejection of man's inherent love of freedom; and the spread of the Communist discipline is a new and more terrible form of imperialism, deadly to the spirit of national independence. Communism thus runs against the grain of humanity and the aspirations of civilized society, and these are formidable obstacles to its ultimate triumph. Yet, armed with a fanatical faith and a program of dogmatic reform in a time of tension and change, already disposing of vast armies and master of a third of the world, forever seeking new strength and new support in the troubled awakening of the great new continents, it is a force we can underestimate only at the risk of our own destruction.

In short, we live in a time of perpetual peril, and the end is not in sight. I won't attempt to guess whether this is a thirty-year war or a hundred-year war. Nor would it be profitable to speculate on how it will eventually turn out. America will have much to do with that. But one thing is certain: it cannot turn out well if the coalition of Western democracies disintegrates either militarily or ideologically. For there are two struggles — the power struggle and the ideological struggle. Essential to both is the steadfast solidarity of the coalition cemented by the United States in the postwar emergency.

Let us consider for a moment the evolution of the power aspects of the struggle. During the war we all hoped that peace might be assured by a harmony of great power interests growing out of wartime co-operation against the Axis and the need for postwar co-operation in reconstructing the ravaged world. This was the central concept of the Security Council of the United Nations. Acting on our hopes and public pressures, we quickly demobilized. In the presidential campaign of 1944, before the war was even over, the Republican candidate called for the release and return of our forces "at the earliest practical moment after victory." And General Eisenhower later assured us that demobilization had not been too fast and that there was no reason to anticipate any conflict of interest with the Soviet Union — which reminds me with a shudder of Cardinal Richelieu's words: "Give me six sentences written by the most innocent of men and I will hang him with them."

At all events, the illusion of peace through harmony crumbled with the realization that Soviet ambitions were unlimited. So in the fateful year of 1947, as we have seen, we turned to another concept — peace through power.

It was the belief of some that the organization and development of the overwhelming economic and military potential of the non-Communist world, added to our atomic monopoly, would produce an opportunity to negotiate peace through a preponderance of power. There followed a series of pacts, arrangements and programs so extensive that it may now be said that the sun never sets on an American commitment.

But, if the effort was to achieve a clear preponderance of power, it was doomed almost as it began. When the North Atlantic Treaty was signed in April, 1949, the Kremlin was already preparing its first atomic test; and, incidentally, communism was consolidating its hold on China. The concept of peace through a preponderance of power became obsolete as soon as our atomic monopoly was broken. Thereafter it became apparent that either side would have the permanent capability of inflicting grievous damage and destruction on the other. The hope of preponderant power faded away in the ghastly vistas of thermonuclear, supersonic war.

Yet the failure to achieve the results intended does not condemn the results achieved. Thanks to American initiative, tired and tried peoples, especially in Europe, turned chaos into order, weakness into strength. Stalin's plan to add the vital industrial centers of Europe to the Communist system failed. Instead, the economy of Western Europe has been restored and production greatly exceeds prewar levels. More than two million men are under arms and many more stand by in trained reserves. And there has been a steady development of political and economic co-operation, even though Americans seem more disappointed with the delays than cheered by the progress.

In short, if we have not been able to establish a preponderance of power in the West, we have succeeded in establishing a *balance* of power. By that I mean recognition on all sides that revision of the status quo in Europe by threat of force is not possible and that revision by force would provoke world war.

The preservation and extension of this balance, attained at such expense and exertion, appears then to be the first order of business, until we can move on to a satisfactory international system for the limitation and control of military power, and ultimately, let us pray, to the realization of our dream of peace by the concerting of all interests among all nations, great and small.

This concept of a balance of power, it should be emphasized, is not a static thing. Once achieved, it does not become ours forever like the tennis tournament cup. Nor can it be maintained merely by words and wishes. It can only be secured by continued labor and sacrifice. And a balance of power between ourselves and our mortal foe requires not only great military strength on our part but a balanced distribution of that strength — a distribution which would enable us to act in a variety of situations and to respond if need be to a variety of threats.

The retaliatory force of air-atomic power is, in my judgment, an indispensable part of our strategy of defense, just as it has been since the last war. But a program of "massive and instantaneous retaliation" is not enough by itself to preserve the balance of power we have so laboriously achieved. Such capacity did not prevent Korea. Nor did it provide us a means of resolving that bitter struggle. Nor has such talk brought about the solution we desire in Indo-China. Many situations may arise where we will be obliged to bring power to bear to arrest subversion or aggression, but not by means of atomic bombing followed

[460]

by counterretaliation and world war in which our allies would be the first victims. If, as many say, atom and hydrogen bombs have made total war an obsolete conception, then conventional weapons and forces may well be of more importance than ever in the clouded days ahead. If atomic power is, in a sense, neutralized, then the coalition will need local strength against local aggression more than ever.

As maintaining the coalition and the power equilibrium will require a sustained and balanced military effort, so developing our ideological strength will require a sustained and balanced moral and diplomatic effort; and for that we shall have to clear the air of the fantasies associated with the idea of dictating our terms or philosophy through a preponderant power which doesn't exist.

Diplomacy, for example, is not the art of asserting ever more emphatically that attitudes should not be what they clearly are. It is not the repudiation of actuality, but the recognition of actuality, and the use of actuality to advance our national interests. Take such vexed problems as neutralism or negotiation. Neutralism sometimes provokes heated demands from our leaders that the uncommitted nations sign on our dotted line or else — as if we ourselves had not practiced neutrality for more than a century. Indeed it is well for us to remember that we intervened in the last two world wars only in the nick of time and only after our territory or rights had been directly assailed.

Neutralism is something we must live with, whether we like it or not. No matter how foolish it is, it is far better for us to have countries neutral than to have them join the Communist bloc. And the great danger is not that we have some neutralism but that we may have much more to contend with if we become divided from our friends.

Similarly with negotiation — a word that in some frenetic circles seems to have become a synonym for appeasement. Of course, we must be prepared to negotiate, where negotiation promises advantage. Negotiation is not only the means, however gradual, of settlement with our adversaries; it is also the means of ascertaining our adversaries' terms of settlement. Moreover, at this stage it is even more important in reassuring our apprehensive friends about our peaceful intentions and thereby strengthening our own coalition.

I have said that there are two struggles taking place within this framework created by the aggressions of communism and the awakening of the underdeveloped peoples — the power struggle and the ideological struggle. While it is impossible to separate the two, it may be said, I think, that in the West the struggle has become primarily a power struggle with ideological undertones. In the East, we have, for the time being, the opposite situation, where the main battle is being fought, except in limited areas, in terms of ideas rather than armies. (This may seem to be contradicted by the long power struggle in Indo-China, but it should be remembered that what has become a Communist aggression started and is still largely sustained by Viet-Namese nationalism and anticolonialism.)

Let us look for a few moments at the West. The division of Europe with all of its implications; the division of Germany, the largest, strongest power in Europe; Anglo-American and Russian forces facing each other in the heart of Europe — all these situations constitute an acute threat to peace. The precarious and uneasy nature of the present balance is revealed by the June, 1953, riots in Berlin and more recently by the disorders which the sudden and ill-fated "solution" provoked in Trieste. And the Berlin Conference made it clear that the Soviet Union will not and the coalition cannot permit an expansion of the other's power in Europe. Even at the risk, indeed the certainty, of higher walls of hatred in Eastern Europe, the Soviet has made it clear again, after an interruption of five years and the death of Stalin, that its objective is a Communist Germany, or at least a susceptible and powerless Germany, and the eviction of Western forces. In other words, its objective is to upset the present balance of power.

I don't know and my guess would be worthless as to the relative weight of the factors of fear and expansionist ambitions in the obdurate attitude of the Soviet. Some will say that Russia fears us as much as we fear them; that they are prisoners of their history and their Communist dogmas about "the crisis of capitalism" and its inevitable ultimate recourse to war. But they are perhaps even more prisoners of their own system of society — a system of tension, held together by calculated fear, in which a committee maintains absolute power at home by invoking a sense of absolute danger from abroad. A society which is unwilling to give its own people a measure of freedom cannot easily risk normal and equable relations with the outside world. Certainly totalitarianism begets a pervasive mood of fear — fear of the world outside, fear of the state, fear of the police, fear of neighbors, fear of one's own innermost thoughts.

And the Soviet leaders can render this fundamental and calculated fear the more plausible by pointing to events of history. Certainly the repeated invasions of the past, the allied intervention after the first war, Hitler's invasion in the second, the present circle of bomber bases and the military strength of the Western coalition must contribute to Soviet apprehension. Nor can there be any doubt that they regard the presence of American, British and French forces in Germany as a threat, just as we regard the Red Army in Eastern Europe as a threat. There seems to be little point in asserting that because we have no aggressive intentions, the Soviet Union should not fear the alliance of an armed and unified Germany with the West or the liberation of the satellites. To the Kremlin the threat inherent in these allied capabilities for action will not be easily erased with words or even guarantees. And it is difficult to argue that they need not fear the passions which would be released if Soviet forces withdraw from Eastern Europe.

Whether Soviet intransigence is the result of fear or ambition, or both, as is probably the case; whether, indeed, it is inherent in their totalitarian system, it is the view of many with whom I have talked around the world that, now confronted with certain and strong resistance, Soviet military adventure in the West is most unlikely. In one important respect it is fortunate that the adversary in the atomic age is totalitarian Bolshevism rather than totalitarian Nazism. The latter, personified by Hitler and unthinkable without him, was suicidally romantic and naïvely irrational. There is good reason to believe that the Kremlin, with or without Stalin, resembles the bookie more than the gambler. It will calculate the odds. It will take risks but it won't risk everything. It will avoid ventures which might involve ruinous losses even if it has to forgo ventures which might yield large gains. As conservative revolutionaries, somewhat sobered by thirty-five years of power, as compared to Hitler's six short years in 1939, they will also liquidate ventures that prove unprofitable or no longer profitable, as in Greece, the Berlin blockade and Korea.

On such an appraisal of a fearful, cautious, stubborn and implacable adversary, the uneasy, unsatisfactory status quo must be maintained until some solution can be found to the basic problem of a divided Europe, which is a divided Germany. Perhaps in time the mounting tensions of a divided Germany will merge into the larger problem of a divided Europe. Perhaps the Soviet rulers may in time conclude that the withdrawal of British-American forces from a united and really independent Europe is safer and better than maintaining Russian garrisons amid the rising tensions of an unnaturally divided Europe.

We should, I believe, be thinking beyond the cold confines of the cold war. Perhaps the ultimate solution will be a declaration of independence for all of Europe, based on the developing strength of the organs of European unity. Perhaps there will evolve the concept of an independent united Europe linked with the United States and Britain on the one hand, and the Soviet Union on the other, in mutual security arrangements pledging common resistance against aggression by any one of the three.

But such remote conjectures are less instructive and important for the present than improving the balance of power and the strength and solidarity of Western Europe on which any permanent and better adjustment must depend. For it is obvious that the Soviet will generate and exploit disunity in our coalition, hoping to deal with its adversaries separately, preferably one against the other.

Their objective, of course, is victory without war. And our objective is neither war nor victory, but an opportunity for all to work out their own destiny in their own way in independence and freedom. To accomplish that, military strength to deter or defeat aggression and economic strength to resist aggression by subversion are the first requirements; and the second is a community of interest and purpose among us in order to keep our strength intact and in order to negotiate as one, not as many. The first phase has been accomplished. America returned to Europe not to intrude but to redress the imbalance of strength and arrest the march of communism. Now the second phase, holding the line, maintaining the coalition and negotiating where possible, is upon us.

And here our adversary has opportunities and advantages in the disunity and multiple sovereignties of the non-Communist world. In Europe, under the Soviet shadow Sweden stands aloof, Italy is weak, Germany is divided and disarmed, France is bedeviled from all sides and demoralized, and, for very good reasons, as wary of a restored Germany as of Russia. Britain is steadfast but her first allegiance is to the Commonwealth. And, to pass for a moment beyond Europe, the Middle East, except for the sturdy Turks and alert little Israel, is largely a power vacuum. So is much of Latin America. India is neutral and Japan disarmed and dependent. The free world comprises many nations, cultures, languages and levels of development which have the effect of subdividing collective power and confusing collective purpose. Our focus is not the same. Our coalition speaks with many voices and many tongues. Intracommunity bickering, conflict and mistrust obscure the steady vision of extracommunity danger. And, as we saw in Europe, first in 1914 and again in 1939, a house divided against itself will fall.

I could go on. But the point is that, in contrast with our divisions and imbalances, we dare not overlook the element of strength in the monolithic unity of the Communist world. Maybe the Russians are just gritting their teeth and holding on, waiting for the collapse of Western power and purpose as foretold by their prophets.

Coalitions are nothing new. There have been several successful ones in modern European history. A coalition frustrated the effort of Louis XIV to impose absolutism on Europe. Napoleon was defeated by a coalition, and so were the Kaiser and Hitler. But the members of a coalition have a way of falling apart after the common danger has passed. And that, of course, is all the greater a hazard to a coalition largely of European states as the immediacy of the danger of general war in Europe subsides and the danger shifts to Asia.

Recognizing the improved posture of the West and the changes wrought in these historic, crowded years, Russian policy is changing too. The intimidation of vast armaments, ceaseless and violent propaganda, a hammer blow here and there, are not enough. Now they will stubbornly hang onto every vantage point and use every device to crack up the coalition, to discourage American participation in European affairs, and to diminish and disrupt the European defense effort. Instead of direct political assault, the Communist parties will make parliamentary alliances with left-wing groups in an attempt to recreate the "popular fronts" of earlier days, always with a view to obstruction and frustration. Soft words and conciliatory gestures are in the repertoire too. Already the Russians have relinquished claims to the Straits, extended the olive branch instead of the pistol to Tito, etc. Moscow is busily negotiating barter agreements and courting Western Europe with the device to which it is most susceptible — trade. As commercial pressure grows, the number of takers may grow too, and with it the dependence of non-Communist economies, particularly in Asia. Proposals such as China's agreement with Ceylon to exchange rice at prices under the market for rubber at prices above the market will be difficult for weak economies and governments to resist.

The propaganda line is changing also. Heretofore the United States, for example, was pictured as a predatory imperialist that had come to Europe to stay with malevolent designs on weaker states. Now, when Europe is nervous about American withdrawal, the Communists tell the Europeans that we are fickle and unreliable and will pull out one of these days and leave them to the mercy of a rearmed Germany. Many more students from non-Communist countries, by no means all of them party members, are being invited to study in the Soviet Union and China, and carefully indoctrinated groups of Russian and Chinese singers, actors, dancers, musicians and athletes are appearing beyond the Iron Curtain.

It should be noted too that the Russian economy may have been expanding at a faster yearly rate of growth than even our own. Already one third the size of ours, it is evidently strong enough now to warrant a change of emphasis to the production and purchase abroad of consumer goods, besides carrying the formidable burden of steadily increasing foreign policy commitments. If the Soviet economy can maintain its present pace of expansion, Russian output may well be from three to four times as great in 1970 as it is today. Should the time come, as some foresee, when the standard of living in the Soviet Union is as good or better than in the democracies of Western Europe, the consequences would be formidable to say the least.

The hazards of internal weakness and instability in many countries have not diminished in recent years. Confronted with a possible loss of cohesion as the immediate danger of general war diminishes, challenged by more resourceful, subtle and flexible exploitation of opportunities by the Soviet, American leadership of the free coalition will face increasingly severe material and moral tests. Certainly any major economic recession here in the United States, which God forbid, would quickly multiply the inherent centrifugal forces of division and recrimination in the coalition, and lend credence to what Stalin used to call "the deepening of the general crisis of capitalism."

Perhaps it is worth a moment to look more closely at some less obvious factors in Europe — and in Asia as well — which contribute both to misunderstanding and hope. Bursts of ill temper and irritation on both sides of the Atlantic obscure for us the genuine appreciation abroad of America's saving role. Nor do we probably appreciate the fact that, with Europe's increasing strength and self-reliance, our postwar relationship is breaking up and Europe is asserting its independence and talking back to us now. We who fought for our independence from Europe should not be surprised when Europe has a similar recoil from advice, direction and domination from across the Atlantic. It should be remembered that multitudes of Americans have been busily mending old Europe's ways with American money and "know-how" and confidence that our methods are best. However benevolent the purpose, however desirable the changes, the reaction was inevitable. It would be the same here if the tables were reversed and Europeans had been impressing us with our deficiencies and the superior merits of their manners, products and way of life. The excesses of McCarthyism, pronouncements of rigid policy by American leaders, intemperance and hysterics of any kind, the growing emphasis on the military aspects of anti-Communist defense, patronizing attitudes and displays of arrogance, wealth and fear, all are exaggerated abroad and summoned as witnesses to prove that America is overbearing and domineering, or erratic and frightened, and not the citadel of freedom, the pattern of perfection and fountain of wisdom after all.

For most Europeans their newspapers, radio and hearsay, and our movies are the source of information about the United States. They know little about us and don't have the same means of evaluating these external impressions of the American scene that we do. That there is much misunderstanding and that we don't look as magnanimous, disinterested and righteous as we do to ourselves is less surprising than the great underlying respect, friendliness and good will.

It seems to me that the rapidly emerging spirit of independence in Europe ("even from its best friends," to use Churchill's phrase), the increasing scrutiny of our policies and critical objectivity about the United States, is wholesome. While it complicates the difficulties of leadership, it will constantly remind us that this is a coalition, a partnership, and the members are not satellites. And certainly we should rejoice that our friends in Europe are not resigned to permanent dependency and henceforth propose to assume a more positive part in the direction of our common concerns.

The European power equilibrium, I have suggested, depends on the maintenance of the coalition; and the coalition, as we have seen, will be pulled this way and that by soft Soviet voices, by resentment of American domination, by healthy aspirations for independence — and also, inevitably, by differing assessments of danger and self-interest.

Where, in all this, does our interest lie? It lies, I believe, in the hope that this emerging self-reliance and spirit may give further momentum to the movement for European unity — a movement which, as it succeeds, will be a factor of incalculable weight in this precariously balanced and dangerously divided world. For separately the enfeebled countries of Western Europe are an invitation to further mistrust and disunion. But together this mighty reservoir of people, skills, industry and culture would be a ponderous weight on the scales.

The dream of a united Europe is as old as the Romans. Conquerors from Charlemagne to Hitler have tried by force and persuasion to hammer or fit the many pieces together again. Countless wars, plans, groupings and blocs wander across the panorama of European history and disappear into thorny thickets of realities. As the center of gravity, power and influence in world affairs ever since Caesar's legions fell slowly back to tottering Rome, there has been little external inducement to arrest the growth of nationalism and separation in Europe. Now in our time the siege from the East and the emergence of the new colossi, Russia and America, are stirring Europe to action, with encouragement from us and interference from beyond the Iron Curtain.

Already the Schuman Plan, a genuine international government for the basic industrial resources of Western Europe, is a going concern. This was a French concept. So also was the European Army which we call the European Defense Community. EDC was born in the emergency. It was a response to Anglo-American insistence on rearming the Germans to shoulder a portion of the defense burden and the French fear of a rearmed, independent Germany. Conceived as a plan to utilize German armed might and still control its use by Germany, which in the past has been more dangerous not only to Europe but to the United States than Russia, the fate of EDC hangs in the balance, as we know. Like the proverbial horse behind the cart, a third project, a constitution for a political community of Europe, has followed, and is under active consideration.

That the progress toward the realization of European union is slow is less of a wonder than that there has been any progress at all, considering the infinite difficulties. The fear of German domination of a military community is echoed in the fear of German economic and political domination so long as Britain hesitates to subordinate its ties with the Commonwealth and participate as part of the new Europe. And there is no minimizing the thousand and one difficulties in the way of even a Western European federation — which, of course, is all that is possible as long as Eastern Europe remains behind the Iron Curtain. Eastern Europe was the food surplus and raw materials areas, and the union of Western Europe would be a union of essentially industrial and highly competitive countries, only two of which, France and Denmark, can feed themselves and leave anything for export. To the need for food and raw materials must be added the need for investment capital and markets for its exports before Western Europe can look forward to the economic good health which is the foundation of successful political, spiritual and defensive integration. It is inevitable that the volume of East-West trade will increase as American aid dries up and especially if we will not, by a policy of trade reform, provide better and more reliable access to the American market.

The important thing is that Europe's anxiety has had the positive effect of helping to unify it. There are heartening signs that the political stability and economic vitality of Europe are to be fostered, not in separate geographic units artifically created by conquest or marriage, but as a whole. For the one situation in Europe that can support an adequate living is Europe itself. An optimist might indeed prophesy that under the pressure of necessity the divisive spirit of nationalism that was born in Europe will die in Europe — with consequences that bode well for enduring resistance to the compulsory unification of communism.

But I strongly suspect that we in America are destined to endure in prolonged and irritable impatience the glacial pace of European integration. And we shall be perplexed and as always impatient with the manifestations of the new forces emerging in Europe: the persistence of large and bold Communist minorities in France and Italy; increasing trade with Russia, China and the satellites; and, of course, the assertiveness of growing self-confidence.

I think we have come to understand better the reasons for the parliamentary instability in peace-hungry France and Italy and the former's stubborn reluctance to face the reality of a threat greater than Germany. But persistence of large Communist political parties in these countries, to which they have become accustomed, makes it hard for them to understand our extreme anxiety about Communists, and in turn creates a complacency which exasperates us who are taxing and spending so heavily to help them fight communism. The explanation, in part at least, is that we don't have the same focus. We are thinking of different things. When we think of "a Communist" we in America think of a hard core, malevolent conspirator dedicated to the overthrow of our government by intrigue if possible and force if necessary. Most Europeans, on the other hand, think of a neighbor, friend, fellow worker or even relative who votes Communist not to express his approval or preference for the Soviet system, but to express his disapproval of the conditions in which he lives and works.

The poverty of the Italian peasant is familiar. Only now with the land reform and development programs is the traditional Italian feudalism breaking up and the intolerable misery of millions abating. In France more than 80 per cent of the housing in the industrial slums was built before our Civil War. In Paris more than 100,000 young couples have no home of their own and little hope of one. The areas of overcrowding, tuberculosis, low income and misery are the areas of Communist strength among masses of people who have been waiting for reform, change and hope — not just for years but for generations. In Catholic Italy the pattern is similar. And to many observers the strange thing is that well-organized, well-financed and disciplined Communist party leadership has been able to do so little with this European legacy of economic stagnation, social irresponsibility, and the shocking disparity between rich and poor.

In our time, the American economy has been constantly changing, constantly converting higher productivity into higher wages, lower prices and greater consumption. We do not, to be sure, have a monopoly on such progress. The recovery of Western Germany since the war, and the way in which that divided and battered country has pressed on to new heights of income and output, is one of the remarkable economic achievements of our time. Britain, the Benelux and the Scandinavian countries have made steady progress and have shown that free people, by their own free decision, can arrange a wide and equitable distribution of the fruits of their common labors. However, elsewhere in Western Europe the picture is less bright. France has been suffering — as has Italy — from the tensions and the rigidities of a traditional capitalism. There one senses the ancient conflict of the "haves" and the "have nots." There social indifference and economies organized around low consumption mean that many people see little chance of bettering themselves and see little hope that their children will have a better life than their own.

However, for all the groans, excursions and lamentations, Europe is, I believe, groping along the path toward unity and strength. Where communism still exerts its influence, it is largely an influence bred in domestic distress which can be remedied, or an influence founded in the dismal conviction that Soviet power is the wave of the future and will inevitably win — and this can be remedied too.

In Western Europe, then, the power struggle appears to be in uneasy balance, with prospects for substantial improvement, and so far as the war of ideas is concerned, Moscow's influence and attraction are ebbing.

But in Asia the situation is reversed. For there the contest is primarily ideological and it would be a bold man indeed who would say that the peril is past and the outcome certain. For Asia is in revolution. Civilizations are very old, but political independence is very young. In the new states the economies are shaky, public administration is weak; they are hungry and poor, sensitive and proud. Nationalism is rampant. And the West, identified with the hated colonialism, is suspect. Utterly occupied with their own overwhelming problems, Asians see little of the world conflict with communism. But they know from experience a lot about colonialism, feudalism, landlords, moneylenders and oppressors, and the theories of Karl Marx sound pretty good to many of their leaders and intellectuals, who know surprisingly little about the ugly realities of communism in practice. Nor is there the perception one would expect of international communism as a new imperialism and a new threat to their independence.

There is little tradition of democracy in these new states, but independence, won at long last, is a passion, which partly accounts in some quarters for their opaque view of Communist China, where to many Asians it appears that the white invaders have at last been thrown out and the ignominy of centuries erased by Asians. There remains a reverent admiration for the ideas of the American Revolution, the Bill of Rights and the great utterances of national independence and human freedom. But they think they see in the current fears and excesses of anti-Communist zeal here at home a contradiction of our professions of faith in individual freedom. So also our alliance and friendship with the Western colonial powers seem to them to make our professed devotion to independence and self-determination hypocritical.

The contest of ideas doesn't mean much to the masses. And our anti-Communist preaching wins few hearts. The Asians want to know what we are for, not just what we are against. And in nations like India, Indonesia and Burma they don't accept the thesis that everyone must choose sides, that they have to be for us or against us, any more than we ourselves did in the midst of threats to world peace and freedom until a dozen or so years ago.

But in spite of all their doubts and difficulties the devotion of the leaders of Asia to the democratic idea of government by consent rather than force is impressive, as is the decisive manner in which so many of the new countries of Asia have dealt with violent Communist insurrections and conspiracies. Their revolutions have not produced Utopia, and they are struggling with infinite difficulties to raise living standards and satisfy the rising tide of expectations. They want rice and respect, and they want to believe in wondrous America that sends money and friendly, earnest people to help them, and that believes in them, and the aspirations of all God's children for peace, dignity and freedom.

Our people and our policy would be deeply concerned with these lands if Marx, Lenin and Stalin had never lived. For poverty, oppression and ignorance have always been our concern, and those who see virtue only in self-interest and self-preservation mistake, I think, our character and misread our history. Besides a policy and attitude narrowly based on self-interest alone will lift no hearts and win no minds in Asia.

A propitious political accident, however, has made our inborn compassion co-ordinate with the national interest; and happily so, for in an area that has known so much of colonialism and condescension, compassion and humility will be our greatest asset in the struggle for the minds of men and the allegiance of uncommitted nations in the decisive area of Asia.

Lenin said "the road to Paris lies through Peiping and Delhi," and the Moscow-Peiping axis will not yield the road to Western ideas and allegiance without an epic struggle for Asia that will sorely try our forbearance, understanding and magnanimity. We shall have to avoid the sins of self-righteousness and self-delusion. Our power is not absolute, nor is our judgment infallible. If we act as if we had a monopoly on all strength and all truth, we will soon discover that ours is the monopoly of hopeless isolation. The tempered use of our power, the sympathetic understanding of people's "yearning to breathe free," the modest proffer of our ideas and faith — these constitute the true resources of America and the treasured hope of our civilization.

Until the long labor is achieved, perpetual peril will be our lot and our condition.

America's Burden

I have suggested that the emergence in Russia of predatory communism does not wholly explain the ferment of change that has convulsed, distorted and reshaped our twentieth-century world. And the elimination of communism as an aggressive, expansive world movement would by no means restore tranquillity, order and security. There would still be with us both the old problem of Russian expansion as well as the new problem of the awakening of continents.

A hundred and fifty years ago Russian leaders were saying that "the mass of Turkish territories in Europe should be divided into separate states, governed locally and bound to each other by a federation, upon which Russia would be able to secure herself a decisive and lawful influence by means of the title of Emperor or Protector of the Slavs of the East which would be accorded to his Imperial Majesty."

What was foreseen 150 years ago has come to pass. Much of that "mass of Turkish territories in Europe," and far more besides, has fallen under Russian control and "satellite" is our Western synonym for what those earlier Russian leaders called "decisive influence." Russian expansion into the Far East, which began even earlier, still goes on, but under slogans and labels better adapted to the modern social revolution. I suspect the Czars would see little new, surprising or distasteful in the aggressions of their successors in the Kremlin. Indeed, reflecting on the frustration of their own plans by the containment policies of nineteenth-century Europe, they might even feel obliged to congratulate the Communist usurpers for their spectacular successes.

It is interesting and perhaps instructive to recall that the Bolshevik Revolution of 1917 was avowedly anti-imperialist; that it renounced the traditional imperial Russian expansionism. But it was not long before the anti-imperialism of the founders of political communism was in turn abandoned and the new Soviet Union reverted to the ancient policies of Imperial Russia.

Two factors perhaps have contributed to our imperfect perception of this continuity in Russian history. For years after the revolution the leaders in the Kremlin were busy perfecting their system, consolidating their position at home, building up the economic and military power of a backward country, catching up with the technological advances of the West, and organizing the world Communist movement. Then we were diverted for some years by the devastating bursts of expansion by violence in Germany, Italy and Japan.

But now, after pausing for revolution, modernization and world war, a stronger Russia is at it again, and we are compelled once more to face the old and half-forgotten reality of Russia's implacable expansionism. Moreover, it seems both reasonable and prudent to assume that the leaders of Russia, whoever they are, will persist in this policy by force or guile until the new age of political enlightenment dawns in the Kremlin.

(One wonders, indeed, if there is a counterpart in the Far East, if Korea and Indo-China are evidence of a reawakened imperial spirit in the new Communist China; one wonders if they imply an approach to problems beyond China's borders which adds revolution to the old Chinese imperial concept of what they called the "tribute states" of Vietnam, Siam, Burma, Korea and parts of Malaya and Indonesia. It seems not unlikely that all of these states and Laos and Cambodia are on Red China's satellite list to insure the security of the borders and the economic well being of the vast homeland.)

At all events, while Russian behavior is consistent with its history, it is clear that something new has been added, and that the new faith of communism is a potent weapon for conquest of the peasant and industrial proletariat, the oppressed and the miserable, especially where poverty is the rule and the recollections of colonialism are painful and fresh. While the promises of emancipation and liberation and the ultimate triumph of socialism and the Communist "people's paradise" are for export only, as the sufferers in all the Russian-occupied countries know so well, the appeal is great to the ignorant and aggrieved. A failure to recognize and to combat the momentum of Russian and Chinese expansion, arrayed in communism's seductive panoply of deliverance for the masses of the Middle East, Asia and Africa, could lose to Western civilization vast areas and peoples which are not dispensable.

As I have pointed out, this fateful struggle in the East is essentially ideological and the burden falls largely on the United States. In the nineteenth century Europe concerted its power to contain Russia. Now this can no longer be done even in Europe, let alone in Asia. As it has fallen to our lot to redress the balance of power in Europe, the hope of security for ourselves, let alone the salvation of the millions who yearn for freedom, devolves on us even more in the East where the Western empires and sources of power have gone with the winds of war and rebellion, and left behind bitter memories of the white man's colonialism and paternalism.

While any inventory of the West's assets and liabilities in the Asian conflict is beyond the scope of this discussion and of my competence, its complexity in comparison with Europe is apparent to any traveler. In Europe the tradition of national independence is old and the more recent development of political democracy rests on a broad basis of literacy, political consciousness and relatively high standards of living. But in the East independence is new, the economies weak, illiteracy high, societies agrarian and stratified, poverty universal, and political consciousness confined to a thin layer. In such circumstances the evolution of the revolution in an orderly way toward the goals of tolerable living standards and the Western democratic concept of government by consent would be difficult and slow at best. But it is made much more difficult and hazardous by Communist interference, incitement, falsehood and pressure.

If anticolonialism and independence are the root passions of the Asian revolution one wonders, sometimes in despair, why international communism should be any problem at all, why with all of Eastern Europe as mute witnesses Asians don't perceive at once that their real enemy is the new Communist imperialism and not the vanishing empires of the West. We can point to the revival of Russia's historical expansionism; we can point to China's seizure of Tibet, invasion of Korea, invasion by proxy of Indo-China, Communist insurrections in Malaya, the Philippines, Burma, Indonesia, and to the built-in fifth columns among the 13 million Chinese living throughout Southeast Asia. We can point, finally, to the consequences of Communist conquest — slavery for the people, submission to the central authority of Moscow or Peiping, and the quick extinction of the dream of genuine national independence. If they point to Yugoslavia's independence of Moscow we can ask them to speculate where Yugoslavia would be were it not for Western help. And we can remind them that China is a next-door neighbor to all of East Asia.

But we have not yet wholly succeeded in clearly identifying the real threat; we have not yet succeeded in marshaling the massive forces of independence against the real enemy. Why not? Can it be done? Can it be done in time? How? These are questions which will plague us for years to come. And if the central problems of the power struggle in Western Europe — the future of Germany, an expanding economy, social reconstruction and unification — are perplexing, they seem relatively simple compared to Asia where we cannot expect to make much progress in the building of a more stable power relationship while the

[474]

ideological struggle is still going on among many states, races and re-ligions.

There are many reasons why perception of the real danger of Communist imperialism is not as distinct in the East as in the West and why, therefore, the ideological struggle is more apparent in Asia than in Europe and its outcome less predictable. Because they are so numerous I will mention only a few of them to indicate the dimensions of the difficulties facing the free world's defenders.

In the first place, of course, is colonialism. It is hard, especially for Americans, to appreciate the depth of this feeling. For centuries resentments have been accumulating among sensitive, proud and ancient peoples for the indignities, exploitation and injuries, real or fancied, of the white man's rule. It will be a long time before this feeling is erased, but it can be reduced. The present cordial relations between Indians and Pakistanis and their former masters, the British, were to me one of the marvels of the East, and evidence of what can be done.

Some of the deep-seated hostility to Western pretensions and condescension has rubbed off on us in spite of our liberation of the Philippines and our traditional anti-imperialism. But curiously it does not seem to rub off on the Russians, probably in part because they are exceedingly inconspicuous in comparison with the Americans who are numerous, visible and closely allied and identified with the Western European colonists. Also it should be remembered that Russia is not a newcomer to Asia; it wasn't brought into Asia by President Roosevelt at Yalta, as some of us seem to think. It has been a great Asian power for 200 years and includes many Asian peoples. It was a part of Asia long before the advent of communism, and the Asian evidently doesn't think of Russians when he thinks and talks of European colonialism.

Moreover, the Russians understand the Orientals, their languages and how they think, better than we, who have a tendency everywhere to expect others to think and act as we do and to appreciate our disinterested and philanthropic righteousness. Finally, it is hard for many peoples, far removed from the struggle in the West, to see any military threat to their independence from a Russia lying beyond the borders of distant Manchuria and the high Himalayas.

The Soviet Union may be far away but political communism is not; and there are no leaders in the new lands anywhere who have not had incessant troubles with native Communist political movements. As I have said, the appeal of Marxist thought is considerable in Asia and even among the leaders, Western-oriented by education and democratic by conviction, there are wonder and respect for the Soviet achievement in industrialization and the rapid development of their country.

For the basic problem of most of the newly independent underdeveloped areas is how to match with performance the promises of their revolutions; how to increase literacy and public health; how to develop their natural resources and reclaim waste areas; how to improve the production of agricultural commodities and consumer goods; how in short, to bring off a delayed industrial revolution and improve the people's lot, quickly — and with little domestic capital and limited national resources to do it.

It is a formidable task to say the least, and it is hardly surprising that the Soviet Union's spectacular achievement in similar circumstances attracts admiring attention and curiosity. Whether the job can be done by the Western methods of consent, or whether impatience, agitation and discontent will drive them to the methods of force and brutal dictatorship, is the big issue. And it is precisely here in the field of economic development and internal improvement where the West and the United States have the advantage both in means and technical experience.

Stability and indigenous strength in what remains of free Asia can only be established in the long run by the will and work of the people themselves. Neither American nor United Nations money, technicians nor advice in any amount is likely to be decisive. But we can help others not just to understand better the deadly deceptions of imperial communism but also to deal more effectively with their own problems and to help themselves. We can contribute greatly to economic improvement and political stability, and to the evolution of healthy governments capable of defending their own interests against outside domination. Indeed we have already done so. But to limit our effort to military strength alone, or to make economic aid contingent on military co-operation, or to penalize and abuse the neutralist nations would be to ignore the basic fact that in large areas of the Middle East, Asia and Africa we have not yet resolved the ideological conflict. Before a reliable and effective defense community can be created there has to be a community purpose.

In Asia, now, India and Japan are the anchors of the free world. With them rests the balance of power; as they are strong and free their non-Communist neighbors will draw increased strength and confidence in the alternative to China and communism. Hence they are the obvious Communist objectives. If either falls most of Asia will be vulnerable and the Communist conspirators will be in sight of their goal of a soft and sympathetic Asia, a neutralized Europe and an isolated America.

India, both because of its decisive weight in South and Southeast Asia and because it is ideologically and militarily less defensible than

Japan, appears to be first on the flexible Communist schedule. The noisy partisan search for scapegoats that has demeaned the American political scene since the Communist conquest of China will be but a preview of the dismal drama — "Who Lost India?" — if enormous India with its enormous problems slips under the Iron Curtain. Responsible and popular opinion in India is deeply anti-Communist as of now. But they don't want *us* to save them from communism, and there is still some ambivalence about acceptance of help which they think has more to do with power politics than with genuine good will and generosity. They want and need and know they need help, but they are also sensitive and sad that it must be so; that they have gained independence and are still dependent.

In addition to the democratic convictions of the new India's leaders there are many other factors working against communism: the tolerance of the Hindu for other ideas, the individualism of the villagers, Gandhi's philosophy of nonviolence, the heritage of British justice, order and responsible government, the large five-year plan for development and economic improvement, and so forth.

But there are many negative factors too, and India's unrealistic but persistent neutralism has been particularly irritating to us. I doubt if the tolerant attitude toward China is so much a reflection of moral indecision or ideological sympathy for communism as an expression of Asian and anticolonial solidarity. But Indians, whether sentimentally bemused or trying to avoid taking sides for practical reasons, must be rapidly learning the facts about life with world communism. And the more they see of situations like the prisoner-of-war conflict in Korea, Communist activity in their own country and along their northern borders, and the more closely Mao follows the Stalinist lead, the more rapidly India's education in realities will spread and her illusions vanish.

We must face the fact that throughout the East the central problem is the attraction and growing power of Communist China. For the first time since British and other naval vessels forced open China's ports to Western trade a century ago, the mainland Chinese, some 500 millions, are now organized under vigorous, fanatical leadership. The Japanese and the Germans have demonstrated the power potential of much smaller and geographically less secure nations when effectively mobilized and industrialized. And that is what China is now doing with Russian and East European help. The spectacular development in thirty-five years of the Soviet Union, today the world's second industrial power, is a sobering reminder of what ruthless totalitarianism can do. China may in time become an even greater influence for good or evil in the world than its partner in the vast Chinese-Russian heartland stretching from the Danube to the Pacific. And someone may yet write a piece or give a lecture entitled "Will Malenkov Become a Tito?"

As young men many of the leaders in Peiping felt the humiliation of the "treaty era" when Westerners treated Chinese as inferiors. The leaders of Communist China now appear to be motivated by multiple compulsions to (1) liberate fellow Asians from what they call "imperialist domination and feudalism," (2) and, as they say, "right the wrongs done China by the Western powers" and restore the nation to her "rightful" status in Asia and the world, and (3) forestall Western-supported action against the Communist regime by creating situations that make such action less possible.

In Asia the intangible weight of probable Communist mistakes is on our side. The Chinese may prove much wiser and cleverer than the Russians under Stalin, but if they perform in the manner of their senior Soviet partners it is predictable that their pressure and obstinacy will alert and arouse the free Asians, even as Soviet intransigence awakened and united Western Europe. Indeed, it is likely that the wholesale defection of Chinese prisoners-of-war in Korea followed by the enlarged operations in Indo-China is spreading the alarm.

The assumption is reasonable and all the evidence confirms that the leaders of Communist China intend to follow the Soviet example and press forward toward their goal of an industrialized and militarily powerful state. But however ruthless and bloodthirsty Mao and his lieutenants may be, to maintain party unity and organize on the centralized Communist system a vast, sprawling, overpopulated empire with primitive communications and limited natural resources is a monstrous undertaking.

While in the past Asian policy of Imperial Russia and even of the Soviets has been little influenced by a feeble, divided China on the other side of the longest boundary in the world, henceforth it is obvious that relations with her Communist neighbor will be a major Soviet concern. One could point out many interesting possibilities here, but I will not speculate on future Soviet-Chinese relations. The only safe assumption for the present, at least, is that they will continue firm and cordial. And there is little doubt that the Soviet Union has made substantial contributions in goods and technical services to China's development, although there is no way of knowing what concessions have been exacted in return. But China's rapid industrial development would seem to require the greatest possible trade with the outside world and for years to come. It would also seem to require a long period of peace.

Our friends both in the East and West who are yearning for more trade point to China's ominous growing commercial dependence on Russia. The 80 million Japanese on their little islands must expand their commerce as our economic support declines. The Germans and British, too, seem to be more eager if anything than Peiping to reopen the trade channels with China. If we don't choose to make markets available here and if we terminate economic aid to our allies, the China market will become more attractive to the nations who must trade to live, and who are also important members of the defensive coalition against communism.

China has it in her power to decide whether and how long the French will bleed in Indo-China and whether and how long we must hold the lines in Korea. To the gathering problems of Indo-China, Korea, Formosa and admission to the United Nations, we shall have to add the rising pressure from our friends for more trade. Hastening industrial development will enhance the strength of China in the Orient, but there is danger too in opposing what our allies need without offering them — as in the trade question — an economic alternative.

All of which highlights the difficulties of leadership, and the further danger of a weakened coalition with the assumption of unilateral responsibilities by a progressively isolated United States. Unilateralism in turn will encourage false hopes at home and neutralism abroad; it will tend to confirm the Communist charge that our purpose is not disinterested co-operation but self-interested domination. The United States will soon have to formulate a reasoned policy with respect to China. We will shortly have to evolve the minimum conditions on which we are willing to live and let live with the Chinese Communists, with the probability that, as in Europe, the ideological contest will go on for a long time.

I have tried to point out that much of the world in Asia, Africa and the Middle East is on the way — somewhere; is trying to telescope centuries into decades, trying to catch up with the Western industrial and technological revolutions overnight and under much more difficult circumstances. And they are trying to accomplish this mighty transformation by the methods of consent, not coercion. A policy based just on anti-communism and military potency is not in the spirit of this great movement of the twentieth century and will win few hearts. The challenge for us is to identify ourselves with this social and human revolution, to encourage, aid and inspire the aspirations of half of mankind for a better life, to guide these aspirations into paths that lead to freedom. To default would be disaster.

The great issue that splits the world in this troubled age, the issue of tyranny or freedom, cannot be reconciled. But need it be forced to a decision? It seems to me the problem is not to find ways to live in harmony with the adversary; it is to find ways to live beside him in the bitter discord of incessant power and ideological competition. In time there will be a break, sooner perhaps than prudence admits.

The infinity of problems we now face, and I have tried to suggest but some of them and their genesis, cannot all be solved quickly. And some of our problems probably can't be solved at all. Our choice is to let time assuage or exacerbate. Emotion in matters of national security is no substitute for intelligence, nor rigidity for prudence. To act coolly, intelligently and prudently in perilous circumstances is the test of a man or nation. The responsibility for organizing and sustaining the great coalition befell us Americans suddenly and before we were prepared for it. But we shall have to learn this job quickly and well. As foreign policy grows out of historical experience and reflects national character, perhaps it is not irrelevant to this task to consider some aspects of our national character and experience.

One of our hardest tasks — if we hope to conduct a successful foreign policy — is to learn a new habit of thought, a new attitude toward the problems of life itself. Fortitude, sobriety and patience as a prescription for combating intolerable evil are cold porridge to Americans who yesterday tamed a continent and tipped the scales decisively in two world wars. Americans have always assumed, subconsciously, that all problems can be solved; that every story has a happy ending; that the application of enough energy and good will can make everything come out right. In view of our history, this assumption is natural enough. As a people, we have never encountered any obstacle that we could not overcome. The Pilgrims had a rough first winter, but after that the colony flourished. Valley Forge was followed naturally by Yorktown. Daniel Boone always found his way through the forest. We crossed the Alleghenies and the Mississippi and the Rockies with an impetus that nothing could stop. The wagon trains got through; the Pony Express delivered the mail; in spite of Bull Run and the Copperheads, the Union was somehow preserved. We never came across a river we couldn't bridge, a depression we couldn't overcome, a war we couldn't win. So far, we have never known the tragedy, frustration and sometimes defeat which are ingrained in the memories of all other peoples.

So when we encounter a problem in foreign policy we naturally assume that it can be solved pretty quick, with enough drive, determination and red corpuscles. "The difficult we do immediately, the impossible takes a little longer." Just pour in enough man power, money and bulldozers, and we can lick it. If one diplomat can't come up with the answer, fire him and hire another — or better yet, hire ten. And if that doesn't solve it, some Americans conclude that there can be only one explanation: treason.

And this raises the question of foreign policy by hindsight. Obviously the British withdrawal from India in 1947 created a power vacuum in that area which was very pleasing to the Kremlin. But did the Conservatives for political advantage charge the Labour government with selling Britain down the river, or being dupes or fellow travelers? Of course not. Remembering the follies of the Chamberlain regime, did Churchill exclude men of Munich from the wartime Cabinet? Of course not. But in our country in recent years we have repeatedly seen policies developed without protest at one time which turned out unsuccessfully, in whole or in part, attacked at a later time for partisan advantage as bumbling and fumbling and even betrayal or treachery. And thereby the door is opened not only to political foul play and demagoguery but to the destruction of public confidence at home and moral authority abroad. No administration can conduct a sound foreign policy when the future sits in judgment on the past and officials are held accountable as dupes, fools or traitors for anything that goes wrong.

Such extreme and cynical political irresponsibility is a problem for the electorate and the press, I suppose; which means that it is a problem of education and character for us. And so are impatience, arrogance and our faith in quick solutions.

As long as this habit of mind persists — and it is fundamentally an unchristian attitude, ignoring the pervasiveness of evil and loaded with arrogance and pride — we shall never be able to face our problems realistically. Our first job, it seems to me, is to school ourselves in cold-eyed humility; to recognize that our wisdom is imperfect and that our capabilities are limited.

Many of the really hard problems in international relations may never be "solved" at all. The conflict between Moslem and Christian, which dominated world politics for some 300 years, was never resolved. Islam and Christianity learned to live together and the problem was submerged in the newer and more urgent problems of the Renaissance, the Age of Discovery, and finally the Industrial Revolution. So with the Thirty Years' War, which also started as a conflict between two ideologies, Protestant and Catholic. The underlying issues were never settled because they were logically irreconcilable; but they did cease to pre-occupy the minds of men, as nationalism and class conflict began to emerge as more pressing issues. Before that war finally petered out, curiously enough, a Catholic Cardinal — Richelieu — was organizing the Protestant League, and a Protestant general was leading the armies of the Holy Roman Empire. The struggle had been transformed from one of religious ideology to one of national ambition.

It is at least conceivable that the ideological conflicts of our own time will defy solution, in similar fashion, but will be replaced by other problems which we cannot now foresee.

So the first step in learning our new role in world affairs is not one which can be taken by technicians in the State Department, or even by political leaders. It has to be taken by individual Americans, in the privacy of their own homes, hearts and souls. It involves a conscious acceptance of Christian humility — a recognition that we are never going to solve many of the hard problems of the world, but will simply have to learn to live with them, for years and maybe for centuries.

When we have accomplished that step, we will no longer call out a posse to find the traitor who was responsible for "our" loss of China; or threaten the French with dire punishment if they don't stop behaving like Frenchmen forthwith. We will no longer be tempted by simple panaceas and total solutions — a blockade of China, or an arms burden that may crush necessary social changes in weak economies and deliver them to the enemy, or unlimited billions for Point Four, or whatever.

On the latter point don't misunderstand me. Point Four and technical assistance are good medicine, in doses which can be absorbed by responsible and genuinely representative governments. However, I am not one of those who think that economic aid is a miracle drug and a sure cure for all ailments, and especially when it is allocated and judged here at home not on its value in building stable, democratic societies, but on its effectiveness in winning a country, India for example, to our side. As I have indicated, I think conformity·with our views and defensive alliances, while highly desirable, is generally not the cause but the consequence of government that has the support of the people so that they will want to defend it against external aggression or internal subversion. It is hard and futile to defend a government whose people won't defend it. We shall have to learn that we cannot buy agreement or effective alliances among the new states of the Middle East and Asia with economic or military aid. All we can do, and in my judgment must do, is to help with the building of free and independent governments whose people will defend them.

All of us, as individuals, have to learn much the same lessons as we approach maturity. In youth, everything seems possible; but we reach a point in the middle years when we realize that we are never going to reach all the shining goals we had set for ourselves. And in the end, most of us reconcile ourselves, with what grace we can, to living with our ulcers and arthritis, our sense of partial failure, our less-than-ideal families — and even our politicians! Maybe America, as a nation, is approaching that point. Maybe we are just now going through that period of emotional protest — so common with individuals in early middle age — which precedes the acceptance of the sad realities of mature responsibility.

In passing, it is noteworthy that other nations have greater patience, especially the Communist ones; and this puts us with our obsessive need for quick solutions at a disadvantage. The Chinese, Russians, Persians, and even British don't mind negotiating for weeks or even years, if necessary. But maybe we too are learning, certainly we showed a good deal of patience in the Korean armistice negotiations, for example. In this connection, however, there would seem to be manifest impatience and even disregard of our friends in such recent impulsive and ill-starred diplomatic maneuvers as the Trieste "solution," the "new look," "massive retaliation," and the sudden cry for "united action" in Indo-China, where a war has been going on and going badly for seven years.

The ordeal of our times, I have suggested, is a challenge to American maturity and American responsibility. Nowhere is this testing more fundamental than in the field of the free mind. For never has an external threat required more clear-headed analysis, more hard and sober thought and more bold and unterrified vision than the threat we confront today. And yet the very existence of that threat has created strains and tensions, anguish and anxiety, which beat upon the free mind, surround it, torment it, and threaten to smother it. It is an irony that unreason should never be more manifest than in the midst of our great planetary effort to make freedom secure.

Senator Fulbright has called anti-intellectualism "that swinish blight so common in our time." This infection has been epidemic, of course, in the totalitarian states. Antireason is the spirit of the shouting, chanting crowds we remember so well in Hitler's Germany. Almost daily we read of new manifestations of unreason, mob emotion and violence in some part of the world. In recent years we have even seen the contagion of unreason and anti-intellectualism spreading among ourselves, inhibiting thought and initiative in government, distorting the emphasis in our public affairs, moving groups to extremes of intolerance, diverting attention from our great concerns and provoking division among us.

Unreason and anti-intellectualism abominate thought. Thinking implies disagreement; and disagreement implies nonconformity; and nonconformity implies heresy; and heresy implies disloyalty — so, obviously, thinking must be stopped. But shouting is not a substitute for thinking and reason is not the subversion but the salvation of freedom.

Another lesson that we shall have to learn is that we cannot deal with questions of foreign policy in terms of moral absolutes. Compromise is not immoral or treasonable. It is the objective of negotiation and negotiation is the means of resolving conflict peacefully. But when we negotiate we have to have something to negotiate *with* as well as *for*. If rigidity and absolutist attitudes deprive our representatives of anything to negotiate *with* then there is nothing they can negotiate *for*. The consequences can be very embarrassing.

We seem to have a current illustration of self-defeating rigidity in the case of China. Because of our justified moral revulsion to the bloodthirsty conspiracy in China, the competition in extreme opinions and arbitrary attitudes among political leaders has virtually deprived us of all flexibility. The Secretary of State was even severely criticized by his own party leaders for even agreeing to join our allies in a meeting with the Chinese.[5] And rigidity known publicly in advance not only embarrasses us with our allies but can be seized upon by our enemies and advertised among the uncommitted peoples to prove our obdurate refusal to make any concessions for peace.

The point is not necessarily that we should support the admission to the United Nations of China or grant recognition or something else in exchange for a settlement in Indo-China, Korea or Formosa. The point is that we must not be imprisoned by our own passions, propaganda or pronouncements; we should not tie the hands of our representatives and hobble ourselves in advance to the adversary's advantage, not ours.

Times change, and rapidly, in this era of change. John Stuart Mill wrote: "That which seems the height of absurdity in one generation often becomes the height of wisdom in the next." Not very long ago there was a lot of "radical" agitation, so called, in this country. What

[5] On January 27, 1954, at the Berlin Big Four conference, Russian Foreign Minister V. M. Molotov proposed that another conference be scheduled for the spring of 1955, which would include the Chinese Communists in a discussion of world disarmament.

did the "radicals" want? They wanted social security, old age pensions, regulation of utilities and securities, government aid for housing and education, a nine-hour day and collective bargaining. Those were heresies not long ago but in 1953 a Republican President raises the welfare state to Cabinet status and asks for an extension of social security.[6]

Similarly a few years ago we were fighting the Germans and Japanese tooth and toenail and calling them names not fit to print. Today we are nourishing them with our money and arming them with our weapons. A few years ago I was doing savage battle with the Communist Yugoslavs in the United Nations. But last summer the same people entertained me like a long lost friend from one end of Yugoslavia to the other.

Passions rise and subside. Absolutes are few and black and white rare colors in international politics. Keeping an open, flexible mind, shedding our passion for crusades and our taste for absolutes that equate compromise with immorality, will be another hard and useful exercise. As Churchill has said: "Guidance in these mundane matters is granted to us only step by step. . . . There is therefore wisdom in reserving one's decisions as long as possible and until all the facts and forces that will be potent are revealed."

The price of inflexibility in foreign policy will be loss of confidence in our leadership first, then the loss of our allies, or worse. We can't have things all our own way. We shall have to face the necessity of compromise not only with our allies but with our enemies, for power factors are realities. And we shall have to learn to expect something less than total success every time, and not slander our officials as suspicious characters at every setback or failure. For if we do we shall soon have no successes.

There are limits to the effectiveness of our nation's foreign policy. For foreign policy is concerned with problems which lie beyond our jurisdiction and about which we cannot legislate. There are only two means available for influencing the actions of other states: persuasion and coercion. As a free society, we must rely primarily on persuasion. We can use coercion only rarely, and usually only as a defensive measure. We cannot have satellites because this depends on the use of coercion. We cannot employ threats and intimidation effectively because our actions are open to free discussion and criticism. Great as our power is, we have only a marginal influence on developments out-

[6] Shortly after taking office, President Eisenhower abolished the Federal Security Agency and transferred its functions to the newly created Department of Health, Education, and Welfare, which was activated on April 11, 1953. Its secretary was given cabinet rank.

side our boundaries. Guatemala is an example. Our power is almost infinite in comparison to Guatemala's. Yet we have been unable to prevent the emergence of Communist influence there.[7]

Like every great power we are always and simultaneously on both the defensive and the offensive. We must adjust our defense to the adversary's strength and should develop our offense to make the most of our strength. The defensive task is to work with our allies and friends to deny the adversary opportunities to win cheap successes. Communism has yet to gain power in any state through free elections. It must gain control of key positions of power by subversion, penetration, or violence — civil war as in Indo-China or direct aggression as in Korea. The defensive task is in large part a military task: to develop and maintain such strength as to deter general war and to deal with violence in local situations. It is partly a political and economic task; for example, military measures alone are inadequate in Indo-China and political and economic measures are necessary now to bring stability to Korea.

The offensive task is to work with allied and friendly countries to create a world environment favorable to the steady growth of free institutions. This means political arrangements which will make possible the unity of action essential to survival but which at the same time are consistent with diversity. It means a healthy international economy. The offensive task never ends. Progress will be slow. We hope that we can leave the world in a little better shape than we found it. But to search for a "solution" prematurely is more likely to produce war than peace. There is no such "solution" now, but our problems may fade away with time and cease to have the importance that they now seem to have.

Because of the nature of free societies, it is of the utmost importance to prevent war, if possible, and if this is not possible, to keep any future war as severely limited in scope as possible. It is a sign of strength, not of weakness, to be able to keep war limited. To generalize hostilities to a world scale would imperil the very institutions we seek to save by war.

Our objective is not the destruction of communism by war. Our objective is not the incitement of others to violence. Our objective is not

[7] In June, 1952, Guatemalan President Jacobo Arbenz Guzmán signed an agrarian reform bill supported by the Communists, and under its provisions the agrarian department in February, 1953, announced a plan to expropriate some seventy-five per cent of the Guatemalan holdings of the United Fruit Company. On October 14, 1953, Assistant Secretary of State John Cabot, charging that Guatemala was "openly playing the Communist game," warned the country it could expect no further U.S. aid. On the day of Stevenson's first Godkin lecture, March 17, 1954, the State Department expressed concern that reported shipments of Communist arms to Guatemala might indicate growing Communist strength there. Later that year the CIA engineered the overthrow of the Arbenz government.

to rectify the boundaries and correct the unnatural divisions that afflict the world by force, but by peaceful processes. Our objective is a peace consistent with decency and justice. And our prayer is that history will not say that we led a noble but a lost cause.

It is doubtful whether in all history two ways of life as different and opposed as the Communist way and our way of life have ever come into contact with one another at so many different points without engaging in mortal conflict.

Experience suggests that it has not been easy for men to learn the wisdom and virtue of tolerance for ideas and ways of life which deeply offend the cherished tenets of their own faith. In times past men of fervent faith regarded religious tolerance as a sign of moral weakness rather than moral strength. It seems that only when warring faiths have become convinced that they must choose between common survival and mutual extinction do they agree to live and let live.

Probably the greatest obstacle in the path of peaceful coexistence is the Soviet belief in the inevitability of conflict between the Communist and the non-Communist worlds. And it is true that Soviet intolerance and unwillingness to abide by the rules of peaceful coexistence have shaken our faith in tolerance and the possibility of peaceful coexistence. But in the atomic era even the most fanatical faith is likely to balk at self-destruction. There is no Iron Curtain that the aggregate sentiments of mankind cannot and will not penetrate in time. Even the most fanatical ambition must adjust itself to demonstrated truth or perish. No faith can long rest on the belief that the world is flat — if its adherents know the world is round. "Great is the truth and mighty above all things."

The hope for peaceful coexistence lies in our ability to convince the rulers of the other world that they cannot extend their system by force, or by stealth, and that unless they use force against us we will not use force against them; that our coalition exists but to serve and to save the imperishable principles of the Charter of the United Nations.

Intolerant power respects power, not weakness. It is imperative therefore to build and better the balance of power. Conspiracy and incitement prosper in disunion and discontent. It is imperative therefore to build and better the unity and well being of the free world. We cannot do it alone. It is imperative therefore to build and better the coalition. And here we encounter our greatest danger and our final task. A coalition built on expedient reaction to the common danger will not stand, because the Sino-Soviet alliance has the power to blow hot and cold, like Boreas and Phoebus in the fable; it has the power to relax or increase the tension as it sees fit. But our coalition cannot live by fits and starts; it must rest on an enduring community of interest. And successful communal relations mean give and take, co-operation, consultation, accommodation — a decent respect for the opinions of others. Our coalition is a partnership, not a dictatorship. We shall have to listen as well as talk; learn as well as teach. And I sometimes think that what America needs more than anything else is a hearing aid. We can encourage the acceptance of our ideas only as we are willing to accept the ideas and suggestions of others. All of this means a large relinquishment of our freedom of action.

There is not the slightest chance of confidence and mutual trust among the members of the free world's coalition if the United States should fail the test of leadership. We have a great and fortuitous advantage, for if there is nothing the Kremlin wants more than to rule the world, there is nothing the United States wants less than to rule the world. To cling to that truth with clarity, sincerity and humility will be our greatest strength in the trials of leadership.

America's greatest contribution to human society has come not from her wealth or weapons or ambitions, but from her ideas; from the moral sentiments of human liberty and human welfare embodied in the Declaration of Independence and the Bill of Rights. We must cling to these truths, for these are everlasting and universal aspirations. In the words of Lincoln: "It was not the mere separation of the colonies from the motherland, but the sentiment in the Declaration of Independence which gave liberty not alone to the people of this country, but hope to all the world. It was that which gave promise that in due time the weights should be lifted from the shoulders of all men, and that all should have an equal chance." Throughout its history, America has given hope, comfort and inspiration to freedom's cause in all lands. The reservoir of good will and respect for America was not built up by American arms or intrigue; it was built upon our deep dedication to the cause of human liberty and human welfare.

All through human history runs a struggle between right and wrong, which is destined to endure, perhaps, to the end of time. Some historians during our materialistic years disavowed this theme. But now in our age of anxiety and time of testing, they are bringing it again within their purview. Arthur Schlesinger, Jr., has stated: "If historians are to understand the fullness of the social dilemma they seek to reconstruct, they must understand that sometimes there is no escape from the implacabilities of moral decisions"; while Allan Nevins notes with approval the emergence in historical writing of "a deepened moral sense much needed in our troubled age."

If the record of man's progress is the chronicle of everlasting struggle between right and wrong, it follows that the solutions of our problems lie largely within ourselves, that only with self-mastery can we hope to master history. The scientific mastery of our environment has brought us not tranquillity but rather unrest and new fears. Knowledge alone is not enough. It must be leavened with magnanimity before it becomes wisdom. And "magnanimity in politics," as Burke has reminded us, "is not seldom the truest wisdom."

America's life story is the record of a marvelous growth of body, mind and character. Now at maturity we shoulder the heaviest burdens of greatness, for in the last analysis the epic struggle for our civilization, for government by consent of the governed, will be determined by what Americans are capable of. In bearing burdens, in ennobling new duties of citizenship, is the greatness of men and nations measured, not in pomp and circumstance.

How shall we bear what Providence has assigned us? In Keat[s]'s *Hyperion* are these lines:

> for to bear all naked truths,
> And to envisage circumstances, all calm,
> That is the top of sovereignty. . . .

And so it is.

Index

Abdullah, king of Jordan, 285, 317
Abdullah, Sheikh Mohammed, 249; AES meets, 201–202, 204–207, 225, 253
Abe, Yoshishige, 37
Acheson, Dean, 121
Adams, Henry, quoted, 438
Adams, John, 435, 451
Adams, Wesley, 220n
Adenauer, Konrad, 376, 378, 382, 383
"Adlai Stevenson Answers Five Questions about Europe" (AES article in *Look*), 373–384
Adlai Stevenson Speaks (phonograph record), 244
Africa, 223, 267, 443, 458
Agar, Mr. and Mrs. Herbert, 400, 401, 402
Agron, Gershon, 301, 304, 310n
Agron, Mrs. Gershon, 310n
Akau, John, Jr., 19
Alaska, 19, 438
Albania, 352
Alexander, Archibald S., 423; letter to, 423
Ali, Mohammed, 222, 225, 241, 246, 252, 253, 254
Ali, General Nasir, 248
Allen, George V., 200, 209, 210, 211, 212, 233, 237n, 240; on Nehru, 221–222; on AES in India, 222, 233n; AES cable to, 225n

Allen, Larry, 97, 110
Amalu, Charles, 20
Amer, Major Abdel Hakim, 275
America. *See* United States
America-Japan Society, AES speech before, 20n, 26–34
American Friends Service Committee, 72
American-Korean Foundation, 45
American Mercury, 422n
American President Lines, 17
American Society for Graphic Arts, 210n
American University of Beirut, 283, 285–286; AES informal speech at, 289–290
American University of Cairo, 275
Ames, John S., III, 213
Amin-ud-Din, Mian, 246–247
Among, Mrs. Haili, 19
An, Tran Van, 104
Anderson, Nancy L. (Mrs. Adlai E. Stevenson III), 214n
Anderson, Mr. and Mrs. Warwick, 214n
Aneta (Indonesian newspaper), 130–136 *passim*
Angkor. *See* Cambodia
Ankara, Treaty of, 321n
Annam, 97, 98
Antara (Indonesian newspaper), 131, 132, 134
anti-Americanism, 369, 375, 429